CEDU(쎄듀)는 A **C**omprehensive **E**nglish e**DU**cation(종합적 영어교육)의 약자입니다.

저자

김기훈 現 ㈜쎄듀 대표이사

現 메가스터디 영어영역 대표강사

前 서울특별시 교육청 외국어 교육정책자문위원회 위원

저서 천일문 / 천일문 Training Book / 천일문 GRAMMAR

어법끝 / 어휘끝 / 첫단추 / 쎈쓰업 / 파워업 / 빈순삽함

쎄듀 본영어 / 문법의 골든룰 101 / ALL쏨 서술형 / 수능실감

천일문 중등 WRITING / Grammar Q / Reading Q / Listening Q 등

쎄듀 영어교육연구센터

쎄듀 영어교육센터는 영어 콘텐츠에 대한 전문지식과 경험을 바탕으로

최고의 교육 콘텐츠를 만들고자 최선의 노력을 다하는 전문가 집단입니다.

장혜승 선임연구원

감수

유원호 (서강대 영미어문과 교수)

마케팅	콘텐츠 마케팅 사업본부
영업	문병구
제작	정승호
인디자인 편집	올댓에디팅
디자인	윤혜영
내지 일러스트	그림숲
영문교열	Janna Christie

LISTENING Q

중학영어듣기
모의고사 24회
❸

PREVIEW

최신 기출을 완벽 분석한 유형별 공략

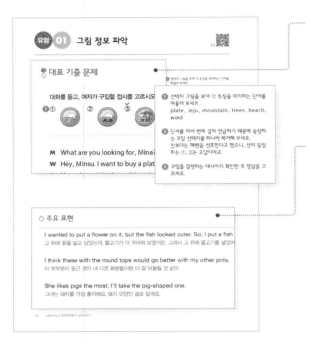

🔔 대표 기출 문제

- 최근 〈시·도교육청 주관 영어듣기능력평가〉에 출제되는 모든 문제 유형을 철저히 분석하여, 유형별 문제 풀이 방법을 제시합니다.
- 오답 함정과 정답 근거를 확인해보며, 각 유형에 대한 이해도를 높일 수 있습니다.

✪ 주요 표현

- 유형별로 가장 많이 출제된 중요 표현을 정리하였습니다.
- 시험 바로 전에 빠르게 훑어볼 수 있습니다.

실전 모의고사로 문제 풀이 감각 익히기

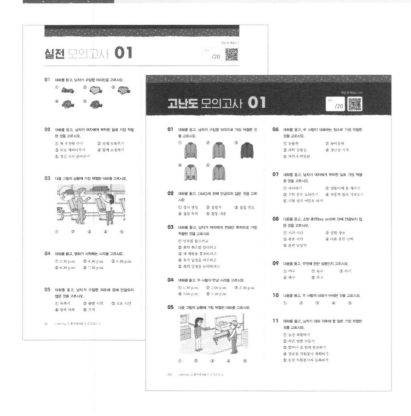

실전 모의고사 20회

- 전국 16개 〈시·도 교육청 주관 영어듣기능력평가〉 최신 5개년 출제 경향이 완벽 반영된 실전 모의고사를 수록했습니다.

- 실전과 동일한 유형 배치 및 엄선된 문항을 통해 영어듣기 평가를 대비하는 동시에 듣기의 기본기를 쌓을 수 있습니다.

고난도 모의고사 4회

- 점진적으로 문제 풀이 능력을 키워나갈 수 있도록 실전보다 높은 난이도의 문제로 실력을 점검합니다.

- 고난도 모의고사 3, 4회는 〈국가수준 학업성취도 평가〉도 대비할 수 있도록 최신 출제 경향이 반영된 모의고사를 수록했습니다.

매회 Dictation 수록

- 문제 풀이에 중요한 단서가 되는 핵심 어휘 및 표현들을 연습할 수 있습니다.

- 들은 내용을 다시 한번 확인하며, 중요 표현들과 놓치기 쉬운 연음 등의 집중적인 학습이 가능합니다.

🔊 Listening Tip

듣기의 기본기를 쌓을 수 있도록, 더 잘 들리는 발음 팁을 수록하였습니다.

＊ 교육부 지정 의사소통 기능

개정교과서에 수록된 의사소통 기능 표현을 정리하였습니다.
중요 표현들이 실제 대화에서 어떻게 쓰이는지 확인할 수 있으며,
다른 예시 문장을 제시하여 응용해 볼 수 있도록 구성했습니다.

학습자 혼자서도 충분한 학습이 가능하도록 자세한 해설과 대본 및 해석을 제공합니다.

CEDU MP3 PLAYER

QR코드 하나로 배속 및 문항 선택 재생

- 〈Listening Q 중학영어듣기 모의고사〉 시리즈는 효율적인 듣기 학습을 위해 MP3 PLAYER 기능이 적용되어 있습니다.

- 교재 안에 있는 QR코드를 휴대전화로 인식하면, 기본 배속과 1.2배속, 1.4배속 세 가지 속도 중에 원하는 속도를 선택하여 음원 재생이 가능합니다.

- 각 문항별 파일도 선택하여 재생 가능하기 때문에 더욱 편리하게 받아쓰기를 연습할 수 있습니다.

무료 부가서비스

www.cedubook.com에서 무료 부가서비스 자료를 다운로드하세요.
- MP3 파일　• 어휘리스트　• 어휘테스트

CONTENTS

PART. 03

고난도 모의고사

[책속책] 정답 및 해설

기출 문제 유형 분석표

2024 ← → 2019

3학년	2024년 2회	2024년 1회	2023년 2회	2023년 1회	2022년 2회	2022년 1회	2021년 2회	2021년 1회	2020년 2회	2020년 1회	2019년 2회
그림 정보 파악	1	1	1	1	1	1	1	1	1	1	1
언급하지 않은 내용 찾기	2	2	2	2	2	2	2	2	2	2	2
목적 파악	2	2	2	2	2	2	2	2	2	2	2
부탁 파악	1	1	1	1	1	1	1	1	1	1	1
숫자 정보 파악 (시각)	1	1	1	1	1	2	2	2	1	1	2
숫자 정보 파악 (금액)	1	1	1	1	1	1	1	1	1	1	1
숫자 정보 파악 (날짜)	1	1	1	1	1				1	1	
심정 추론	1	1	1	1	1	1	1		1	1	
그림 상황에 적절한 대화 고르기	1	1	1	1	1	1	1	1	1	1	1
화제 추론	1	1	1	1	1	1	1	1	1	1	1
어색한 대화 고르기	1	1	1	1	1	1	1	1	1	1	1
할 일 파악	1	1	1	1	1	1	1	1	1	1	1
한 일 파악	1	1	1	1	1	1	1	1	1	1	1
도표 정보 파악	1	1	1	1	1	1			1	1	
위치 찾기							1	1			1
특정 정보 파악											
직업 추론											
대화 장소 추론								1			1
관계 추론											
의도 파악											
요지 파악											
이어질 응답 찾기	3	3	3	3	3	3	3	3	3	3	3
가장 적절한 말 고르기	1	1	1	1	1	1	1	1	1	1	1

기출 문제 유형 분석표

2019년 ~ 2024년

Study Planner

●● 영어듣기평가 **D-25일**

1일차 유형공략 ◯월 ◯일	2일차 실전 모의고사 1회 ◯월 ◯일 _____점	3일차 실전 모의고사 2회 ◯월 ◯일 _____점	4일차 실전 모의고사 3회 ◯월 ◯일 _____점	5일차 실전 모의고사 4회 ◯월 ◯일 _____점
6일차 실전 모의고사 5회 ◯월 ◯일 _____점	7일차 실전 모의고사 6회 ◯월 ◯일 _____점	8일차 실전 모의고사 7회 ◯월 ◯일 _____점	9일차 실전 모의고사 8회 ◯월 ◯일 _____점	10일차 실전 모의고사 9회 ◯월 ◯일 _____점
11일차 실전 모의고사 10회 ◯월 ◯일 _____점	12일차 실전 모의고사 11회 ◯월 ◯일 _____점	13일차 실전 모의고사 12회 ◯월 ◯일 _____점	14일차 실전 모의고사 13회 ◯월 ◯일 _____점	15일차 실전 모의고사 14회 ◯월 ◯일 _____점
16일차 실전 모의고사 15회 ◯월 ◯일 _____점	17일차 실전 모의고사 16회 ◯월 ◯일 _____점	18일차 실전 모의고사 17회 ◯월 ◯일 _____점	19일차 실전 모의고사 18회 ◯월 ◯일 _____점	20일차 실전 모의고사 19회 ◯월 ◯일 _____점
21일차 실전 모의고사 20회 ◯월 ◯일 _____점	22일차 고난도 모의고사 1회 ◯월 ◯일 _____점	23일차 고난도 모의고사 2회 ◯월 ◯일 _____점	24일차 고난도 모의고사 3회 ◯월 ◯일 _____점	25일차 고난도 모의고사 4회 ◯월 ◯일 _____점

●● 영어듣기평가 **D-15일**

1일차 유형공략 ◯월 ◯일	2일차 실전 모의고사 1, 2회 ◯월 ◯일 ____점 / ____점	3일차 실전 모의고사 3, 4회 ◯월 ◯일 ____점 / ____점	4일차 실전 모의고사 5, 6회 ◯월 ◯일 ____점 / ____점	5일차 실전 모의고사 7, 8회 ◯월 ◯일 ____점 / ____점
6일차 실전 모의고사 9, 10회 ◯월 ◯일 ____점 / ____점	7일차 실전 모의고사 11, 12회 ◯월 ◯일 ____점 / ____점	8일차 실전 모의고사 13, 14회 ◯월 ◯일 ____점 / ____점	9일차 실전 모의고사 15, 16회 ◯월 ◯일 ____점 / ____점	10일차 실전 모의고사 17, 18회 ◯월 ◯일 ____점 / ____점
11일차 실전 모의고사 19, 20회 ◯월 ◯일 ____점 / ____점	12일차 고난도 모의고사 1회 ◯월 ◯일 _____점	13일차 고난도 모의고사 2회 ◯월 ◯일 _____점	14일차 고난도 모의고사 3회 ◯월 ◯일 _____점	15일차 고난도 모의고사 4회 ◯월 ◯일 _____점

PART. 01

Listening Q

^^^

중학영어듣기 모의고사

유형공략

×

영어듣기능력 평가에 자주 출제되는
14가지 대표 유형을 기출문제와 함께 살펴보자!

유형 01 그림 정보 파악

🏅 대표 기출 문제

대화를 듣고, 여자가 구입할 접시를 고르시오.

① ② ③✓ ④   ⑤

✕ 오답 함정　○ 정답 근거

M What are you looking for, Mina?

W Hey, Minsu. I want to buy a plate from Jeju for my mom.

M How about this plate with a picture of a mountain on it? It has snow at the top. It looks like Halla Mountain.

W Well, ❷ my mom likes beaches more than mountains.

M Then, how about this one? It has a beach with two trees.

W Perfect. And I like that it has the word, "JEJU", too.
❸ I'll buy this one.
　➔ 해변과 나무 두 그루, 글자 JEJU가 있는 접시를 사겠다는 내용이에요.

❶ 선택지 그림을 보며 각 특징을 의미하는 단어를 떠올려 보세요.
plate, Jeju, mountain, trees, beach, word

❷ 단서를 여러 번에 걸쳐 언급하기 때문에 등장하는 오답 선택지를 하나씩 제거해 보세요.
산보다는 해변을 선호한다고 했으니, 산이 등장하는 ①, ②는 오답이에요.

❸ 구입을 결정하는 대사까지 확인한 후 정답을 고르세요.

남　무엇을 찾고 있니, 미나야?
여　안녕, 민수야. 우리 엄마에게 드릴 제주에서 만든 접시를 사려고 해.
남　접시 위에 산 그림이 그려진 이건 어때? 꼭대기에 눈이 있어. 한라산처럼 보이잖아.
여　음, 우리 엄마는 산보다는 해변을 더 좋아하셔.
남　그러면 이건 어떠니? 해변과 나무 두 그루가 있어.
여　아주 좋네. 그리고 'JEJU'라는 글자가 있는 게 마음에 들어. 이걸로 살게.

✪ 주요 표현

I wanted to put a flower on it, but the fish looked cuter. So, I put a fish on it.
그 위에 꽃을 넣고 싶었는데, 물고기가 더 귀여워 보였거든. 그래서 그 위에 물고기를 넣었어.

I think these with the round tops would go better with my other pots.
이 윗부분이 둥근 것이 내 다른 화분들이랑 더 잘 어울릴 것 같아.

She likes pigs the most. I'll take the pig-shaped one.
그녀는 돼지를 가장 좋아해요. 돼지 모양인 걸로 살게요.

Sorry, I don't like the word "GARDEN". I'll take the one with only a leaf on it.
죄송하지만, 전 'GARDEN'이라는 단어가 마음에 안 들어요. 그 위에 나뭇잎만 있는 걸로 살게요.

They're not bad, but I think the round cushions would look better with my chair.
그것들은 나쁘지 않지만, 둥근 쿠션이 제 의자와 더 잘 어울릴 것 같아요.

I'm afraid that those patterns are not to my taste.
저 무늬는 제 취향이 아닌 것 같아요.

대표 기출 문제

1. 대화를 듣고, Glory Sale에 관해 언급되지 <u>않은</u> 것을 고르시오.

① 행사 목적   ② 개최 요일   ③ 행사 장소
④ 판매 물품   ⑤ 참가 신청 방법

✕오답 함정   O정답 근거

W   David, have you heard about the Glory Sale?

M   Yeah, it's a charity sale **to help children in need**, right?
→ ① 어려운 아이들을 돕기 위한 바자회예요.

W   Yes, it'll be **next Friday**. Why don't we join as sellers and
→ ② 다음 주 금요일에 열려요.
help them?

M   Good idea! Where will it be held?

W   **In the school gym.**
→ ③ 학교 체육관에서 진행돼요.

M   Okay, how can we sign up to join it?

W   We need to **go to the library and talk to Ms. Kim.**
→ ⑤ 도서관에 가서 선생님에게 말해서 신청하는 거예요.

M   Let's go there now.

① 주어진 선택지를 보면서 어떤 내용들이 등장하는지 미리 예상해 보세요.

② 선택지가 등장한 순서대로 대화가 이루어져요. 대화를 들으면서 언급되는 항목을 선택지에서 하나씩 제거해 보세요.

여 David, Glory Sale에 대해 들어본 적 있니?
남 응, 어려운 아이들을 돕는 자선 바자회잖아, 그렇지?
여 응, 다음 주 금요일에 있을 거야. 판매자로 참가해서 그들을 돕는 게 어때?
남 좋은 생각이야! 어디서 열리니?
여 학교 체육관에서 열려.
남 알았어, 참가 신청하려면 어떻게 하면 돼?
여 도서관에 가서 김 선생님에게 말해야 해.
남 지금 거기로 가자.

2. 다음을 듣고, Book Fair에 관해 언급되지 <u>않은</u> 것을 고르시오.

① 시작 연도   ② 행사 기간   ③ 활동 내용
④ 신청 방법   ⑤ 참가 선물

✕오답 함정   O정답 근거

M   Hi, students. I'm Andrew from the book club. Our Book Fair is coming soon. It has been 12 years since it **first started in 2008**. This year's event will be held next week
→ 시작 연도: 2008년
from Monday to Friday in the library. You can **exchange**
→ 행사 기간: 월요일부터 금요일까지
books with each other and have a talk with famous
→ 활동 내용: 책을 교환하고 유명 작가들과 얘기 나눌 수 있음.
writers through this event. All participants will be **given a**
bookmark as a gift. Come and enjoy!
→ 참가 선물: 책갈피

① 주어진 선택지를 보면서 어떤 내용들이 등장하는지 미리 예상해 보세요.
first started in, from A to B, give, gift

② 선택지가 등장한 순서대로 대화가 이루어져요. 대화를 들으면서 언급되는 항목을 선택지에서 하나씩 제거해 보세요.

남 학생 여러분, 안녕하세요. 저는 독서 클럽의 Andrew입니다. 저희 도서 박람회가 곧 열립니다. 2008년에 처음 시작한 이래로 12년째 계속되고 있습니다. 올해 행사는 다음 주 월요일부터 금요일까지 도서관에서 열립니다. 이번 행사를 통해서 서로 책을 교환하실 수 있고 유명한 작가들과 이야기를 나눌 수 있습니다. 모든 참가자에게는 선물로 책갈피가 주어집니다. 와서 즐기세요!

 **목적 파악**

대표 기출 문제

1. 대화를 듣고, ❶ 남자가 여자에게 전화한 목적으로 가장 적절한 것을 고르시오.

❷① 입상 소식을 통보하려고　　✓② 대회 장소 변경을 안내하려고
③ 작품 제출 여부를 확인하려고　　④ 제출된 미술 작품을 돌려주려고
⑤ 전시회 개최 날짜를 공지하려고

✗오답 함정　o정답 근거

[Cell phone rings.]

W Hello.

M Hello. This is Vision Art Center. Is this Emma Taylor?

W Yes, speaking.

M Oh, I want to inform you that ❸ **the location of the 2020**
➜ 대회 장소가 변경되었다고 하네요.
art contest has been changed.

W It was supposed to be in auditorium A at your center,
wasn't it?

M Yes, it was. But it'll **be held in auditorium D instead.**
➜ 변경된 대회 장소에 대해 알려주고 있어요.

W Oh, I see. Is there any change to the date or time?

M No. Those are the same. Thank you for understanding.

W No problem.

❶ 지시문에서 누가 전화한 것인지 확인하세요. 남자가 전화를 걸었으니, 남자의 말에 집중하세요.

❷ 선택지 내용을 확인한 후, 관련 단어들을 미리 떠올려 보세요.
announce, inform, change, location, contest, artwork, return, date

❸ 대화 초반에 섣불리 정답을 선택하지 않도록 유의하세요. 오답 선택지의 일부 내용이 언급되기도 하므로, 대화를 들으면서 전체 상황을 정확하게 파악하는 것이 중요해요.

[휴대전화가 울린다.]
여 여보세요.
남 여보세요. Vision 아트센터인데요. Emma Taylor신가요?
여 네, 접니다.
남 아, 2020년 미술 대회가 열리는 위치가 변경되었음을 알려드리려고 합니다.
여 센터의 A 강당에서 열리기로 했었죠, 그렇지 않나요?
남 네, 그랬습니다. 하지만 D 강당에서 대신 열릴 예정입니다.
여 아, 그렇군요. 날짜나 시간은 변경이 없나요?
남 없습니다. 날짜와 시간은 동일합니다. 이해해 주셔서 감사합니다.
여 아닙니다.

---

2. 다음을 듣고, 방송의 목적으로 가장 적절한 것을 고르시오.

❶① 다음 정차역을 알리려고　　② 지하철 내 예절을 안내하려고
③ 열차 도착지연을 공지하려고　　④ 열차 내 편의 시설을 홍보하려고
⑤ 분실물 보관소 위치를 설명하려고

✗오답 함정　o정답 근거

W Good afternoon, passengers! May I have your attention?
Please keep ❷ **the following manners in mind while on**
the subway train. First, don't stand in front of the door. It
➜ 지하철 내 예절에 대해서 소개하고 있어요.
blocks people getting on or off the train. **Second, please**
use earphones to listen to music or watch videos. Please
keep these manners in mind for everyone's safety and
➜ 왜 지하철 내 예절이 중요한지 이유를 설명하네요.
comfort. Thank you.

❶ 선택지 내용을 확인한 후, 관련 단어들을 미리 떠올려 보세요.
next stop, station, subway, manners, delays, lost and found, location

❷ 대화 초반에 정답 근거의 일부만 듣고 섣불리 정답을 선택하지 않도록 유의하세요.
초반에 등장하는 근거를 놓쳤더라도, 이어지는 내용을 듣고, 중심 내용을 파악한다면 쉽게 정답을 찾을 수 있어요.

여 안녕하세요, 승객 여러분! 주목해 주시겠어요? 지하철에 있을 때 다음과 같이 예절을 지켜주시기 바랍니다. 우선, 문 근처에 서지 마세요. 열차에 타거나 내리는 사람들을 막습니다. 두 번째로, 음악을 청취하시거나 영상을 시청하실 경우 이어폰을 사용해 주세요. 우리 모두의 안전과 편안함을 위해 이 예절을 명심해 주세요. 감사합니다.

🎖 대표 기출 문제

1. 대화를 듣고, ❶ 여자가 예약한 시티투어버스의 출발 시각을 고르시오.

① 11 a.m. ② 12 p.m. ③ 1 p.m.
④ 2 p.m. ⑤ 3 p.m.

✕ 오답 함정 ○ 정답 근거

M Welcome to the Tourist Information Center. How can I help you?

W I'd like to book a seat on your city tour bus tomorrow.

M The first bus of the day ❷ leaves at 11 a.m.

W That's a bit early for me. When is the next bus?

M The next bus is at 1 p.m., but it's fully booked.

W Then, what other times are available?

M We still have seats for the 2 p.m. and 3 p.m. buses.

W Can you put ❸ my name on the list for the 2 p.m. bus?
It's Claire Choi.
➡ 여자가 오후 2시 버스 좌석을 신청했어요.

M Sure. That's one ticket for the 2 p.m. bus.
➡ 남자가 버스 시각을 다시 언급하여 예약을 확인해요.

❶ 어떤 숫자 정보를 파악해야 하는지 지시문을 확인하세요.
book a seat, city tour bus

❷ 여러 번 다른 시각을 언급하기 때문에 대화를 들으면서 시각과 내용을 메모하세요.

❸ 이어지는 상대방의 응답까지 확인한 후에, 정답을 고르세요.

남 관광객 안내소에 오신 것을 환영합니다. 무엇을 도와드릴까요?
여 내일 이용 할 시티투어버스 좌석을 예약하려고 합니다.
남 첫 차는 오전 11시에 출발합니다.
여 저한테는 조금 이르네요. 다음 버스는 언제인가요?
남 다음 버스는 오후 1시에 있습니다만, 예약이 마감되었습니다.
여 그러면 가능한 다른 시간대는 언제인가요?
남 오후 2시와 3시 버스에 아직 좌석이 남아있습니다.
여 오후 2시 버스 명단에 제 이름을 올려주시겠어요? Claire Choi입니다.
남 물론이죠. 오후 2시 버스에 좌석 한 개입니다.

2. 대화를 듣고, 여자가 지불할 금액을 고르시오.

① $10 ② $20 ③ $30 ④ $40 ⑤ $50

✕ 오답 함정 ○ 정답 근거

M How may I help you?

W I'd like to pay for the group study room.

M Which room did you use?

W We used Room A.

M Okay, you stayed there for two hours, so it's ❶ 20 dollars for the room. Did you borrow a laptop?

W Yes, we borrowed one.

M Okay, it's ❷ ten dollars for the laptop and 20 dollars for the room.
➡ 노트북 컴퓨터 사용료가 추가되었어요.

W All right. Here you are.

❶ 대화를 들으면서 언급되는 가격을 메모하세요.

❷ 지불해야 할 총금액이 언급되지 않고 계산을 요구하네요. 앞서 메모한 내용을 토대로 차근히 계산해 보세요.
두 시간 이용 금액: $20
노트북 컴퓨터 사용료: $10
총금액: $30 = $20 + $10

남 어떻게 도와드릴까요?
여 그룹 스터디 룸 사용료를 결제하고 싶습니다.
남 어느 방을 이용하셨나요?
여 A실을 이용했습니다.
남 네, 2시간 동안 이용하셨으니 방 이용료는 20달러입니다. 노트북 컴퓨터를 빌리셨나요?
여 네, 한 개 빌렸습니다.
남 네, 노트북 컴퓨터는 10달러이고 방 이용료는 20달러입니다.
여 알겠습니다. 여기 있습니다.

🎖 대표 기출 문제

대화를 듣고, ① 남자의 심정으로 가장 적절한 것을 고르시오.

② ① bored ② upset ✓ ③ excited

④ scared ⑤ disappointed

✗ 오답 함정 ○ 정답 근거

W Fred, you look happy today.

M Yeah. You know my best friend Sujin, right?

W Of course. I remember she moved to another town.

M But she's coming to see me this weekend.

W Wow! Lucky you! You must ❸ **be looking forward to seeing her again.**

M Yes, I can't wait!

W Well, have a great time this weekend.

M Okay, I will.

① 남자의 심정을 묻고 있으므로, 남자의 말에 집중하세요.

② 영문인 선택지를 확인하고, 해당 어휘의 의미를 떠올려 보세요.
지루한, 속상한, 신이 난, 겁먹은, 실망한

❸ 상황이나 분위기를 파악하면 쉽게 심정을 파악할 수 있어요. 심정을 간접적으로 나타내는 표현들을 미리 익혀 두면 쉽게 정답을 찾을 수 있어요.

> 기출 기대를 나타내는 표현
> look forward to: ~을 기대하다, 즐거운 마음으로 기다리다
> can't wait to-v: 너무 ~하고 싶다

여 Fred, 너 오늘 즐거워 보인다.
남 응. 너 내 가장 친한 친구 수진이 알지, 그렇지?
여 물론이지. 나는 걔가 다른 도시로 이사 갔다는 것을 기억해.
남 그런데 이번 주말에 걔가 나를 보러 온대.
여 와! 잘됐네! 너 걔를 다시 보기를 기대하겠구나.
남 응, 빨리 보고 싶어!
여 자, 이번 주말 잘 보내.
남 알겠어, 그렇게.

① 지루한 ② 속상한 ③ 신이 난 ④ 겁먹은 ⑤ 실망한

⚙ 주요 어휘 및 표현

frustrated 좌절한, 실망한	A: I'm afraid that's not possible. The deadline was last Friday. 그건 불가능합니다. 마감 일자는 지난 금요일이었습니다. B: Oh no! I can't believe that I made such a big mistake. 이런! 제가 그런 실수를 했다니 믿어지지 않아요.
excited 신이 난	A: In addition, they provide a lot of interesting field trips for the volunteers. 게다가 봉사자들에게 재미있는 현장 학습을 많이 제공합니다. B: That's wonderful. I can't wait! Thank you so much! 잘됐네요. 기대되네요! 정말 감사합니다!
annoyed 짜증이 난	A: My cell phone screen was broken, so I had it fixed. 내 휴대전화 화면이 고장이 나서 그걸 고쳤어. B: So is it working now? 그래서 지금은 작동되니? A: The screen is fixed, but now I can't hear any sound. 화면은 고쳤는데 이제 소리가 나지 않아.
regretful 후회하는	A: If I had known that it was going to be noisy like this, I would have never moved here. 내가 이곳이 이렇게 시끄러운 곳인 줄 알았다면, 여기로 이사 오지 않았을 거야. B: That's a pity. I don't know what to say. 그것 참 안됐다. 뭐라고 위로해야 할지 모르겠네.

📀 대표 기출 문제

다음 그림의 상황에 가장 적절한 대화를 고르시오.

1

①   ②   ③   ④   ✓⑤

✕ 오답 함정   O 정답 근거

① **W**   What's wrong? You don't look so good.

   M   I have a stomachache.

② **W**   Where did you buy your hat?

   M   I bought it at the market.

③ **W**   Smile! I'm about to take a picture.

   M   Okay. I'm ready. Go ahead.

④ **W**   Excuse me, how can I get to the bakery?

   M   Go straight and turn left at the building over there.

⑤ **W**   **How do you like the cookie?**

   M   Wow! It's ❷ **so delicious.**

     ➜ 엄지손가락을 들고 맛있다는 표시를 했어요.

❶ 주어진 그림을 보면서 어떤 상황인지 확인하세요. 어떤 상황인지 미리 예측하면 정답을 쉽게 찾을 수 있어요.

삽화 안에 강조되는 부분은 중요한 근거가 될 수 있으니, 영어로 미리 떠올려 보세요.
cookies, delicious

❷ 그림에서 강조된 부분이 언급되는 대화가 정답인 경우가 많아요.
기출 의견을 물을 때
How do you like ~? ~ 어때요?

① 여   무슨 일 있어? 안 좋아 보이네.
    남   나 배가 아파.
② 여   네 모자를 어디서 샀니?
    남   가게에서 샀어.
③ 여   미소 지으세요! 사진을 찍겠습니다.
    남   알겠어요. 준비되었습니다. 찍으세요.
④ 여   실례합니다만 빵집에 어떻게 가나요?
    남   직진하셔서 저쪽에 있는 건물에서 왼쪽으로 도세요.
⑤ 여   쿠키 어떤 것 같니?
    남   와! 너무 맛있어.

그림 안에서 강조되는 부분을 활용한 오답 함정이 등장하기도 해요. 부분적인 내용보다는 전체 상황을 정확히 파악해야 해요.

✕ 오답 함정   O 정답 근거

① **A**   I'm writing a card for Bella's birthday.

   B   Really? I want to write something on it, too.

② **A**   Honey, you are driving too fast.

   B   Sorry. I didn't know.

✓③ **A**   How would you like to pay, cash or card?

   B   I'll pay by card. Here you are.

🎖 대표 기출 문제

대화를 듣고, ❶ 여자가 남자에게 부탁한 일로 가장 적절한 것을 고르시오.

❷ ① 인물화 그리기   ② 교우 관계 상담하기
  ③ 미술 준비물 알려 주기   ④ 박물관 방문 예약하기
  ✓⑤ 동아리 지도 교사 되어 주기

✗오답 함정 **○정답 근거**

W   Hello, Mr. Park. Do you have a minute?

M   Hi, Sally. What's up?

W   My friends and I want to start a ❸ drawing club, and we're looking for **a teacher to advise us.**

M   Well, what would you like to do with your drawing club?

W   We're planning to meet once a week to practice drawing. Also, we'll **visit art museums** to see different drawing styles.

M   Sounds like a great plan.

W   Then, Mr. Park, ❹ **would you be our club advisor?**
                  ➜ 지도 교사가 되어달라고 부탁하고 있어요.

M   All right. I'd be happy to do it.

❶ 지시문에서 누가 누구에게 부탁하는 것인지 확인하세요.

❷ 선택지 내용을 확인한 후, 관련 단어들을 미리 떠올려 보세요.

❸ 오답 선택지 내용이 등장하는 경우가 있어요. 오답을 유도하는 함정일 뿐이니 정답으로 선택하지 않도록 주의하세요.

❹ 부탁할 때 자주 쓰이는 표현을 미리 익혀 두세요.
  기출 Would[Will] you ~? ~ 해주시겠어요?

여 안녕하세요, 박 선생님. 시간 있으신가요?
남 안녕, Sally. 무슨 일이니?
여 제 친구와 제가 그림 그리기 동아리를 시작하고 싶은데요. 저희를 지도해 주실 선생님을 찾고 있어요.
남 음, 그림 그리기 동아리에서 무엇을 하고 싶니?
여 저희는 일주일에 한 번 모여서 그림 그리는 연습을 하려고 계획하고 있어요. 또, 다양한 그림체를 보기 위해 미술관을 방문하려고 해요.
남 아주 훌륭한 계획 같구나.
여 그러면 박 선생님, 저희 동아리 지도 교사가 되어 주시겠어요?
남 알겠다. 기꺼이 그렇게 하마.

⭐ 주요 표현

So, could you attend the meeting instead of me? 그래서, 저 대신에 회의에 참석해 주실 수 있나요?

Could you put one of these posters on the community center board for me? 이 포스터 중 하나를 지역 센터 게시판에 붙여 줄 수 있어?

I don't think it's serious. Can you just bring me some ice for my arm? 심각하지 않은 것 같아요. 제 팔에 올려둘 얼음만 조금 가져다 줄래요?

Then, can you buy some oil from the supermarket? 그러면, 슈퍼마켓에서 기름만 좀 사다 줄래요?

Could you pass this letter to Susan for me? 이 편지를 Susan에게 전달해 줄래?

Could you choose the clothes for the play? 연극에 입을 옷을 골라 줄래?

Will you give them a ride to school for the next three days? 앞으로 3일 동안 그들을 학교까지 태워다 주시겠어요?

Can you make a list of participants for each game? 각 게임의 참가자들 목록을 만들어 줄래요?

대표 기출 문제

1. 다음을 듣고, 어떤 직업에 관한 설명인지 고르시오.

① 교사   ② 기자   ③ 의사

④ 건축가   ⑤ 소방관

×오답 함정 **O**정답 근거

W People who have this job ❷ **tell us about what's happening in the world.** When an event happens, they go to the site right away and **find out facts about the event.** They also **interview people** about events. Then they write articles for the Internet and newspapers, and **report on TV.**

❶ 선택지를 보고 관련 단어나 표현을 떠올려 보세요.
teach, students, report, write, news, treat, sick people, design, buildings, save, from a fire, fire truck

❷ 간접적으로 설명하는 내용으로 시작하다가 점차 후반에는 결정적인 정답 근거를 제시해요. 언급된 특징을 모두 종합하여 정답을 찾으세요.

여 이 직업을 가진 사람들은 우리에게 세상에서 무슨 일이 일어나는지 알려 줍니다. 한 사건이 발생하면 그들은 그 현장에 가서 사건에 대한 사실을 알아냅니다. 그들은 사건에 대해 사람들을 인터뷰하기도 합니다. 그러고 나서 인터넷과 신문에 싣기 위해 기사를 작성하고 TV에서 보도합니다.

2. 다음을 듣고, 무엇에 관한 설명인지 고르시오.

① 리모컨   ② 이어폰   ③ 손전등

④ 에어컨   ⑤ 텔레비전

×오답 함정 **O**정답 근거

W This is a very useful device. We can ❷ **hold it in one hand very easily.** It is usually **long and thin with some buttons on it.** With this, we can **control another device from a distance without touching it.** For example, we can **turn on** an air-conditioner or **change the channels of a TV.** We simply **point to the other device** with it and **push buttons to control** that device.

❶ 선택지를 보고 관련 단어나 표현을 떠올려 보세요.
hold, hand, buttons, ear, listen, light, carry, cool, dry, screen, programs

❷ 언급되는 정답 근거를 들으면서 오답을 걸러내세요.
hold it in one hand very easily
→ ④, ⑤ 오답
control another device from a distance
→ ②, ③ 오답

여 이것은 매우 유용한 기구입니다. 우리는 이것을 한 손에 아주 쉽게 잡을 수 있습니다. 그것은 보통 여러 버튼을 가지고 있으며, 길고 얇습니다. 이것으로 우리는 또 다른 장치를 만지지 않고 멀리서 조정할 수 있습니다. 예를 들면, 우리는 에어컨을 실행시키거나 TV의 채널을 바꿀 수 있습니다. 우리는 단지 그것으로 다른 장치를 가리키고 조정하기 위해 버튼을 누릅니다.

🎖 대표 기출 문제

다음을 듣고, 두 사람의 대화가 <u>어색한</u> 것을 고르시오.

①   ②   ✓③   ④   ⑤

✗ 오답 함정   ○ 정답 근거

① **W**   Are you ready for the dance festival next week?

   M   Yes. I'm very excited about it.

② **W**   Is it okay to take pictures here?

   M   Sure, but not with a flash.

③ **W**   Wow! **That green color looks really nice on you!**

   M   ❶ **The park is next to City Hall.**

     → 초록색이 잘 어울린다는 말에 이어서 공원의 위치를 설명하는 응답은 어색해요.

④ **W**   How's the weather going to be this weekend?

   M   It's going to be sunny all weekend.

⑤ **W**   Hey, what's the matter? You look sad.

   M   I lost my cell phone.

❶ '질문-대답'으로 이루어진 대화가 등장하거나, 평서문으로 일반적인 대화 내용이 등장해요.

질문 또는 평서문에 등장하는 중심 내용에서 벗어난 응답이 어색한 대화예요.

① 여   다음 주에 댄스 축제에 갈 준비됐니?
   남   응. 정말 기대돼.
② 여   여기서 사진을 찍어도 되나요?
   남   네, 그런데 플래시는 터뜨리지 마세요.
③ 여   와! 그 초록색이 너하고 정말 잘 어울려!
   남   공원은 시청 옆에 있습니다.
④ 여   이번 주말 날씨는 어떤가요?
   남   주말 내내 화창할 거예요.
⑤ 여   얘, 무슨 일 있니? 너 슬퍼 보여.
   남   내 휴대전화를 잃어버렸어.

⭐ 주요 표현

평서문	A: You have so many plants in your house. 당신 집에는 식물들이 정말 많군요. B: Yes. I like growing plants. 네. 저는 식물 기르는 것을 좋아해요. A: I heard that John had a car accident yesterday. 어제 John이 차 사고가 났다고 들었어. B: Really? I'm sorry to hear that. 정말? 그 소식을 듣게 되어 유감이네.
질문-대답	A: Is it possible for you to join the race? 너 경주에 참가할 수 있니? B: I'm not sure. My leg still hurts. 잘 모르겠어요. 아직 다리가 아파서요. A: How long will it take to get to Busan? 부산에 가는 데 얼마나 걸릴까요? B: I think it'll take about two hours by car. 차로는 약 두 시간 정도 걸릴 것 같아요.
부탁, 제안	A: Can you take care of my dog this afternoon? 오늘 오후에 우리 개 좀 돌봐 줄래? B: I'm afraid I can't. 안 될 것 같아. A: Why don't we get some rest? 우리 좀 쉴까? B: That sounds great! 그거 좋겠다! A: Would you like a cup of coffee? 커피 한 잔 하시겠어요? B: No, thanks. I've already had some. 괜찮아요. 이미 좀 마셨어요.

유형 10 한 일·할 일 파악

🏅 대표 기출 문제

1. 대화를 듣고, ① 여자가 어제 한 일로 가장 적절한 것을 고르시오.

② ① 친구 만나기 　 ✓② 이삿짐 정리하기 　 ③ 택배 보내기

④ 여행 가방 꾸리기 　 ⑤ 가구 구입하기

✗오답 함정 　O정답 근거

M　Lisa, you look tired.

W　Hi, Hojin. I was so busy yesterday.

M　Oh, what did you do?

W　You know I moved into a new house, right?

M　Yeah, I remember. That was a week ago.

W　I didn't ③ **have time to organize my things** when I
moved, but I finally **did it yesterday.**
　　➜ 정리할 시간이 없었는데 어제 드디어 했다고 해요.

M　Oh, why didn't you call me to ask for help?

W　Well, I didn't want to bother you, but thanks for the offer.

---

① 누가, 언제 한 일을 묻고 있는 지 확인하세요.
여자, yesterday

② 선택지 내용을 영어로 떠올려 보세요.
met friends, organized, sent packages,
packed, bought, furniture

③ 지시문에서 묻고 있는 때는 어제이므로,
yesterday가 등장할 때까지 여자의 말에 집중
하세요.

남　Lisa, 너 피곤해 보인다.
여　안녕, 호진아. 나 어제 너무 바빴어.
남　아, 무엇을 했는데?
여　내가 새 집으로 이사 간 거 알고 있지, 그렇지?
남　응, 기억해. 일주일 전이였잖아.
여　이사했을 때 내 물건들을 정리할 시간이 없었는데, 어
제 마침내 정리를 다 했어.
남　아, 왜 나한테 전화해서 도움을 요청하지 않았니?
여　음, 널 귀찮게 하고 싶지 않았거든. 제안해 줘서 고마워.

---

2. 대화를 듣고, ① 남자가 할 일로 가장 적절한 것을 고르시오.

② ✓① 음식 만들기 　 ② 케이크 사기 　 ③ 물건 환불하기

④ 선물 포장하기 　 ⑤ 식당 예약하기

✗오답 함정 　O정답 근거

W　Hi, Jiho! What did you buy?

M　Hi, Kate! I ③ **bought** some tomatoes and mushrooms to
make spaghetti.

W　You really like spaghetti, don't you?

M　Actually, this time, it's not just for me. ④ **I'm going to**
cook for my mom.
　　➜ 요리할 예정이라고 해요.

W　Is it a special day for her?

M　Yes, today is her birthday and ④ **I'll cook for her this**
evening. ➜ 이유를 설명하면서 남자가 할 일에 대해 한 번 더 말하네요.

W　I hope she likes your food.

---

① 누구의 할 일을 묻는지 확인하세요.

② 선택지 내용을 영어로 떠올려 보세요.
make food, buy[get] a cake, refund,
wrap gifts, make a reservation

③ 선택지의 일부 내용이 대화에 등장해요. 오답 함
정에 빠지지 않도록 유의하세요.

④ 미래를 나타내는 표현이나 조동사를 사용하여
할 일을 표현하기도 하지만, 의무를 나타내는 표
현으로 앞으로 할 일을 표현하기도 해요.

여　안녕, 지호야! 무엇을 샀니?
남　안녕, Kate! 나는 스파게티를 만들려고 토마토하고 버
섯을 좀 샀어.
여　너는 정말로 스파게티를 좋아하는구나, 그렇지 않니?
남　사실 이번에는 나만을 위한 게 아니야. 우리 엄마를 위
해서 요리를 하려고 해.
여　그분에게 특별한 날이니?
남　응, 오늘이 엄마의 생신이어서 오늘 저녁에 요리해 드
릴 거야.
여　너희 엄마가 네 요리를 마음에 들어 하셨으면 좋겠네.

유형 11 위치 찾기, 도표 정보 파악

🎖 대표 기출 문제

1. 다음 주차장 배치도를 보면서 대화를 듣고, 두 사람이 선택할 주차 구역을 고르시오.

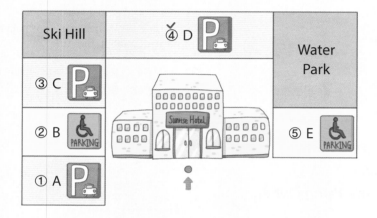

*✗오답 함정 *○정답 근거

W Honey, let's stop at this sign to see where to park.

M Okay. Well, how about ❷ parking area B?

W **We can't.** Parking area B is **for the disabled.**

M Oh, I didn't see that. Then, we cannot park in parking area E, either.

W You're right. How about ❸ **parking near the ski hill**?

M **Good idea.** It'll be easier for us to carry our skis.

W Right, but there are still two options.

M You said you'd like to swim, too. We'd better choose the parking area **closest to the water park.**

W Perfect.

---

❶ 배치도에서 선택지가 있는 위치를 확인하고, 위치 기준을 확인하세요.
Ski Hill, Water Park

❷ 제안에 이어지는 응답을 확인하여, 정답인지 아닌지를 파악해야 해요. 오답을 걸러내면서 정답을 찾아보세요.
parking area B는 장애인 전용
➔ ②, ⑤는 오답임을 알 수 있어요.

❸ 새로 언급되는 정보를 통해 정답을 조금씩 좁혀가세요.
near the ski hill ➔ ① 오답
closest to the water park ➔ ③ 오답

여 여보, 이 표지판을 보고 어디에 주차할지 확인해요.
남 알겠어요. 음, B 주차 구역에 주차하는 게 어때요?
여 그럴 수 없어요. B 주차 구역은 장애인 전용이에요.
남 아, 그걸 못 봤네요. 그러면 E 주차 구역에도 주차할 수 없겠네요.
여 맞아요. 스키 언덕 근처에 주차하는 건 어때요?
남 좋은 생각이에요. 우리가 스키를 가지고 다니기도 훨씬 편할 거예요.
여 맞아요, 그런데 여전히 두 가지 선택 사항이 남았어요.
남 당신이 수영도 하고 싶다고 했잖아요. 워터 파크에 가장 가까운 주차 구역을 선택하는 게 좋을 것 같아요.
여 아주 좋아요.

2. 다음 표를 보면서 대화를 듣고, 두 사람이 관람할 쇼를 고르시오.

	Show	Length	Time
①	Magic show	1 hour	12:00 p.m.
②	Magic show	2 hours	3:00 p.m.
③	Animal show	1 hour	12:00 p.m.
④	Animal show	2 hours	1:00 p.m.
⑤	Animal show	1 hour	3:00 p.m.

× 오답 함정 ○ 정답 근거

M Sarah, which show do you want to see?

W How about ② an animal show? I love animals more than magic.

M Okay. **Animal shows are better for me, too.** Then, which one would you like to see?

W Well, wouldn't a two-hour show be too long for us?

M I agree. There are one-hour shows at 12 p.m. and 3 p.m.

W It's 11:30 a.m. now. Why don't we have lunch first and go to the show after 2 p.m.?

M Sounds great! Let's see the show after lunch.

---

① 도표 안에 주어진 정보를 확인하면서 이어질 대화의 내용을 예상해 보세요.

② 대화의 진행은 도표에 나열된 순서대로 진행되고 있어요. 선택되지 않는 항목들을 하나씩 제거해 보면서 정답을 조금씩 좁혀가세요.

여자는 Animal show를 제안했고, 남자도 그게 더 낫다고 응답했으니, 두 사람은 Animal show를 관람할 거예요. ➡ ①, ② 오답

두 시간 쇼는 너무 길어서 한 시간 쇼를 보기로 했어요. ➡ ④ 오답

점심을 먼저 먹자는 여자의 제안에 남자가 동의했어요. ➡ ③ 오답

남 Sarah, 어떤 쇼를 보고 싶니?
여 동물 쇼는 어때? 난 마술보다는 동물이 더 좋거든.
남 알겠어. 동물 쇼가 나한테도 더 좋아. 그러면 어떤 걸 보고 싶어?
여 음, 두 시간 쇼는 우리한테 너무 길지 않을까?
남 나도 동의해. 한 시간 쇼는 오후 12시랑 3시에 있어.
여 지금 오전 11시 30분이야. 우리 먼저 점심을 먹고 오후 2시 이후에 있는 쇼를 보는 게 어때?
남 좋은 것 같아! 점심 먹은 후에 쇼를 보자.

대표 기출 문제

1. 대화를 듣고, 여자의 마지막 말에 대한 남자의 응답으로 가장 적절한 것을 고르시오.

Man: _____

❶ ① I'm really sorry to hear that.
② You'll be a great movie director.
③ There's nothing to get angry about.
④ You can trust yourself and go for it.
✓⑤ I'll upload videos mostly on passing skills.

✕오답 함정 ○정답 근거

W Summer vacation is coming. Are you going to play soccer during this vacation, too?

M Well, I'll play soccer a lot, but I have another plan as well.

W Oh, what is it?

M I'm going to make videos to teach soccer skills and upload them online.

W Sounds great. I think you can make useful content since you know so much about soccer.

M Yeah, I want to share how to play soccer well using my videos.

W ❷ What skills will you especially focus on?

M _____

❶ 선택지가 영문으로 제시되기 때문에 미리 훑어 보는 것이 중요해요.

❷ 마지막 말이 의문사 의문문일 경우, 의문사는 결정적인 정답 근거예요.
축구를 좋아하는 남자의 방학 계획에 대해 설명하는 상황이에요. 어떤 기술인지 묻고 있으므로, 이어지는 응답에서 어떤 기술인지 설명하는 내용이 등장해야 해요.

여 여름 방학이 오고 있어. 이번 방학에도 축구를 할 거니?
남 글쎄, 축구를 많이 할 건데, 다른 계획도 있어.
여 아, 그게 뭔데?
남 축구 기술을 가르치는 영상을 만들어서 온라인에 올릴 거야.
여 좋은 생각이다. 너는 축구에 대해 아는 게 많으니까 유용한 내용을 만들 거라고 생각해.
남 응, 내 영상을 활용해서 축구를 하는 법을 공유할 거야.
여 특히 어떤 기술에 중점을 둘 거니?
남 _____

① 정말 유감이야.
② 너는 훌륭한 영화감독이 될 거야.
③ 화낼 이유가 전혀 없어.
④ 너는 너 자신을 믿고 도전하면 돼.
⑤ 나는 주로 패스 기술에 대한 영상을 올릴 거야.

2. 대화를 듣고, 남자의 마지막 말에 대한 여자의 응답으로 가장 적절한 것을 고르시오.

Woman: _____

1 ① You should take a walk with your dog every day.

✓② Thanks for telling me. I'll apply for it right now.

③ Great. I'm looking forward to my birthday.

④ Please tell me where you found my cat.

⑤ I'm really sorry. It was all my fault.

1 선택지를 훑어보고 어떤 내용의 대화가 이어질지 예상해 보세요.

2 전체 대화 흐름을 통해, 상황을 정확하게 파악하여 마지막 말에 대한 응답을 찾는 것이 중요해요.

✗오답 함정 o 정답 근거

M Bella! Read this! The animal care center needs someone to work with their animals now.

W Is that so? **2** **I've always wanted a job like that. Can I see it?**
　　　　　　　→ 늘 관심이 있었다고 말해요.

M Here you go. You've done volunteer work feeding animals before, right?

W Yes. I also participated in an animal care workshop to learn more about them.

M Really? Then your experience will help you get the job.

W I hope so. **I'm sure I can look after the animals well.**

M This will be the perfect job! **But applications close**

tomorrow. → 대화를 통해, 여자는 매우 관심이 있다는 걸 알 수 있어요.
　　　　　내일이 지원 마감이면 오늘이나 지금 지원하겠다는 내용이 이어져야 해요.

W _____

남 Bella! 이걸 읽어봐! 지금 동물 돌봄 센터에서 동물들과 일할 사람이 필요한가 봐.

여 그래? 나는 늘 그런 일을 하고 싶었어. 그걸 좀 봐도 될까?

남 여기 있어. 너는 전에 동물들에게 먹이를 주는 봉사활동을 한 적이 있었지, 그렇지?

여 응. 나는 그것에 대해 더 배우려고 동물 돌봄 워크숍에도 참가했었어.

남 정말? 그럼 네 경험이 그 일자리를 얻는 데 도움이 될 거야.

여 그랬으면 좋겠어. 내가 동물들을 잘 돌볼 거라 확신해.

남 아주 딱 맞는 직업이 될 거야! 그런데 등록이 내일 마감이네.

여 _____

① 너는 매일 너희 집 개를 산책시켜야 해.
② 알려 줘서 고마워. 지금 당장 지원할게.
③ 잘됐다. 내 생일만을 기다리고 있었어.
④ 내 고양이를 어디에서 찾았는지 말해 줘.
⑤ 정말 미안해. 모두 내 잘못이야.

🎖 대표 기출 문제

1. 대화를 듣고, ❶ 두 사람이 봉사 활동을 하기로 한 날짜를 고르시오.

❷① 5월 2일 ② 5월 9일 ③ 5월 16일
④ 5월 23일 ⑤ 5월 30일

✕오답 함정 ㅇ정답 근거

M Suji, have you decided where to volunteer?

W Not yet. I'm still thinking about it. What about you, Ben?

M I'm thinking of volunteering at a local recycling center on ❸ May 2nd. Would you like to join me?

W I'd love to, but I have to go see my dentist that day. How about May 16th?

M I have a family trip on May 16th. What about May 23rd?

W ❹ May 23rd works for me! Thanks, Ben.

❶ 지시문에서 묻고 있는 특정 정보가 무엇인지 확인하고 영어로 떠올려 보세요.
volunteer

❷ 선택지 내용을 확인한 후, 관련 단어들을 미리 떠올려 보세요.

❸ 대화를 들으면서 언급되는 날짜를 메모하세요.
May 2nd: 여자가 치과에 가야 하는 날
May 16th: 남자가 가족 여행 가는 날

❹ 두 사람이 같이 일정을 조율하는 상황이므로, 제안한 날짜에 이어지는 상대방의 응답을 꼭 확인한 후, 정답을 고르세요.

남 수지야, 어디서 봉사 활동할지 결정했니?
여 아직 안 했어. 아직도 생각 중이야. 너는 결정했니, Ben?
남 나는 5월 2일에 지역 재활용 센터에서 봉사 활동하려고 해. 나랑 같이 할래?
여 좋은데, 그날 치과에 가야 해. 5월 16일은 어떠니?
남 나는 5월 16일에 가족 여행이 있어. 5월 23일은 어떠니?
여 5월 23일은 가능해! 고마워, Ben.

---

2. 대화를 듣고, ❶ 여자가 무용실을 사용할 요일을 고르시오.

❷① 월요일 ② 화요일 ③ 수요일
④ 목요일 ⑤ 금요일

✕오답 함정 ㅇ정답 근거

W Hello, Mr. Thompson. I'd like to use the dancing room after school next week.

M Okay. Which day do you need the room?

W Is it available ❸ on Monday?

M No, sorry. The school band practices every Monday. How about next Tuesday?
➜ 월요일에는 학교 밴드 연습이 있어서 화요일을 제안하네요.

W I'm afraid I can't. Is it free on Thursday?
➜ 여자가 안 된다고 하면서 목요일을 물어봐요.

M Let me see. [Pause] Yes, you can use it on Thursday.

W Great. I'll use it then. Thank you.
➜ 그때 사용하겠다고 여자가 말하네요.

❶ 지시문에서 묻고 있는 특정 정보가 무엇인지 확인하고 영어로 떠올려 보세요.

❷ 선택지 내용을 확인한 후, 관련 단어들을 미리 떠올려 보세요.

❸ 오답을 유도하는 내용이 등장하기도 해요. 이어지는 응답에서 오답인지, 정답인지 꼭 확인하세요.

여 안녕하세요, Thompson 선생님. 다음 주 방과 후에 무용실을 사용하고 싶어서요.
남 그래. 무슨 요일에 무용실이 필요하니?
여 월요일에 가능한가요?
남 미안하지만 안 되는구나. 학교 밴드 연습이 매주 월요일에 있거든. 다음 주 화요일은 어떠니?
여 그날은 안 될 것 같아요. 목요일에는 가능할까요?
남 어디 보자. [잠시 후] 그래, 목요일에 사용해도 돼.
여 잘됐네요. 그럼 그날 사용할게요. 감사합니다.

대표 기출 문제

다음 상황 설명을 듣고, ❶ Amy가 소년에게 할 말로 가장 적절한 것을 고르시오.

Amy: _____

❷ ① Can you stop kicking my seat?
② Which team won the soccer match?
③ Are you interested in being a director?
④ Why don't you turn off your cell phone?
⑤ How long does it take to finish a report?

✕오답 함정 ○정답 근거

W Amy is at the ❸ **theater** to watch a movie. Not long after the movie starts, a boy sitting behind her starts kicking the back of her seat. At first, she waits for him to stop, but he keeps doing it. So, she wants to ❹ **ask him to stop kicking her seat.** In this situation, what would Amy most likely say to the boy?

→ 여자가 소년에게 그만하라고 말하고 싶어 하는 상황이에요.

❶ 지시문에서 누가 누구에게 할 말인지 확인하세요.

❷ 선택지에 등장하는 내용을 훑어보고 어떤 상황일지 미리 예상해 보세요.

❸ 담화에 등장하는 일부 단어를 활용한 오답 선택지가 있어요. 전체 상황 파악이 가장 중요하니, 일부 내용만 듣고 섣불리 정답으로 선택하지 않도록 하세요.

❹ 상황에 대한 설명이 이어지다가 후반부에 결정적인 정답 근거가 등장해요.

여 Amy는 영화를 보기 위해 극장에 있다. 영화가 시작하고 얼마 지나지 않아, 그녀의 뒤에 앉은 한 소년이 그녀의 좌석 뒤쪽을 발로 차기 시작한다. 처음에 그녀는 그가 멈추기를 기다리지만 그는 계속 발로 찬다. 그래서 그녀는 그에게 좌석을 그만 차라고 요청하려고 한다. 이러한 상황에서 Amy가 소년에게 할 말로 적절한 것은 무엇인가?

Amy _____

① 내 좌석 좀 그만 차 줄래요?
② 어느 팀이 축구 경기에서 이겼나요?
③ 감독이 되는 것에 관심이 있나요?
④ 휴대폰을 꺼 주실래요?
⑤ 과제를 끝내는 데 얼마나 걸리나요?

주요 표현

상황 설명		상황에 적절한 말
He wants to ask the girl to be quiet. 그는 그 여자아이에게 조용히 해달라고 요청하고 싶어 한다.	→	Could you be quiet, please? 조용히 해주시겠어요?
Crystal decides to tell Brian not to be late for practice again. Crystal은 Brian에게 다시는 연습에 늦지 말라고 말하기로 결심한다.	→	Don't be late for practice again. 다시는 연습에 늦지 마.
He decides to call Sally and suggest that she take warm clothes. 그는 Sally에게 전화해서 따뜻한 옷을 가져올 것을 제안하기로 결심한다.	→	Why don't you take a warm jacket with you? 따뜻한 재킷을 가져가는 게 어때?
She decides to ask Mr. Jung where the music room is. 그녀는 정 선생님에게 음악실이 어디에 있는지 묻기로 결심한다.	→	Could you tell me where the music room is? 음악실이 어디에 있는지 알려 주시겠어요?
He wants to ask if he could get his money back. 그는 그의 돈을 돌려받을 수 있는지 묻고 싶어 한다.	→	I'm sorry, but I want to get a refund. 죄송하지만, 전 환불하고 싶어요.
Susan would like to ask if he is the owner of the wallet. Susan은 그가 지갑의 주인인지 묻고 싶어 한다.	→	Excuse me, are you looking for your wallet? 실례합니다. 혹시 지갑을 찾고 계신가요?

PART. 02

Listening Q

^^^

중학영어듣기 모의고사

실전 모의고사

실제 시험과 동일한 실전 모의고사 20회로 문제 풀이 감각을 익히고,
받아쓰기 훈련으로 듣기 실력 UP!

실전 모의고사 **01**

점수 /20

---

01 대화를 듣고, 남자가 구입할 머리핀을 고르시오.

①   ②   ③

④   ⑤

02 대화를 듣고, 남자가 여자에게 부탁한 일로 가장 적절한 것을 고르시오.

① 책 추천해 주기　　② 숙제 도와주기
③ 차로 데려다주기　　④ 함께 쇼핑하기
⑤ 점심 식사 준비하기

03 다음 그림의 상황에 가장 적절한 대화를 고르시오.

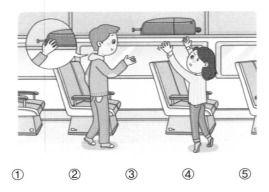

① 　② 　③ 　④ 　⑤

04 대화를 듣고, 영화가 시작하는 시각을 고르시오.

① 3:30 p.m.　② 4:30 p.m.　③ 5:30 p.m.
④ 6:30 p.m.　⑤ 7:30 p.m.

05 대화를 듣고, 남자가 구입한 차표에 관해 언급되지 않은 것을 고르시오.

① 목적지　② 출발 시각　③ 소요 시간
④ 왕복 여부　⑤ 가격

06 대화를 듣고, 두 사람이 대화하는 장소로 가장 적절한 곳을 고르시오.

① 공원　　② 꽃가게　　③ 체육관
④ 식당　　⑤ 스포츠 용품점

07 다음을 듣고, 두 사람의 대화가 어색한 것을 고르시오.

①　　②　　③　　④　　⑤

08 대화를 듣고, 여자가 남자에게 부탁한 일로 가장 적절한 것을 고르시오.

① 잔디 깎기　　② 옷 정리하기
③ 가방 만들어 주기　　④ 식물에 물 주기
⑤ 미술 숙제 도와주기

09 다음을 듣고, 무엇에 관한 안내 방송인지 고르시오.

① 할인 판매　　② 영업시간
③ 문화센터 등록　　④ 주차비 정산
⑤ 분실물 습득

10 대화를 듣고, 남자가 지불할 금액을 고르시오.

① $15　　② $17　　③ $22
④ $25　　⑤ $27

11 대화를 듣고, 남자가 할 일로 가장 적절한 것을 고르시오.

① 딸 데리러 가기
② 여행 가방 찾기
③ 도시락 싸기
④ 제주도 날씨 알아보기
⑤ 세탁소에서 옷 찾아오기

12 다음을 듣고, 불꽃놀이 축제(Fireworks Festival)에 관해 언급되지 않은 것을 고르시오.

① 개최 날짜   ② 참가국 수   ③ 개최 장소
④ 교통편   ⑤ 입장료

13 다음 표를 보면서 대화를 듣고, 두 사람이 선택할 등산로를 고르시오.

	Course	Difficulty	Reach the Top	Hiking Time
①	A	Steep and rough	○	1 hr. and 30 min.
②	B	Gentle	○	3 hrs. and 30 min.
③	C	Gentle	×	2 hrs.
④	D	Steep and rough	×	45 min.
⑤	E	Gentle	○	2 hrs. and 30 min.

14 다음을 듣고, 무엇에 관한 설명인지 고르시오.

① 천둥   ② 번개   ③ 해일
④ 무지개   ⑤ 허리케인

15 대화를 듣고, 여자가 대화 직후에 할 일로 가장 적절한 것을 고르시오.

① 차 마시기   ② 선물 포장하기
③ 엄마에게 전화하기   ④ 감사 카드 만들기
⑤ 휴대전화 케이스 사기

16 대화를 듣고, 여자가 치과를 예약한 시각을 고르시오.

① 10 a.m.   ② 11 a.m.   ③ 12 p.m.
④ 1 p.m.   ⑤ 2 p.m.

17 대화를 듣고, 남자의 마지막 말에 대한 여자의 응답으로 가장 적절한 것을 고르시오.

Woman: _____

① Thanks. That's very kind of you.
② Right. I had a math test yesterday.
③ Yes. I have been to the history museum.
④ Great. How about going to the museum?
⑤ Sorry, I have other plans this afternoon.

18 대화를 듣고, 여자의 마지막 말에 대한 남자의 응답으로 가장 적절한 것을 고르시오.

Man: _____

① I agree. Let's take a taxi.
② Okay, I'll do that. See you soon.
③ How about meeting at the theater?
④ No. I don't think the subway will be faster.
⑤ Good idea! Let's go to the movies tonight.

19 대화를 듣고, 남자의 마지막 말에 대한 여자의 응답으로 가장 적절한 것을 고르시오.

Woman: _____

① That's great. How much is it?
② I'd like to have it wrapped, please.
③ You mean buy one and get one free?
④ Good. Can I use this discount coupon?
⑤ Okay, I understand. Thank you for your help.

20 다음 상황 설명을 듣고, Peter가 여자에게 할 말로 가장 적절한 것을 고르시오.

Peter: _____

① Please take my seat.
② Do you have the time?
③ Can I help you carry your bag?
④ You should get off at this station.
⑤ It will take over an hour by subway.

Dictation 01

◇ 다시 듣고, 빈칸에 들어갈 알맞은 단어를 써보세요.

정답 및 해설 p.2

01 그림 정보 파악

대화를 듣고, 남자가 구입할 머리핀을 고르시오.

① ② ③ ④ ⑤

W Mike, what are you going to buy?
M I'm looking for a hairpin for my sister.
W How about this one _____ _____ _____ _____?
M She already has one just like it. I think she wants something with crystals.
W Then, how about this heart-shaped one with a lot of _____ _____ _____ _____?
M Oh, that's really pretty. _____ _____ _____ the rose-shaped one with crystals.
W _____ _____. I'm sure she'll like it.

02 부탁 파악

대화를 듣고, 남자가 여자에게 부탁한 일로 가장 적절한 것을 고르시오.

① 책 추천해 주기 ② 숙제 도와주기
③ 차로 데려다 주기 ④ 함께 쇼핑하기
⑤ 점심 식사 준비하기

M Mom, are you busy this afternoon?
W Yes, I'm _____ _____ _____ _____. Why?
M Well, I want to go to Bandi Bookstore. I have to buy some books for my science homework.
W Do you want me to _____ _____ _____ the books?
M No. Actually, I just wanted you to _____ _____ _____ _____ there.
W Okay. How about leaving at 2? _____ _____ _____ there on my way to the mall.
M Okay. Thank you.

03 그림 상황에 적절한 대화 찾기

다음 그림의 상황에 가장 적절한 대화를 고르시오.

① ② ③ ④ ⑤

① M Did you pack your bag for the trip?
    W Sure. _____ _____ _____.
② M _____ _____ _____ _____ I sit here?
    W No, go ahead.
③ M May I help you to _____ _____ _____ _____?

W Thank you. You're so kind.

④ **M** Have you been waiting long?

W No, I just arrived a few minutes ago.

⑤ **M** Do you have _____ _____

_____ _____ this vacation?

W Yes, I'm planning to go backpacking for a month.

---

04 숫자 정보 파악 (시각)

대화를 듣고, 영화가 시작하는 시각을 고르시오.

① 3:30 p.m.　　② 4:30 p.m.
③ 5:30 p.m.　　④ 6:30 p.m.
⑤ 7:30 p.m.

🔊 **Listening Tip**

half에서 l은 소리가 안 나서 '해프'로 발음되며, 첫 단어의 끝 자음과 두 번째 단어의 첫 자음의 소리가 비슷할 경우 앞의 자음소리는 탈락되므로 past three는 '패스 뜨리'와 같이 발음되어요.

M What time is it, Mom?

W It's 🔊 half past 3. Why do you ask?

M Because I have to meet my friend at 4:30.

W Then you've _____ _____ _____

_____ . You'd better get ready.

M It's okay. I'm meeting him at the cafe near our house.

W You didn't forget that we're _____ _____

_____ _____ tonight, did you?

M Oh, right. What time _____ _____

_____ ?

W _____ _____ _____ 7:30 p.m.

Don't be late.

M Okay, I won't.

---

05 언급하지 않은 내용 찾기

대화를 듣고, 남자가 구입한 차표에 관해 언급되지 않은 것을 고르시오.

① 목적지　　② 출발 시각
③ 소요 시간　　④ 왕복 여부
⑤ 가격

M I'd like a ticket for the 7 o'clock train to London.

W I'm sorry, the 7 o'clock train to London is delayed

_____ _____ .

M What time will that train arrive?

W _____ _____ 30 minutes

late and leave at 7:40.

M Then can you give me a ticket _____

_____ _____ ?

W Do you want a one-way ticket or a round-trip ticket?

M A one-way ticket, please.

W Here is your ticket, _____ _____

_____ $25.

M Okay. Here you are.

06 장소 추론

대화를 듣고, 두 사람이 대화하는 장소로 가장 적절한 곳을 고르시오.

① 공원   ② 꽃가게   ③ 체육관
④ 식당   ⑤ 스포츠 용품점

M The weather is perfect for a picnic.

W It is. Let's place a mat _____ _____ _____.

M Okay. There are a lot of people here today.

W Yes. _____ _____ _____ _____ crowded on weekends.

M Well, it really is a beautiful place _____ _____ _____ _____ and flowers.

W Yes. Look! There are some children riding bicycles _____ _____ _____.

M Let's ride bicycles next week. I brought badminton rackets today. Would you like to play?

W Sure. That sounds fun.

07 어색한 대화 찾기

다음을 듣고, 두 사람의 대화가 어색한 것을 고르시오.

①   ②   ③   ④   ⑤

① W Did you study a lot for the tests?

   M I _____ _____ _____, but I'm still worried.

② W _____ _____ _____ _____ the milk and cheese?

   M You should call her now. She is around here somewhere.

③ W What are you going to have for lunch?

   M Well, I _____ _____ _____.

④ W How can I get to World Cup Stadium?

   M You can take the subway.

⑤ W *I wonder why Brian isn't answering his cell phone.

   M He said _____ _____ _____ _____.

> ✻ **교육부 지정 의사소통 기능: 궁금증 표현하기**   동(이) 기|천(이) 4|미 4|능(양) 5|Y(송) 7|금 6|다 5
>
> **I wonder ~. 나는 ~가 궁금해.**
> • **I wonder** why he is running. 나는 그가 왜 뛰고 있는지 궁금해.
> • **I wonder** where the bus stop is. 나는 버스 정류장이 어디에 있는지 궁금해.

08 부탁 파악

대화를 듣고, 여자가 남자에게 부탁한 일로 가장 적절한 것을 고르시오.

① 잔디 깎기   ② 옷 정리하기
③ 가방 만들어 주기   ④ 식물에 물 주기
⑤ 미술 숙제 도와주기

W Mason, are you busy right now?

M I'm still doing my art homework.

W Do you mean making a bag with old clothes?

M Yes. I think I'll be able to _____ _____

_____ _____.

W Can you help me _____ _____

_____ _____ after

finishing your homework?

M Do you want me to cut the grass?

W No, _____ _____ _____ of the

plants.

M Okay, I will.

09 주제 추론

다음을 듣고, 무엇에 관한 안내 방송인지 고르시오.

① 할인 판매   ② 영업시간
③ 문화 센터 등록   ④ 주차비 정산
⑤ 분실물 습득

W Attention all shoppers! We _____ _____

_____. It is light blue and there are some books and

a tablet PC in it. We found it _____ _____

_____ _____ on the 5th floor. If

_____ _____ _____

_____, please come to the customer service center

on the 9th floor. We hope you're enjoying your shopping.

Thank you.

10 숫자 정보 파악 (금액)

대화를 듣고, 남자가 지불할 금액을 고르시오.

① $15   ② $17   ③ $22
④ $25   ⑤ $27

M Excuse me. What time does the _Avengers_ movie start?

W There is a showing at 3:00 and another at 5:00.

M How much are the tickets?

W _____ _____ _____ $10 and

children's tickets are $7.

M I need tickets for 2 _____ _____

_____ _____ for the 5:00 showing.

W Okay, _____ _____ _____ $27 in

total.

M Can I use this discount coupon?

W Sure. _____ _____ _____ $5 off

the total.

M Great. Here you are.

대화를 듣고, 남자가 할 일로 가장 적절한 것을 고르시오.

① 딸 데리러 가기
② 여행 가방 찾기
③ 도시락 싸기
④ 제주도 날씨 알아보기
⑤ 세탁소에서 옷 찾아오기

M Honey, something smells good! What are you making?

W I'm making Judy's lunch _____ _____ _____ _____ tomorrow.

M She's going to Jeju-do, isn't she?

W Yes. She's very excited about the trip. Oh, can I ask a favor?

M Sure. What do I have to do?

W Would you _____ _____ _____ _____ from the cleaner's? Judy needs it for her trip.

M Okay, I will go and _____ _____ _____ .

다음을 듣고, 불꽃놀이 축제(Fireworks Festival)에 관해 언급되지 않은 것을 고르시오.

① 개최 날짜 ② 참가국 수 ③ 개최 장소
④ 교통편   ⑤ 입장료

M Hello, everyone. I'm happy to inform you about the annual Fireworks Festival. This year, it _____ _____ _____ _____ October 5. More than 30 nations _____ _____ _____ in the festival. You can enjoy the festival at Yeouido Hangang Park from 2 to 9:30 p.m. You can watch amazing fireworks and _____ _____ _____ of street foods, too. There is _____ _____ _____ _____ the event. Come and enjoy the festival!

다음 표를 보면서 대화를 듣고, 두 사람이 선택할 등산로를 고르시오.

	Course	Difficulty	Reach the Top	Hiking Time
①	A	Steep and rough	○	1 hr. and 30 min.
②	B	Gentle	○	3 hrs. and 30 min.
③	C	Gentle	×	2 hrs.
④	D	Steep and rough	×	45 min.
⑤	E	Gentle	○	2 hrs. and 30 min.

M Look at the board. There are several courses to _____ _____ _____ .

W Oh, that's good. Which course is best for us?

M Well, I think we'd better not try the steep and rough courses.

W I agree. _____ _____ a gentle course.

M Okay. Do you want to reach the top?

W It'll be difficult, but I want to _____ _____ _____ of the mountain.

M So do I. But I don't want to _____ _____ _____ _____ 3 hours.

W Okay. Let's take this course.

다음을 듣고, 무엇에 관한 설명인지 고르시오.

① 천둥　② 번개　③ 해일
④ 무지개　⑤ 허리케인

W This is a kind of natural phenomenon. When there is a big storm, you will sometimes see this. It is a very _____ _____ in the sky. After this, you'll _____ _____ _____. This can be beautiful, but it _____ _____ _____ _____ because this is actually electricity. Every year, _____ _____ _____ by this and sometimes people are killed by this.

---

15 할 일 파악

대화를 듣고, 여자가 대화 직후에 할 일로 가장 적절한 것을 고르시오.

① 차 마시기
② 선물 포장하기
③ 엄마에게 전화하기
④ 감사 카드 만들기
⑤ 휴대전화 케이스 사기

W Eric, have you bought a present for Parents' Day?
M Of course. I got cell phone cases. How about you?
W I bought teacups. My parents like to _____ _____ _____ _____.
M I'm sure they will like them.
W Oh, I haven't made a thank-you card yet.
M Neither have I. _____ _____ _____ _____.
W That's right. I think _____ _____ _____ right now. I _____ _____ _____ _____ carnations after that.

---

16 숫자 정보 파악 (시각)

대화를 듣고, 여자가 치과를 예약한 시각을 고르시오.

① 10 a.m.　② 11 a.m.　③ 12 p.m.
④ 1 p.m.　⑤ 2 p.m.

[Telephone rings.]

M Thank you for calling Miller's Dental Clinic. How may I help you?
W Hello. This is Emily Blunt. I'd like to make an appointment on Tuesday.
M There is _____ _____ _____ _____ 11 a.m.
W I don't think I can make it at 11 a.m. How about the next day?

M Let me check. [Pause] You _____ _____ _____ _____ 10 a.m. if you'd like.

W I have an important meeting at that time. _____ _____ _____ in the afternoon.

M Then, how about at 2 p.m.?

W _____ _____ .

M All right. I'll see you then.

17 이어질 응답 찾기

대화를 듣고, 남자의 마지막 말에 대한 여자의 응답으로 가장 적절한 것을 고르시오.

Woman: _____

① Thanks. That's very kind of you.
② Right. I had a math test yesterday.
③ Yes. I have been to the history museum.
④ Great. How about going to the museum?
⑤ Sorry, I have other plans this afternoon.

W Minho, what are you doing?

M I'm reading a book about Korean history.

W Are you interested in history?

M Yes. History is _____ _____ _____ .

W Really? I don't like history. It's so boring.

M I like _____ _____ _____ _____ . What's your favorite subject?

W I like math the most. I enjoy _____ _____ _____ _____ .

M Oh, really? I'm bad at math. Can you help me _____ _____ _____ _____ after school?

18 이어질 응답 찾기

대화를 듣고, 여자의 마지막 말에 대한 남자의 응답으로 가장 적절한 것을 고르시오.

Man: _____

① I agree. Let's take a taxi.
② Okay, I'll do that. See you soon.
③ How about meeting at the theater?
④ No. I don't think the subway will be faster.
⑤ Good idea! Let's go to the movies tonight.

[Cell phone rings.]

M Hello.

W Hey, Steve, are you _____ _____ _____ _____ the theater?

M Yes, but the traffic is really heavy.

W What? Aren't you coming by subway?

M No, I'm coming by taxi. I took this taxi half an hour ago.

W Why did you take a taxi? The subway is _____ _____ _____ at this time of the day.

M I didn't know that. I thought a taxi _____ _____ _____ .

W Why don't you get out of the taxi now _____ _____ _____ _____ ? It will be faster.

19 이어질 응답 찾기

대화를 듣고, 남자의 마지막 말에 대한 여자의 응답으로 가장 적절한 것을 고르시오.

Woman: _____

① That's great. How much is it?
② I'd like to have it wrapped, please.
③ You mean buy one and get one free?
④ Good. Can I use this discount coupon?
⑤ Okay, I understand. Thank you for your help.

M Hello. May I help you?

W I'm just looking, thanks.

M All winter clothing is on sale _____ _____ _____ _____.

W Oh, really? Are these winter coats also on sale?

M Yes, they are on sale _____ _____ _____ _____.

W Hmm... I like this blue coat with a hood. Do you have it _____ _____ _____ _____?

M I'm sorry. That's _____ _____ _____. There isn't a lot left in stock because it's on sale.

20 상황에 적절한 말 찾기

다음 상황 설명을 듣고, Peter가 여자에게 할 말로 가장 적절한 것을 고르시오.

Peter: _____

① Please take my seat.
② Do you have the time?
③ Can I help you carry your bag?
④ You should get off at this station.
⑤ It will take over an hour by subway.

M Peter is on the subway and _____ _____ _____. Fortunately, he finds an empty seat and sits there. After a few minutes, an old woman with a heavy bag gets on the subway. The woman _____ _____ _____, and there are _____ _____ _____ for her. So, Peter decides to _____ _____ _____ to her. In this situation, what would Peter most likely say to the woman?

실전 모의고사 **02**

01 대화를 듣고, 여자가 구입할 거울을 고르시오.

02 대화를 듣고, 여자가 남자에게 부탁한 일로 가장 적절한 것을 고르시오.

① 파티 준비하기　　② 상자 운반하기
③ 생일 선물 고르기　④ 상자 잡아주기
⑤ 포장지 사다 주기

03 다음 그림의 상황에 가장 적절한 대화를 고르시오.

① 　② 　③ 　④ 　⑤

04 대화를 듣고, 남자의 경주가 끝나는 시각을 고르시오.

① 9:00 a.m. 　② 9:30 a.m. 　③ 10:00 a.m.
④ 10:30 a.m. 　⑤ 11:30 a.m.

05 대화를 듣고, 현장 학습에 관해 언급되지 않은 것을 고르시오.

① 교통편 　② 만나는 시각 　③ 입장료
④ 복장 　⑤ 준비물

06 대화를 듣고, 두 사람이 대화하는 장소로 가장 적절한 곳을 고르시오.

① 공항 　　② 기차역 　　③ 경찰서
④ 우체국 　⑤ 백화점

07 다음을 듣고, 두 사람의 대화가 어색한 것을 고르시오.

① 　　② 　　③ 　　④ 　　⑤

08 대화를 듣고, 남자가 여자에게 부탁한 일로 가장 적절한 것을 고르시오.

① 팬 미팅 함께 가기　　② 사인 받아 주기
③ 선생님께 연락하기　　④ 레슨 시간 변경하기
⑤ 바이올린 가르쳐 주기

09 다음을 듣고, 무엇에 관한 안내 방송인지 고르시오.

① 주말 날씨 　② 경기 취소 　③ 도로 상황
④ 야구팀 소개 　⑤ 태풍 피해 현황

10 대화를 듣고, 여자가 지불할 금액을 고르시오.

① $25 　　② $30 　　③ $40
④ $45 　　⑤ $50

11 대화를 듣고, 여자가 할 일로 가장 적절한 것을 고르시오.

① 식당 예약하기　　② 영화표 예매하기
③ 인터넷 쇼핑하기　　④ 보고서 작성하기
⑤ 스마트폰 수리 맡기기

12 다음을 듣고, 교내 미술 대회에 관해 언급되지 <u>않은</u> 것을 고르시오.

① 참가 대상　　② 작품 주제　　③ 작품 크기
④ 출품 마감일　　⑤ 수상자 상품

13 다음 표를 보면서 대화를 듣고, 두 사람이 선택할 꽃바구니를 고르시오.

	Flower Basket	Flower	Price	Size
①	A	Rose	$30	Small
②	B	Rose	$50	Large
③	C	Lily	$25	Small
④	D	Lily	$30	Medium
⑤	E	Lily	$40	Large

14 다음을 듣고, 무엇에 관한 설명인지 고르시오.

① 버스　　② 택시　　③ 기차
④ 지하철　　⑤ 비행기

15 대화를 듣고, 남자가 대화 직후에 할 일로 가장 적절한 것을 고르시오.

① 수영 강습 가기　　② 팬케이크 만들기
③ 숙제 끝마치기　　④ 저녁 식사하기
⑤ 방 청소하기

16 대화를 듣고, 남자가 여동생을 데리러 가야 할 시각을 고르시오.

① 6 p.m.　　② 7 p.m.　　③ 8 p.m.
④ 9 p.m.　　⑤ 10 p.m.

17 대화를 듣고, 여자의 마지막 말에 대한 남자의 응답으로 가장 적절한 것을 고르시오.

Man: _____

① Then you have to practice hard.
② Cheer up! You'll do better next time.
③ That's too bad. I'm sorry to hear that.
④ Great. I hope you have a great time there.
⑤ I'll take part in the English speech contest, too.

18 대화를 듣고, 남자의 마지막 말에 대한 여자의 응답으로 가장 적절한 것을 고르시오.

Woman: _____

① Green will be fine.
② I don't have paper to write on.
③ Can I use your colored pencils?
④ I watched the whole *Star Wars* series.
⑤ Right. My hobby is collecting figures.

19 대화를 듣고, 여자의 마지막 말에 대한 남자의 응답으로 가장 적절한 것을 고르시오.

Man: _____

① I can't wait to eat some pizza.
② Honestly, I'm not good at cooking.
③ Good idea. I like spicy Korean food!
④ I hope to visit the country someday.
⑤ No, I've never eaten Chinese food before.

20 다음 상황 설명을 듣고, Olivia가 Julia에게 할 말로 가장 적절한 것을 고르시오.

Olivia: Julia, _____

① let's try to get along from now on.
② you should clean up your things.
③ you'd better take a shower more often.
④ I promise that I'll be a good sister to you.
⑤ how about decorating our room with these things?

Dictation 02

◆ 다시 듣고, 빈칸에 들어갈 알맞은 단어를 써보세요.

정답 및 해설 p.9

---

01 그림 정보 파악

대화를 듣고, 여자가 구입할 거울을 고르시오.

① ② ③ ④ ⑤

M   Excuse me, would you like some help with mirrors?

W   Yes, I'd like to buy a mirror to _____ _____ _____ _____ in my room.

M   How about this round one? It's the most popular one.

W   It's too simple. I don't like shapes that _____ _____ _____ _____.

M   Then how about this egg-shaped one with lights _____ _____ _____?

W   Oh, it looks nice. I'll take it. Could you please _____ _____ _____ for me?

M   Sure.

---

02 부탁 파악

대화를 듣고, 여자가 남자에게 부탁한 일로 가장 적절한 것을 고르시오.

① 파티 준비하기
② 상자 운반하기
③ 생일 선물 고르기
④ 상자 잡아 주기
⑤ 포장지 사다 주기

M   Angela, what is in this box?

W   It's a birthday present for my dad. I need your help to wrap it.

M   Hmm... I'm _____ _____ _____ _____ that.

W   Don't worry. I'm going to _____ _____ _____ _____.

M   Oh, I see. What do you _____ _____ _____ _____?

W   Can you _____ _____ _____ while I wrap it with the paper?

M   Okay.

---

03 그림 상황에 적절한 대화 찾기

다음 그림의 상황에 가장 적절한 대화를 고르시오.

① ② ③ ④ ⑤

① W   How would you like your steak?

　 M   I'd like to have it medium rare, please.

② W   I'm _____ _____ _____ _____.

　 M   Me, too. Let's turn on the air conditioner.

③ W   Look at the castle-shaped 🔊ice sculpture.

　 M   Wow! _____ a

◀)) **Listening Tip**

동일한 자음이 연달아 나올 때는 하나는 탈락되어 발음되어요. 따라서 ice sculpture는 /아이스 스컬쳐/가 아니라 /아이스컬쳐/와 같이 발음되어요.

real castle.

④ W Do you want me to _____ _____

_____ _____ your drink?

M Yes, please.

⑤ W Would you like something to drink?

M Yes. I'd like _____ _____

_____ _____.

---

04 숫자 정보 파악 (시각)

대화를 듣고, 남자의 경주가 끝나는 시각을 고르시오.

① 9:00 a.m.   ② 9:30 a.m.
③ 10:00 a.m.   ④ 10:30 a.m.
⑤ 11:30 a.m.

W Hey, Mark. Are you running in tomorrow's race?

M Yes. Are you coming to see me?

W Of course! You begin at 9 o'clock, right?

M Actually, that's when the marathon starts. But the 10-kilometer _____ _____ _____ 9:30.

W Oh, I see. And how long _____ _____

_____ _____?

M We're only running 10 kilometers, so we'll _____

_____ _____ 2 hours.

W I see. Then do you want to do _____ _____

_____ _____?

M Sure. Let's go for lunch.

---

05 언급하지 않은 내용 찾기

대화를 듣고, 현장 학습에 관해 언급되지 <u>않은</u> 것을 고르시오.

① 교통편   ② 만나는 시각
③ 입장료   ④ 복장
⑤ 준비물

M I'm so excited about the field trip this Thursday.

W Me, too. We're going to the science park, right?

M Yes. Do you want to go there together?

W Sure. What's the best way _____ _____

_____?

M By subway. It's a 10-minute walk from City Hall Station.

W Okay. _____ _____ _____ 10 a.m. in front of the ticket office, right?

M Right. Well, do we have to wear _____

_____ _____ on that day?

W Yes. And *don't forget to bring _____

_____ and _____ _____.

M Okay.

＊ 교육부 지정 의사소통 기능: **상기시켜 주기**   능(김) 6 l 능(양) 7

Don't forget to ~. 반드시 ~해라, ~하는 거 잊지 마.
• **Don't forget to** put the lid on. 뚜껑을 반드시 닫아라.
• **Don't forget to** you bring the science book. 과학 책 가지고 오는 거 잊지 마.

06 장소 추론

대화를 듣고, 두 사람이 대화하는 장소로 가장 적절한 곳을 고르시오.

① 공항   ② 기차역   ③ 경찰서
④ 우체국   ⑤ 백화점

W Excuse me, sir. Do you need any help?

M I can't find my suitcase.

W _____ _____ _____

_____ _____?

M It was KO 747 from New York.

W Did you check the baggage claim area?

M Yes. I waited for my luggage _____ _____

_____ _____ more than 30 minutes.

W Oh, really? I'll check for you. *[Pause]* There were some problems with the baggage on that flight. So your suitcase will arrive on _____ _____ _____ from New York.

M I see. How long do I have to wait?

W It'll arrive in an hour.

07 어색한 대화 찾기

다음을 듣고, 두 사람의 대화가 <u>어색한</u> 것을 고르시오.

①   ②   ③   ④   ⑤

① M How about pizza or spaghetti for lunch?

W Sorry, I don't like _____ _____ _____.

② M This tennis match is really exciting.

W I feel _____ _____ _____.

③ M _____ _____ _____ _____ me with these bags?

W Don't forget to write your name on the bags.

④ M Do you have _____ _____ _____?

W Well, I want a striped shirt.

⑤ M I'm sorry, but ＊can you say that again?

W Okay. The number is 345-1234.

Can[Could] you say that again? 너는 다시 말해줄 수 있니?
A: Who's calling? 누구세요?
B: This is Brian. May I speak to Jenny? 저 Brian이에요. Jenny와 통화할 수 있을까요?
A: Sorry, **can you say that again?** I can't hear you.
죄송해요, 다시 말씀해주실래요? 잘 안 들리네요.

---

08 부탁 파악

대화를 듣고, 남자가 여자에게 부탁한 일로 가장 적절한 것을 고르시오.

① 팬 미팅 함께 가기
② 사인 받아 주기
③ 선생님께 연락하기
④ 레슨 시간 변경하기
⑤ 바이올린 가르쳐 주기

W Hey, Gary. Are you going to Black Pearl's fan meeting tomorrow?

M No, I can't. I have _____ _____ _____.

W Oh, that's too bad.

M Yes, I was really looking forward to it.

W Why don't you ask your teacher to _____ _____ _____ of the lesson?

M I already did, but my teacher said no. If possible, _____ _____ _____ _____ their autographs?

W Sure. I'll do that for you!

M Thanks so much.

---

09 주제 추론

다음을 듣고, 무엇에 관한 안내 방송인지 고르시오.

① 주말 날씨   ② 경기 취소
③ 도로 상황   ④ 야구팀 소개
⑤ 태풍 피해 현황

M Ladies and gentlemen, I have an announcement. There is a heavy typhoon coming this way. The weather report says it will bring a thunderstorm _____ _____ _____ _____. So, I'm sorry to tell you we have to _____ _____ _____ _____ between AB Tigers and KO Dragons today. Thank you for your understanding and patience. _____ _____ _____ _____.

---

10 숫자 정보 파악 (금액)

대화를 듣고, 여자가 지불할 금액을 고르시오.

① $25   ② $30   ③ $40
④ $45   ⑤ $50

M May I help you?

W Yes. How much is this shirt?

M The shirt is $25.

W Do you have the same shirt _____ _____ _____ _____?

M Yes, it comes in white, blue, green, and black.

W I'll take one white shirt and one blue shirt. Can I
_____ _____ _____ for these
shirts?

M Yes. You get 10 percent _____ _____
_____ _____ if you buy 2 shirts.

W Great. I'll pay by card.

---

11 할 일 파악

대화를 듣고, 여자가 할 일로 가장 적절한 것을 고르시오.

① 식당 예약하기   ② 영화표 예매하기
③ 인터넷 쇼핑하기   ④ 보고서 작성하기
⑤ 스마트폰 수리 맡기기

W Tom, did you _____ _____ _____
for tonight?

M No, I didn't. I was too busy.

W Have you decided which movie we are going to watch?

M Sorry, but I haven't done that, either.

W Hmm... Then I'll look for _____ _____
_____ to watch and get the tickets on my
smartphone.

M Thank you so much. I have to finish writing this report
_____ _____ _____.

W No problem. I have _____ _____
_____ now.

---

12 언급하지 않은 내용 찾기

다음을 듣고, 교내 미술 대회에 관해 언급되지 않은 것을 고르시오.

① 참가 대상   ② 작품 주제
③ 작품 크기   ④ 출품 마감일
⑤ 수상자 상품

W Hi, students! I'm pleased to announce the school art contest.
The contest is _____ _____
_____ _____ at our school. Participants
should create artwork that shows his or her dream. The
artwork _____ _____ _____ on
white paper with watercolors. Participants must hand in
their artworks to the school art club by May 15th. The top
3 winners _____ _____ _____
and tablet PCs will be _____ _____
_____ _____ them. Thank you for
listening.

13 도표 정보 파악

다음 표를 보면서 대화를 듣고, 두 사람이 선택할 꽃바구니를 고르시오.

Flower Basket	Flower	Price	Size
① A	Rose	$30	Small
② B	Rose	$50	Large
③ C	Lily	$25	Small
④ D	Lily	$30	Medium
⑤ E	Lily	$40	Large

W Paul, what should we buy for Grandma's birthday present?

M How about a flower basket? She loves flowers.

W That sounds good! _____ _____ _____ _____ roses and lilies.

M She has a lot of roses in her garden, so let's _____ _____ _____ _____.

W Okay. How much do we have?

M We only have $30. We have to choose the size.

W Let's _____ _____ _____ _____.

M Okay. I hope she loves our gift.

14 화제 추론

다음을 듣고, 무엇에 관한 설명인지 고르시오.
① 버스　　② 택시　　③ 기차
④ 지하철　　⑤ 비행기

M This is a type of public transportation. It's _____ _____ _____ _____ _____. The driver takes you _____ _____ _____ to go. You should _____ _____ _____ when you arrive at your destination. People call this a 'cab' in several countries, such as England and America. New York is _____ _____ _____ _____ cabs. You can call this through a smartphone app these days.

15 할 일 파악

대화를 듣고, 남자가 대화 직후에 할 일로 가장 적절한 것을 고르시오.
① 수영 강습 가기　　② 팬케이크 만들기
③ 숙제 끝마치기　　④ 저녁 식사하기
⑤ 방 청소하기

🔊 **Listening Tip**
can't의 t는 거의 발음되지 않으므로 can과 can't는 거의 똑같이 들려요. can은 /컨/과 같이 모음이 약하게 발음되는 반면 can't는 /캔ㅌ/와 같이 모음이 강하게 발음되는 것을 생각하며 구분해야 해요. 그리고 wait to와 같이 앞 단어의 끝 자음과 뒷 단어의 첫 자음이 같을 경우 하나는 탈락되어 /웨이투/로 발음됩니다.

M Mom, I'm so hungry. I 🔊 can't wait to eat until dinnertime.

W Well, _____ _____ _____ _____ go to your swimming lesson?

M No, it's Tuesday. I don't have any lessons today.

W Oh, that's right. So do you want _____ _____ _____ now?

M Yes. Can you make me some pancakes, please?

W No problem. But make sure that _____ _____ _____ while I'm cooking.

M Okay, _____ _____ _____.

16 숫자 정보 파악 (시각)

대화를 듣고, 남자가 여동생을 데리러 가야 할 시각을 고르시오.

① 6 p.m. ② 7 p.m. ③ 8 p.m.
④ 9 p.m. ⑤ 10 p.m.

W _____ _____ _____ the lecture about Korean films with me tonight?

M I'd love to go, but I'm not sure I can. What time does it start?

W It starts at 6 p.m. The speaker is a famous film director. He directed *Parasite*.

M That sounds really interesting, but I _____ _____ _____ my sister from the airport at 9.

W I'm sure the lecture _____ _____ _____ _____ 7:30.

M Okay. Then I _____ _____ _____.

W Great!

17 이어질 응답 찾기

대화를 듣고, 여자의 마지막 말에 대한 남자의 응답으로 가장 적절한 것을 고르시오.

Man: _____

① Then you have to practice hard.
② Cheer up! You'll do better next time.
③ That's too bad. I'm sorry to hear that.
④ Great. I hope you have a great time there.
⑤ I'll take part in the English speech contest, too.

M Mina, you look so happy.

W Oh, I am. I _____ _____ _____ in the speech contest.

M That's amazing. Congratulations! That's why you are happy.

W Well, that's not all. I have _____ _____ _____.

M What is it?

W A friend of mine in England _____ _____ _____ _____ at her house.

M That's amazing. Are you going with your parents?

W No, I'm going alone. My parents said no at first. But since I won first prize in the contest, they _____ _____ _____.

18 이어질 응답 찾기

대화를 듣고, 남자의 마지막 말에 대한 여자의 응답으로 가장 적절한 것을 고르시오.

Woman: _____

① Green will be fine.
② I don't have paper to write on.
③ Can I use your colored pencils?
④ I watched the whole *Star Wars* series.
⑤ Right. My hobby is collecting figures.

W Do you have video games?

M Yes, we do. _____ _____ _____ _____ _____?

W *Star Wars*.

M It's right here. And it's on sale today for $20.

W Great! I'll take it. It's a gift for my friend, so _____ _____ _____ _____ gift-wrapped?

M Sure, you can. _____ _____
_____ would you like?

W Hmm... Do you have blue paper?

M Sorry, but there's _____ _____
_____ . I have red, green, or yellow paper.

19 이어질 응답 찾기

대화를 듣고, 여자의 마지막 말에 대한 남자의 응답으로 가장 적절한 것을 고르시오.

Man: _____

① I can't wait to eat some pizza.
② Honestly, I'm not good at cooking.
③ Good idea. I like spicy Korean food!
④ I hope to visit the country someday.
⑤ No, I've never eaten Chinese food before.

W It's already 1 p.m. Let's hurry to the library. I have many things to do.

M I am so hungry. _____ _____
_____ _____ before going to the library?

W Okay. What are we going to have?

M Well, how about Chinese food?

W Sorry, but I don't _____ _____
_____ . How about pizza or spaghetti?

M I had Italian food yesterday.

W Then _____ _____ _____
_____ the Korean restaurant which opened last week? I heard the _____ _____
_____ _____ .

20 상황에 적절한 말 찾기

다음 상황 설명을 듣고, Olivia가 Julia에게 할 말로 가장 적절한 것을 고르시오.

Olivia: Julia, _____

① let's try to get along from now on.
② you should clean up your things.
③ you'd better take a shower more often.
④ I promise that I'll be a good sister to you.
⑤ how about decorating our room with these things?

W Olivia has a sister, Julia, who is 2 years younger than her. They share a room. They _____ _____
_____ , and they have a good relationship. But there is one thing that Olivia doesn't _____
_____ _____ _____ . Julia never cleans up her things, so their _____ _____
_____ _____ . So Olivia decides to tell her sister to _____ _____ _____
_____ . In this situation, what would Olivia most likely say to Julia?

실전 모의고사 03

점수 /20

01 대화를 듣고, 남자가 만든 학습 플래너 표지를 고르시오.

①   ②   ③

④   ⑤

02 대화를 듣고, 남자가 구입한 시계에 관해 언급되지 <u>않은</u> 것을 고르시오.

① 기능　　② 색상　　③ 제조사
④ 가격　　⑤ 보증 기간

03 대화를 듣고, 여자가 남자에게 전화한 목적으로 가장 적절한 것을 고르시오.

① 집에 초대하려고
② 과학책을 빌리려고
③ 약속을 취소하려고
④ 약속을 상기시키려고
⑤ 박람회장 위치를 물으려고

04 대화를 듣고, 남자가 탈 기차의 출발 시각을 고르시오.

① 10:30 a.m.　② 11:00 a.m.　③ 1:00 p.m.
④ 2:00 p.m.　⑤ 2:30 p.m.

05 다음 그림의 상황에 가장 적절한 대화를 고르시오.

①　　②　　③　　④　　⑤

06 대화를 듣고, 두 사람이 대화하는 장소로 가장 적절한 곳을 고르시오.

① 경찰서　　　　② 백화점
③ 버스 정류장　　④ 차량 정비소
⑤ 분실물 센터

07 대화를 듣고, 여자가 남자에게 부탁한 일로 가장 적절한 것을 고르시오.

① 소포 부치기　　② 우유 사 오기
③ 빨래 걷기　　　④ 병원 데려가기
⑤ 약 사 오기

08 다음을 듣고, 돌고래 관광 투어(Dolphin Watching Tour)에 관해 언급되지 <u>않은</u> 것을 고르시오.

① 소요 시간　　　② 투어 장소
③ 식사 제공 여부　④ 신청 방법
⑤ 투어 비용

09 다음을 듣고, 무엇에 관한 설명인지 고르시오.

① 모니터　　② 키보드　　③ 프린터
④ 스피커　　⑤ 마우스

10 다음을 듣고, 두 사람의 대화가 <u>어색한</u> 것을 고르시오.

①　　②　　③　　④　　⑤

11 대화를 듣고, 여자가 할 일로 가장 적절한 것을 고르시오.

① 축하 문자 보내기　　② 성적표 확인하기
③ 시험지 제출하기　　④ 이메일 주소 알려주기
⑤ 이메일로 과제 보내기

12 대화를 듣고, 두 사람이 만나기로 한 시각을 고르시오.

① 12:00 p.m.　② 12:30 p.m.　③ 1:00 p.m.

④ 1:30 p.m.　⑤ 2:00 p.m.

13 다음 공원 배치도를 보면서 대화를 듣고, 두 사람이 선택할 구역을 고르시오.

Parking Lot	① A	Restroom		② B
		Lake		Food Stands
	③ C	④ D	Fountain	⑤ E

14 대화를 듣고, 남자가 어제 한 일로 가장 적절한 것을 고르시오.

① 동물원 가기　　② 영화 보기

③ 책상 정리하기　④ 포스터 그리기

⑤ 유리창 청소하기

15 다음을 듣고, 방송의 목적으로 가장 적절한 것을 고르시오.

① 수업 일정 변경을 공지하려고

② 식목일의 유래를 설명하려고

③ 정원 가꾸는 법을 소개하려고

④ 식목일 학교 행사를 안내하려고

⑤ 환경 미화 우수 학급을 발표하려고

16 대화를 듣고, 남자가 지불할 금액을 고르시오.

① $5　　　② $6　　　③ $7

④ $8　　　⑤ $9

17 대화를 듣고, 여자의 마지막 말에 대한 남자의 응답으로 가장 적절한 것을 고르시오.

Man: _____

① You're right. I'll try to do that.

② No. You have to exercise more.

③ I don't think I can eat any more.

④ Okay. Let's go to the fast food restaurant.

⑤ Right. You'd better eat more vegetables and fruits.

18 대화를 듣고, 남자의 마지막 말에 대한 여자의 응답으로 가장 적절한 것을 고르시오.

Woman: _____

① Yes, I'd like a large coke.

② Of course not. Go ahead.

③ No, thank you. I'm really full.

④ Sure. I'll be right back with one.

⑤ No, I've never been to New York before.

19 대화를 듣고, 여자의 마지막 말에 대한 남자의 응답으로 가장 적절한 것을 고르시오.

Man: _____

① I don't like playing games.

② I agree. I really liked her acting.

③ Instead, I bought some gifts for her.

④ Yes. We had a great time at the theater.

⑤ Really? Maybe I should do that right now.

20 다음 상황 설명을 듣고, Mason이 Chloe에게 할 말로 가장 적절한 것을 고르시오.

Mason: Chloe, _____

① you'd better wear warm clothes.

② don't forget to bring your umbrella.

③ do you enjoy riding roller coasters?

④ have you been to the amusement park?

⑤ why don't we watch a movie at home instead?

Dictation 03

◇ 다시 듣고, 빈칸에 들어갈 알맞은 단어를 써보세요.

정답 및 해설 p.16

01 그림 정보 파악

대화를 듣고, 남자가 만든 학습 플래너 표지를 고르시오.

① ② ③ ④ ⑤

W Hey, Peter. What are you doing?

M I'm making a study planner for my sister. She'll _____ _____ _____ next year.

W That's why you wrote the sentence "Dreams come true!" _____ _____ _____.

M Yes. My sister likes flowers, but I _____ _____ _____ _____ instead under the title.

W Why did you add balloons?

M They stand for hope. I wanted to _____ _____ _____ for her.

W I see. I hope your sister likes it.

02 언급하지 않은 내용 찾기

대화를 듣고, 남자가 구입한 시계에 관해 언급되지 <u>않은</u> 것을 고르시오.

① 기능 ② 색상 ③ 제조사
④ 가격 ⑤ 보증 기간

W Hello, how may I help you?

M I'd like to buy a smartwatch.

W How about this one? You can listen to music and _____ _____ _____ with it.

M Great. Does it come in different colors?

W It comes in red and blue.

M Then I'll take a blue one. How much does it cost?

W It is $400. You can _____ _____ _____ for free for one year.

M Okay. I will _____ _____ _____. Here is the money.

03 목적 파악

대화를 듣고, 여자가 남자에게 전화한 목적으로 가장 적절한 것을 고르시오.

① 집에 초대하려고
② 과학책을 빌리려고
③ 약속을 취소하려고
④ 약속을 상기시키려고
⑤ 박람회장 위치를 물으려고

[Cell phone rings.]

M Hello.

W Hi, Mark. We're still going to the book fair, right?

M Oh, right. I _____ _____ _____. When is the book fair?

W The book fair is this Saturday. It starts at 9 a.m.

M I see. Do I need to bring anything?

W You need to bring your student ID. _____ _____, you have to pay $5.

M Okay. Thanks _____ _____ _____ _____.

W That's why I called. I wanted _____ _____ _____ about it.

M I won't forget about it.

04 숫자 정보 파악 (시각)

대화를 듣고, 남자가 탈 기차의 출발 시각을 고르시오.

① 10:30 a.m.　　② 11:00 a.m.
③ 1:00 p.m.　　④ 2:00 p.m.
⑤ 2:30 p.m.

M Excuse me. What time does the next train for Busan leave?

W _____ _____ at 10:30 a.m. and it arrives in Busan at 2:30 p.m.

M I need to arrive in Busan before 2 p.m. Is there _____ _____ _____ to get there?

W Let me check. *[Pause]* There is _____. _____ _____ at 11 a.m., and it arrives in Busan at 1:30 p.m.

M Oh, I see. Can I get one ticket _____ _____ _____ _____?

W Okay. The ticket for the express train is $60.

M Here you are.

05 그림 상황에 적절한 대화 찾기

다음 그림의 상황에 가장 적절한 대화를 고르시오.

①　②　③　④　⑤

① M You look so tired.

　W I've been so busy _____ _____ _____ _____.

② M Please wait! _____ _____ the elevator.

　W Okay. ◀》Take your time.

③ M I think this elevator is _____ _____ _____.

　W Oh no! Then we must take the stairs.

④ M Which floor are you going to?

　W _____ _____ _____ the 5th floor.

⑤ M May I try this suit on?

　W Sure. There's a fitting room over there.

◀》 Listening Tip

자음과 you가 만나면 연음현상이 일어나서 take your는 /테이크 유어/가 아니라 /테이큐어/와 같이 발음되어요.

대화를 듣고, 두 사람이 대화하는 장소로 가장 적절한 곳을 고르시오.

① 경찰서   ② 백화점
③ 버스 정류장   ④ 차량 정비소
⑤ 분실물 센터

W Excuse me. Is this wallet yours?

M Oh, yes, it's mine. Thank you. Where did you get that?

W It was right _____ _____ _____.
What bus are you waiting for?

M Bus number 95. _____ _____
_____ _____.

W Don't worry. _____ _____ _____
_____ 5 minutes.

M That's true. Oh, here _____ _____
_____ _____. Thanks again and have a
nice day.

W You have a good day, too.

대화를 듣고, 여자가 남자에게 부탁한 일로 가장 적절한 것을 고르시오.

① 소포 부치기   ② 우유 사 오기
③ 빨래 걷기   ④ 병원 데려가기
⑤ 약 사 오기

[Cell phone rings.]

M Hello.

W Honey, where are you?

M I just left the post office. I _____ _____
_____ and now I'm going to the supermarket
to get some milk.

W Okay. Can I ask you to get something for me?

M Sure. What is it?

W I _____ _____ _____. Can you
_____ _____ _____ for me?

M Okay. I'll _____ _____ _____
_____ before I go home.

W Thank you.

다음을 듣고, 돌고래 관광 투어(Dolphin Watching Tour)에 관해 언급되지 <u>않은</u> 것을 고르시오.

① 소요 시간   ② 투어 장소
③ 식사 제공 여부   ④ 신청 방법
⑤ 투어 비용

W Hello, visitors! Do you want to experience something
amazing? Then join our Dolphin Watching Tour. This
_____ _____ _____
_____ 3 hours, including dolphin watching and a
lunch party. A luxury boat will take you to the eastern coast
of Saipan. There, you will _____ _____
_____ _____ and _____
_____ _____ _____ on the boat.

_____ _____ _____ $50 for adults and $30 for children. Thanks for listening and enjoy your time in Saipan.

09 화제 추론

다음을 듣고, 무엇에 관한 설명인지 고르시오.

① 모니터 ② 키보드 ③ 프린터
④ 스피커 ⑤ 마우스

M This is the device that all the computer users use _____ _____ _____ _____. This device was invented in 1964. Until then people controlled their computers by typing commands _____ _____ _____. By using this, however, today's computer users can not only _____, _____, _____ _____ their files but also draw or paint something _____ _____ _____.

10 어색한 대화 찾기

다음을 듣고, 두 사람의 대화가 <u>어색한</u> 것을 고르시오.

①   ②   ③   ④   ⑤

🔊 **Listening Tip**

sold out의 out처럼 모음으로 시작하는 단어는 앞 단어의 끝 자음과 연결해서 말해요. 즉 /솔드아웃/이 아니라 /솔다웃/으로 발음하지요.

① M _____ _____ _____ _____ in this blue jacket?
   W You look wonderful.
② M Can you make it on Wednesday at 3 p.m.?
   W Yes, that's fine.
③ M I want 2 tickets for the movie that starts at 7.
   W Sorry, but _____ _____ _____ for 7 are 🔊 sold out.
④ M _____ _____ _____ take a picture of me?
   W Sure. Say cheese!
⑤ M Excuse me. _____ _____ _____ _____ ?
   W You can take the number 10 bus from here.

11 할 일 파악

대화를 듣고, 여자가 할 일로 가장 적절한 것을 고르시오.

① 축하 문자 보내기
② 성적표 확인하기
③ 시험지 제출하기
④ 이메일 주소 알려주기
⑤ 이메일로 과제 보내기

[Cell phone rings.]
W Hello.
M Hi, Jenny. This is Mr. Stevens. I'm calling you about your final project.
W Oh, hello, Mr. Stevens. Is there something wrong with it?
M I didn't get it from you today.

W Are you sure? I _____ _____

_____ _____ by e-mail.

M Maybe you sent it to the wrong e-mail address. Can you

_____ _____ _____

_____ _____ ?

W No problem.

M I'll text you my e-mail address. I want you to send your

project _____ _____ _____

_____ .

W Okay. I'll _____ _____ _____

_____ .

12 **숫자 정보 파악 (시각)**

대화를 듣고, 두 사람이 만나기로 한 시각을 고르시오.

① 12:00 p.m.　　② 12:30 p.m.
③ 1:00 p.m.　　④ 1:30 p.m.
⑤ 2:00 p.m.

M Sarah, do you _____ _____ _____

_____ this Saturday?

W Nothing special. Why?

M I have 2 tickets to the baseball game between the Lions and Twins. Would you like to go with me?

W I'd love to. What time _____ _____

_____ ?

M At 2 p.m.

W Well, how about meeting 30 minutes _____

_____ _____ at the stadium?

M I don't think that is enough time. We should buy some snacks to eat during the game. Let's _____

_____ _____ _____ the game.

W Okay. See you then.

13 **위치 찾기**

다음 공원 배치도를 보면서 대화를 듣고, 두 사람이 선택할 구역을 고르시오.

Parking Lot	① A	Restroom	② B
	Lake		Food Stands
	③ C	④ D Fountain	⑤ E

M The weather is really good today.

W I agree. It's a perfect day for a picnic. Where should we sit down?

M Let's _____ _____ _____ .
The two sections near the parking lot seem noisy and dusty.

W How about near the food stands? We didn't bring any food.

M Okay. Let's buy _____ _____

_____ _____ there. Which section do you

want to go to?

W Well, I don't want to sit _____ _____

_____.

M Okay. Let's place our picnic mat here. It'll be _____

_____ _____ _____ the fountain.

14 한 일 파악

대화를 듣고, 남자가 어제 한 일로 가장 적절한 것
을 고르시오.

① 동물원 가기　② 영화 보기
③ 책상 정리하기　④ 포스터 그리기
⑤ 유리창 청소하기

W Hey, Ken. What are you doing?

M I'm hanging up _____ _____

_____ of *The Lion King*.

W I heard a lot about the movie. Where did you get the poster?

M I _____ _____ _____ last night

and I got it at the theater. Can you help me hang this poster?

W Sure. Are you going to put it _____ _____

_____?

M No. I _____ _____ on the wall by the

window.

W That's a good idea.

15 목적 파악

다음을 듣고, 방송의 목적으로 가장 적절한 것을
고르시오.

① 수업 일정 변경을 공지하려고
② 식목일의 유래를 설명하려고
③ 정원 가꾸는 법을 소개하려고
④ 식목일 학교 행사를 안내하려고
⑤ 환경 미화 우수 학급을 발표하려고

W Hello, students. As you know, this Friday is Arbor Day. So I'd

like to tell you about what _____ _____

_____ _____ at school then. On Friday, we

won't have regular classes. Instead, we're going to plant

_____ _____ _____

_____ to make the Earth a better place. Please

_____ _____ _____

_____ or small trees. We really need your help.

Thank you.

16 숫자 정보 파악 (금액)

대화를 듣고, 남자가 지불할 금액을 고르시오.

① $5　② $6　③ $7
④ $8　⑤ $9

W May I take your order?

M Yes, I'd like a large coke and a medium popcorn, please.

W Would you like cheese or caramel popcorn?

M Well, do I need to _____ _____

_____ _____?

W Yes. _____ _____ _____
_____ dollar.

M With the caramel one, how much does it come to?

W _____ _____ _____ $7 in total.

M *Is it okay if I use this $1 discount coupon?

W Sure. You can get $1 off the total price.

M Great. Here are the money _____ _____
_____.

17 이어질 응답 찾기

대화를 듣고, 여자의 마지막 말에 대한 남자의 응답으로 가장 적절한 것을 고르시오.

Man: _____

① You're right. I'll try to do that.
② No. You have to exercise more.
③ I don't think I can eat any more.
④ Okay. Let's go to the fast food restaurant.
⑤ Right. You'd better eat more vegetables and fruits.

M I run and swim almost every day but I'm gaining weight. It's strange.

W Hmm... That really is strange. Do you like eating fast food?

M Yes. I eat _____ _____ _____
_____ 3 times a week.

W Do you also enjoy _____ _____
_____?

M Yes. I often eat instant noodles at night.

W You should eat less fast food _____ _____
_____ late night snacks.

18 이어질 응답 찾기

대화를 듣고, 남자의 마지막 말에 대한 여자의 응답으로 가장 적절한 것을 고르시오.

Woman: _____

① Yes, I'd like a large coke.
② Of course not. Go ahead.
③ No, thank you. I'm really full.
④ Sure. I'll be right back with one.
⑤ No, I've never been to New York before.

W Excuse me, sir. Please fasten your seat belt. The emergency _____ _____ _____.

M Oh, I'm sorry. I didn't see it.

W Could you put your bag _____ _____
_____? You're not allowed to leave things in the aisle.

M Okay, I will. Well, when _____ _____
_____ _____ New York?

W We'll _____ _____ _____

_____ in about an hour.

M Then would you do me a favor?

W I'd be glad to. What is it?

M _____ _____ _____

_____ soda, please?

19 이어질 응답 찾기

대화를 듣고, 여자의 마지막 말에 대한 남자의 응답으로 가장 적절한 것을 고르시오.

Man: _____

① I don't like playing games.
② I agree. I really liked her acting.
③ Instead, I bought some gifts for her.
④ Yes. We had a great time at the theater.
⑤ Really? Maybe I should do that right now.

W I saw Amy on the way, and she _____

_____ _____.

M I think I know why.

W Did _____ _____ _____ you

two?

M Well, she _____ _____ _____

_____, but I didn't answer the phone.

W Why didn't you?

M I was busy playing computer games, so I didn't know she called me.

W I don't think that's why Amy is upset. Why don't you

_____ _____ _____

_____ why she called?

20 상황에 적절한 말 찾기

다음 상황 설명을 듣고, Mason이 Chloe에게 할 말로 가장 적절한 것을 고르시오.

Mason: Chloe, _____

① you'd better wear warm clothes.
② don't forget to bring your umbrella.
③ do you enjoy riding roller coasters?
④ have you been to the amusement park?
⑤ why don't we watch a movie at home instead?

M The final exams are finished, and Mason and Chloe have some time to rest. They are planning to go to an amusement park tomorrow. However, the weather forecast says that there is _____ _____ _____

_____ _____ and it'll be cold with strong winds tomorrow. So, Mason _____ _____

_____ and wants to _____ _____

_____ _____ _____ instead of

going to an amusement park. In this situation, what would Mason most likely say to Chloe?

정답 및 해설 p.23

실전 모의고사 04

점수 /20

01 대화를 듣고, 여자가 만든 이름표를 고르시오.

02 대화를 듣고, 여자가 기르는 반려동물에 관해 언급되지 <u>않은</u> 것을 고르시오.
① 종류 ② 털 색깔 ③ 나이
④ 먹이 ⑤ 이름

03 대화를 듣고, 남자가 여자에게 전화한 목적으로 가장 적절한 것을 고르시오.
① 뮤지컬 표를 예매하려고
② 예매한 표를 변경하려고
③ 예매한 표를 취소하려고
④ 뮤지컬 시간을 확인하려고
⑤ 좌석 별 가격을 문의하려고

04 대화를 듣고, 여자가 테니스 코트를 사용할 시각을 고르시오.
① 10 a.m. ② 11 a.m. ③ 2 p.m.
④ 3 p.m. ⑤ 4 p.m.

05 다음 그림의 상황에 가장 적절한 대화를 고르시오.

① ② ③ ④ ⑤

06 대화를 듣고, 두 사람이 대화하는 장소로 가장 적절한 곳을 고르시오.
① 도서관 ② 은행 ③ 영화관
④ 체육관 ⑤ 학교 교실

07 대화를 듣고, 남자가 여자에게 부탁한 일로 가장 적절한 것을 고르시오.
① 함께 낚시 가기 ② 책 구매하기
③ 소포 대신 받기 ④ 인터넷 쇼핑하기
⑤ 집에 일찍 오기

08 다음을 듣고, Love Pet Club에 관해 언급되지 <u>않은</u> 것을 고르시오.
① 회장 이름 ② 모임 시간
③ 모임 장소 ④ 봉사 활동 장소
⑤ 회원 가입 자격

09 다음을 듣고, 무엇에 관한 설명인지 고르시오.
① 장기 ② 오목 ③ 체스
④ 바둑 ⑤ 부루 마불

10 다음을 듣고, 두 사람의 대화가 <u>어색한</u> 것을 고르시오.
① ② ③ ④ ⑤

11 대화를 듣고, 남자가 할 일로 가장 적절한 것을 고르시오.
① 넥타이 사기 ② 빵집 가기
③ 케이크 만들기 ④ 생일상 차리기
⑤ 아빠에게 전화하기

12 대화를 듣고, 두 사람이 만나기로 한 시각을 고르시오.

① 12 p.m. ② 2 p.m. ③ 3 p.m.
④ 4 p.m. ⑤ 5 p.m.

13 다음 좌석 배치도를 보면서 대화를 듣고, 두 사람이 선택할 구역을 고르시오.

	Stage		
1F	① A	② B	
2F	③ C	④ D	⑤ E	Entrance

14 대화를 듣고, 여자가 어제 한 일로 가장 적절한 것을 고르시오.

① 병원 가기 ② 자전거 타기
③ 어깨 마사지 받기 ④ 도서관 가기
⑤ 엄마 심부름하기

15 다음을 듣고, 방송의 목적으로 가장 적절한 것을 고르시오.

① 비행기 탑승을 안내하려고
② 출발 지연 항공편을 알리려고
③ 좌석 선택 방법을 안내하려고
④ 응급 상황 대처 방법을 설명하려고
⑤ 입국 신고서 작성 방법을 설명하려고

16 대화를 듣고, 여자가 지불할 금액을 고르시오.

① $100 ② $105 ③ $110
④ $115 ⑤ $120

17 대화를 듣고, 남자의 마지막 말에 대한 여자의 응답으로 가장 적절한 것을 고르시오.

Woman: _____

① Because I need some rest.
② Why not? You can do anything.
③ I'm really excited to have a long vacation.
④ Good. Let's book the hotel near the beach.
⑤ I want to stay in a room facing the beach.

18 대화를 듣고, 여자의 마지막 말에 대한 남자의 응답으로 가장 적절한 것을 고르시오.

Man: _____

① I'm looking for a striped shirt.
② You can find them at the corner.
③ What did you do last Wednesday?
④ I think it'll take 3 days from today.
⑤ Okay. I'll pick you up at the airport.

19 대화를 듣고, 남자의 마지막 말에 대한 여자의 응답으로 가장 적절한 것을 고르시오.

Woman: _____

① Great! I'm glad that you enjoyed it.
② Wow, you had a wonderful vacation!
③ That's too bad. I hope you have fun next time.
④ I'm sorry to hear that. I hope she'll get well soon.
⑤ Okay. Where do you want to go for sightseeing?

20 다음 상황 설명을 듣고, Angela가 남자에게 할 말로 가장 적절한 것을 고르시오.

Angela: _____

① Can I take a seat here?
② Is it okay to switch our seats?
③ I need some paint for my art homework.
④ Will you save a seat for me at the library?
⑤ Don't sit on the bench. The paint is still wet.

01 그림 정보 파악

대화를 듣고, 여자가 만든 이름표를 고르시오.

① ② ③ ④ ⑤

W I made a name tag for my dog Happy. Look!

M It _____ _____ _____
_____. It's very cute.

W Thanks. Actually, I wanted to make it in a heart shape, but I
_____ _____ _____. Happy really
likes bones.

M He will love it. Oh, I think you should write your phone
_____ _____ _____
_____.

W That's a good idea. I'll write my number right away. *[Pause]*
What do you think?

M It's perfect.

02 언급하지 않은 내용 찾기

대화를 듣고, 여자가 기르는 반려동물에 관해 언급되지 않은 것을 고르시오.

① 종류 ② 털 색깔 ③ 나이
④ 먹이 ⑤ 이름

M Emily, what are you doing?

W I'm looking at pictures of my cat.

M Oh, do you have a cat?

W Yes. She has blue eyes _____ _____
_____.

M Wow, she looks so lovely. How old is she?

W She is 3 months old. My aunt's cat _____
_____ _____ 2 kittens and she gave one of
them to me.

M What's _____ _____ _____?

W Scarlett. I _____ _____ _____ the
famous actress Scarlett Johansson.

M I think the name suits her well.

03 목적 파악

대화를 듣고, 남자가 여자에게 전화한 목적으로 가장 적절한 것을 고르시오.

① 뮤지컬 표를 예매하려고
② 예매한 표를 변경하려고
③ 예매한 표를 취소하려고
④ 뮤지컬 시간을 확인하려고
⑤ 좌석 별 가격을 문의하려고

[Telephone rings.]

W Hello, Wonder Park Ticket. May I help you?

M Hello. I 🔊booked 2 musical tickets for *Ghost* last month.

W Okay. Is there a problem?

M I _____ _____ _____ the 3 o'clock
showing, but I'd like to _____ _____

🔊 **Listening Tip**

booked의 ed는 [t]로 발음 되어 뒤에 오는 two와 동일한 음이 이어지므로 하나는 발음이 탈락되어 /북투/와 같이 발음되어요.

_____ the 7 o'clock one. Are there any seats available?

W Oh, I'm sorry. Both showings are _____

_____ _____.

M I see. I think I have to keep my original tickets then.

W _____ _____ _____.

M Thanks for your help.

---

04 숫자 정보 파악 (시각)

대화를 듣고, 여자가 테니스 코트를 사용할 시각을 고르시오.

① 10 a.m. ② 11 a.m. ③ 2 p.m.
④ 3 p.m. ⑤ 4 p.m.

[Telephone rings.]

M Hello, CS Sports Center. How may I help you?

W I'd like to _____ _____ _____

_____ for this Saturday.

M Okay. How long are you going to play?

W For one hour. _____ _____

_____ from 10 a.m. to 11 a.m.?

M Let me check. _[Pause]_ Sorry, but they're all booked until noon. How about 2 p.m.?

W I _____ _____

_____. Is it possible to use one at 3 p.m. or 4 p.m.?

M You can use one at 4 p.m.

W Great. _____ _____ _____ for then.

---

05 그림 상황에 적절한 대화 찾기

다음 그림의 상황에 가장 적절한 대화를 고르시오.

① ② ③ ④ ⑤

① **W** What did you have for lunch?

   M I ate potato pizza.

② **W** I'd like to make a reservation for 3 for 7 o'clock tonight.

   M Sorry, _____ _____

   _____ for tonight.

③ **W** That pizza is delicious. How is your meal?

   M *I'm not satisfied with my salad. _____

   _____ _____ _____.

④ **W** What would you like to drink?

   M I want a small coke.

⑤ **W** Excuse me. _____ _____

   _____ _____ leftovers into a box for me?

   M Sure. Please _____ _____

   _____.

I'm not satisfied with ~. 나는 ~가 마음에 들지 않아.

• **I'm not satisfied with** the result. 나는 결과가 마음에 들지 않아.
• **I'm not satisfied with** the customer service. 나는 고객 서비스가 마음에 들지 않아.

---

06 장소 추론

대화를 듣고, 두 사람이 대화하는 장소로 가장 적절한 곳을 고르시오.

① 도서관　　② 은행　　③ 영화관
④ 체육관　　⑤ 학교 교실

W Tony, I didn't expect to see you here.

M Oh, hi, Jenny. It's nice to see ＿＿＿＿＿＿ ＿＿＿＿＿＿ ＿＿＿＿＿＿ ＿＿＿＿＿＿. Do you come here often?

W Yes. I'm a ＿＿＿＿＿＿ ＿＿＿＿＿＿ ＿＿＿＿＿＿ ＿＿＿＿＿＿. I've been working out here since last year.

M That's why you always look healthy and slim.

W Oh, thanks. How long have you been ＿＿＿＿＿＿ ＿＿＿＿＿＿ ＿＿＿＿＿＿?

M Actually, I signed up here last week.

W Why did you start working out?

M Well, I want to ＿＿＿＿＿＿ ＿＿＿＿＿＿ ＿＿＿＿＿＿.

---

07 부탁 파악

대화를 듣고, 남자가 여자에게 부탁한 일로 가장 적절한 것을 고르시오.

① 함께 낚시 가기　　② 책 구매하기
③ 소포 대신 받기　　④ 인터넷 쇼핑하기
⑤ 집에 일찍 오기

W Honey, are you going fishing again on the weekend?

M Yes. Do you want to come with me?

W No, thanks. I'd rather ＿＿＿＿＿＿ ＿＿＿＿＿＿ ＿＿＿＿＿＿ ＿＿＿＿＿＿.

M If you are going to stay home, can I ask you a favor?

W Sure. What is it?

M ＿＿＿＿＿＿ ＿＿＿＿＿＿ ＿＿＿＿＿＿ ＿＿＿＿＿＿ Saturday afternoon. Can you ＿＿＿＿＿＿ ＿＿＿＿＿＿ ＿＿＿＿＿＿ ＿＿＿＿＿＿?

W Of course. Did you order something online?

M Yes, I ＿＿＿＿＿＿ ＿＿＿＿＿＿ ＿＿＿＿＿＿.

---

08 언급하지 않은 내용 찾기

다음을 듣고, Love Pet Club에 관해 언급되지 않은 것을 고르시오.

① 회장 이름　　② 모임 시간
③ 모임 장소　　④ 봉사 활동 장소
⑤ 회원 가입 자격

W Hi, students! I'm Lily Collins, president of Love Pet Club. If you love animals, I'd like to invite you to join our club. We ＿＿＿＿＿＿ ＿＿＿＿＿＿ ＿＿＿＿＿＿ from 2 p.m. to 4 p.m. We learn ＿＿＿＿＿＿ ＿＿＿＿＿＿ ＿＿＿＿＿＿ ＿＿＿＿＿＿ and handle many kinds of pets. And we go to the ＿＿＿＿＿＿ ＿＿＿＿＿＿

_____ _____ on the last Friday of every month. Anyone who is 15 years of age or older _____ _____ _____

_____ . Please come and join us.

09 화제 추론

다음을 듣고, 무엇에 관한 설명인지 고르시오.

① 장기　　② 오목　　③ 체스
④ 바둑　　⑤ 부루 마불

M This is _____ _____ _____

_____ _____ . This was invented in China more than 3,000 years ago. In this game, the player

_____ _____ _____

_____ than the other player is the winner. The playing pieces, or stones, are white and black. One player

_____ _____ _____

_____ and the other uses the black stones. The players take turns _____ _____

_____ _____ on the empty places of a board.

10 어색한 대화 찾기

다음을 듣고, 두 사람의 대화가 어색한 것을 고르시오.

①　　②　　③　　④　　⑤

① M Please _____ _____ _____ your parents for me.

　W Thank you, I will.

② M How much will it cost me to go to the airport?

　W If you go by bus, it will cost $10.

③ M Could _____ _____ _____

_____ the TV?

　W Sorry, I didn't know you were studying.

④ M What kind of movies do you like best?

　W _____ _____ _____ popcorn and Coke.

⑤ M Are there any more trains for Gangnam today?

　W No. The last one just left _____ _____

_____ _____ .

11 할 일 파악

대화를 듣고, 남자가 할 일로 가장 적절한 것을 고르시오.

① 넥타이 사기　　② 빵집 가기
③ 케이크 만들기　　④ 생일상 차리기
⑤ 아빠에게 전화하기

M Mom, is there anything that I _____ _____

_____ _____ ?

W Not really. I'm ◀ almost done. Look.

M Wow, it's a great birthday dinner. I'm sure Dad will be very happy.

W I hope so. Did you _____ _____ _____ for him?

M Yes. I got a necktie for him. Oh, where is the birthday cake?

W Oh no. I need to _____ _____ _____ from Momo's Bakery.

M Don't worry. _____ _____ _____ right now.

---

12 숫자 정보 파악 (시각)

대화를 듣고, 두 사람이 만나기로 한 시각을 고르시오.

① 12:00 p.m. ② 2:00 p.m.
③ 3:00 p.m. ④ 4:00 p.m.
⑤ 5:00 p.m.

M Do you want to go out and play badminton with me today?

W Sure, but I have a dentist appointment at 2 p.m.

M _____ _____ _____ _____ ?

W No, I'll probably be done by 3 p.m. _____ _____ _____ _____ 4 p.m.?

M Sorry, I can't. I have to go to a guitar lesson at 4:30. _____ _____ _____ _____ your dentist appointment?

W Okay. _____ _____ _____ _____ .

M That's fine.

---

13 위치 찾기

다음 좌석 배치도를 보면서 대화를 듣고, 두 사람이 선택할 구역을 고르시오.

Stage		
1F	① A	② B
2F	③ C	④ D	⑤ E	Entrance

M Let's book the BTB concert tickets online. Where do you want to sit?

W I'd like to sit in one of the front sections _____ _____ _____ _____ .

M Well, the first floor only has a standing area. We have to stand and watch the concert there.

W Oh, I don't think I can stand for 3 hours. Then, let's sit in the central section on the second floor.

M Sure. *[Pause]* Oh, we're too late. All the seats in that section _____ _____ _____ _____ . There are 2 sections left.

W Then this one seems better than the one _____ _____ _____ .

M Okay. _____ _____ _____ for this section.

14 한 일 파악

대화를 듣고, 여자가 어제 한 일로 가장 적절한 것을 고르시오.

① 병원 가기　　② 자전거 타기
③ 어깨 마사지 받기　　④ 도서관 가기
⑤ 엄마 심부름하기

M Emily, is there something wrong with your right shoulder?

W Yes. _____ _____ _____.

M What happened?

W Oh, I fell down hard _____ _____ _____ _____ yesterday.

M Did you see a doctor?

W Not yet. After school, I'll ask my mom to _____ _____ _____ _____ _____.

M I hope you _____ _____ _____.

W Thank you.

15 목적 파악

다음을 듣고, 방송의 목적으로 가장 적절한 것을 고르시오.

① 비행기 탑승을 안내하려고
② 출발 지연 항공편을 알리려고
③ 좌석 선택 방법을 안내하려고
④ 응급 상황 대처 방법을 설명하려고
⑤ 입국 신고서 작성 방법을 설명하려고

W Attention all passengers for Flight 747 to Frankfurt. _____ _____ _____ _____ in a minute. Please _____ _____ _____ and passports. Passengers with first-class tickets may board first. Passengers in rows 10 through 25 will be _____ _____ _____. If you are in rows 26 to 40, _____ _____ _____ the next announcement. Thank you very much for your cooperation.

16 숫자 정보 파악 (금액)

대화를 듣고, 여자가 지불할 금액을 고르시오.

① $100　　② $105　　③ $110
④ $115　　⑤ $120

W Excuse me. I'm looking for a handbag for my mom.

M How about this red one with a gold chain? It is _____ _____ _____ _____.

W It's nice. How much does it cost?

M The original price is $110, but _____ _____ _____.

W That sounds good. What is the sale price?

M It's $10 _____ _____ _____.

W Great. I'll take it.

M Would you like it gift-wrapped?

W Yes. Is there an extra charge for that?

M No, we _____ _____ _____
_____ .

---

17 이어질 응답 찾기

대화를 듣고, 남자의 마지막 말에 대한 여자의 응
답으로 가장 적절한 것을 고르시오.

Woman: _____

① Because I need some rest.
② Why not? You can do anything.
③ I'm really excited to have a long
vacation.
④ Good. Let's book the hotel near the
beach.
⑤ I want to stay in a room facing the
beach.

W Honey, what are you doing?

M I'm looking for a hotel for our vacation.

W Did you _____ _____ _____
_____ for us?

M Yes, I found 2 hotels that I want to stay at. One is called the
Paradise Inn. The other is called Oasis Hotel. Which do you
prefer?

W I don't know. Which one is _____ _____ ?

M The Paradise Inn costs a little more because it's

_____ _____ _____
_____ .

W Then let's choose the Paradise Inn.

M Why do you want to _____ _____
_____ _____ ?

---

18 이어질 응답 찾기

대화를 듣고, 여자의 마지막 말에 대한 남자의 응
답으로 가장 적절한 것을 고르시오.

Man: _____

① I'm looking for a striped shirt.
② You can find them at the corner.
③ What did you do last Wednesday?
④ I think it'll take 3 days from today.
⑤ Okay. I'll pick you up at the airport.

M Hello, how may I help you?

W I'd like to _____ _____ _____
dry-cleaned.

M Okay. What do you have?

W I have 2 jackets and a pair of pants. How much is each one?

M $7 for each jacket and $5 for the pants.

W _____ _____ _____
_____ ?

M No, you can pay later when _____ _____
_____ _____ .

W It's Wednesday today. _____ _____
_____ _____ _____ ?

---

19 이어질 응답 찾기

대화를 듣고, 남자의 마지막 말에 대한 여자의 응답으로 가장 적절한 것을 고르시오.

Woman: _____

① Great! I'm glad that you enjoyed it.
② Wow, you had a wonderful vacation!
③ That's too bad. I hope you have fun next time.
④ I'm sorry to hear that. I hope she'll get well soon.
⑤ Okay. Where do you want to go for sightseeing?

W Jiho, how was your weekend?
M I visited Busan with my family.
W Did you _____ _____ _____ _____ there?
M No. It was really boring!
W I thought there were many things to enjoy in Busan. Why _____ _____ _____ _____?
M I had a _____ _____ on the first day.
W Oh, I'm sorry to hear that. So what did you do there?
M I stayed at a hotel and just _____ _____ _____ _____ while my family went sightseeing.

20 상황에 적절한 말 찾기

다음 상황 설명을 듣고, Angela가 남자에게 할 말로 가장 적절한 것을 고르시오.

Angela: _____

① Can I take a seat here?
② Is it okay to switch our seats?
③ I need some paint for my art homework.
④ Will you save a seat for me at the library?
⑤ Don't sit on the bench. The paint is still wet.

M Angela feels tired, so she sits on a bench and takes a break. After a while, she finds out that there is _____ _____ _____ _____ _____. She stands up and tries to remove the paint off her pants. Then, a man _____ _____ _____ _____ and tries to _____ _____. She wants to tell him _____ _____ _____ _____ _____. In this situation, what would Angela most likely say to the man?

정답 및 해설 p.30

실전 모의고사 **05**

01 대화를 듣고, 여자가 구입할 바지로 가장 적절한 것을 고르시오.

①   ②   ③

④ ⑤

02 대화를 듣고, 여자가 남자에게 전화한 목적으로 가장 적절한 것을 고르시오.

① 모임 일정을 알리려고
② 모임이 취소됐음을 알리려고
③ 학생이 결석한 이유를 알리려고
④ 남자의 도착 시간을 물어보려고
⑤ 모임 장소가 변경됐음을 알리려고

03 다음 그림의 상황에 가장 적절한 대화를 고르시오.

① ② ③ ④ ⑤

04 대화를 듣고, 두 사람이 놀이공원에 가기로 한 요일을 고르시오.

① 월요일 ② 화요일 ③ 금요일
④ 토요일 ⑤ 일요일

05 대화를 듣고, 카페에 관해 언급되지 <u>않은</u> 것을 고르시오.

① 위치 ② 이름
③ 개점한 시기 ④ 애완동물 출입
⑤ 직원 수

06 대화를 듣고, 두 사람의 관계로 가장 적절한 것을 고르시오.

① 남편 – 아내
② 교통경찰 – 운전자
③ 자동차 판매원 – 고객
④ 자동차 정비사 – 손님
⑤ 백화점 직원 – 손님

07 다음을 듣고, 두 사람의 대화가 <u>어색한</u> 것을 고르시오.

① ② ③ ④ ⑤

08 대화를 듣고, 여자가 남자에게 부탁한 일로 가장 적절한 것을 고르시오.

① 책 읽어 주기 ② 치약 건네주기
③ 읽을 책 권하기 ④ 숙제 도와주기
⑤ 새 칫솔 찾아 주기

09 대화를 듣고, 여자의 마지막 말에 담긴 의도로 가장 적절한 것을 고르시오.

① 사과 ② 충고 ③ 위로
④ 불만 ⑤ 제안

10 대화를 듣고, 남자가 지불할 금액을 고르시오.

① $100 ② $130 ③ $140
④ $170 ⑤ $180

11 대화를 듣고, 남자가 할 일로 가장 적절한 것을 고르시오.

① 한식 주문하기 ② 피자 주문하기
③ 쿠폰 가져다주기 ④ 스파게티 만들기
⑤ 야구 경기 보러 가기

12 다음을 듣고, New York City Library에 관해 언급되지 <u>않은</u> 것을 고르시오.

① 위치　　　　　　② 특징
③ 개관 시간　　　　④ 기록물 관람 요일
⑤ 휴게실 위치

13 다음 표를 보면서 대화를 듣고, 두 사람이 관람할 영화를 고르시오.

	Movie	Genre	Time	Screen
①	A	Horror	1 p.m.	2D
②	B	Horror	3 p.m.	3D
③	C	Romantic comedy	5 p.m.	2D
④	D	Romantic comedy	7 p.m.	3D
⑤	E	Romantic comedy	8 p.m.	2D

14 다음을 듣고, 무엇에 관한 설명인지 고르시오.

① 망고　　　　② 바나나　　　　③ 오렌지
④ 파인애플　　⑤ 참외

15 대화를 듣고, 남자가 할 일로 가장 적절한 것을 고르시오.

① 뮤지컬 보러 가기
② 뮤지컬 티켓 사기
③ 영화 다운로드하기
④ 온라인으로 물건 사기
⑤ 동생과 약속 정하기

16 대화를 듣고, 두 사람이 구입할 물건을 고르시오.

① cake　　　　　　② toaster
③ alarm clock　　　④ candle
⑤ toilet paper

17 대화를 듣고, 여자의 마지막 말에 이어질 남자의 말로 가장 적절한 것을 고르시오.

Man: _____

① Santa Claus really doesn't exist.
② I'm going to bring a cheesecake.
③ You can bring your sister to the party.
④ I'm having a birthday party next Thursday.
⑤ I'll remember to send out all the invitations.

18 대화를 듣고, 남자의 마지막 말에 이어질 여자의 말로 가장 적절한 것을 고르시오.

Woman: _____

① I know. We should buy a new bed.
② You can fix the bathroom tomorrow.
③ I think I'm coming down with a cold.
④ I'll feel much better after I take a bath.
⑤ It's okay. This is the cheapest hotel in the area.

19 대화를 듣고, 여자의 마지막 말에 이어질 남자의 말로 가장 적절한 것을 고르시오.

Man: _____

① I went to your cookie shop last weekend.
② I'll have to bake more cookies for you then.
③ I'm so glad to hear that you like my cookies.
④ I can't tell you where I bought these cookies.
⑤ I promise that I will be a regular customer.

20 다음 상황 설명을 듣고, Rachel이 여자에게 할 말로 가장 적절한 것을 고르시오.

Rachel: _____

① I don't think I've met you before.
② How long have you been working?
③ I think you look beautiful in that dress.
④ Do you want to pay by cash or credit card?
⑤ You can't return this because it's already been used.

Dictation 05

◇ 다시 듣고, 빈칸에 들어갈 알맞은 단어를 써보세요.

정답 및 해설 p.30

01 그림 정보 파악

대화를 듣고, 여자가 구입할 바지로 가장 적절한 것을 고르시오.

① ② ③
④ ⑤

W Excuse me, where can I find girls' clothing?

M I'll show you where. Please follow me.

W Thank you. *[Pause]* These are all shorts. Do you _____ _____ _____?

M Yes, we do. Pants are over here.

W Great. I know it's summer, but my daughter needs a pair of pants.

M I understand. The ones _____ _____ _____ are on sale for $10.

W Oh, that's really cheap, but she needs _____ _____ _____ _____.

M Then how about the ones _____ _____ _____ _____?

W They are really pretty. I'll take a pair of them.

02 목적 파악

대화를 듣고, 여자가 남자에게 전화한 목적으로 가장 적절한 것을 고르시오.

① 모임 일정을 알리려고
② 모임이 취소됐음을 알리려고
③ 학생이 결석한 이유를 알리려고
④ 남자의 도착 시간을 물어보려고
⑤ 모임 장소가 변경됐음을 알리려고

[Telephone rings.]

M Hello.

W Hello. May I speak to Mr. Thompson?

M This is he. May I ask _____ _____?

W Hi, Mr. Thompson. This is Sandy Johnson from Crossroad Middle School.

M Hi, Ms. Johnson. _____ _____ _____ _____ the parent meeting?

W No, but I'm calling you about the meeting place.

M Isn't it at the cafeteria?

W That was the original plan, but the meeting _____ _____ _____ _____ the auditorium.

M *Thank you for _____ _____ _____. I'll be there on time.

Thank you for ~. ~해 주셔서 감사합니다.
- **Thank you for** lending the book. 저에게 책을 빌려주셔서 감사합니다.
- **Thank you for** inviting me. 초대해 주셔서 고맙습니다.

---

03 그림 상황에 적절한 대화 찾기

다음 그림의 상황에 가장 적절한 대화를 고르시오.

① ② ③ ④ ⑤

① M Should I _____ _____ _____ _____ ?

W Yes, please. I'm almost done cooking.

② M Excuse me. You dropped your purse.

W I don't think _____ _____ .

③ M Do you need help with your backpack?

W Thank you so much. It's really heavy.

④ M _____ _____ _____ _____ I sit next to you?

W I'm sorry, but someone's sitting here.

⑤ M Can you show me your passport?

W Sure, let me _____ _____ _____ _____ my bag.

---

04 특정 정보 파악

대화를 듣고, 두 사람이 놀이공원에 가기로 한 요일을 고르시오.

① 월요일　　② 화요일　　③ 금요일
④ 토요일　　⑤ 일요일

W Have you been to the amusement park in Gyeongju?

M Not yet, but I've _____ _____ _____ _____ there.

W I'm thinking about going there this Saturday with Kate. Do you want to come with us?

M Sure, but don't you think it's going to _____ _____ _____ _____ ?

W I guess you're right. Why don't we go _____ _____ _____ _____ ?

M That's a good idea. We _____ _____ _____ _____ next Tuesday.

W Okay, then it's a plan.

---

05 언급하지 않은 내용 찾기

대화를 듣고, 카페에 관해 언급되지 **않은** 것을 고르시오.

① 위치　　　　② 이름
③ 개점한 시기　④ 애완동물 출입
⑤ 직원 수

W Have you been to the new cafe on 5th Avenue?

M Are you talking about the one _____ _____ _____ _____ 5th Avenue and Main Street?

W Yes, it's called Orange Cafe.

M I've passed by it, but I've never _____ _____ _____.

W It opened last week, and you can bring your pet there.

M _____ _____ _____ _____ so much about that cafe?

W I actually _____ _____ _____ yesterday.

M I see. I'm sure it'll be a very good experience for you.

---

06 관계 추론

대화를 듣고, 두 사람의 관계로 가장 적절한 것을 고르시오.

① 남편 – 아내
② 교통경찰 – 운전자
③ 자동차 판매원 – 고객
④ 자동차 정비사 – 손님
⑤ 백화점 직원 – 손님

🔊 **Listening Tip**

look at에서 at처럼 모음으로 시작하는 단어는 앞 단어의 끝 자음과 연결해서 말해요. 그렇다면 /룩 앳/이 아니라 /루캣/으로 연음된다는 것인데, 실제 원어민들은 강세가 없는 음절의 'k, p, t'는 된소리로 말하는 경향이 있어서 /루깻/으로 발음하는 경우가 많아요.

W Can you take a 🔊look at my tires?

M Sure, do you have a flat tire?

W One of the front tires _____ _____ _____.

M Let me check. *[Pause]* Oh, all of your tires need to be replaced. They're very old.

W Are they? How much would it _____ _____ _____ _____ _____?

M It's $100 each, so it'll be $400.

W _____ _____ _____ _____ a look at the brakes?

M Yes, I'll examine them while _____ _____ _____ _____.

---

07 어색한 대화 찾기

다음을 듣고, 두 사람의 대화가 어색한 것을 고르시오.

①   ②   ③   ④   ⑤

① **M** Would you like something to drink?

  W Yes, please. _____ _____ _____ _____ milk?

② **M** I have to buy a new car. Mine is really old.

  W What kind of car do you want?

③ **M** Did you get a good night's sleep?

  W Yes, I _____ _____ _____ _____.

④ **M** How often do you play tennis?

  W I play at least _____ _____ _____.

⑤ **M** Could you give me a ride home?

  W Yes, _____ _____ _____.

대화를 듣고, 여자가 남자에게 부탁한 일로 가장 적절한 것을 고르시오.

① 책 읽어 주기　② 치약 건네주기
③ 읽을 책 권하기　④ 숙제 도와주기
⑤ 새 칫솔 찾아 주기

W　Honey, are you awake?

M　Yes. I was about to read a book ＿＿＿＿＿＿
＿＿＿＿＿ ＿＿＿＿＿ ＿＿＿＿＿.

W　Can I ask you a favor?

M　Sure. What is it?

W　I have some e-mails to write, but I think it'll ＿＿＿＿＿
＿＿＿＿＿ ＿＿＿＿＿.

M　Okay. Do you need ＿＿＿＿＿ ＿＿＿＿＿
＿＿＿＿＿ ＿＿＿＿＿?

W　No, that's okay. But Sandy is not sleeping at all. Can you
＿＿＿＿＿ ＿＿＿＿＿ ＿＿＿＿＿
＿＿＿＿＿ until she falls asleep?

M　Of course. I'll do that.

대화를 듣고, 여자의 마지막 말에 담긴 의도로 가장 적절한 것을 고르시오.

① 사과　② 충고　③ 위로
④ 불만　⑤ 제안

M　I'm so happy that spring is finally here.

W　I know. It was an unusually cold winter.

M　Aren't you glad ＿＿＿＿＿ ＿＿＿＿＿
＿＿＿＿＿ to the park today?

W　Yes, I am. I thought it'd still be a little chilly, but it's really warm.

M　Look at all those beautiful flowers.

W　Wow, they're so lovely.

M　＿＿＿＿＿ ＿＿＿＿＿ ＿＿＿＿＿
＿＿＿＿＿ of the flowers for you.

W　That's not a good idea. We ＿＿＿＿＿ ＿＿＿＿＿
＿＿＿＿＿ ＿＿＿＿＿ enjoy their beauty, too.

대화를 듣고, 남자가 지불할 금액을 고르시오.

① $100　② $130　③ $140
④ $170　⑤ $180

M　Excuse me. How much is this skateboard?

W　Let me see. That's $100.

M　Do you have a ＿＿＿＿＿ ＿＿＿＿＿
＿＿＿＿＿?

W　No, that's the cheapest model we have.

M Okay. I _____ _____ _____ _____. How much is this one?

W That's $40. _____ _____ _____ _____ buy a pair of protective gloves, too.

M How much are they?

W They are $30 a pair.

M Hmm... It's all right. _____ _____ _____ the skateboard and the helmet.

11 할 일 파악

대화를 듣고, 남자가 할 일로 가장 적절한 것을 고르시오.

① 한식 주문하기　② 피자 주문하기
③ 쿠폰 가져다주기　④ 스파게티 만들기
⑤ 야구 경기 보러 가기

M What should we eat for dinner tonight?

W I _____ _____ _____ _____ _____ Korean food.

M I can cook spaghetti if you want.

W Why don't we eat out? It's been a long time _____ _____ _____ _____.

M We could, but there's a baseball game I want to watch at 7.

W Okay, then I'll just order a pizza for us. I think we _____ _____ _____ for Johnny's Pizza. Can you _____ _____ _____ _____?

M Sure. I will.

12 언급하지 않은 내용 찾기

다음을 듣고, New York City Library에 관해 언급되지 <u>않은</u> 것을 고르시오.

① 위치　② 특징
③ 개관 시간　④ 기록물 관람 요일
⑤ 휴게실 위치

W Welcome everyone to the New York City Library. We're located in the heart of the city, _____ _____ _____ the city hall. Unlike other libraries, this unique building is not only a library _____ _____ _____ _____. It keeps and displays various historical records of the city. The records are _____ _____ _____ _____ only on Wednesdays. Eating or drinking is not allowed in the library _____ _____ _____ on the first floor.

13 도표 정보 파악

다음 표를 보면서 대화를 듣고, 두 사람이 관람할 영화를 고르시오.

	Movie	Genre	Time	Screen
①	A	Horror	1 p.m.	2D
②	B	Horror	3 p.m.	3D
③	C	Romantic comedy	5 p.m.	2D
④	D	Romantic comedy	7 p.m.	3D
⑤	E	Romantic comedy	8 p.m.	2D

M What kind of movie do you want to watch, Michelle?

W I hate _____ _____. Let's watch a romantic comedy.

M That sounds good to me.

W Let's have dinner at 6 before the movie.

M Okay. By the way, do you want to watch the movie on a 2D or a 3D screen?

W _____ _____ _____ when I watch a movie on a 3D screen.

M Okay, then _____ _____ _____ _____ on a 2D screen.

W All right. Then we have only one choice.

14 화제 추론

다음을 듣고, 무엇에 관한 설명인지 고르시오.
① 망고 ② 바나나 ③ 오렌지
④ 파인애플 ⑤ 참외

M This is a tropical fruit _____ _____ _____ _____ and a soft flesh. The color of this _____ _____ _____ _____ when it is ripe and green when it is not ripe. Many people like to eat this fruit because it is low in calories _____ _____ _____ _____. All you have to do is _____ _____ _____ your hands.

15 할 일 파악

대화를 듣고, 남자가 할 일로 가장 적절한 것을 고르시오.

① 뮤지컬 보러 가기
② 뮤지컬 티켓 사기
③ 영화 다운로드하기
④ 온라인으로 물건 사기
⑤ 동생과 약속 정하기

🔊 **Listening** Tip

weekend의 'k'처럼 [p], [t], [k]가 강세가 있는 음절의 첫 음이 아닐 때는 된소리인 /쁘, 뜨, 끄/로 발음돼요. 그래서 weekend는 /위크엔드/가 아니라 /위껜드/에 가깝게 발음해요.

M What are you doing this 🔊weekend, Jennifer?

W I'm going to see the musical *Cats* with my dad.

M Oh, I _____ _____ _____ last year.

W I did, too. And I really wanted to see the musical version of it.

M The musical is _____ _____ _____ _____ the movie, isn't it?

W Usually, yes. But if you buy 2 or more tickets online, you get 15 percent off.

M _____ _____ _____ _____. I'll buy 2 tickets for me and my sister right now.

특정 정보 파악

대화를 듣고, 두 사람이 구입할 물건을 고르시오.

① cake
② toaster
③ alarm clock
④ candle
⑤ toilet paper

W We need to buy a present before we go to your uncle's housewarming party.

M How about buying some toilet paper?

W No, I don't want to do that. Let's get him _____ _____ _____.

M Okay, Mom. He said he needed a toaster.

W I already gave him our toaster because we never used it.

M Then _____ _____ _____ an alarm clock. He's _____ _____ _____ _____.

W _____ _____ _____ _____!

M Okay, let's go to the mall then.

---

17 **이어질 응답 찾기**

대화를 듣고, 여자의 마지막 말에 이어질 남자의 말로 가장 적절한 것을 고르시오.

Man: _____

① Santa Claus really doesn't exist.
② I'm going to bring a cheesecake.
③ You can bring your sister to the party.
④ I'm having a birthday party next Thursday.
⑤ I'll remember to send out all the invitations.

W When are we having our Christmas party?

M It's next Thursday. We only have 5 days left.

W I heard our teacher _____ _____ _____ _____ Santa Claus.

M That's right. I can't wait!

W Oh, we should bring _____ _____ _____ _____ with our classmates, right?

M Yes. _____ _____ _____ if everyone brings something.

W What are _____ _____ _____ _____, Jake?

---

18 **이어질 응답 찾기**

대화를 듣고, 남자의 마지막 말에 이어질 여자의 말로 가장 적절한 것을 고르시오.

Woman: _____

① I know. We should buy a new bed.
② You can fix the bathroom tomorrow.
③ I think I'm coming down with a cold.
④ I'll feel much better after I take a bath.
⑤ It's okay. This is the cheapest hotel in the area.

M This is the worst hotel I've ever stayed in.

W What's wrong, honey? We just got here.

M There's _____ _____ _____ in the bathroom.

W It's okay. I don't need hot water now. _____ _____ _____ _____ the staff tomorrow.

M I thought you wanted to take a bath.

W No. I'm just going to _____ _____ _____ and go to bed. I'm really tired.

M I'm sorry. *Do you want me to _____ _____ _____ _____ tomorrow?

19 이어질 응답 찾기

대화를 듣고, 여자의 마지막 말에 이어질 남자의 말로 가장 적절한 것을 고르시오.

Man: _____

① I went to your cookie shop last weekend.
② I'll have to bake more cookies for you then.
③ I'm so glad to hear that you like my cookies.
④ I can't tell you where I bought these cookies.
⑤ I promise that I will be a regular customer.

W I have something for your birthday, Michael.

M What is it? [Pause] Wow, these cookies are so cute. Where did you get them?

W I _____ _____ _____.

M Really? I didn't know _____ _____ _____ _____.

W I became interested in baking about 2 years ago.

M Let me try one of them. [Pause] This is so good. I think you should _____ _____ _____ _____.

W Thank you. I hope I _____ _____ _____ _____ cookie shop in the future.

20 상황에 적절한 말 찾기

다음 상황 설명을 듣고, Rachel이 여자에게 할 말로 가장 적절한 것을 고르시오.

Rachel: _____

① I don't think I've met you before.
② How long have you been working?
③ I think you look beautiful in that dress.
④ Do you want to pay by cash or credit card?
⑤ You can't return this because it's already been used.

W Rachel works at the customer service desk _____ _____ _____ _____. One day, a woman comes up to the desk with a bottle of shampoo. The bottle is _____ _____ _____. She says she wants to return the product and _____ _____ _____. Customers _____ _____ _____ _____ have already been used. In this situation, what would Rachel most likely say to the woman?

실전 모의고사 06

01 대화를 듣고, 여자가 구입할 신발로 가장 적절한 것을 고르시오.

① 　② 　③

④ 　⑤

02 대화를 듣고, 남자가 여자에게 부탁한 일로 가장 적절한 것을 고르시오.

① 사과 씻어 주기
② 신발 끈 매주기
③ 아침 식사 차리기
④ 학교까지 태워 주기
⑤ 선생님에게 전화하기

03 다음 그림의 상황에 가장 적절한 대화를 고르시오.

①　　②　　③　　④　　⑤

04 대화를 듣고, 두 사람이 쇼핑하기로 한 요일을 고르시오.

① 월요일　　② 화요일　　③ 수요일
④ 금요일　　⑤ 토요일

05 대화를 듣고, Sandwich King에 관해 언급되지 <u>않은</u> 것을 고르시오.

① 위치　　　　　　② 음식 맛
③ 음식 가격　　　　④ 특별 행사 품목
⑤ 주재료

06 대화를 듣고, 두 사람이 대화하는 장소로 가장 적절한 것을 고르시오.

① 백화점　　② 제과점　　③ 구내식당
④ 요리 강습소　　⑤ 호텔

07 다음을 듣고, 두 사람의 대화가 <u>어색한</u> 것을 고르시오.

①　　　②　　　③　　　④　　　⑤

08 대화를 듣고, 여자가 남자에게 부탁한 일로 가장 적절한 것을 고르시오.

① TV 그만 보기　　　② 숙제 끝내기
③ 동생과 놀아 주기　　④ 개 산책시키기
⑤ 실내 환기시키기

09 다음을 듣고, 무엇에 관한 안내 방송인지 고르시오.

① 공동 구역 환경 미화
② 층간 소음 문제 예방
③ 공동 주택 관리 법규
④ 놀이터 건축 설계 공모
⑤ 놀이터 운영 시간 변경

10 대화를 듣고, 여자가 지불할 금액을 고르시오.

① $100　　② $110　　③ $120
④ $130　　⑤ $140

11 대화를 듣고, 남자가 할 일로 가장 적절한 것을 고르시오.

① 병원에 함께 가기　　② 두통약 먹기
③ 부모님께 전화하기　　④ 약속 취소하기
⑤ 식당 예약 확인하기

12 다음을 듣고, Sejong School에 관해 언급되지 <u>않은</u> 것을 고르시오.

① 교장 이름　　② 설립 연도　　③ 사용 언어
④ 모집 인원　　⑤ 개학 날짜

13 다음 게스트 하우스의 배치도를 보면서 대화를 듣고, 두 사람이 머물 방의 위치를 고르시오.

	① Room A	② Room B	③ Room C	
Kitchen	Yard			◀ Entrance
	④ Room D	Restroom	⑤ Room E	

14 다음을 듣고, 무엇에 관한 설명인지 고르시오.

① 코알라　　② 캥거루　　③ 말
④ 타조　　⑤ 너구리

15 대화를 듣고, 여자가 대화 직후에 할 일로 가장 적절한 것을 고르시오.

① 공원에 가기　　　　② 연 날리기
③ 슈퍼마켓에 가기　　④ 연 만들기
⑤ 겨울옷 꺼내기

16 대화를 듣고, 다음 테니스 경기가 열리는 날짜를 고르시오.

① April 23rd　　　　② April 24th
③ May 1st　　　　④ May 10th
⑤ May 11th

17 대화를 듣고, 여자의 마지막 말에 대한 남자의 응답으로 가장 적절한 것을 고르시오.

Man: _____

① You should've come with us.
② Well, I don't have a favorite car.
③ We had to stop by City Hall.
④ It's hard to say. I liked all of them.
⑤ My dad gave us a ride to the park.

18 대화를 듣고, 남자의 마지막 말에 대한 여자의 응답으로 가장 적절한 것을 고르시오.

Woman: _____

① I got up at 10 o'clock this morning.
② Yes, I'll be fine. I'll sleep on the plane.
③ Don't worry. I will be fine by myself.
④ I can't hear you. The connection is really bad.
⑤ No, you don't have to wait for me at the airport.

19 대화를 듣고, 여자의 마지막 말에 대한 남자의 응답으로 가장 적절한 것을 고르시오.

Man: _____

① I'm sorry, but we'll be closed this Friday.
② If you cannot stay awake, drink more coffee.
③ Too much sleep can hurt your health as well.
④ I'll give you something for the pain in your eyes.
⑤ Your health is more important than doing well on your exam.

20 다음 상황 설명을 듣고, Tim이 Jennifer에게 할 말로 가장 적절한 것을 고르시오.

Tim: Jennifer, _____

① we have a meeting at 4.
② can you introduce yourself?
③ you should work out every day.
④ how was your meeting with Mr. Smith?
⑤ please turn on your computer before 4 o'clock.

◆ 다시 듣고, 빈칸에 들어갈 알맞은 단어를 써보세요.

정답 및 해설 p.37

01 그림 정보 파악

대화를 듣고, 여자가 구입할 신발로 가장 적절한 것을 고르시오.

① ② ③ ④ ⑤

W Hi, I'm looking for a pair of shoes.
M You've come to the right place. What are you looking for?
W I need casual shoes.
M Okay. How about _____ _____ _____?
W They have shoelaces. I'd prefer _____ _____ _____.
M Then these might be what you're looking for.
W They look good, but the _____ _____ _____ _____.
M How about these?
W They're perfect. _____ _____ _____.

02 부탁 파악

대화를 듣고, 남자가 여자에게 부탁한 일로 가장 적절한 것을 고르시오.

① 사과 씻어 주기
② 신발 끈 매주기
③ 아침 식사 차리기
④ 학교까지 태워 주기
⑤ 선생님에게 전화하기

W You're going to be late for school _____ _____ _____ _____, James.
M What time is it, Mom?
W It's 7:30. Hurry up and eat your breakfast.
M Oh no. I'm already late.
W What do you mean? School starts at 8:30.
M Mr. Johnson asked me to _____ _____ _____ _____ 8 today.
W Oh, then you need to leave right now.
M Can you just _____ _____ _____ _____ _____? I'll just eat that for breakfast.
W Okay, I'll do that while _____ _____ _____ your shoes.

03 그림 상황에 적절한 대화 찾기

다음 그림의 상황에 가장 적절한 대화를 고르시오.

① ② ③ ④ ⑤

① M Did you make a reservation?

W Yes, I _____ _____ _____

2 days ago.

② M Where can I find the restroom?

W _____ _____ _____

_____ the main entrance.

③ M Why don't you take my seat?

W It's okay. We're getting off _____ _____

_____ _____.

④ M Would you like _____ _____

_____ ?

W No, thank you. I've had enough to eat.

⑤ M Do you need more time to decide?

W Yes, _____ _____ _____

_____ in 5 minutes?

04 특정 정보 파악

대화를 듣고, 두 사람이 쇼핑하기로 한 요일을 고르시오.

① 월요일   ② 화요일   ③ 수요일
④ 금요일   ⑤ 토요일

W When is John's birthday?

M It's January 7th, which is next Wednesday.

W So that's why he's having his birthday party _____

_____.

M That's right. You're going to the party, too, aren't you?

W Yes. Did you get _____ _____

_____ _____ a present for him?

M No, I am going to go to the mall _____

_____ _____ _____.

W Oh, let's go to the mall together. I need to buy a present for him, too.

M _____ _____ _____.

05 언급하지 않은 내용 찾기

대화를 듣고, Sandwich King에 관해 언급되지 않은 것을 고르시오.

① 위치   ② 음식 맛
③ 음식 가격   ④ 특별 행사 품목
⑤ 주재료

W What's your favorite fast food restaurant?

M My favorite is 🔊 Sandwich King. There's one _____

_____ _____.

W Why do you like Sandwich King so much?

M The food _____ _____ _____,

and everything is at a reasonable price.

◀)) **Listening Tip**

sandwiches처럼 명사 뒤에 -(e)s가 붙어서 복수형이 되지요. -(e)s는 유성음 뒤에서는 [z]로, 무성음 뒤에서는 [s]로 발음하며, [s], [z], [ʃ], [ʤ], [tʃ] 소리 다음에 올 때는 [iz]로 발음해요. sandwich에서 'ch'는 [tʃ]로 발음되므로 뒤에 오는 -es는 [iz]로 발음해요.

W Really? I think their sandwiches are too expensive.

M _____ _____ _____

_____ their $1 special deals?

W Yes, I do. They are cheap, but you get _____

_____ _____ _____.

M Well, *I'm with you on that.

> ✳ 교육부 지정 의사소통 기능: **동의하기**   동(이) 4
>
> **I'm with you on that.** 나도 그것에 동의해.
>
> A: I think reading books on a smartphone is good. We can read anytime.
>   스마트폰으로 독서하는 것은 좋은 것 같아. 우리는 언제든지 책을 읽을 수 있잖아.
> B: **I'm with you on that.** 나도 그것에 동의해.

---

06 장소 추론

대화를 듣고, 두 사람이 대화하는 장소로 가장 적절한 것을 고르시오.

① 백화점   ② 제과점
③ 구내식당   ④ 요리 강습소
⑤ 호텔

M *Have you ever been here before, Linda?

W Yes, I have. I've _____ _____

_____ _____.

M How were they?

W They were okay. But they were _____

_____ _____ _____ I expected.

M That's because this place is actually _____

_____ _____.

W Are you going to buy a cake today?

M No, I'm actually _____ _____

_____ _____ for breakfast tomorrow.

W Oh, I should do that, too.

> ✳ 교육부 지정 의사소통 기능: **경험 묻고 답하기**   동(윤) 1
>
> **Have you ever ~?** ~해 본 적이 있니?
>
> A: **Have you ever** seen the rainbow? 무지개를 본 적이 있니?
> B: No, I haven't. 아니. 없어.

---

07 어색한 대화 찾기

다음을 듣고, 두 사람의 대화가 어색한 것을 고르시오.

①   ②   ③   ④   ⑤

① M Don't worry. He'll _____ _____

_____.

W Thank you. I hope he will.

② M I'm so tired that I can't move.

W _____ _____ _____ just fine

to me.

③ **M** Can you _____ _____ _____

_____ back?

W Yes, as soon as she gets home.

④ **M** Excuse me. Do you have the time?

W Yes, it's a quarter to 3.

⑤ **M** Would you like coffee or tea?

W _____ _____ _____, please.

---

08 부탁 파악

대화를 듣고, 여자가 남자에게 부탁한 일로 가장
적절한 것을 고르시오.

① TV 그만 보기   ② 숙제 끝내기
③ 동생과 놀아 주기   ④ 개 산책시키기
⑤ 실내 환기시키기

W Are you still watching TV, Paul?

M It's Saturday, Mom. I don't _____ _____

_____ to do.

W You've been watching TV for over 3 hours.

M I had a very busy week. I just don't _____

_____ _____ _____.

W Okay, I guess you deserve to be lazy for a day.

M Thanks, Mom.

W But can you at least _____ _____

_____? He's been inside the house all day.

M Yes, I can do that. I want to _____ _____

_____ _____, too.

---

09 화제 추론

다음을 듣고, 무엇에 관한 안내 방송인지 고르시
오.

① 공동 구역 환경 미화
② 층간 소음 문제 예방
③ 공동 주택 관리 법규
④ 놀이터 건축 설계 공모
⑤ 놀이터 운영 시간 변경

W Attention, residents. There is a change in operating

_____ _____ _____

_____ in our apartment complex. The management

has received a lot of complaints about some _____

_____ _____ _____ on the

playgrounds _____ _____ _____.

Starting tomorrow, the new operating hours of all the

playgrounds _____ _____ _____

10 a.m. to 9 p.m. We thank you in advance for your

cooperation.

대화를 듣고, 여자가 지불할 금액을 고르시오.

① $100   ② $110   ③ $120
④ $130   ⑤ $140

🔊 **Listening Tip**

traveling처럼 't'로 시작하는 단어에서 't' 다음에 'r'이
바로 오면 /트/가 아니라 /추/로 발음하는 경우가 많아요.
tree를 /트리/ 또는 /추리/라고 발음하듯 말이지요.
traveling은 /추래블링/에 가깝게 발음해요.

M   Good morning. How can I help you?

W   I'd like to rent a car for 2 days.

M   What kind of car would you like to rent?

W   I'll be 🔊traveling by myself, so I don't need a big car.

M   Then this car _____ _____ _____
_____ . It's $50 a day.

W   Does it come with a GPS system?

M   No, there is a $10 _____ _____
_____ _____ for a GPS system.

W   Okay, I'll _____ _____ _____
_____ a GPS system for 2 days.

---

11 할 일 파악

대화를 듣고, 남자가 할 일로 가장 적절한 것을 고
르시오.

① 병원에 함께 가기
② 두통약 먹기
③ 부모님께 전화하기
④ 약속 취소하기
⑤ 식당 예약 확인하기

M   Are you ready, honey? We'll be late for dinner.

W   I'm ready, John, but I have a terrible headache.

M   Oh no. Do you want me to _____ _____
_____ _____ ?

W   Yes, please. And I think we should tell your parents we're
_____ _____ _____
_____ .

M   We _____ _____ _____ if you're
not feeling too well.

W   I think I'll be fine if I just lie down for 10 minutes.

M   Okay, _____ _____ _____
_____ and let them know.

W   Yes, thank you.

---

12 언급하지 않은 내용 찾기

다음을 듣고, Sejong School에 관해 언급되지
않은 것을 고르시오.

① 교장 이름   ② 설립 연도
③ 사용 언어   ④ 모집 인원
⑤ 개학 날짜

M   Welcome to our orientation session, everyone. My name is
Rick Kim, and _____ _____
_____ _____ of this school. Sejong School
was established in 2010, and it is _____
_____ _____ school in the state. Students
will learn half of their subjects in Korean and the other half
in English. _____ _____ _____
_____ 100 new students this year, and you can start
applying on Monday the 20th.

다음 게스트 하우스의 배치도를 보면서 대화를 듣고, 두 사람이 머물 방의 위치를 고르시오.

	① Room A	② Room B	③ Room C	
Kitchen		Yard		◀ Entrance
	④ Room D	Restroom	⑤ Room E	

W   I'm so excited to stay at Hanok Guesthouse.

M   Me, too. Which room would you like to stay in?

W   Well, I don't like _____ _____ _____ _____ the restroom.

M   Okay. What about a room _____ _____ _____? It will be easier to move around because we have many bags.

W   I don't think that's a good idea. It could _____ _____ _____, so we won't be able to sleep.

M   I see. Then, we have 2 rooms left.

W   How about _____ _____ _____ _____ _____? We can cook and eat faster.

M   Great. Let's stay there then.

다음을 듣고, 무엇에 관한 설명인지 고르시오.

① 코알라   ② 캥거루   ③ 말
④ 타조   ⑤ 너구리

W   This animal is usually found in Australia. In fact, it is _____ _____ _____ Australia and even appears on some Australian money. This animal _____ _____ _____ _____, and it also has a long tail for balancing. It is the only large animal that _____ _____ _____. This animal is famous for having a pouch and _____ _____ _____ in it.

대화를 듣고, 여자가 대화 직후에 할 일로 가장 적절한 것을 고르시오.

① 공원에 가기   ② 연 날리기
③ 슈퍼마켓에 가기   ④ 연 만들기
⑤ 겨울옷 꺼내기

M   It's such a beautiful day. Do you want to go to the park, Cindy?

W   Now? Can we go tomorrow instead, Dad?

M   Sure, we can. But it's going to _____ _____ _____ _____ tomorrow.

W   I know. I want to _____ _____ _____ at the park tomorrow.

M   Oh, that's why you asked me to get some glue this morning.

W   Yes, I'm going to _____ _____ _____ _____ _____.

M   Do you want me to help you?

W   No, thanks, Dad. I want to do it by myself.

16 숫자 정보 파악 (날짜)

대화를 듣고, 다음 테니스 경기가 열리는 날짜를 고르시오.

① April 23rd   ② April 24th
③ May 1st   ④ May 10th
⑤ May 11th

M Are you ready for the next tennis matches, Donna?
W I don't know. I still have to watch _____ _____ _____ of the other team.
M Aren't you playing against the Newtown High School players on May 1st? That's only 3 days away.
W We _____ _____ _____ them on April 24th, Dad.
M Oh, I meant to say Riverside High School.
W _____ _____ _____ them on May 11th.
M I _____ _____ _____ the dates and schools.

17 이어질 응답 찾기

대화를 듣고, 여자의 마지막 말에 대한 남자의 응답으로 가장 적절한 것을 고르시오.

Man: _____

① You should've come with us.
② Well, I don't have a favorite car.
③ We had to stop by City Hall.
④ It's hard to say. I liked all of them.
⑤ My dad gave us a ride to the park.

W Have you been to Fantasy World, the new amusement park?
M Yes, I have. I went with my brother 2 weeks ago.
W It's _____ _____ _____, isn't it?
M Yes, it's the best amusement park I've ever been to.
W Were you able to _____ _____ _____ _____ _____ ?
M Yes, we were very lucky.
W What was _____ _____ _____ ?

18 이어질 응답 찾기

대화를 듣고, 남자의 마지막 말에 대한 여자의 응답으로 가장 적절한 것을 고르시오.

Woman: _____

① I got up at 10 o'clock this morning.
② Yes, I'll be fine. I'll sleep on the plane.
③ Don't worry. I will be fine by myself.
④ I can't hear you. The connection is really bad.
⑤ No, you don't have to wait for me at the airport.

M It's 9:30 right now. What time is your flight, Sally?
W The departure time is 10:30 a.m.
M I don't see any flights that _____ _____ _____ 10:30 a.m.
W That can't be right. Let me see.
M Are you flying American Air?
W Yes, Dad. It says the flight has been delayed. _____ _____ _____ is 11:30 a.m.
M Oh, I see. Do you want me _____ _____ _____ _____ ?

이어질 응답 찾기

대화를 듣고, 여자의 마지막 말에 대한 남자의 응답으로 가장 적절한 것을 고르시오.

Man: _____

① I'm sorry, but we'll be closed this Friday.
② If you cannot stay awake, drink more coffee.
③ Too much sleep can hurt your health as well.
④ I'll give you something for the pain in your eyes.
⑤ Your health is more important than doing well on your exam.

W Dr. Jackson, my eyes are really red.
M Let me take a look. Do they hurt?
W No. I _____ _____ _____. My eyes have been dry for _____ _____ _____ _____.
M Have you been sleeping well?
W No, I haven't.
M That's why. Your eyes are telling you that you need to _____ _____ _____ _____.
W But I can't rest. There's _____ _____ _____ _____ this Friday.

상황에 적절한 말 찾기

다음 상황 설명을 듣고, Tim이 Jennifer에게 할 말로 가장 적절한 것을 고르시오.

Tim: Jennifer, _____

① we have a meeting at 4.
② can you introduce yourself?
③ you should work out every day.
④ how was your meeting with Mr. Smith?
⑤ please turn on your computer before 4 o'clock.

M Tim is the leader of a debate club. He holds a club meeting at 4 p.m. every Wednesday. _____ _____ _____ _____ 10 minutes late because one of the club members, Jennifer, _____ _____ _____ _____ her computer. She needs to take notes on her computer, but everyone else _____ _____ _____ _____. So, Tim wants to _____ _____ _____ _____ her computer before the meeting. In this situation, what would Tim most likely say to Jennifer?

실전 모의고사 **07**

점수
/20

01 대화를 듣고, 여자가 구입할 셔츠로 가장 적절한 것을 고르시오.

① ② ③

④ ⑤

02 대화를 듣고, 농구공에 관해 언급되지 <u>않은</u> 것을 고르시오.

① 크기 ② 가격 ③ 재질
④ 색상 ⑤ 무게

03 대화를 듣고, 남자가 여자에게 전화한 목적으로 가장 적절한 것을 고르시오.

① 환불을 요청하려고
② 배송 상황을 확인하려고
③ 구매 이력을 확인하려고
④ 책상 크기를 문의하려고
⑤ 가구 배달 일정을 조정하려고

04 대화를 듣고, 두 사람이 만나기로 한 시각을 고르시오.

① 4:30 p.m. ② 5:30 p.m. ③ 6:00 p.m.
④ 6:30 p.m. ⑤ 7:00 p.m.

05 대화를 듣고, 두 사람이 대화하는 장소로 가장 적절한 것을 고르시오.

① 기차 안 ② 경기장 앞 ③ 지하철역
④ 모자 가게 ⑤ 커피숍

06 다음 그림의 상황에 가장 적절한 대화를 고르시오.

① ② ③ ④ ⑤

07 대화를 듣고, 여자가 남자에게 부탁한 일로 가장 적절한 것을 고르시오.

① 일찍 귀가하기 ② 여행 가방 싸기
③ 우편함 확인하기 ④ 보고서 작성 도와주기
⑤ 시장에서 물건 사 오기

08 다음을 듣고, 캠핑장에 관해 언급되지 <u>않은</u> 것을 고르시오.

① 불 피우는 장소 ② 주차 공간
③ 화장실 위치 ④ 체크아웃 시각
⑤ 사용료

09 다음을 듣고, 무엇에 관한 설명인지 고르시오.

① 배드민턴 라켓 ② 셔틀콕
③ 야구 글러브 ④ 탁구 라켓
⑤ 럭비공

10 다음을 듣고, 두 사람의 대화가 <u>어색한</u> 것을 고르시오.

① ② ③ ④ ⑤

11 대화를 듣고, 여자가 할 일로 가장 적절한 것을 고르시오.

① 화장지 사오기
② 동영상 제작하기
③ 비디오카메라 수리 맡기기
④ 화장실에 포스터 붙이기
⑤ 포스터 디자인하기

12 다음 표를 보면서 대화를 듣고, 두 사람이 관람할 뮤지컬을 고르시오.

	Musical	Day	Time	Price
①	A	Saturday	7 p.m.	$100
②	B	Saturday	8 p.m.	$80
③	C	Saturday	8 p.m.	$100
④	D	Sunday	8 p.m.	$80
⑤	E	Sunday	7 p.m.	$100

13 대화를 듣고, 화재가 처음 발생한 날짜를 고르시오.

① September 23rd   ② September 30th
③ October 7th   ④ October 14th
⑤ October 21st

14 대화를 듣고, 남자가 어제 한 일로 가장 적절한 것을 고르시오.

① 가구 수리 맡기기   ② 진통제 사오기
③ 책상 조립하기   ④ 책상 주문하기
⑤ 허리 치료하기

15 다음을 듣고, 방송의 목적으로 가장 적절한 것을 고르시오.

① 여름 캠프를 홍보하려고
② 운동의 필요성을 강조하려고
③ 환경 보존의 중요성을 알리려고
④ 게임 중독의 위험성을 일깨우려고
⑤ 야외 활동에 학부모들을 참여시키려고

16 대화를 듣고, 여자가 지불할 금액을 고르시오.

① $10   ② $18   ③ $20
④ $27   ⑤ $30

17 대화를 듣고, 여자의 마지막 말에 대한 남자의 응답으로 가장 적절한 것을 고르시오.

Man: _____

① I like him at least as much as you like him.
② I've only recently learned about him.
③ I don't like him because he is a bad actor.
④ He's handsome, but he is not such a nice person.
⑤ I like him because he donates to charities every year.

18 대화를 듣고, 남자의 마지막 말에 대한 여자의 응답으로 가장 적절한 것을 고르시오.

Woman: _____

① Do you know how to fix the computer?
② Perfect! We're finally done preparing.
③ You still have 10 minutes to finish the exam.
④ No problem. I can fix your phone right away.
⑤ Really? I'll ask Mr. Kim to bring a new one.

19 대화를 듣고, 여자의 마지막 말에 대한 남자의 응답으로 가장 적절한 것을 고르시오.

Man: _____

① No, it's April 1st.
② Yes. We should be careful.
③ It's not possible to play jokes on teachers.
④ Well, I've always celebrated April Fools' Day.
⑤ Having fun is more important than telling the truth.

20 다음 상황 설명을 듣고, Jason이 남자에게 할 말로 가장 적절한 것을 고르시오.

Jason: Excuse me, _____

① is there a supermarket near here?
② where do you go grocery shopping?
③ I didn't know you were working here.
④ you need to go to the end of the line.
⑤ how much did you pay for the basket?

◆ 다시 듣고, 빈칸에 들어갈 알맞은 단어를 써보세요.

정답 및 해설 p.44

01 그림 정보 파악

대화를 듣고, 여자가 구입할 셔츠를 가장 적절한 것을 고르시오.

① ② ③ ④ ⑤

M Hello, how may I help you?

W Where can I find boys' shirts?

M Oh, they're right over there. This way, please.

W Thanks.

M Are you _____ _____ _____ in particular?

W I'm looking for a unique shirt. My son needs to wear it for his school play.

M Then, how about this one _____ _____ _____ _____?

W It looks good, but this one with lots of stars on it _____ _____ _____.

M I'm sure he'll like it, ma'am.

W _____ _____ _____, _____. I'll take it.

02 언급하지 않은 내용 찾기

대화를 듣고, 농구공에 관해 언급되지 <u>않은</u> 것을 고르시오.

① 크기   ② 가격   ③ 재질
④ 색상   ⑤ 무게

W Welcome to Richard's Sporting Goods. Can I help you find anything?

M I'm looking for a basketball.

W Sure, this is the most popular basketball we have.

M That is too big. I'm looking for _____ _____. It's for my son in second grade.

W Then size 6 _____ _____ _____ _____. This one's only $15.

M Is it _____ _____ _____?

W Yes, and it comes in 2 different colors, black and brown.

M Okay. I'll _____ _____ _____ _____.

03 목적 파악

대화를 듣고, 남자가 여자에게 전화한 목적으로 가장 적절한 것을 고르시오.

① 환불을 요청하려고
② 배송 상황을 확인하려고
③ 구매 이력을 확인하려고
④ 책상 크기를 문의하려고
⑤ 가구 배달 일정을 조정하려고

[Telephone rings.]

W Thank you for calling Jane's Furniture. How may I help you?

M I have a question about _____ _____ _____ _____ last week.

W Can I have your order number?

M Yes, it's 655789.

W Okay, let me check. *[Pause]* A bed frame and _____ _____ _____ _____ 3 days ago.

M Yes, that's correct. Could I return the desk and get a refund for it?

W Is there _____ _____ _____ the desk?

M It is too big for my room.

W Okay. You can return it and get a refund. But you'll have to _____ _____ _____.

M That's not a problem.

04 숫자 정보 파악 (시각)

대화를 듣고, 두 사람이 만나기로 한 시각을 고르시오.

① 4:30 p.m.   ② 5:30 p.m.
③ 6:00 p.m.   ④ 6:30 p.m.
⑤ 7:00 p.m.

W Hey, Peter. Are you excited about going to the baseball game tonight?

M Of course, I am. It's the final game of the season.

W We're meeting at 5:30 p.m. at the bus stop, right?

M Right. But I think we need to meet _____ _____ _____.

W _____ _____ _____? The game starts at 7, right?

M There are pre-game activities that all the fans can participate in. _____ _____ _____ 6 p.m.

W Really? Then _____ _____ _____ _____ 4:30.

M That sounds good.

05 장소 추론

대화를 듣고, 두 사람이 대화하는 장소로 가장 적절한 것을 고르시오.

① 기차 안   ② 경기장 앞
③ 지하철역   ④ 모자 가게
⑤ 커피숍

M Wow, it's so crowded in here.

W I know. This happens _____ _____ _____ a concert at the stadium.

M Oh, is that why so many people are waiting in line?

W Yes. All these people are trying to get home after watching a boy group's concert.

M Will we be able to _____ _____ _____ _____ _____?

W Probably not. If we can't, _____ _____ _____ _____ the one after that.

M _____ _____ _____ _____ 5 minutes, right?

W Yes. We're lucky we only have 2 stops to go.

06 그림 상황에 적절한 대화 찾기

다음 그림의 상황에 가장 적절한 대화를 고르시오.

① ② ③ ④ ⑤

① **M** _____ _____ _____ _____ go swimming?

W I go swimming every day.

② **M** How much are these flowers?

W They are $20 a dozen.

③ **M** Look out! _____ _____ _____ the ice.

W Oh, thank you! I didn't see it.

④ **M** What would you like to drink?

W _____ _____ a glass of iced tea.

⑤ **M** Where can I park my car?

W You can _____ _____ _____ _____.

07 부탁 파악

대화를 듣고, 여자가 남자에게 부탁한 일로 가장 적절한 것을 고르시오.

① 일찍 귀가하기
② 여행 가방 싸기
③ 우편함 확인하기
④ 보고서 작성 도와주기
⑤ 시장에서 물건 사 오기

[Cell phone rings.]

M Hello.

W Hi, John. Are you _____ _____ _____ _____ ?

M Yes, Mom. I should be home in about 10 minutes.

W Did you get all your schoolwork done?

M Yes, _____ _____ _____ _____ finish my report before I left.

W Good. I'll _____ _____ _____.

M Do you want me to pick up anything from the supermarket?

W No. We have everything we need. Could you just _____ _____ _____ ?

M Okay, I will.

다음을 듣고, 캠핑장에 관해 언급되지 <u>않은</u> 것을 고르시오.

① 불 피우는 장소　　② 주차 공간
③ 화장실 위치　　　④ 체크아웃 시각
⑤ 사용료

M Hello, campers. This is a short announcement reminding you of the rules for all the guests. Fires are allowed only _____ _____. Each campsite has one parking spot, and parking is _____ _____ _____ the grass. Bathrooms are 🔊located _____ _____ _____ _____ _____. Please, remember that _____ _____ _____ is 12 p.m. Make sure to be polite to other campers, and I hope you enjoy your stay!

09 화제 추론

다음을 듣고, 무엇에 관한 설명인지 고르시오.

① 배드민턴 라켓　　② 셔틀콕
③ 야구 글러브　　　④ 탁구 라켓
⑤ 럭비공

W This is shaped like a cone. It has a round end and 16 or more _____ _____ _____ _____. It is used when you play badminton. In badminton, each player _____ _____ _____ a racket and sends it _____ _____ _____ to the other player. If the other player _____ _____ _____, you win a point.

10 어색한 대화 찾기

다음을 듣고, 두 사람의 대화가 <u>어색한</u> 것을 고르시오.

①　　②　　③　　④　　⑤

① M I'll call you _____ _____ _____ _____.

W Of course. You can use my phone.

② M Did you _____ _____ _____ ?

W No, I didn't get it.

③ M Are you from 🔊 Philadelphia?

W I was born and _____ _____.

④ M How often do you watch TV?

W I don't _____ _____ _____ _____.

⑤ M Can I help you find anything?

W Yes, I'm looking for a green hat.

대화를 듣고, 여자가 할 일로 가장 적절한 것을 고르시오.

① 화장지 사오기
② 동영상 제작하기
③ 비디오카메라 수리 맡기기
④ 화장실에 포스터 붙이기
⑤ 포스터 디자인하기

M Judy, can we talk about our project now?

W Sure. We are going to _____ _____ _____ about using less toilet paper, right?

M Yes. But we don't have enough time to make a video. So, how about _____ _____ _____?

W Okay. What do you want to do?

M *I'm thinking of making a poster instead. Can you _____ _____ _____? I brought you paper and a pencil.

W Sure. _____ _____ _____ _____.

M Thanks.

> ＊ **교육부 지정 의사소통 기능: 의향 말하기**   미 1
>
> **I'm thinking of ~.** 나는 ~ 할까 생각 중이야.
> • **I'm thinking of** keeping a bird. 나는 새를 한 마리 키울까 생각 중이야.
> • **I'm thinking of** learning Spanish. 나는 스페인어를 배울 것을 고려하고 있어.

다음 표를 보면서 대화를 듣고, 두 사람이 관람할 뮤지컬을 고르시오.

	Musical	Day	Time	Price
①	A	Saturday	7 p.m.	$100
②	B	Saturday	8 p.m.	$80
③	C	Saturday	8 p.m.	$100
④	D	Sunday	8 p.m.	$80
⑤	E	Sunday	7 p.m.	$100

M Honey, let's go to a musical this weekend.

W Sure. I have _____ _____ _____.

M Great. I'll buy the tickets right now.

W Make sure to leave enough time for dinner before the musical starts.

M I will. The one we saw last month started at 7 p.m., right?

W Right. We _____ _____ _____ _____.

M We have 2 musicals to choose from. Which one do you want to see?

W This musical is _____ _____ than that one, but I've read _____ _____ _____ about it.

M Okay. This one _____ _____ _____ then.

13 숫자 정보 파악 (날짜)

대화를 듣고, 화재가 처음 발생한 날짜를 고르시오.

① September 23rd
② September 30th
③ October 7th
④ October 14th
⑤ October 21st

M Did you see the news about the huge fire in California?

W Yes, I did. Wildfires often happen in autumn, but this one is really bad.

M I know. It's terrible. Do you know _____ _____ _____ _____ ?

W I _____ _____ _____ _____ October 7th.

M That's over 2 weeks ago. _____ _____ _____ _____ October 14th?

W Well, the 7th is what I heard on the 8 o'clock news yesterday.

M Let's check the news on the Internet. [Pause] Oh, _____ _____ . It started 2 weeks ago.

W It is really sad, isn't it?

14 한 일 파악

대화를 듣고, 남자가 어제 한 일로 가장 적절한 것을 고르시오.

① 가구 수리 맡기기 ② 진통제 사오기
③ 책상 조립하기 ④ 책상 주문하기
⑤ 허리 치료하기

W Jack, are you going somewhere?

M I'm going to the pharmacy _____ _____ _____ _____ .

W Why? Are you feeling okay?

M No, I think I _____ _____ _____ . It's killing me.

W Oh no. What happened?

M I ordered a new desk a few days ago and it was delivered yesterday. So I spent _____ _____ _____ _____ _____ .

W That sounds like a lot of work. I hope you feel better soon.

M Thanks.

15 목적 파악

다음을 듣고, 방송의 목적으로 가장 적절한 것을 고르시오.

① 여름 캠프를 홍보하려고
② 운동의 필요성을 강조하려고
③ 환경 보존의 중요성을 알리려고
④ 게임 중독의 위험성을 일깨우려고
⑤ 야외 활동에 학부모들을 참여시키려고

M Hello, parents. _____ _____ _____ _____ a summer camp for your children? The JC Baseball Camp is _____ _____ _____ young players to improve their skills, work hard and make new friends. Most importantly, _____ _____

_____ valuable life skills they'll need for the rest of their lives. _____ _____ _____ , please visit our website, www.jcbaseballcamp.com.

16 숫자 정보 파악 (금액)

16 숫자 정보 파악 (금액)

대화를 듣고, 여자가 지불할 금액을 고르시오.

① $10   ② $18   ③ $20
④ $27   ⑤ $30

M Welcome to the Natural History Museum. How may I help you?

W I'd like to _____ _____ _____ 4 people, please.

M Are there _____ _____ _____ 12?

W Yes, there are 2 children.

M For adults, it's $10, and for children, it's $5.

W I see. _____ _____ _____ _____ ?

M The total is $30. But on Wednesdays only, we offer a _____ _____ _____ _____ . So today you get a 10% discount.

W That's great. Here is my card.

17 이어질 응답 찾기

대화를 듣고, 여자의 마지막 말에 대한 남자의 응답으로 가장 적절한 것을 고르시오.

Man: _____

① I like him at least as much as you like him.
② I've only recently learned about him.
③ I don't like him because he is a bad actor.
④ He's handsome, but he is not such a nice person.
⑤ I like him because he donates to charities every year.

W Who's your favorite actor, Andy?

M It's hard to _____ _____ _____ . Hmm... I think I like Michael Smith best.

W He's one of my favorite actors, too.

M Did you see his blockbuster movie this summer?

W Of course, I did. I've seen _____ _____ _____ _____ since 2010.

M Wow, you _____ _____ _____ _____ .

W Yes, I do. I think he's very handsome. _____ _____ _____ _____ him so much?

18 이어질 응답 찾기

대화를 듣고, 남자의 마지막 말에 대한 여자의 응답으로 가장 적절한 것을 고르시오.

Woman: _____

① Do you know how to fix the computer?
② Perfect! We're finally done preparing.
③ You still have 10 minutes to finish the exam.
④ No problem. I can fix your phone right away.
⑤ Really? I'll ask Mr. Kim to bring a new one.

M Have we finished preparing for our school festival?
W I'm not sure. Let's do a final check.
M Sure. How much time _____ _____ _____ _____ ?
W We should be done preparing in about 10 minutes.
M You should make sure that _____ _____ _____ _____ .
W Yes, it's working fine. _____ _____ _____ the microphone for me?
M Okay. [Pause] There seems to be _____ _____ _____ this microphone.

19 이어질 응답 찾기

대화를 듣고, 여자의 마지막 말에 대한 남자의 응답으로 가장 적절한 것을 고르시오.

Man: _____

① No, it's April 1st.
② Yes. We should be careful.
③ It's not possible to play jokes on teachers.
④ Well, I've always celebrated April Fools' Day.
⑤ Having fun is more important than telling the truth.

W Did you hear anything interesting at school today?
M No, I didn't. _____ _____ _____ _____ ?
W Didn't you know? Today's April Fools' Day.
M Oh, I wasn't aware of that. Did anyone play a joke on someone at your school?
W No, _____ _____ _____ .
M Good. _____ _____ _____ jokes or stupid lies.
W I agree. It might _____ _____ _____ .

20 상황에 적절한 말 찾기

다음 상황 설명을 듣고, Jason이 남자에게 할 말로 가장 적절한 것을 고르시오.

Jason: Excuse me, _____

① is there a supermarket near here?
② where do you go grocery shopping?
③ I didn't know you were working here.
④ you need to go to the end of the line.
⑤ how much did you pay for the basket?

W Jason goes grocery shopping at a big supermarket every Friday evening. Last Friday, there were _____ _____ _____ _____ at the supermarket because it was right before a long weekend. He _____ _____ _____ _____ because the waiting line for a cashier was too long. A few minutes later, a man with a small basket _____ _____ _____ _____ him. In this situation, what would Jason most likely say to the man?

실전 모의고사 08

01 대화를 듣고, 여자가 잃어버린 물건으로 가장 적절한 것을 고르시오.

① ② ③

④ ⑤

02 대화를 듣고, Vincent van Gogh에 관해 언급되지 않은 것을 고르시오.

① 국적　　　② 사망 연도　　　③ 대표작
④ 가족 관계　　⑤ 종교

03 대화를 듣고, 남자가 여자에게 전화한 목적으로 가장 적절한 것을 고르시오.

① 같이 볼 영화를 정하려고
② 여자의 안부를 물으려고
③ 커피숍에 대해 홍보하려고
④ 프로젝트 일정을 확인하려고
⑤ 촬영 구경 가자고 제안하려고

04 대화를 듣고, 지하철 막차가 떠나는 시각을 고르시오.

① 10:00 p.m.　② 10:30 p.m.　③ 11:00 p.m.
④ 11:30 p.m.　⑤ 12:00 a.m.

05 대화를 듣고, 두 사람이 대화하는 장소로 가장 적절한 것을 고르시오.

① 커피숍　　　　② 호텔
③ 미용실　　　　④ 의료 기기 가게
⑤ 치과

06 다음 그림의 상황에 가장 적절한 대화를 고르시오.

① ② ③ ④ ⑤

07 대화를 듣고, 남자가 여자에게 부탁한 일로 가장 적절한 것을 고르시오.

① 휴가 내기　　　　② 어깨 마사지 해 주기
③ 이메일 확인하기　　④ 혼자 있게 내버려 두기
⑤ 위로해 주기

08 다음을 듣고, 독서 주간에 관해 언급되지 않은 것을 고르시오.

① 기간　　　　　　② 읽어야 할 도서 종류
③ 독후감 제출 방법　④ 읽을 책의 분량
⑤ 초대 손님

09 다음을 듣고, 무엇에 관한 설명인지 고르시오.

① 케이블카　　　　② 러닝머신
③ 엘리베이터　　　④ 킥보드
⑤ 에스컬레이터

10 다음을 듣고, 두 사람의 대화가 어색한 것을 고르시오.

① ② ③ ④ ⑤

11 대화를 듣고, 남자가 대화 직후에 할 일로 가장 적절한 것을 고르시오.

① 체육관 가기　　　② 잡초 뽑기
③ 식사 준비하기　　④ 엄마와 대화하기
⑤ 지하실 가기

12 다음 표를 보면서 대화를 듣고, 두 사람이 탈 기차를 고르시오.

	Train	Destination	Arrival Time	Seat
①	A	Yeosu	12 p.m.	Economy
②	B	Mokpo	1 p.m.	First class
③	C	Mokpo	12 p.m.	First class
④	D	Mokpo	12 p.m.	Economy
⑤	E	Yeosu	10 p.m.	First class

13 대화를 듣고, 여자가 미용실에 가기로 한 날짜를 고르시오.

① July 10th   ② July 11th

③ July 12th   ④ July 13th

⑤ July 14th

14 대화를 듣고, 남자가 어제 한 일로 가장 적절한 것을 고르시오.

① 쇼핑하기   ② 요리 연습하기

③ 집에서 휴식하기   ④ 호텔에서 외식하기

⑤ 음식 축제 다녀오기

15 다음을 듣고, 방송의 목적으로 가장 적절한 것을 고르시오.

① 날씨를 예보하려고

② 이메일 활용을 장려하려고

③ 허리케인 피해를 접수하려고

④ 비상 연락망을 활성화하려고

⑤ 허리케인 대비 행동 요령을 안내하려고

16 대화를 듣고, 남자가 지불할 금액을 고르시오.

① $1,000   ② $1,400   ③ $1,600

④ $1,800   ⑤ $2,000

17 대화를 듣고, 여자의 마지막 말에 대한 남자의 응답으로 가장 적절한 것을 고르시오.

Man: _____

① Perfect! I'll wake you up in 2 hours.

② We should keep going since we're late.

③ Oh, good. I was getting really worried.

④ We need to find a restroom, not a gas station.

⑤ Okay, I'll call you when I arrive at the station.

18 대화를 듣고, 남자의 마지막 말에 대한 여자의 응답으로 가장 적절한 것을 고르시오.

Woman: _____

① I won't be able to graduate this year.

② I think I'll take his class next semester.

③ I've never studied European history.

④ I think you should take another history class.

⑤ He's not interesting, but his class is very organized.

19 대화를 듣고, 여자의 마지막 말에 대한 남자의 응답으로 가장 적절한 것을 고르시오.

Man: _____

① I learned it from my mom.

② I think baking bread is much more difficult.

③ Most people say rice is better than noodles.

④ It was really hot when I went to Vietnam.

⑤ Rice noodles taste much better than other noodles.

20 다음 상황 설명을 듣고, Jake가 Terry에게 할 말로 가장 적절한 것을 고르시오.

Jake: _____

① Where did you get your bicycle?

② Did your father buy a present for you?

③ Can you teach me how to ride a bicycle?

④ Is your bicycle more expensive than mine?

⑤ What do you want for your birthday present?

Dictation 08

◆ 다시 듣고, 빈칸에 들어갈 알맞은 단어를 써보세요.

정답 및 해설 p.51

01 그림 정보 파악

대화를 듣고, 여자가 잃어버린 물건으로 가장 적절한 것을 고르시오.

①   ②   ③

④   ⑤

[Telephone rings.]

M Thanks for calling Michelle's Diner. How may I help you?

W Hi. I had lunch there today, and I think I left my watch in the restroom.

M What does it look like?

W It's a digital watch, and it _____ _____ _____ _____.

M We haven't found _____ _____ _____, so can you call back tomorrow?

W Yes, I will. Oh, it _____ _____ _____ _____ K. J. Y. on it.

M Okay, _____ _____ _____ _____ to look for your watch, ma'am.

02 언급하지 않은 내용 찾기

대화를 듣고, Vincent van Gogh에 관해 언급되지 않은 것을 고르시오.

① 국적   ② 사망 연도
③ 대표작   ④ 가족 관계
⑤ 종교

W Do you have a favorite painter?

M Yes, my favorite painter is Vincent van Gogh. He's a Dutch painter.

W He is my favorite, too. It's too bad that he wasn't famous at all when he was alive.

M I know. _____ _____ _____ 1890, but his paintings became really popular 11 years later.

W Yes, that's right. So, which one of his paintings is your favorite?

M It's _____ _____ _____ _____. I like *The Starry Night* and *Sunflowers* the most.

W I heard he was really close _____ _____ _____, but did he get married?

M No, he didn't. That's why he _____ _____ _____ children.

목적 파악

대화를 듣고, 남자가 여자에게 전화한 목적으로
가장 적절한 것을 고르시오

① 같이 볼 영화를 정하려고
② 여자의 안부를 물으려고
③ 커피숍에 대해 홍보하려고
④ 프로젝트 일정을 확인하려고
⑤ 촬영 구경 가자고 제안하려고

[Cell phone rings.]

M Hello.

M Hey, Samantha. It's Thomas.

W Hey, Thomas. What's up?

M Do you know the new cafe near the bus terminal?

W Sure. I went there once _____ _____

_____ _____. What about it?

M I heard that Tom Cruise is coming to that cafe next week.

He is going to _____ _____ _____

there. We should go!

W But the cafe is going to be closed, isn't it?

M Yes. But don't worry. My uncle is one of _____

_____ _____. We can get _____

_____ _____ _____

_____.

W That's great! I hope we can see Tom Cruise.

---

04 **숫자 정보 파악 (시각)**

대화를 듣고, 지하철 막차가 떠나는 시각을 고르
시오.

① 10:00 p.m.   ② 10:30 p.m.
③ 11:00 p.m.   ④ 11:30 p.m.
⑤ 12:00 a.m.

🔊 **Listening Tip**
last train처럼 앞 단어의 끝부분과 뒤에 있는 단어의 앞부
분에 같은 자음이 오면 앞의 자음은 발음이 되지 않아요.
따라서 /래스트 트레인/이 아니라 /래스~ 츄레인/으로 발
음해요.

M It's getting really late. We _____ _____

_____ _____, Amy.

W Let's stay a little longer, Dad. It's your retirement party.

M It's already 10 p.m. We'll miss the 🔊last train.

W The subway _____ _____ _____

_____ 11 p.m.

M Are you sure? We should check the subway schedule to make

sure.

W Okay, let's do that.

M *[Pause]* Oh, _____ _____ _____

_____ here at 11:30 p.m.

W See? Can we _____ _____ _____

_____ then?

M Yes, of course.

---

05 **장소 추론**

대화를 듣고, 두 사람이 대화하는 장소로 가장 적
절한 것을 고르시오.

① 커피숍   ② 호텔
③ 미용실   ④ 의료 기기 가게
⑤ 치과

M Ms. Jensen, the total amount for your visit today comes out
to be $67.

W Okay, I'll pay by credit card.

M We _____ _____ _____

_____ your next visit.

W Right. _____ _____ _____ I need to come back in about 2 weeks.

M Will April 17th work for you?

W How long will my next visit take?

M The doctor needs to check _____ _____ _____ _____ again. So it'll take at least an hour.

W I can come in at 4 p.m. on the 17th.

M Okay, Ms. Jensen. We'll _____ _____ _____ _____ the 17th.

---

06 그림 상황에 적절한 대화 찾기

다음 그림의 상황에 가장 적절한 대화를 고르시오.

① ② ③ ④ ⑤

① M _____ _____ _____ _____ Iceland?

W Yes, I have. It's a beautiful country.

② M Did you catch a lot of fish?

W Yes, _____ _____ _____ 20 fish already.

③ M Why don't we go fishing this weekend?

W Sure. *I'm really looking forward to it.

④ M Would you like some dessert?

W No, thanks. Can I _____ _____ _____, please?

⑤ M Did you clean your room?

W No, I didn't. I'll do it tomorrow.

＊ 교육부 지정 의사소통 기능: 기대 표현하기　　　　동(이) 5ㅣ천(이) 5ㅣ천(정) 3ㅣY(박) 5

I'm looking forward to ~. 나는 ~을 기대하고 있어.
- **I'm looking forward to** your visit. 당신이 방문해 주기를 기대합니다.
- **I'm looking forward to** my vacation. 나는 휴가를 기대하고 있어.

---

07 부탁 파악

대화를 듣고, 남자가 여자에게 부탁한 일로 가장 적절한 것을 고르시오.

① 휴가 내기
② 어깨 마사지 해 주기
③ 이메일 확인하기
④ 혼자 있게 내버려 두기
⑤ 위로해 주기

W How was your day, honey?

M I had _____ _____ _____ _____ at the office.

W Did something bad happen?

M Well, 3 people _____ _____ _____ _____ today, so I had to answer all the e-mails from customers by myself.

W Oh, I'm sorry to hear that. Is there anything I can do for you?

M _____ _____ _____ _____ a shoulder massage? My shoulders hurt a little bit.

W Sure. _____ _____ _____ over here.

08 언급하지 않은 내용 찾기

다음을 듣고, 독서 주간에 관해 언급되지 않은 것을 고르시오.

① 기간   ② 읽어야 할 도서 종류
③ 독후감 제출 방법   ④ 읽을 책의 분량
⑤ 초대 손님

M Happy Friday, everyone. This is your English teacher Mr. Jenner speaking. Reading Week this year _____ _____ Monday the 20th and _____ _____ Sunday the 26th. All of you are required _____ _____ _____ _____. The book of your choice _____ _____ _____ at least 100 pages long. To celebrate this year's Reading Week, we will _____ _____ _____ _____, a famous author, visit on Wednesday.

09 화제 추론

다음을 듣고, 무엇에 관한 설명인지 고르시오.

① 케이블카   ② 러닝머신
③ 엘리베이터   ④ 킥보드
⑤ 에스컬레이터

W This is something that _____ _____ _____, but it's not a vehicle. It takes you from _____ _____ _____. You will see many of these in large buildings. For example, a department store has at least one of these on every floor. This _____ _____, so you need to be careful when you get on it. This moving object _____ _____ _____.

10 어색한 대화 찾기

다음을 듣고, 두 사람의 대화가 어색한 것을 고르시오.

①   ②   ③   ④   ⑤

① M _____ _____ _____ _____ the movie?

W I liked it a lot. It was really good.

② M I'm starving. What about you?

W I'm really hungry, too.

③ M My eyes are _____ _____
_____ _____.

W Why don't you take a break?

④ M Do you have a runny nose?

W Yes, I _____ _____ _____.

⑤ M You shouldn't go to bed so late.

W I know. It is _____ _____
_____.

11 할 일 파악

대화를 듣고, 남자가 대화 직후에 할 일로 가장 적절한 것을 고르시오.

① 체육관 가기   ② 잡초 뽑기
③ 식사 준비하기   ④ 엄마와 대화하기
⑤ 지하실 가기

M It's raining now. Did you see my raincoat?

W Why do you need a raincoat, Dad?

M I just remembered what your mother said about rainy days.

W Oh, we should _____ _____
_____ _____ outside when it's raining,
right?

M Yes, _____ _____ _____
I'm going to do.

W Why don't you _____ _____
_____ for your raincoat? I think I saw it there.

M Okay, I will. Thanks.

12 도표 정보 파악

다음 표를 보면서 대화를 듣고, 두 사람이 탈 기차를 고르시오.

	Train	Destination	Arrival Time	Seat
①	A	Yeosu	12 p.m.	Economy
②	B	Mokpo	1 p.m.	First class
③	C	Mokpo	12 p.m.	First class
④	D	Mokpo	12 p.m.	Economy
⑤	E	Yeosu	10 p.m.	First class

M You wanted to go to Yeosu this Saturday, right?

W Yes, but can we go to Mokpo instead? I heard it'll rain in
Yeosu this weekend.

M Sure, what time do you want to get there?

W I want to have lunch there, so _____ _____
_____ _____ 12 p.m.

M Then we'll _____ _____ _____
around 9 a.m.

W That's fine. Do you want to take economy or first class?

M Let's _____ _____ _____. It's a lot
more comfortable.

W I agree. It's _____ _____, but it's definitely
worth it.

대화를 듣고, 여자가 미용실에 가기로 한 날짜를 고르시오.

① July 10th   ② July 11th
③ July 12th   ④ July 13th
⑤ July 14th

[Telephone rings.]

M Thank you for calling Janet's Beauty Salon. How may I help you?

W Hi, I'd like to make an appointment for a haircut.

M Okay. When would you like to come in?

W I'd like to ＿＿＿＿＿ ＿＿＿＿＿ ＿＿＿＿＿ July 12th.

M I'm sorry, but Janet ＿＿＿＿＿ ＿＿＿＿＿ ＿＿＿＿＿ ＿＿＿＿＿ the 12th. Would July 10th work for you?

W I don't think I can come in on the 10th. ＿＿＿＿＿ ＿＿＿＿＿ ＿＿＿＿＿ ＿＿＿＿＿?

M July 11th? There is ＿＿＿＿＿ ＿＿＿＿＿ ＿＿＿＿＿ 2 o'clock. Is that all right with you?

W That's perfect. Thank you very much.

대화를 듣고, 남자가 어제 한 일로 가장 적절한 것을 고르시오.

① 쇼핑하기
② 요리 연습하기
③ 집에서 휴식하기
④ 호텔에서 외식하기
⑤ 음식 축제 다녀오기

M How was your weekend, Monica?

W It was good. I ＿＿＿＿＿ ＿＿＿＿＿ ＿＿＿＿＿ my friends.

M Did you buy the boots you wanted?

W Yes, they were on sale, so I got a very good deal. Did you ＿＿＿＿＿ ＿＿＿＿＿ ＿＿＿＿＿ last weekend?

M Yes, I went to ＿＿＿＿＿ ＿＿＿＿＿ ＿＿＿＿＿ with my sister yesterday.

W Your sister is a chef at a hotel restaurant, isn't she?

M Yes, she's ＿＿＿＿＿ ＿＿＿＿＿ ＿＿＿＿＿ Chinese food.

다음을 듣고, 방송의 목적으로 가장 적절한 것을 고르시오

① 날씨를 예보하려고
② 이메일 활용을 장려하려고
③ 허리케인 피해를 접수하려고
④ 비상 연락망을 활성화하려고
⑤ 허리케인 대비 행동 요령을 안내하려고

M Hurricane season is here, and we all should be aware of what to do ＿＿＿＿＿ ＿＿＿＿＿ ＿＿＿＿＿ ＿＿＿＿＿. During a hurricane, please follow these guidelines. ＿＿＿＿＿ ＿＿＿＿＿ ＿＿＿＿＿ ＿＿＿＿＿ from windows and glass doors. You ＿＿＿＿＿ ＿＿＿＿＿ ＿＿＿＿＿ and keep curtains and blinds closed.

If necessary, stay in a small room or a closet. You could also

_____ _____ _____

_____ under a table.

16
숫자 정보 파악 (금액)

대화를 듣고, 남자가 지불할 금액을 고르시오.

① $1,000 ② $1,400 ③ $1,600
④ $1,800 ⑤ $2,000

M Welcome to Mattress King. How may I help you?

W I saw the advertisement about _____

_____ _____ _____.

M Oh, yes. If you buy a mattress and a bed frame together, you will get a 30% discount _____ _____

_____ _____.

W That sounds great. How much is this mattress?

M That mattress is $1,000.

W How about this bed frame?

M That bed frame is also $1,000.

W Okay, I'll get this _____ _____

_____ _____ _____, too.

M Okay. _____ _____ _____ the 30% discount.

17
이어질 응답 찾기

대화를 듣고, 여자의 마지막 말에 대한 남자의 응답으로 가장 적절한 것을 고르시오.

Man: _____

① Perfect! I'll wake you up in 2 hours.
② We should keep going since we're late.
③ Oh, good. I was getting really worried.
④ We need to find a restroom, not a gas station.
⑤ Okay, I'll call you when I arrive at the station.

W How long have we been on the road, Dad?

M I think it's been about 2 hours.

W _____ _____ _____

_____ a gas station? I need to go to the restroom.

M Sure. I was about to look for a gas station because

_____ _____ _____

_____.

W _____ _____ _____ we run out of gas?

M I hope that doesn't happen.

W Look! The sign over there *says there's a gas station within 3 kilometers.

* 교육부 지정 의사소통 기능: **보고하기**   동(이) 7

A says ~. A에 ~라고 나와 있어.

• The article **says** scientists have discovered a new plant.
  그 기사에는 과학자가 새로운 식물을 발견했다고 나와 있어.
• The weather forecast **says** it will rain tomorrow. 일기 예보는 내일 비가 올 것이라 나와 있어.

18 이어질 응답 찾기

대화를 듣고, 남자의 마지막 말에 대한 여자의 응답으로 가장 적절한 것을 고르시오.

Woman: _____

① I won't be able to graduate this year.
② I think I'll take his class next semester.
③ I've never studied European history.
④ I think you should take another history class.
⑤ He's not interesting, but his class is very organized.

M　How's your semester coming along, Kate?

W　I think I'm doing _____ _____ _____ _____ last semester.

M　That's good. _____ _____ Mr. Kim's European history class, right?

W　Yes, I am. Didn't you take that class last year?

M　I did, and I got a B+.

W　I heard that _____ _____ _____ to get an A in that class.

M　I heard that, too. _____ _____ _____ _____ about his teaching style?

19 이어질 응답 찾기

대화를 듣고, 여자의 마지막 말에 대한 남자의 응답으로 가장 적절한 것을 고르시오.

Man: _____

① I learned it from my mom.
② I think baking bread is much more difficult.
③ Most people say rice is better than noodles.
④ It was really hot when I went to Vietnam.
⑤ Rice noodles taste much better than other noodles.

M　Do you like noodles, Mary?

W　Yes, I love noodles.

M　I love noodles, too. In fact, I eat noodles _____ _____ _____ _____ I eat bread or rice.

W　Really? What kind of noodles do you like?

M　My favorite is Korean cold noodles. What about you?

W　My favorite is Vietnamese rice noodles. _____ _____ _____ Vietnamese noodles before?

M　Of course, I have. I _____ _____ _____ _____ quite often.

W　I didn't know you cooked. _____ _____ _____ _____ to cook them?

20 상황에 적절한 말 찾기

다음 상황 설명을 듣고, Jake가 Terry에게 할 말로 가장 적절한 것을 고르시오.

Jake: _____

① Where did you get your bicycle?
② Did your father buy a present for you?
③ Can you teach me how to ride a bicycle?
④ Is your bicycle more expensive than mine?
⑤ What do you want for your birthday present?

W　Jake wants a bicycle for his birthday present. Jake's father will buy him any bicycle he wants this weekend. Jake _____ _____ the perfect bicycle for himself yet. One day, he sees his friend Terry _____ _____ _____. Jake really likes Terry's bicycle and wants to _____ _____ he bought it. In this situation, what would Jake most likely say to Terry?

실전 모의고사 09

점수 /20

01 대화를 듣고, 여자가 구입할 잠옷으로 가장 적절한 것을 고르시오.

① ② ③

④ ⑤

02 대화를 듣고, 레오나르도 다빈치(Leonardo da Vinci)에 관해 언급되지 <u>않은</u> 것을 고르시오.

① 출생지   ② 사망한 나이
③ 대표 작품   ④ 성격
⑤ 다양한 직업

03 대화를 듣고, 남자가 여자에게 전화한 목적으로 가장 적절한 것을 고르시오.

① 환불을 요구하려고
② 항공편을 예약하려고
③ 여행 일정을 변경하려고
④ 여행 상품을 문의하려고
⑤ 직원에 대한 불만을 말하려고

04 대화를 듣고, 남자가 식당을 예약한 시각을 고르시오.

① 5:30 p.m.   ② 6:00 p.m.   ③ 6:30 p.m.
④ 7:00 p.m.   ⑤ 7:30 p.m.

05 대화를 듣고, 두 사람이 대화하는 장소로 가장 적절한 것을 고르시오.

① 우체국   ② 도서관   ③ 은행
④ 경찰서   ⑤ 시청

06 다음 그림의 상황에 가장 적절한 대화를 고르시오.

①   ②   ③   ④   ⑤

07 대화를 듣고, 남자가 여자에게 부탁한 일로 가장 적절한 것을 고르시오.

① 생일 케이크 굽기   ② 요리 강좌 수강하기
③ 집에 일찍 들어오기   ④ 생일 카드 만들기
⑤ 케이크 만들 재료 사 오기

08 다음을 듣고, 박물관에 관해 언급되지 <u>않은</u> 것을 고르시오.

① 개관 시기   ② 위치   ③ 입장료
④ 주차료   ⑤ 소장품

09 다음을 듣고, 무엇에 관한 설명인지 고르시오.

① 딸기   ② 사과   ③ 자두
④ 수박   ⑤ 토마토

10 다음을 듣고, 두 사람의 대화가 <u>어색한</u> 것을 고르시오.

①   ②   ③   ④   ⑤

11 대화를 듣고, 남자가 할 일로 가장 적절한 것을 고르시오.

① 운전하기   ② 커피 마시기
③ 사진 출력하기   ④ 여행 가방 싸기
⑤ 카메라 가져다주기

12 다음 표를 보면서 대화를 듣고, 남자가 구입할 스마트폰을 고르시오.

	Model	Screen Size	Storage Space	Color
①	A	5-inch	32GB	black
②	B	5-inch	64GB	red
③	C	6-inch	64GB	black
④	D	6-inch	64GB	red
⑤	E	6-inch	128GB	black

13 대화를 듣고, 여자가 로봇 경진 대회에 참가할 날짜를 고르시오.

① June 1st   ② June 5th   ③ June 6th
④ June 7th   ⑤ June 15th

14 대화를 듣고, 남자가 어제 한 일로 가장 적절한 것을 고르시오.

① 농구 연습하기   ② 블로그 개설하기
③ 드론 구입하기   ④ 동영상 편집하기
⑤ 드론으로 촬영하기

15 다음을 듣고, 방송의 목적으로 가장 적절한 것을 고르시오

① 봄방학 일정을 통보하려고
② 현장 학습 연기를 공지하려고
③ 회의 참석 인원을 점검하려고
④ 화재 예방의 중요성을 강조하려고
⑤ 소방관들의 노고에 감사를 표하려고

16 대화를 듣고, 남자가 지불할 금액을 고르시오.

① $30   ② $40   ③ $50
④ $60   ⑤ $70

17 대화를 듣고, 남자의 마지막 말에 대한 여자의 응답으로 가장 적절한 것을 고르시오.

Woman: _____

① I'd like to book a smaller one.
② No problem. I'll do it online now.
③ Didn't you already have breakfast?
④ This hotel is cheaper than the other one.
⑤ I'll call the hotel and cancel our reservation.

18 대화를 듣고, 여자의 마지막 말에 대한 남자의 응답으로 가장 적절한 것을 고르시오.

Man: _____

① I met him 3 days ago.
② Sorry, I should have called you.
③ I'm sorry, but I'm not a good speaker.
④ It's not a good idea to tell someone's secret.
⑤ I already did, but he didn't accept my apology.

19 대화를 듣고, 남자의 마지막 말에 대한 여자의 응답으로 가장 적절한 것을 고르시오.

Woman: _____

① Okay. I'll take you there by car.
② Of course. Take as long as you need.
③ I'm sure you'll do your best at school.
④ You have to finish your homework now.
⑤ I need to decide where to go out for dinner.

20 다음 상황 설명을 듣고, Claire가 웨이터에게 할 말로 가장 적절한 것을 고르시오.

Claire: _____

① I'll show you how I start my work.
② Do you have to go to work by 9:30?
③ I'm afraid that's not what I ordered.
④ This is the best apple pie I've ever had.
⑤ What kind of coffee do you have today?

Dictation 09

◇ 다시 듣고, 빈칸에 들어갈 알맞은 단어를 써보세요.

정답 및 해설 p.58

01 그림 정보 파악

대화를 듣고, 여자가 구입할 잠옷으로 가장 적절한 것을 고르시오.

①   ②   ③

④   ⑤

M Welcome to Good House. Can I help you find anything?

W Yes, please. I'm looking for women's pajamas.

M Do you have anything in mind?

W Hmm... I _____ _____ _____ _____ pants.

M Okay. How about these ones with dinosaurs on them?

W They're cute, but I don't like dinosaurs. Oh, these ones _____ _____ _____ _____.

M They are popular. They're also on sale for $30.

W Great. I'll take them.

M Okay. Would you like _____ _____ _____ _____? They are just $5 more.

W Yes, please.

02 언급하지 않은 내용 찾기

대화를 듣고, 레오나르도 다빈치(Leonardo da Vinci)에 관해 언급되지 <u>않은</u> 것을 고르시오.

① 출생지
② 사망한 나이
③ 대표 작품
④ 성격
⑤ 다양한 직업

W What are you reading, Mike?

M I'm reading a book on Leonardo da Vinci.

W Oh, I know him. _____ _____ _____ _____ Italy, right?

M Yes. He _____ _____ _____ _____ 67.

W He created _____ _____ _____, including *The Mona Lisa* and *The Last Supper*.

M I know. Did you know that he was also a great engineer and an inventor?

W Really? _____ _____ _____ _____.

03 목적 파악

대화를 듣고, 남자가 여자에게 전화한 목적으로 가장 적절한 것을 고르시오.

① 환불을 요구하려고
② 항공편을 예약하려고
③ 여행 일정을 변경하려고
④ 여행 상품을 문의하려고
⑤ 직원에 대한 불만을 말하려고

🔊 **Listening Tip**

would you처럼 앞 단어가 [d] 소리로 끝나고 바로 뒤에 y로 시작하는 단어가 오면 두 소리가 합쳐져 /쥬/로 발음됩니다. 따라서 would you는 /위쥬/에 가깝게 발음됩니다.

[Telephone rings.]

W   World Travel. This is Linda Shaw speaking.

M   Hello, Ms. Shaw. This is Paul Kay.

W   Good morning, Mr. Kay. How can I help you?

M   I'm calling about the travel plans I made yesterday.

W   Yes. I remember helping you to ＿＿＿＿＿ ＿＿＿＿＿ ＿＿＿＿＿ ＿＿＿＿＿.

M   I'm supposed to leave for France this Friday, ＿＿＿＿＿ ＿＿＿＿＿ ＿＿＿＿＿.

W   🔊 Would you like to ＿＿＿＿＿ ＿＿＿＿＿ ＿＿＿＿＿?

M   Yes, please. Can I leave next Friday instead?

W   I can certainly ＿＿＿＿＿ ＿＿＿＿＿ ＿＿＿＿＿ for you, sir.

04 숫자 정보 파악 (시각)

대화를 듣고, 남자가 식당을 예약한 시각을 고르시오.

① 5:30 p.m.   ② 6:00 p.m.
③ 6:30 p.m.   ④ 7:00 p.m.
⑤ 7:30 p.m.

[Telephone rings.]

W   Thanks for calling Top Restaurant. How may I help you?

M   Hello. Do you take reservations for Friday evening?

W   I'm sorry, sir. Friday evening ＿＿＿＿＿ ＿＿＿＿＿ ＿＿＿＿＿.

M   Then, can I make a reservation for 7 p.m. on Thursday?

W   Of course. How many ＿＿＿＿＿ ＿＿＿＿＿ ＿＿＿＿＿ ＿＿＿＿＿?

M   It's for 8 people.

W   I'm terribly sorry, but ＿＿＿＿＿ ＿＿＿＿＿ ＿＿＿＿＿ ＿＿＿＿＿ for a party of 5 or more is 6:30 p.m.

M   Oh, that's fine. We can get ＿＿＿＿＿ ＿＿＿＿＿ ＿＿＿＿＿ ＿＿＿＿＿.

W   Thank you so much for your understanding.

05 장소 추론

대화를 듣고, 두 사람이 대화하는 장소로 가장 적절한 것을 고르시오.

① 우체국   ② 도서관   ③ 은행
④ 경찰서   ⑤ 시청

M   Can I help the next person, please?

W   Hi. I'd like to ＿＿＿＿＿ ＿＿＿＿＿ ＿＿＿＿＿ ＿＿＿＿＿.

M   Of course. May I see your ID?

W Yes. Here is my driver's license.

M Thanks. Can you write down _____ _____ _____ here?

W Of course. *[Pause]* Here you are.

M It looks like your _____ _____ _____ _____ was already sent to the old address by mail.

W That's fine. My parents live there. I'll pick it up later.

M Okay. Your address has been updated. Is there anything else?

W Oh, can you put this money _____ _____ _____ _____, too?

M Sure.

---

06 그림 상황에 적절한 대화 찾기

다음 그림의 상황에 가장 적절한 대화를 고르시오.

① ② ③ ④ ⑤

① M What kind of tree is that?

   W I think that's an oak tree.

② M Can I help you find anything?

   W Yes, _____ _____ _____ cameras?

③ M I think someone _____ _____ _____.

   W Why don't you call the police?

④ M Could you _____ _____ _____ _____ us?

   W Certainly.

⑤ M _____ _____ _____ the pepper, please?

   W Sure, here you are.

---

07 부탁 파악

대화를 듣고, 남자가 여자에게 부탁한 일로 가장 적절한 것을 고르시오.

① 생일 케이크 굽기
② 요리 강좌 수강하기
③ 집에 일찍 들어오기
④ 생일 카드 만들기
⑤ 케이크 만들 재료 사 오기

W What are you doing, Dad?

M I'm making a birthday cake for your mom.

W Really? Where did you learn to do that?

M I _____ _____ _____ for the last 6 months after work. I wanted to surprise your mom.

W Do you want me to _____ _____ _____ _____?

M Yes, could you _____ _____

_____ _____ for her? I forgot to get a card.

W Sure. I can do that.

---

08 언급하지 않은 내용 찾기

다음을 듣고, 박물관에 관해 언급되지 <u>않은</u> 것을
고르시오.

① 개관 시기   ② 위치   ③ 입장료
④ 주차료   ⑤ 소장품

M Welcome everyone to the Payne Museum. _____
_____ _____ _____ January 28,
2006, and its purpose is to teach others about the visual arts.
It's _____ _____ _____
_____ any admission fees. We do, however,
_____ _____ _____
_____ of $10. The Payne Museum has
_____ _____ _____
_____ European paintings, sculptures, and photos
by world-famous artists. I hope you enjoy your visit.

---

09 화제 추론

다음을 듣고, 무엇에 관한 설명인지 고르시오.

① 딸기   ② 사과   ③ 자두
④ 수박   ⑤ 토마토

🔊 **Listening Tip**

whether는 wh-로 시작하는 단어로 [h] 소리가 발음되지
않고 '날씨'를 뜻하는 weather와 비슷하게 들린다는 점에
유의하세요. 하지만 whole은 [h] 소리가 발음된다는 것도
잊지 마세요.

W This is something that we eat. It's usually _____
_____ _____. Everybody agrees that this
is good for us, _____ _____
_____ _____ 🔊 whether this is a fruit or a
vegetable. Some people consider this a vegetable because this
_____ _____ _____
_____ other fruits. So, people don't usually eat this
as a dessert. Instead, they cook this _____
_____ _____ such as in a soup or sauce.

---

10 어색한 대화 찾기

다음을 듣고, 두 사람의 대화가 어색한 것을 고르
시오.

①   ②   ③   ④   ⑤

① M Did you call your mother?

   W I did, but _____ _____ _____.

② M Do you like to watch TV?

   W I like it a lot.

③ M The phone's ringing, Cindy.

   W Okay. I'll get it.

④ M Can you _____ _____ _____
_____?

W No. We're open from 10 to 7 every day.

⑤ M _____ _____ _____
_____ Ms. Taylor?

W This is she. How can I help you?

---

11 할 일 파악

대화를 듣고, 남자가 할 일로 가장 적절한 것을 고르시오.

① 운전하기
② 커피 마시기
③ 사진 출력하기
④ 여행 가방 싸기
⑤ 카메라 가져다주기

M The coffee smells really nice, honey.

W Did you sleep well? I didn't want to _____
_____ _____.

M I did. I guess I was really tired.

W I'm sure you were. _____ _____
_____ 10 hours yesterday.

M It was a great trip, wasn't it?

W Yes, it was. Did you _____ _____
_____? I'm going to print out some of the pictures
we took.

M Your camera is in my backpack. _____
_____ _____ _____ to you.

W Thanks.

---

12 도표 정보 파악

다음 표를 보면서 대화를 듣고, 남자가 구입할 스마트폰을 고르시오.

	Model	Screen Size	Storage Space	Color
①	A	5-inch	32GB	black
②	B	5-inch	64GB	red
③	C	6-inch	64GB	black
④	D	6-inch	64GB	red
⑤	E	6-inch	128GB	black

W How may I help you?

M I'd like to buy a smartphone. Can you help me choose one?

W Of course. _____ _____ _____
_____ something in particular?

M I want the screen to be big. My old smartphone had a 5-inch
screen, and it was _____ _____
_____ _____.

W I see. How about storage space?

M I don't take many pictures or videos. So, I don't
_____ _____ _____ 64GB.

W All right. How about this model? It comes in two different
colors, black and red.

M This model is perfect for me. I'll _____
_____ _____ _____.

13 숫자 정보 파악 (날짜)

대화를 듣고, 여자가 로봇 경진 대회에 참가할 날짜를 고르시오.

① June 1st   ② June 5th
③ June 6th   ④ June 7th
⑤ June 15th

M I heard you're going to enter the robot competition. Are you ready for it, Michelle?

W I'm not ready yet, but I will be.

M Isn't the competition _____ _____ _____ June 5th? That's tomorrow.

W Yes. But it's held for 3 days from June 5th to 7th.

M Right. So, _____ _____ _____ _____ the competition?

W _____ _____ _____ on June 6th.

M I see. Well, I hope you'll win!

W Thanks.

14 한 일 파악

대화를 듣고, 남자가 어제 한 일로 가장 적절한 것을 고르시오.

① 농구 연습하기   ② 블로그 개설하기
③ 드론 구입하기   ④ 동영상 편집하기
⑤ 드론으로 촬영하기

W What are you doing, Rick?

M I'm editing a video.

W Wow, it's our school! Did you take _____ _____ _____ _____?

M Yes. I took it to post on my blog.

W I see. Where did you learn how to shoot videos?

M I learned it from my father.

W Cool. So, _____ _____ _____ _____ our school campus?

M I used my drone to _____ _____ _____ _____ yesterday.

W Wow, I didn't know our school was this beautiful.

15 목적 파악

다음을 듣고, 방송의 목적으로 가장 적절한 것을 고르시오.

① 봄방학 일정을 통보하려고
② 현장 학습 연기를 공지하려고
③ 회의 참석 인원을 점검하려고
④ 화재 예방의 중요성을 강조하려고
⑤ 소방관들의 노고에 감사를 표하려고

M Hello, students. This is your principal speaking. I wanted to tell you that our field trip to the City Fire Department this Friday _____ _____ _____ _____ bad weather. Because of this change, classes on Friday will _____ _____ _____ _____. I'll let you know when we _____ _____ _____. Thank you all for your attention.

16 숫자 정보 파악 (금액)

대화를 듣고, 남자가 지불할 금액을 고르시오.

① $30   ② $40   ③ $50
④ $60   ⑤ $70

M Hi, I'd like to rent an electric bicycle.

W Okay. _____ _____ _____ _____ going to rent it?

M For 3 hours.

W Sure. It's $10 an hour.

M Oh, this sign here says that it's $8 an hour _____ _____ _____ _____.

W That was last year, but the price _____ _____ _____ $10 this year.

M All right. I'll rent 2 bicycles for 3 hours then.

W Sure.

17 이어질 응답 찾기

대화를 듣고, 남자의 마지막 말에 대한 여자의 응답으로 가장 적절한 것을 고르시오.

Woman: _____

① I'd like to book a smaller one.
② No problem. I'll do it online now.
③ Didn't you already have breakfast?
④ This hotel is cheaper than the other one.
⑤ I'll call the hotel and cancel our reservation.

M Amy, I need to talk to you about our club trip to Gyeongju this Saturday.

W Oh, did something happen?

M We have more people participating _____ _____ _____, so we have to make a reservation for a bigger room.

W Okay. I _____ _____ _____ that can take more than 20 people. And it's cheap.

M That's good. Can you _____ _____ _____ right now? We don't _____ _____ _____.

18 이어질 응답 찾기

대화를 듣고, 여자의 마지막 말에 대한 남자의 응답으로 가장 적절한 것을 고르시오.

Man: _____

① I met him 3 days ago.
② Sorry, I should have called you.
③ I'm sorry, but I'm not a good speaker.
④ It's not a good idea to tell someone's secret.
⑤ I already did, but he didn't accept my apology.

W Did you have a fight with Chris yesterday?

M How do you know that, Mom?

W Your sister told me this morning. So, what happened between you and Chris?

M I thought Chris broke my bike _____ _____ _____. So we had an argument.

W Did _____ _____ _____ _____?

M No. Actually, the bike wasn't broken at all. _____

_____ _____. *I should have believed

him.

W Chris must be very upset. _____ _____

_____ and apologize to him.

---

19 이어질 응답 찾기

대화를 듣고, 남자의 마지막 말에 대한 여자의 응답으로 가장 적절한 것을 고르시오.

Woman: _____

① Okay. I'll take you there by car.

② Of course. Take as long as you need.

③ I'm sure you'll do your best at school.

④ You have to finish your homework now.

⑤ I need to decide where to go out for dinner.

W Can I talk to you for a second, Rick?

M Sure, Mom. What's up?

W Your teacher _____ _____ _____.

M Oh, I didn't know that. What did she say?

W She told me to think about sending you to Horton Science High School.

M Horton Science High School? I don't know if I'm

_____ _____ _____

_____ there.

W Well, I think you will be fine there. But I'm worried that the school is _____ _____ _____

_____.

M I see. Well, can you _____ _____

_____ _____ to think about it?

---

20 상황에 적절한 말 찾기

다음 상황 설명을 듣고, Claire가 웨이터에게 할 말로 가장 적절한 것을 고르시오.

Claire: _____

① I'll show you how I start my work.

② Do you have to go to work by 9:30?

③ I'm afraid that's not what I ordered.

④ This is the best apple pie I've ever had.

⑤ What kind of coffee do you have today?

W Claire eats her breakfast _____ _____

_____ _____ every morning. She needs to

be at work by 9:30, so she arrives at the diner at 8:50 every

morning. _____ _____ _____ a

cup of coffee and a slice of apple pie. This morning, she

ordered _____ _____ _____, but

_____ _____ _____

_____ a slice of cherry pie. In this situation, what

would Claire most likely say to the server?

정답 및 해설 p.65

실전 모의고사 10

점수

/20

01 대화를 듣고, 남자가 만든 에코백으로 가장 적절한 것을 고르시오.

① 　② 　③

④ 　⑤

02 대화를 듣고, 버클리(Berkeley) 시에 관해 언급되지 않은 것을 고르시오.

① 위치　　② 명소　　③ 날씨
④ 인구수　⑤ 도시 이름의 유래

03 대화를 듣고, 남자가 여자에게 전화한 목적으로 가장 적절한 것을 고르시오.

① Atlanta에 대해 물어 보려고
② 취업 소식을 전하려고
③ 졸업식 행사에 초청하려고
④ 감사의 뜻을 전하려고
⑤ 이사한 곳 주소를 알려 주려고

04 대화를 듣고, 여자가 일어날 시각을 고르시오.

① 2:30 p.m.　② 3:00 p.m.　③ 3:30 p.m.
④ 4:00 p.m.　⑤ 4:30 p.m.

05 대화를 듣고, 남자의 심정으로 가장 적절한 것을 고르시오.

① scared　　② jealous　　③ annoyed
④ satisfied　⑤ thankful

06 다음 그림의 상황에 가장 적절한 대화를 고르시오.

①　　②　　③　　④　　⑤

07 대화를 듣고, 여자가 남자에게 부탁한 일로 가장 적절한 것을 고르시오.

① 꽃 보내기　　　② 날씨 알아보기
③ 집 청소하기　　④ 잎과 가지 줍기
⑤ 정원에 물 주기

08 다음을 듣고, Lesson Paradise에 관해 언급되지 않은 것을 고르시오.

① 위치　　　　② 운영 시간
③ 악기 종류　④ 강사 수
⑤ 수업료 할인율

09 다음을 듣고, 무엇에 관한 설명인지 고르시오.

① 헬멧　　② 고글　　③ 털장갑
④ 귀마개　⑤ 마스크

10 다음을 듣고, 두 사람의 대화가 어색한 것을 고르시오.

①　　②　　③　　④　　⑤

11 대화를 듣고, 여자가 할 일로 가장 적절한 것을 고르시오.

① 캠핑 짐 싸기　　② 옷 갈아입기
③ 보고서 완성하기　④ 차 태워 주기
⑤ 쇼핑몰 위치 확인하기

12 다음 표를 보면서 대화를 듣고, 남자가 선택할 방과 후 교실 수업을 고르시오.

	Class	Day	Time	Subject
①	A	Thur.	3 p.m.	Chess
②	B	Thur.	4 p.m.	Chess
③	C	Tue.	5 p.m.	Swimming
④	D	Thur.	4 p.m.	Guitar
⑤	E	Thur.	5 p.m.	Guitar

13 대화를 듣고, 텔레비전이 배송되는 날짜를 고르시오.

① August 12th   ② August 14th
③ August 16th   ④ August 18th
⑤ August 20th

14 대화를 듣고, 남자가 어제 한 일로 가장 적절한 것을 고르시오.

① 숙제하기   ② 병원 진료 받기
③ 컴퓨터 구입하기   ④ 선생님과 상담하기
⑤ 이메일 보내기

15 다음을 듣고, 방송의 목적으로 가장 적절한 것을 고르시오.

① 식당 수리 상황을 알리려고
② 성적 우수 학생을 칭찬하려고
③ 단축 수업 계획을 공지하려고
④ 올바른 식습관을 소개하려고
⑤ 점심시간 주의 사항을 전하려고

16 대화를 듣고, 여자가 지불할 금액을 고르시오.

① $20   ② $40   ③ $60
④ $80   ⑤ $120

17 대화를 듣고, 남자의 마지막 말에 대한 여자의 응답으로 가장 적절한 것을 고르시오.

Woman: _____

① I left my science book on my desk.
② Why do you keep your books so clean?
③ I hope these notes help me pass the test.
④ You can borrow my science book today.
⑤ I like to read a book while having lunch.

18 대화를 듣고, 여자의 마지막 말에 대한 남자의 응답으로 가장 적절한 것을 고르시오.

Man: _____

① No, I don't want to read this book.
② Right. That's exactly what I'm going to do.
③ No, we already have enough clean water.
④ Well, no one will be able to drink this book.
⑤ Yes, I need to drink at least 8 glasses of water.

19 대화를 듣고, 남자의 마지막 말에 대한 여자의 응답으로 가장 적절한 것을 고르시오.

Woman: _____

① You can meet him in person.
② I don't think he is famous at all.
③ You need to work as hard as he does.
④ I forgot to watch the news last night.
⑤ It's impossible for a soccer player to become famous.

20 다음 상황 설명을 듣고, David가 James에게 할 말로 가장 적절한 것을 고르시오.

David: _____

① Did you enjoy cooking dinner?
② Have you gone camping before?
③ What is your favorite outdoor activity?
④ When did you first learn to play the guitar?
⑤ It's too late. You shouldn't be playing the guitar.

Dictation 10

◇ 다시 듣고, 빈칸에 들어갈 알맞은 단어를 써보세요.

01 그림 정보 파악

대화를 듣고, 남자가 만든 에코백으로 가장 적절한 것을 고르시오.

① ② ③
④ ⑤

W What is that?

M I made an eco-friendly bag, Mom.

W Did you _____ _____ _____ one of your T-shirts?

M Yes, I did. You can _____ _____ _____ from the T-shirt here.

W _____ _____ _____ _____? Did you draw it?

M I did.

W Why didn't you _____ _____ _____ on it?

M This is for my girlfriend Sara, not me.

02 언급하지 않은 내용 찾기

대화를 듣고, 버클리(Berkeley) 시에 관해 언급되지 않은 것을 고르시오.
① 위치   ② 명소   ③ 날씨
④ 인구수   ⑤ 도시 이름의 유래

W Have you been to Berkeley?

M No, I haven't. _____ _____ _____?

W It's in Northern California. _____ _____ _____ the University of California, Berkeley.

M Isn't San Francisco in Northern California too?

W Yes, Berkeley is very close to San Francisco.

M Then the weather _____ _____ _____ _____ in Berkeley.

W Yes, the weather is really nice there. Oh, and the city _____ _____ _____ _____ the 18th-century Irish philosopher George Berkeley.

M That's very interesting.

03 목적 파악

대화를 듣고, 남자가 여자에게 전화한 목적으로 가장 적절한 것을 고르시오.
① Atlanta에 대해 물어 보려고
② 취업 소식을 전하려고
③ 졸업식 행사에 초청하려고
④ 감사의 뜻을 전하려고
⑤ 이사한 곳 주소를 알려 주려고

[Cell phone rings.]

W Hello.

M Aunt Mary, this is Tim.

W Tim? Oh, it's so nice to hear your voice again. _____ _____ _____?

M I've been great. How have you and Uncle Jack been doing?

W We've been just fine. I heard that you'll be graduating from college in June.

M Yes, I will, and I _____ _____ _____ to share with you.

W Really? What is it?

M I'll _____ _____ at a bank in Atlanta this summer.

W That's great. _____ _____ _____ _____ to where we live, then.

M That's right. I'll be seeing you a lot more often.

04 숫자 정보 파악 (시각)

대화를 듣고, 여자가 일어날 시각을 고르시오.

① 2:30 p.m.   ② 3:00 p.m.
③ 3:30 p.m.   ④ 4:00 p.m.
⑤ 4:30 p.m.

🔊 **Listening Tip**

hour의 h는 묵음으로 소리가 나지 않아요. 그래서 /아워/처럼 들리는데 h로 시작하는 honest, honor도 마찬가지로 묵음이에요.

W I'm going to take a nap, Dad.

M Okay. Do you want me to wake you up in an 🔊hour?

W Hmm... It's 2:30 right now, so can you wake me up at 4:30?

M You _____ _____ _____ _____ sleep at night if you take a 2-hour nap.

W But I'm really tired right now. I haven't _____ _____ for the past few days.

M Don't you _____ _____ _____ at 4:00 today?

W Oh, you're right. I completely forgot about that. I should get up _____ _____ _____, then.

05 심정 추론

대화를 듣고, 남자의 심정으로 가장 적절한 것을 고르시오.

① scared   ② jealous   ③ annoyed
④ satisfied   ⑤ thankful

M Hello. I have 2 tickets _____ _____ _____ _____ Jackson Kim.

W Okay. May I see your ID, please?

M Sure. [Pause] Oh no. I think I left my ID at home. Can I just get the tickets?

W _____ _____ _____ _____. We need to check your ID _____ _____ _____ _____ the theater.

M Can I show you my friend's ID instead?

W No. We need to see your ID because you _____ _____ _____.

M I _____ _____ _____ _____ my ID. Now we'll miss the show.

W I'm sorry, but there's _____ _____

_____ _____.

06 그림 상황에 적절한 대화 찾기

다음 그림의 상황에 가장 적절한 대화를 고르시오.

① ② ③ ④ ⑤

① M _____ _____ _____ my pencil case?

W Yes, I put it in your backpack.

② M Do you _____ _____ _____ here?

W No, sir. We only offer piano lessons.

③ M Excuse me. What time is it right now?

W I'm sorry. I don't know the time.

④ M I have a sore throat. I think I'm _____

_____ _____.

W I see. The doctor will be with you shortly.

⑤ M She _____ _____ _____, doesn't she?

W Yes, she does. Let's buy one of her CDs.

07 부탁 파악

대화를 듣고, 여자가 남자에게 부탁한 일로 가장 적절한 것을 고르시오.

① 꽃 보내기
② 날씨 알아보기
③ 집 청소하기
④ 잎과 가지 줍기
⑤ 정원에 물 주기

W The weather's been really nice these days.

M I know. It's been really warm and sunny.

W When was the last time _____ _____

_____ _____?

M I think it rained about 2 weeks ago.

W Now that spring is finally here, we should start

_____ _____ _____ our garden.

M Yes, we should.

W Can you _____ _____ _____

_____? I'll pick up the leaves and branches.

M Sure, _____ _____ _____

_____ right away.

08 언급하지 않은 내용 찾기

다음을 듣고, Lesson Paradise에 관해 언급 되지 않은 것을 고르시오.

① 위치
② 운영 시간
③ 악기 종류
④ 강사 수
⑤ 수업료 할인율

W Do you want to improve your musical skills? You should come to the Lesson Paradise. We _____

_____ _____ the corner of 3rd street and Palm Avenue. We're _____ _____

_____ from 10 a.m. to 10 p.m. We provide music lessons for all levels and ages, and _____ _____ _____ 30 instructors. If you sign up now, you'll get a 10% _____ _____ _____. If you have any questions, we'll be more than happy to answer them.

09 화제 추론

다음을 듣고, 무엇에 관한 설명인지 고르시오.

① 헬멧　　② 고글　　③ 털장갑
④ 귀마개　　⑤ 마스크

M This is something that you _____ _____ _____ _____. It can completely cover your face, or it can cover only part of your face, including the nose and the mouth. People wear this _____ _____ _____. Some people wear this because they think this is stylish, and others wear this _____ _____ _____ _____ in the winter. But it is important that you wear this if _____ _____ _____ _____ or the flu.

10 어색한 대화 찾기

다음을 듣고, 두 사람의 대화가 <u>어색한</u> 것을 고르시오.

①　　②　　③　　④　　⑤

① M Can I see you in my office?
  W Sure, I'll _____ _____ _____.
② M Hello, _____ _____ _____?
  W Yes, I'm coming.
③ M Should I do the dishes?
  W Yes, _____ _____ _____ _____.
④ M I'm sleepy. Can we go to bed?
  W Okay, _____ _____ _____ a cup of coffee.
⑤ M Do you like chocolate cake?
  W No, I don't like sweet things.

11 할 일 파악

대화를 듣고, 여자가 할 일로 가장 적절한 것을 고르시오.

① 캠핑 짐 싸기　　② 옷 갈아입기
③ 보고서 완성하기　　④ 차 태워 주기
⑤ 쇼핑몰 위치 확인하기

W Are you busy now, Dad?
M No, it's all right. Do you need something?
W Can you _____ _____ _____ _____ to the mall if you have time?
M Sure. What are you getting at the mall?

🔊 Listening Tip

모음으로 시작하는 단어는 앞 단어의 끝부분 자음과 연음이 되어 붙어서 발음돼요. 그리고 pick의 [k] 발음은 강세가 없는 단어이므로 경음화가 진행되어 /피겁/보다는 /피껍/으로 소리 나요.

W I need to 🔊pick up a few things _____
_____ _____ trip next week.

M I see. _____ _____ _____ 10 minutes.

W All right. Then I'll _____ _____
_____ first.

---

12 도표 정보 파악

다음 표를 보면서 대화를 듣고, 남자가 선택할 방과 후 교실 수업을 고르시오.

	Class	Day	Time	Subject
①	A	Thur.	3 p.m.	Chess
②	B	Thur.	4 p.m.	Chess
③	C	Tue.	5 p.m.	Swimming
④	D	Thur.	4 p.m.	Guitar
⑤	E	Thur.	5 p.m.	Guitar

M Mom, I need to decide which class to take after school.

W You have swimming lessons on Tuesday, so _____
_____ _____ _____ on Thursday.

M You're right. Should I take a 4 o'clock or 5 o'clock class?

W Well, what time does your last class end on Thursdays?

M It ends at 3:30 p.m. So _____ _____
_____ 3:30 is good.

W Why don't you _____ _____
_____ _____? You like music, don't you?

M I do, but I'm taking piano lessons. I _____
_____ _____ _____ another
instrument right now.

W Okay, then you have only one choice.

---

13 숫자 정보 파악 (날짜)

대화를 듣고, 텔레비전이 배송되는 날짜를 고르시오.

① August 12th   ② August 14th
③ August 16th   ④ August 18th
⑤ August 20th

[Telephone rings.]

W Hello.

M Hello. May I speak to Tara Taylor, please?

W This is she. Who's calling?

M I'm calling from Best Electronics. You bought a TV last week from us.

W That's right. Is there something wrong?

M I'm very sorry, but the delivery date _____
_____ _____ _____.

W Really? To when?

M The date _____ _____ _____
_____ August 12th or 14th.

W I see. Both dates are not good for me. I'm going away for
a few days. _____ _____ _____
the 16th would be better.

M Then how about the 18th?

W _____ _____ _____ .

14 한 일 파악

대화를 듣고, 남자가 어제 한 일로 가장 적절한 것을 고르시오.

① 숙제하기 ② 병원 진료 받기
③ 컴퓨터 구입하기 ④ 선생님과 상담하기
⑤ 이메일 보내기

M Mrs. Robinson, may I talk to you for a minute?

W Of course, Jake. What is it?

M Well, could you give me _____ _____ _____ _____ my history homework?

W Was it _____ _____ _____ _____ ?

M That's not it. I haven't started it yet.

W Oh, did something happen?

M Yes, Mrs. Robinson. I had a terrible stomachache yesterday and went _____ _____ _____ _____ . Here is the doctor's note.

W I see. Then can you finish it and _____ _____ _____ _____ ?

M Sure, I will. Thank you very much.

15 목적 파악

다음을 듣고, 방송의 목적으로 가장 적절한 것을 고르시오.

① 식당 수리 상황을 알리려고
② 성적 우수 학생을 칭찬하려고
③ 단축 수업 계획을 공지하려고
④ 올바른 식습관을 소개하려고
⑤ 점심시간 주의 사항을 전하려고

W Hello, everyone. I'm sorry to interrupt your class, but I have an important announcement to make. At noon today, the mayor of our city _____ _____ _____ _____ _____ . He's going to _____ _____ _____ some of our teachers in the cafeteria. I know that many of you run around and speak loudly during lunchtime, but _____ _____ _____ _____ _____ as much as possible. Thank you.

16 숫자 정보 파악 (금액)

대화를 듣고, 여자가 지불할 금액을 고르시오.

① $20 ② $40 ③ $60
④ $80 ⑤ $120

M Hi, do you need any help?

W Yes, how much are these T-shirts?

M They are $20 each.

W Oh, that's a reasonable price. How about these?

M Those are $40 each. They are a little more expensive, so we _____ _____ _____ _____ on them.

W _____ _____ _____ _____ do you have on them?

M If you buy two of them, you can get _____ _____ _____ _____ free.

W That's good. Then I'll get 2 _____ _____ _____.

---

17 이어질 응답 찾기

대화를 듣고, 남자의 마지막 말에 대한 여자의 응답으로 가장 적절한 것을 고르시오.

Woman: _____

① I left my science book on my desk.
② Why do you keep your books so clean?
③ I hope these notes help me pass the test.
④ You can borrow my science book today.
⑤ I like to read a book while having lunch.

M I'm starving. Why don't we go and get something to eat, Judy?

W _____ _____ _____ _____?

M Yes, it's 12:30. You've been _____ _____ _____ 3 hours already.

W We came to the library at 10:30, James.

M Did we? Anyway, you're too serious about studying.

W I have to be. I don't want to _____ _____ _____ _____ again.

M You won't. You _____ _____ _____ _____ really hard for it.

---

18 이어질 응답 찾기

대화를 듣고, 여자의 마지막 말에 대한 남자의 응답으로 가장 적절한 것을 고르시오.

Man: _____

① No, I don't want to read this book.
② Right. That's exactly what I'm going to do.
③ No, we already have enough clean water.
④ Well, no one will be able to drink this book.
⑤ Yes, I need to drink at least 8 glasses of water.

W That's an interesting title for a book, *Drinkable Book*. What is that about?

M Well, it's not a book we can read. There's something very special about it.

W Really? _____ _____ _____ about this book?

M You use the book to drink water.

W What? You _____ _____ _____ _____?

M No. You can tear out a page of this book and use it _____ _____ _____ _____.

W Oh, it would be _____ _____ _____ drinkable books to villages in Africa.

대화를 듣고, 남자의 마지막 말에 대한 여자의 응답으로 가장 적절한 것을 고르시오.

Woman: _____

① You can meet him in person.
② I don't think he is famous at all.
③ You need to work as hard as he does.
④ I forgot to watch the news last night.
⑤ It's impossible for a soccer player to become famous.

M Did you see the amazing goal by Son Heung-min?

W Yes, I did. It's _____ _____ _____

_____.

M I'm so proud of him. He's _____ _____

_____ _____ soccer players in the world.

W There's no doubt about that. What a great soccer player he is!

M *I wish I could become as famous as he is.

W Well, you're only 16 years old. You still have time.

M You think so? What do you think _____

_____ _____ to become famous?

✱ **교육부 지정 의사소통 기능: 바람·소원 표현하기**   미 7|비 8|Y(박) 9|지 7|금 3|다 7

I wish I could ~. 내가 ~ 할 수 있다면 좋겠다.
• **I wish I could** speak French. 프랑스어를 할 수 있다면 좋겠어.
• **I wish I could** make it to the party. 파티에 갈 수 있으면 좋을 텐데.

다음 상황 설명을 듣고, David가 James에게 할 말로 가장 적절한 것을 고르시오.

David: _____

① Did you enjoy cooking dinner?
② Have you gone camping before?
③ What is your favorite outdoor activity?
④ When did you first learn to play the guitar?
⑤ It's too late. You shouldn't be playing the guitar.

M David loves outdoor activities, and he goes camping once every other week. He usually _____ _____

_____ one of his friends, and this week he goes with James. After dinner, they talk for a while, and David is getting ready to go to sleep. Then, James _____

_____ _____ _____ and starts playing. _____ _____ _____

_____, and David is worried that he _____

_____ _____ _____. In this situation, what would David most likely say to James?

실전 모의고사 11

점수 /20

01 대화를 듣고, 남자가 구입한 카드로 가장 적절한 것을 고르시오.

①   ②   ③

④   ⑤

02 대화를 듣고, 팬케이크에 관해 언급되지 <u>않은</u> 것을 고르시오.

① 두께　　　② 냄새　　　③ 맛
④ 가격　　　⑤ 재료

03 대화를 듣고, 남자가 여자에게 전화한 목적으로 가장 적절한 것을 고르시오.

① 병원에 같이 가려고
② 약속을 취소하려고
③ 숙제를 확인하려고
④ 출발을 재촉하려고
⑤ 약속 시간을 변경하려고

04 대화를 듣고, 두 사람이 만날 시각을 고르시오.

① 5:00 p.m　② 5:30 p.m　③ 6:30 p.m
④ 7:00 p.m　⑤ 7:30 p.m

05 대화를 듣고, 두 사람이 대화하는 장소로 가장 적절한 것을 고르시오.

① 공원　　　② 도서관　　　③ 백화점
④ 레스토랑　⑤ 커피숍

06 다음 그림의 상황에 가장 적절한 대화를 고르시오.

①　　②　　③　　④　　⑤

07 대화를 듣고, 여자가 남자에게 부탁한 일로 가장 적절한 것을 고르시오.

① 초대 전화하기　　　② 상 차리기
③ 계란 삶기　　　　　④ 장 봐 오기
⑤ 집 청소하기

08 다음을 듣고, 실내 운동용 자전거에 관해 언급되지 <u>않은</u> 것을 고르시오.

① 이름　　　② 무게　　　③ 사용법
④ 가격　　　⑤ 구매 방법

09 다음을 듣고, 무엇에 관한 설명인지 고르시오.

① 농구　　　② 탁구　　　③ 배구
④ 테니스　　⑤ 배드민턴

10 다음을 듣고, 두 사람의 대화가 <u>어색한</u> 것을 고르시오.

①　　②　　③　　④　　⑤

11 대화를 듣고, 남자가 할 일로 가장 적절한 것을 고르시오.

① 휴식 취하기　　　② 파티 장소 예약하기
③ 파티 참석하기　　④ 만날 약속 변경하기
⑤ 파티 음식 준비하기

12 다음 표를 보면서 대화를 듣고, 두 사람이 선택할 여행 패키지를 고르시오.

	Package	Destination	Duration	Price
①	A	Bangkok	7 days	$2,500
②	B	Bangkok	5 days	$2,000
③	C	Singapore	7 days	$3,500
④	D	Singapore	7 days	$3,000
⑤	E	Singapore	5 days	$2,000

13 대화를 듣고, 추석 연휴가 시작되는 날짜를 고르시오.

① September 30th　　② October 1st
③ October 2nd　　④ October 3rd
⑤ October 4th

14 대화를 듣고, 남자가 어제 한 일로 가장 적절한 것을 고르시오.

① 직업 박람회 가기
② 자기소개서 쓰기
③ 선생님과 상담하기
④ 대학교 입학 원서 내기
⑤ 고등학교 졸업식 참석하기

15 다음을 듣고, 방송의 목적으로 가장 적절한 것을 고르시오.

① 특별 점심 메뉴를 안내하려고
② 칠면조 소비를 장려하려고
③ 바람직한 식습관을 강조하려고
④ 추수 감사절의 유래를 알리려고
⑤ 각국의 다양한 명절을 소개하려고

16 대화를 듣고, 남자가 지불할 금액을 고르시오.

① $60　　② $70　　③ $80
④ $90　　⑤ $100

17 대화를 듣고, 여자의 마지막 말에 대한 남자의 응답으로 가장 적절한 것을 고르시오.

Man: _____

① I bought my first ukulele in China.
② Most guitar shops also have ukuleles.
③ I thought I was too big to play the ukulele.
④ I taught myself by watching videos on the Internet.
⑤ String instruments are easier to play than the piano.

18 대화를 듣고, 남자의 마지막 말에 대한 여자의 응답으로 가장 적절한 것을 고르시오.

Woman: _____

① I wish I had studied a little harder, too.
② I feel like I wasted 3 years of my life.
③ Middle school was a really difficult time.
④ You will make more money in high school.
⑤ I'm sorry I missed your graduation ceremony.

19 대화를 듣고, 여자의 마지막 말에 대한 남자의 응답으로 가장 적절한 것을 고르시오.

Man: _____

① No, my favorite subject is science.
② Good. You need to get some sleep.
③ You shouldn't play games too much.
④ I understand. I'll go to sleep after this video.
⑤ I've been uploading these videos since last month.

20 다음 상황 설명을 듣고, Patrick이 여자에게 할 말로 가장 적절한 것을 고르시오.

Patrick: Excuse me, _____

① I believe this is yours.
② you may run around the bus.
③ would you like to get a coffee?
④ can I see your driver's license?
⑤ this bus will take you to the library.

Dictation 11

◈ 다시 듣고, 빈칸에 들어갈 알맞은 단어를 써보세요.

정답 및 해설 p.72

01 그림 정보 파악

대화를 듣고, 남자가 구입한 카드로 가장 적절한 것을 고르시오.

① ② ③
④ ⑤

🔊 **Listening Tip**

t가 모음 사이에 오고 이 부분에 강세가 없을 경우 [r]로 발음됩니다. bottom 은 /바텀/보다는 /바럼/으로 발음됩니다. later, water도 마찬가지 경우입니다.

M I bought a Christmas card for our parents, Jane. Let's write in it together.

W Good. Oh, _____ _____ _____ a Christmas tree.

M Yes, I thought it looked cute.

W It does, but do you think it _____ _____ _____ for us to write on?

M Yes, it's big enough to write something inside.

W Good. Can we write anything on the front?

M No, _____ _____ _____ "Merry Christmas" at the 🔊bottom of the card. So we _____ _____ _____.

W Oh, okay.

02 언급하지 않은 내용 찾기

대화를 듣고, 팬케이크에 관해 언급되지 <u>않은</u> 것을 고르시오.

① 두께 ② 냄새 ③ 맛
④ 가격 ⑤ 재료

W Are you making pancakes for breakfast, Dad?

M Yes, I am. Try these pancakes.

W [Pause] They're very _____ _____ _____ _____ vanilla.

M They do, don't they? Do you like them?

W They _____ _____ _____.
They are not sweet enough.

M I knew you would say that.

W Why do _____ _____ _____?

M That's because I used _____ _____ _____ _____.

03 목적 파악

대화를 듣고, 남자가 여자에게 전화한 목적으로 가장 적절한 것을 고르시오.

① 병원에 같이 가려고
② 약속을 취소하려고
③ 숙제를 확인하려고
④ 출발을 재촉하려고
⑤ 약속 시간을 변경하려고

[Cell phone rings.]

W Hello.

M Hi, Sarah.

W Will, are you already there? I'm almost ready. It _____ _____ to get there.

M No. I'm still at home.

W Oh, that's good. Can we meet 30 minutes later?

M Actually, I was calling to ask you if we could _____ _____ _____ _____ .

W Of course. That's not a problem. Did something happen?

M _____ _____ _____ _____ , and I think I should get some rest.

W Okay, I understand. I hope you _____ _____ _____ .

04 숫자 정보 파악 (시각)

대화를 듣고, 두 사람이 만날 시각을 고르시오.

① 5:00 p.m   ② 5:30 p.m
③ 6:30 p.m   ④ 7:00 p.m
⑤ 7:30 p.m

W What are you doing tonight, Mike?

M Nothing special. How about you?

W Do you want to go bowling with me? I'm _____ _____ _____ my friends at 7:30 p.m.

M Sure. That sounds fun. What time _____ _____ _____ ?

W I can meet anytime after 6:00 p.m.

M Why don't we meet at 6:30 then? Let's _____ _____ _____ _____ before we go bowling.

W Okay. Where do you want to meet?

M Let's meet at Central Station.

05 장소 추론

대화를 듣고, 두 사람이 대화하는 장소로 가장 적절한 것을 고르시오.

① 공원   ② 도서관   ③ 백화점
④ 레스토랑   ⑤ 커피숍

M What do you _____ _____ _____ , Rebecca?

W I don't need anything right now.

M Then can you find a table _____ _____ _____ _____ ?

W All the tables are taken on the first floor, so I'll check the second floor.

M Okay. Are you sure you don't need anything?

W Yes, I'm sure. I _____ _____ _____ _____ this morning.

M Okay. I'll go upstairs after I _____ _____ _____ .

06 그림 상황에 적절한 대화 찾기

다음 그림의 상황에 가장 적절한 대화를 고르시오.

① ② ③ ④ ⑤

🔊 **Listening Tip**

Go ahead.(어서 하세요.)는 대화 중에 아주 많이 쓰이는 표현인데 두 단어가 연음이 되어 ahead의 [ɑ] 발음은 거의 들리지 않고 생략됩니다.

① M Excuse me. _____ _____
_____?

W No, I'm still working on it.

② M *Do you mind if I _____ _____
_____?

W 🔊 Go ahead. No one's sitting there.

③ M Do you want me to move this table?

W Yes, please. It is _____ _____
_____ _____.

④ M It's time to go to bed, honey.

W Okay, can you read me a book?

⑤ M Is _____ _____ _____
_____?

W Yes, you get a 15% discount on that chair.

✱ 교육부 지정 의사소통 기능: 허락 요청하기　　　　천(이) 6 | 미 2 | Y(송) 6

Do you mind if I ~? 제가 ~해도 될까요?

• **Do you mind if I** sit here? 제가 여기 앉아도 될까요?
• **Do you mind if I** open the window? 제가 창문을 좀 열어도 될까요?

---

07 부탁 파악

대화를 듣고, 여자가 남자에게 부탁한 일로 가장 적절한 것을 고르시오.

① 초대 전화하기　　② 상 차리기
③ 계란 삶기　　　　④ 장 봐 오기
⑤ 집 청소하기

M Are you still cooking, honey?

W Yes, but _____ _____ _____.

M I'm sorry I invited so many people.

W It's okay. The more, the better.

M Is there anything I can do to help? Do you want me
_____ _____ _____
_____?

W No, I'll do that later. But can you _____
_____ _____ for me?

M Of course. That's _____ _____
_____ how to do for sure.

다음을 듣고, 실내 운동용 자전거에 관해 언급되지 않은 것을 고르시오.

① 이름   ② 무게   ③ 사용법
④ 가격   ⑤ 구매 방법

W Hello, everyone. If you'd like to stay fit during winter time, consider buying an exercise bike from us. Our exercise bike is 100 centimeters ＿＿＿＿＿ ＿＿＿＿＿ ＿＿＿＿＿ ＿＿＿＿＿ than 28 kilograms. All you have to do is ＿＿＿＿＿ ＿＿＿＿＿ ＿＿＿＿＿ ＿＿＿＿＿ 20 minutes a day. This amazing piece of equipment is only $200, and the only way to buy this product is ＿＿＿＿＿ ＿＿＿＿＿ ＿＿＿＿＿ ＿＿＿＿＿ the next 60 minutes. So, hurry and don't miss this great opportunity.

다음을 듣고, 무엇에 관한 설명인지 고르시오.

① 농구   ② 탁구   ③ 배구
④ 테니스   ⑤ 배드민턴

M This is a sport that is usually played by 2 individuals. It ＿＿＿＿＿ ＿＿＿＿＿ ＿＿＿＿＿ ＿＿＿＿＿ by 2 teams, and each team ＿＿＿＿＿ ＿＿＿＿＿ 2 players. In order to play this sport, you need to have a ball and a racket. The ball is made of rubber and is usually ＿＿＿＿＿ ＿＿＿＿＿ ＿＿＿＿＿. This sport can be played on an ＿＿＿＿＿ ＿＿＿＿＿ ＿＿＿＿＿ ＿＿＿＿＿ which has a net in the middle.

다음을 듣고, 두 사람의 대화가 어색한 것을 고르시오.

①   ②   ③   ④   ⑤

① **M** Can I ＿＿＿＿＿ ＿＿＿＿＿ ＿＿＿＿＿, please?
    W Yes, I'll bring it right away.

② **M** Is that your sister in the picture?
    W No, she's ＿＿＿＿＿ ＿＿＿＿＿.

③ **M** Be careful. The coffee is really hot.
    W Thank you. I'll just ＿＿＿＿＿ ＿＿＿＿＿ ＿＿＿＿＿.

④ **M** How many times have you read this book?
    W I ＿＿＿＿＿ ＿＿＿＿＿ ＿＿＿＿＿ ＿＿＿＿＿ than 5 times.

⑤ **M** May I have your name?
    W Yes, ＿＿＿＿＿ ＿＿＿＿＿ the T-bone steak.

11 **할 일 파악**

대화를 듣고, 남자가 할 일로 가장 적절한 것을 고르시오.

① 휴식 취하기 　 ② 파티 장소 예약하기
③ 파티 참석하기 　 ④ 만날 약속 변경하기
⑤ 파티 음식 준비하기

M You look tired, Erica. Is everything all right?

W I've been really ＿＿＿＿＿＿ ＿＿＿＿＿＿ ＿＿＿＿＿＿ the class party next week.

M You're not ＿＿＿＿＿＿ ＿＿＿＿＿＿ ＿＿＿＿＿＿ ＿＿＿＿＿＿ all by yourself, are you?

W Yes, I am. Everyone else in my class is busy with other work.

M But that's too much work for one person. I can help if you want.

W Then can you ＿＿＿＿＿＿ ＿＿＿＿＿＿ ＿＿＿＿＿＿ ＿＿＿＿＿＿ ＿＿＿＿＿＿ for the party for me? I'll give you the number.

M Okay. I will do it now.

12 **도표 정보 파악**

다음 표를 보면서 대화를 듣고, 두 사람이 선택할 여행 패키지를 고르시오.

	Package	Destination	Duration	Price
①	A	Bangkok	7 days	$2,500
②	B	Bangkok	5 days	$2,000
③	C	Singapore	7 days	$3,500
④	D	Singapore	7 days	$3,000
⑤	E	Singapore	5 days	$2,000

M Honey, let's decide on our summer vacation package today.

W Sure. Where do you want to go?

M How about Singapore? I want to visit the Botanic Gardens.

W I ＿＿＿＿＿＿ ＿＿＿＿＿＿ ＿＿＿＿＿＿ ＿＿＿＿＿＿, too. How long are we going to stay there?

M How about staying ＿＿＿＿＿＿ ＿＿＿＿＿＿ ＿＿＿＿＿＿ ＿＿＿＿＿＿?

W Great. Then we only have 2 options to choose from.

M Why is this one more expensive than the other one?

W That's because this one includes ＿＿＿＿＿＿ ＿＿＿＿＿＿ ＿＿＿＿＿＿ ＿＿＿＿＿＿.

M Let's choose this package then. I ＿＿＿＿＿＿ ＿＿＿＿＿＿ ＿＿＿＿＿＿ ＿＿＿＿＿＿ a good hotel.

W That sounds good.

13 **숫자 정보 파악 (날짜)**

대화를 듣고, 추석 연휴가 시작되는 날짜를 고르시오.

① September 30th 　 ② October 1st
③ October 2nd 　 ④ October 3rd
⑤ October 4th

M When is Chuseok this year?

W It's October 1st. That's a Thursday.

M That's perfect! Then we have a 5-day holiday this year.

W You're right. The Chuseok ＿＿＿＿＿＿ ＿＿＿＿＿＿ ＿＿＿＿＿＿ September 30th.

M Do you have any plans _____ _____

_____ _____ ?

W My grandmother's birthday is October 4th, so we'll

_____ _____ _____

_____ during the entire holiday.

14 한 일 파악

대화를 듣고, 남자가 어제 한 일로 가장 적절한 것을 고르시오.

① 직업 박람회 가기
② 자기소개서 쓰기
③ 선생님과 상담하기
④ 대학교 입학 원서 내기
⑤ 고등학교 졸업식 참석하기

W What do you want to do after you _____

_____ _____ _____ ?

M Well, I'm not going to university. I'm planning to get a job right away.

W Really? _____ _____ _____

_____ do you want to have?

M I want to be either a mechanic or an engineer.

W Wow, you already decided what to become. That's amazing.

M I went _____ _____ _____

_____ yesterday, and I found out a lot about myself.

W I'd like to go there, too.

15 목적 파악

다음을 듣고, 방송의 목적으로 가장 적절한 것을 고르시오.

① 특별 점심 메뉴를 안내하려고
② 칠면조 소비를 장려하려고
③ 바람직한 식습관을 강조하려고
④ 추수 감사절의 유래를 알리려고
⑤ 각국의 다양한 명절을 소개하려고

W May I have your attention, please? As you all know, Thanksgiving is _____ _____

_____ _____ . I'm sure most of you will have a big Thanksgiving dinner with friends and family. But some of you may not _____ _____

_____ _____ eating turkey _____

_____ _____ . So we have prepared our own turkey and _____ _____

_____ as a special lunch today. I hope you enjoy it!

16 숫자 정보 파악 (금액)

대화를 듣고, 남자가 지불할 금액을 고르시오.

① $60   ② $70   ③ $80
④ $90   ⑤ $100

M Excuse me. How much is this soccer ball?

W That one is $80.

M Wow, it's expensive. Do you have any less expensive ones?

W Sure. This ball is $50. The quality is about the same.

M That's good. _____ _____ _____

_____ . I also need some pairs of soccer socks.

W Of course. These ones are $10 per pair.

M Great. I'll take 2 _____ _____

_____ _____ .

W Okay. _____ _____ _____

_____ the payment over there.

17 이어질 응답 찾기

대화를 듣고, 여자의 마지막 말에 대한 남자의 응답으로 가장 적절한 것을 고르시오.

Man _____

① I bought my first ukulele in China.
② Most guitar shops also have ukuleles.
③ I thought I was too big to play the ukulele.
④ I taught myself by watching videos on the Internet.
⑤ String instruments are easier to play than the piano.

W What are you carrying, Sam?

M This is a ukulele.

W I thought it was a guitar. That's a big ukulele.

M Yes, it is. There are about 5 different sizes, and this is

_____ _____ _____ .

W Ukuleles only have 4 strings, right?

M Yes, they do, and guitars have 6 strings. So, ukuleles are

_____ _____ _____

_____ than guitars.

W _____ _____ _____

_____ to play the ukulele?

18 이어질 응답 찾기

대화를 듣고, 남자의 마지막 말에 대한 여자의 응답으로 가장 적절한 것을 고르시오.

Woman _____

① I wish I had studied a little harder, too.
② I feel like I wasted 3 years of my life.
③ Middle school was a really difficult time.
④ You will make more money in high school.
⑤ I'm sorry I missed your graduation ceremony.

W I can't believe we're graduating in 3 weeks.

M I know. It feels _____

_____ that I started middle school.

W We had a great time, didn't we? It was the best 3 years of my life.

M I _____ _____ _____

_____ , but I wish I had done a few things

differently.

W It's _____ _____ _____

_____ a few regrets, Paul.

M I don't think I've made enough friends or _____

_____ _____ .

대화를 듣고, 여자의 마지막 말에 대한 남자의 응답으로 가장 적절한 것을 고르시오.

Man _____

① No, my favorite subject is science.
② Good. You need to get some sleep.
③ You shouldn't play games too much.
④ I understand. I'll go to sleep after this video.
⑤ I've been uploading these videos since last month.

W Are you still sitting at your computer, Jack? It's

_____ _____ _____ .

M Okay, Mom. I'll go to bed in 5 minutes.

W You know you're not supposed to play computer games on school nights.

M I wasn't playing games. I _____ _____

_____ online.

W What were you watching?

M Something for science class tomorrow. This video is about a science experiment.

W Okay, but I still don't want you _____

_____ _____ _____ .

다음 상황 설명을 듣고, Patrick이 여자에게 할 말로 가장 적절한 것을 고르시오.

Patrick: Excuse me, _____

① I believe this is yours.
② you may not run around the bus.
③ would you like to get a coffee?
④ can I see your driver's license?
⑤ this bus will take you to the library.

M Patrick is a regular customer at a cafe near the bus stop. He drinks his coffee while he _____ _____

_____ _____ to work. One day, he orders his coffee and starts to drink it. Then he sees a woman

_____ _____ _____ and leave the cafe. Patrick grabs the wallet and _____

_____ _____ . When she is about to get on a bus, he finally _____ _____

_____ _____ . In this situation, what would Patrick most likely say to the woman?

실전 모의고사 **12**

점수
/20

01 대화를 듣고, 남자가 구입할 케이크로 가장 적절한 것을 고르시오.

①   ②   ③

④   ⑤

02 대화를 듣고, Lantern Parade에 관해 언급되지 않은 것을 고르시오.

① 개최 요일   ② 시작 장소   ③ 종료 시각
④ 참가비   ⑤ 참가자 의상

03 대화를 듣고, 남자가 여자에게 전화한 목적으로 가장 적절한 것을 고르시오.

① 진료 예약을 확인하려고
② 진료비에 대해 문의하려고
③ 직원용 입구를 사용하려고
④ 병원 가는 교통편을 문의하려고
⑤ 병원에 들어가는 방법을 물어보려고

04 대화를 듣고, 남자가 기차를 탈 시각을 고르시오.

① 11:00 a.m.   ② 12:00 p.m.   ③ 1:00 p.m.
④ 2:00 p.m.   ⑤ 3:00 p.m.

05 대화를 듣고, 두 사람이 대화하는 장소로 가장 적절한 것을 고르시오.

① 야외 수영장   ② 휴대전화 수리점
③ 호텔 로비   ④ 가전제품 판매점
⑤ 공원 매표소

06 다음 그림의 상황에 가장 적절한 대화를 고르시오.

① ② ③ ④ ⑤

07 대화를 듣고, 남자가 여자에게 부탁한 일로 가장 적절한 것을 고르시오.

① 우산 가져다주기   ② 점심 차리기
③ 야구 방망이 찾기   ④ 야구 경기 구경하기
⑤ 친구들과 놀러 가게 허락하기

08 다음을 듣고, Swim Boston에 관해 언급되지 않은 것을 고르시오.

① 위치   ② 개장 시간   ③ 휴무일
④ 등록 조건   ⑤ 등록 기간

09 다음을 듣고, 무엇에 관한 설명인지 고르시오.

① 시금치   ② 무   ③ 고구마
④ 양파   ⑤ 당근

10 다음을 듣고, 두 사람의 대화가 어색한 것을 고르시오.

① ② ③ ④ ⑤

11 대화를 듣고, 남자가 대화 직후에 할 일로 가장 적절한 것을 고르시오.

① 이사 준비하기   ② 영화관 가기
③ 반려견 돌보기   ④ 숙소 알아보기
⑤ 등산 갈 준비하기

12 다음 표를 보면서 대화를 듣고, 남자가 구입할 이어폰을 고르시오.

	Earphones	Wire	Color	Price
①	A	○	Black	$50
②	B	○	Red	$60
③	C	○	Black	$70
④	D	×	White	$100
⑤	E	×	Black	$100

13 대화를 듣고, 부산 국제 영화제가 시작되는 날짜를 고르시오.

① September 7th ② September 16th
③ October 7th ④ October 10th
⑤ October 16th

14 대화를 듣고, 남자가 어제 한 일로 가장 적절한 것을 고르시오.

① 생일 파티 가기 ② TV 시청하기
③ 안과 병원 가기 ④ 강연 듣기
⑤ 친구 도와주기

15 다음을 듣고, 방송의 목적으로 가장 적절한 것을 고르시오.

① 구인 앱을 홍보하려고
② 수학의 중요성을 강조하려고
③ 구직자들에게 정보를 제공하려고
④ 스마트폰 사용법을 안내하려고
⑤ 새로운 앱 사용법을 설명하려고

16 대화를 듣고, 여자가 지불할 금액을 고르시오.

① $10 ② $11 ③ $12
④ $13 ⑤ $14

17 대화를 듣고, 여자의 마지막 말에 대한 남자의 응답으로 가장 적절한 것을 고르시오.

Man: _____

① I heard she was in Korea last week.
② You may not cancel your reservation.
③ She's going to China next week instead.
④ I wish I went to the concert with you.
⑤ I'm sure she'll come as soon as she can.

18 대화를 듣고, 남자의 마지막 말에 대한 여자의 응답으로 가장 적절한 것을 고르시오.

Woman: _____

① You're the fastest runner I know.
② I'll be cheering for you this Friday.
③ I can't pick you up after school today.
④ Yes, I am. I'm running in the relay race.
⑤ No, I won't be able to come to your game.

19 대화를 듣고, 여자의 마지막 말에 대한 남자의 응답으로 가장 적절한 것을 고르시오.

Man: _____

① Sorry, I don't know where the village is.
② Let's go to a higher place to fly the drone.
③ That's great. I hope the pictures turn out great.
④ Do you want me to take a picture of the drone?
⑤ I already took a few pictures of the whole village.

20 다음 상황 설명을 듣고, Paul이 여자에게 할 말로 가장 적절한 것을 고르시오.

Paul: Excuse me, _____

① where did you buy all your blankets?
② how much is this washing machine?
③ how long have you been living in this city?
④ what time does this coin laundry close today?
⑤ can you show me how to use this washing machine?

Dictation 12

◆ 다시 듣고, 빈칸에 들어갈 알맞은 단어를 써보세요.

---

01 그림 정보 파악

대화를 듣고, 남자가 구입할 케이크로 가장 적절한 것을 고르시오.

① ② Happy Birthday ③ Happy Birthday Kore
④ Happy Birthday Kore ⑤ Happy Birthday

W Hello, how may I help you?
M Hi, I'm looking for a birthday cake for my daughter.
W Sure. We have many different kinds here.
M I like this heart-shaped one. Can you _____ _____ _____ _____ on it?
W I'm sorry, but this cake is _____ _____ _____ _____ anything on it.
M I see. How about this one?
W Yes, _____ _____ _____ is big enough.
M If you could write "_____ _____, _____" on the cake, that would be great.
W No problem. Just give me a few minutes.

---

02 언급하지 않은 내용 찾기

대화를 듣고, Lantern Parade에 관해 언급되지 않은 것을 고르시오.

① 개최 요일 ② 시작 장소
③ 종료 시각 ④ 참가비
⑤ 참가자 의상

W What are you making, Jake?
M I'm making a lantern.
W Are you going to participate in the Lantern Parade _____ _____ ?
M Yes, I am. _____ _____ _____ the sports stadium and ends at the city hall.
W What time does the parade start?
M It starts at 7 p.m. _____ _____ _____ 11:30 p.m.
W It ends pretty late. How much do you have to pay to participate?
M _____ _____ _____. You just need to show up with your own lantern.

---

03 목적 파악

대화를 듣고, 남자가 여자에게 전화한 목적으로 가장 적절한 것을 고르시오.

① 진료 예약을 확인하려고
② 진료비에 대해 문의하려고
③ 직원용 입구를 사용하려고
④ 병원 가는 교통편을 문의하려고
⑤ 병원에 들어가는 방법을 물어보려고

[Telephone rings.]
W Riverside Hospital, how can I help you?
M Hi, I have a 3:30 appointment with Dr. Taylor. I'm at the entrance, but _____ _____ _____ _____.
W Are you on Peachtree Street right now?

M Yes, I am. Isn't that where you're located?

W You're _____ _____ _____

_____. The front entrance is on Elm Street.

M Do I have to enter through the front entrance?

W Yes, sir. The back entrance is _____ _____

_____.

M I see. Then _____ _____ _____

the front entrance.

04 숫자 정보 파악 (시각)

대화를 듣고, 남자가 기차를 탈 시각을 고르시오.

① 11:00 a.m. ② 12:00 p.m.
③ 1:00 p.m.   ④ 2:00 p.m.
⑤ 3:00 p.m.

W Paul, what are you still doing at home?

M I'm not done packing yet.

W But it's already 11 o'clock. You should be _____

_____ _____ _____ soon.

M I know, Mom. Don't worry. I still have enough time.

W Don't you have a 12 o'clock train to catch?

M No, I changed _____ _____

_____ _____ 2 o'clock in the afternoon.

W Why did you do that?

M My friend Jake said he _____ _____

_____ _____ 1 o'clock today.

W Okay. Then you'll _____ _____

_____ _____, too.

05 장소 추론

대화를 듣고, 두 사람이 대화하는 장소로 가장 적
절한 것을 고르시오.

① 야외 수영장   ② 휴대전화 수리점
③ 호텔 로비   ④ 가전제품 판매점
⑤ 공원 매표소

W Can you check this for me?

M Sure. What's wrong with it?

W I dropped it in the pool. So I _____ _____

_____ and let the cell phone dry for a few days.

M Oh, I see. What else did you do?

W I tried to turn it on. But the _____ _____

_____ _____.

M I have to open it and check the inside. But there is a chance
that your cell phone might not work again.

W I understand, but I'd _____ _____

_____ _____ than buy a new one.

M All right. I'll _____ _____ _____

_____.

06 그림 상황에 적절한 대화 찾기

다음 그림의 상황에 가장 적절한 대화를 고르시오.

① ② ③ ④ ⑤

① M Can you _____ _____ _____ ?

   W Sorry, I can't. I'm a little cold.

② M What would you like to order?

   W Can you give me a minute? _____

   _____ _____ _____ .

③ M Could you give me the menu?

   W Of course, sir. Here it is.

④ M Where can I find toilet paper?

   W I'm sorry. We're _____ _____

   _____ _____ right now.

⑤ M Do you want to _____ _____

   _____ ?

   W No, I need to take a break.

07 부탁 파악

대화를 듣고, 남자가 여자에게 부탁한 일로 가장 적절한 것을 고르시오.

① 우산 가져다주기
② 점심 차리기
③ 야구 방망이 찾기
④ 야구 경기 구경하기
⑤ 친구들과 놀러 가게 허락하기

🔊 **Listening Tip**

will 은 /윌/ 보다는 /위을/에 가깝게 발음되므로 I will은 /아 위을/처럼 들립니다. 반면 I will의 축약형인 I'll은 /아 을/에 가깝게 들린다는 것에 유의하세요.

W The rain has finally stopped.

M I know. _____ _____ _____

   _____ again, so I'm going to the park.

W Are you going to play baseball with your friends today?

M Yes, I'm meeting with them _____ _____

   _____ _____ .

W Then you should hurry up and finish your lunch.

M Okay, 🔊 I will. Oh, can _____ _____

   _____ my baseball bat? I don't see it anywhere.

W Okay. 🔊 I'll go and _____ _____

   _____ _____ .

08 언급하지 않은 내용 찾기

다음을 듣고, Swim Boston에 관해 언급되지 않은 것을 고르시오.

① 위치   ② 개장 시간   ③ 휴무일
④ 등록 조건   ⑤ 등록 기간

M Welcome to Swim Boston, everyone. If you want to become a better swimmer, you've come to the right place. _____ _____ _____ 6 a.m. to 10 p.m. from Monday to Saturday. We're _____ _____ _____ . If you want to take swim lessons, you must _____ _____ _____ _____ with one of our instructors. Anyone who wants to take lessons _____ _____ _____ _____ the 1st and 5th of each month.

09 화제 추론

다음을 듣고, 무엇에 관한 설명인지 고르시오.

① 시금치   ② 무   ③ 고구마
④ 양파   ⑤ 당근

W This is a root vegetable that looks like a stick. This is _____ _____ _____ vitamin A, so it can _____ _____ _____ _____. Many people like to put this vegetable in many dishes because it _____ _____ _____ _____. Though many children don't like this very much, animals _____ _____ _____ enjoy it.

10 어색한 대화 찾기

다음을 듣고, 두 사람의 대화가 <u>어색한</u> 것을 고르시오.

①   ②   ③   ④   ⑤

🔊 **Listening Tip**

대화체에서는 축약형을 쓰는 경우가 많아요. I would의 축약형인 I'd는 /아이드/로, I have의 축약형인 I've는 /아이브/에 가깝게 발음해요.

① M It's 4:15. You're late again.
   W I thought _____ _____ _____ 4:30.
② M What would you like to do tonight?
   W 🔊 I'd like a cheeseburger and a coke.
③ M I feel terrible and I think I _____ _____.
   W Let me take your temperature.
④ M Could you take a picture of us?
   W Sure. Do I _____ _____ _____ ?
⑤ M _____ _____ _____ _____ Rome in Italy?
   W No, I've never been abroad.

11 할 일 파악

대화를 듣고, 남자가 대화 직후에 할 일로 가장 적절한 것을 고르시오.

① 이사 준비하기   ② 영화관 가기
③ 반려견 돌보기   ④ 숙소 알아보기
⑤ 등산 갈 준비하기

W Dad, why don't we do something fun together more often?
M We went hiking last weekend. Wasn't it fun?
W Well, it was _____ _____ _____.
M Oh, I didn't see it that way. Do you want to go to the movies this weekend then?
W How about _____ _____ _____ _____ ?
M That's a good idea. We _____ _____ _____ _____ a few days.

W Great! Mom will love that, too.

M In fact, I know exactly where we should go. I'll look for

_____ _____ _____

_____ .

12 도표 정보 파악

12 도표 정보 파악

다음 표를 보면서 대화를 듣고, 남자가 구입할 이어폰을 고르시오.

	Earphones	Wire	Color	Price
①	A	○	Black	$50
②	B	○	Red	$60
③	C	○	Black	$70
④	D	×	White	$100
⑤	E	×	Black	$100

M Excuse me. Can you help me choose earphones?

W Of course. Would you like wired ones or wireless ones?

M I heard wireless ones are really convenient. But I

_____ _____ _____ .

W Sure. Do you have any particular color in mind?

M Black. I don't want my earphones _____

_____ _____ _____ .

W I understand. There are 2 models to choose from.

M Hmm... I don't want to _____ _____

_____ $60.

W Then these ones are _____ _____

_____ for you.

13 숫자 정보 파악 (날짜)

대화를 듣고, 부산 국제 영화제가 시작되는 날짜를 고르시오.

① September 7th   ② September 16th
③ October 7th   ④ October 10th
⑤ October 16th

M What are you doing this weekend, Rachel?

W I'm going to Busan with my family.

M Are you visiting your grandparents in Busan?

W Yes, we are, and we're _____ _____

_____ the Busan International Film Festival on

Saturday the 10th.

M Oh, right. The festival is held _____ _____

_____ _____ , isn't it?

W Yes. This year _____ _____ _____

on the 7th.

M Really? Why does it _____ _____

_____ _____ ?

W The festival runs for 10 days, so it _____

_____ _____ _____ the 16th.

M Oh, I see. I hope you have fun!

대화를 듣고, 남자가 어제 한 일로 가장 적절한 것을 고르시오.

① 생일 파티 가기　② TV 시청하기
③ 안과 병원 가기　④ 강연 듣기
⑤ 친구 도와주기

W The meeting was really long today.

M I know. I couldn't ＿＿＿＿＿＿ ＿＿＿＿＿＿

　　＿＿＿＿＿＿ ＿＿＿＿＿＿.

W Do you want to go and get some coffee?

M Yes. Let's go to the donut place near the subway station.

W The donut place? I've ＿＿＿＿＿＿ ＿＿＿＿＿＿

　　＿＿＿＿＿＿ ＿＿＿＿＿＿ before. Is it new?

M Yes. One of my friends ＿＿＿＿＿＿ ＿＿＿＿＿＿

　　＿＿＿＿＿＿. I went there ＿＿＿＿＿＿ ＿＿＿＿＿＿

　　＿＿＿＿＿＿.

W That's great. Can we get a discount?

M Of course. ＿＿＿＿＿＿ ＿＿＿＿＿＿ ＿＿＿＿＿＿

　　donuts for you.

다음을 듣고, 방송의 목적으로 가장 적절한 것을 고르시오.

① 구인 앱을 홍보하려고
② 수학의 중요성을 강조하려고
③ 구직자들에게 정보를 제공하려고
④ 스마트폰 사용법을 안내하려고
⑤ 새로운 앱 사용법을 설명하려고

M Hello, listeners. Have you been looking for a more efficient

　　way to ＿＿＿＿＿＿ ＿＿＿＿＿＿ ＿＿＿＿＿＿?

　　＿＿＿＿＿＿ ＿＿＿＿＿＿ ＿＿＿＿＿＿

　　＿＿＿＿＿＿ "Find Employees Fast" and you will be able

　　to find more people. As a result, you will have a better

　　chance ＿＿＿＿＿＿ ＿＿＿＿＿＿ ＿＿＿＿＿＿

　　＿＿＿＿＿＿ for your job. The smart filtering tools in our

　　app will help you ＿＿＿＿＿＿ ＿＿＿＿＿＿

　　＿＿＿＿＿＿ ＿＿＿＿＿＿ in no time!

대화를 듣고, 여자가 지불할 금액을 고르시오.

① $10　　② $11　　③ $12
④ $13　　⑤ $14

M Good morning, and welcome to Rick's Bagels.

W How much are these plain bagels?

M One plain bagel is $1.

W Okay, I'll get 10 of them.

M If you want 10 plain bagels, you ＿＿＿＿＿＿

　　＿＿＿＿＿＿ ＿＿＿＿＿＿ ＿＿＿＿＿＿ a dozen of

　　them.

W Why is that?

M Because you get 13 bagels ＿＿＿＿＿＿ ＿＿＿＿＿＿

　　＿＿＿＿＿＿ ＿＿＿＿＿＿ 12 bagels.

W Does that mean I get one more bagle?

M Yes, that's right. It's called _____ _____ _____.

W _____ _____ _____. I'll get a baker's dozen then.

17 이어질 응답 찾기

대화를 듣고, 여자의 마지막 말에 대한 남자의 응답으로 가장 적절한 것을 고르시오.

Man: _____

① I heard she was in Korea last week.
② You may not cancel your reservation.
③ She's going to China next week instead.
④ I wish I went to the concert with you.
⑤ I'm sure she'll come as soon as she can.

W I can't believe this is happening.

M What's wrong, Samantha?

W Have you heard _____ _____ _____ _____ Taylor's world tour concerts?

M Oh, yes. They suddenly got canceled. How disappointing!

W I know. She _____ _____ _____ _____ to Korea next week.

M I heard she's in the hospital in Japan now. *I hope she recovers soon.

W _____ _____ _____ _____ she'll be able to come to Korea?

> ✱ 교육부 지정 의사소통 기능: **기원하기**   동(윤) 1 | 동(이) 8 | 지 1
>
> **I hope ~. 나는 ~하기를 바라.**
> • **I hope** you'll pass the test. 나는 네가 그 시험에 합격하길 바라.
> • **I hope** everything goes well. 나는 모든 것이 잘 되기를 바라.

18 이어질 응답 찾기

대화를 듣고, 남자의 마지막 말에 대한 여자의 응답으로 가장 적절한 것을 고르시오.

Woman: _____

① You're the fastest runner I know.
② I'll be cheering for you this Friday.
③ I can't pick you up after school today.
④ Yes, I am. I'm running in the relay race.
⑤ No, I won't be able to come to your game.

M Sports day is this Friday, right?

W Yes, it is. Are you participating in any event?

M Yes. I'm _____ _____ _____ _____ for my class.

W Is your team going to play in _____ _____ _____ this Friday?

M Oh, we're having our semi-final match after school today. We have to win today to go to the finals.

W Wow, your team _____ _____ _____ _____. Good luck on your match today.

M Thank you. How about you? Are you _____ _____ _____ _____?

19 이어질 응답 찾기

대화를 듣고, 여자의 마지막 말에 대한 남자의 응답으로 가장 적절한 것을 고르시오.

Man: _____

① Sorry, I don't know where the village is.
② Let's go to a higher place to fly the drone.
③ That's great. I hope the pictures turn out great.
④ Do you want me to take a picture of the drone?
⑤ I already took a few pictures of the whole village.

W This place is so beautiful, isn't it?

M It really is. _____ _____ _____

_____ such a beautiful and peaceful place as this

before.

W Did you take many pictures of the village?

M I took a few, but I need to go to a higher place.

W Why do you need to do that?

M I want to take a picture _____ _____

_____ _____ .

W Well, _____ _____ _____

_____ this drone. We can take pictures of the

_____ _____ _____

_____ here.

20 상황에 적절한 말 찾기

다음 상황 설명을 듣고, Paul이 여자에게 할 말로 가장 적절한 것을 고르시오.

Paul: Excuse me, _____

① where did you buy all your blankets?
② how much is this washing machine?
③ how long have you been living in this city?
④ what time does this coin laundry close today?
⑤ can you show me how to use this washing machine?

W Paul is in a coin laundry. He _____ _____

_____ _____ a different city and has never

been to this particular coin laundry. He needs to wash all his

blankets but _____ _____ _____

_____ to use big washing machines. He

_____ _____ _____

_____ if he can get some help. Then he

_____ _____ _____

_____ her laundry in one of the big washing

machines. In this situation, what would Paul most likely say

to the woman?

실전 모의고사 **13**

점수 /20

01 대화를 듣고, 남자가 구입할 수면 안대를 고르시오.

①   ②   ③

④   ⑤

02 대화를 듣고, 남자의 새 집에 관해 언급되지 <u>않은</u> 것을 고르시오.

① 주소　　　② 지붕　　　③ 층수
④ 침실 개수　⑤ 마당

03 대화를 듣고, 남자가 여자에게 전화한 목적으로 가장 적절한 것을 고르시오.

① 책을 빌리려고
② 친구 집에 같이 가려고
③ 시험공부를 함께 하려고
④ 집 주소를 알려 주려고
⑤ 친구 집 전화번호를 물어보려고

04 대화를 듣고, 두 사람이 공연을 볼 시각을 고르시오.

① 3:00 p.m.　② 4:00 p.m.　③ 5:00 p.m.
④ 6:00 p.m.　⑤ 7:00 p.m.

05 다음 그림의 상황에 가장 적절한 대화를 고르시오.

①　　②　　③　　④　　⑤

06 대화를 듣고, 두 사람이 대화하는 장소로 가장 적절한 곳을 고르시오.

① 부엌　　　② 음식점　　③ 도서관
④ 서점　　　⑤ 옷 가게

07 대화를 듣고, 남자가 여자에게 부탁한 일로 가장 적절한 것을 고르시오.

① 여행 가방 싸기　　② 환전하기
③ 날씨 확인하기　　④ 여권 찾아 주기
⑤ 우산 찾아 주기

08 다음을 듣고, 구겐하임 박물관(Guggenheim Museum)에 관해 언급되지 <u>않은</u> 것을 고르시오.

① 위치　　　② 건물 설계자　③ 건물 외형
④ 주요 전시물　⑤ 일일 투어

09 다음을 듣고, 무엇에 관한 설명인지 고르시오.

① 학생증　　　② 여권　　　③ 운전면허증
④ 항공권　　　⑤ 주민 등록증

10 다음을 듣고, 두 사람의 대화가 <u>어색한</u> 것을 고르시오.

①　　②　　③　　④　　⑤

11 대화를 듣고, 남자가 할 일로 가장 적절한 것을 고르시오.

① 방 청소하기　　　② 개 산책시키기
③ 개 집 만들기　　　④ 땅콩버터 사 오기
⑤ 개 목욕시키기

12 대화를 듣고, 두 사람이 보기로 한 텔레비전 프로그램이 시작하는 시간을 고르시오.

① 5:00 p.m.　② 5:10 p.m.　③ 5:15 p.m.
④ 5:20 p.m.　⑤ 5:30 p.m.

13 다음 도서관 배치도를 보면서 대화를 듣고, 남자가 선택할 구역을 고르시오.

Children's Books	③	History Books	④
②			Magazine
①		Information Desk　↑ Entrance	⑤

14 대화를 듣고, 여자가 어제 한 일로 가장 적절한 것을 고르시오.

① 병원 가기　　② 배구하기
③ 기타 치기　　④ 콘서트 가기
⑤ 노래 연습하기

15 다음을 듣고, 방송의 목적으로 가장 적절한 것을 고르시오.

① 할인 소식을 알리려고
② 매장 개업을 홍보하려고
③ 현명한 소비를 권장하려고
④ 유기농 식품을 장려하려고
⑤ 행운권 추첨 결과를 공지하려고

16 대화를 듣고, 남자가 지불할 금액을 고르시오.

① $500　　② $600　　③ $700
④ $800　　⑤ $900

17 대화를 듣고, 남자의 마지막 말에 대한 여자의 응답으로 가장 적절한 것을 고르시오.

Woman: _____

① What do you do in Korea on that day?
② I'm really looking forward to that day.
③ So what are you going to do tomorrow?
④ I love the fireworks best. I always watch them.
⑤ That's because I don't need to go to school.

18 대화를 듣고, 여자의 마지막 말에 대한 남자의 응답으로 가장 적절한 것을 고르시오.

Man: _____

① Now I know what it is.
② I will. Can I go now?
③ Okay. I'll fasten my seat belt.
④ It's not fair to give me a ticket.
⑤ Thank you so much for your help.

19 대화를 듣고, 여자의 마지막 말에 대한 남자의 응답으로 가장 적절한 것을 고르시오.

Man: _____

① I can't forget about it.
② It will be the perfect gift for him.
③ Your advice is always helpful to me.
④ It means you should focus on today.
⑤ Thanks for helping me with the presentation.

20 다음 상황 설명을 듣고, Jacob이 엄마에게 할 말로 가장 적절한 것을 고르시오.

Jacob: Mom, _____

① why don't we eat out?
② what would you like to drink?
③ do you mind if I sit next to you?
④ what are we going to eat for dinner?
⑤ do you want me to get you anything?

Dictation 13

◇ 다시 듣고, 빈칸에 들어갈 알맞은 단어를 써보세요.

정답 및 해설 p.86

01 그림 정보 파악

대화를 듣고, 남자가 구입할 수면 안대를 고르시오.

① ② ③ ④ ⑤

W Hello. May I help you?

M Yes, please. I'm looking for a sleep mask for travelers. I can't sleep well on planes.

W Is there any particular design you want?

M Well, I want one that ＿＿＿＿＿＿ ＿＿＿＿＿＿ ＿＿＿＿＿＿ ＿＿＿＿＿＿ my eyes while I sleep.

W Okay. Is there anything else?

M I want one ＿＿＿＿＿＿ ＿＿＿＿＿＿ ＿＿＿＿＿＿ ＿＿＿＿＿＿.

W Then how about these ones with the pictures of eyes ＿＿＿＿＿＿ ＿＿＿＿＿＿ ＿＿＿＿＿＿ ＿＿＿＿＿＿?

M They're not bad, but I think ＿＿＿＿＿＿ ＿＿＿＿＿＿ ＿＿＿＿＿＿ ＿＿＿＿＿＿ on it is better. I'll take that one.

02 언급하지 않은 내용 찾기

대화를 듣고, 남자의 새 집에 관해 언급되지 않은 것을 고르시오.

① 주소   ② 지붕   ③ 층수
④ 침실 개수 ⑤ 마당

M Look. This is a picture of my new house.

W Oh, ＿＿＿＿＿＿ ＿＿＿＿＿＿ ＿＿＿＿＿＿ ＿＿＿＿＿＿ now?

M At 120 Pine Street.

W It's a two-story house, isn't it?

M Yes. ＿＿＿＿＿＿, ＿＿＿＿＿＿ ＿＿＿＿＿＿ a living room, a kitchen and a guest room.

W How about upstairs?

M There are 2 ＿＿＿＿＿＿ ＿＿＿＿＿＿ ＿＿＿＿＿＿.

W Do you have a yard?

M Yes, I ＿＿＿＿＿＿ ＿＿＿＿＿＿ ＿＿＿＿＿＿. And there's a small swimming pool in it.

W Nice! I'd like to visit your house sometime.

대화를 듣고, 남자가 여자에게 전화한 목적으로 가장 적절한 것을 고르시오.

① 책을 빌리려고
② 친구 집에 같이 가려고
③ 시험공부를 함께 하려고
④ 집 주소를 알려 주려고
⑤ 친구 집 전화번호를 물어보려고

🔊 **Listening Tip**

I called him에서 I와 him은 대명사로 역할어라서 강세가 없어요. 역할어 him에서 처음에 오는 'h'는 발음하지 않고 모음 'i'도 약화되어서 /어/에 가깝게 발음하므로 I called him은 /아 콜 덤/으로 발음하게 돼요.

[Cell phone rings.]

W Hello.

M Hi, Jane. This is Paul. _____ _____ _____ _____ Chris is?

W I think he's at home now. He has to study for an exam.

M 🔊 I called him on his cell phone to borrow his book, _____ _____ _____ _____ _____. Do you know his home number?

W Let me check. *[Pause]* Yes, I have his home number. _____ _____ _____ _____?

M Yes, please. Can you _____ _____ _____ _____ by text message right away?

W Sure.

대화를 듣고, 두 사람이 공연을 볼 시각을 고르시오.

① 3:00 p.m.   ② 4:00 p.m.
③ 5:00 p.m.   ④ 6:00 p.m.
⑤ 7:00 p.m.

M The tickets for Teen Music Fest _____ _____ _____ _____.

W Let's book the tickets online right away.

M Okay. *[Pause]* There are still tickets left for 3 o'clock on Saturday and 7 o'clock on Sunday.

W Really? I want to go to the festival on Saturday. How about you?

M Oh, I have a swimming lesson this Saturday until 5. Can we go to the festival _____ _____ _____?

W Sure. Sunday is fine with me.

M _____ _____ _____ 2 tickets for the 7 o'clock showing.

W Okay. I _____ _____ _____ go to the festival!

다음 그림의 상황에 가장 적절한 대화를 고르시오.

① ② ③ ④ ⑤

① M You can _____ _____ _____
_____ .

W Oh, I see. How convenient!

② M What would you like to drink?

W I'd like a glass of mango juice.

③ M Shall we try that new Vietnamese restaurant?

W Sure. I hope there isn't _____ _____
_____ right now.

④ M Are you enjoying your meal?

W Not really. This steak is _____ _____
_____ _____ .

⑤ M Do you mind if I sit here?

W Sorry, but _____ _____ _____
my friend.

대화를 듣고, 두 사람이 대화하는 장소로 가장 적절한 곳을 고르시오.

① 부엌   ② 음식점   ③ 도서관
④ 서점   ⑤ 옷 가게

M Hello. How may I help you?

W I'm looking for a Thai cookbook. _____
_____ _____ _____ ?

M Okay. Have you ever cooked Thai food?

W No, I haven't, but I love eating Thai food.

M Well, we have some Thai _____ _____
_____ . Come this way, please.

W [Pause] Oh, how about this one? This book _____
_____ _____ _____ .

M Good choice. And it's 20% off now.

W Great! Thank you so much. _____ _____
_____ .

대화를 듣고, 남자가 여자에게 부탁한 일로 가장 적절한 것을 고르시오.

① 여행 가방 싸기   ② 환전하기
③ 날씨 확인하기   ④ 여권 찾아 주기
⑤ 우산 찾아 주기

W Billy, are you ready for your trip tomorrow?

M Yes, but I _____ _____ _____
_____ something.

W Oh, where did you put your passport?

M It's in my backpack.

W Good. Did _____ _____ _____ ?

M No, but I'm going to do that at the airport.

W Okay. You checked the weather in Rome before you packed your clothes, right?

M Of course, I did. *[Pause]* Oh, I forgot to pack an umbrella and a raincoat. Can you _____ _____ a small umbrella?

W Sure. _____ _____ _____ _____ in the closet.

M Okay. Thanks, Mom.

08 언급하지 않은 내용 찾기

다음을 듣고, 구겐하임 박물관(Guggenheim Museum)에 관해 언급되지 않은 것을 고르시오.

① 위치 ② 건물 설계자
③ 건물 외형 ④ 주요 전시물
⑤ 일일 투어

M Welcome to the Guggenheim Museum _____ _____ _____. You'll find beautiful works of art here, but the building itself is a work of art. Frank Lloyd Wright, an American architect, _____ _____ _____ to be such a unique shape. The outside _____ _____ _____ _____. If you go inside, you'll feel like you're walking in a big sculpture. If you want to know more about this museum, join the daily tour _____ _____ _____ _____.

09 화제 추론

다음을 듣고, 무엇에 관한 설명인지 고르시오.

① 학생증 ② 여권
③ 운전면허증 ④ 항공권
⑤ 주민 등록증

W This is an official document that identifies you. This contains your photo, name, date of birth, your nationality, and some _____ _____ _____ _____. If you don't have this when you're _____ _____ _____ _____, you have to go to a city hall _____ _____ _____. When you leave your country and enter another country at an airport, _____ _____ _____ _____.

10 어색한 대화 찾기

다음을 듣고, 두 사람의 대화가 어색한 것을 고르시오.

① ② ③ ④ ⑤

① M Hi, Sandy. What a surprise!
   W Hi, Jimin. I'm glad we're _____ _____ _____ _____.

② M I think chocolate is the greatest invention.
   W I agree. It _____ _____ _____ _____.

③ **M** You look so worried.

W I'm nervous that I might make a mistake in the school play.

④ **M** Ben ＿＿＿＿＿＿ ＿＿＿＿＿＿ ＿＿＿＿＿＿ ＿＿＿＿＿＿ the quiz show.

W Really? I'm so happy for him.

⑤ **M** ＿＿＿＿＿＿ ＿＿＿＿＿＿ ＿＿＿＿＿＿ ＿＿＿＿＿＿ the camp?

W I like to go hiking because I can see wild birds.

---

11 할 일 파악

대화를 듣고, 남자가 할 일로 가장 적절한 것을 고르시오.

① 방 청소하기　　② 개 산책시키기
③ 개 집 만들기　　④ 땅콩버터 사 오기
⑤ 개 목욕시키기

M Mom, where is Buddy? I want to take him for a walk.

W I think I ＿＿＿＿＿＿ ＿＿＿＿＿＿ ＿＿＿＿＿＿ ＿＿＿＿＿＿ your bedroom.

M Oh no! I left a jar of peanut butter on my desk.

W Hurry before he makes a mess in your room.

M ＿＿＿＿＿＿ ＿＿＿＿＿＿ ＿＿＿＿＿＿. Look at him. He has peanut butter ＿＿＿＿＿＿ ＿＿＿＿＿＿ ＿＿＿＿＿＿ ＿＿＿＿＿＿.

W It's your fault to leave peanut butter in your room. You should give him a bath now. I don't want Buddy ＿＿＿＿＿＿ ＿＿＿＿＿＿ ＿＿＿＿＿＿ ＿＿＿＿＿＿ peanut butter on him.

M Okay, I will.

---

12 숫자 정보 파악 (시각)

대화를 듣고, 두 사람이 보기로 한 텔레비전 프로그램이 시작하는 시간을 고르시오.

① 5:00 p.m.　　② 5:10 p.m.
③ 5:15 p.m.　　④ 5:20 p.m.
⑤ 5:30 p.m.

M What's on TV right now?

W *My Girl*. It's really interesting. ＿＿＿＿＿＿ ＿＿＿＿＿＿ ＿＿＿＿＿＿.

M No, thanks. I don't like watching dramas.

W Okay. There's ＿＿＿＿＿＿ ＿＿＿＿＿＿ ＿＿＿＿＿＿ ＿＿＿＿＿＿ later.

M What is it?

W It's *Kim's Kitchen* and it's a popular show. A ＿＿＿＿＿＿ ＿＿＿＿＿＿ ＿＿＿＿＿＿ a pop-up Korean restaurant in Turkey.

M I like _____ _____ _____. Let's watch that instead. What time is it on?

W It's on at 5:20.

M Oh, it's 5:15 now. What channel is the show on?

W It's on channel 6. I'll change the channel with the remote control.

13 위치 찾기

다음 도서관 배치도를 보면서 대화를 듣고, 남자가 선택할 구역을 고르시오.

Children's Books	③	History Books		④
②				Magazine
①		Information Desk	↑ Entrance	⑤

M Hello, Ms. Lee.

W Hi, Ben. How may I help you?

M I want to read a mystery novel. Can you recommend a good book?

W Sure. There's Steve King's new book, *The Dark House*.

M Great! I'm a big fan of his. _____ _____ _____ _____ the book?

W It's in the "New Arrivals" section. The section is _____ _____ the "History Books" section.

M Is it _____ _____ the "Children's Books" section?

W No. You have to go to _____ _____ _____ the "Magazine" section.

M Thank you for your help. I hope the book is still there.

14 한 일 파악

대화를 듣고, 여자가 어제 한 일로 가장 적절한 것을 고르시오.

① 병원 가기　　② 배구하기
③ 기타 치기　　④ 콘서트 가기
⑤ 노래 연습하기

M Sena, can you _____ _____ _____ _____?

W What is it?

M I'm going to participate in the K-pop contest next week.

W That's great, Paul!

M So, can you _____ _____ _____ while I sing in the contest?

W I'd love to, but I can't. I hurt my right hand while I _____ _____ _____ yesterday.

M Oh, that's too bad.

W _____ _____ _____ _____ Hajun instead? He's good at playing the guitar, too.

15 목적 파악

다음을 듣고, 방송의 목적으로 가장 적절한 것을 고르시오.

① 할인 소식을 알리려고
② 매장 개업을 홍보하려고
③ 현명한 소비를 권장하려고
④ 유기농 식품을 장려하려고
⑤ 행운권 추첨 결과를 공지하려고

🔊 **Listening Tip**

variety에서 't'처럼 모음 사이에 오는 강세가 없는 음절의 't'나 'd'는 / ㄹ /로 발음해요. 따라서 variety는 /버롸이어리/처럼 발음하게 돼요.

M Hello, shoppers. Here's _____ _____ _____! Today is Joe's Supermarket's Special Price Day. Fresh organically grown fruits and vegetables _____ _____ _____. A bag of oranges is only $2. A bag of delicious apples is $3. In addition, we are selling a 🔊variety of other products at _____ _____ _____. These amazing prices are _____ _____ _____. Enjoy shopping!

16 숫자 정보 파악 (금액)

대화를 듣고, 남자가 지불할 금액을 고르시오.

① $500   ② $600   ③ $700
④ $800   ⑤ $900

M Excuse me, how much is this laptop?
W That's $800.
M Do you have any cheaper ones?
W Sure. The ones _____ _____ _____ are cheaper. This is $600, and that is $700.
M What's _____ _____ _____ the two models?
W The one that is $600 has a 5-hour battery life, and _____ _____ _____ _____ a 7-hour battery life.
M I see. I don't need a long battery life. I'll _____ _____ _____ _____.
W That's a very good choice.

17 이어질 응답 찾기

대화를 듣고, 남자의 마지막 말에 대한 여자의 응답으로 가장 적절한 것을 고르시오.

Woman: _____

① What do you do in Korea on that day?
② I'm really looking forward to that day.
③ So what are you going to do tomorrow?
④ I love the fireworks best. I always watch them.
⑤ That's because I don't need to go to school.

M I _____ _____ _____ tomorrow.
W Really? Why not?
M It's the National Foundation Day of Korea.
W Oh, I see. We also have Australia Day. It's on January 26th.
M Is that _____ _____ _____ _____ Australia, too?
W Yes. There's no school or work. Everyone has a day off.
M What events do you have?
W _____ _____ _____ a street parade, a concert, and fireworks.
M That sounds exciting. _____ _____ _____ _____?

대화를 듣고, 여자의 마지막 말에 대한 남자의 응답으로 가장 적절한 것을 고르시오.

Man: _____

① Now I know what it is.
② I will. Can I go now?
③ Okay. I'll fasten my seat belt.
④ It's not fair to give me a ticket.
⑤ Thank you so much for your help.

W Excuse me, sir. Let me see your driver's license.
M Here you are, Officer. What did _____ _____ _____ ?
W You were speeding.
M I was speeding?
W Yes. I'm going to have to _____ _____ _____ _____ .
M Oh no. How fast was I going?
W You were going 90 kilometers per hour. This road has _____ _____ _____ _____ 60 kilometers per hour.
M I'm sorry. I didn't know that.
W [Pause] Here's your license. _____ _____ .

대화를 듣고, 여자의 마지막 말에 대한 남자의 응답으로 가장 적절한 것을 고르시오.

Man: _____

① I can't forget about it.
② It will be the perfect gift for him.
③ Your advice is always helpful to me.
④ It means you should focus on today.
⑤ Thanks for helping me with the presentation.

M What's the matter? Are you all right?
W I was just thinking about my presentation _____ _____ _____ .
M What about it?
W Well, I think I _____ _____ _____ _____ .
M Don't worry about it. I didn't notice them at all.
W I don't know. I wish I could _____ _____ _____ and do it again.
M Have you heard "Today is a gift" before?
W No. _____ _____ _____ _____ ?

다음 상황 설명을 듣고, Jacob이 엄마에게 할 말로 가장 적절한 것을 고르시오.

Jacob: Mom, _____

① why don't we eat out?
② what would you like to drink?
③ do you mind if I sit next to you?
④ what are we going to eat for dinner?
⑤ do you want me to get you anything?

W Jacob comes home from school at 3 o'clock and finds his mother in the living room. She is not supposed to _____ _____ _____ 7 p.m., but she is home already. He notices that she is drinking hot tea and _____ _____ _____ _____ . He thinks that she is _____ _____ _____ . So he wants to ask her if there is anything to _____ _____ _____ _____ . In this situation, what would Jacob most likely say to his mom?

실전 모의고사 **14**

01 대화를 듣고, 남자가 만든 팔찌를 고르시오.

①   ②   ③

④   ⑤

02 대화를 듣고, 남자가 볼 오페라에 관해 언급되지 <u>않은</u> 것을 고르시오.

① 제목   ② 줄거리   ③ 작곡가
④ 공연 요일   ⑤ 공연 장소

03 대화를 듣고, 남자가 여자에게 전화한 목적으로 가장 적절한 것을 고르시오.

① 축구 경기를 미루려고
② 경기 장소를 바꾸려고
③ 내일 날씨를 확인하려고
④ 부족한 팀원을 충원하려고
⑤ 미세 먼지에 대해 경고하려고

04 대화를 듣고, 여자가 영화를 볼 시각을 고르시오.

① 3:00 p.m.   ② 3:30 p.m.   ③ 4:00 p.m.
④ 5:00 p.m.   ⑤ 5:30 p.m.

05 다음 그림의 상황에 가장 적절한 대화를 고르시오.

①   ②   ③   ④   ⑤

06 대화를 듣고, 두 사람이 대화하는 장소로 가장 적절한 곳을 고르시오.

① 공원   ② 자전거 판매점
③ 병원   ④ 헬스클럽
⑤ 경찰서

07 대화를 듣고, 남자가 여자에게 부탁한 일로 가장 적절한 것을 고르시오.

① 쿠키 맛보기   ② 우유 사 오기
③ 쿠키 포장하기   ④ 벼룩시장 가기
⑤ 어린이집에서 봉사하기

08 다음을 듣고, FUNDaFIELD에 관해 언급되지 <u>않은</u> 것을 고르시오.

① 설립자   ② 설립 계기   ③ 설립 시기
④ 주요 활동   ⑤ 참여 방법

09 다음을 듣고, 무엇에 관한 설명인지 고르시오.

① 잠자리   ② 모기   ③ 개미
④ 꿀벌   ⑤ 나비

10 다음을 듣고, 두 사람의 대화가 <u>어색한</u> 것을 고르시오.

①   ②   ③   ④   ⑤

11 대화를 듣고, 남자가 할 일로 가장 적절한 것을 고르시오.

① 물건 수리하기
② 환불 요청하기
③ 배터리 교체하기
④ 교환 신청서 작성하기
⑤ 새로운 모델 알아보기

12 대화를 듣고, 남자가 내일 일어날 시각을 고르시오.

① 5:00 a.m.   ② 6:00 a.m.   ③ 7:00 a.m.

④ 8:00 a.m.   ⑤ 9:00 a.m.

13 다음 박물관 배치도를 보면서 대화를 듣고, 여자가 찾아갈 곳을 고르시오.

Gift Shop	②	③	Restroom
①	Information Desk ↑ Entrance		④
			Cafeteria
			⑤

14 다음을 듣고, 남자가 어제 한 일로 가장 적절한 것을 고르시오.

① 병원 가기   ② 유리창 닦기

③ 태권도 연습하기   ④ 안경 사러 가기

⑤ 엄마와 쇼핑하기

15 다음을 듣고, 방송의 목적으로 가장 적절한 것을 고르시오.

① 강도 용의자를 신고하게 하려고

② 범죄 예방 방법을 알려 주려고

③ 총기 사용 금지법을 공지하려고

④ 감시 카메라의 필요성을 알리려고

⑤ 새로운 기능의 휴대전화를 소개하려고

16 대화를 듣고, 남자가 지불할 금액을 고르시오.

① $20   ② $25   ③ $30

④ $35   ⑤ $40

17 대화를 듣고, 남자의 마지막 말에 대한 여자의 응답으로 가장 적절한 것을 고르시오.

Woman: _____

① I want a cheaper one.

② I don't want a black car.

③ Then this is the right car for you.

④ I'm looking for a brand-new car.

⑤ What car colors are popular these days?

18 대화를 듣고, 여자의 마지막 말에 대한 남자의 응답으로 가장 적절한 것을 고르시오.

Man: _____

① Two tickets are 16 dollars.

② I think that works for me.

③ I can't wait to see the concert!

④ I don't like romantic movies.

⑤ I'm really into horror movies these days.

19 대화를 듣고, 남자의 마지막 말에 대한 여자의 응답으로 가장 적절한 것을 고르시오.

Woman: _____

① Do you want me to help you?

② What should we do for the ocean?

③ Great. Let's get more cups for the party.

④ And it is also important to wash your hands.

⑤ Good idea. Taking simple actions like these can help.

20 다음 상황 설명을 듣고, Emily가 Ben에게 할 말로 가장 적절한 것을 고르시오.

Emily: _____

① You did a very good job.

② I'll try my best for the race.

③ I'm sorry to hear about the race.

④ I think you should practice harder.

⑤ You should enjoy yourself on Sports Day.

Dictation 14

◇ 다시 듣고, 빈칸에 들어갈 알맞은 단어를 써보세요.

정답 및 해설 p.93

---

01 그림 정보 파악

대화를 듣고, 남자가 만든 팔찌를 고르시오.

① ② ③ ④ ⑤

M Maya, this is a gift for you.

W Wow, what a pretty bracelet! Where did you buy it?

M I _____ _____ _____ in our craft club.

W Really? How did you make it?

M After wrapping the leather strap a few times _____ _____ _____, I tied a knot and cut it. And I _____ _____ _____ _____ you like.

W That sounds easy, but you made the world's coolest bracelet.

M I'm glad you like it.

---

02 언급하지 않은 내용 찾기

대화를 듣고, 남자가 볼 오페라에 관해 언급되지 않은 것을 고르시오.

① 제목 ② 줄거리
③ 작곡가 ④ 공연 요일
⑤ 공연 장소

W Luke, what are you going to do this weekend?

M I'm going to watch the opera *Turandot*.

W *Turandot*? _____ _____ _____ _____?

M It's about a Chinese princess and a brave prince who falls in love with her.

W That sounds interesting. Who composed it?

M Giacomo Puccini. He was a _____ _____ composer.

W Cool. I want to see an opera someday.

M Oh, really? Then why don't you _____ _____ _____ _____?

W I'd love to, but I can't. I have other plans this weekend.

M Okay. Maybe next time.

---

03 목적 파악

대화를 듣고, 남자가 여자에게 전화한 목적으로 가장 적절한 것을 고르시오.

① 축구 경기를 미루려고
② 경기 장소를 바꾸려고
③ 내일 날씨를 확인하려고
④ 부족한 팀원을 충원하려고
⑤ 미세 먼지에 대해 경고하려고

[Cell phone rings.]

W Hello.

M Hi, Kate. It's Harry. Did you hear the weather forecast for tomorrow?

W No, I didn't. _____ _____ _____ _____?

M It said the fine dust level will be very high and outdoor activities _____ _____ _____.

W Oh no. We're supposed to play soccer tomorrow.

M Yes. I think _____ _____ _____ another day.

W You're right. Then we should let the other members know.

M I'll _____ _____ _____ _____ of our team right now.

W That would be good.

---

04 숫자 정보 파악 (시각)

대화를 듣고, 여자가 영화를 볼 시각을 고르시오.

① 3:00 p.m.   ② 3:30 p.m.
③ 4:00 p.m.   ④ 5:00 p.m.
⑤ 5:30 p.m.

W Can I get 2 tickets for *Girlhood* for 3 o'clock?

M I'm afraid _____ _____ _____ _____ for 3 o'clock, but there are some seats left for 5:30.

W We don't want to wait so long to see it.

M We have _____ _____ _____ _____ playing around 3. They are *Space* and *Jump Shot*.

W Oh, we'll watch one of them, then.

M If you like action, I recommend *Jump Shot*. _____ _____ _____ 3:30.

W _____ _____ _____. I'd like 2 tickets for *Jump Shot*, please.

M Okay.

---

05 그림 상황에 적절한 대화 찾기

다음 그림의 상황에 가장 적절한 대화를 고르시오.

① ② ③ ④ ⑤

① M Are there _____ _____ _____ _____ nearby?

W The closest one is just around the corner.

② M _____ _____ _____ your new bike?

W Sorry, but it's not my bike. It's my brother's.

③ M You should wear a helmet when you ride a bike.

W Okay. Then I'll go back _____ _____ _____ _____.

④ M Oh no! Are you okay?

W I think so. I _____ _____ _____ _____ and hit it.

⑤ M We need to make a bicycle parking space at school.

W That's a good idea.

06 장소 추론

대화를 듣고, 두 사람이 대화하는 장소로 가장 적절한 곳을 고르시오.

① 공원   ② 자전거 판매점
③ 병원   ④ 헬스클럽
⑤ 경찰서

W Well, your arm is _____ _____ _____.

M Oh, that's good news. When will you take off my cast?

W I _____ _____ _____ in a week if you don't hurt yourself again.

M Yes, I'll be careful.

W It _____ _____ _____ _____ use your arm for a while after the cast is off.

M Then what should I do?

W I _____ _____ _____ _____ a physical therapy program here.

M Okay, I will. Thank you so much.

07 부탁 파악

대화를 듣고, 남자가 여자에게 부탁한 일로 가장 적절한 것을 고르시오.

① 쿠키 맛보기   ② 우유 사 오기
③ 쿠키 포장하기   ④ 벼룩시장 가기
⑤ 어린이집에서 봉사하기

W Bill, are you baking cookies? Can I try one?

M Go ahead. *[Pause]* What do you think?

W Wow, it's really good. It's _____ _____ _____ _____ cookie.

M Thanks. I'm glad you like it.

W You're baking so many cookies. Are you _____ _____ _____ _____?

M No, they're _____ _____ _____ at the day-care center.

W Oh, I see. Do you need any help?

M Sure. Please _____ _____ _____ _____ the gift boxes. 5 cookies in each box.

W Okay.

08 언급하지 않은 내용 찾기

다음을 듣고, FUNDaFIELD에 관해 언급되지 않은 것을 고르시오.

① 설립자　　② 설립 계기
③ 설립 시기　④ 주요 활동
⑤ 참여 방법

M Hi, I'm Kyle Weiss. At the 2006 World Cup games in Germany, I _____ _____ _____ from Africa. During that time, I realized that soccer helps _____ _____ and teaches kids important values and life skills. So, 2 years after the German World Cup, I created an organization with my brother _____ _____ _____ _____ for children in Africa. We provide a safe field with equipment to play soccer. I hope you will help us at FUNDaFIELD.

09 화제 추론

다음을 듣고, 무엇에 관한 설명인지 고르시오.

① 잠자리　② 모기　③ 개미
④ 꿀벌　⑤ 나비

🔊 **Listening Tip**

social과 small은 모두 's'로 시작하지만 's'의 발음을 약간 다르게 해요. 모음 앞에 오는 's'는 /ㅆ/로 발음하고 자음 앞에 오는 것은 /스/로 발음해요. social은 /쏘우셜/로 small은 /스몰/로 발음해요.

W These are flying insects, and they help flowers, fruits, and vegetables grow. When they collect food, they go _____ _____ _____ _____. They also carry fine powder from one flower to another flower. This helps _____ _____ and fruits. They are called 🔊 social insects because they _____ _____ _____ _____ as a community. Each of them makes hundreds of trips to produce a 🔊 small _____ _____ _____.

10 어색한 대화 찾기

다음을 듣고, 두 사람의 대화가 <u>어색한</u> 것을 고르시오.

①　②　③　④　⑤

① M What would you like to _____ _____ _____?

W I'd like to have some apple pie.

② M Why don't we go fishing tomorrow?

W That's a good idea.

③ M Can you tell me _____ _____ _____ _____ is?

W It's about 120 years old.

④ M Why do you like K-pop?

W I'd like to _____ _____ _____ _____.

⑤ M Need any help, ma'am?

W Yes, please. Where's the Museum of Modern Art?

11 할 일 파악

대화를 듣고, 남자가 할 일로 가장 적절한 것을 고르시오.

① 물건 수리하기
② 환불 요청하기
③ 배터리 교체하기
④ 교환 신청서 작성하기
⑤ 새로운 모델 알아보기

W Hello, sir. What can I do for you?

M I bought this smartwatch only 2 weeks ago, but the battery is _____ _____ _____ _____.

W May I have a look at it?

M Here you are.

W *[Pause]* I'm sorry, but I think it'll _____ _____ _____ to fix it.

M Well, I'm not satisfied with the watch. I'd like to return it.

W You can't return it, but you _____ _____ _____ _____ a new one.

M I see. Then *I'd like to exchange it for a new one, please.

W Of course. You need to _____ _____ _____ _____. Here is a pen.

M Thanks.

＊ 교육부 지정 의사소통 기능: 교환 요청하기   동(윤) 4

I'd like to exchange ~. 저는 ~을 교환하고 싶어요.
• **I'd like to exchange** this sweater. 저는 이 스웨터를 교환하고 싶어요.
• **I'd like to exchange** this shirt for a smaller one. 저는 셔츠를 작은 것으로 교환하고 싶어요.

---

12 숫자 정보 파악 (시각)

대화를 듣고, 남자가 내일 일어날 시각을 고르시오.

① 5 a.m.   ② 6 a.m.   ③ 7 a.m.
④ 8 a.m.   ⑤ 9 a.m.

M Mom, what time are we going to visit grandmother tomorrow?

W We're going to leave around 9 in the morning.

M Aren't we going to _____ _____ _____ _____ for her?

W Yes. I'm going to bake it before we go.

M Should I _____ _____ _____ _____ help you?

W _____ _____ _____ _____ you could help me.

M What time should I get up?

W I'm going to get up around 6 o'clock to prepare for baking. You _____ _____ _____ _____ 7 and help me make the cake.

M Okay. Good night, Mom.

13 위치 찾기

다음 박물관 배치도를 보면서 대화를 듣고, 여자가 찾아갈 곳을 고르시오.

Gift Shop	②	③	Restroom
①	Information Desk		④
			Cafeteria
	↑ Entrance		⑤

W Excuse me.

M Hello. How can I help you?

W Is it okay to take ＿＿＿＿＿＿＿＿＿＿ ＿＿＿＿＿＿＿＿＿＿ ＿＿＿＿＿＿＿＿＿＿ in here?

M I'm afraid large bags ＿＿＿＿＿＿＿＿＿＿ ＿＿＿＿＿＿＿＿＿＿ ＿＿＿＿＿＿＿＿＿＿ ＿＿＿＿＿＿＿＿＿＿ the museum.

W I see. Are there any lockers I can leave my backpack in?

M Sure. Do you see the ＿＿＿＿＿＿＿＿＿＿ ＿＿＿＿＿＿＿＿＿＿ ＿＿＿＿＿＿＿＿＿＿ ＿＿＿＿＿＿＿＿＿＿?

W Yes.

M ＿＿＿＿＿＿＿＿＿＿ ＿＿＿＿＿＿＿＿＿＿ ＿＿＿＿＿＿＿＿＿＿ ＿＿＿＿＿＿＿＿＿＿ the cafeteria and the restroom.

W I see. Thank you so much.

14 한 일 파악

다음을 듣고, 남자가 어제 한 일로 가장 적절한 것을 고르시오.

① 병원 가기　　② 유리창 닦기
③ 태권도 연습하기　　④ 안경 사러 가기
⑤ 엄마와 쇼핑하기

W Ouch! You ＿＿＿＿＿＿＿＿＿＿ ＿＿＿＿＿＿＿＿＿＿ ＿＿＿＿＿＿＿＿＿＿ ＿＿＿＿＿＿＿＿＿＿ again.

M Oh, I'm sorry. Are you okay?

W Yes, but this is the second time you did that today.

M I ＿＿＿＿＿＿＿＿＿＿ ＿＿＿＿＿＿＿＿＿＿ ＿＿＿＿＿＿＿＿＿＿ because I'm not wearing my glasses today.

W What happened to your glasses?

M I ＿＿＿＿＿＿＿＿＿＿ ＿＿＿＿＿＿＿＿＿＿ ＿＿＿＿＿＿＿＿＿＿ ＿＿＿＿＿＿＿＿＿＿ practicing Taekwondo yesterday. I'm going to ＿＿＿＿＿＿＿＿＿＿ ＿＿＿＿＿＿＿＿＿＿ ＿＿＿＿＿＿＿＿＿＿ this afternoon.

W I see. You should be careful until then.

15 목적 파악

다음을 듣고, 방송의 목적으로 가장 적절한 것을 고르시오.

① 강도 용의자를 신고하게 하려고
② 범죄 예방 방법을 알려 주려고
③ 총기 사용 금지법을 공지하려고
④ 감시 카메라의 필요성을 알리려고
⑤ 새로운 기능의 휴대전화를 소개하려고

🔊 **Listening Tip**

전치사 of의 [v] 발음은 뒤에 자음이 오면 발음하지 않아요. 그래서 one of the는 /원 오브 더/가 아니라 /워 너 더/로 발음해요.

M Good evening and welcome to DBS News. The police ＿＿＿＿＿＿＿＿＿＿ ＿＿＿＿＿＿＿＿＿＿ ＿＿＿＿＿＿＿＿＿＿ 2 men who robbed a mobile phone store this morning on East Broad Street. Police released a video showing 🔊 one of the men. The man is wearing a medical mask and is about 180 centimeters tall. He is ＿＿＿＿＿＿＿＿＿＿ ＿＿＿＿＿＿＿＿＿＿ ＿＿＿＿＿＿＿＿＿＿ and has long blond hair. If you ＿＿＿＿＿＿＿＿＿＿ ＿＿＿＿＿＿＿＿＿＿ ＿＿＿＿＿＿＿＿＿＿ about the robbers, please ＿＿＿＿＿＿＿＿＿＿ ＿＿＿＿＿＿＿＿＿＿ ＿＿＿＿＿＿＿＿＿＿.

대화를 듣고, 남자가 지불할 금액을 고르시오.

① $20 ② $25 ③ $30
④ $35 ⑤ $40

[Telephone rings.]

W Hot Chicken. Can I take your order?

M Yes, I'd like a 12-piece original chicken with mashed potatoes and a green salad.

W All right. _____ _____ _____ $25.

M Is that with or without _____ _____ ?

W Without. _____ _____ _____ _____ $5 for the delivery. What's your address, please?

M It's 30 Lake Street, apartment 7.

W Okay. Is your phone number 3232-7740?

M That's correct.

W It'll be $30 _____ _____, and your food will _____ _____ _____ 40 minutes.

M Thank you.

---

17 이어질 응답 찾기

대화를 듣고, 남자의 마지막 말에 대한 여자의 응답으로 가장 적절한 것을 고르시오.

Woman: _____

① I want a cheaper one.
② I don't want a black car.
③ Then this is the right car for you.
④ I'm looking for a brand-new car.
⑤ What car colors are popular these days?

M Hello. How may I help you?

W I'm looking _____ _____ _____ _____ .

M Okay. Do you want an automatic car?

W Yes, please. It's easier for me to drive.

M Okay. How much are you _____ _____ _____ ?

W I don't want _____ _____ _____ $7,000.

M What about the color? The 3 _____ _____ _____ _____ black, white, and gray.

---

18 이어질 응답 찾기

대화를 듣고, 여자의 마지막 말에 대한 남자의 응답으로 가장 적절한 것을 고르시오.

Man: _____

① Two tickets are 16 dollars.
② I think that works for me.
③ I can't wait to see the concert!
④ I don't like romantic movies.
⑤ I'm really into horror movies these days.

M Emma, why don't we stay at home and watch a movie tonight?

W Well, _____ _____ _____ _____ to the theater.

M Okay. What movie would you like to watch?

W How about *Friday the 13th*?

M No way! You know I _____ _____ _____

_____ _____.

W I'm sorry. I forgot. Then, how about *Forever Love*?

M I don't enjoy romantic movies, either. _____

_____ _____ _____?

W Well, then how about _____ _____

_____? *My Spy* is also playing.

대화를 듣고, 남자의 마지막 말에 대한 여자의 응답으로 가장 적절한 것을 고르시오.

Woman: _____

① Do you want me to help you?
② What should we do for the ocean?
③ Great. Let's get more cups for the party.
④ And it is also important to wash your hands.
⑤ Good idea. Taking simple actions like these can help.

M Sandy, did you see the TV program *A Plastic Ocean*?

W Yes, I did. I learned that plastic waste is _____

_____ _____ sea animals from that

program.

M Me, too. I was really shocked to see sea animals suffer.

W We have to do _____ _____

_____ _____.

M You're right. How can we reduce plastic waste?

W We should _____ _____ _____

to use less of them.

M Sure. We can also _____ _____

_____ _____ instead of plastic ones.

다음 상황 설명을 듣고, Emily가 Ben에게 할 말로 가장 적절한 것을 고르시오.

Emily: _____

① You did a very good job.
② I'll try my best for the race.
③ I'm sorry to hear about the race.
④ I think you should practice harder.
⑤ You should enjoy yourself on Sports Day.

W Sports Day is next Wednesday. Emily is looking forward to it,

but Ben isn't. He is _____ _____

_____ _____ because he's the last runner

in the relay race. He's also afraid that his team will

_____ _____ _____

_____. So, Emily wants to tell him Sports Day is

_____ _____ _____. She wants

Ben to relax a little and _____ _____

_____ _____. In this situation, what would

Emily most likely say to Ben?

실전 모의고사 15

01 대화를 듣고, 여자가 선택한 학급 티셔츠를 고르시오.

①   ②   ③

④   ⑤

02 대화를 듣고, 남자가 여자에게 전화한 목적으로 가장 적절한 것을 고르시오.

① 책을 추천받으려고
② 영화 평을 들으려고
③ 어제 일을 사과하려고
④ 함께 영화를 보러 가려고
⑤ 빌려준 책을 돌려받으려고

03 다음 그림의 상황에 가장 적절한 대화를 고르시오.

①   ②   ③   ④   ⑤

04 대화를 듣고, 여자가 가장 좋아하는 달을 고르시오.

① 5월   ② 6월   ③ 7월
④ 8월   ⑤ 9월

05 다음을 듣고, 〈위대한 개츠비(The Great Gatsby)〉에 관해 언급되지 않은 것을 고르시오.

① 원작   ② 배경   ③ 주인공
④ 결말   ⑤ 상영 시간

06 대화를 듣고, 두 사람의 관계로 가장 적절한 것을 고르시오.

① 서점 직원 – 고객
② 택시 기사 – 승객
③ 옷 가게 점원 – 고객
④ 관광 안내원 – 관광객
⑤ 벼룩시장 상인 – 손님

07 다음을 듣고, 두 사람의 대화가 어색한 것을 고르시오.

①   ②   ③   ④   ⑤

08 대화를 듣고, 여자가 남자에게 부탁한 일로 가장 적절한 것을 고르시오.

① 낮잠 깨우기   ② 휴대전화 찾아 주기
③ 시험공부 도와주기   ④ 약 먹도록 알려 주기
⑤ 집에 전화하라고 말하기

09 대화를 듣고, 남자의 마지막 말에 담긴 의도로 가장 적절한 것을 고르시오.

① 칭찬   ② 축하   ③ 동의
④ 격려   ⑤ 거절

10 대화를 듣고, 여자가 지불할 금액을 고르시오.

① $3   ② $4   ③ $5
④ $6   ⑤ $7

11 대화를 듣고, 남자가 할 일로 가장 적절한 것을 고르시오.

① 사진 고르기   ② 포스터 만들기
③ 사진첩 만들기   ④ 신문 기사 쓰기
⑤ 동물 보호 단체 가입하기

12 다음을 듣고, 흰긴수염고래(blue whale)에 관해 언급되지 <u>않은</u> 것을 고르시오.

① 서식지 　② 개체 수 　③ 먹이
④ 멸종 이유 　⑤ 보호 대책

13 다음 표를 보면서 대화를 듣고, 두 사람이 관람할 연극을 고르시오.

	Play	Place	Time	Price
①	A	Apollo Theater	1 p.m.	$40
②	B	Apollo Theater	3 p.m.	$60
③	C	Apollo Theater	7 p.m.	$20
④	D	Shakespeare Theater	3 p.m.	$40
⑤	E	Shakespeare Theater	7 p.m.	$20

14 다음을 듣고, 무엇에 관한 설명인지 고르시오.

① 화전 　② 송편 　③ 가래떡
④ 빈대떡 　⑤ 수정과

15 대화를 듣고, 여자가 대화 직후에 할 일로 가장 적절한 것을 고르시오.

① 이삿짐 싸기 　② 사진집 만들기
③ 온라인 쇼핑하기 　④ 선물 목록 만들기
⑤ 친구와 화상 채팅하기

16 대화를 듣고, 여자가 교환할 옷의 색을 고르시오.

① orange 　② yellow 　③ purple
④ blue 　⑤ red

17 대화를 듣고, 남자의 마지막 말에 대한 여자의 응답으로 가장 적절한 것을 고르시오.

Woman: _____

① Because it made me try harder.
② You don't have to worry about it.
③ I put too much pressure on myself.
④ Don't worry. You're good at science.
⑤ Because I was lucky to have many good friends.

18 대화를 듣고, 여자의 마지막 말에 대한 남자의 응답으로 가장 적절한 것을 고르시오.

Man: _____

① No, thanks. I'm not thirsty.
② Let me have the check, please.
③ I'm not satisfied with this pasta.
④ Then I'd like some chocolate cake.
⑤ Do you have strawberry ice cream?

19 대화를 듣고, 남자의 마지막 말에 대한 여자의 응답으로 가장 적절한 것을 고르시오.

Woman: _____

① No, thanks. Maybe later.
② I hope you have a nice trip.
③ Do you want me to join you?
④ Sorry, but I have other plans.
⑤ Great. Thanks for inviting me.

20 다음 상황 설명을 듣고, Jason이 은지에게 할 말로 가장 적절한 것을 고르시오.

Jason: _____

① I'll get the popcorn.
② Do you like action movies?
③ How did you like the movie?
④ Why don't we see a movie tomorrow?
⑤ How many times have you seen that movie?

Dictation 15

◆ 다시 듣고, 빈칸에 들어갈 알맞은 단어를 써보세요.

정답 및 해설 p.100

01 그림 정보 파악

대화를 듣고, 여자가 선택한 학급 티셔츠를 고르시오.

① ② ③
④ ⑤

W Dad, can you help me decide on the design for my class T-shirt? We're going to wear the T-shirt on Sports Day in June.

M Sure. Let me see _____ _____ _____ _____.

W How about this red one with short sleeves?

M Wasn't the class T-shirt last year red? How about this one _____ _____ _____ on it?

W It's not bad, but I want _____ _____ _____.

M How about this one with _____ _____ _____ _____? You can change those to the faces of your classmates.

W That's a great idea!

02 목적 파악

대화를 듣고, 남자가 여자에게 전화한 목적으로 가장 적절한 것을 고르시오.

① 책을 추천받으려고
② 영화 평을 들으려고
③ 어제 일을 사과하려고
④ 함께 영화를 보러 가려고
⑤ 빌려준 책을 돌려받으려고

[Cell phone rings.]

W Hello.

M Hi, Becky. I had a great time with you yesterday. Did you _____ _____ _____ as well?

W Yes. I am a big fan of mystery movies.

M Since I watched the movie, I started _____ _____ _____ the books by Agatha Christie, the original author.

W That sounds great. Many of her novels have been made into movies, too.

M I know you're a big fan of her. _____ _____ _____ _____ of her books?

W Of course. I've read all of her mystery books. And I _____ _____ _____ _____ some books I have.

M Thanks. I'm sure I'll like her books, too.

다음 그림의 상황에 가장 적절한 대화를 고르시오.

① ② ③ ④ ⑤

① **W** Dad, I'm a bit hungry.

M Do you _____ _____ _____ _____ a pizza for you?

② **W** I'm late for school. Could you give me a ride, please?

M Sure. _____ _____ _____ _____.

③ **W** Do you mind if I open the window?

M No, not at all.

④ **W** Why don't you take a walk every day?

M Okay. _____ _____ _____ _____.

⑤ **W** Dad, is something wrong? You look tired.

M I _____ _____ _____ _____ this morning.

대화를 듣고, 여자가 가장 좋아하는 달을 고르시오.
① 5월　　② 6월　　③ 7월
④ 8월　　⑤ 9월

W Jake, what's your favorite month?

M Hmm... Let's see. I think I _____ _____ _____.

W Why?

M My birthday is July 10th. I get a lot of presents and have a fun party on that day.

W Really? My birthday is on the 10th, too. But August 10th.

M I see. Then is August _____ _____ _____ of the year?

W Yes, but _____ _____ _____ why I like August best.

M What is it?

W That's the month when my parents _____ _____ _____ _____. So we go on vacation then.

다음을 듣고, 〈위대한 개츠비(The Great Gatsby)〉에 관해 언급되지 않은 것을 고르시오.
① 원작　　② 배경　　③ 주인공
④ 결말　　⑤ 상영 시간

W The beautiful movie *The Great Gatsby* is based on F. Scott Fitzgerald's 1925 _____ _____ _____ _____. The movie tells the story of neighbors _____ _____ _____ _____ New York's Long Island in

1922. _____ _____ _____ Jay
Gatsby, who is very rich, falls in love with Daisy, but

_____ _____ _____

_____ tragedy. After the movie is over, you will

never forget the party scenes in the movie.

---

06 관계 추론

대화를 듣고, 두 사람의 관계로 가장 적절한 것을
고르시오.

① 서점 직원 – 고객
② 택시 기사 – 승객
③ 옷 가게 점원 – 고객
④ 관광 안내원 – 관광객
⑤ 벼룩시장 상인 – 손님

🔊 **Listening Tip**

sounds great에서 보면 ds는 합쳐져서 /ㅊ/로 발음하여
'nds'와 'g'가 세 개의 자음을 나란히 발음하게 되지요. 이럴
때는 중간에 있는 소리는 발음하지 않아요. sounds great
는 /싸운즈 그레이트/가 아니라 /싸운 그렛/에 가깝게 발
음해요.

W Hello. How may I help you?
M Hi. I'd like to get _____ _____
   _____ of the city.
W Are there any special places you want to go?
M Yes. I want to _____ _____ _____
   _____.
W Oh, there are many flea markets held in London. The biggest
   one in London is Portobello Market. It opens every day.
M That 🔊 sounds great. Do you know any specific ones for
   clothes and accessories?
W Then go to Black Lane Market. _____
   _____ _____.
M How can I get there?
W Just _____ _____ _____ you see
   a subway station. Then turn right at the corner, and the
   market should be there.

---

07 어색한 대화 찾기

다음을 듣고, 두 사람의 대화가 <u>어색한</u> 것을 고르
시오.

①   ②   ③   ④   ⑤

① M I'm going to enter the model airplane contest.
   W Me, too. I'm _____ _____
      _____ it.
② M _____ _____ _____
      _____ to school?
   W I go to school early in the morning.
③ M You look disappointed.
   W I failed the audition _____ _____
      _____ _____.
④ M How do I get to the bank?
   W _____ _____ _____
      _____ and turn left at the traffic light.
⑤ M Do you have any brothers or sisters?
   W Yes, I have 2 brothers and a sister.

08 부탁 파악

대화를 듣고, 여자가 남자에게 부탁한 일로 가장 적절한 것을 고르시오.

① 낮잠 깨우기
② 휴대전화 찾아 주기
③ 시험공부 도와주기
④ 약 먹도록 알려주기
⑤ 집에 전화하라고 말하기

[Cell phone rings.]

M Hello?

W Hi, James. This is Mark's mom. Is he with you?

M Oh, hello, ma'am. Yes, he is. We're studying for the exam together. Do you need something?

W No, I ＿＿＿＿ ＿＿＿＿ ＿＿＿＿ his cell phone, but he wasn't answering.

M Oh, he's ＿＿＿＿ ＿＿＿＿ ＿＿＿＿ now. I'll wake him up.

W No, you don't have to.

M Then I'll ＿＿＿＿ ＿＿＿＿ ＿＿＿＿ that you called when he wakes up.

W Sure. Also, tell him not to forget to take ＿＿＿＿ ＿＿＿＿ ＿＿＿＿ ＿＿＿＿.

09 의도 파악

대화를 듣고, 남자의 마지막 말에 담긴 의도로 가장 적절한 것을 고르시오.

① 칭찬　　② 축하　　③ 동의
④ 격려　　⑤ 거절

W Peter, do you hear the music ＿＿＿＿ ＿＿＿＿ ＿＿＿＿ ＿＿＿＿?

M Yes. Is it Korean traditional music?

W Yes, it's called nongak.

M Nongak? *Can you explain more about it?

W Sure. It's a form of traditional farmers' music. It has been performed to cheer up farmers and to wish ＿＿＿＿ ＿＿＿＿ ＿＿＿＿ ＿＿＿＿.

M I see. I like the sound of it.

W Look! Many people are dancing to the rhythm together. ＿＿＿＿ ＿＿＿＿ ＿＿＿＿ ＿＿＿＿ ＿＿＿＿, too?

M ＿＿＿＿ ＿＿＿＿ ＿＿＿＿! Why not?

✱ 교육부 지정 의사소통 기능: **설명 요청하기**　　미 4 l 능(김) 기능(양) 6 l 금 6

Can[could] you explain ~? ～을 설명해 주시겠어요?

• **Can you explain** more about the book? 그 책에 대해 좀 더 설명해 주시겠어요?
• **Could you explain** how to get there? 그곳으로 어떻게 가는지 설명해 주시겠어요?

10 숫자 정보 파악 (금액)

대화를 듣고, 여자가 지불할 금액을 고르시오.

① $3   ② $4   ③ $5
④ $6   ⑤ $7

W   Hello, I'd like a hot dog with fries.

M   Okay. _____ _____ _____
_____ $5.

W $5? Isn't it supposed to be $4?

M   That's only _____ _____.

W   Okay, I see. Oh, how much is a large drink?

M   The large one is $2.

W   All right. _____ _____ _____
a large coke.

M   Let me _____ _____ _____.
One hot dog with fries and one large drink, correct?

W   That's right.

11 할 일 파악

대화를 듣고, 남자가 할 일로 가장 적절한 것을 고르시오.

① 사진 고르기   ② 포스터 만들기
③ 사진첩 만들기   ④ 신문 기사 쓰기
⑤ 동물 보호 단체 가입하기

W   Paul, are you busy now? Can you help me with something?

M   I'm not busy at all. What do you need help with?

W   I _____ _____ _____
_____ my article in the school newspaper.

M   What is your story about?

W   It's about endangered animals. We _____
_____ _____ _____
_____ see some animals in the near future.

M   I see. I am interested in saving them, too.

W   Great. I need to _____ _____
_____ _____ out of these four. Which one
should I pick?

M   Let me see.

12 언급하지 않은 내용 찾기

다음을 듣고, 흰긴수염고래(blue whale)에 관해 언급되지 않은 것을 고르시오.

① 서식지   ② 개체 수   ③ 먹이
④ 멸종 이유   ⑤ 보호 대책

M   Hello. I'd like to tell you why we save blue whales and how.
Blue whales are the largest animals in the world. They
_____ _____ _____ all the
oceans of the world. They were numerous in the past, but
today only between 10,000 and 25,000 of _____
_____ _____. That's because people have
_____ _____ _____
_____, food, and clothing. To protect them, we
should support conservation programs and avoid any
products _____ _____ _____.

13 도표 정보 파악

다음 표를 보면서 대화를 듣고, 두 사람이 관람할 연극을 고르시오.

	Play	Place	Time	Price
①	A	Apollo Theater	1 p.m.	$40
②	B	Apollo Theater	3 p.m.	$60
③	C	Apollo Theater	7 p.m.	$20
④	D	Shakespeare Theater	3 p.m.	$40
⑤	E	Shakespeare Theater	7 p.m.	$20

W Jack, do you want to go and see a play today?

M There are 2 famous theaters in town. Which one should we go to?

W I've already been to the Shakespeare Theater. Can we go to _____ _____ _____ today?

M Of course, I don't really mind.

W I also need to _____ _____ by 7 p.m. today. Will we have enough time?

M Yes, the plays are about 2 _____ _____.

W I see. Then you can choose which one to watch. I don't really mind either one.

M Okay, then let's choose _____ _____ _____.

W Good choice.

14 화제 추론

다음을 듣고, 무엇에 관한 설명인지 고르시오.

① 화전　　② 송편　　③ 가래떡
④ 빈대떡　　⑤ 수정과

W This is a traditional Korean food. We _____ _____ _____ _____ the Korean Thanksgiving Day, Chuseok. It has a half-moon shape, and it is _____ _____ sesame seeds, sugar, chestnuts, or beans. You _____ _____ _____ pine needles. That's why _____ _____ _____ pine trees. Its name _____ _____ the use of pine trees and it translates to "pine cakes."

15 할 일 파악

대화를 듣고, 여자가 대화 직후에 할 일로 가장 적절한 것을 고르시오.

① 이삿짐 싸기
② 사진집 만들기
③ 온라인 쇼핑하기
④ 선물 목록 만들기
⑤ 친구와 화상 채팅하기

M Sura, is something wrong? _____ _____ _____ _____.

W I'm feeling very sad. My best friend Jamie is moving to Toronto next week.

M I'm sorry to hear that.

W We promised to have video chats online every day, but _____ _____ _____ _____.

◄)) Listening Tip

don't you에서처럼 [t] 소리로 끝나는 단어 뒤에 'y'로 시
작되는 단어가 오면 두 소리가 합쳐져서 /츄/로 발음해요.
don't you는 /돈트 유/가 아니라 /돈 츄/로 발음되지요.

M Then why ◄) don't you make Jamie _____
_____ _____ _____
_____ her and your pictures?

W That's a good idea. I'm sure it will be a meaningful gift.

M _____ _____ _____ right now. I'll
help you.

W Thanks.

---

16 특정 정보 파악

대화를 듣고, 여자가 교환할 옷의 색을 고르시오.

① orange ② yellow ③ purple
④ blue ⑤ red

M Hello, ma'am. How may I help you?

W I got this blouse as a gift yesterday, but the color
_____ _____ _____ _____
me.

M Oh, I see. This blouse comes in 3 other colors.

W Great. _____ _____ _____
_____ orange?

M I'm sorry, but there are yellow, purple, and blue ones. How
about this purple one?

W It looks good, but I think _____ _____
_____ _____. Do you have a blue one in
medium?

M Of course. I'll _____ _____ _____
_____ it.

---

17 이어질 응답 찾기

대화를 듣고, 남자의 마지막 말에 대한 여자의 응
답으로 가장 적절한 것을 고르시오.

Woman: _____

① Because it made me try harder.
② You don't have to worry about it.
③ I put too much pressure on myself.
④ Don't worry. You're good at science.
⑤ Because I was lucky to have many
   good friends.

W Are you studying, Henry? Have some of these cookies.

M Thanks, Mom. I'm studying _____ _____
_____ _____, but I'm so worried.

W I understand. I used to feel that way before exams, too.

M Really? You did well in school, didn't you?

W I tried my best, but _____ _____
_____ me out. But a little stress _____
_____ for me.

M _____ _____ _____
_____ _____ ?

18 이어질 응답 찾기

대화를 듣고, 여자의 마지막 말에 대한 남자의 응답으로 가장 적절한 것을 고르시오.

Man: _____

① No, thanks. I'm not thirsty.
② Let me have the check, please.
③ I'm not satisfied with this pasta.
④ Then I'd like some chocolate cake.
⑤ Do you have strawberry ice cream?

W Good evening, sir. Can I take your order?
M Good evening. I'd like some pasta with fresh mushrooms.
W Okay. Would you like _____ _____
_____ _____ ?
M Yes, please. I'd like some water with lemon.
W Okay. Anything else?
M _____ _____
_____ bread and cheese?
W Yes, of course. Is that all then?
M I'd like some mango ice cream for dessert.
W I'm sorry, but there isn't _____ _____
_____ _____ .

19 이어질 응답 찾기

대화를 듣고, 남자의 마지막 말에 대한 여자의 응답으로 가장 적절한 것을 고르시오.

Woman: _____

① No, thanks. Maybe later.
② I hope you have a nice trip.
③ Do you want me to join you?
④ Sorry, but I have other plans.
⑤ Great. Thanks for inviting me.

M Amy, where are you going to go on vacation this summer break?
W I'm not sure yet. What about you?
M I'm going to go to Ulleung-do with my friends.
_____ _____ _____ its peaceful blue waves and beautiful scenery.
W I heard that, too. _____ _____
_____ _____ wanted to go.
M Then would you like to come with us?
W Wow! That sounds awesome. Are you sure _____
_____ _____ join you and your friends?
M Of course. It will be _____ _____
_____ _____ .

20 상황에 적절한 말 찾기

다음 상황 설명을 듣고, Jason이 은지에게 할 말로 가장 적절한 것을 고르시오.

Jason: _____

① I'll get the popcorn.
② Do you like action movies?
③ How did you like the movie?
④ Why don't we see a movie tomorrow?
⑤ How many times have you seen that movie?

M Jason is _____ _____ _____
_____ action movies. He watched the new movie that he had waited for with Eunji today. The thrilling action movie _____ _____ _____
_____ the edge of his seat throughout it. The main characters were great and the special effects were amazing. Jason loved the movie, _____ _____
_____ _____ Eunji liked it. In this situation, what would Jason most likely say to Eunji?

실전 모의고사 16

01 대화를 듣고, 여자가 구입할 쟁반을 고르시오.

① ② ③

④ ⑤

02 대화를 듣고, 남자가 전화한 목적으로 가장 적절한 것을 고르시오.

① 중고차 시세를 확인하려고
② 자동차 사고를 신고하려고
③ 자동차 수리를 예약하려고
④ 수리가 끝났는지 확인하려고
⑤ 주말 영업시간을 문의하려고

03 다음 그림의 상황에 가장 적절한 대화를 고르시오.

① ② ③ ④ ⑤

04 대화를 듣고, 여자가 저녁 식사로 먹게 될 음식을 고르시오.

① 피자 ② 카레 ③ 불고기
④ 스파게티 ⑤ 생선 초밥

05 다음을 듣고, 기장의 방송 내용 속에 언급되지 않은 것을 고르시오.

① 목적지 ② 비행시간
③ 도착 예정 시각 ④ 비행 속도
⑤ 날씨

06 대화를 듣고, 두 사람의 관계로 가장 적절한 것을 고르시오.

① 경찰관 – 시민 ② 은행원 – 고객
③ 버스 운전사 – 승객 ④ 여행사 직원 – 관광객
⑤ 분실물 센터 직원 – 방문자

07 다음을 듣고, 두 사람의 대화가 <u>어색한</u> 것을 고르시오.

① ② ③ ④ ⑤

08 대화를 듣고, 여자가 남자에게 부탁한 일로 가장 적절한 것을 고르시오.

① 잡지 구독하기 ② 휴가 계획 취소하기
③ 해변 상태 취재하기 ④ 경치 사진 찍어 오기
⑤ 휴가 일정 알려 주기

09 대화를 듣고, 여자의 마지막 말에 담긴 의도로 가장 적절한 것을 고르시오.

① 사과 ② 충고 ③ 불만
④ 거절 ⑤ 위로

10 대화를 듣고, 여자가 지불할 금액을 고르시오.

① $9 ② $10 ③ $12
④ $15 ⑤ $18

11 대화를 듣고, 대화 직후에 남자가 할 일로 가장 적절한 것을 고르시오.

① 대출 도서 반납하기
② 도서 구입 주문하기
③ 대출 예약 서식 작성하기
④ 재고 도서 목록 작성하기
⑤ 도서관 아르바이트 신청하기

12 다음을 듣고, 마추픽추(Machu Picchu)에 대해 언급되지 <u>않은</u> 것을 고르시오.

① 위치   ② 건설 시기   ③ 건설 목적

④ 발견 시기   ⑤ 발견자

13 다음 표를 보면서 대화를 듣고, 여자가 선택할 강좌를 고르시오.

	Class	Level	Day	Time
①	A	Basic	Mon., Wed., Fri.	2:00 p.m. ~ 3:00 p.m.
②	B	Basic	Tue., Thu., Sat.	8:00 a.m. ~ 9:00 a.m.
③	C	Basic	Tue., Thu., Sat.	2:00 p.m. ~ 3:00 p.m.
④	D	Intermediate	Mon., Wed., Fri.	8:00 a.m. ~ 9:00 a.m.
⑤	E	Advanced	Tue., Thu.	2:00 p.m. ~ 3:00 p.m.

14 다음을 듣고, 무엇에 관한 설명인지 고르시오.

① 옥수수   ② 대나무   ③ 야자수

④ 소나무   ⑤ 유칼립투스

15 대화를 듣고, 여자가 대화 직후에 할 일로 가장 적절한 것을 고르시오.

① 모닝콜하기   ② 객실 청소하기

③ 수건 전달하기   ④ 햄버거 배달하기

⑤ 프런트에 대신 요청하기

16 대화를 듣고, 두 사람이 만날 시각을 고르시오

① 1:00 p.m.   ② 1:30 p.m.   ③ 2:00 p.m.

④ 3:00 p.m.   ⑤ 4:00 p.m.

17 대화를 듣고, 남자의 마지막 말에 대한 여자의 응답으로 가장 적절한 것을 고르시오.

Woman: _____

① Who should he call?

② I will tell you his phone number.

③ I'm looking forward to your visit.

④ Sorry, but you have the wrong number.

⑤ I'll give him the message as soon as he's back.

18 대화를 듣고, 여자의 마지막 말에 대한 남자의 응답으로 가장 적절한 것을 고르시오.

Man: _____

① Be confident, please.

② No, I'll be a good pianist.

③ Right, you'll be successful.

④ Thanks, I hope you're right.

⑤ You should have started practicing earlier.

19 대화를 듣고, 남자의 마지막 말에 대한 여자의 응답으로 가장 적절한 것을 고르시오.

Woman: _____

① I'd like to go shopping there, too.

② Where is the new shopping mall?

③ How much did you spend in total?

④ You'd better not go shopping anymore.

⑤ The new T-shirt doesn't look good on me.

20 다음 상황 설명을 듣고, Bill이 Amy에게 할 말로 가장 적절한 것을 고르시오.

Bill: _____

① Bye, see you tomorrow.

② You can share mine if you want.

③ Don't worry, it will clear up soon.

④ Thank you for being my good friend.

⑤ Why didn't you bring your umbrella?

Dictation 16

◇ 다시 듣고, 빈칸에 들어갈 알맞은 단어를 써보세요.

정답 및 해설 p.107

01 그림 정보 파악

대화를 듣고, 여자가 구입할 쟁반을 고르시오.

① ② ③ HAPPY
④ ⑤

M Hello, ma'am. Can I help you?

W Hello. I'm looking for a tray.

M Round ones are popular these days. _____ _____ _____ _____ _____ this round one with the word "Happy" in the center?

W Hmm... *I prefer square ones to round ones.

M I see. Then how about this one with flowers in the center?

W Actually, this is not bad, but do you have _____ _____ _____ _____ a band of flowers around the edge?

M Oh, you _____ _____ _____ _____ something like this.

W This is perfect. _____ _____ _____.

★ 교육부 지정 의사소통 기능: **선호 표현하기**   능(김) 6 | 급 7

I prefer A to B. 나는 B보다 A를 더 좋아해.

• **I prefer** sports **to** singing. 나는 노래 부르는 것보다 스포츠를 더 좋아해.

• **I prefer** the white shoes **to** the black shoes. 나는 검은 신발보다 흰 신발을 더 좋아해.

---

02 목적 파악

대화를 듣고, 남자가 전화한 목적으로 가장 적절한 것을 고르시오.

① 중고차 시세를 확인하려고
② 자동차 사고를 신고하려고
③ 자동차 수리를 예약하려고
④ 수리가 끝났는지 확인하려고
⑤ 주말 영업시간을 문의하려고

[Telephone rings.]

W Johnny's Auto Repair Shop, what can I do for you?

M Hello, I'm Larry Jackson. I took my car there yesterday afternoon _____ _____ _____ _____. Is the repair complete?

W Let me check. *[Pause]* Oh, Mr. Jackson, it seems like your car is _____ _____ _____.

M I see. When should I come in?

W Your car _____ _____ _____ _____ this afternoon, around 5 p.m.

M Okay. How late are you open today?

W _____ _____ _____ 6 p.m.

M All right. I'll come by around 5:30.

---

03 그림 상황에 적절한 대화 찾기

다음 그림의 상황에 가장 적절한 대화를 고르시오.

① ② ③ ④ ⑤

① W _____ _____ _____

_____ the volume? I can't hear the TV.

M I'm sorry. I didn't know it _____ _____

_____.

② W Can I get you something to drink?

M I'd like a Coke, please.

③ W Would you like an aisle seat or a window seat?

M A window seat, please.

④ W Excuse me, can you tell me _____

_____ _____ the ATM?

M Don't worry, I'll help you.

⑤ W Do you mind if I _____ _____

_____ _____ ?

M Sorry, but I'm trying to concentrate.

---

04 특정 정보 파악

대화를 듣고, 여자가 저녁 식사로 먹게 될 음식을 고르시오.

① 피자   ② 카레   ③ 불고기
④ 스파게티   ⑤ 생선 초밥

W There is nothing to cook with in the kitchen. Do you want to eat out?

M Sure. Maybe we should go grocery shopping after dinner.

W Then let's go to one of the restaurants _____

_____ _____ _____.

M Okay. We could go to a Japanese or an Indian restaurant.

W Well, _____ _____ _____

_____ ?

M Let me think. How about Ted's Pizza? The pizza is really good there.

W Does _____ _____ _____

_____ other than pizza?

M There are spaghetti and steaks, too.

W _____ _____ _____ then.

다음을 듣고, 기장의 방송 내용 속에 언급되지 않은 것을 고르시오.

① 목적지   ② 비행시간
③ 도착 예정 시각   ④ 비행 속도
⑤ 날씨

M Good evening, ladies and gentlemen. This is your captain speaking. The crew would like to welcome you all aboard. _____ _____ _____ _____ Rome today will be 11 hours and 25 minutes. _____ _____ _____ _____ an altitude of 43,000 feet and our airspeed is 520 miles an hour. _____ _____ _____ _____ _____, so relax and enjoy the rest of the flight. Thank you.

06 관계 추론

대화를 듣고, 두 사람의 관계로 가장 적절한 것을 고르시오.

① 경찰관 – 시민
② 은행원 – 고객
③ 버스 운전사 – 승객
④ 여행사 직원 – 관광객
⑤ 분실물 센터 직원 – 방문자

M Good afternoon. How may I help you?
W Hello. I need to _____ _____ _____ _____.
M I see. Do you have an account with our bank?
W Yes. I lost my wallet and everything in it. So, I'd like to _____ _____ _____ _____ I had.
M I see. Then can you _____ _____ this form?
W All right. How long _____ _____ _____ to get a new card?
M If you choose to pick it up _____ _____ _____, it'll take 2 to 3 business days.

07 어색한 대화 찾기

다음을 듣고, 두 사람의 대화가 어색한 것을 고르시오.

①   ②   ③   ④   ⑤

① **M** How often do you practice the piano?
    W I usually practice 3 or 4 times a week.
② **M** Have you been to Paris before?
    W No, but I hope to _____ _____ _____ _____.
③ **M** What do you do for a living?
    W Well, I _____ _____ _____ _____.
④ **M** _____ _____ _____ _____?
    W Yes, there are only 10 minutes left until class.

⑤ M Why don't you join the music club?

W Sure. ＿＿＿＿＿＿ ＿＿＿＿＿＿ ＿＿＿＿＿＿ to learn to sing.

대화를 듣고, 여자가 남자에게 부탁한 일로 가장 적절한 것을 고르시오.

① 잡지 구독하기
② 휴가 계획 취소하기
③ 해변 상태 취재하기
④ 경치 사진 찍어 오기
⑤ 휴가 일정 알려 주기

W Tom, where are you going on vacation this summer?

M I'm going to a beach in the South Pacific.

W Really? Are you ＿＿＿＿＿＿ ＿＿＿＿＿＿ ＿＿＿＿＿＿?

M Not really. I just want to relax and enjoy the scenery.

W I see. Oh, can you do me a favor?

M What is it? I hope ＿＿＿＿＿＿ ＿＿＿＿＿＿ ＿＿＿＿＿＿ ＿＿＿＿＿＿.

W Can you ＿＿＿＿＿＿ ＿＿＿＿＿＿ ＿＿＿＿＿＿ the beautiful scenery there? I want to put them in my magazine.

M No problem. You know I am ＿＿＿＿＿＿ ＿＿＿＿＿＿ ＿＿＿＿＿＿ ＿＿＿＿＿＿.

대화를 듣고, 여자의 마지막 말에 담긴 의도로 가장 적절한 것을 고르시오.

① 사과　② 충고　③ 불만
④ 거절　⑤ 위로

W Jack! Look at your room.

M What about my room, Mom?

W It's a mess. Your dirty clothes are everywhere.

M I'll ＿＿＿＿＿＿ ＿＿＿＿＿＿ ＿＿＿＿＿＿ ＿＿＿＿＿＿ ＿＿＿＿＿＿ room in a minute.

W And all this trash?

M I'll put it in the can and clean the room.

W It's very important to ＿＿＿＿＿＿ ＿＿＿＿＿＿ ＿＿＿＿＿＿ ＿＿＿＿＿＿ and organized. It's also good for your health.

M But there is too much to clean.

W ＿＿＿＿＿＿ ＿＿＿＿＿＿ ＿＿＿＿＿＿ a habit of cleaning and organizing a little each day.

대화를 듣고, 여자가 지불할 금액을 고르시오.

① $9　② $10　③ $12
④ $15　⑤ $18

W ＿＿＿＿＿＿ ＿＿＿＿＿＿ ＿＿＿＿＿＿ the tickets for the tour bus?

M $6 for adults and $3 for children under 8.

W How often does the tour bus run on Sundays?

M It runs _____ _____ _____.
The next one leaves at 4 o'clock.

W How long does it _____ _____
_____ _____ the K-Tower?

M About an hour and a half. Would you like a ticket?

W Yes. I _____ _____ _____
2 adults and a child, please.

M All right.

11 할 일 파악

대화를 듣고, 대화 직후에 남자가 할 일로 가장 적절한 것을 고르시오.

① 대출 도서 반납하기
② 도서 구입 주문하기
③ 대출 예약 서식 작성하기
④ 재고 도서 목록 작성하기
⑤ 도서관 아르바이트 신청하기

W Hi, can I help you?

M Yes. Do you have the latest *World Geographic*?

W I'll check for you. *[Pause]* I'm afraid it _____
_____ _____ _____ next week.
Somebody else already borrowed it.

M Oh no! I really need it now.

W It's one of the most popular magazines in this library.

M Hmm... What _____ _____
_____ _____ _____ now?

W Fill out this form. We'll send you a text message as soon as
_____ _____ _____
_____.

M Okay.

12 언급하지 않은 내용 찾기

다음을 듣고, 마추픽추(Machu Picchu)에 대해 언급되지 않은 것을 고르시오.

① 위치   ② 건설 시기
③ 건설 목적   ④ 발견 시기
⑤ 발견자

W Machu Picchu is an Inca city in Peru. Many researchers
believe that the city _____ _____
_____ 1450 AD. It is about 2,430 meters above sea
level. For centuries, it was buried in the jungle. In 1911, it
_____ _____ _____ American
historian Hiram Bingham and became _____
_____ _____ _____. Machu
Picchu has been one of the most famous tourist attractions
in the world ever since its discovery.

다음 표를 보면서 대화를 듣고, 여자가 선택할 강좌를 고르시오.

	Class	Level	Day	Time
①	A	Basic	Mon., Wed., Fri.	2:00 p.m. ~ 3:00 p.m.
②	B	Basic	Tue., Thu., Sat.	8:00 a.m. ~ 9:00 a.m.
③	C	Basic	Tue., Thu., Sat.	2:00 p.m. ~ 3:00 p.m.
④	D	Intermediate	Mon., Wed., Fri.	8:00 a.m. ~ 9:00 a.m.
⑤	E	Advanced	Tue., Thu.	2:00 p.m. ~ 3:00 p.m.

🔊 **Listening Tip**

'n' 뒤에 오는 't'는 발음하지 않으므로 center는 /쎄널/처럼 들립니다. Internet, winter, disappointing도 마찬가지 예입니다.

W Hello, I'd like to take table tennis lessons here at the sports 🔊 center.

M Okay. What level are you going to take?

W Well, since I'm a beginner, I have to _____ _____ _____ _____.

M For basic, you have to come 3 times a week.

W Well, I can _____ _____ _____ _____ Mondays.

M Okay. _____ _____ _____ to come in the morning or afternoon?

W _____ _____ _____, please.

M All right.

다음을 듣고, 무엇에 관한 설명인지 고르시오.

① 옥수수 ② 대나무
③ 야자수 ④ 소나무
⑤ 유칼립투스

🔊 **Listening Tip**

often은 원어민에 따라 [t] 발음을 살려서 하기도 하고 생략하고 발음하기도 해요.

M This is a plant. This _____ _____ _____ 30 meters tall and be 30 centimeters in diameter. This is 🔊 often used to _____ _____ _____, furniture, tools, and even weapons. Young ones _____ _____ _____ _____ a food ingredient. Stems of this are hard and light. People in many Asian countries use them to cook food like rice and soup. Pandas love to _____ _____ _____ _____ 18 kilograms of it each day.

대화를 듣고, 여자가 대화 직후에 할 일로 가장 적절한 것을 고르시오.

① 모닝콜하기 ② 객실 청소하기
③ 수건 전달하기 ④ 햄버거 배달하기
⑤ 프런트에 대신 요청하기

[Telephone rings.]

W Room service. How can I help you?

M I'd like to order a hamburger, please.

W Of course, sir. It'll _____ _____ _____ 20 minutes. Is there anything else?

M I also would like a wake-up call at 5:30 tomorrow morning.

W I'm sorry. For wake-up calls, you have to call the front desk.

M I see. I also need some towels. Should I _____

_____ _____ _____ about that, too?

W Yes. But since it's your first time, I'll let the front desk clerk _____ _____ _____ _____ right away.

M Thank you very much.

---

16 숫자 정보 파악 (시각)

대화를 듣고, 두 사람이 만날 시각을 고르시오

① 1:00 p.m.　　② 1:30 p.m.
③ 2:00 p.m.　　④ 3:00 p.m.
⑤ 4:00 p.m.

[Telephone rings.]

W Hello.

M Hello. I'm calling about the 3-bedroom apartment you advertised.

W Of course. What time would you like to _____ _____ _____ _____ ?

M I'd like to be there at 1 o'clock tomorrow afternoon.

W I'm sorry, but I _____ _____ _____ at 1:30 tomorrow afternoon.

M How about 3 o'clock then?

W Sorry. There _____ _____ _____ _____ home around 3 o'clock. Is 4 o'clock okay?

M _____ _____ _____ _____ . See you then.

---

17 이어질 응답 찾기

대화를 듣고, 남자의 마지막 말에 대한 여자의 응답으로 가장 적절한 것을 고르시오.

Woman: _____ _____

① Who should he call?
② I will tell you his phone number.
③ I'm looking forward to your visit.
④ Sorry, but you have the wrong number.
⑤ I'll give him the message as soon as he's back.

[Telephone rings.]

W Hello. This is Anderson's Law Office. How can I help you?

M Hello. _____ _____ _____ _____ Mr. David Greene, please?

W I'm afraid he's not here at the moment.

M Can I leave him a message?

W Sure. May I _____ _____ _____ , please?

M Eric Koppel. Please tell him I am _____ _____ _____ in Berlin at 8 p.m. tomorrow.

W All right. Does he have your number?

M Yes, he does. He can _____ _____ _____ _____ .

대화를 듣고, 여자의 마지막 말에 대한 남자의 응답으로 가장 적절한 것을 고르시오.

Man: _____

① Be confident, please.
② No, I'll be a good pianist.
③ Right, you'll be successful.
④ Thanks, I hope you're right.
⑤ You should have started practicing earlier.

W How are your violin lessons going?
M My teacher says I'm getting better, but I'm not sure.
W How long have _____ _____
   _____ _____?
M For 6 months.
W Do you enjoy playing the violin?
M No, I find it boring and difficult. I'm not confident that I should _____ _____ _____
   _____.
W You _____ _____ _____
   _____. Keep practicing and you'll be able to enjoy playing the violin.

대화를 듣고, 남자의 마지막 말에 대한 여자의 응답으로 가장 적절한 것을 고르시오.

Woman: _____

① I'd like to go shopping there, too.
② Where is the new shopping mall?
③ How much did you spend in total?
④ You'd better not go shopping anymore.
⑤ The new T-shirt doesn't look good on me.

M How do I look in my new T-shirt?
W Wow, you look wonderful. _____ _____
   _____ your shirt?
M It was just $10.
W That's a very good price.
M I think so, too. It's still _____ _____ now.
   And I also got _____ _____ _____,
   too.
W Where did you get them?
M At _____ _____ _____
   _____ across the street.

다음 상황 설명을 듣고, Bill이 Amy에게 할 말로 가장 적절한 것을 고르시오.

Bill: _____

① Bye, see you tomorrow.
② You can share mine if you want.
③ Don't worry, it will clear up soon.
④ Thank you for being my good friend.
⑤ Why didn't you bring your umbrella?

W Amy comes to school without an umbrella. When she sees Bill carrying an umbrella, she asks him _____
   _____ _____. Bill says heavy rain is
   _____ _____ _____ _____.
   Amy gets worried because she has no one to bring her an umbrella. So Bill wants to tell her he can _____
   _____ with her since _____
   _____ _____. In this situation, what would Bill most likely say to Amy?

실전 모의고사 **17**

01 대화를 듣고, 두 사람이 구입할 욕실 매트를 고르시오.

①   ②   ③

④   ⑤

02 대화를 듣고, 여자가 남자에게 전화한 목적으로 가장 적절한 것을 고르시오.

① 방문 약속을 하려고
② 사고를 신고하려고
③ 방문 예약을 취소하려고
④ 친구에게 안부를 전하려고
⑤ 경찰서 위치를 물어보려고

03 다음 그림의 상황에 가장 적절한 대화를 고르시오.

① ② ③ ④ ⑤

04 대화를 듣고, 두 사람이 만나기로 한 요일을 고르시오.

① 수요일　② 목요일　③ 금요일
④ 토요일　⑤ 일요일

05 다음을 듣고, Rainbow 20에 관해 언급되지 <u>않은</u> 것을 고르시오.

① 출시일　② 크기　③ 기능
④ 색상　⑤ 가격

06 대화를 듣고, 여자의 심정으로 가장 적절한 것을 고르시오.

① bored　② jealous　③ regretful
④ excited　⑤ surprised

07 다음을 듣고, 두 사람의 대화가 <u>어색한</u> 것을 고르시오.

① ② ③ ④ ⑤

08 대화를 듣고, 여자가 남자에게 부탁한 일로 가장 적절한 것을 고르시오.

① 매점 확장하기
② 음료 가져다주기
③ 음료 캔 재활용하기
④ 새 자판기로 교체하기
⑤ 자판기에 대해 논의하기

09 대화를 듣고, 여자의 마지막 말에 담긴 의도로 가장 적절한 것을 고르시오.

① 충고　② 거절　③ 칭찬
④ 동의　⑤ 제안

10 대화를 듣고, 여자가 지불할 금액을 고르시오.

① $10　② $15　③ $30
④ $50　⑤ $60

11 대화를 듣고, 여자가 할 일로 가장 적절한 것을 고르시오.

① 점심 먹기　② 수영하러 가기
③ 체육 수업 듣기　④ 배드민턴 치기
⑤ 테니스 수업 신청하기

12 다음을 듣고, School Picnic Day에 관해 언급되지 않은 것을 고르시오.

① 장소　　② 놀이 활동　　③ 준비물
④ 출발 시간　　⑤ 옷차림

13 다음 표를 보면서 대화를 듣고, 여자가 탑승할 비행 편을 고르시오.

	Destination	Direct	Departure Time	Fare
①	Chicago	×	9:30 a.m.	$730
②	Chicago	○	10:00 a.m.	$830
③	Chicago	○	11:15 a.m.	$970
④	Chicago	○	3:15 p.m.	$1,250
⑤	Los Angeles	×	3:15 p.m.	$1,350

14 다음을 듣고, 무엇에 관한 설명인지 고르시오.

① 공항　　② 극장　　③ 도서관
④ 백화점　　⑤ 박물관

15 대화를 듣고, 여자가 주말에 할 일로 가장 적절한 것을 고르시오.

① 쇼핑하기　　② 산책하기
③ 집에서 쉬기　　④ 병원에 가기
⑤ 스케이트보드 타기

16 대화를 듣고, 영화가 끝나는 시각을 고르시오.

① 7:30 p.m.　② 8:00 p.m.　③ 9:00 p.m.
④ 10:00 p.m.　⑤ 11:00 p.m.

17 대화를 듣고, 남자의 마지막 말에 대한 여자의 응답으로 가장 적절한 것을 고르시오.

Woman: _____

① That's fine with me. See you then.
② Sorry, but I don't have any free time.
③ That sounds great. What time is good?
④ I have a good plan to sell our products.
⑤ I have another appointment tomorrow morning.

18 대화를 듣고, 여자의 마지막 말에 대한 남자의 응답으로 가장 적절한 것을 고르시오.

Man: _____

① They are $5 in all.
② I'll attend the meeting.
③ I will pay by credit card.
④ I'll stay here until 1 o'clock.
⑤ They'll be ready in 20 minutes.

19 대화를 듣고, 남자의 마지막 말에 대한 여자의 응답으로 가장 적절한 것을 고르시오.

Woman: _____

① Sorry, I don't know you.
② Nobody knows where it is.
③ That's the first place I checked.
④ Yes, I'll put it in the desk drawer.
⑤ Be sure to lock the desk drawer next time.

20 다음 상황 설명을 듣고, Sophia가 배달원에게 할 말로 가장 적절한 것을 고르시오.

Sophia: _____

① Great! Come in, please.
② How much is it all together?
③ Why didn't you come earlier?
④ I'm sorry, but I want a refund.
⑤ Please leave it in front of the door.

Dictation 17

◇ 다시 듣고, 빈칸에 들어갈 알맞은 단어를 써보세요.

정답 및 해설 p.114

01 그림 정보 파악

대화를 듣고, 두 사람이 구입할 욕실 매트를 고르시오.

① ② ③
④ ⑤

W   Let's go in here. I need a mat for our bathroom.
M   Okay. They have many kinds of mats on the shelf.
W   I like this flower design. It's soft and the price is reasonable.
M   That one is good. But I like ＿＿＿＿＿＿ ＿＿＿＿＿＿ ＿＿＿＿＿＿ ＿＿＿＿＿＿.
W   But it's more expensive. Why do you prefer it?
M   It's made of 100% cotton and it's thicker. So I think ＿＿＿＿＿＿ ＿＿＿＿＿＿ ＿＿＿＿＿＿.
W   I see what you mean. Should we get the striped one then?
M   Yes. I think ＿＿＿＿＿＿ ＿＿＿＿＿＿ ＿＿＿＿＿＿ for a long time.
W   All right. ＿＿＿＿＿＿ ＿＿＿＿＿＿ ＿＿＿＿＿＿ ＿＿＿＿＿＿ the cash register.

02 목적 파악

대화를 듣고, 여자가 남자에게 전화한 목적으로 가장 적절한 것을 고르시오.

① 방문 약속을 하려고
② 사고를 신고하려고
③ 방문 예약을 취소하려고
④ 친구에게 안부를 전하려고
⑤ 경찰서 위치를 물어보려고

[Telephone rings.]
M   Nine-one-one. What's your emergency?
W   I want to ＿＿＿＿＿＿ ＿＿＿＿＿＿ ＿＿＿＿＿＿.
M   Can you describe the accident?
W   A truck has just ＿＿＿＿＿＿ ＿＿＿＿＿＿ ＿＿＿＿＿＿ ＿＿＿＿＿＿!
M   Are you hurt?
W   No, but ＿＿＿＿＿＿ ＿＿＿＿＿＿ ＿＿＿＿＿＿ ＿＿＿＿＿＿.
M   Where did it happen?
W   At the corner of Pearl Street and 10th Street.
M   What's your name?
W   Mary Adams.
M   All right. I'll ＿＿＿＿＿＿ ＿＿＿＿＿＿ ＿＿＿＿＿＿ right away.

03 그림 상황에 적절한 대화 찾기

다음 그림의 상황에 가장 적절한 대화를 고르시오.

① ② ③ ④ ⑤

🔊 **Listening Tip**

make it에서 'e'는 발음 과정에서 생략되고 [k]와 [it]이
연음되어 /메이킽/으로 한 단어처럼 발음돼요.

① W _____ _____ _____
_____ ?

  M No, it isn't. Go ahead.

② W What's the matter with it?

  M It's the engine. It's making a loud noise.

③ W Could you _____ _____ _____
_____ , please?

  M Yes, of course.

④ W This Christmas tree is so beautiful.

  M I know. _____ _____ _____
🔊 make it very beautiful.

⑤ W Can you teach me _____ _____
_____ _____ _____ ?

  M Sure. Let me take a look first.

04 특정 정보 파악

대화를 듣고, 두 사람이 만나기로 한 요일을 고르시오.

① 수요일   ② 목요일   ③ 금요일
④ 토요일   ⑤ 일요일

[Cell phone rings.]

W Hello.

M Hello, Susan. This is Eric.

W Hi, Eric. What's up?

M _____ _____ _____ play tennis
this Friday. Do you want to join me?

W Sorry, I can't. I'm going to volunteer at a nursing home.
_____ _____ _____
_____ ?

M Saturday? I have other plans that day. Is Sunday okay with
you?

W _____ _____ _____ .

M Great! I'll _____ _____ _____
_____ tonight after I reserve a tennis court.

05 언급하지 않은 내용 찾기

다음을 듣고, Rainbow 20에 관해 언급되지 않은 것을 고르시오.

① 출시일   ② 크기   ③ 기능
④ 색상   ⑤ 가격

W Let me introduce our new smartphone, the Rainbow 20. It
_____ _____ _____ March 2020.
There are 3 models based on size: basic, plus, and ultra. It
has an amazing camera. _____ _____
_____ _____ 100 times larger. Rainbow 20

실전 모의고사 17   191

has 5 colors: black, white, blue, red, and gray. _____

_____ _____ 30% off today only. Buy one.

_____ _____ _____

_____ !

06 심정 추론

대화를 듣고, 여자의 심정으로 가장 적절한 것을 고르시오.

① bored　　② jealous　　③ regretful
④ excited　　⑤ surprised

M   I heard you got a new smartphone. Can I see it?

W   Sure. Here it is.

M   Aren't you excited to _____ _____

_____ _____ ?

W   Not really. _____ _____ _____

_____ with it.

M   This one doesn't look so bad. Why are you not satisfied with it?

W   Well, a better version of this phone is _____

_____ _____ _____.

It comes with much more space and a better camera.

M   When did you get yours?

W   I got this a week ago. I _____ _____

_____ next week.

07 어색한 대화 찾기

다음을 듣고, 두 사람의 대화가 <u>어색한</u> 것을 고르시오.

①　　②　　③　　④　　⑤

① M   My sister is very sick.

　 W   I'm sorry to hear that.

② M   Please _____ _____ _____

_____ .

　 W   Thanks. Your house is very lovely.

③ M   Would you like something to _____

_____ _____ _____ ?

　 W   Yes, please. I'll have a glass of water.

④ M   _____ _____ _____

_____ ?

　 W   No. Please stand behind the yellow line.

⑤ M   That was close!

　 W   You'd better be careful when _____

_____ _____ _____ .

대화를 듣고, 여자가 남자에게 부탁한 일로 가장 적절한 것을 고르시오.

① 매점 확장하기
② 음료 가져다주기
③ 음료 캔 재활용하기
④ 새 자판기로 교체하기
⑤ 자판기에 대해 논의하기

🔊 **Listening Tip**

soft drinks처럼 [t] 소리가 끝에 오고 다음 단어가 자음으로 시작되면, 끝소리는 다음 단어의 첫 소리에 흡수되어 거의 들리지 않아요. 따라서 /소프드링크쓰/와 같이 들리게 돼요.

W Excuse me, Mr. Pine. Do you have a moment?

M Sure, Lisa. Come on in.

W There is something I'd like to _____ _____

_____ _____ .

M Okay. What is it?

W There are many vending machines in our office building. However, they only have coffee and 🔊 soft drinks.

M I see. Would you like to _____ _____

_____ ?

W I think those vending machines should have more healthy drinks like juice. _____ _____

_____ this at the next staff meeting?

M Of course. _____ _____ _____

at the next meeting.

대화를 듣고, 여자의 마지막 말에 담긴 의도로 가장 적절한 것을 고르시오.

① 충고   ② 거절   ③ 칭찬
④ 동의   ⑤ 제안

W Hi, David. It's been a long time since we last met.

M I know. Almost 10 years _____ _____

_____ we graduated from middle school.

W Time really flies, right?

M It sure does.

W You look slimmer now than in middle school. Do you work out often?

M Yes. I lost a lot of weight. And I _____

_____ _____ since then.

W Wow, that's great. And you don't wear glasses any longer.

M I'm wearing contact lenses instead. You look great, too. You _____ _____ _____

_____ .

W Thanks. _____ _____ _____

_____ the others. I can't wait to see them all.

대화를 듣고, 여자가 지불할 금액을 고르시오.

① $10   ② $15   ③ $30
④ $50   ⑤ $60

W Tomorrow is my sister's birthday. I want to buy a present for her.

M _____ _____ _____

_____ ? She likes music.

W Right. Maybe I'll get her the second album of John Mendes. He is her favorite singer.

M Isn't it expensive? _____ _____ _____ _____ $30.

W It was, but it's on sale now. I can get it _____ _____ _____.

M Oh, that's cool!

W I know. My sister will be so happy when she sees the album.

---

11 할 일 파악

대화를 듣고, 여자가 할 일로 가장 적절한 것을 고르시오.

① 점심 먹기
② 수영하러 가기
③ 체육 수업 듣기
④ 배드민턴 치기
⑤ 테니스 수업 신청하기

M Where are you going?

W I'm going to the gym _____ _____ _____ _____ a class.

M What class are you planning to take next month?

W Well, I'm deciding between badminton and tennis.

M Why don't we take a swimming class together?

W I took a swimming class last month. It was interesting, but I don't want _____ _____ _____ _____.

M How about signing up for _____ _____ _____? I took it last month, and it was fun.

W All right. I'll go and sign up for it.

---

12 언급하지 않은 내용 찾기

다음을 듣고, School Picnic Day에 관해 언급되지 않은 것을 고르시오.

① 장소   ② 놀이 활동
③ 준비물   ④ 출발 시간
⑤ 옷차림

M Good morning, everyone. Don't forget that tomorrow is _____ _____ _____ _____ Olympic Park. Please bring your own lunch and $3 _____ _____ _____ _____. Please come to school by 9:20. The buses _____ _____ _____ 9:30. Don't be late! You don't need to wear school uniforms. You can come _____ _____ _____. Oh, don't forget to bring some drinking water. See you tomorrow!

---

13 도표 정보 파악

다음 표를 보면서 대화를 듣고, 여자가 탑승할 비행 편을 고르시오.

	Destination	Direct	Departure Time	Fare
①	Chicago	×	9:30 a.m.	$730
②	Chicago	○	10:00 a.m.	$830
③	Chicago	○	11:15 a.m.	$970
④	Chicago	○	3:15 p.m.	$1,250
⑤	Los Angeles	×	3:15 p.m.	$1,350

M How may I help you?

W I'd like to get a ticket to Chicago from Los Angeles on July 4th.

M Of course. Would you _____ _____ _____ _____ ?

W Yes, please. I don't want a stopover. It will _____ _____ _____ _____ .

M Okay. Would you like to leave in the morning or afternoon?

W _____ _____ _____ is fine with me.

M It seems like there are 2 flights with 2 different prices.

W I'll go _____ _____ _____ _____ , please.

14 화제 추론

다음을 듣고, 무엇에 관한 설명인지 고르시오.

① 공항 ② 극장 ③ 도서관
④ 백화점 ⑤ 박물관

W This is a building. In the building, there are rooms with many chairs for people to sit. _____ _____ _____ this building to watch something _____ _____ _____ _____ . During that time, everyone _____ _____ _____ _____ their cell phones, be quiet and _____ _____ _____ disturb others.

15 할 일 파악

대화를 듣고, 여자가 주말에 할 일로 가장 적절한 것을 고르시오.

① 쇼핑하기 ② 산책하기
③ 집에서 쉬기 ④ 병원에 가기
⑤ 스케이트보드 타기

M What's the matter with you?

W I feel so blue. I go to work early in the morning and I _____ _____ _____ at night every day.

M I have an idea to make you feel better.

W Oh, really? What's that?

M Let's go skateboarding this weekend.

W You know how much I _____ _____ _____ .

M When you feel bad, doing something different might _____ _____ _____ .

W I don't know how to skateboard. I could hurt myself.

M You _____ _____ _____ if you wear protective gear. What is important is that you have some fun on the weekend.

W Okay. Just this once.

---

16 숫자 정보 파악 (시각)

대화를 듣고, 영화가 끝나는 시각을 고르시오.

① 7:30 p.m.　　② 8:00 p.m.
③ 9:00 p.m.　　④ 10:00 p.m.
⑤ 11:00 p.m.

W Dad, I'm going out tonight.

M With whom? Are you going on a date?

W I am. *Don't worry. He's a nice person.

M What are you going to do tonight? Are you _____ _____ _____ _____?

W Yes. But before that, we're going to have dinner at an Italian restaurant.

M Okay. Make sure you come home by 8:00.

W 8:00? The movie _____ _____ _____ 7:30.

M How long does the movie run?

W For 2 and a half hours.

M Okay. _____ _____ _____ 11:00.

W I will. Thanks, Dad.

---

* 교육부 지정 의사소통 기능: **안심시키기**　　　　　　Y(송) 2 | 비 6

Don't worry. 걱정하지 마. / **Don't worry about ~.** ~에 대해 걱정하지 마.

• **Don't worry.** You'll make many friends at the new school.
  걱정하지 마. 너는 새 학교에서 많은 친구를 사귈 거야.
• **Don't worry about** making mistakes. 실수하는 것에 대해 걱정하지 마.

---

17 이어질 응답 찾기

대화를 듣고, 남자의 마지막 말에 대한 여자의 응답으로 가장 적절한 것을 고르시오.

Woman: _____

① That's fine with me. See you then.
② Sorry, but I don't have any free time.
③ That sounds great. What time is good?
④ I have a good plan to sell our products.
⑤ I have another appointment tomorrow morning.

M Carol, we need to review our sales plan.

W Okay. How long do we need to talk?

M Maybe half an hour.

W Let me check my schedule. Is Thursday okay?

M Sure. Do _____ _____ _____ _____ in the morning or in the afternoon?

W In the afternoon. I'm _____ _____ _____ in the morning.

M _____ _____ _____ _____ 2:00 p.m.?

W I already have another meeting then.

M Then, will 4:00 _____ _____?

대화를 듣고, 여자의 마지막 말에 대한 남자의 응답으로 가장 적절한 것을 고르시오.

Man: _____

① They are $5 in all.
② I'll attend the meeting.
③ I will pay by credit card.
④ I'll stay here until 1 o'clock.
⑤ They'll be ready in 20 minutes.

W Excuse me, I'd like some help, please.
M What can I do for you?
W I'd like to _____ _____ _____.
M No problem. _____ _____ _____ do you want?
W I'd like 5 copies of these documents.
M How many pages are there?
W 10. How much _____ _____ _____?
M It is 10 cents per page.
W _____ _____ _____ _____ _____? I have a class at 1 o'clock.

대화를 듣고, 남자의 마지막 말에 대한 여자의 응답으로 가장 적절한 것을 고르시오.

Woman: _____

① Sorry, I don't know you.
② Nobody knows where it is.
③ That's the first place I checked.
④ Yes, I'll put it in the desk drawer.
⑤ Be sure to lock the desk drawer next time.

W Do you know _____ _____ _____?
M Your passport? Where are you going?
W I have to go to India next week on business, and I can't find my passport.
M Next week? This is so sudden.
W I know. I only found out about the business trip this morning.
M Then, when are _____ _____ _____?
W On Tuesday. Anyway, do you remember where I put it?
M _____ _____ _____ _____ the desk drawer?

다음 상황 설명을 듣고, Sophia가 배달원에게 할 말로 가장 적절한 것을 고르시오.

Sophia: _____

① Great! Come in, please.
② How much is it all together?
③ Why didn't you come earlier?
④ I'm sorry, but I want a refund.
⑤ Please leave it in front of the door.

M Sophia is _____ _____ _____ her family has gone out. Suddenly, someone _____ _____ _____ at Sophia's home. Sophia asks who he is. He's _____ _____ _____ _____ an online marketplace and asking her to open the door. Sophia feels uneasy _____ _____ _____ _____, so she decides to tell him to leave the package by the door. In this situation, what would Sophia most likely say to the delivery man?

정답 및 해설 p.121

실전 모의고사 18

01 대화를 듣고, 여자가 주문한 소파를 고르시오.

① 　② 　③

④ 　⑤

02 대화를 듣고, 여자가 남자에게 전화한 목적으로 가장 적절한 것을 고르시오.

① 예약을 취소하려고
② 테니스 라켓을 팔려고
③ 테니스 라켓을 빌리려고
④ 테니스 코트를 예약하려고
⑤ 경기 관람표를 구입하려고

03 다음 그림의 상황에 가장 적절한 대화를 고르시오.

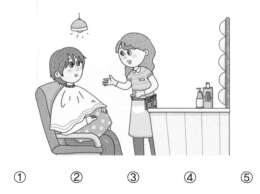

①　　②　　③　　④　　⑤

04 대화를 듣고, 두 사람이 만나기로 한 요일을 고르시오.

① 월요일　　② 화요일　　③ 수요일
④ 목요일　　⑤ 금요일

05 다음을 듣고, Sky World에 관해 언급되지 <u>않은</u> 것을 고르시오.

① 개장일　　② 위치　　③ 부대 시설
④ 입장료　　⑤ 영업시간

06 대화를 듣고, 두 사람의 관계로 가장 적절한 것을 고르시오.

① 집주인 – 집 수리업자
② 아파트 경비원 – 주민
③ 건축 설계사 – 의뢰인
④ 부동산 중개인 – 고객
⑤ 택배 기사 – 물품 구매자

07 다음을 듣고, 두 사람의 대화가 <u>어색한</u> 것을 고르시오.

①　　②　　③　　④　　⑤

08 대화를 듣고, 남자가 여자에게 부탁한 일로 가장 적절한 것을 고르시오.

① 메시지 전해 주기
② 소포 돌려보내기
③ 요금 대신 지불하기
④ 실수에 대해 사과하기
⑤ Smith 씨에게 소포 전달하기

09 대화를 듣고, 여자의 마지막 말에 담긴 의도로 가장 적절한 것을 고르시오.

① 동의　　② 요청　　③ 거절
④ 제안　　⑤ 위로

10 대화를 듣고, 여자가 지불할 금액을 고르시오.

① $10　　② $12　　③ $14
④ $16　　⑤ $18

11 대화를 듣고, 남자가 할 일로 가장 적절한 것을 고르시오.

① 신발 신어보기　　② 창고 정리하기
③ 신발장 구입하기　　④ 다른 신발 보여주기
⑤ 창고에서 신발 찾기

12 다음을 듣고, Summer Sale에 관해 언급되지 않은 것을 고르시오.

① 행사 기간　　② 할인 품목　　③ 제외 품목
④ 할인율　　　⑤ 사은품

13 다음 표를 보면서 대화를 듣고, 두 사람이 관람할 공연을 고르시오.

	Location	Show	Price	Time
①	Blue Square	Dolphin Show	$10	11:30
②	Blue Square	Mermaid Show	$15	12:30
③	Blue Square	Fish in Wonderland	$12	13:00
④	Rainbow Rounge	Fish in Wonderland	$15	16:30
⑤	Blue Square	Dolphin Show	$10	17:30

14 다음을 듣고, 무엇에 관한 설명인지 고르시오.

① 거북　　　② 앵무새　　　③ 햄스터
④ 고양이　　⑤ 고슴도치

15 대화를 듣고, 여자가 할 일로 가장 적절한 것을 고르시오.

① 수영복 사기　　　　② 건강 검진 받기
③ 강사 자격증 따기　　④ 수영하러 가기
⑤ 에어로빅 강습 신청하기

16 대화를 듣고, 여자가 일을 시작하는 시각을 고르시오.

① 10 a.m.　　② 12 p.m.　　③ 3 p.m.
④ 7 p.m.　　⑤ 11 p.m.

17 대화를 듣고, 남자의 마지막 말에 대한 여자의 응답으로 가장 적절한 것을 고르시오.

Woman: _____

① When is a convenient time?
② Sorry. I'm busy this Saturday.
③ You should come back next Friday.
④ Please stop by my house at 7 o'clock.
⑤ Can you pick it up in front of my house?

18 대화를 듣고, 여자의 마지막 말에 대한 남자의 응답으로 가장 적절한 것을 고르시오.

Man: _____

① You have to check out by 11 a.m.
② I'm sorry. I'll give you the new bill.
③ Sorry, but we can't extend your stay.
④ I'm afraid I can't find your reservation.
⑤ According to this, you made four calls.

19 대화를 듣고, 남자의 마지막 말에 대한 여자의 응답으로 가장 적절한 것을 고르시오.

Woman: _____

① I'm sorry to hear that.
② I said she just came in.
③ She is on the other line.
④ She wants to speak to you.
⑤ Why didn't you talk about it?

20 다음 상황 설명을 듣고, Tiffany가 John에게 할 말로 가장 적절한 것을 고르시오.

Tiffany: _____

① I'd like to go, but I can't.
② What's wrong with your sister?
③ Can we change the time to 7:20?
④ Buy the tickets online at this time.
⑤ How about watching a movie this evening?

01 그림 정보 파악

대화를 듣고, 여자가 주문한 소파를 고르시오.

① ② ③

④ ⑤

M Where do you want to put this sofa?

W In the living room, please. Next to the window would be perfect.

M No problem.

W Wait! This is not _____ _____ _____ _____. It's not even the same color. I ordered a black one.

M Are you sure?

W Yes. I ordered a sofa _____ _____ _____. This one has _____, _____ _____. This is not the right sofa.

M I'm sorry. It seems like there has been a mistake.

W Please _____ _____ _____ _____ and bring me the one I ordered.

02 목적 파악

대화를 듣고, 여자가 남자에게 전화한 목적으로 가장 적절한 것을 고르시오.

① 예약을 취소하려고
② 테니스 라켓을 팔려고
③ 테니스 라켓을 빌리려고
④ 테니스 코트를 예약하려고
⑤ 경기 관람표를 구입하려고

[Cell phone rings.]

M Hello.

W Hello, is this Brian Jones?

M Yes, this is he. Who's calling?

W I'm Jenny Davis. You left a message about _____ _____ _____ I put up for sale.

M That's right. Is it in good shape?

W It's _____ _____ _____ _____. I only used it once.

M How much do you want for it?

W It's $70.

M $70? It's a little more expensive than I thought.

W Well, how about $60?

M Okay. _____ _____ _____.

03 그림 상황에 적절한 대화 찾기

다음 그림의 상황에 가장 적절한 대화를 고르시오.

① ② ③ ④ ⑤

🔊 **Listening** Tip

fitting에서 'tt'는 양쪽의 모음, 즉 'i'와 'i'의 영향으로 [t]보다 부드러운 발음인 [r]로 발음돼요.

① W How would you like your hair cut?
   M I want to ＿＿＿＿＿＿ ＿＿＿＿＿＿ ＿＿＿＿＿＿.
② W *Do you know how to use this machine?
   M Sorry. You have to ask somebody else.
③ W I ＿＿＿＿＿＿ ＿＿＿＿＿＿ ＿＿＿＿＿＿ hairstyle.
   M Thank you. I'm glad you like it.
④ W Where is the 🔊 fitting room?
   M It's over there.
⑤ W Can I ＿＿＿＿＿＿ ＿＿＿＿＿＿ ＿＿＿＿＿＿
     ＿＿＿＿＿＿?
   M Sure. Would you ＿＿＿＿＿＿ ＿＿＿＿＿＿
     ＿＿＿＿＿＿ ＿＿＿＿＿＿ and sit here?

✻ **교육부 지정 의사소통 기능: 방법 묻기**   동(윤) 기 동(이) 2 금 2

Do you know how to ~? 너는 ~하는 방법을 아니?
• **Do you know how to** solve the problem? 너는 그 문제를 푸는 방법을 아니?
• **Do you know how to** use chopsticks? 너는 젓가락을 쓰는 방법을 아니?

---

04 특정 정보 파악

대화를 듣고, 두 사람이 만나기로 한 요일을 고르시오.

① 월요일　② 화요일　③ 수요일
④ 목요일　⑤ 금요일

M I heard that you're going back to Korea soon. Would you like to go out for dinner before you go?
W That's a great idea, ＿＿＿＿＿＿ ＿＿＿＿＿＿ ＿＿＿＿＿＿ Monday. I have to study for the final exam.
M Me, too, but I am free on Tuesday. How about going out that night?
W I am afraid I can't. I'm going out for dinner with Nancy. How about Wednesday night?
M I have a meeting for the band club. Are you busy on ＿＿＿＿＿＿ ＿＿＿＿＿＿?
W No. I'm free.
M ＿＿＿＿＿＿ ＿＿＿＿＿＿ ＿＿＿＿＿＿. I'll take you to the best restaurant in town.
W Okay.

---

05 언급하지 않은 내용 찾기

다음을 듣고, Sky World에 관해 언급되지 않은 것을 고르시오.

① 개장일　② 위치　③ 부대 시설
④ 입장료　⑤ 영업시간

M Do you want to experience something exciting? Come to Sky World. ＿＿＿＿＿＿ ＿＿＿＿＿＿ ＿＿＿＿＿＿ May 1st. It's located in Blue City, which has a beautiful lake. You'll find 2 ＿＿＿＿＿＿ ＿＿＿＿＿＿ and a variety of shops here. You can have fun, and _____

_____ _____, too. It's open every day from

9 a.m to 10 p.m. Experience a lot of fun and excitement in

this place _____ _____ _____

_____ .

06 관계 추론

대화를 듣고, 두 사람의 관계로 가장 적절한 것을
고르시오.

① 집주인 – 집 수리업자
② 아파트 경비원–주민
③ 건축 설계사 – 의뢰인
④ 부동산 중개인 – 고객
⑤ 택배 기사–물품 구매자

[Telephone rings.]

W Hello.

M Hi. This is Jack. I'm calling about the apartment

_____ _____ _____

_____ .

W Hi, Jack. Did you find any good places?

M Yes, I think I _____ _____ _____

_____ the perfect apartment.

W Really? Tell me about it.

M It's on Sunshine Street. And it's on the third floor.

W Is it new?

M No. It's not very new, but the floors and walls have been

changed recently.

W Does _____ _____ _____ ?

M Yes, it does. It is very clean. It also has a _____

_____ _____ _____ the park.

07 어색한 대화 찾기

다음을 듣고, 두 사람의 대화가 <u>어색한</u> 것을 고르
시오.

①   ②   ③   ④   ⑤

① M Go ahead. _____ _____ _____

this soup.

W No, thanks. I've had more than enough.

② M What time _____ _____ _____ ?

W How about 10 o'clock?

③ M Do you mind if I sit here?

W No, I _____ _____ at all.

④ M I'm looking for White Hospital.

W It's two blocks from here.

⑤ M I'm sure that our team will win.

W _____ _____ _____

_____ . It can't be.

대화를 듣고, 남자가 여자에게 부탁한 일로 가장
적절한 것을 고르시오.

① 메시지 전해 주기
② 소포 돌려보내기
③ 요금 대신 지불하기
④ 실수에 대해 사과하기
⑤ Smith 씨에게 소포 전달하기

[Telephone rings.]

W Hello.

M Hello. I'm Tom Collins. Is Mr. Smith in?

W I'm sorry. He just went out.

M When will he be back?

W He _____ _____ _____
_____. Would you like to leave a message?

M No, but would you _____ _____
_____ _____?

W What is it?

M I sent a package to Mr. Smith but there's been a mistake.
I put another client's document in it. When the package
arrives, would you _____ _____
_____ _____ _____?

W Okay. But will you pay the return fee?

M Of course. Thank you.

대화를 듣고, 여자의 마지막 말에 담긴 의도로 가
장 적절한 것을 고르시오.

① 동의   ② 요청   ③ 거절
④ 제안   ⑤ 위로

M Hi, Sally.

W Oh, it's Harry, right?

M Yeah. We met at Daniel's birthday party last Friday night.

W Oh, I remember. You sang for Daniel that day. By the way,
what brings you here?

M I'm going to _____ _____ _____
_____ a restaurant nearby.

W I see. Have a good time.

M Thanks. Oh, wait. Do you have any plans this Saturday?
There's a great exhibition downtown at a gallery.

W Sorry. I have _____ _____ at an animal
shelter that day.

M How about this Sunday? We _____ _____
_____ and then see the exhibition.

W _____ _____. I'm not interested in art.

10 숫자 정보 파악 (금액)

대화를 듣고, 여자가 지불할 금액을 고르시오.

① $10 ② $12 ③ $14
④ $16 ⑤ $18

M May I help you?
W Yes, please. I want some oranges.
M Here they are. They're very fresh and sweet.
W How much are they?
M One is $2. Buy 6, and you'll get 1 _____ _____.
W Do you mean I get 7 oranges _____ _____ _____ _____ 6 oranges?
M _____ _____.
W Then I'll have 7 oranges, please.
M Of course. Did you _____ _____ _____ _____ ?
W No. Please put them in a plastic bag. Here is the money.
M Thank you.

11 할 일 파악

대화를 듣고, 남자가 할 일로 가장 적절한 것을 고르시오.

① 신발 신어보기
② 창고 정리하기
③ 신발장 구입하기
④ 다른 신발 보여주기
⑤ 창고에서 신발 찾기

M May I help you?
W Yes. Do you _____ _____ _____ _____ a size 6?
M I'm not sure. If you can't find them on the rack, they may be _____ _____ _____.
W I really like these shoes. I'm sorry, but could you please look them up?
M Sure. _____ _____ _____ _____ in the stockroom.
W Thanks. I'd like to _____ _____ _____ _____ if you have them.
M Okay. I'll be right back.

12 언급하지 않은 내용 찾기

다음을 듣고, Summer Sale에 관해 언급되지 않은 것을 고르시오.

① 행사 기간 ② 할인 품목 ③ 제외 품목
④ 할인율 ⑤ 사은품

W May I have your attention, please? Starting May 31st, we are going to _____ _____ our spring items. This sale _____ _____ _____ June 10th. Most clothing stores will reduce _____ _____ _____ _____ _____, from socks to jackets, by 20 to 50%. Customers who spend over $100 will _____ _____ _____ _____. If you want to know more about the sale, visit the customer service center.

다음 표를 보면서 대화를 듣고, 두 사람이 관람할 공연을 고르시오.

	Location	Show	Price	Time
①	Blue Square	Dolphin Show	$10	11:30
②	Blue Square	Mermaid Show	$15	12:30
③	Blue Square	Fish in Wonderland	$12	13:00
④	Rainbow Rounge	Fish in Wonderland	$15	16:30
⑤	Blue Square	Dolphin Show	$10	17:30

M Wow! This aquarium is very large. I've never been to such a large aquarium before.

W Me neither. There are a lot of things to see.

M Oh, look! There is the list for the shows here at Blue Square.

W How about watching the "Mermaid Show"? It's the most popular show here.

M Can we _____ _____?
I want to see sea animals.

W Then, what are our options?

M There are 2 shows to choose from. They are "Dolphin Show" and "Fish in Wonderland."

W I've always wanted to see the "Dolphin Show." I heard it's fantastic. In addition, it's _____ _____ _____ _____ "Fish in Wonderland."

M Let me see. It's 2:30. So let's _____ _____ _____ _____.

다음을 듣고, 무엇에 관한 설명인지 고르시오.

① 거북   ② 앵무새   ③ 햄스터
④ 고양이   ⑤ 고슴도치

M They are wonderful pets because they are lovely and cute. They are also _____ _____ _____. They don't like eating much, so they are not expensive to have around. People who _____ _____ prefer them. Some people are _____ _____ _____ _____, so they can't have them. Interestingly, they think their owners are _____ _____. Having them can make your home a happy place.

대화를 듣고, 여자가 할 일로 가장 적절한 것을 고르시오.

① 수영복 사기
② 건강 검진 받기
③ 강사 자격증 따기
④ 수영하러 가기
⑤ 에어로빅 강습 신청하기

W Would you like to exercise with me?

M Good idea. My new year's resolution is _____ _____ _____ _____.

W Get in shape? You're already in good shape.

M Yes, but I'm going to enter a Taekwondo competition next fall. I have to lose more weight.

W I want to be fit, too. I need your advice. *Can you recommend _____ _____ _____ _____?

M In my opinion, an aerobic program would be good for you.

W Then _____ _____ _____ _____ it. I am determined to look good in my swimming suit this summer.

✽ 교육부 지정 의사소통 기능: **추천 요청하기**   천(이) 5

Can[Could] you recommend ~? ~을 추천해 주시겠어요?

• **Can you recommend** some good books to me? 나에게 좋은 책을 추천해 줄래?
• **Could you recommend** a good place to visit? 방문하기 좋은 곳을 추천해 주시겠어요?

16 숫자 정보 파악 (시각)

대화를 듣고, 여자가 일을 시작하는 시각을 고르시오.

① 10 a.m.   ② 12 p.m.   ③ 3 p.m.
④ 7 p.m.   ⑤ 11 p.m.

M How do you spend your day?

W Well, I get up around 10 on weekdays. Then I read the newspaper and have lunch at about noon.

M Really? What time do you go to work?

W I _____ _____ _____ 3 p.m.

M You start working so late. _____ _____ _____ _____ exactly?

W I _____ _____ _____ on an evening news show.

M I'm sorry, I didn't know that. When do _____ _____ _____?

W _____ _____ _____ 11 p.m.

17 이어질 응답 찾기

대화를 듣고, 남자의 마지막 말에 대한 여자의 응답으로 가장 적절한 것을 고르시오.

Woman: _____

① When is a convenient time?
② Sorry. I'm busy this Saturday.
③ You should come back next Friday.
④ Please stop by my house at 7 o'clock.
⑤ Can you pick it up in front of my house?

M How may I help you?

W Hi, _____ _____ _____ _____ _____ on it. Can you get the stain out?

M Let me see. [Pause] Hmm... It is a tough one, and it _____ _____ _____. Is that okay with you?

W Of course. It's my favorite jacket, so it doesn't matter how much it costs.

M Okay. It'll _____ _____ _____ though.

W No problem.

M Please write down your name and your phone number here.

W Sure. [Pause] _____ _____ _____ _____ _____?

18 이어질 응답 찾기

대화를 듣고, 여자의 마지막 말에 대한 남자의 응답으로 가장 적절한 것을 고르시오.

Man: _____

① You have to check out by 11 a.m.
② I'm sorry. I'll give you the new bill.
③ Sorry, but we can't extend your stay.
④ I'm afraid I can't find your reservation.
⑤ According to this, you made four calls.

W Good morning. I'd like to check out. My room number is 703.

M _____ _____ _____. Oh, I got it. Are you Natalie Brown?

W Yes.

M Here's your room bill.

W Hmm, this is strange. The amount is _____ _____ _____ _____.

M I believe you had room service yesterday.

W I ordered breakfast yesterday morning, but _____ _____ _____ a few minutes later.

19 이어질 응답 찾기

대화를 듣고, 남자의 마지막 말에 대한 여자의 응답으로 가장 적절한 것을 고르시오.

Woman: _____

① I'm sorry to hear that.
② I said she just came in.
③ She is on the other line.
④ She wants to speak to you.
⑤ Why didn't you talk about it?

[Cell phone rings.]

W Hello.

M Hello. Is this Susan?

W No. This is Susie. Who's this?

M Oh, Susie. This is Andy. Can I talk to Susan?

W Sorry, _____ _____ _____ _____.

M Is she expected home soon?

W Maybe in about an hour. Shall I _____ _____ _____ _____ back?

M Yes. I'd rather speak to her directly.

W *[Pause]* Oh, I think she just stepped in.

M _____ _____ _____ _____?

20 상황에 적절한 말 찾기

다음 상황 설명을 듣고, Tiffany가 John에게 할 말로 가장 적절한 것을 고르시오.

Tiffany: _____

① I'd like to go, but I can't.
② What's wrong with your sister?
③ Can we change the time to 7:20?
④ Buy the tickets online at this time.
⑤ How about watching a movie this evening?

W John and Tiffany are friends in middle school. John asks Tiffany to _____ _____ _____ _____ with him because he has 2 free movie tickets. So they agree to meet _____ _____ _____ at 7 p.m. Tiffany comes home, but she finds out she has to _____ _____ _____ _____ 7 p.m. Now Tiffany decides to call John and tell him _____ _____ _____ 7:20 instead. In this situation, what would Tiffany most likely say to John?

정답 및 해설 p.128

실전 모의고사 **19**

점수

/20

---

01 대화를 듣고, 여자가 취해야 할 동작을 고르시오.

02 대화를 듣고, 여자가 남자에게 부탁한 일로 가장 적절한 것을 고르시오.

① 시계 수리하기　　② 함께 학교 가기
③ 모닝콜 해주기　　④ 알람 시계 사 오기
⑤ 수리점에 시계 맡기기

03 다음 그림의 상황에 가장 적절한 대화를 고르시오.

① ② ③ ④ ⑤

04 대화를 듣고, 여자가 남자의 집에 방문할 요일을 고르시오.

① 월요일　　② 화요일　　③ 수요일
④ 목요일　　⑤ 금요일

05 대화를 듣고, 여자가 사려는 집에 관해 언급되지 않은 것을 고르시오.

① 침실의 개수　② 주차장 유무　③ 주변 시설
④ 층수　　　　⑤ 주변 환경

06 대화를 듣고, 두 사람이 대화하는 장소로 가장 적절한 곳을 고르시오.

① 호텔　　　　② 병원　　　　③ 회의장
④ 도서관　　　⑤ 주차장

07 다음을 듣고, 두 사람의 대화가 <u>어색한</u> 것을 고르시오.

① ② ③ ④ ⑤

08 대화를 듣고, 남자가 여자에게 부탁한 일로 가장 적절한 것을 고르시오.

① 설거지하기　　　② 식사 준비하기
③ 공부 도와주기　　④ 숙제 자료 조사하기
⑤ 농구 연습 같이 하기

09 다음을 듣고, 무엇에 관한 안내 방송인지 고르시오.

① 시 전시회 개최
② 도서관 수리 안내
③ 시 쓰기 대회 홍보
④ 필독 도서 목록 소개
⑤ 도서관 열람 시간 변경

10 대화를 듣고, 여자가 지불할 금액을 고르시오.

① $45　　　　② $50　　　　③ $80
④ $90　　　　⑤ $100

11 대화를 듣고, 남자가 할 일로 가장 적절한 것을 고르시오.

① 승강장 찾기　　　② 기차표 사기
③ 화장실 가기　　　④ 현금 인출하기
⑤ 간식거리 사기

12 다음을 듣고, Parkwoods Flea Market에 관해 언급되지 <u>않은</u> 것을 고르시오.

① 개최 장소 　② 개최 날짜 　③ 행사 목적
④ 판매 품목 　⑤ 간식 메뉴

13 대화를 듣고, 두 사람이 사용할 사무실을 고르시오.

① Room A	② Room B	Exit	③ Room C	
		↑		Cafe
Restroom	④ Room D	Elevator	⑤ Room E	

14 다음을 듣고, 무엇에 관한 설명인지 고르시오.

① 비 　② 우유 　③ 물
④ 혈액 　⑤ 탄산수

15 대화를 듣고, 여자가 대화 직후에 할 일로 가장 적절한 것을 고르시오.

① 청소하기 　② 하이킹하기
③ 정원 손질하기 　④ 날씨 확인하기
⑤ 친구와 약속 정하기

16 대화를 듣고, 두 사람이 영화를 볼 날짜를 고르시오.

① April 23rd 　② April 24th
③ April 25th 　④ April 26th
⑤ April 27th

17 대화를 듣고, 남자의 마지막 말에 대한 여자의 응답으로 가장 적절한 것을 고르시오.

Woman: _____

① How often does the bus come?
② You had better not take the bus.
③ That's good. I appreciate your help.
④ Have you ever been to the museum?
⑤ That's okay. I'm used to morning traffic jams.

18 대화를 듣고, 여자의 마지막 말에 대한 남자의 응답으로 가장 적절한 것을 고르시오.

Man: _____

① It'll board at Gate 202 at 5:30.
② Let's meet at the check-in counter.
③ Your train will depart from platform 7.
④ It will take four hours and thirty minutes.
⑤ You'd better wait in the lounge for 30 minutes.

19 대화를 듣고, 남자의 마지막 말에 대한 여자의 응답으로 가장 적절한 것을 고르시오.

Woman: _____

① It's 8:30 now.
② 9 to 5, Monday through Friday.
③ I'd like to, but I have to go now.
④ He'll be able to go there in time.
⑤ I'm busy. I'll go to the hospital later.

20 다음 상황 설명을 듣고, Ben의 어머니가 Ben에게 할 말로 가장 적절한 것을 고르시오.

Ben's mother: _____

① Can I call you back later?
② Math is my favorite subject, too.
③ You should study hard for the test.
④ It's okay to skip math for one day.
⑤ Can I borrow your notes from yesterday's class?

Dictation 19

◇ 다시 듣고, 빈칸에 들어갈 알맞은 단어를 써보세요.

정답 및 해설 p.128

01 그림 정보 파악

대화를 듣고, 여자가 취해야 할 동작을 고르시오.

① ② ③
④ ⑤

W Ouch!

M What's the matter?

W I was standing all day long, and my legs really hurt.

M Why don't you ＿＿＿＿＿＿ ＿＿＿＿＿＿ ＿＿＿＿＿＿ ＿＿＿＿＿＿ your leg muscles?

W Okay. What exercises should I do?

M ＿＿＿＿＿＿ ＿＿＿＿＿＿ ＿＿＿＿＿＿ ＿＿＿＿＿＿ ＿＿＿＿＿＿ both of your heels.

W Okay.

M Then ＿＿＿＿＿＿ ＿＿＿＿＿＿ ＿＿＿＿＿＿ for 15 seconds and repeat it 3 times.

W Oh, ＿＿＿＿＿＿ ＿＿＿＿＿＿ ＿＿＿＿＿＿ ＿＿＿＿＿＿. Thanks.

02 부탁 파악

대화를 듣고, 여자가 남자에게 부탁한 일로 가장 적절한 것을 고르시오.

① 시계 수리하기　　② 함께 학교 가기
③ 모닝콜 해주기　　④ 알람 시계 사 오기
⑤ 수리점에 시계 맡기기

W I was late for work today.

M Again?

W I overslept. My alarm clock didn't ＿＿＿＿＿＿ ＿＿＿＿＿＿ this morning, even though I set it last night.

M Your clock never works. Perhaps you should buy a new one.

W You're right. I'll ＿＿＿＿＿＿ ＿＿＿＿＿＿ ＿＿＿＿＿＿ ＿＿＿＿＿＿ this weekend.

M What will you do until this weekend?

W Since my alarm clock doesn't work, ＿＿＿＿＿＿ ＿＿＿＿＿＿ ＿＿＿＿＿＿ a wake-up call until then?

M Okay. ＿＿＿＿＿＿ ＿＿＿＿＿＿ ＿＿＿＿＿＿ ＿＿＿＿＿＿ at 6 in the morning.

W I'd really appreciate that.

다음 그림의 상황에 가장 적절한 대화를 고르시오.

① ② ③ ④ ⑤

① W What are ＿＿＿＿＿ ＿＿＿＿＿ ＿＿＿＿＿?

　 M I'm looking for my dog.

② W What kind of dog do you want?

　 M I like gentle ones. They are easy to take care of.

③ W What kind of pet would ＿＿＿＿＿ ＿＿＿＿＿ ＿＿＿＿＿ ＿＿＿＿＿?

　 M Dogs are the best.

④ W Have you ever raised a dog?

　 M No, I haven't.

⑤ W Would you mind looking after my dog ＿＿＿＿＿ ＿＿＿＿＿ ＿＿＿＿＿?

　 M No, not at all.

대화를 듣고, 여자가 남자의 집에 방문할 요일을 고르시오.

① 월요일　　② 화요일　　③ 수요일
④ 목요일　　⑤ 금요일

W Sam, can I borrow your guitar?

M Sure. But it's at home. You have to come over to get it. Is that all right?

W That's fine. ＿＿＿＿＿ ＿＿＿＿＿ ＿＿＿＿＿ ＿＿＿＿＿ your house at 5 p.m. on Tuesday?

M Oh, sorry. I won't be home at that time.

W Then how about 4:30 p.m. on Wednesday?

M 4:30 p.m.? I have to meet Jake at 4.

W Well, how about ＿＿＿＿＿ ＿＿＿＿＿ ＿＿＿＿＿ ＿＿＿＿＿? 10 a.m.?

M ＿＿＿＿＿ ＿＿＿＿＿ ＿＿＿＿＿.

W Okay. See you then.

대화를 듣고, 여자가 사려는 집에 관해 언급되지 않은 것을 고르시오.

① 침실의 개수　　② 주차장 유무
③ 주변 시설　　④ 층수
⑤ 주변 환경

M Hello, Mrs. Baker. I've found a house you will want to buy.

W Oh, terrific! What's it like?

M It has 3 bedrooms and 2 bathrooms. There is also a big garage, so you can ＿＿＿＿＿ ＿＿＿＿＿ ＿＿＿＿＿ ＿＿＿＿＿ ＿＿＿＿＿.

W That sounds good.

M The house has been renovated, so it is as good as new.

W All right. Then, what about the hospital and the shopping center?

M They're ＿＿＿＿＿ ＿＿＿＿＿ ＿＿＿＿＿

the house. The house is also in very _____

_____ _____ surroundings.

W Okay. Could I see it tomorrow afternoon?

M Sure.

---

06 장소 추론

대화를 듣고, 두 사람이 대화하는 장소로 가장 적절한 곳을 고르시오.

① 호텔 ② 병원 ③ 회의장
④ 도서관 ⑤ 주차장

🔊 **Listening Tip**

dress, true처럼 'dr', 'tr'에서 'd'와 't'는 각각 우리말의 /쥬/, /츄/와 같이 발음돼요.

M Hello, ma'am. How may I help you?

W Hello. Is there _____ _____ _____

for tonight?

M Oh, do you not have a reservation?

W No, I don't. I called about a month ago, but the front desk said we didn't need one.

M During this time of year, that's usually 🔊true. However, because of a conference being held near here, we have

_____ _____ _____

_____. Are you alone?

W No. My husband is bringing our 2 daughters.

M I'm sorry, but all we have _____ _____

_____ is a room for 2. Would you like to stay

anyway?

W Well, it's better than spending the night in our car.

---

07 어색한 대화 찾기

다음을 듣고, 두 사람의 대화가 <u>어색한</u> 것을 고르시오.

① ② ③ ④ ⑤

① **W** *How do you like your new home?

M I love it! It's _____ _____ _____.

② **W** What time are you leaving for China?

M At 3 o'clock this afternoon.

③ **W** _____ _____. Let's do something.

M Okay. How about taking a walk in the park?

④ **W** Have you ever been to London?

M No, I haven't. I really want to _____

_____ _____.

⑤ **W** What do you want to do after you graduate from school?

M I am planning to _____ _____

_____ at the airport.

✱ **교육부 지정 의사소통 기능: 의견 묻기**   능(김) 1│능(양) 2│비 7│Y(박) 8│지 4│다 1

How do you like ~? ~는 어떻게 생각해?

• **How do you like** my new coat? 내 새 코트 어때?
• **How do you like** this plan? 이 계획을 어떻게 생각해?

대화를 듣고, 남자가 여자에게 부탁한 일로 가장
적절한 것을 고르시오.

① 설거지하기
② 식사 준비하기
③ 공부 도와주기
④ 숙제 자료 조사하기
⑤ 농구 연습 같이 하기

W You look tired. What's the matter?

M I _____ _____ _____ 3 a.m.
studying for the exam. I got up early in the morning and
went to school. Then I took the exam from 9 to 11. Then I
had basketball practice from 1 to 3.

W It sounds like _____ _____ _____
_____ _____ .

M Yes. Could you _____ _____
_____ _____ ? I know it's my turn, but
I am too tired.

W Sure. You can _____ _____ _____
_____ tomorrow night.

M It's a deal. Thanks.

다음을 듣고, 무엇에 관한 안내 방송인지 고르시오.

① 시 전시회 개최
② 도서관 수리 안내
③ 시 쓰기 대회 홍보
④ 필독 도서 목록 소개
⑤ 도서관 열람 시간 변경

W Good morning, students. Our school library _____
_____ _____ _____ a Poem
Writing Contest. Students will have to write 3 poems on the
subjects _____ _____ _____
_____ _____ . Three winners will be
chosen, and _____ _____ _____
will receive a gift card as a reward. If you want to
_____ _____ _____ , please bring
your application form to the library office. Thank you.

대화를 듣고, 여자가 지불할 금액을 고르시오.

① $45   ② $50   ③ $80
④ $90   ⑤ $100

M May I help you?

W Yes, please. I'm looking for a pair of shoes.

M Okay, ma'am. Take your time.

W How much are those red ones?

M They're $50, but they are _____ _____
_____ 10% off.

W Do you have them _____ _____
_____ , too?

M We also have them in black.

W All right. I'll take _____ _____ _____ _____, and one in red.

M _____ _____ _____ _____ separately?

W Yes, please.

---

11 할 일 파악

대화를 듣고, 남자가 할 일로 가장 적절한 것을 고르시오.

① 승강장 찾기　② 기차표 사기
③ 화장실 가기　④ 현금 인출하기
⑤ 간식거리 사기

W Peter, _____ _____ _____ _____. We are about to board.

M Okay. Wait a minute.

W What's the matter?

M I can't find the tickets.

W Oh no! The train leaves in 10 minutes. I _____ _____ _____ _____ this morning, remember?

M Yes. I put them in the pocket of my jacket and now _____ _____ _____.

W Look again.

M I'm afraid I left them at home. _____ _____ _____ _____ now.

---

12 언급하지 않은 내용 찾기

다음을 듣고, Parkwoods Flea Market에 관해 언급되지 않은 것을 고르시오.

① 개최 장소　② 개최 날짜
③ 행사 목적　④ 판매 품목
⑤ 간식 메뉴

🔊 **Listening Tip**

it will be는 /잇 윌 비/라고 한 단어씩 발음하기보다는 /이를비/처럼 연음하여 발음하는 경우가 더 많아요.

M Hello, students. I'm Robert Clark, the president of the Art Club. I'm happy to introduce the Parkwoods Flea Market. 🔊It will be _____ _____ _____ _____ the main building at the school on September 7th. We've prepared this event in order _____ _____ _____ _____ poor children who want to study art. _____ _____ such as books and clothes at this event. You can _____ _____ _____ _____ in the cafeteria. Please come and get some good things at a low price. Thank you.

13 위치 찾기

대화를 듣고, 두 사람이 사용할 사무실을 고르시오.

① Room A	② Room B	Exit	③ Room C	
		↑		Cafe
Restroom	④ Room D	Elevator	⑤ Room E	

M Emily, which room is good for our office?

W How about Room A? I think it's quiet because it's in the corner.

M _____ _____ _____ _____, too. But the room looks old. We would need to spend some money on remodeling.

W What about using one of the rooms _____ _____ _____ _____? You're a coffee lover.

M But the cafe is crowded and music plays all day long. So those rooms _____ _____ _____.

W You're right. Then, we have 2 rooms left, Room B and Room D.

M Let's _____ _____ _____ _____ next to the restroom.

W Okay.

14 화제 추론

다음을 듣고, 무엇에 관한 설명인지 고르시오.

① 비 ② 우유 ③ 물
④ 혈액 ⑤ 탄산수

W This is a clear liquid. It has _____ _____ _____ _____ _____. It is very necessary for most plant and animal life. Without this, almost all of the _____ _____ _____ _____ would die. It freezes at 0°C and boils at 100°C. In fact, _____ _____ _____ _____ of the earth. Also, this makes up a large part of living things. About 60 to 70 percent of the human body is this. Because this is necessary for life, it's important that we _____ _____ _____.

15 할 일 파악

대화를 듣고, 여자가 대화 직후에 할 일로 가장 적절한 것을 고르시오.

① 청소하기 ② 하이킹하기
③ 정원 손질하기 ④ 날씨 확인하기
⑤ 친구와 약속 정하기

W Larry, I'm going hiking in the mountains this weekend. Do you want to come?

M This weekend? Are you sure?

W Is there something wrong?

M I heard that it _____ _____ _____ _____.

W Well, I checked the weather a few days ago, but there was

_____ _____ _____

_____ this weekend.

M I might be mistaken. _____ _____

_____ _____ again to make sure.

W You're right. I'll do that right now.

16 숫자 정보 파악 (날짜)

대화를 듣고, 두 사람이 영화를 볼 날짜를 고르시오.

① April 23rd   ② April 24th
③ April 25th   ④ April 26th
⑤ April 27th

[Cell phone rings.]

W Hello.

M Hi, Cindy. It's Mark.

W Hi, Mark. What's up?

M Did you buy the tickets to the movie for this Wednesday?

W Not yet. Why?

M Actually, I don't think I can _____ _____

_____ _____ _____ . I forgot

April 25th is my grandmother's birthday.

W That's okay. Are you _____ _____

_____ _____ ?

M Yes. Do you want to see the movie on that day instead?

W Sure. Then I will _____ _____

_____ _____ Thursday.

M Okay. See you on Thursday.

17 이어질 응답 찾기

대화를 듣고, 남자의 마지막 말에 대한 여자의 응답으로 가장 적절한 것을 고르시오.

Woman: _____

① How often does the bus come?
② You had better not take the bus.
③ That's good. I appreciate your help.
④ Have you ever been to the museum?
⑤ That's okay. I'm used to morning traffic jams.

W Excuse me. I'd like to go to the National Museum of Korea. How can I get there?

M Then you need to take bus number 400.

W Where _____ _____ _____

_____ _____ ?

M You can catch it over there across the street.

W Right on that corner?

M Yes. You can _____ _____ _____

at the crosswalk.

W Thanks a lot.

M It runs about every 15 minutes, so you shouldn't have to

_____ _____ _____ .

대화를 듣고, 여자의 마지막 말에 대한 남자의 응답으로 가장 적절한 것을 고르시오.

Man: _____

① It'll board at Gate 202 at 5:30.
② Let's meet at the check-in counter.
③ Your train will depart from platform 7.
④ It will take four hours and thirty minutes.
⑤ You'd better wait in the lounge for 30 minutes.

M May I see your passport, please?
W Here you go.
M Do you have _____ _____ _____, Ms. Anderson?
W I'd like an aisle seat. One with extra legroom, _____ _____.
M I have _____ _____ _____ _____ the emergency exit.
W Oh, that would be good!
M Here's your boarding pass.
W Thank you. _____ _____ _____ _____ _____ and gate number?

대화를 듣고, 남자의 마지막 말에 대한 여자의 응답으로 가장 적절한 것을 고르시오.

Woman: _____

① It's 8:30 now.
② 9 to 5, Monday through Friday.
③ I'd like to, but I have to go now.
④ He'll be able to get there in time.
⑤ I'm busy. I'll go to the hospital later.

M Excuse me. Where's Dr. Miller's office?
W It's on the fifth floor.
M Is there an elevator here?
W Yes. Go this way, and the elevator is _____ _____ _____.
M Thanks.
W No problem. But you should hurry. It's almost _____ _____.
M _____ _____ _____ _____ _____?

다음 상황 설명을 듣고, Ben의 어머니가 Ben에게 할 말로 가장 적절한 것을 고르시오.

Ben's mother: _____

① Can I call you back later?
② Math is my favorite subject, too.
③ You should study hard for the test.
④ It's okay to skip math for one day.
⑤ Can I borrow your notes from yesterday's class?

M Ben is not doing well in math class. To get better grades in math class, he listens to the teacher and _____ _____ _____ _____. This morning, when he wakes up, he starts to feel dizzy. His mother tells him to stay home today. However, Ben wants to go to school _____ _____ _____ _____ he is. He is very worried about a math test next week. He is afraid that if he misses a math class, he _____ _____ _____ _____. His mother is worried about him, so she decides to tell him _____ _____ _____ the test. In this situation, what would Ben's mother most likely say to Ben?

실전 모의고사 **20**

점수 /20

01 대화를 듣고, 여자가 취해야 할 동작을 고르시오.

① ② ③

④ ⑤

02 대화를 듣고, 여자가 남자에게 부탁한 일로 가장 적절한 것을 고르시오.

① 책 빌려주기　　　　② 함께 공부하기
③ 숙제 도와주기　　　　④ 수학 과제 제출하기
⑤ 수행평가 자료 수집하기

03 다음 그림의 상황에 가장 적절한 대화를 고르시오.

①　　　②　　　③　　　④　　　⑤

04 대화를 듣고, 남자가 컴퓨터 게임을 할 수 있는 요일을 고르시오.

① 월요일　　　② 화요일　　　③ 수요일
④ 목요일　　　⑤ 금요일

05 대화를 듣고, 스웨터에 관해 언급되지 <u>않은</u> 것을 고르시오.

① 디자인　　　② 가격　　　③ 재료
④ 색깔　　　⑤ 사이즈

06 대화를 듣고, 두 사람이 대화하는 장소로 가장 적절한 곳을 고르시오.

① 식당　　　② 호텔　　　③ 은행
④ 가구점　　　⑤ 옷 가게

07 다음을 듣고, 두 사람의 대화가 <u>어색한</u> 것을 고르시오.

①　　　②　　　③　　　④　　　⑤

08 대화를 듣고, 여자가 남자에게 부탁한 일로 가장 적절한 것을 고르시오.

① 설탕 사 오기　　　　② 날씨 확인하기
③ 쇼핑 목록 만들기　　　　④ 차로 데리러 오기
⑤ 음식 배달 주문하기

09 다음을 듣고, 무엇에 관한 안내 방송인지 고르시오.

① 하이킹 참여 권유　　　② 분실물 습득 공고
③ 중고 자전거 판매　　　④ 동아리 회원 모집
⑤ 자전거 최신 모델 홍보

10 대화를 듣고, 남자가 지불할 금액을 고르시오.

① $70　　　② $77　　　③ $90
④ $100　　　⑤ $110

11 대화를 듣고, 남자가 할 일로 가장 적절한 것을 고르시오.

① 건전지 사기　　　　② 시계 수리하기
③ 시계 빌려주기　　　　④ 건전지 가져오기
⑤ 사무실 문 잠그기

12 다음을 듣고, Seoul Charity Concert에 관해 언급되지 않은 것을 고르시오.

① 날짜　　　② 장소　　　③ 공연자
④ 관람료　　⑤ 행사 목적

13 대화를 듣고 여자가 갈 매장을 고르시오.

①　Shop A	Exit	②　Shop B	③　Shop C
	↑		
④　Shop D	Elevator	Restroom	⑤　Shop E

14 다음을 듣고, 무엇에 관한 설명인지 고르시오.

① 표 발권기　　　　② 자동판매기
③ 동전 교환기　　　④ 현금 지급기
⑤ 셀프 주유기

15 대화를 듣고, 여자가 대화 직후에 할 일로 가장 적절한 것을 고르시오.

① 딸기 씻기　　　　② 저녁 준비하기
③ 숙제 도와주기　　④ 과자 사러 가기
⑤ 샌드위치 만들기

16 대화를 듣고, 여자가 집에 돌아오는 날짜를 고르시오.

① January 9th　　　② January 10th
③ January 11th　　④ January 12th
⑤ January 13th

17 대화를 듣고, 남자의 마지막 말에 대한 여자의 응답으로 가장 적절한 것을 고르시오.

Woman: _____

① May I take your order now?
② Would you like to change tables?
③ Sure. I'll take it back to the kitchen.
④ I think there's a mistake on our check.
⑤ Okay. I'll call you when your table's ready.

18 대화를 듣고, 여자의 마지막 말에 대한 남자의 응답으로 가장 적절한 것을 고르시오.

Man: _____

① I'm sorry to hear that.
② What makes you say that?
③ Could you do me a favor?
④ I don't know how you spend money.
⑤ That sounds like a perfect way to spend money.

19 대화를 듣고, 남자의 마지막 말에 대한 여자의 응답으로 가장 적절한 것을 고르시오.

Woman: _____

① Yes, I'll buy a blue jacket.
② Yes, it's the most popular one.
③ Okay. I will give you a refund.
④ Sure. I'll exchange it for a new one.
⑤ Sorry, but that is the final price.

20 다음 상황 설명을 듣고, Kate가 Tim에게 할 말로 가장 적절한 것을 고르시오.

Kate: _____

① You'd better work harder.
② You're in good shape now.
③ I think you should get some rest.
④ Shall we jog together in the park?
⑤ How about going to the gym earlier?

Dictation 20

◈ 다시 듣고, 빈칸에 들어갈 알맞은 단어를 써보세요.

정답 및 해설 p.135

01 그림 정보 파악

대화를 듣고, 여자가 취해야 할 동작을 고르시오.

① ② ③
④ ⑤

W Ugh, my back really hurts.

M I know an easy and _____ _____ _____ _____.

W Okay. What is that?

M First _____ _____ _____ _____ with both legs out straight.

W And then?

M Extend your arms. Then _____ _____ _____ by bending at the waist.

W Oh, my back feels better already.

M _____ _____ _____ _____ 30 seconds and repeat this three times.

02 부탁 파악

대화를 듣고, 여자가 남자에게 부탁한 일로 가장 적절한 것을 고르시오.

① 책 빌려주기
② 함께 공부하기
③ 숙제 도와주기
④ 수학 과제 제출하기
⑤ 수행평가 자료 수집하기

M Hey, what's on your mind?

W The mid-term exams. I'm not fully prepared yet.

M Well, you still have 3 days.

W Yeah, but 3 days are not _____ _____ _____ for several classes.

M Which classes are _____ _____ _____ for you?

W Math and science. It's really hard for me to study alone. _____ _____ _____ _____ _____?

M Of course. I hope I can help you.

W You will. *I am really worried about those exams.

M Don't worry so much. Just study hard and _____ _____ _____.

★ **교육부 지정 의사소통 기능: 걱정 표현하기**   동(이) 2 | 미 5

I'm worried about ~. 나는 ~가 걱정돼.

• **I'm worried about** global warming. 나는 지구 온난화가 걱정돼.
• **I'm worried about** my future. 나는 나의 미래가 걱정돼.

03 그림 상황에 적절한 대화 찾기

다음 그림의 상황에 가장 적절한 대화를 고르시오.

① ② ③ ④ ⑤

① M Could you _____ _____ _____ ?

W Of course. Here you are.

② M What are you doing now?

W I'm writing a letter to my parents.

③ M How do you want to send the package?

W I'd like to _____ _____ _____ _____ .

④ M I'd like to send this package.

W Could _____ _____ _____ the package on the scale?

⑤ M Where can I send the package?

W There is a post office _____ _____ _____ _____ .

04 특정 정보 파악

대화를 듣고, 남자가 컴퓨터 게임을 할 수 있는 요일을 고르시오.

① 월요일   ② 화요일   ③ 수요일
④ 목요일   ⑤ 금요일

🔊 **Listening Tip**

special, film과 같이 /l/ 소리가 음절 끝이나 음절 끝의 자음 앞에 올 경우에는 /으/가 첨가된 것처럼 발음돼요.

M Mom, can I play some computer games this week?

W _____ _____ _____ _____ to play computer games?

M Maybe on Wednesday, after school.

W Well, you shouldn't do it on that day. You _____ _____ _____ _____ .

M What about Monday?

W Monday? You have a dentist's appointment.

M Then _____ _____ _____ ?

W _____ _____ _____ _____ . I don't think you have anything 🔊 special to do on that day.

05 언급하지 않은 내용 찾기

대화를 듣고, 스웨터에 관해 언급되지 <u>않은</u> 것을 고르시오.

① 디자인   ② 가격   ③ 재료
④ 색깔   ⑤ 사이즈

W Oh, that sweater looks good.

M That turtleneck sweater with flowers? Girls really love it.

W I think _____ _____ _____ _____ would look good on my daughter. How much is it?

M It's $50. It's on sale now.

W It's a little expensive.

M It is very warm because _____ _____

_____ _____.

W Do you have it in a different color?

M _____ _____ _____ pink, yellow,

and green.

W I'll take 2, one in pink and one in yellow.

M Okay. I'll _____ _____ _____

_____ _____.

06 장소 추론

대화를 듣고, 두 사람이 대화하는 장소로 가장 적절한 곳을 고르시오.

① 식당　　② 호텔　　③ 은행
④ 가구점　　⑤ 옷 가게

M This sofa set is on sale this week. It's a very good deal.

W It's really nice and so comfortable.

M And for only $300 more, you _____ _____

_____ _____ leather.

W Leather! I've always wanted a leather sofa.

M If you buy it today, you'll get _____ _____

_____ _____ _____.

W I really need a coffee table, too.

M You won't find a deal _____ _____

_____ _____.

W Okay, _____ _____ _____.

M Great! You won't regret it.

07 어색한 대화 찾기

다음을 듣고, 두 사람의 대화가 어색한 것을 고르시오.

①　　②　　③　　④　　⑤

① M Ann, will you do me a favor?

W Sure, what is it?

② M I'm really nervous about _____ _____

_____ _____.

W Don't be. You're the best singer in our school.

③ M Can I _____ _____ _____

_____ ?

W Sure, I can. Thanks for helping me.

④ M Excuse me, can you _____ _____

_____ _____ _____ Pearl

Bookstore?

W Sorry, but I'm a visitor here, too.

⑤ M What do you want to be in the future?

W I'm _____ _____ _____ , so I

want to be a math teacher.

08 부탁 파악

대화를 듣고, 여자가 남자에게 부탁한 일로 가장 적절한 것을 고르시오.

① 설탕 사 오기
② 날씨 확인하기
③ 쇼핑 목록 만들기
④ 차로 데리러 오기
⑤ 음식 배달 주문하기

[Cell phone rings.]

M   Hello.

W   Hello, Robin. It's me. Where are you?

M   I am still in the supermarket.

W   Great! Did you find ＿＿＿＿＿＿＿＿ ＿＿＿＿＿＿＿＿ ＿＿＿＿＿＿＿＿ ＿＿＿＿＿＿＿＿ ＿＿＿＿＿＿＿＿ I gave you?

M   Everything except milk. I am on my way to pick it up.

W   Great. Actually, I'm calling because I forgot to add sugar on the list. We're running out of it. Can you ＿＿＿＿＿＿＿＿ ＿＿＿＿＿＿＿＿ ＿＿＿＿＿＿＿＿?

M   Of course. Anything else?

W   ＿＿＿＿＿＿＿＿ ＿＿＿＿＿＿＿＿ ＿＿＿＿＿＿＿＿ ＿＿＿＿＿＿＿＿. Thanks.

09 화제 추론

다음을 듣고, 무엇에 관한 안내 방송인지 고르시오.

① 하이킹 참여 권유
② 분실물 습득 공고
③ 중고 자전거 판매
④ 동아리 회원 모집
⑤ 자전거 최신 모델 홍보

W   Do you enjoy outdoor sports? ＿＿＿＿＿＿＿＿ ＿＿＿＿＿＿＿＿ ＿＿＿＿＿＿＿＿ ＿＿＿＿＿＿＿＿ our bike club? You can ride your bike and make new friends. Also, we can breathe in fresh air! We are ＿＿＿＿＿＿＿＿ ＿＿＿＿＿＿＿＿ ＿＿＿＿＿＿＿＿ ＿＿＿＿＿＿＿＿ now! Anyone who is interested in bike riding can join. If you want to join, come to the school playground at 4 o'clock tomorrow. We meet every Saturday ＿＿＿＿＿＿＿＿ ＿＿＿＿＿＿＿＿ ＿＿＿＿＿＿＿＿ ＿＿＿＿＿＿＿＿. Oh, and one more thing. You must have your own bike.

10 숫자 정보 파악 (금액)

대화를 듣고, 남자가 지불할 금액을 고르시오.

① $70   ② $77   ③ $90
④ $100   ⑤ $110

[Telephone rings.]

W   Hello. Sunnyside Hotel. How may I help you?

M   I'd like to reserve a room on the 21st of March.

W   Okay. Let me ＿＿＿＿＿＿＿＿ ＿＿＿＿＿＿＿＿ ＿＿＿＿＿＿＿＿ ＿＿＿＿＿＿＿＿. *[Pause]* Well, we have only one room available.

M   How much is it?

W It's $100, plus a 10% room tax.

M Oh, that's _____ _____ _____
_____ . Do you have a cheaper room available?

W We have a few _____ _____
_____ the 20th.

M How much are they?

W They are $70, plus the 10% room tax.

M Okay, _____ _____ _____
_____ _____ .

11 할 일 파악

대화를 듣고, 남자가 할 일로 가장 적절한 것을 고
르시오.

① 건전지 사기   ② 시계 수리하기
③ 시계 빌려주기   ④ 건전지 가져오기
⑤ 사무실 문 잠그기

M There is something wrong with this clock.

W What's the problem?

M Well, _____ _____ _____ .

W Really? Let me have a look. Maybe the battery
_____ _____ _____
_____ .

M Do you have any extra batteries?

W I _____ _____ _____ in one of
my desk drawers.

M Which drawer should I look in?

W _____ _____ _____
_____ . The batteries should be in there.

12 언급하지 않은 내용 찾기

다음을 듣고, Seoul Charity Concert에 관
해 언급되지 않은 것을 고르시오.

① 날짜   ② 장소   ③ 공연자
④ 관람료   ⑤ 행사 목적

M Hello. The Seoul Charity Concert will _____
_____ _____ Sunday, May 10th at the
Seoul Art Center. Many famous singers and performers
_____ _____ _____
_____ will perform in this concert. It's held for
African children in need. Many children there are
_____ _____ _____
_____ _____ . Your help is needed, more
than ever. So come and join us for this meaningful event.

13 위치 찾기

대화를 듣고 여자가 갈 매장을 고르시오.

① Shop A	Exit	② Shop B	③ Shop C
	↑		
④ Shop D	Elevator	Restroom	⑤ Shop E

🔊 **Listening Tip**

get off에서 전치사 off는 매우 약하게 발음되어 잘 들리지 않아요. 내용어인 동사에 비해 기능어인 전치사는 강세가 들어가지 않기 때문이에요.

W Excuse me. Do you know any _____ _____ _____ art supplies?

M Yes, there's a new place, Art Complex, on the 3rd floor of this building.

W This is my first time visiting this building. _____ _____ _____ _____ the 3rd floor?

M 🔊 Get off the elevator and _____ _____. Keep walking past the restroom. You'll see it _____ _____ _____.

W I see. Thank you so much.

M Don't mention it.

14 화제 추론

다음을 듣고, 무엇에 관한 설명인지 고르시오.

① 표 발권기 ② 자동판매기
③ 동전 교환기 ④ 현금 지급기
⑤ 셀프 주유기

W This is a machine, and you can see it everywhere. It's so easy to use this machine. First, just _____ _____ _____ _____ it. Second, _____ _____ _____ of the product you want. Then, take it out from the machine. You can use either coins or paper bills _____ _____ _____ _____. You can get lots of things, such as coffee, juice, snacks, and even some food.

15 할 일 파악

대화를 듣고, 여자가 대화 직후에 할 일로 가장 적절한 것을 고르시오.

① 딸기 씻기 ② 저녁 준비하기
③ 숙제 도와주기 ④ 과자 사러 가기
⑤ 샌드위치 만들기

M Mom, I'm a little hungry. Can I have a snack?

W There are some strawberries and milk in the refrigerator.

M I don't feel like _____ _____ _____ _____. Can I have something else?

W Would you like to have a sandwich and orange juice?

M Yes, please. The sandwiches that you make are really good.

W Wait a minute. _____ _____ _____ _____ right away.

M Thank you.

16 숫자 정보 파악 (날짜)

대화를 듣고, 여자가 집에 돌아오는 날짜를 고르시오.

① January 9th　② January 10th
③ January 11th　④ January 12th
⑤ January 13th

[Cell phone rings.]

M Hello.

W Hi, Peter. It's me, Julia.

M Oh, Julia! Are you enjoying your winter vacation in Pyeongchang?

W Of course, I am. I went snowboarding yesterday. Today, I'll visit a sheep ranch. I'm ＿＿＿＿＿ ＿＿＿＿＿ ＿＿＿＿＿ it.

M That's great! How long have you been there?

W I arrived here on January 3rd and I've been ＿＿＿＿＿ ＿＿＿＿＿ ＿＿＿＿＿ ＿＿＿＿＿.

M When will you come back to Gwangju?

W ＿＿＿＿＿ ＿＿＿＿＿ ＿＿＿＿＿ ＿＿＿＿＿ 2 days.

M Okay. See you soon.

17 이어질 응답 찾기

대화를 듣고, 남자의 마지막 말에 대한 여자의 응답으로 가장 적절한 것을 고르시오.

Woman: ＿＿＿＿＿＿＿＿＿＿＿＿

① May I take your order now?
② Would you like to change tables?
③ Sure. I'll take it back to the kitchen.
④ I think there's a mistake on our check.
⑤ Okay. I'll call you when your table's ready.

W Good evening. Did you make a reservation?

M I'm afraid we didn't.

W How many are ＿＿＿＿＿ ＿＿＿＿＿ ＿＿＿＿＿?

M There are 4 of us.

W I'm sorry, but we are ＿＿＿＿＿ ＿＿＿＿＿ ＿＿＿＿＿ ＿＿＿＿＿.

M How long do we have to wait?

W ＿＿＿＿＿ ＿＿＿＿＿ ＿＿＿＿＿ ＿＿＿＿＿ a table is about 20 minutes. Is that okay?

M ＿＿＿＿＿ ＿＿＿＿＿ ＿＿＿＿＿ ＿＿＿＿＿ the lounge.

18 이어질 응답 찾기

대화를 듣고, 여자의 마지막 말에 대한 남자의 응답으로 가장 적절한 것을 고르시오.

Man: ＿＿＿＿＿＿＿＿＿＿＿＿

① I'm sorry to hear that.
② What makes you say that?
③ Could you do me a favor?
④ I don't know how you spend money.
⑤ That sounds like a perfect way to spend money.

W Dad, please give me my allowance. Today is Monday.

M Oh, I forgot about that. How much do I owe you?

W $100.

M $100? Do I ＿＿＿＿＿ ＿＿＿＿＿ ＿＿＿＿＿ ＿＿＿＿＿?

W You keep forgetting to give me my allowance, ＿＿＿＿＿ ＿＿＿＿＿ ＿＿＿＿＿ ＿＿＿＿＿ piling up.

M What are you planning to do with the money?

W I'm going to put _____ _____

_____ _____, donate some to poor people,

and use the rest to buy books.

---

19 이어질 응답 찾기

대화를 듣고, 남자의 마지막 말에 대한 여자의 응답으로 가장 적절한 것을 고르시오.

Woman: _____

① Yes, I'll buy a blue jacket.
② Yes, it's the most popular one.
③ Okay. I will give you a refund.
④ Sure. I'll exchange it for a new one.
⑤ Sorry, but that is the final price.

W May I help you?

M I got this jacket last week, and I _____

_____ _____ I could return or exchange it.

W You can do either. May I ask why?

M I really like this jacket, but _____ _____

_____ _____.

W All right. [Pause] Here, try this one. It's a little larger.

M Thanks. This is good, but it seems to be a little longer.

W I'm afraid _____ _____ _____

_____ in that style and size.

M Then I guess I _____ _____

_____ _____. I have the receipt right here.

---

20 상황에 적절한 말 찾기

다음 상황 설명을 듣고, Kate가 Tim에게 할 말로 가장 적절한 것을 고르시오.

Kate: _____

① You'd better work harder.
② You're in good shape now.
③ I think you should get some rest.
④ Shall we jog together in the park?
⑤ How about going to the gym earlier?

W Tim always gets up around 4 o'clock. He usually

_____ _____ _____

_____. Then he does his weight training for 2 hours

_____ _____ _____

_____ his house. After that, he comes home, takes a

shower, and eats breakfast. After he reads the newspaper, he

goes to work at 9 o'clock. He _____ _____

_____ _____ during this time. His wife

Kate is really worried that he is _____

_____ _____ _____. In this

situation, what would Kate most likely say to Tim?

PART. 03

Listening Q

^^^

중학영어듣기 모의고사

고난도 모의고사

✕

실전 모의고사보다 한 단계 높은 고난도 모의고사 4회로
듣기 모의고사 만점을 향해 Listening Q!

정답 및 해설 p.142

고난도 모의고사 01

01 대화를 듣고, 남자가 구입할 재킷으로 가장 적절한 것을 고르시오.

①   ②   ③

④   ⑤

02 대화를 듣고, OMG에 관해 언급되지 <u>않은</u> 것을 고르시오

① 정식 명칭 ② 설립자 ③ 설립 연도
④ 설립 목적 ⑤ 활동 내용

03 대화를 듣고, 남자가 여자에게 전화한 목적으로 가장 적절한 것을 고르시오

① 안부를 물으려고
② 회의 취소를 알리려고
③ 새 제품을 홍보하려고
④ 휴가 일정을 바꾸려고
⑤ 회의 일정을 논의하려고

04 대화를 듣고, 두 사람이 만날 시각을 고르시오.

① 1:30 p.m. ② 2:00 p.m. ③ 2:30 p.m.
④ 3:00 p.m. ⑤ 3:30 p.m.

05 다음 그림의 상황에 가장 적절한 대화를 고르시오.

① ② ③ ④ ⑤

06 대화를 듣고, 두 사람이 대화하는 장소로 가장 적절한 것을 고르시오.

① 동물원 ② 놀이공원
③ 과학 실험실 ④ 장난감 가게
⑤ 자연사 박물관

07 대화를 듣고, 남자가 여자에게 부탁한 일로 가장 적절한 것을 고르시오.

① 세차하기 ② 양동이에 물 채우기
③ 수학 공부 도와주기 ④ 자동차 열쇠 가져오기
⑤ 시험 성적 비밀로 하기

08 다음을 듣고, 소방 훈련(fire drill)에 관해 언급되지 <u>않은</u> 것을 고르시오.

① 시작 시각 ② 집합 장소
③ 종료 시각 ④ 다음 훈련 날짜
⑤ 훈련 담당자

09 다음을 듣고, 무엇에 관한 설명인지 고르시오.

① 야구 ② 농구 ③ 하키
④ 배구 ⑤ 축구

10 다음을 듣고, 두 사람의 대화가 <u>어색한</u> 것을 고르시오.

① ② ③ ④ ⑤

11 대화를 듣고, 남자가 대화 직후에 할 일로 가장 적절한 것을 고르시오.

① 농장 체험하기
② 작은 텃밭 만들기
③ 할머니 집 함께 방문하기
④ 양로원 자원 봉사 계획하기
⑤ 농장 자원 봉사자 등록하기

12 대화를 듣고, 두 사람이 공항 셔틀버스를 탈 시각을 고르시오.

① 11:00 a.m.　② 11:30 a.m.　③ 12:00 p.m.
④ 1:30 p.m.　⑤ 2:00 p.m.

13 다음 배치도를 보면서 대화를 듣고, 두 사람이 선택할 구역을 고르시오.

	Screen		
Entrance	① Section A	② Section B	③ Section C
	④ Section D	Section E	⑤ Section F

14 대화를 듣고, 여자가 어제 한 일로 가장 적절한 것을 고르시오.

① 소개팅하기　　　② 영화사 면접 보기
③ 남자친구 만나기　④ 학교 밴드와 공연하기
⑤ 밴드 오디션 참가하기

15 다음을 듣고, 방송의 목적으로 가장 적절한 것을 고르시오

① 마을 회의를 공지하려고
② 집을 안전하게 하도록 권고하려고
③ 이웃 간의 이해를 촉구하기 위해서
④ 도난 사건에 대한 신고를 받으려고
⑤ 휴가를 알차게 보내는 방법을 알리려고

16 대화를 듣고, 여자가 지불할 금액을 고르시오.

① $200　　② $225　　③ $250
④ $275　　⑤ $300

17 대화를 듣고, 여자의 마지막 말에 대한 남자의 말로 가장 적절한 것을 고르시오.

Man: _____

① Unfortunately, it wasn't my lucky day.
② No problem. I'll catch up with you later.
③ This is the biggest fish I have ever caught.
④ You can ask your parents to join us, too.
⑤ I caught a cold, so I stayed at home all day.

18 대화를 듣고, 남자의 마지막 말에 대한 여자의 말로 가장 적절한 것을 고르시오.

Woman: _____

① I've never had Mexican food before.
② You really need to stop eating too much.
③ I should first find out where the restaurant is.
④ I know where we can get better Mexican food.
⑤ But we can't go there unless we have a reservation.

19 대화를 듣고, 여자의 마지막 말에 대한 남자의 말로 가장 적절한 것을 고르시오.

Man: _____

① I don't know where my pajamas are.
② I think their children have gone to bed.
③ Okay, I'll apologize to her for the noise.
④ Well, you should have told me that sooner.
⑤ How long did it take you to bake this cake?

20 다음 상황 설명을 듣고, Sean이 웨이터에게 할 말로 가장 적절한 것을 고르시오.

Sean: Excuse me, _____

① can we have the menu please?
② I'm afraid this is not what we ordered.
③ Why hasn't our food been served yet?
④ would you like to have dinner with us?
⑤ when are we getting the high chair we asked for?

Dictation 01

◆ 다시 듣고, 빈칸에 들어갈 알맞은 단어를 써보세요.

정답 및 해설 p.142

01 그림 정보 파악

대화를 듣고, 남자가 구입할 재킷으로 가장 적절한 것을 고르시오.

① ② ③
④ ⑤

M Can I get some help?

W Sure, what can I do for you?

M I really like this jacket, but do you have this style ＿＿＿＿＿＿ ＿＿＿＿＿＿ ＿＿＿＿＿＿?

W Let me see. *[Pause]* Is this what you're looking for?

M Thank you. Let me try it on.

W I think you would look better if you put on ＿＿＿＿＿＿ ＿＿＿＿＿＿ ＿＿＿＿＿＿ a hood.

M Really? What do you think about this one then? This one has 2 zippers.

W That one's actually the most popular style.

M There's no hood, and there are ＿＿＿＿＿＿ ＿＿＿＿＿＿, ＿＿＿＿＿＿.

W That's true. That's ＿＿＿＿＿＿ ＿＿＿＿＿＿ ＿＿＿＿＿＿ ＿＿＿＿＿＿ these days.

M Okay, I'll take this.

02 언급하지 않은 내용 찾기

대화를 듣고, OMG에 관해 언급되지 않은 것을 고르시오

① 정식 명칭 ② 설립자 ③ 설립 연도
④ 설립 목적 ⑤ 활동 내용

🔊 **Listening Tip**

people에는 두 개의 'p'가 나오는데 앞의 'p'처럼 강세가 있는 음절의 첫 음일 때는 /ㅍ/로 발음하지만 뒤의 'p'처럼 강세가 없는 음절에 올 때는 /ㅃ/로 발음해요. 그래서 people을 잘 들어보면 /피쁠/에 가깝게 들릴 거예요.

W Have you heard of an organization called OMG?

M Does OMG ＿＿＿＿＿＿ ＿＿＿＿＿＿ ＿＿＿＿＿＿?

W Yes, it stands for One More Generation.

M Oh, I've heard of it. It's a non-profit organization that 2 kids started, right?

W Right, their names are Carter and Olivia Ries.

M What is the organization for?

W It's for ＿＿＿＿＿＿ ＿＿＿＿＿＿ ＿＿＿＿＿＿ like wild cheetahs in South Africa.

M What does the organization do to save animals?

W 🔊 People there try to raise awareness ＿＿＿＿＿＿ ＿＿＿＿＿＿ ＿＿＿＿＿＿ ＿＿＿＿＿＿.

M Really? Why is that important?

W Because many animals die _____ _____

_____ _____.

M Oh, I see.

---

03 목적 파악

대화를 듣고, 남자가 여자에게 전화한 목적으로 가장 적절한 것을 고르시오

① 안부를 물으려고
② 회의 취소를 알리려고
③ 새 제품을 홍보하려고
④ 휴가 일정을 바꾸려고
⑤ 회의 일정을 논의하려고

[Cell phone rings.]

W Hello.

M Hello, Michelle? This is Jake.

W Hi, Jake. How are you?

M I'm good. Thanks. How are you feeling?

W I'm feeling much better.

M Great. I'm calling to ask you when it would be good to

_____ _____ _____

_____ _____ Mr. Taylor.

W I'm sorry that you had to delay the meeting with him.

M It's perfectly fine.

W I should be able to _____ _____

_____ _____ _____.

M Will 3 p.m. on Friday work for you?

W Yes, _____ _____ _____

_____. I'll see you then.

---

04 숫자 정보 파악 (시각)

대화를 듣고, 두 사람이 만날 시각을 고르시오.

① 1:30 p.m. ② 2:00 p.m.
③ 2:30 p.m. ④ 3:00 p.m.
⑤ 3:30 p.m.

W Do you remember my older sister Rachel?

M Of course, I do. Isn't she _____ _____

this month?

W Yes, her wedding is this Saturday. Do you want to come?

M Sure. What time is the ceremony?

W _____ _____ _____ 3 p.m. at

Grace Wedding Hall.

M Okay. Can I go there and meet you at 2?

W You don't have to come too early. _____ _____ _____ 2:30 in front of the wedding hall.

M Sure. See you then.

다음 그림의 상황에 가장 적절한 대화를 고르시오.

① ② ③ ④ ⑤

① M Did you order pizza, ma'am?

　 W Yes, can you put it _____ _____ _____, please?

② M Excuse me. Are TVs on sale?

　 W Yes, you get a 20% _____ _____ _____ _____.

③ M Where do you want this table?

　 W Can you put it in the living room _____ _____ _____ _____?

④ M I'm tired. I can't run any more.

　 W Why don't you take a 5-minute break?

⑤ M Did you finish your art project?

　 W No, _____ _____ _____ after dinner tonight.

대화를 듣고, 두 사람이 대화하는 장소로 가장 적절한 것을 고르시오.

① 동물원　　　② 놀이공원
③ 과학 실험실　　④ 장난감 가게
⑤ 자연사 박물관

M Excuse me. Do you have any dinosaurs here?

W Yes, of course. We have a _____ _____ _____ dinosaurs.

M Can you show me _____ _____ _____?

W Sure, follow me, please.

M *[Pause]* Oh, there they are. You have so many _____ _____ _____ _____ _____.

W Yes, we do. Who is the dinosaur for?

M It's for my little brother. His birthday is tomorrow.

W We also offer gift-wrapping service for $1. It's at _____ _____ _____ near the counter.

M All right. Thank you for your help.

대화를 듣고, 남자가 여자에게 부탁한 일로 가장
적절한 것을 고르시오.

① 세차하기
② 양동이에 물 채우기
③ 수학 공부 도와주기
④ 자동차 열쇠 가져오기
⑤ 시험 성적 비밀로 하기

W Where are you going, Bill?

M I'm going outside _____ _____
_____ _____, Mom.

W What? Why would you do that?

M I promised Dad something and I am trying to keep it.

W What kind of _____ _____ _____
_____?

M I promised that I'd wash the car if I _____
_____ _____ _____ my math
exam.

W Oh, I see. *Can I give you a hand?

M Yes, please. Can you _____ _____
_____ _____ _____, please?

W Okay. I'll do that right now.

✳ 교육부 지정 의사소통 기능: 도움 제안하기   능(양) 6급 3

Can I give you a hand? 내가 도와줄까?

A: **Can I give you a hand?** 내가 도와줄까?
B: Yes, please. Can you help me carry this box?
   응, 부탁할게. 내가 이 상자를 옮길 수 있게 도와줄래?

다음을 듣고, 소방 훈련(fire drill)에 관해 언급되
지 않은 것을 고르시오.

① 시작 시각   ② 집합 장소
③ 종료 시각   ④ 다음 훈련 날짜
⑤ 훈련 담당자

M Good morning, students. This is your principal speaking.
I want to remind all of you that we're having a fire drill
_____ _____ _____. When you
hear the alarm, all of you need to leave your classrooms
and _____ _____ _____
_____ the main building. You'll be asked to
_____ _____ _____ your
classrooms when the drill ends at 12:30. The next fire
drill _____ _____
_____ June 10th. That's the only message I have for
you this morning. I hope you have a great day.

09 화제 추론

다음을 듣고, 무엇에 관한 설명인지 고르시오.

① 야구 ② 농구 ③ 하키
④ 배구 ⑤ 축구

W This is a team sport. In order to play this sport, you need to have at least _____ _____, _____ _____, and gloves. You score a point when you bat at home plate and touch all 4 bases. The person who _____ _____ _____ is called a pitcher, and the person who _____ _____ _____ is called a batter. There are 9 _____ _____ _____ _____, and they play 9 innings. This is a very popular sport in many countries, such as Korea, Japan, Taiwan, and the U.S.

10 어색한 대화 찾기

다음을 듣고, 두 사람의 대화가 어색한 것을 고르시오.

① ② ③ ④ ⑤

① M Will you dry the dishes, please?
   W Of course. Let me get a _____ _____ _____, first.
② M Could I speak to you in private?
   W Yes, _____ _____ _____ a private school.
③ M How do you _____ _____ _____?
   W I try to run 30 minutes every day.
④ M Did you want to talk to me?
   W Yes, do you have a minute?
⑤ M I'm sorry. Did I interrupt you?
   W No, you didn't. I _____ _____ _____.

11 할 일 파악

대화를 듣고, 남자가 대화 직후에 할 일로 가장 적절한 것을 고르시오.

① 농장 체험하기
② 작은 텃밭 만들기
③ 할머니 집 함께 방문하기
④ 양로원 자원 봉사 계획하기
⑤ 농장 자원 봉사자 등록하기

M How was your weekend, Samantha?
W It was great. I volunteered to work at a farm.
M That sounds interesting. What did you do there?
W I planted tomatoes and potatoes _____ _____ _____ _____.
M I've always wanted to do that, too. How did you volunteer there?
W Oh, it's not difficult _____ _____ _____ _____ at a farm.

M Really? I didn't know that.

W Just _____ _____ _____ _____ _____ on the website helpingfarmers.org, and you'll get a list of places to volunteer.

M Thanks for the information. I'll _____ _____ _____ _____ .

대화를 듣고, 두 사람이 공항셔틀버스를 탈 시각을 고르시오.

① 11:00 a.m.   ② 11:30 a.m.
③ 12:00 p.m.   ④ 1:30 p.m.
⑤ 2:00 p.m.

W How are we getting to the airport tomorrow, Dad?

M I'm planning to drive there.

W Why don't we take the shuttle bus since we only have 2 bags?

M That's a good idea. _____ _____ _____ the 12 o'clock shuttle.

W Our plane leaves at 2 o'clock, Dad. _____ _____ _____ _____ the 11 o'clock shuttle?

M _____ _____ _____ about 30 minutes to get to the airport. Besides, we don't have to go to the airport that early. We're only going to Jeju-do.

W I thought we had to _____ _____ _____ _____ at least 2 hours before the departure time.

M That's for an international flight.

W Oh, I see. Then I guess we don't have to _____ _____ _____ .

다음 배치도를 보면서 대화를 듣고, 두 사람이 선택할 구역을 고르시오.

Entrance	Screen		
	① Section A	② Section B	③ Section C
	④ Section D	Section E	⑤ Section F

M We're still going to the movies this Saturday, right?

W Yes. I'll buy the tickets right away.

M I was actually doing that now. We just need to decide _____ _____ _____ .

W Oh, I see. One section is _____ _____ .

M Yes, unfortunately. You don't want to _____ _____ _____ the screen, do you?

W No, I don't. My _____ _____ if I sit too close to the screen.

M Okay, then we only have 2 sections to choose from.

W I don't want to _____ _____ _____ _____ the entrance. It might not be easy to go to the restroom during the movie.

M Okay. Let's sit there.

14 한 일 파악

대화를 듣고, 여자가 어제 한 일로 가장 적절한 것을 고르시오.

① 소개팅하기
② 영화사 면접 보기
③ 남자친구 만나기
④ 학교 밴드와 공연하기
⑤ 밴드 오디션 참가하기

M You seem to be in a good mood today, Aunt Ann.

W Well, I'm just waiting for a _____ _____ _____ _____.

M A phone call? From who? Your boyfriend?

W No. He is busy with work right now.

M You met your boyfriend in college, right?

W Yes, we were in the school band.

M Right, you _____ _____ _____ and he was the drummer.

W That's right. Actually, I auditioned for _____ _____ _____ _____ yesterday, and I think it went really well.

M Oh, that's who you are waiting for a phone call from.

W Yes. If everything goes well, I'll _____ _____ _____ _____ for the band next week.

M I'm sure you'll get it.

15 목적 파악

다음을 듣고, 방송의 목적으로 가장 적절한 것을 고르시오

① 마을 회의를 공지하려고
② 집을 안전하게 하도록 권고하려고
③ 이웃 간의 이해를 촉구하기 위해서
④ 도난 사건에 대한 신고를 받으려고
⑤ 휴가를 알차게 보내는 방법을 알리려고

M Hello, neighbors. I understand that many of you are planning on visiting your parents and relatives outside the city during the holiday season. So, I want to remind you of _____ _____ _____ your homes against possible break-ins while you're away. Please make sure to _____ _____ _____ _____, lock all the doors, and activate your home security system. We try our best to _____ _____ _____ _____ for everyone. You should also do your part by securing your homes as best as you can.

대화를 듣고, 여자가 지불할 금액을 고르시오.

① $200　　② $225　　③ $250
④ $275　　⑤ $300

[Telephone rings.]

M Thank you for calling Kids' World. How may I help you?

W Hi, I have some questions about your admission prices.

M Sure. The admission for adults is $100, and the admission for children under 13 is $50.

W I have a 4-year-old son. Do I ＿＿＿＿＿ ＿＿＿＿＿ ＿＿＿＿＿ ＿＿＿＿＿ him?

M No, ma'am. There is ＿＿＿＿＿ ＿＿＿＿＿ ＿＿＿＿＿ ＿＿＿＿＿ who's 5 or younger.

W I also have a 10-year-old daughter. Do you have any special discounts for families?

M Yes, we do. We have a 10% ＿＿＿＿＿ ＿＿＿＿＿ ＿＿＿＿＿ with children between 6 and 12.

W Great! My family can get the discount, right?

M Yes, then ＿＿＿＿＿ ＿＿＿＿＿ ＿＿＿＿＿ 2 adults and 1 child. And ＿＿＿＿＿ ＿＿＿＿＿ a 10% discount.

W Perfect. Can I purchase the tickets over the phone?

M Sure. I can help you with that.

대화를 듣고, 여자의 마지막 말에 대한 남자의 말로 가장 적절한 것을 고르시오.

Man: ＿＿＿＿＿＿＿＿＿＿＿＿＿＿＿＿＿

① Unfortunately, it wasn't my lucky day.
② No problem. I'll catch up with you later.
③ This is the biggest fish I have ever caught.
④ You can ask your parents to join us, too.
⑤ I caught a cold, so I stayed at home all day.

W How was your weekend, Mike?

M It was awesome. How was yours?

W I just stayed at home. I wasn't feeling too well. What did you do?

M I ＿＿＿＿＿ ＿＿＿＿＿ ＿＿＿＿＿ my dad on Saturday.

W Really? I've ＿＿＿＿＿ ＿＿＿＿＿ ＿＿＿＿＿ before.

M Oh, if you want, I can ask my dad to ＿＿＿＿＿ ＿＿＿＿＿ ＿＿＿＿＿ ＿＿＿＿＿.

W That would be great! Where did you go fishing on Saturday?

M We went to a river near my grandparents' house.

W ＿＿＿＿＿ ＿＿＿＿＿ ＿＿＿＿＿ did you catch?

대화를 듣고, 남자의 마지막 말에 대한 여자의 말로 가장 적절한 것을 고르시오.

Woman: _____

① I've never had Mexican food before.
② You really need to stop eating too much.
③ I should first find out where the restaurant is.
④ I know where we can get better Mexican food.
⑤ But we can't go there unless we have a reservation.

M I heard there's a very famous restaurant near your house.
W Are you talking about Joe's Mexican Restaurant?
M Yes, that's the name. _____ _____ _____, right?
W Of course, I have.
M How's the food? Is it really good?
W It's the best Mexican restaurant I've ever been to.
M Is the food really that good? I _____ _____ _____ _____ _____.
W You'll love it.
M All right, then there's only one way to find out. _____ _____ _____ right now.

대화를 듣고, 여자의 마지막 말에 대한 남자의 말로 가장 적절한 것을 고르시오.

Man: _____

① I don't know where my pajamas are.
② I think their children have gone to bed.
③ Okay, I'll apologize to her for the noise.
④ Well, you should have told me that sooner.
⑤ How long did it take you to bake this cake?

W Where are you going, honey? It's almost 10 p.m.
M I _____ _____ _____ _____ any more.
W Are you going to talk to the Wilsons about the noise?
M Yes, I am. They shouldn't _____ _____ _____ _____ around like that after 9 p.m.
W No, don't. Mrs. Wilson _____ _____ _____ _____ and told me that this would happen.
M What do you mean?
W It's her youngest daughter's birthday today, and they're having a pajama party.
M Oh, that makes more sense.
W Mrs. Wilson also brought us this cake and _____ _____ _____.

다음 상황 설명을 듣고, Sean이 웨이터에게 할 말로 가장 적절한 것을 고르시오.

Sean: Excuse me, _____

① can we have the menu please?
② I'm afraid this is not what we ordered.
③ Why hasn't our food been served yet?
④ would you like to have dinner with us?
⑤ when are we getting the high chair we asked for?

W Sean is going out for dinner with his family today. They go to his favorite Korean restaurant, which _____ _____ _____ on Fridays. They have to wait for over an hour to get a table. He and his family finally sit down, and he _____ _____ _____ _____ _____ for his 5-year-old son. The waiter says that he will be right back with a high chair, _____ _____ _____ _____. All the food is served, but the waiter _____ _____ _____ _____ a high chair. In this situation, what would Sean most likely say to the waiter?

고난도 모의고사 02

점수 /20

01 대화를 듣고, 여자가 구입할 자전거로 가장 적절한 것을 고르시오.

02 대화를 듣고, K Mobile에 관해 언급되지 <u>않은</u> 것을 고르시오

① 점포 위치   ② 서비스 품질
③ 특별 할인 행사   ④ 인터넷 요금
⑤ 인터넷 속도

03 대화를 듣고, 남자가 여자에게 전화한 목적으로 가장 적절한 것을 고르시오.

① 점포 위치를 알려주려고
② 배송 방법에 대해 상의하려고
③ 배송 실수에 대해 사과하려고
④ 두고 간 물건이 있음을 알려주려고
⑤ 배달 서비스 만족도를 확인하려고

04 대화를 듣고, 두 사람이 만날 시각을 고르시오.

① 5:00 p.m.   ② 5:30 p.m.   ③ 6:00 p.m.
④ 6:30 p.m.   ⑤ 7:00 p.m.

05 다음 그림의 상황에 가장 적절한 대화를 고르시오.

①   ②   ③   ④   ⑤

06 대화를 듣고, 두 사람이 대화하는 장소로 가장 적절한 것을 고르시오.

① 과일가게   ② 디저트 카페
③ 생물 실험실   ④ 현지 여행사
⑤ 열대 식물원

07 대화를 듣고, 여자가 남자에게 부탁한 일로 가장 적절한 것을 고르시오.

① 상 차리기   ② 재료 다듬기
③ 소스 맛보기   ④ 요리법 검색하기
⑤ 파스타 주문하기

08 다음을 듣고, 달리기 대회에 관해 언급되지 <u>않은</u> 것을 고르시오.

① 개최 횟수   ② 대회 일시
③ 총 코스 거리   ④ 우승 상품
⑤ 참가 복장

09 다음을 듣고, 무엇에 관한 설명인지 고르시오.

① 드론   ② 열기구   ③ 인공위성
④ 헬리콥터   ⑤ UFO

10 다음을 듣고, 두 사람의 대화가 <u>어색한</u> 것을 고르시오.

①   ②   ③   ④   ⑤

11 대화를 듣고, 남자가 대화 직후에 할 일로 가장 적절한 것을 고르시오.

① 집 청소하기
② TV 모델 비교하기
③ 창고에서 재고 확인하기
④ 무선 청소기 조작법 배우기
⑤ 온라인으로 청소기 주문하기

12 대화를 듣고, 남자가 받을 요가 수업이 시작하는 시각을 고르시오.

① 7:30 a.m.　② 8:30 a.m.　③ 9:30 a.m.
④ 10:30 a.m.　⑤ 11:30 a.m.

13 다음 배치도를 보면서 대화를 듣고, 두 사람이 선택할 구역을 고르시오.

①	Restroom	②	③
Convenience Store	Lake		Food Trucks
	④	⑤	

14 대화를 듣고, 여자가 어제 한 일로 가장 적절한 것을 고르시오.

① 집들이하기　　② 벼룩시장 가기
③ 커피메이커 사기　④ 여행 기념품 사기
⑤ 동료와 쇼핑몰 가기

15 다음을 듣고, 방송의 목적으로 가장 적절한 것을 고르시오

① 응급 처치법을 설명하려고
② 독감 예방법을 알려주려고
③ 겨울방학 일정을 공지하려고
④ 효과적인 손 씻는 방법을 소개하려고
⑤ 겨울방학을 유익하게 보내도록 권장하려고

16 대화를 듣고, 여자가 지불할 금액을 고르시오.

① $550　　② $600　　③ $650
④ $700　　⑤ $750

17 대화를 듣고, 남자의 마지막 말에 대한 여자의 응답으로 가장 적절한 것을 고르시오.

Woman: _____

① I think someone smoked in this room.
② Your request is not as specific as mine.
③ Why haven't I received the ice I asked for?
④ I'd like to reserve this room for three nights.
⑤ This room has a great view of the ocean.

18 대화를 듣고, 여자의 마지막 말에 대한 남자의 응답으로 가장 적절한 것을 고르시오.

Man: _____

① Right. I became famous with my songs.
② I want to speak French more fluently.
③ I came to Korea to study K-pop music.
④ I lived in England for 3 years when I was young.
⑤ I watched many movies and TV shows in English.

19 대화를 듣고, 남자의 마지막 말에 대한 여자의 응답으로 가장 적절한 것을 고르시오.

Woman: _____

① I've already told you who I voted for.
② I won't be able to vote because I am 18.
③ The candidate I voted for is a good person.
④ If I were you, I would vote for any of the candidates.
⑤ We'd better start paying attention now that we can vote.

20 다음 상황 설명을 듣고, Peter가 여자에게 할 말로 가장 적절한 것을 고르시오.

Peter: _____

① Can I help you with the desk?
② Are you back from the gym already?
③ I don't think this is the desk I ordered.
④ Can I borrow your car? I'm running late.
⑤ I'm sorry, but I'm the driver of the truck.

Dictation 02

◆ 다시 듣고, 빈칸에 들어갈 알맞은 단어를 써보세요.

정답 및 해설 p.150

01 그림 정보 파악

대화를 듣고, 여자가 구입할 자전거로 가장 적절한 것을 고르시오.

① ② ③
④ ⑤

M Hello, how can I help you?

W I'm looking for a bicycle for my daughter. She's turning 7 next month.

M Okay, then this should be ＿＿＿＿＿＿ ＿＿＿＿＿＿ ＿＿＿＿＿＿ ＿＿＿＿＿＿ her.

W Is the front wheel bigger than the back wheel?

M Yes, it is. This is a very popular model.

W Okay, do you have that model ＿＿＿＿＿＿ ＿＿＿＿＿＿ ＿＿＿＿＿＿?

M Sure, this one has 2 small ＿＿＿＿＿＿ ＿＿＿＿＿＿ ＿＿＿＿＿＿ the back wheel.

W It ＿＿＿＿＿＿ ＿＿＿＿＿＿ ＿＿＿＿＿＿, too. Can we take the training wheels off later?

M Of course, you can.

W Good! ＿＿＿＿＿＿ ＿＿＿＿＿＿ ＿＿＿＿＿＿ ＿＿＿＿＿＿.

02 언급하지 않은 내용 찾기

대화를 듣고, K Mobile에 관해 언급되지 않은 것을 고르시오

① 점포 위치　　② 서비스 품질
③ 특별 할인 행사　　④ 인터넷 요금
⑤ 인터넷 속도

🔊 Listening Tip

Internet의 발음을 잘 들어보면 /인터넷/이 아니라 /이널넷/으로 들릴 거예요. 이처럼 'n' 뒤에 오는 't'는 보통 발음하지 않아요.

W I need to find a new 🔊Internet provider.

M What's wrong with the one you have right now?

W It's too slow. I'm going to check out the new store right ＿＿＿＿＿＿ ＿＿＿＿＿＿ ＿＿＿＿＿＿ ＿＿＿＿＿＿ ＿＿＿＿＿＿.

M You mean K Mobile? That's my Internet provider.

W Really? I heard the ＿＿＿＿＿＿ ＿＿＿＿＿＿ ＿＿＿＿＿＿ is really good.

M Yes, and ＿＿＿＿＿＿ ＿＿＿＿＿＿ ＿＿＿＿＿＿ $30 a month for the Internet service.

W Wow! That's $10 less than what I'm paying.

M Then you should switch because the Internet ＿＿＿＿＿＿ ＿＿＿＿＿＿ ＿＿＿＿＿＿ ＿＿＿＿＿＿.

W I should have talked to you about my Internet provider sooner.

대화를 듣고, 남자가 여자에게 전화한 목적으로 가장 적절한 것을 고르시오.

① 점포 위치를 알려주려고
② 배송 방법에 대해 상의하려고
③ 배송 실수에 대해 사과하려고
④ 두고 간 물건이 있음을 알려주려고
⑤ 배달 서비스 만족도를 확인하려고

[Telephone rings.]

W Hello.

M Hello, my name is Rick Price, and I'm the store manager of Best Furniture. May I speak to Ms. Miller?

W Hi, Mr. Price. This is she. I was just about to call the store. I think there's been a mistake.

M Yes, Ms. Miller. _____ _____ _____ I am calling you.

W I told the delivery person that we didn't order a table, but he _____ _____.

M I sincerely apologize for _____ _____ _____, Ms. Miller.

W When will I be getting the desk I ordered?

M It will be _____ _____ _____ tomorrow, ma'am.

W All right. Please make sure that I _____ _____ _____ _____ this time.

대화를 듣고, 두 사람이 만날 시각을 고르시오.

① 5:00 p.m.　　② 5:30 p.m.
③ 6:00 p.m.　　④ 6:30 p.m.
⑤ 7:00 p.m.

W I can't believe it's Christmas again.

M I know. Time flies.

W What time is our dinner reservation tomorrow? Is it at 7 p.m.?

M Actually, I _____ _____ _____ _____ for us tomorrow. I called too late.

W That's okay. We can get there early and wait for a table.

M Do you want to meet at the restaurant at 6 p.m.?

W Shouldn't we _____ _____ _____ _____? How about 5 p.m.?

M That might be a little too early. We _____ _____ _____ _____ 5:30.

W That's fine. I don't _____ _____ _____ _____.

M Okay, then let's do that.

05 그림 상황에 적절한 대화 찾기

다음 그림의 상황에 가장 적절한 대화를 고르시오.

①   ②   ③   ④   ⑤

① **M**   Are you going to take the elevator?

   W   No, I'm _____ _____ _____.

② **M**   Do you work here at the department store?

   W   Yes, I've been working here since 2010.

③ **M**   Does your child know how to read?

   W   Yes, he _____ _____

      every day.

④ **M**   Can I talk to you for a second?

   W   Sure, let me just _____ _____

      _____ _____.

⑤ **M**   Do you want me _____ _____

      _____ _____ for you?

   W   That would be great. I appreciate that.

06 장소 추론

대화를 듣고, 두 사람이 대화하는 장소로 가장 적절한 것을 고르시오.

① 과일가게   ② 디저트 카페
③ 생물 실험실   ④ 현지 여행사
⑤ 열대 식물원

M   Margaret, do you know what that is?

W   I'm not sure. Is it a watermelon?

M   Well, it is _____ _____ _____

     _____, but it is certainly not a watermelon.

W   I knew it was _____ _____ _____

     _____ a watermelon. What is it then?

M   It's called a honeydew melon.

W   I guess _____ _____ _____

     _____ its name has the word "honey" in it.

M   Yes, it is sweet. It's one of my favorite fruits, and it's a really popular fruit in this country.

W   _____ _____ _____. I want to try it.

M   Sure. I think you'll love them since they're so delicious.

W   *I can't wait to try it. _____ _____

     _____ _____ how much it is.

✱ 교육부 지정 의사소통 기능: **기대 표현하기**   능(김) 5 | 비 2

I can't wait to ~. 나는 빨리 ~하고 싶어.

• **I can't wait to** see you. 나는 빨리 널 보고 싶어.
• **I can't wait to** visit there. 나는 빨리 그곳을 방문하고 싶어.

대화를 듣고, 여자가 남자에게 부탁한 일로 가장
적절한 것을 고르시오.

① 상 차리기 ② 재료 다듬기
③ 소스 맛보기 ④ 요리법 검색하기
⑤ 파스타 주문하기

M Something smells good. What are you cooking, Mom?

W I'm cooking creamy garlic pasta.

M I don't think we've ever had that at home.

W You're right. I'm making this ＿＿＿＿＿＿ ＿＿＿＿＿＿ ＿＿＿＿＿＿ ＿＿＿＿＿＿.

M Where did you ＿＿＿＿＿＿ ＿＿＿＿＿＿ ＿＿＿＿＿＿ ＿＿＿＿＿＿?

W One of my friends showed me how to make this the other day.

M Well, I hope it tastes ＿＿＿＿＿＿ ＿＿＿＿＿＿ ＿＿＿＿＿＿ ＿＿＿＿＿＿ ＿＿＿＿＿＿.

W Can you ＿＿＿＿＿＿ ＿＿＿＿＿＿ ＿＿＿＿＿＿ to see if it's any good?

M Yes, but I'm sure it's good. You've always been a good cook.

W Thanks.

다음을 듣고, 달리기 대회에 관해 언급되지 않은
것을 고르시오.

① 개최 횟수 ② 대회 일시
③ 총 코스 거리 ④ 우승 상품
⑤ 참가 복장

M Hello, everyone. If you haven't signed up for our 10th ＿＿＿＿＿＿ ＿＿＿＿＿＿ ＿＿＿＿＿＿ yet, you must do so by 9 a.m. tomorrow in order to participate in the event. It ＿＿＿＿＿＿ ＿＿＿＿＿＿ ＿＿＿＿＿＿ this Saturday, and the first group will start at 8 a.m. ＿＿＿＿＿＿ ＿＿＿＿＿＿ ＿＿＿＿＿＿ 5 kilometers as this is a short race. Make sure to ＿＿＿＿＿＿ ＿＿＿＿＿＿ ＿＿＿＿＿＿ and running shoes. However, *you are not allowed to wear jeans. If you have any questions or concerns about the race, please don't hesitate to email me.

＊ 교육부 지정 의사소통 기능: 금지하기　　　동(이) 6

You are not allowed to ~. 너는 ~하면 안 돼.
• **You are not allowed to** feed birds here. 너는 여기서 새들에게 먹이를 주면 안 돼.
• **You are not allowed to** watch TV past 11 p.m. 너는 밤 11시 지나서 TV를 시청하면 안 돼.

다음을 듣고, 무엇에 관한 설명인지 고르시오.

① 드론 ② 열기구
③ 인공위성 ④ 헬리콥터
⑤ UFO

M This is a flying object that comes in various sizes and shapes. This can ＿＿＿＿＿＿ ＿＿＿＿＿＿ ＿＿＿＿＿＿, but this has no pilots or passengers. This can ＿＿＿＿＿＿ ＿＿＿＿＿＿ ＿＿＿＿＿＿ military purposes such as dropping a bomb in enemy territory, but this can also be used for commercial purposes such as

_____ _____ _____

_____ . Many people like to fly one of these objects

_____ _____ _____ , too. You can

learn to fly one by yourself, or you can take lessons at a

special school.

---

10 어색한 대화 찾기

다음을 듣고, 두 사람의 대화가 <u>어색한</u> 것을 고르시오.

①   ②   ③   ④   ⑤

① M   Do you think I _____ _____

    _____ _____ ?

   W   I would if I were you.

② M   Could I talk to you for a second?

   W   Can it wait? I'm busy right now.

③ M   I'll call you as soon as I'm done.

   W   _____ _____ _____ .

④ M   I don't think I can eat any more.

   W   You _____ _____ _____ finish

    it then.

⑤ M   Do you know where the post office is?

   W   Sure, _____ _____ _____

    _____ my office tomorrow.

---

11 할 일 파악

대화를 듣고, 남자가 대화 직후에 할 일로 가장 적절한 것을 고르시오.

① 집 청소하기
② TV 모델 비교하기
③ 창고에서 재고 확인하기
④ 무선 청소기 조작법 배우기
⑤ 온라인으로 청소기 주문하기

🔊 **Listening Tip**

shipped에서처럼 무성음([p]) 다음에 과거형을 만드는 -ed가 오면 -ed의 발음은 [t]가 됩니다. 따라서 shipped는 /쉽트/로 발음해요.

M   Excuse me, do you know where I can find vacuum cleaners?

W   Yes, you'll find them next to the TVs.

M   Do you have cordless vacuum cleaners?

W   Oh, we just _____ _____ _____

    _____ we had in stock.

M   When do you think you'll _____ _____

    _____ _____ again?

W   We'll probably have them in about 10 days.

M   That's not good. I'm having a party at my place this weekend.

W   If you _____ _____ _____

    _____ right now, it'll be 🔊 shipped to your place in 2 days.

M Will there be an extra charge for shipping?

W No, shipping is always free.

M Great! Then I'll _____ _____

_____. I should be able to use it before the party.

대화를 듣고, 남자가 받을 요가 수업이 시작하는 시각을 고르시오.

① 7:30 a.m.   ② 8:30 a.m.
③ 9:30 a.m.   ④ 10:30 a.m.
⑤ 11:30 a.m.

[Telephone rings.]

W Thanks for calling California Fitness. How may I help you?

M Hi, I'd like to register for one of your yoga classes.

W Sure. We have _____ _____ _____

_____ 9:30 a.m. and 11:30 a.m.

M Don't you have a class that starts at 10:30 a.m.?

W Yes, we do, but that class is currently full.

M Can you add me _____ _____

_____ _____ for that class?

W Sure, but it may take over a month before you can sign up.

M Oh, I _____ _____ _____

_____ that long.

W Then you'll have to choose between the 2 classes.

M Okay, then I'll just sign up _____ _____

_____ _____.

다음 배치도를 보면서 대화를 듣고, 두 사람이 선택할 구역을 고르시오.

①	Restroom	②	③
Convenience Store	Lake		Food Trucks
	④	⑤	

M This is such a beautiful park, isn't it?

W It's an amazing park. I don't know how they made

_____ _____ in the middle of this city.

M I don't, either, but I'm glad that we have it.

W Where should we have our picnic?

M Well, we shouldn't be _____ _____

_____.

W I agree. We packed _____ _____, right?

M Yes, we have more than enough food.

W Then we don't really have to be near _____

_____ _____.

M That's right. It would be better to be near the convenience store.

W Okay, then there's _____ _____ _____ left.

---

14 한 일 파악

대화를 듣고, 여자가 어제 한 일로 가장 적절한 것을 고르시오.

① 집들이하기
② 벼룩시장 가기
③ 커피메이커 사기
④ 여행 기념품 사기
⑤ 동료와 쇼핑몰 가기

M You have such a beautiful apartment, Janice.

W Thanks, Mike. I'm so glad that all our coworkers were able to come.

M Yes, everyone was _____ _____ _____ _____ to your housewarming party.

W And thank you so much for the coffeemaker. Where did you get it?

M Oh, I _____ _____ _____ the shopping mall near my house.

W Can you take me there some time? I need to get a few things for my apartment.

M Sure. By the way, _____ _____ _____ _____ all these interesting mugs and glasses?

W I _____ _____ _____ _____ _____ yesterday and bought most of them there.

M Really? They look very exotic.

---

15 목적 파악

다음을 듣고, 방송의 목적으로 가장 적절한 것을 고르시오

① 응급 처치법을 설명하려고
② 독감 예방법을 알려주려고
③ 겨울방학 일정을 공지하려고
④ 효과적인 손 씻는 방법을 소개하려고
⑤ 겨울방학을 유익하게 보내도록 권장하려고

M Hello, everyone. Today is the last day of school as winter break starts next week. Before I let you go today, I wanted to tell you about what you can do to prevent yourself _____ _____ _____ _____. First, you should _____ _____ _____ _____. Second, you should avoid touching your eyes, nose, or mouth. Lastly, try to avoid close contact with _____ _____ _____ _____. And if you get sick, it is very _____ _____ _____ _____ at home. I hope all of you have a great winter break!

대화를 듣고, 여자가 지불할 금액을 고르시오.

① $550 ② $600 ③ $650
④ $700 ⑤ $750

[Telephone rings.]

M The Greatest World Tour. How can I help you?

W Hi, I'm calling about the Vietnam package tour that I saw in the newspaper.

M Yes, that's our most popular package tour.

W Is it $500 per person?

M Yes, that's correct, but the $500 doesn't _____
_____ _____ _____ .

W If I buy an airline ticket from you, it'll be $200 extra, right?

M Right, but you can purchase your ticket from the airline directly.

W I see. I'll be _____ _____ _____ ,
so I only need one room.

M Oh, then you'll be _____ _____
_____ $50.

W I see. I'll sign up for one person, and I'll buy _____
_____ _____ from you, too.

---

17 이어질 응답 찾기

대화를 듣고, 남자의 마지막 말에 대한 여자의 응답으로 가장 적절한 것을 고르시오.

Woman: _____

① I think someone smoked in this room.
② Your request is not as specific as mine.
③ Why haven't I received the ice I asked for?
④ I'd like to reserve this room for 3 nights.
⑤ This room has a great view of the ocean.

[Telephone rings.]

M This is the front desk. How may I help you?

W Hi, my name is Kathy Smith, and I'm in room 1705.

M Yes, Ms. Smith. We're going to get you the ice you
_____ _____ _____
_____ _____ . We're very sorry for the delay.

W Oh, I just received the bucket of ice. Thank you.

M You're very welcome. Is there anything else I can do for you?

W Would it be possible _____ _____
_____ _____ to a different room?

M If there are any vacancies, you can move. But it will take a while for me to check.

W Well, can you _____ _____ _____
_____ ? I don't think I can stay in this room any longer.

M Oh, is there _____ _____ _____
_____ _____ ?

대화를 듣고, 여자의 마지막 말에 대한 남자의 응답으로 가장 적절한 것을 고르시오.

Man: _____

① Right. I became famous with my songs.
② I want to speak French more fluently.
③ I came to Korea to study K-pop music.
④ I lived in England for 3 years when I was young.
⑤ I watched many movies and TV shows in English.

W Welcome to England, Justin. How was your concert last night?
M It was great. A lot of _____ _____ _____ and supported me.
W You've become one of the most famous singers in the world almost overnight.
M I'm just _____ _____ _____ everyone else, and I'm really thankful to all my fans in the world.
W You're 23 years old and _____ _____ _____ _____ an English-speaking country. Is that right?
M That is correct. I've been living in Korea ever since I was born.
W Yet, you speak English so well. _____ _____ _____ _____ to learn English?

대화를 듣고, 남자의 마지막 말에 대한 여자의 응답으로 가장 적절한 것을 고르시오.

Woman: _____

① I've already told you who I voted for.
② I won't be able to vote because I am 18.
③ The candidate I voted for is a good person.
④ If I were you, I would vote for any of the candidates.
⑤ We'd better start paying attention now that we can vote.

W How old are you, William?
M I'm turning 18 next month.
W Are you going to vote in April?
M Don't I have to be at least 19 in order to vote?
W No, the law _____ _____ _____. You only have to be 18 to vote.
M I didn't know that. You turned 18 last month, right?
W Yes, I _____ _____ _____ _____, too.
M Do you know whom you're going to vote for in this election?
W That's the problem. I know I can vote, but I don't know _____ _____ _____ _____ _____.
M I don't know any of the candidates. I've _____ _____ _____ _____ to politics.

다음 상황 설명을 듣고, Peter가 여자에게 할 말로 가장 적절한 것을 고르시오.

Peter: _____

① Can I help you with the desk?
② Are you back from the gym already?
③ I don't think this is the desk I ordered.
④ Can I borrow your car? I'm running late.
⑤ I'm sorry, but I'm the driver of the truck.

W Peter sees a moving truck in front of his apartment building. It's blocking his car and he _____ _____ _____ _____ _____ soon. He looks around to find the driver of the truck but _____ _____ _____ _____. He comes back after taking a shower and sees a young woman trying to take a desk out of the truck by herself. He wants to _____ _____ _____ _____ _____ before he asks her to move her truck. In this situation, what would Peter most likely to say to the woman?

고난도 모의고사 03

정답 및 해설 p.158

점수 /18

01 대화를 듣고, 여자가 구입할 장난감을 고르시오.

①   ②   ③

④   ⑤

02 대화를 듣고, 두 사람이 대화하는 장소로 가장 적절한 곳을 고르시오.

① 택시 승강장 　　② 공항 접수대
③ 호텔 접수대 　　④ 음식점 계산대
⑤ 셔틀버스 탑승장

03 대화를 듣고, 여자의 심정으로 가장 적절한 것을 고르시오.

① happy 　　② afraid 　　③ proud
④ shocked 　　⑤ disappointed

04 다음을 듣고, Siam Thai Cooking School에 관한 내용과 일치하지 않는 것을 고르시오.

① 채소와 허브 키우는 법을 배운다.
② 구시가지의 중심에 있다.
③ 두 가지 과정이 있다.
④ 반나절 과정은 4시간이 걸린다.
⑤ 태국 요리 식당도 운영한다.

05 대화를 듣고, 여자의 조언으로 가장 적절한 것을 고르시오.

① 따뜻한 물을 많이 마셔라.
② 카페인이 든 음료를 줄여라.
③ 커피 대신 에너지 드링크를 마셔라.
④ 공부할 때는 집중력이 필요하다.
⑤ 맑은 공기가 목을 튼튼하게 한다.

06 다음을 듣고, 무엇에 관한 내용인지 고르시오.

① 전통 떡의 유래 　　② 떡 만드는 과정
③ 위생 관리 중요성 　　④ 조리 실습 시 유의점
⑤ 요리사 직업 체험 일정

07 다음을 보면서 대화를 듣고, 내용과 일치하지 않는 것을 고르시오.

> **Happy Dog Volunteer Project**
>
> ① **When:** Saturday, 10 a.m. ~ 4 p.m.
> ② **Where:** the Animal Center
> 　**Activities:**
> ③ • walk the dogs
> ④ • give the dogs a bath
> ⑤ • make dog houses
>
> *Come and make friends with the poor dogs!*

08 대화를 듣고, Michael이 일을 그만둔 이유로 가장 적절한 것을 고르시오.

① 건강이 좋지 않아서
② 업무가 너무 많아서
③ 급여에 불만이 있어서
④ 일이 적성에 맞지 않아서
⑤ 상사와 사이가 좋지 않아서

09 대화를 듣고, 여자가 전화를 건 목적으로 가장 적절한 것을 고르시오.

① 한복을 빌리려고
② 관광 안내를 부탁하려고
③ 안내해 준 것에 감사하려고
④ 기차 출발 시간을 알려주려고
⑤ 한옥마을 위치를 물어보려고

10 다음을 듣고, 여자가 한 일을 순서대로 배열한 것 고르시오.

(A)  (B)  (C)

① (A) − (B) − (C)　② (A) − (C) − (B)
③ (B) − (A) − (C)　④ (B) − (C) − (A)
⑤ (C) − (A) − (B)

11 다음을 듣고, 방송의 목적으로 가장 적절한 것을 고르시오.

① 도시 관광 안내　② 비행기 구조 소개
③ 비행기 도착 안내　④ 공공장소 예의 안내
⑤ 승무원 직업 체험 홍보

12 대화를 듣고, 여자의 마지막 말에 대한 남자의 응답으로 가장 적절한 것을 고르시오.

① You're right. Let's just run.
② I can't wait to see the movie.
③ We were lucky to get the tickets.
④ I'm sorry, but I didn't listen to you.
⑤ See? We shouldn't have taken the bus.

13 대화를 듣고, 남자의 마지막 말에 대한 여자의 응답으로 가장 적절한 것을 고르시오.

① Let's go another time, then.
② How long does the hiking course take?
③ How about going on a picnic this afternoon?
④ Okay. What time should I meet up with you?
⑤ I'm thinking of going to Dobong Mountain.

14 다음을 듣고, 주어진 상황에서 할 말로 가장 적절한 것을 고르시오.

① I promise I'll do my best.
② Mom won't understand me.
③ Can you repeat what you said?
④ I'm sure I'll be a great scientist.
⑤ I will learn how to sing and dance.

15 다음을 듣고, 남자가 주장하는 내용으로 가장 적절한 것을 고르시오.

① Happiness is always near you.
② Children always make us laugh.
③ Traveling makes our heart sing.
④ Don't forget to enjoy your work.
⑤ When we get something hard to get, we are happy.

[서답형 1] 대화를 듣고, 빈칸에 적절한 말을 주어진 철자로 시작하여 한 단어로 쓰시오.

Oliver's Restaurant

Our Operating Hours are:

• Monday to Friday	11 a.m. to 9 p.m. (Last order 8 p.m.)
• Saturday	11 a.m. to 10:30 p.m.
• S_____ Break	4 p.m. to 5:30 p.m.

We are closed on Sundays.

[서답형 2] 다음을 듣고, 질문에 대한 답이 되도록 빈칸에 적절한 말을 주어진 철자로 시작하여 한 단어로 쓰시오.

Question: What does the woman suggest to make your dreams come true?

➡ She suggests that we believe in our t_____ and dreams to make our dreams come true.

[서답형 3] 다음을 듣고, 남자가 말한 내용과 일치하도록 빈칸에 적절한 말을 주어진 철자로 시작하여 한 단어로 쓰시오.

Sometimes, it's easier to tell a s_____ something very personal.

Dictation 03

◆ 다시 듣고, 빈칸에 들어갈 알맞은 단어를 써보세요.

정답 및 해설 p.158

---

01 그림 정보 파악

대화를 듣고, 여자가 구입할 장난감을 고르시오.

① ② ③ ④ ⑤

M Hello. May I help you?

W Yes, please. I want to buy a toy for my dog.

M How about these balls? Many dogs like to play with balls.

W He already _____ _____ _____.

M Okay. This chicken-shaped one _____ _____ _____ _____ is popular.

W He doesn't like that kind of toy.

M What does your dog like to do?

W He likes to _____ _____ _____ _____.

M Then how about this shoe-shaped toy? You won't have to worry about your shoes any more.

W Great! _____ _____ _____.

---

02 장소 추론

대화를 듣고, 두 사람이 대화하는 장소로 가장 적절한 곳을 고르시오.

① 택시 승강장　　② 공항 접수대
③ 호텔 접수대　　④ 음식점 계산대
⑤ 셔틀버스 탑승장

M Good morning. May I check out?

W Sure. Was _____ _____ _____?

M Yes, it was very nice.

W That's great. Did you _____ _____ _____ the minibar?

M No, I didn't.

W Okay. Here's your bill.

M Thanks. By the way, I need to _____ _____ _____ _____.

W I see. A free airport shuttle is leaving in half an hour.

M Great. _____ _____ _____ _____. Thank you so much.

---

03 심정 추론

대화를 듣고, 여자의 심정으로 가장 적절한 것을 고르시오.

① happy　　② afraid
③ proud　　④ shocked
⑤ disappointed

W Dad, look at that bag in the window. Isn't it nice?

M Oh, it's very nice.

W That's the most popular style these days.

M But I think it's _____ _____ _____

you.

W That's okay. I need a small bag. * I wonder how much it is.

M Why don't we go in and check it out? If the price is reasonable, I'll buy it _____ _____ _____ _____.

W Really? Thank you so much, Dad. _____ _____ _____.

04 일치하지 않는 내용 찾기

다음을 듣고, Siam Thai Cooking School 에 관한 내용과 일치하지 **않는** 것을 고르시오.

① 채소와 허브 키우는 법을 배운다.
② 구시가지의 중심에 있다.
③ 두 가지 과정이 있다.
④ 반나절 과정은 4시간이 걸린다.
⑤ 태국 요리 식당도 운영한다.

🔊 **Listening Tip**
'-ed'는 유성음 뒤에서는 [d]로, 무성음 뒤에서는 [t]로 발음하고, 'd'나 't' 뒤에서는 [id]로 발음하지요. 따라서 located는 /로케이티드/로 발음해야 하는데 모음 사이에 있는 't'는 / ㄹ /로 발음하게 되어 /로케이릳/처럼 발음해요.

W Welcome to Siam Thai Cooking School. We are not just a cooking school where you simply cook and eat. You can also learn _____ _____ _____ _____ and herbs here. The school is 🔊located in _____ _____ _____ the old town of Chiang Mai. We have 2 courses. A full-day course is 8 hours long, and a half-day course is 4 hours long. We _____ _____ _____. We're sure you will never forget your time here.

05 조언 파악

대화를 듣고, 여자의 조언으로 가장 적절한 것을 고르시오.

① 따뜻한 물을 많이 마셔라.
② 카페인이 든 음료를 줄여라.
③ 커피 대신 에너지 드링크를 마셔라.
④ 공부할 때는 집중력이 필요하다.
⑤ 맑은 공기가 목을 튼튼하게 한다.

W What's wrong?

M I cough a lot and sometimes _____ _____ _____, Doctor.

W [Pause] Hmm, you don't have a fever. Do you drink a lot of coffee or energy drinks?

M I always drink energy drinks to _____ _____ _____ _____.

W Those drinks contain a lot of caffeine, and too much caffeine can _____ _____ _____.

M Oh, I didn't know that.

W You need to _____ _____ _____ _____ with caffeine in them so that your throat can get better.

M I see. Thank you, Doctor.

---

06 주제 추론

다음을 듣고, 무엇에 관한 내용인지 고르시오.

① 전통 떡의 유래
② 떡 만드는 과정
③ 위생 관리 중요성
④ 조리 실습 시 유의점
⑤ 요리사 직업 체험 일정

M Hello, everyone. Today you're going to make traditional Korean rice cake. Make groups of 4 people and sit around the tables. _____ _____ _____, there are a few things I want you to _____ _____ _____. First, make sure you wash your hands. Second, be careful when you _____ _____ _____. Lastly, _____ _____ _____ when you cook. All right, let's start.

---

07 도표와 일치하지 않는 내용 찾기

다음을 보면서 대화를 듣고, 내용과 일치하지 <u>않는</u> 것을 고르시오.

Happy Dog Volunteer Project

① **When:** Saturday, 10 a.m. ~ 4 p.m.
② **Where:** the Animal Center
 Activities:
③ • walk the dogs
④ • give the dogs a bath
⑤ • make dog houses

Come and make friends with the poor dogs!

[Telephone rings.]

M Thanks for calling Happy Dog. What can I help you with?

W Hi, I'd like to join your volunteer project with dogs.

M *Why do you _____ _____ _____ _____?

W When I saw some poor dogs on TV, I wanted to help them.

M We work at the Animal Center _____ _____ _____ 10 a.m. to 4 p.m. Is that okay?

W Sure. What can I do there?

M You can walk the dogs, give them _____ _____, and _____ _____ _____.

W No problem. I'll do my best.

M Thank you for joining us. See you this Saturday.

✳ 교육부 지정 의사소통 기능: **이유 묻기**   비 5 | 지 4

Why do you ~? 너는 왜 ~하니?

• **Why do you** want to go there? 너는 왜 거기에 가려고 하니?
• **Why do you** think so? 너는 왜 그렇게 생각하니?

08 이유 파악

대화를 듣고, Michael이 일을 그만둔 이유로 가장 적절한 것을 고르시오.

① 건강이 좋지 않아서
② 업무가 너무 많아서
③ 급여에 불만이 있어서
④ 일이 적성에 맞지 않아서
⑤ 상사와 사이가 좋지 않아서

W Hey, Peter! I heard Michael quit his job. Is that true?

M I didn't know that. Where did you hear that?

W I heard that from his friend.

M Did Michael work overtime?

W I don't think so. He _____ _____ _____ _____ every day.

M Then _____ _____ _____ _____ his job?

W I heard he worked hard and his salary was good, but he didn't _____ _____ _____ his boss.

M Did Michael do something wrong?

W _____ _____ _____ _____ _____. His boss wanted to focus on sales, and Michael wanted to focus on quality.

09 목적 파악

대화를 듣고, 여자가 전화를 건 목적으로 가장 적절한 것을 고르시오.

① 한복을 빌리려고
② 관광 안내를 부탁하려고
③ 안내해 준 것에 감사하려고
④ 기차 출발 시간을 알려주려고
⑤ 한옥마을 위치를 물어보려고

🔊 **Listening** Tip

did you에서처럼 [d] 소리로 끝나는 단어 뒤에 'y'로 시작하는 단어가 오면 두 소리가 연음되어 /쥬/로 발음하게 돼요. 그래서 /디드 유/가 아니라 /디쥬/로 발음해요.

[Cell phone rings.]

M Hello.

W Hi, Jiho. _____ _____ _____ _____. My train is leaving in 10 minutes.

M Great. I hope you _____ _____ _____ _____.

W I really enjoyed it.

M Which place 🔊did you like most in my town?

W I liked the Jeonju Hanok Village most. I enjoyed walking around in hanbok.

M Yes, that was _____ _____ _____ _____!

W I'm calling to thank you _____ _____ _____ _____.

M I enjoyed it, too.

그림 순서 배열

다음을 듣고, 여자가 한 일을 순서대로 배열한 것 고르시오.

(A)　　　(B)　　　(C)

① (A) – (B) – (C)　　② (A) – (C) – (B)
③ (B) – (A) – (C)　　④ (B) – (C) – (A)
⑤ (C) – (A) – (B)

W I had fun today. I had no school because today is my school's 30th anniversary. My dad and I decided _____ _____ _____ _____, so he took the afternoon off for me. _____ _____ _____ _____, we had lunch together. I had pasta and it was delicious! Then we _____ _____ _____ the musical and it was amazing. We both liked it very much. When we came home, I felt a little tired. But before I went to bed, I _____ _____ _____.

11 목적 파악

다음을 듣고, 방송의 목적으로 가장 적절한 것을 고르시오.

① 도시 관광 안내
② 비행기 구조 소개
③ 비행기 도착 안내
④ 공공장소 예의 안내
⑤ 승무원 직업 체험 홍보

M Good afternoon, everyone. We are _____ _____ _____ Istanbul International Airport. It is 4:30 in the afternoon. It is _____ _____ and the temperature is 25 degrees Celsius. You can't use the restroom from now on. Please make sure you _____ _____ _____ _____ and fasten your seat belts until we _____ _____ _____ _____. Thank you.

12 이어질 응답 찾기

대화를 듣고, 여자의 마지막 말에 대한 남자의 응답으로 가장 적절한 것을 고르시오.

① You're right. Let's just run.
② I can't wait to see the movie.
③ We were lucky to get the tickets.
④ I'm sorry, but I didn't listen to you.
⑤ See? We shouldn't have taken the bus.

W Hurry up, Leo.
M One minute. I can't run any more.
W We don't _____ _____ _____ _____. The movie starts in 15 minutes.
M This is your fault. You said it would be _____ _____ _____ _____.
W You said _____ _____ _____, too. We shouldn't have stopped for a hamburger.
M I wish we could fly to the theater.
W Come on. We _____ _____ _____ _____ _____ about that.

13 이어질 응답 찾기

대화를 듣고, 남자의 마지막 말에 대한 여자의 응답으로 가장 적절한 것을 고르시오.

① Let's go another time, then.
② How long does the hiking course take?
③ How about going on a picnic this afternoon?
④ Okay. What time should I meet up with you?
⑤ I'm thinking of going to Dobong Mountain.

M Anna, what are you going to do this Sunday?

W I'm not sure yet. What about you?

M I'm going to go hiking with my brother. Do you _____ _____ _____ _____?

W I'd love to. Where are you going?

M We're going to Bukhan Mountain. The scenery there is really beautiful this time of year.

W That sounds great. But I'm not good at hiking. _____ _____ _____ _____?

M Of course. The mountain is _____ _____ _____ _____ _____ and it is not dangerous. And my brother and I _____ _____ _____ _____.

14 상황에 적절한 말 찾기

다음을 듣고, 주어진 상황에서 할 말로 가장 적절한 것을 고르시오.

① I promise I'll do my best.
② Mom won't understand me.
③ Can you repeat what you said?
④ I'm sure I'll be a great scientist.
⑤ I will learn how to sing and dance.

W When you graduate from middle school, you want to go to a design high school. You tell your mother about it for the first time. Your mother is _____ _____ _____ _____ that because she thought you were interested in science. She says that it's not easy to _____ _____ _____, so you should focus more on _____ _____ _____ _____. However, you hope that your mother _____ _____ _____ _____ _____ a design school. In this situation, what would you say to your mother?

15 주장 파악

다음을 듣고, 남자가 주장하는 내용으로 가장 적절한 것을 고르시오.

① Happiness is always near you.
② Children always make us laugh.
③ Traveling makes our heart sing.
④ Don't forget to enjoy your work.
⑤ When we get something hard to get, we are happy.

M Where do _____ _____ _____? Here's the story of 2 children who set out to find a bluebird. They _____ _____ _____ _____ _____ for a long time, but they can't find it. Surprisingly, however, when they return home, they find it _____ _____ _____ backyard. The story explains that happiness is found when you _____ _____ _____

_____. Happiness is _____ _____

_____, but within you.

1

대화를 듣고, 빈칸에 적절한 말을 주어진 철자로
시작하여 한 단어로 쓰시오.

Oliver's Restaurant

Our Operating Hours are:
- **Monday to Friday**
  11 a.m. to 9 p.m.
  (Last order 8 p.m.)
- **Saturday**
  11 a.m. to 10:30 p.m.
- **S_____ Break**
  4 p.m. to 5:30 p.m.

We are closed on Sundays.

[Telephone rings.]

M Oliver's Restaurant. How may I help you?

W What are _____ _____ _____

_____ Friday?

M We are open from 11 a.m. to 9 p.m. on weekdays and take

_____ _____ _____ 8 p.m.

W How about on the weekend?

M From 11 a.m. to 10:30 p.m. on Saturdays. But we are closed
on Sundays.

W I see. Can I _____ _____ _____

for 3 people at 5 o'clock this Saturday?

M I'm sorry. We take an hour and a half off _____

_____ _____ 4 p.m.

W Then how about 5:30?

M Okay. May I have your name?

2

다음을 듣고, 질문에 대한 답이 되도록 빈칸에 적
절한 말을 주어진 철자로 시작하여 한 단어로 쓰
시오.

Question: What does the woman
suggest to make your dreams come
true?

➡ She suggests that we believe in our
t_____ and dreams to make our
dreams come true.

W Have you ever read a novel written by Park Wansuh? She was
one of the greatest novelists in Korea. She wrote 15 novels
and 10 short story collections after she became a writer

_____ _____ _____

_____ 40. When she was young, she could not show

her _____ _____ _____

_____ because of war and poverty. However, she

believed in _____ _____ _____

_____, so she finally became a famous writer. If you

believe in _____ _____ _____

_____ _____ and what you want to do,

you can make your dreams come true someday.

다음을 듣고, 남자가 말한 내용과 일치하도록 빈 칸에 적절한 말을 주어진 철자로 시작하여 한 단어로 쓰시오.

Sometimes, it's easier to tell a
s_____ something very personal.

M   Why do _____ _____ _____
_____ personal details, thoughts, and emotions
online with people they've never met? Why do some people
tell _____ _____ _____ their
problems? This is called the "stranger on the train" effect. It's
about 2 people meeting on the train, having a personal
conversation, and leaving _____ _____
_____ _____ ever again. That's because
_____ _____ _____
_____ worry about being judged or seeing them the
next day. They even feel better because of this experience.

고난도 모의고사 **04**

점수
/18

01 대화를 듣고, 남자가 구입할 시계를 고르시오.

02 대화를 듣고, 두 사람이 대화하고 있는 장소로 가장 적절한 것을 고르시오.

① 서점 　　② 교실 　　③ 도서관
④ 여행사 　　⑤ 영화관

03 대화를 듣고, 남자의 심정으로 가장 적절한 것을 고르시오.

① proud 　　② angry 　　③ excited
④ worried 　　⑤ disappointed

04 다음을 듣고, Golden Cinema Week에 관한 내용과 일치하지 않는 것을 고르시오.

① 옛날 영화를 상영한다.
② 하루에 두 편 상영한다.
③ 마지막 영화가 10시 55분에 끝난다.
④ 회원의 입장료는 10달러이다.
⑤ 첫 영화 상영 30분 전에 극장 문을 연다.

05 대화를 듣고, 여자의 조언으로 가장 적절한 것을 고르시오.

① 수업 시간에 집중해라.
② 친구에게 언제나 솔직해라.
③ 부모님의 말씀을 잘 따라라.
④ 자신을 너무 괴롭게 하지 마라.
⑤ 괴롭힘을 당하는 친구를 도와주어라.

06 다음을 듣고, 무엇에 관한 내용인지 고르시오.

① 노령기의 질병 　　② 청년 일자리 부족
③ 노령 인구의 증가 　　④ 노인 돌봄 서비스
⑤ 자연 환경 오염의 원인

07 다음을 보면서, 대화를 듣고, 내용과 일치하지 않는 것을 고르시오.

> **Winter Ski Camp**
>
> ① **When:** January 15 – 16
> ② **Where:** White Resort
> ③ **Program:**
> • Ski and snowboard lessons
> • A dance competition
> • Face painting
> • A campfire
> ④ **What to Bring:** Extra clothes and gloves
> ⑤ We will go to the resort by school bus. You must arrive at school by 9:00. Please don't be late!

08 대화를 듣고, 남자가 이곳에 온 이유로 가장 적절한 것을 고르시오.

① 숙제를 하기 위해서
② 책을 빌리기 위해서
③ 번역을 부탁하기 위해서
④ 봉사활동을 하기 위해서
⑤ 동생을 데려가기 위해서

09 대화를 듣고, 남자가 전화를 건 목적으로 가장 적절한 것을 고르시오.

① 잡지를 구독하려고
② 인터뷰를 요청하려고
③ 여자를 집에 초대하려고
④ 친구의 안부를 물으려고
⑤ 면접에 대해 물어보려고

10 다음을 듣고, 남자가 한 일을 순서대로 배열한 것을 고르시오.

 (A)    (B)    (C)

① (A) − (C) − (B)   ② (B) − (A) − (C)
③ (B) − (C) − (A)   ④ (C) − (A) − (B)
⑤ (C) − (B) − (A)

11 다음을 듣고, 방송의 목적으로 가장 적절한 것을 고르시오.

① 기차역 공사 안내   ② 선상 시설 이용 안내
③ 열차 운행 취소 안내   ④ 구명조끼 착용법 소개
⑤ 응급구조 교육 참가자 모집

12 대화를 듣고, 여자의 마지막 말에 대한 남자의 응답으로 가장 적절한 것을 고르시오.

① Thanks! I'll do my best.
② I don't have enough time to visit her.
③ Sorry, but I am a stranger here myself.
④ I'll be waiting for her in front of her house.
⑤ No, that's okay. Can you tell her to call me back?

13 대화를 듣고, 남자의 마지막 말에 대한 여자의 응답으로 가장 적절한 것을 고르시오.

① Sure, you can't miss it.
② Okay, I'll give you a hand.
③ Why don't you get some rest?
④ It is, but it makes me feel good.
⑤ Yes, there is one around the corner.

14 다음을 듣고, 주어진 상황에서 할 말로 가장 적절한 것을 고르시오.

① Thank you for helping me.
② How do you like your meal?
③ I haven't seen you in a long time.
④ I'm sorry. I mistook you for my friend.
⑤ I'm sorry to have kept you waiting so long.

15 다음을 듣고, 여자가 주장하는 내용으로 가장 적절한 것을 고르시오.

① Buy a new keyboard.
② Don't use the keyboard.
③ Clean your keyboard often.
④ Stay away from the keyboard.
⑤ Wear gloves before you use the keyboard.

[서답형 1] 대화를 듣고, 빈칸에 적절한 말을 주어진 철자로 시작하여 한 단어로 쓰시오.

Swimming Class

Student Name: Bora Kim
- **Level:** ☑ Beginner ☐ Intermediate ☐ Advanced
- **Class:** ☐ Free Swimming (Monday ~ Sunday)
  ☑ Lessons
  (☐ Monday ☑ Wednesday ☐ Friday)
- **Price:** 70,000 won a month
  (including the l_____)
- **Purpose:** 1. *To overcome fear of water*
  2. *To get in shape*

[서답형 2] 다음을 듣고, 질문에 대한 답이 되도록 빈칸에 적절한 말을 주어진 철자로 시작하여 한 단어로 쓰시오.

Question: What does the man suggest to develop creativity?

➡ He suggests that we should read f_____ in order to develop creativity.

[서답형 3] 다음을 듣고, 여자가 말한 내용과 일치하도록 빈칸에 적절한 말을 주어진 철자로 시작하여 한 단어로 쓰시오.

You should remember that j_____ can be considered a medicine to relieve your stress.

Dictation 04

다시 듣고, 빈칸에 들어갈 알맞은 단어를 써보세요.

정답 및 해설 p.165

01 그림 정보 파악

대화를 듣고, 남자가 구입할 시계를 고르시오.

① ② ③ ④ ⑤

🔊 **Listening Tip**

this square에서처럼 두 단어의 끝 자음과 앞 자음의 소리가 같은 경우에는 [s]를 하나 탈락시켜 /디스퀘얼/처럼 발음해요.

M Emma, what clock would look good in my office?

W I think the triangle one _____ _____ _____. What do you think?

M I don't like the design. What about the long, narrow one?

W It _____ _____ _____ _____ your office.

M You're right. Since the office is small, maybe I should get a small one.

W Yes. These round ones are not bad. How about _____ _____ _____ _____?

M They are too common. I wanted to get something different this time.

W How about 🔊this square one then? It would be _____ _____ _____ _____.

M Okay. I'll get it.

02 장소 추론

대화를 듣고, 두 사람이 대화하고 있는 장소로 가장 적절한 것을 고르시오.

① 서점　　② 교실　　③ 도서관
④ 여행사　　⑤ 영화관

M Excuse me. I'm _____ _____ _____ _____. Can you help me find them, please?

W Yes, of course. Let me see your list.

M Here it is. I was only able to find one of the 3 books that I was looking for.

W I'm sorry, I can't _____ _____ _____. What does it say?

M It's _____ _____ _____ *How to Become a Good Teacher.*

W Let me check if we have these books.

M Thank you.

W *[Pause]* Sorry, but these books _____ _____ _____.

M Does that mean you don't have them at the moment?

W _____ _____ _____.

03 심정 추론

대화를 듣고, 남자의 심정으로 가장 적절한 것을 고르시오.

① proud ② angry ③ excited
④ worried ⑤ disappointed

W Paul, did you catch the soccer match last night?

M I did. The game was not _____ _____. The referees made so many mistakes.

W No, they didn't. They were completely right.

M They made mistakes and it should have been _____ _____ _____ _____.

W Why do you say that? The other team won fair and square.

M Do you remember the last game? We _____ _____ _____ because of the referee's one-sided judgment.

W You're right about that game, but not about this one.

M No way. Those referees must be replaced!

04 일치하지 않는 내용 찾기

다음을 듣고, Golden Cinema Week에 관한 내용과 일치하지 않는 것을 고르시오.

① 옛날 영화를 상영한다.
② 하루에 두 편 상영한다.
③ 마지막 영화가 10시 55분에 끝난다.
④ 회원의 입장료는 10달러이다.
⑤ 첫 영화 상영 30분 전에 극장 문을 연다.

M Hello. We have the Golden Cinema event at ABC Theater this week. You can enjoy movies _____ _____ _____ _____ _____. During the week, there will be 2 _____ _____ _____ _____. Tonight, the first is *Casablanca*. It starts at 7:00 and ends at 8:40. The second is *Breakfast at Tiffany's*, starring Audrey Hepburn. It starts at 9:00 and ends at 10:55. The admission _____ _____ _____ is $7, and it is $10 for non-members. Doors open at 30 minutes _____ _____ _____.

05 조언 파악

대화를 듣고, 여자의 조언으로 가장 적절한 것을 고르시오.

① 수업 시간에 집중해라.
② 친구에게 언제나 솔직해라.
③ 부모님의 말씀을 잘 따라라.
④ 자신을 너무 괴롭게 하지 마라.
⑤ 괴롭힘을 당하는 친구를 도와주어라.

W Tony, is something troubling you?

M No, everything's fine, Ms. Brown.

W Well, you _____ _____ _____ _____ in school or talk to anybody in class. Is there anything I can help you with?

M I think this is my own problem to solve.

W I understand that it is _____ _____ _____ _____ open and talk about what's on your mind at first. But once you get it off your chest, you'll feel so much better.

M All right. Here it goes. *[Pause]* My parents _____ _____ _____ _____ me. I feel like I can't live up to their expectations.

W Your parents will love you no matter what. Please don't _____ _____ _____ _____ yourself.

---

06 화제 추론

다음을 듣고, 무엇에 관한 내용인지 고르시오.

① 노령기의 질병
② 청년 일자리 부족
③ 노령 인구의 증가
④ 노인 돌봄 서비스
⑤ 자연 환경 오염의 원인

W The world is getting older and older. Not the planet, but _____ _____ _____ _____ _____ . A new report shows that the global population of older people is _____ _____ _____ _____ . Today, there are about 700 million people aged 65 or older. However, researchers predict the number will be _____ _____ 1.5 billion by 2050. They also say _____ _____ _____ _____ outnumber the young. This will have a big impact on society.

---

07 도표와 일치하지 않는 내용 찾기

다음을 보면서 대화를 듣고, 내용과 일치하지 <u>않는</u> 것을 고르시오.

Winter Ski Camp

① **When:** January 15 – 16
② **Where:** White Resort
③ **Program:**
  • Ski and snowboard lessons
  • A dance competition
  • Face painting
  • A campfire
④ **What to Bring:** Extra clothes and gloves
⑤ We will go to the resort by school bus. You must arrive at school by 9:00. Please don't be late!

M Look at this poster. We're going to go to a Winter Ski Camp.

W Yay! It _____ _____ _____ _____ January 15th and 16th.

M It will be a fun event. It's held at White Resort.

W What can we do there?

M We can _____ _____ _____ _____ _____ . And there are special activities like a dance competition, face painting, and a campfire.

W Oh, they all sound very interesting. What do we need to take?

M We must bring _____ _____ _____ _____ .

W Does it say how and when we should go there?

M We will go to the resort by school bus. We must

_____ _____ _____ by 8.

08 이유 파악

대화를 듣고, 남자가 이곳에 온 이유로 가장 적절한 것을 고르시오.

① 숙제를 하기 위해서
② 책을 빌리기 위해서
③ 번역을 부탁하기 위해서
④ 봉사활동을 하기 위해서
⑤ 동생을 데려가기 위해서

W Hello. What can I do for you?

M My name is Daniel. I called earlier this week _____

_____ _____.

W Oh, that's right. I'm Janet. We talked over the telephone.

M Nice to meet you, Janet. So *what do you want me to do?

W Today, could you _____ _____

_____ to the children?

M No problem. Is there anything else?

W That's all for today. Oh, you mentioned you speak Korean, correct?

M Yes. Do you _____ _____ _____

_____ Korean, too?

W No. There are a few kids who speak Korean in this hospital. If you can, can you _____ _____

_____ _____ _____ for them?

M Sure. That's not a problem.

✱ 교육부 지정 의사소통 표현: **원하는 행동 묻기**   동(이) 3

What do you want me to do? 제가 뭘 하기를 원하세요?

A: **What do you want me to do?** 제가 뭘 하기를 원하세요?
B: Please put the clothes into the box. 그 상자 안에 옷을 넣어주세요.

---

09 목적 파악

대화를 듣고, 남자가 전화를 건 목적으로 가장 적절한 것을 고르시오.

① 잡지를 구독하려고
② 인터뷰를 요청하려고
③ 여자를 집에 초대하려고
④ 친구의 안부를 물으려고
⑤ 면접에 대해 물어보려고

[Telephone rings.]

W Hello.

M Hello. Is this Maggie Jones?

W No, this is Olivia, her sister. May I _____

_____ _____?

M This is Matt Cooper, and I work for *Happy Life* magazine. I was wondering _____ _____

_____ _____ Ms. Jones.

W Well, you're going to have to ask her yourself, but she's not here at the moment.

M Could you tell me _____ _____ _____ _____?

W She has some personal business to take care of. Please _____ _____ _____ at the beginning of next week.

M Okay. Thank you.

10 그림 순서 배열

다음을 듣고, 남자가 한 일을 순서대로 배열한 것을 고르시오.

(A) (B) (C)

① (A) – (C) – (B) ② (B) – (A) – (C)
③ (B) – (C) – (A) ④ (C) – (A) – (B)
⑤ (C) – (B) – (A)

M Last weekend, I had a fantastic time with my family. On Saturday, I went to a safari _____ _____ _____ _____, crocodiles, lions, elephants, and other wildlife. On Sunday afternoon, we _____ _____ _____ _____ on a beautiful lake. I saw hundreds of birds there. I _____ _____ _____ _____ the birds. And in the evening on that day, we shared experiences of the day _____ _____ _____ on a campground surrounded by tall pine trees. It was a really good trip.

11 목적 파악

다음을 듣고, 방송의 목적으로 가장 적절한 것을 고르시오.

① 기차역 공사 안내
② 선상 시설 이용 안내
③ 열차 운행 취소 안내
④ 구명조끼 착용법 소개
⑤ 응급구조 교육 참가자 모집

M May I have your attention, please? This announcement is for passengers who are waiting on Platform 4. We are sorry to announce that the 6:30 train to Incheon _____ _____ _____. This is due to an engine checkup. Please do not _____ _____ _____ on Platform 4. We ask you to catch the 6:40 train to Incheon at Platform 7 instead. Once again, the 6:40 train to Incheon will _____ _____ Platform 7. We apologize for the inconvenience. Thank you for your understanding.

12 이어질 응답 찾기

대화를 듣고, 여자의 마지막 말에 대한 남자의 응답으로 가장 적절한 것을 고르시오.

① Thanks! I'll do my best.
② I don't have enough time to visit her.
③ Sorry, but I am a stranger here myself.
④ I'll be waiting for her in front of her house.
⑤ No, that's okay. Can you tell her to call me back?

[Telephone rings.]

W Hello.

M Hello. Is this Star Travel?

W Yes, it is.

M I'd like to _____ _____ _____ _____ there.

W Who would you like to speak to?

M I'd like to speak to Ms. Parker, please.

W May I ask _____ _____ ?

M My name is Christian Russell.

W Hold on, please. *[Pause]* Sorry, Mr. Russell. She's on another line. Would you like to _____ _____ _____ ?

13 이어질 응답 찾기

대화를 듣고, 남자의 마지막 말에 대한 여자의 응답으로 가장 적절한 것을 고르시오.

① Sure, you can't miss it.
② Okay, I'll give you a hand.
③ Why don't you get some rest?
④ It is, but it makes me feel good.
⑤ Yes, there is one around the corner.

M Do you have any plans for this weekend?

W Yes, I have to go to a soup kitchen.

M A soup kitchen? What is that?

W It's a place that _____ _____ _____ _____ .

M Do you volunteer there?

W Yes, I do.

M _____ _____ _____ _____ do you do?

W Well, I make sandwiches or I _____ _____ , things like that.

M Wow, _____ _____ _____ _____ _____ .

14 상황에 적절한 말 찾기

다음을 듣고, 주어진 상황에서 할 말로 가장 적절한 것을 고르시오.

① Thank you for helping me.
② How do you like your meal?
③ I haven't seen you in a long time.
④ I'm sorry. I mistook you for my friend.
⑤ I'm sorry to have kept you waiting so long.

W You _____ _____ _____ _____ your friend Bill at a restaurant in the shopping mall. But you are already 15 minutes late. When you step into the restaurant, you see Bill _____ _____ and French fries. So you think _____ _____ _____ _____ from behind. Then you _____ _____ _____ _____ Bill's shoulder and _____ _____. But you find

out _____ _____ _____

_____, not Bill. In this situation, what would you

say to the man?

15 주장 파악

다음을 듣고, 여자가 주장하는 내용으로 가장 적절한 것을 고르시오.

① Buy a new keyboard.
② Don't use the keyboard.
③ Clean your keyboard often.
④ Stay away from the keyboard.
⑤ Wear gloves before you use the keyboard.

W Your computer keyboards _____ _____

_____ _____ your health. A company

asked some researchers to check 30 keyboards in

_____ _____ _____

_____. The results were shocking. They showed the

keyboards were 5 times dirtier than a toilet seat. The

researchers said the germs from the keyboards could

_____ _____

_____ _____. Thus, you should

_____ _____ _____

_____ in order to stay healthy.

서답형

1

대화를 듣고, 빈칸에 적절한 말을 주어진 철자로 시작하여 한 단어로 쓰시오.

Swimming Class

Student Name: Bora Kim
- **Level:** ☑ Beginner
  ☐ Intermediate
  ☐ Advanced
- **Class:** ☐ Free Swimming
  (Monday ~ Sunday)
  ☑ Lessons
  (☐ Monday ☑ Wednesday
  ☐ Friday)
- **Price:** 70,000 won a month
  (including the l_____)
- **Purpose:** 1. *To overcome fear of water*
  2. *To get in shape*

W Can I sign up for your swimming class?

M Sure. I'll ask you some questions to fill out this form. _____ _____ _____ to swim before?

W No. I've always wanted to, but I'm afraid of water.

M You _____ _____ _____.

W That's right. When do you have classes?

M The classes are on Mondays, Wednesdays, and Fridays. But you may use the pool every day. It's 70,000 won a month _____ _____ _____.

W I'll take the class on Wednesdays.

M Okay. Why do you want to learn swimming?

W I want to overcome my fear of water. Also, it'll help me _____ _____ _____.

2

다음을 듣고, 질문에 대한 답이 되도록 빈칸에 적절한 말을 주어진 철자로 시작하여 한 단어로 쓰시오.

> **Question:** What does the man suggest to develop creativity?

➡ He suggests that we should read
f_____ in order to develop
creativity.

M Books about real events, real people, and facts are important as they can teach us about history, important people that we should know about, and scientific facts. However, we should _____ _____ _____ _____ of books. So *I suggest you should also read fiction. _____ _____ _____ _____ _____ non-fiction because it can help us to _____ _____ _____.
Of course, knowing history and facts is essential in life, but imagination and creativity _____ _____ _____ _____ to dream about the future as well.

> **✳ 교육부 지정 의사소통 기능: 제안, 권유하기** 동(윤) 5| Y(박) 6
> **I suggest (that) you (should) ~.** 나는 네가 ~할 것을 제안해.
> • **I suggest that you should** attend the party. 나는 네가 파티에 참석할 것을 제안해.
> • **I suggest you** exercise regularly. 나는 네가 규칙적으로 운동할 것을 제안해.

3

다음을 듣고, 여자가 말한 내용과 일치하도록 빈칸에 적절한 말을 주어진 철자로 시작하여 한 단어로 쓰시오.

> You should remember that
> j_____ can be considered a
> medicine to relieve your stress.

🔊 **Listening Tip**
instead of에서 instead의 [d]가 양쪽 모음의 영향으로 [r]로 발음되면서 of와 연음되어 /인스레로브/처럼 들려요.

W There has been increasing interest in health. Today, _____ _____ _____ _____ _____, using our brains 🔊instead of our bodies. Every day, we find ourselves under pressure from our jobs and just living in a modern urban environment. In this sense, _____ _____ _____ _____ upon as medicine. Also, while a person _____ _____ _____, he has time to enjoy himself alone. Moreover, it can _____ _____ _____ _____, and you don't have to spend a lot of money to do it.

MEMO

MEMO

쎄듀
본영어

<쎄듀 종합영어> 개정판

고등영어의
근본을
바로 세운다!

◈ **문법편**

1 내신·수능 대비 문법/어법

2 올바른 해석을 위한 독해 문법

3 내신·수능 빈출 포인트 수록

4 서술형 문제 강화

◈ **문법적용편**

1 문법편에서 학습한 내용을
   문법/어법 문제에 적용하여 완벽 체화

2 내신·서술형·수능으로 이어지는
   체계적인 3단계 구성

◈ **독해적용편**

1 문법편에서 학습한 내용을
   독해 문제에 적용하여 독해력 완성

2 대의 파악을 위한 수능 유형과 지문 전체를
   리뷰하는 내신 유형의 이원화된 구성

'나'에게 딱! 맞는 암기&문제모드만 골라서 학습!

5가지 암기모드

8가지 문제모드

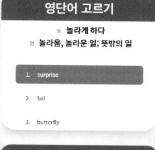

 암기모드를 선택하면, 최적의 문제 모드를 자동 추천!

2 **미암기 단어는 단어장에! 외워질 때까지 반복 학습 GO!**

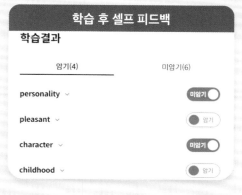

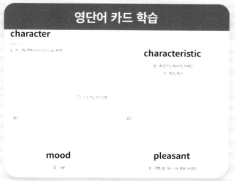

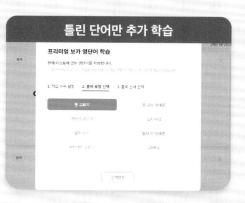

LISTENING Q

중학영어듣기
모의고사 24회

3

[리스닝 큐]

김기훈 | 쎄듀 영어교육연구센터

정답 및 해설

쎄듀

LISTENING Q

중학영어듣기
모의고사 24회

3

정답 및 해설

실전 모의고사 01

p. 28

01 ⑤	02 ③	03 ③	04 ⑤	05 ③	06 ①	07 ②
08 ④	09 ⑤	10 ③	11 ⑤	12 ④	13 ⑤	14 ②
15 ④	16 ⑤	17 ⑤	18 ②	19 ⑤	20 ①	

01 ⑤

해설 장미 모양에 작은 크리스털이 들어간 머리핀이 더 마음에 든다고 했다.

어휘 hairpin[hέərpìn] 머리핀
crystal[krístəl] 크리스털, 수정
prefer[prifə́ːr] 더 좋아하다
choice[tʃɔis] 선택

W Mike, what are you going to buy?
M I'm looking for a hairpin for my sister.
W How about this one with a big ribbon?
M She already has one just like it. I think she wants something with crystals.
W Then, how about this heart-shaped one with a lot of small crystals on it?
M Oh, that's really pretty. But I prefer the rose-shaped one with crystals.
W Good choice. I'm sure she'll like it.

여 Mike, 무엇을 살 거니?
남 여동생을 위한 머리핀을 찾고 있어.
여 큰 리본이 달린 이건 어때?
남 걔가 그것과 비슷한 걸 이미 갖고 있어. 크리스털이 있는 걸 원할 것 같아.
여 그럼, 작은 크리스털이 많이 박힌 이 하트 모양 핀은 어때?
남 아, 정말 예쁘네. 하지만 크리스털이 달린 장미 모양 핀이 더 마음에 들어.
여 좋은 선택이야. 분명 마음에 들어 할 거야.

02 ③

해설 남자가 여자에게 차로 서점에 데려다 달라고 부탁했다.

어휘 actually[ǽktʃuəli] 사실은
give A a ride A를 태워주다

M Mom, are you busy this afternoon?
W Yes, I'm going shopping after lunch. Why?
M Well, I want to go to Bandi Bookstore. I have to buy some books for my science homework.
W Do you want me to help you choose the books?
M No. Actually, I just wanted you to give me a ride there.
W Okay. How about leaving at 2? I'll take you there on my way to the mall.
M Okay. Thank you.

남 엄마, 오늘 오후에 바쁘세요?
여 응, 점심 먹고 나서 쇼핑하러 갈 거야. 왜?
남 저, Bandi 서점에 가려고 하는데요. 과학 숙제를 위한 책을 좀 사야 하거든요.
여 책 고르는 거 도와줄까?
남 아니요, 실은, 거기에 데려다주시기만 하면 돼요.
여 알겠어. 2시에 나가는 게 어떠니? 쇼핑몰에 가는 길에 그곳으로 데려다줄게.
남 알겠어요. 감사해요.

03 ③

해설 여자가 선반의 짐을 꺼내려고 애쓰고 있고 남자가 도와주려는 상황이 적절하다.

어휘 pack[pæk] (짐을) 싸다, 꾸리다
go backpacking 배낭여행을 가다

① M Did you pack your bag for the trip?
   W Sure. Everything's all set.
② M Would you mind if I sit here?
   W No, go ahead.
③ M May I help you to take your bag down?
   W Thank you. You're so kind.
④ M Have you been waiting long?
   W No, I just arrived a few minutes ago.
⑤ M Do you have any special plans for this vacation?
   W Yes, I'm planning to go backpacking for a month.

① 남 여행을 위한 짐을 다 챙겼니?
   여 물론이죠. 모든 게 준비 완료예요.
② 남 여기에 앉아도 될까요?
   여 네, 앉으세요.
③ 남 가방 내리는 걸 도와드릴까요?
   여 감사해요. 정말 친절하시네요.
④ 남 오래 기다렸니?
   여 아니, 조금 전에 막 도착했어.
⑤ 남 이번 방학에 특별한 계획이 있니?
   여 응, 한 달 동안 배낭여행을 갈 계획이야.

04 ⑤

해설 영화 시작 시각이 7시 30분이라고
했다.

어휘 half[hæf] 30분
near[niər] ~에서 가까운

M What time is it, Mom?
W It's half past 3. Why do you ask?
M Because I have to meet my friend at 4:30.
W Then you've <u>only</u> <u>got</u> <u>an</u> <u>hour</u>. You'd better get ready.
M It's okay. I'm meeting him at the cafe near our house.
W You didn't forget that we're <u>going</u> <u>to</u> <u>the</u> <u>movies</u> tonight, did you?
M Oh, right. What time <u>does</u> <u>the</u> <u>movie</u> <u>start</u>?
W <u>It</u> <u>starts</u> <u>at</u> 7:30 p.m. Don't be late.
M Okay, I won't.

남 지금 몇 시예요, 엄마?
여 3시 30분이야. 왜 물어보니?
남 4시 30분에 친구를 만나기로 했거든요.
여 그럼 한 시간밖에 안 남았구나. 준비하는 게 좋겠네.
남 괜찮아요. 우리 집 근처에 있는 카페에서 만나거든요.
여 우리 오늘 밤에 영화 보러 가기로 한 거 잊지 않았지?
남 아, 맞아요. 영화가 몇 시에 시작하죠?
여 7시 30분에 시작해. 늦지 마라.
남 알겠어요, 늦지 않을게요.

05 ③

해설 목적지(London), 출발 시각(7시
40분), 왕복 여부(편도), 가격(25달러)에
대한 언급은 있지만 소요 시간에 대한 언
급은 없다.

어휘 delay[diléi] 미루다, 연기하다
heavy snow 폭설
one-way[wʌ́n-wéi] 편도의
round-trip[ráund-tríp] 왕복 여행의

M I'd like a ticket for the 7 o'clock train to London.
W I'm sorry, the 7 o'clock train to London is delayed <u>because</u> <u>of</u> <u>heavy</u> <u>snow</u>.
M What time will that train arrive?
W <u>It</u> <u>will</u> <u>arrive</u> 30 minutes late and leave at 7:40.
M Then can you give me a ticket <u>for</u> <u>that</u> <u>train</u>?
W Do you want a one-way ticket or a round-trip ticket?
M A one-way ticket, please.
W Here is your ticket, <u>and</u> <u>that'll</u> <u>be</u> $25.
M Okay. Here you are.

남 런던 행 7시 기차표 주세요.
여 죄송하지만 폭설 때문에 런던 행 7시 기차가 연착되었어요.
남 그 기차는 몇 시에 도착하나요?
여 30분 늦게 도착해서 7시 40분에 출발할 거예요.
남 그럼 그 기차표 한 장 주시겠어요?
여 편도요 아니면 왕복이요?
남 편도로 주세요.
여 여기 표 있습니다. 25달러예요.
남 알겠습니다. 여기 있습니다.

06 ①

해설 나무와 꽃들이 있고 호수 주위로
자전거를 타는 아이들이 보이며 배드민턴
을 칠 수 있는 장소라고 했으므로 공원임
을 알 수 있다.

어휘 place[pleis] 놓다, 두다; 장소
mat[mæt] 돗자리
crowded[kráudid] 붐비는, 혼잡한
along[əlɔ́(ː)ŋ] ~을 따라서
racket[rǽkit] 라켓

M The weather is perfect for a picnic.
W It is. Let's place a mat <u>under</u> <u>the</u> <u>big</u> <u>tree</u>.
M Okay. There are a lot of people here today.
W Yes. <u>This</u> <u>place</u> <u>is</u> <u>always</u> crowded on weekends.
M Well, it really is a beautiful place <u>with</u> <u>all</u> <u>the</u> <u>trees</u> and flowers.
W Yes. Look! There are some children riding bicycles <u>along</u> <u>the</u> <u>lake</u>.
M Let's ride bicycles next week. I brought badminton rackets today. Would you like to play?
W Sure. That sounds fun.

남 소풍 가기에 딱 좋은 날씨네.
여 맞아. 저 큰 나무 아래에 돗자리를 깔자.
남 좋아. 오늘 여기에 사람들이 정말 많네.
여 그래. 이곳은 주말이면 항상 붐벼.
남 음, 이곳이 나무와 꽃들로 정말 아름다운 곳이잖아.
여 맞아. 봐! 호수를 따라 자전거를 타는 아이들이 있어.
남 다음 주에는 자전거를 타자. 나 오늘 배드민턴 라켓 가져왔는데. 칠래?
여 좋아. 재밌겠다.

07 ②

[해설] 우유와 치즈가 있는 위치를 묻는데 그녀가 여기 어딘가에 있다고 응답하는 것은 어색하다.

[어휘] somewhere[sʌ́mhwɛ̀ər] 어딘가에
get to ~에 도착하다
stadium[stéidiəm] 경기장

① W Did you study a lot for the tests?
　 M I studied all night, but I'm still worried.
② W Where can I find the milk and cheese?
　 M You should call her now. She is around here somewhere.
③ W What are you going to have for lunch?
　 M Well, I haven't decided yet.
④ W How can I get to World Cup Stadium?
　 M You can take the subway.
⑤ W I wonder why Brian isn't answering his cell phone.
　 M He said he lost it yesterday.

① 여 시험공부 많이 했니?
　 남 밤새워 공부했는데 여전히 걱정돼.
② 여 우유와 치즈는 어디에서 찾을 수 있나요?
　 남 지금 그녀에게 전화해 봐요. 그녀는 여기 어딘가에 있어요.
③ 여 점심으로 뭘 먹을 거니?
　 남 글쎄, 아직 결정하지 못했어.
④ 여 월드컵 경기장에 어떻게 갈 수 있나요?
　 남 지하철을 타면 돼요.
⑤ 여 Brian이 왜 휴대전화를 안 받는지 궁금해.
　 남 어제 전화기를 잃어버렸다고 그러더라.

08 ④

[해설] 여자는 남자에게 정원 가꾸는 것을 도와 달라고 하면서, 식물에 물 주는 것을 부탁했다.

[어휘] take care of ~을 돌보다
garden[gáːrdən] 정원
grass[græs] 잔디(밭)
water[wɔ́ːtər] 물을 주다
plant[plænt] 식물, 나무

W Mason, are you busy right now?
M I'm still doing my art homework.
W Do you mean making a bag with old clothes?
M Yes. I think I'll be able to finish in an hour.
W Can you help me take care of the garden after finishing your homework?
M Do you want me to cut the grass?
W No, just water some of the plants.
M Okay, I will.

여 Mason, 지금 바쁘니?
남 아직 미술 숙제를 하고 있어요.
여 헌 옷으로 가방 만드는 거 말이니?
남 네, 한 시간이면 끝낼 수 있을 것 같아요.
여 숙제 다 하고 정원 가꾸는 것 좀 도와줄 수 있니?
남 제가 잔디를 깎을까요?
여 아니, 식물에 물만 좀 주면 돼.
남 알겠어요, 그럴게요.

09 ⑤

[해설] 쇼핑객이 분실한 가방을 보관하고 있으므로 찾아가라고 안내하는 방송이다.

[어휘] Attention! (안내 방송에서) 알립니다! 주목하세요!
shopper[ʃápər] 쇼핑객
backpack[bǽkpæ̀k] 배낭
floor[flɔ́ːr] 층
customer[kʌ́stəmər] 고객

W Attention all shoppers! We found a backpack. It is light blue and there are some books and a tablet PC in it. We found it at a sports shop on the 5th floor. If you lost this bag, please come to the customer service center on the 9th floor. We hope you're enjoying your shopping. Thank you.

여 쇼핑객 여러분 모두 주목해 주세요! 저희는 가방을 보관하고 있습니다. 하늘색이고 안에 책 몇 권과 태블릿 PC가 들어 있습니다. 5층에 있는 스포츠 용품점에서 습득했습니다. 이 가방을 분실하셨다면 9층에 있는 고객 서비스 센터로 오시기 바랍니다. 즐거운 쇼핑하시길 바랍니다. 감사합니다.

10 ③

[해설] 총금액은 27달러인데 5달러를 할인받을 수 있다고 했으므로 22달러를 지불할 것이다.

[어휘] avenger[əvénddʒər] 원수를 갚는 사람
showing[ʃóuiŋ] 상영

M Excuse me. What time does the *Avengers* movie start?
W There is a showing at 3:00 and another at 5:00.
M How much are the tickets?
W Adult tickets are $10 and children's tickets are $7.

남 실례합니다. 〈어벤져스〉 영화 몇 시에 시작하나요?
여 3시에 상영하는 것과 5시에 상영하는 것이 있습니다.
남 티켓 가격은 얼마인가요?
여 성인은 10달러이고, 어린이는 7달러예요.

adult[ədʌ́lt] 성인
in total 합계하여
discount[dískaunt] 할인
coupon[kú:pan] 쿠폰

M I need tickets for 2 <u>adults and a child</u> for the 5:00 showing.
W Okay, <u>then that costs</u> $27 in total.
M Can I use this discount coupon?
W Sure. <u>You can get</u> $5 off the total.
M Great. Here you are.

남 5시에 상영하는 영화에 성인 두 명과 아이 한 명 티켓 주세요.
여 네, 전부 27달러입니다.
남 이 할인 쿠폰을 사용할 수 있나요?
여 물론이죠. 총금액에서 5달러 할인받을 수 있어요.
남 좋네요. 여기 있습니다.

11 ⑤

해설 여자가 세탁소에서 재킷을 찾아다 달라고 부탁하자 남자가 수락했다.

어휘 smell[smel] 냄새가 나다
excited[iksáitid] 흥분한
ask a favor 부탁하다
pick up 찾아오다

M Honey, something smells good! What are you making?
W I'm making Judy's lunch <u>for her school trip</u> tomorrow.
M She's going to Jeju-do, isn't she?
W Yes. She's very excited about the trip. Oh, can I ask a favor?
M Sure. What do I have to do?
W Would you <u>pick up her jacket</u> from the cleaner's? Judy needs it for her trip.
M Okay, I will go and <u>pick it up</u>.

남 여보, 좋은 냄새가 나는데! 뭘 만들고 있어요?
여 내일 Judy가 가는 수학여행에서 먹을 점심을 만들고 있어요.
남 우리 딸이 제주도에 가는 거 맞죠?
여 맞아요. 그 애는 여행 때문에 무척 들떠있어요. 아, 부탁 하나만 해도 될까요?
남 그럼요. 뭘 해야 해요?
여 세탁소에서 Judy의 재킷을 찾아와줄래요? 걔가 여행에서 그 재킷을 입어야 해서요.
남 알겠어요, 내가 가서 찾아올게요.

12 ④

해설 개최 날짜(10월 5일), 참가국 수(30개 나라 이상), 개최 장소(여의도 한강 공원), 입장료(무료)에 대한 언급은 있으나 교통편에 대한 언급은 없다.

어휘 inform[infɔ́:rm] 알리다
annual[ǽnjuəl] 매년의, 연례의
firework[fáiərwə̀:rk] 불꽃(놀이)
participate in ~에 참가하다, 참여하다
entrance fee 입장료

M Hello, everyone. I'm happy to inform you about the annual Fireworks Festival. This year, it <u>will be held on</u> October 5. More than 30 nations <u>will be participating</u> in the festival. You can enjoy the festival at Yeouido Hangang Park from 2 to 9:30 p.m. You can watch amazing fireworks and <u>taste different kinds</u> of street foods, too. There is <u>no entrance fee for</u> the event. Come and enjoy the festival!

남 안녕하세요, 여러분. 연례 불꽃 축제에 관해 알려 드리게 되어 기쁩니다. 올해, 불꽃 축제는 10월 5일에 열립니다. 30개 이상의 나라가 축제에 참여할 것입니다. 여러분들은 여의도 한강 공원에서 오후 2시부터 9시 30분까지 축제를 즐기실 수 있습니다. 멋진 불꽃을 볼 수 있고 다양한 종류의 길거리 음식을 맛볼 수도 있습니다. 이 행사는 입장료가 없습니다. 오셔서 축제를 즐기시기 바랍니다!

13 ⑤

해설 완만한 경로로 정상까지 오를 수 있고, 3시간 이상 걸리지 않는 등산로를 선택하기로 했다.

어휘 board[bɔ:rd] (안내)판
several[sévərəl] 몇몇의
hike up a mountain 등산하다, 산에 오르다
had better not-v ~하지 않는 것이 좋다
steep[sti:p] 가파른
rough[rʌf] 거친, 험한
gentle[dʒéntl] 완만한

M Look at the board. There are several courses to <u>hike up this mountain</u>.
W Oh, that's good. Which course is best for us?
M Well, I think we'd better not try the steep and rough courses.
W I agree. <u>Let's take</u> a gentle course.
M Okay. Do you want to reach the top?
W It'll be difficult, but I want to <u>reach the top</u> of the mountain.
M So do I. But I don't want to <u>hike for more than</u> 3 hours.
W Okay. Let's take this course.

남 안내판을 봐. 등산하는 경로가 몇 군데 있어.
여 아, 잘됐다. 어느 경로가 가장 좋을까?
남 글쎄, 가파르고 험한 경로로는 가지 않는 게 좋을 것 같아.
여 동의해. 완만한 경로로 가자.
남 그래. 너는 정상까지 오르고 싶니?
여 힘들겠지만 산꼭대기를 밟고 싶어.
남 나도 그래. 하지만 세 시간 이상 등산하고 싶지는 않아.
여 좋아. 이 경로로 가자.

14 ②

해설 일종의 자연 현상으로 하늘에서 일어나는 빛의 번쩍임이며 이로 인해 화재가 일어나거나 사람들이 죽는다고 했으므로 번개가 알맞다.

어휘 natural[nǽtʃərəl] 자연의
phenomenon[finámənàn] 현상
storm[stɔːrm] 폭우, 폭풍우
flash[flæʃ] 섬광, 번쩍임
dangerous[déindʒərəs] 위험한
electricity[ilektrísəti] 전기

W This is a kind of natural phenomenon. When there is a big storm, you will sometimes see this. It is a very <u>bright flash</u> <u>of</u> <u>light</u> in the sky. After this, you'll <u>hear</u> <u>a</u> <u>loud</u> <u>noise</u>. This can be beautiful, but it <u>can</u> <u>also</u> <u>be</u> <u>dangerous</u> because this is actually electricity. Every year, <u>fires</u> <u>are</u> <u>started</u> by this and sometimes people are killed by this.

여 이것은 일종의 자연 현상이에요. 큰 폭풍우가 있을 때 가끔 이것을 볼 수 있어요. 이것은 하늘에서 번쩍이는 아주 밝은 빛이에요. 이것이 일어난 후에 당신은 시끄러운 소리를 들을 거예요. 이것은 아름다울 수 있지만 사실은 전기이기 때문에 위험할 수도 있어요. 매년 이것으로 인해 화재가 일어나고 때로 사람들이 죽기도 해요.

15 ④

해설 감사 카드를 지금 만들 거라고 했다.

어휘 present[prézənt] 선물
teacup[tíkəp] 찻잔
meal[miːl] 식사
neither[níːðər] ~도 또한 …아니다
carnation[kɑːrnéiʃən] 카네이션

W Eric, have you bought a present for Parents' Day?
M Of course. I got cell phone cases. How about you?
W I bought teacups. My parents like to <u>drink</u> <u>tea</u> <u>after</u> <u>meals</u>.
M I'm sure they will like them.
W Oh, I haven't made a thank-you card yet.
M Neither have I. <u>Making</u> <u>cards</u> <u>is</u> <u>not</u> <u>easy</u>.
W That's right. I think <u>I'll</u> <u>make</u> <u>one</u> right now. I <u>should</u> <u>also</u> <u>buy</u> <u>some</u> carnations after that.

여 Eric, 어버이날 선물을 샀니?
남 물론이지. 휴대폰 케이스를 샀어. 너는?
여 나는 찻잔을 샀어. 부모님이 식사 후에 차 마시는 걸 좋아하시거든.
남 부모님이 분명 좋아하실 거야.
여 아, 나 아직 감사 카드를 안 만들었네.
남 나도. 카드 만드는 건 쉽지 않아.
여 맞아. 지금 만들어야겠어. 카드 만들고 나서 카네이션도 사야 하거든.

16 ⑤

해설 오후 중에는 괜찮다는 여자의 말에 남자는 2시를 제안했으며, 여자는 이를 수락했다.

어휘 opening[óupəniŋ] 빈자리
at that time 그때에
available[əvéiləbl] 시간[여유]이 있는

[Telephone rings.]
M Thank you for calling Miller's Dental Clinic. How may I help you?
W Hello. This is Emily Blunt. I'd like to make an appointment on Tuesday.
M There is <u>only</u> <u>one</u> <u>opening</u> at 11 a.m.
W I don't think I can make it at 11 a.m. How about the next day?
M Let me check. [Pause] You <u>can</u> <u>come</u> <u>in</u> <u>at</u> 10 a.m. if you'd like.
W I have an important meeting at that time. <u>I'll</u> <u>be</u> <u>available</u> in the afternoon.
M Then, how about at 2 p.m.?
W <u>That's</u> <u>fine</u>.
M All right. I'll see you then.

[전화벨이 울린다.]
남 Miller 치과에 전화주셔서 감사합니다. 어떻게 도와드릴까요?
여 여보세요. 저는 Emily Blunt인데요. 화요일에 예약을 하고 싶어요.
남 오전 11시에만 비어 있습니다.
여 11시에는 갈 수 없을 것 같네요. 그 다음 날은 어떤가요?
남 확인해 볼게요. [잠시 후] 원하시면 오전 10시에 오셔도 됩니다.
여 그 시간에 중요한 회의가 있어요. 오후에는 가능할 것 같아요.
남 그럼, 오후 2시는 어떠세요?
여 좋아요.
남 네, 그럼 그때 뵙겠습니다.

17 ⑤

해설 방과 후에 수학 숙제하는 것을 도와 달라는 남자의 말에 이를 수락하거나 거절하는 응답이 이어져야 한다.

W Minho, what are you doing?
M I'm reading a book about Korean history.
W Are you interested in history?

여 민호야, 뭐하고 있니?
남 한국사에 관한 책을 읽고 있어.
여 넌 역사에 관심이 있니?

어휘 subject[sʌ́bdʒikt] 과목
boring[bɔ́:riŋ] 따분한, 지루한
past[pæst] 과거
be bad at ~을 잘 못하다
help A with B A의 B를 돕다

M Yes. History is my favorite subject.
W Really? I don't like history. It's so boring.
M I like learning about the past. What's your favorite subject?
W I like math the most. I enjoy solving difficult math problems.
M Oh, really? I'm bad at math. Can you help me with my math homework after school?
W Sorry, I have other plans this afternoon.

남 응. 역사는 내가 가장 좋아하는 과목이야.
여 정말? 난 역사를 싫어해. 너무 따분하거든.
남 나는 과거에 대해 배우는 게 좋아. 네가 가장 좋아하는 과목은 뭐니?
여 난 수학을 가장 좋아해. 어려운 수학 문제 푸는 것을 즐기거든.
남 아, 정말? 나는 수학을 못해. 방과 후에 내 수학 숙제 좀 도와줄 수 있니?
여 미안하지만 오늘 오후에 다른 계획이 있어.

① 고마워. 넌 정말 친절하구나.
② 맞아. 나는 어제 수학 시험을 봤어.
③ 그래. 나는 역사박물관에 가 본 적이 있어.
④ 잘됐다. 박물관에 가는 게 어때?

18 ②

해설 택시를 타고 극장에 가고 있는 남자가 차가 많이 막힌다고 하자 여자가 택시에서 내려서 지하철을 타라고 했으므로 이 제안에 대해 승낙하거나 거절하는 것이 자연스럽다.

어휘 on A's way to ~로 가는 길에
traffic[trǽfik] 교통
heavy[hévi] (양·정도 등이) 많은
quick[kwik] 빠른
at this time of the day 하루 중 이 시간에
get out of ~에서 나오다

[Cell phone rings.]
M Hello.
W Hey, Steve, are you on your way to the theater?
M Yes, but the traffic is really heavy.
W What? Aren't you coming by subway?
M No, I'm coming by taxi. I took this taxi half an hour ago.
W Why did you take a taxi? The subway is a lot quicker at this time of the day.
M I didn't know that. I thought a taxi would be faster.
W Why don't you get out of the taxi now and take the subway? It would be faster.
M Okay, I'll do that. See you soon.

[휴대전화가 울린다.]
남 여보세요.
여 안녕, Steve, 너 극장에 오는 길이지?
남 응. 그런데 차가 너무 막혀.
여 뭐라고? 너 지하철 타고 오고 있는 거 아니야?
남 응. 택시 타고 가고 있어. 이 택시 30분 전에 탔거든.
여 왜 택시를 탔니? 이 시간대에는 지하철이 훨씬 더 빠른데.
남 몰랐어. 택시가 더 빠를 거라고 생각했거든.
여 지금 택시에서 내려서 지하철을 타는 게 어때? 그게 더 빠를 것 같은데.
남 알겠어. 그렇게. 곧 보자.

① 동의해. 택시를 타자.
③ 극장에서 만나는 게 어때?
④ 아니. 난 지하철이 더 빠를 거라고 생각하지 않아.
⑤ 좋은 생각이야! 오늘 밤에 영화 보러 가자.

19 ⑤

해설 세일 기간이어서 재고가 없다는 남자의 말에 이어질 응답으로 상황상 알겠다고 말하는 것이 가장 적절하다.

어휘 clothing[klóuðiŋ] 옷, 의복
on sale 세일 중인
except[iksépt] 제외하고는
scarf[ska:rf] 스카프
hood[hud] (외투에 달린) 모자
in stock 재고로, 비축되어

M Hello. May I help you?
W I'm just looking, thanks.
M All winter clothing is on sale except gloves and scarves.
W Oh, really? Are these winter coats also on sale?
M Yes, they are on sale with a big discount.
W Hmm... I like this blue coat with a hood. Do you have it in a bigger size?

남 안녕하세요. 도와드릴까요?
여 그냥 둘러보는 중이에요. 감사합니다.
남 장갑과 스카프를 제외하고 모든 겨울 의류는 세일 중이에요.
여 아, 정말요? 이 겨울 코트들도 세일하나요?
남 네. 그것들은 할인을 많이 해서 판매 중이에요.
여 음… 모자가 달린 이 파란색 코트가 마음에 드네요. 이걸로 더 큰 사이즈가 있나요?

M I'm sorry. That's all we have. There isn't a lot left in stock because it's on sale.

W Okay, I understand. Thank you for your help.

남 죄송해요. 이게 저희가 가지고 있는 전부예요. 세일 기간이라서 재고가 많이 남아 있지 않거든요.

여 네, 알겠습니다. 도와주셔서 감사해요.

① 정말 좋네요. 얼마인가요?
② 그걸 포장해 주세요.
③ 하나 사면 하나가 공짜라는 말씀인가요?
④ 좋네요. 이 할인 쿠폰을 사용할 수 있나요?

20 ①

해설 붐비는 지하철에 무거운 가방을 들고 탄 할머니에게 Peter가 자신의 자리를 양보하려는 상황이다.

어휘 crowded[kráudid] 붐비는
fortunately[fɔ́ːrtʃənitli] 다행히
get on (지하철·버스 등을) 타다
seat[siːt] 자리, 좌석
empty[émpti] 빈, 비어 있는
situation[sìtʃuéiʃən] 상황

M Peter is on the subway and it's very crowded. Fortunately, he finds an empty seat and sits there. After a few minutes, an old woman with a heavy bag gets on the subway. The woman looks very tired, and there are no empty seats for her. So, Peter decides to give his seat to her. In this situation, what would Peter most likely say to the woman?

Peter Please take my seat.

남 Peter는 지하철을 타고 있는데 무척 붐빈다. 다행히, 그는 빈자리를 발견하고 거기에 앉는다. 몇 분 뒤에 무거운 가방을 든 한 나이든 여자가 지하철에 탄다. 그녀는 무척 피곤해 보이지만 앉을 빈자리가 없다. 그래서 Peter는 그녀에게 자신의 자리를 양보하려고 한다. 이러한 상황에서 Peter가 그 여자에게 할 말로 가장 적절한 것은 무엇인가?

Peter 제 자리에 앉으세요.

② 지금 몇 시인지 아세요?
③ 가방 드는 것 도와 드릴까요?
④ 이번 역에서 내리셔야 해요.
⑤ 지하철로 한 시간 넘게 걸릴 거예요.

실전 모의고사
02
p. 38

01 ⑤	02 ④	03 ④	04 ⑤	05 ③	06 ①	07 ③
08 ②	09 ②	10 ④	11 ②	12 ③	13 ④	14 ②
15 ③	16 ④	17 ④	18 ①	19 ③	20 ②	

01 ⑤

해설 남자가 가장자리에 전구가 달린 타원형 거울을 추천하자 좋다고 했다.

어휘 **mirror**[mírər] 거울
hang[hæŋ] 걸다
simple[símpl] 단순한
shape[ʃeip] 모양
square[skwɛər] 정사각형의
edge[edʒ] 가장자리
wrap up 싸다, 포장하다

M Excuse me, would you like some help with mirrors?
W Yes, I'd like to buy a mirror to hang on a wall in my room.
M How about this round one? It's the most popular one.
W It's too simple. I don't like shapes that are round or square.
M Then how about this egg-shaped one with lights around the edges?
W Oh, it looks nice. I'll take it. Could you please wrap it up for me?
M Sure.

남 실례합니다. 거울 찾는 것을 도와 드릴까요?
여 네, 제 방 벽에 걸 거울을 사고 싶어요.
남 이 원형 거울 어떠세요? 가장 인기 있는 거예요.
여 그건 너무 단순해요. 원형이나 정사각형 모양을 좋아하지 않아요.
남 그럼 가장자리에 전구들이 달린 이 달걀 모양의 거울은 어떠세요?
여 아, 멋지네요. 그걸로 살게요. 포장해 주실 수 있나요?
남 그럼요.

02 ④

해설 선물 상자를 포장하는 동안 상자를 잡아달라고 부탁했다.

어휘 **wrap**[ræp] 포장하다
hold[hould] 잡다
while[hwail] ~하는 동안

M Angela, what is in this box?
W It's a birthday present for my dad. I need your help to wrap it.
M Hmm... I'm not good at doing that.
W Don't worry. I'm going to do the wrapping myself.
M Oh, I see. What do you want me to do?
W Can you hold the box while I wrap it with the paper?
M Okay.

남 Angela, 이 상자는 뭐니?
여 아빠에게 드릴 생일 선물이야. 그걸 포장하는 데 네 도움이 필요해.
남 음… 나는 포장을 잘 못해.
여 걱정하지 마. 포장은 내가 직접 할 거야.
남 아, 알겠어. 내가 뭘 해 주면 될까?
여 포장지로 그걸 싸는 동안 상자를 잡아줄래?
남 알겠어.

03 ④

해설 패스트푸드점에서 음료에 얼음을 넣을 것인지 묻는 상황이다.

어휘 **steak**[steik] 스테이크
rare[rɛər] 살짝 익힌
heat[hiːt] 더위, 열기
air conditioner 에어컨
sculpture[skʌ́lptʃər] 조각(물)
castle[kǽsl] 성

① W How would you like your steak?
  M I'd like to have it medium rare, please.
② W I'm dying from the heat.
  M Me, too. Let's turn on the air conditioner.
③ W Look at the castle-shaped ice sculpture.
  M Wow! It looks like a real castle.
④ W Do you want me to put some ice in your drink?
  M Yes, please.
⑤ W Would you like something to drink?
  M Yes. I'd like a cup of coffee.

① 여 스테이크를 어떻게 해 드릴까요?
  남 미디엄 레어로 해주세요.
② 여 더워 죽겠어.
  남 나도 그래. 에어컨을 켜자.
③ 여 성 모양의 얼음 조각을 봐.
  남 와! 진짜 성처럼 보여.
④ 여 음료에 얼음 넣어 드릴까요?
  남 네, 넣어 주세요.
⑤ 여 마실 것 좀 드릴까요?
  남 네. 커피 한 잔 주세요.

04 ⑤

해설 10km 경주는 9시 30분에 시작하며, 두 시간 후면 끝날 거라고 했으므로 남자의 경주는 11시 30분에 끝날 것이다.

어휘 race[reis] 경주, 달리기
actually[ǽktʃuəli] 사실은
marathon[mǽrəθὰn] 마라톤
last[læst] 지속하다

W Hey, Mark. Are you running in tomorrow's race?
M Yes. Are you coming to see me?
W Of course! You begin at 9 o'clock, right?
M Actually, that's when the marathon starts. But the 10-kilometer race begins at 9:30.
W Oh, I see. And how long will the race last?
M We're only running 10 kilometers, so we'll be done in 2 hours.
W I see. Then do you want to do something after the race?
M Sure. Let's go for lunch.

여 안녕, Mark. 너 내일 경주에서 뛸 거지?
남 그럼. 나 보러 올 거니?
여 물론이지! 9시에 시작하는 거 맞지?
남 사실, 그건 마라톤이 시작하는 시간이야. 하지만 10km 경주는 9시 30분에 시작해.
여 아, 알겠어. 경주는 얼마나 걸리니?
남 10킬로미터만 뛰는 거니까 두 시간 후면 끝날 거야.
여 그렇구나. 그럼 경주 끝나고 뭐라도 하고 싶니?
남 물론이지. 점심 먹으러 가자.

05 ③

해설 교통편(지하철), 만나는 시각(오전 10시), 복장(교복), 준비물(노트와 펜)에 대한 언급은 있지만 입장료에 대한 언급은 없다.

어휘 field trip 현장 학습
ticket office 매표소
school uniform 교복

M I'm so excited about the field trip this Thursday.
W Me, too. We're going to the science park, right?
M Yes. Do you want to go there together?
W Sure. What's the best way to get there?
M By subway. It's a 10-minute walk from City Hall Station.
W Okay. We'll meet at 10 a.m. in front of the ticket office, right?
M Right. Well, do we have to wear our school uniform on that day?
W Yes. And don't forget to bring a notebook and a pen.
M Okay.

남 이번 주 목요일에 현장 학습을 가게 되어 너무 신이 나.
여 나도. 과학 공원에 가는 거 맞지?
남 응. 거기에 같이 갈래?
여 좋아. 거기에 가는 가장 좋은 방법이 뭐니?
남 지하철로 가는 거야. 시청역에서 걸어서 10분 걸리거든.
여 알겠어. 매표소 앞에서 오전 10시에 만나는 거지, 맞지?
남 맞아. 참, 그날 교복을 입어야 하니?
여 그래. 그리고 노트와 펜 가져오는 거 잊지 마.
남 알겠어.

06 ①

해설 여행 가방을 찾지 못한 남자에게 타고 온 항공편을 물은 뒤 그 가방의 도착 일정에 대해 설명해 주고 있는 상황으로 보아 공항에서 이루어지는 대화임을 알 수 있다.

어휘 suitcase[sjúːtkèis] 여행 가방
flight[flait] 항공편
luggage[lʌ́gidʒ] 짐, 수하물
baggage claim area
(공항의) 수하물 찾는 곳
baggage[bǽgidʒ] 짐, 수하물

W Excuse me, sir. Do you need any help?
M I can't find my suitcase.
W What flight were you on?
M It was KO 747 from New York.
W Did you check the baggage claim area?
M Yes. I waited for my luggage to come out for more than 30 minutes.
W Oh, really? I'll check for you. [Pause] There were some problems with the baggage on that flight. So your suitcase will arrive on the next flight from New York.
M I see. How long do I have to wait?
W It'll arrive in an hour.

여 실례합니다. 도움이 필요하신가요?
남 제 여행 가방을 찾을 수 없어요.
여 어느 항공편으로 오셨나요?
남 뉴욕에서 온 KO 747이에요.
여 짐 찾는 곳을 확인해 보셨나요?
남 네. 30분도 넘게 제 짐이 나오길 기다렸어요.
여 아, 정말요? 제가 확인해 보겠습니다. [잠시 후] 그 비행기의 수하물 처리에 문제가 있었습니다. 그래서 고객님의 가방은 뉴욕에서 오는 다음 비행편으로 도착할 예정입니다.
남 그렇군요. 얼마나 기다려야 하나요?
여 한 시간 후에 도착할 것입니다.

07 ③

① M How about pizza or spaghetti for lunch?
  W Sorry, I don't like either of them.
② M This tennis match is really exciting.
  W I feel the same way.
③ M Would you mind helping me with these bags?
  W Don't forget to write your name on the bags.
④ M Do you have something in mind?
  W Well, I want a striped shirt.
⑤ M I'm sorry, but can you say that again?
  W Okay. The number is 345-1234.

① 남 점심으로 피자나 스파게티를 먹는 게 어때?
  여 미안하지만 나는 둘 다 좋아하지 않아.
② 남 이 테니스 경기는 정말 흥미로워.
  여 나도 그렇게 생각해.
③ 남 이 가방들 드는 것 좀 도와주시겠어요?
  여 가방에 이름 쓰는 것을 잊지 마세요.
④ 남 마음에 두신 것이 있나요?
  여 음, 줄무늬 셔츠를 원해요.
⑤ 남 미안하지만 다시 말해 줄래?
  여 알겠어. 번호는 345-1234야.

08 ②

W Hey, Gary. Are you going to Black Pearl's fan meeting tomorrow?
M No, I can't. I have a violin lesson.
W Oh, that's too bad.
M Yes, I was really looking forward to it.
W Why don't you ask your teacher to change the date of the lesson?
M I already did, but my teacher said no. If possible, could you get me their autographs?
W Sure. I'll do that for you!
M Thanks so much.

여 안녕, Gary. 내일 Black Pearl의 팬 미팅에 갈 거지?
남 아니, 못 가. 바이올린 레슨이 있거든.
여 아, 안됐다.
남 맞아, 난 정말 그걸 기대하고 있었거든.
여 선생님께 레슨 날짜를 바꿔 달라고 부탁하는 게 어때?
남 이미 했는데 선생님이 안 된다고 하셨어. 가능하다면 사인을 받아줄 수 있니?
여 물론이지. 너를 위해서 받아 줄게!
남 정말 고마워.

09 ②

M Ladies and gentlemen, I have an announcement. There is a heavy typhoon coming this way. The weather report says it will bring a thunderstorm along with heavy wind. So, I'm sorry to tell you we have to cancel the baseball game between AB Tigers and KO Dragons today. Thank you for your understanding and patience. Please drive home safely.

남 관중 여러분, 안내 말씀 드립니다. 강력한 태풍이 이쪽으로 몰려오고 있습니다. 일기 예보에 따르면 강한 바람과 함께 천둥 번개와 몰려올 거라고 합니다. 그래서 오늘 AB Tigers와 KO Dragons와의 야구 경기는 취소하게 됨을 말씀드리게 되어 죄송합니다. 여러분의 이해와 양해에 감사드립니다. 안전 운전하시기 바랍니다.

10 ④

해설 25달러짜리 셔츠를 두 개를 구매하면 전체 금액(50달러)에서 10퍼센트를 할인을 받을 수 있다고 했으므로 남자는 45달러를 지불할 것이다.

어휘 get a discount 할인을 받다
off[ɔːf] 할인되어
total[tóutl] 전체의, 총

M May I help you?
W Yes. How much is this shirt?
M The shirt is $25.
W Do you have the same shirt in a different color?
M Yes, it comes in white, blue, green, and black.
W I'll take one white shirt and one blue shirt. Can I get a discount for these shirts?
M Yes. You get 10 percent off the total price if you buy 2 shirts.
W Great. I'll pay by card.

남 도와드릴까요?
여 네. 이 셔츠는 얼마인가요?
남 그 셔츠는 25달러입니다.
여 같은 셔츠로 다른 색상도 있나요?
남 네, 흰색, 파란색, 초록색, 검정색으로 나와요.
여 흰색 셔츠와 파란색 셔츠를 하나씩 살게요. 이 셔츠들을 할인받을 수 있나요?
남 네. 두 개를 사시면, 전체 금액에서 10퍼센트 할인해 드려요.
여 좋네요. 카드로 계산할게요.

11 ②

해설 여자는 오늘 밤에 볼 영화를 찾아서 예매하겠다고 했다.

어휘 book[buk] 예매[예약]하다
not ~ either ~도 또한 아닌
finish v-ing ~하는 것을 끝내다

W Tom, did you book movie tickets for tonight?
M No, I didn't. I was too busy.
W Have you decided which movie we are going to watch?
M Sorry, but I haven't done that, either.
W Hmm... Then I'll look for a good movie to watch and get the tickets on my smartphone.
M Thank you so much. I have to finish writing this report by this afternoon.
W No problem. I have nothing to do now.

여 Tom, 오늘 밤에 볼 영화표 예매했니?
남 아니, 못했어. 너무 바빴거든.
여 어떤 영화를 볼지는 결정했니?
남 미안하지만 그것도 못 했어.
여 음… 그럼 내가 스마트폰으로 볼만한 좋은 영화를 찾아보고 표를 예매할게.
남 정말 고마워. 오늘 오후까지 이 보고서를 끝내야 하거든.
여 괜찮아. 난 지금 할 일이 없는걸.

12 ③

해설 참가 대상(모든 학생), 작품 주제(자신의 꿈), 출품 마감일(5월 15일), 수상자 상품(태블릿 PC)에 대해서는 언급이 있지만 작품 크기에 대한 언급은 없다.

어휘 pleased[pliːzd] 기쁜
announce[ənáuns] 발표하다, 알리다
participant[pɑːrtísəpənt] 참가자
create[kriéit] 창조하다, 만들다
artwork[áːrtwə̀ːrk] 미술품
watercolor[wɔ́tərkə̀lər] 수채화 그림 물감
hand in 제출하다
award[əwɔ́ːrd] 수여하다

W Hi, students! I'm pleased to announce the school art contest. The contest is open to all students at our school. Participants should create artwork that shows his or her dream. The artwork must be painted on white paper with watercolors. Participants must hand in their artworks to the school art club by May 15th. The top 3 winners will be chosen and tablet PCs will be awarded to all of them. Thank you for listening.

여 안녕하세요, 학생 여러분! 교내 미술 대회를 알리게 되어 기쁩니다. 대회는 우리 학교 학생들이라면 모두 참가할 수 있습니다. 참가자들은 자신의 꿈을 표현하는 미술 작품을 만들어야 합니다. 작품은 수채화 물감으로 흰 종이에 그려져야 합니다. 참가자들은 5월 15일까지 학교 미술 동아리에 작품을 제출해야 합니다. 상위 3명을 선정해서 모두에게 태블릿 PC를 수여할 것입니다. 들어주셔서 감사합니다.

13 ④

해설 꽃은 백합이어야 하며, 30달러 이하인 꽃바구니 중에서 크기가 큰 것을 선택할 것이다.

어휘 basket[bǽskit] 바구니
lily[líli] 백합

W Paul, what should we buy for Grandma's birthday present?

M How about a flower basket? She loves flowers.

W That sounds good! <u>Her favorite flowers are</u> roses and lilies.

M She has a lot of roses in her garden, so let's <u>go for lilies instead</u>.

W Okay. How much do we have?

M We only have $30. We have to choose the size.

W Let's <u>get a bigger one</u>.

M Okay. I hope she loves our gift.

여 Paul, 할머니 생신 선물로 뭘 사야 할까?

남 꽃바구니가 어때? 할머니는 꽃을 좋아하시잖아.

여 좋아! 가장 좋아하시는 꽃은 장미와 백합이야.

남 할머니 정원에 장미꽃이 많이 있으니까 대신에 백합으로 사자.

여 좋아. 우리 얼마를 가지고 있지?

남 우리 30달러만 있어. 크기를 골라야 해.

여 큰 것으로 사자.

남 그래. 할머니께서 우리 선물을 좋아하셨으면 좋겠다.

14 ②

해설 원하는 장소에 운전사가 데려다주고 몇몇 나라에서는 'cab'이라고도 부른다고 했으므로 택시가 알맞다.

어휘 public[pʌ́blik] 공공의, 대중의
transportation[trænspərtéiʃən] 운송수단; 수송
arrive at ~에 도착하다
destination[dèstənéiʃən] 목적지
cab[kæb] 택시
several[sévrəl] 몇몇의
through[θru:] ~을 통해서

M This is a type of public transportation. It's <u>a car with a driver</u>. The driver takes you <u>anywhere you want</u> to go. You should <u>pay the driver</u> when you arrive at your destination. People call this a 'cab' in several countries, such as England and America. New York is <u>famous for its yellow</u> cabs. You can call this through a smartphone app these days.

남 이것은 일종의 대중교통수단이에요. 이것은 운전사가 있는 자동차예요. 운전사는 당신이 원하는 곳으로 데려다줘요. 목적지에 도착하면 운전사에게 돈을 지불해야 하지요. 영국이나 미국과 같은 몇몇 나라에서는 이것을 'cab'이라고 불러요. 뉴욕은 노란 cab들로 유명해요. 요즘에는 이것을 스마트폰 앱을 통해서 부를 수도 있어요.

15 ③

해설 여자는 남자에게 팬케이크를 만드는 동안 숙제를 끝내라고 했고, 남자는 알겠다고 했다.

어휘 dinnertime[dínərtàim] 저녁 식사 시간
be supposed to-v ~하기로 되어 있다
pancake[pǽnkèik] 팬케이크

M Mom, I'm so hungry. I can't wait to eat until dinnertime.

W Well, <u>aren't you supposed to</u> go to your swimming lesson?

M No, it's Tuesday. I don't have any lessons today.

W Oh, that's right. So do you want <u>something to eat</u> now?

M Yes. Can you make me some pancakes, please?

W No problem. But make sure that <u>you finish your homework</u> while I'm cooking.

M Okay, <u>I'll do that</u>.

남 엄마, 엄청 배고파요. 저녁 시간까지 먹는 걸 기다릴 수가 없어요.

여 음, 너 수영 강습받으러 가야 하는 거 아니니?

남 아니요, 오늘 화요일이잖아요. 오늘은 아무 수업도 없어요.

여 아, 맞다. 그래서 지금 뭔가 좀 먹고 싶다는 거니?

남 네. 팬케이크를 좀 만들어 주실 수 있나요?

여 그래. 하지만 내가 요리하는 동안 숙제를 꼭 끝내야 해.

남 알겠어요, 그럴게요.

16 ④

해설 9시에 공항으로 여동생을 데리러 가야 한다고 했다.

어휘 attend[əténd] 참석하다
lecture[léktʃər] 강의, 강연
director[diréktər] 감독
direct[dirékt] (영화를) 감독하다
parasite[pǽrəsàit] 기생충
pick up 데리러 가다
be over 끝나다

W Will you attend the lecture about Korean films with me tonight?
M I'd love to go, but I'm not sure I can. What time does it start?
W It starts at 6 p.m. The speaker is a famous film director. He directed *Parasite*.
M That sounds really interesting, but I have to pick up my sister from the airport at 9.
W I'm sure the lecture will be over by 7:30.
M Okay. Then I have enough time.
W Great!

여 오늘 밤에 나랑 한국 영화에 대한 강연을 들으러 갈래?
남 가고는 싶은데 갈 수 있을지 모르겠어. 몇 시에 시작해?
여 저녁 6시에 시작해. 강사가 유명한 영화감독이야. 그는 〈기생충〉을 감독했어.
남 정말 흥미롭게 들리는데, 9시에 공항으로 여동생을 데리러 가야 해.
여 강연은 7시 30분까지는 틀림없이 끝날 거야.
남 알겠어. 그럼 시간이 충분하겠다.
여 잘됐다!

17 ④

해설 영국에 가게 된 배경을 설명하는 여자의 말에 좋은 시간을 보내길 바란다는 응답이 가장 적절하다.

어휘 win first prize 1등 상을 타다
amazing[əméiziŋ] 놀라운, 대단한
invite[inváit] 초대하다
change A's mind 마음을 바꾸다

M Mina, you look so happy.
W Oh, I am. I won first prize in the speech contest.
M That's amazing. Congratulations! That's why you are happy.
W Well, that's not all. I have more good news.
M What is it?
W A friend of mine in England invited me to stay at her house.
M That's amazing. Are you going with your parents?
W No, I'm going alone. My parents said no at first. But since I won first prize in the contest, they changed their minds.
M Great. I hope you have a great time there.

남 미나야, 너 무척 행복해 보여.
여 아, 행복해. 말하기 대회에서 1등을 했거든.
남 놀랍다. 축하해! 그래서 네가 행복한 거구나.
여 음, 그게 다가 아니야. 좋은 소식이 더 있어.
남 뭔데?
여 영국에 사는 내 친구 중 한 명이 그녀의 집에 나를 초대했어.
남 놀라운데. 부모님과 함께 가니?
여 아니, 혼자 갈 거야. 부모님이 처음에는 안 된다고 하셨거든. 하지만 내가 대회에서 1등을 해서 마음을 바꾸셨어.
남 잘됐다. 그곳에서 좋은 시간을 보내길 바라.

① 그럼 너는 열심히 연습해야 해.
② 기운 내! 다음에는 더 잘할 거야.
③ 안됐다. 그 말을 들으니 유감이다.
⑤ 나도 영어 말하기 대회에 참가하기로 했어.

18 ①

해설 파란색 포장지는 없고 빨간색, 초록색, 노란색 종이가 있다는 남자의 말에 세 가지 색 중 하나를 고르는 응답이 적절하다.

어휘 on sale 할인 중인
gift-wrap[gift-ræp] 선물용으로 포장하다

W Do you have video games?
M Yes, we do. What are you looking for?
W *Star Wars*.
M It's right here. And it's on sale today for $20.
W Great! I'll take it. It's a gift for my friend, so can I have it gift-wrapped?
M Sure, you can. What colored paper would you like?
W Hmm... Do you have blue paper?

여 비디오 게임이 있나요?
남 네. 어떤 것을 찾고 계신가요?
여 Star Wars요.
남 바로 여기 있습니다. 오늘 세일해서 20달러예요.
여 잘됐네요! 그걸로 살게요. 제 친구 선물이니까 선물 포장해 주시겠어요?
남 물론이죠, 어떤 색의 종이를 원하세요?
여 음… 파란색 종이가 있나요?

M Sorry, but there's <u>no blue paper</u>. I have red, green, or yellow paper.
W <u>Green will be fine.</u>

남 죄송하지만 파란색 종이는 없어요. 빨간색, 초록색 아니면 노란색 종이가 있어요.
여 초록색이 좋을 것 같아요.

② 나는 글을 쓸 종이가 없어.
③ 네 색연필을 사용해도 되니?
④ 나는 〈스타워즈〉 시리즈를 전부 다 봤어요.
⑤ 맞아. 내 취미는 피겨를 모으는 거야.

19 ③

[해설] 여자가 새로 오픈한 한식당에 가자고 제안했으므로 제안을 수락하거나 거절하는 응답이 이어져야 한다.

[어휘] already[ɔ:lrédi] 이미, 벌써
Shall we ~ ? 우리 ~할까?
open[óupən] 열다, 개장하다
[선택지]
honestly[ánistli] 솔직히
spicy[spáisi] 매운
someday[sʌ́mdei] 언젠가, 훗날

W It's already 1 p.m. Let's hurry to the library. I have many things to do.
M I am so hungry. <u>Can we have lunch</u> before going to the library?
W Okay. What are we going to have?
M Well, how about Chinese food?
W Sorry, but I don't <u>like Chinese food</u>. How about pizza or spaghetti?
M I had Italian food yesterday.
W Then <u>shall we go to</u> the Korean restaurant which opened last week? I heard the <u>food there is amazing</u>.
M Good idea. I like spicy Korean food!

여 벌써 오후 1시네. 도서관으로 서두르자. 할 일이 많거든.
남 나 너무 배고파. 도서관에 가기 전에 점심을 먹을래?
여 그래. 뭘 먹을까?
남 음, 중국 음식은 어때?
여 미안하지만 난 중국 음식을 안 좋아해. 피자나 스파게티 어때?
남 어제 난 이탈리아 음식을 먹었어.
여 그럼, 지난주에 오픈한 한식당에 갈까? 거기 음식이 끝내준다고 들었어.
남 좋은 생각이야. 나는 매운 한국 음식 좋아해!

① 빨리 피자를 먹고 싶어.
② 솔직히, 나는 요리를 잘 못해.
④ 나도 언젠가 그 나라에 가고 싶어.
⑤ 아니, 나는 전에 중국 음식을 먹어본 적이 없어.

20 ②

[해설] 자신의 물건을 치우지 않는 동생에게 물건을 치우라고 말하고 싶은 상황이다.

[어휘] share[ʃɛər] ~을 같이 쓰다
get along well 사이좋게 지내다
relationship[riléiʃənʃip] 관계
clean up 치우다
messy[mési] 지저분한
[선택지]
from now on 이제부터
decorate[dékərèit] 장식하다

W Olivia has a sister, Julia, who is 2 years younger than her. They share a room. They <u>get along well</u>, and they have a good relationship. But there is one thing that Olivia doesn't <u>like about her sister</u>. Julia never cleans up her things, so their <u>room is always messy</u>. So Olivia decides to tell her sister to <u>clean up her things</u>. In this situation, what would Olivia most likely say to Julia?

Olivia Julia, <u>you should clean up your things.</u>

여 Olivia는 그녀보다 두 살 어린 여동생 Julia가 있다. 그들은 함께 방을 쓴다. 그들은 사이좋게 지내고 원만한 관계를 유지한다. 하지만 Olivia가 그녀의 여동생에 대해 마음에 들어 하지 않는 점이 한 가지 있다. Julia는 자신의 물건을 절대 치우지 않아서 방이 항상 지저분하다. 그래서 Olivia는 여동생에게 그녀의 물건을 정리하라고 말하기로 결심한다. 이러한 상황에서 Olivia가 Julia에게 할 말로 가장 적절한 것은 무엇인가?

Olivia Julia, 넌 네 물건들을 치워야 해.

① 이제부터 사이좋게 지내자.
③ 너는 더 자주 샤워를 하는 게 좋겠어.
④ 너에게 좋은 언니가 되겠다고 약속할게.
⑤ 이것들로 우리 방을 꾸미는 게 어때?

01 ①	02 ③	03 ④	04 ②	05 ②	06 ③	07 ⑤
08 ④	09 ⑤	10 ⑤	11 ⑤	12 ③	13 ⑤	14 ②
15 ④	16 ②	17 ①	18 ④	19 ⑤	20 ⑤	

01 ①

[해설] 'Dreams come true!'라고 쓰여진 문장 아래 여러 풍선들을 추가했다고 했다.

[어휘] enter[éntər] 입학하다, 들어가다
sentence[séntəns] 문장
come true 이루어지다, 실현되다
cover[kʌ́vər] 표지
add[sǽd] 추가하다
stand for ~을 상징하다

W Hey, Peter. What are you doing?
M I'm making a study planner for my sister. She'll enter middle school next year.
W That's why you wrote the sentence "Dreams come true!" on the cover.
M Yes. My sister likes flowers, but I added a few balloons instead under the title.
W Why did you add balloons?
M They stand for hope. I wanted to make it special for her.
W I see. I hope your sister likes it.

여 안녕, Peter. 뭐 하고 있니?
남 여동생에게 줄 학습 플래너를 만들고 있어. 걔가 내년에 중학교에 입학하거든.
여 그래서 플래너에 '꿈은 이루어진다!'라는 문장을 썼구나.
남 맞아. 내 동생은 꽃을 좋아하기는 하지만 문구 아래에 풍선 여러 개를 대신 추가했어.
여 왜 풍선을 추가했어?
남 그건 희망을 상징하거든. 동생을 위해 특별하게 만들고 싶었어.
여 그렇구나. 네 동생이 좋아했으면 좋겠네.

02 ③

[해설] 기능(음악 듣기, 스케줄 확인), 색상(파란색), 가격(400달러), 보증 기간(1년)에 대한 언급은 있지만 제조사에 대한 언급은 없다.

[어휘] schedule[skédʒuːl] 스케줄, 일정
cost[kɔːst] (비용이) ~들다
for free 무상으로, 무료로
repair[ripέər] 수리하다, 고치다
in cash 현금으로

W Hello, how may I help you?
M I'd like to buy a smartwatch.
W How about this one? You can listen to music and check your schedule with it.
M Great. Does it come in different colors?
W It comes in red and blue.
M Then I'll take a blue one. How much does it cost?
W It is $400. You can get it repaired for free for one year.
M Okay. I will pay in cash. Here is the money.

여 어서 오세요, 도와드릴까요?
남 스마트 시계를 사려고요.
여 이건 어떠세요? 음악을 듣거나 스케줄을 확인할 수 있어요.
남 좋네요. 다른 색상으로도 나오나요?
여 빨간색과 파란색으로 나와요.
남 그럼 파란색으로 살게요. 얼마인가요?
여 400달러입니다. 1년간 무상으로 수리를 받을 수 있어요.
남 알겠습니다. 현금으로 낼게요. 여기 돈 있습니다.

03 ④

[해설] 이번 주에 같이 가기로 한 도서전에 대해 다시 한번 알려주기 위해 전화했다.

[어휘] book fair 도서전
forget[fərgét] 잊어버리다
(forget-forgot-forgotten)
student ID 학생증
without[wiðáut] ~ 없이
remind[rimáind] 다시 한 번 알려주다, 상기시키다

[Cell phone rings.]
M Hello.
W Hi, Mark. We're still going to the book fair, right?
M Oh, right. I forgot about it. When is the book fair?
W The book fair is this Saturday. It starts at 9 a.m.
M I see. Do I need to bring anything?
W You need to bring your student ID. Without it, you have to pay $5.
M Okay. Thanks for letting me know.

[휴대전화가 울린다.]
남 여보세요.
여 안녕, Mark. 우리 도서전에 가는 거지, 맞지?
남 아, 맞아. 깜빡했어. 도서전이 언제야?
여 도서전은 이번 주 토요일이야. 오전 9시에 시작해.
남 그렇구나. 내가 뭘 챙겨야 하니?
여 학생증을 가져와야 해. 그게 없으면 5달러를 내야 하거든.
남 알겠어. 알려 줘서 고마워.

W	That's why I called. I wanted to remind you about it.	여 그래서 내가 전화 한거야. 다시 한 번 알려 주고 싶었거든.
M	I won't forget about it.	남 잊지 않을게.

04 ②

해설 남자는 11시에 출발하여 1시 30분에 부산에 도착하는 급행열차를 탄다고 했다.

어휘 check[tʃek] 확인하다
express[iksprés] 급행의, 신속한

M	Excuse me. What time does the next train for Busan leave?	남 실례합니다. 다음 부산행 열차가 몇 시에 출발하나요?
W	The next one leaves at 10:30 a.m. and it arrives in Busan at 2:30 p.m.	여 다음 열차는 오전 10시 30분에 떠나고 부산에는 오후 2시 30분에 도착해요.
M	I need to arrive in Busan before 2 p.m. Is there any faster way to get there?	남 전 오후 2시 전에는 부산에 가야 하는데요. 그곳에 가는 더 빠른 방법이 있나요?
W	Let me check. [Pause] There is an express train at 11 a.m., and it arrives in Busan at 1:30 p.m.	여 확인해 볼게요. [잠시 후] 오전 11시에 급행열차가 있는데 그건 오후 1시 30분에 부산에 도착해요.
M	Oh, I see. Can I get one ticket for the express one?	남 아, 그렇군요. 급행열차로 표 1장 주실래요?
W	Okay. The ticket for the express train is $60.	여 알겠습니다. 급행열차 표는 60달러입니다.
M	Here you are.	남 여기에 있습니다.

05 ②

해설 엘리베이터를 같이 타기 위해 출발하지 않도록 다급하게 요청하고 있는 상황이다.

어휘 be busy v-ing ~하느라 바쁘다
work on ~ 작업을 하다
get on 올라타다 (↔ get off 내리다)
elevator[éləvèitər] 승강기, 엘리베이터
out of order 고장이 난
stair[ster] 계단
floor[flɔːr] 층
suit[suːt] 정장, 수트
fitting room 탈의실

① M	You look so tired.	① 남 너 무척 피곤해 보여.
W	I've been so busy working on my reports.	여 보고서를 쓰느라 바쁘게 작업하고 있거든.
② M	Please wait! I'm getting on the elevator.	② 남 기다려 주세요! 저도 엘리베이터에 탈 거예요.
W	Okay. Take your time.	여 알겠습니다. 천천히 하세요.
③ M	I think this elevator is out of order.	③ 남 이 엘리베이터는 고장 난 것 같군요.
W	Oh no! Then we must take the stairs.	여 이런! 그럼 계단을 이용해야겠네요.
④ M	Which floor are you going to?	④ 남 몇 층에 가세요?
W	I'm getting off at the 5th floor.	여 5층에서 내릴 거예요.
⑤ M	May I try this suit on?	⑤ 남 이 정장을 입어 봐도 될까요?
W	Sure. There's a fitting room over there.	여 물론이죠. 저쪽에 탈의실이 있어요.

06 ③

해설 버스 시간에 대해 대화를 나누고 있고, 버스가 오자 대화가 마무리되는 상황으로 보아 대화 장소는 버스 정류장임을 알 수 있다.

어휘 wallet[wάlit] 지갑
bench[bentʃ] 벤치, 긴 의자
miss[mis] 놓치다
every[évri] ~마다

W	Excuse me. Is this wallet yours?	여 실례합니다. 혹시 이 지갑의 주인이신가요?
M	Oh, yes, it's mine. Thank you. Where did you get that?	남 아, 네. 제 거예요. 감사합니다. 어디서 주우셨어요?
W	It was right under the bench. What bus are you waiting for?	여 바로 벤치 아래에 있었어요. 어느 버스를 기다리시나요?
M	Bus number 95. I just missed it.	남 95번 버스요. 근데 방금 놓쳤어요.
W	Don't worry. That bus comes every 5 minutes.	여 걱정 마세요. 그 버스는 5분마다 오거든요.
M	That's true. Oh, here comes the next bus. Thanks again and have a nice day.	남 맞네요. 아, 다음 버스가 오네요. 다시 한 번 감사하고 좋은 하루 보내세요.
W	You have a good day, too.	여 좋은 하루 보내세요.

07 ⑤

해설 여자는 머리가 아파서 남자에게 약을 사다 달라고 부탁했다.

어휘 package[pǽkidʒ] 소포
supermarket[súpərmàrkit] 슈퍼마켓
headache[hédèik] 두통
medicine[médisn] 약
stop by 들르다
drugstore[drʌ́gstɔ̀ːr] 약국

[Cell phone rings.]

M Hello.

W Honey, where are you?

M I just left the post office. I sent some packages and now I'm going to the supermarket to get some milk.

W Okay. Can I ask you to get something for me?

M Sure. What is it?

W I have a headache. Can you buy some medicine for me?

M Okay. I'll stop by the drugstore before I go home.

W Thank you.

[휴대전화가 울린다.]

남 여보세요.

여 여보, 지금 어디예요?

남 우체국에서 막 나왔어요. 소포를 부치고 지금은 우유를 사러 슈퍼마켓에 가는 길이에요.

여 알겠어요. 저 뭐 하나만 사 오라고 부탁해도 돼요?

남 물론이죠. 그게 뭐예요?

여 머리가 아파서요. 약 좀 사다 줄래요?

남 알겠어요. 집에 가기 전에 약국에 들릴게요.

여 고마워요.

08 ④

해설 소요 시간(약 3시간), 투어 장소(사이판 동부 해안), 식사 제공 여부(선상 점심 식사 포함), 투어 비용(어른 50달러, 어린이 30달러)에 관해 언급되었지만 신청 방법에 대한 언급은 없다.

어휘 visitor[vízitər] 방문객
experience[ikspíəriəns] 경험하다
amazing[əméiziŋ] 놀라운
including[inklúːdiŋ] ~을 포함하여
luxury[lʌ́kʃəri] 호화로움, 사치
eastern coast 동해안

W Hello, visitors! Do you want to experience something amazing? Then join our Dolphin Watching Tour. This tour will take about 3 hours, including dolphin watching and a lunch party. A luxury boat will take you to the eastern coast of Saipan. There, you will watch wild dolphins swimming and have a nice meal on the boat. A tour costs $50 for adults and $30 for children. Thanks for listening and enjoy your time in Saipan.

여 안녕하세요, 방문객 여러분! 뭔가 놀라운 것을 경험하고 싶으신가요? 그렇다면 저희 돌고래 관람 투어와 함께 하세요. 이 투어는 돌고래 관람과 점심 파티를 포함하여 약 3시간이 소요될 겁니다. 호화로운 보트가 여러분을 사이판의 동부 해안으로 데려갈 것입니다. 그곳에서, 야생의 돌고래가 유영하는 것을 보고 선상에서 맛있는 식사를 할 것입니다. 투어는 성인 50달러, 어린이는 30달러의 비용이 듭니다. 들어주셔서 감사하며, 사이판에서 즐거운 시간 보내세요.

09 ⑤

해설 컴퓨터 작동을 위해 사용하는 것으로 파일을 열고 닫고 복사하거나 무언가를 그리거나 칠할 수도 있는 장치는 마우스이다.

어휘 device[diváis] 장치, 도구
control[kəntróul] 제어하다, 조절하다
machine[məʃíːn] 기계
invent[invént] 발명하다
type[taip] 입력하다, 타자를 치다
command[kəmǽnd] 명령어; 명령
keyboard[kíbɔ̀ːrd] 키보드

M This is the device that all the computer users use to control their machines. This device was invented in 1964. Until then people controlled their computers by typing commands on their keyboards. By using this, however, today's computer users can not only open, close, and copy their files, but also draw or paint something on their screens.

남 이것은 모든 컴퓨터 사용자들이 자신의 기계를 제어하기 위해 사용하는 장치예요. 이 장치는 1964년에 발명되었어요. 그때까지 사람들은 키보드로 명령어를 쳐서 자신의 컴퓨터를 제어했어요. 하지만, 오늘날의 컴퓨터 사용자들은 이것을 사용하지만 파일을 열고 닫고 복사할 수 있을 뿐만 아니라 화면에 무언가를 그리거나 칠할 수도 있어요.

10 ⑤

해설 옆자리에 앉아도 되는지 묻는 말에 교통편을 안내해 주는 응답은 어색하다.

어휘 sold out 매진된
seat[siːt] (앉을 수 있는) 자리, 좌석

① M How do I look in this blue jacket?
　 W You look wonderful.
② M Can you make it on Wednesday at 3 p.m.?
　 W Yes, that's fine.
③ M I want 2 tickets for the movie that starts at 7.
　 W Sorry, but all the tickets for 7 are sold out.
④ M Would you please take a picture of me?
　 W Sure. Say cheese!
⑤ M Excuse me. Is this seat taken?
　 W You can take the number 10 bus from here.

① 남　이 파란색 재킷이 내게 어울리니?
　 여　정말 멋져 보여.
② 남　수요일 오후 3시에 시간 되세요?
　 여　네, 가능해요.
③ 남　7시에 시작하는 영화표 두 장 주세요.
　 여　죄송하지만 7시 표는 모두 매진되었어요.
④ 남　사진 한 장만 찍어 주시겠어요?
　 여　물론이죠. 웃으세요!
⑤ 남　실례합니다. 여기 자리 있나요?
　 여　여기서 10번 버스를 타시면 돼요.

11 ⑤

해설 남자가 다시 보내주는 이메일 주소로 과제를 보내 달라고 하자 여자는 지금 당장 보내겠다고 했다.

어휘 project[práːdʒekt] 과제
send[send] 보내다 (send-sent-sent)
text[tekst] (휴대전화로) 문자를 보내다
as soon as possible 되도록 빨리

[Cell phone rings.]
W Hello.
M Hi, Jenny. This is Mr. Stevens. I'm calling you about your final project.
W Oh, hello, Mr. Stevens. Is there something wrong with it?
M I didn't get it from you today.
W Are you sure? I sent it to you by e-mail.
M Maybe you sent it to the wrong e-mail address. Can you send it to me again?
W No problem.
M I'll text you my e-mail address. I want you to send your project as soon as possible.
W Okay. I'll do it right away.

[휴대전화가 울린다.]
여　여보세요.
남　안녕, Jenny. Stevens 선생님이야. 네 기말 과제 때문에 전화 걸었어.
여　아, 안녕하세요, Stevens 선생님. 뭐가 잘못 되었나요?
남　너한테서 오늘 받지 못 했단다.
여　정말이세요? 제가 이메일로 선생님께 보내드렸는데요.
남　아마 잘못된 이메일 주소로 보낸 것 같구나. 나한테 다시 보내 줄래?
여　그럴게요.
남　내 이메일 주소를 문자로 보낼게. 되도록 빨리 과제를 보냈으면 좋겠구나.
여　알겠어요. 지금 바로 보낼게요.

12 ③

해설 오후 2시 경기가 시작하기 한 시간 전에 만나기로 했으므로 두 사람은 오후 1시에 만날 것이다.

어휘 special[ispéʃəl] 특별한
between A and B A와 B 사이에
enough[ináf] 충분한
during[djúəriŋ] ~ 동안

M Sarah, do you have any plans for this Saturday?
W Nothing special. Why?
M I have 2 tickets to the baseball game between the Lions and Twins. Would you like to go with me?
W I'd love to. What time does it start?
M At 2 p.m.
W Well, how about meeting 30 minutes before the game at the stadium?
M I don't think that is enough time. We should buy some snacks to eat during the game. Let's meet an hour before the game.
W Okay. See you then.

남　Sarah, 이번 주 토요일에 특별한 계획 있니?
여　특별한 건 없어. 왜?
남　Lions와 Twins 간의 야구 경기 표가 두 장 있거든. 나와 같이 갈래?
여　그렇게 할게. 몇 시에 시작하는데?
남　오후 2시에.
여　그럼, 경기 시작 30분 전에 경기장에서 만날까?
남　시간이 충분하지 않은 것 같아. 경기를 볼 동안 먹을 간식을 사야 하거든. 경기 한 시간 전에 만나자.
여　좋아. 그때 보자.

13 ⑤

해설 화장실에서 가깝지 않고 음식 가판대와 분수대에서 가까운 곳에 매트를 둔다고 했다.

어휘 farther[fáːrðər] 더 멀리
inside[ìnsáid] 안에, 안으로
section[sékʃən] 구역
parking lot 주차장
noisy[nɔ́izi] 소란스러운
dusty[dʌ́sti] 먼지가 많은
food stand 음식 가판대
restroom[réstrù(ː)m] 화장실
place[pleis] 두다, 놓다
fountain[fáuntən] 분수(대)

M The weather is really good today.
W I agree. It's a perfect day for a picnic. Where should we sit down?
M Let's go farther inside. The two sections near the parking lot seem noisy and dusty.
W How about near the food stands? We didn't bring any food.
M Okay. Let's buy some food and drinks there. Which section do you want to go to?
W Well, I don't want to sit near the restroom.
M Okay. Let's place our picnic mat here. It'll be nice to sit near the fountain.

남 오늘 날씨 정말 좋다.
여 맞아. 피크닉 하기에 완벽한 날이야. 어디에 앉을까?
남 좀 더 안쪽으로 들어가자. 주차장과 가까이에 있는 두 구역은 시끄럽고 먼지가 많을 것 같아.
여 음식 가판대 근처는 어때? 우리 음식을 하나도 안 가져 왔잖아.
남 좋아. 그곳에서 음식과 음료를 좀 사자. 어느 구역으로 가고 싶니?
여 음, 난 화장실 가까이에는 앉고 싶지 않아.
남 좋아. 여기에 피크닉 매트를 깔자. 분수대 근처에 앉는 게 좋을 거야.

14 ②

해설 남자는 어제 영화를 보았고 그 영화의 포스터를 지금 걸고 있다.

어휘 hang up (그림·옷 등을) 걸다
poster[póustər] 포스터

W Hey, Ken. What are you doing?
M I'm hanging up this movie poster of *The Lion King*.
W I heard a lot about the movie. Where did you get the poster?
M I watched the movie last night and I got it at the theater. Can you help me hang this poster?
W Sure. Are you going to put it over your desk?
M No. I want it on the wall by the window.
W That's a good idea.

여 안녕, Ken. 뭐하고 있니?
남 〈라이온 킹〉 영화 포스터를 걸고 있어.
여 그 영화에 대해 많이 들었어. 그 포스터는 어디서 난거야?
남 어젯밤에 영화를 봤는데 극장에서 그것을 샀어. 이 포스터 거는 걸 도와줄래?
여 그래. 책상 위에 걸 거니?
남 아니. 창문 옆 벽에 두고 싶어.
여 좋은 생각이야.

15 ④

해설 학생들을 대상으로 식목일에 있을 학교 행사를 안내하는 방송이다.

어휘 Arbor Day 식목일
regular[régjələr] 규칙적인, 정기적인
plant[plænt] 심다
seed[siːd] 씨, 씨앗

W Hello, students. As you know, this Friday is Arbor Day. So I'd like to tell you about what we're going to do at school then. On Friday, we won't have regular classes. Instead, we're going to plant some trees and flowers to make the Earth a better place. Please bring some flower seeds or small trees. We really need your help. Thank you.

여 안녕하세요, 학생 여러분. 아시다시피, 이번 주 금요일은 식목일입니다. 그래서 그날 학교에서 우리가 어떤 활동을 할지에 대해 말씀드리려고 합니다. 금요일에 정규 수업은 하지 않습니다. 대신 지구를 더 멋진 장소로 만들기 위해서 나무와 꽃을 심을 것입니다. 꽃씨나 묘목을 가져오시기 바랍니다. 여러분들의 도움이 정말 필요합니다. 감사합니다.

16 ②

해설 총 7달러인데 1달러 할인 쿠폰을 사용하면 할인 받을 수 있다고 했으므로 지불할 금액은 6달러이다.

W May I take your order?
M Yes, I'd like a large coke and a medium popcorn, please.

여 주문하시겠어요?
남 네, 콜라 큰 것 하나와 중간 크기의 팝콘 하나 주세요.

어휘 order[ɔ́:rdər] 주문
medium[mí:diəm] 중간의
pay[pei] 지불하다
extra[ékstrə] 추가의
in total 통틀어
discount[dískaunt] 할인
coupon[kú:pan] 쿠폰
total price 총 가격

W Would you like cheese or caramel popcorn?
M Well, do I need to pay more for them?
W Yes. They cost an extra dollar.
M With the caramel one, how much does it come to?
W It will be $7 in total.
M Is it okay if I use this $1 discount coupon?
W Sure. You can get $1 off the total price.
M Great. Here are the money and the coupon.

여 치즈나 캐러멜 팝콘을 원하세요?
남 글쎄요, 그것에 돈을 더 지불해야 하나요?
여 네. 추가로 1달러 비용이 듭니다.
남 캐러멜 팝콘으로 하면 얼마인가요?
여 총 7달러 되겠습니다.
남 이 1달러 할인 쿠폰 사용해도 될까요?
여 네. 총 가격에서 1달러 할인 받으실 수 있어요.
남 잘됐네요. 여기 돈과 쿠폰 있습니다.

17 ①

해설 살이 찌는 것을 걱정하는 사람에게 건강한 식습관을 갖도록 조언하고 있으므로 이에 동의하고 다짐하는 내용의 응답이 자연스럽다.

어휘 gain weight 체중이 늘다
strange[streindʒ] 이상한
at least 적어도, 최소한
late night snack 야식
instant noodle 라면
quit[kwit] 그만두다

M I run and swim almost every day but I'm gaining weight. It's strange.
W Hmm... That really is strange. Do you like eating fast food?
M Yes. I eat fast food at least 3 times a week.
W Do you also enjoy late night snacks?
M Yes. I often eat instant noodles at night.
W You should eat less fast food and quit eating late night snacks.
M You're right. I'll try to do that.

남 거의 매일 달리기와 수영을 하는데 체중은 늘고 있어. 이상해.
여 음… 정말 이상하네. 너 패스트푸드 먹는 거 좋아하니?
남 응. 일주일에 적어도 세 번은 패스트푸드를 먹어.
여 야식도 먹고?
남 응. 종종 밤에 라면을 먹어.
여 넌 패스트푸드를 적게 먹고 야식 먹는 것을 끊어야 해.
남 네 말이 맞아. 그렇게 하려고 노력할게.

② 아니. 너는 운동을 더 많이 해야 해.
③ 나는 더 이상 먹을 수 없을 것 같아.
④ 좋아. 패스트푸드 음식점으로 가자.
⑤ 맞아. 너는 채소와 과일을 더 많이 먹는 게 좋겠어.

18 ④

해설 탄산음료를 하나 더 달라고 요청하는 남자의 말에 여자가 수락하거나 거절하는 응답이 이어져야 한다.

어휘 fasten A's seat belt 안전벨트를 매다
emergency light 비상등
be allowed to-v ~하도록 허용되다
aisle[ail] 복도, 통로
land[lænd] 착륙하다
arrive at ~에 도착하다
favor[féivər] 부탁

W Excuse me, sir. Please fasten your seat belt. The emergency light is on.
M Oh, I'm sorry. I didn't see it.
W Could you put your bag under your seat? You're not allowed to leave things in the aisle.
M Okay, I will. Well, when are we landing in New York?
W We'll arrive at the airport in about an hour.
M Then would you do me a favor?
W I'd be glad to. What is it?
M May I have another soda, please?
W Sure. I'll be right back with one.

여 실례합니다, 선생님. 안전벨트를 매 주세요. 비상등이 켜졌습니다.
남 아, 죄송해요. 못 봤어요.
여 가방을 좌석 아래에 두시겠어요? 통로에 물건을 두는 건 허용되지 않습니다.
남 알겠습니다. 그런데, 언제 New York에 착륙하나요?
여 한 시간쯤 후에 공항에 도착할 거예요.
남 그럼 부탁 하나만 들어주시겠어요?
여 물론이죠. 뭔가요?
남 탄산음료 하나만 더 주시겠어요?
여 알겠습니다. 금방 하나 가져다 드릴게요.

① 네, 콜라 큰 것 하나 주세요.
② 물론 괜찮아요. 어서 하세요.
③ 고맙지만 사양할게요. 정말 배불러요.
⑤ 아니요, 전에 뉴욕에 가 본 적 없어요.

[해설] 화가 난 이유가 다른 데에 있는 것 같다며 전화해서 물어보라고 했으므로 전화해 보겠다고 하는 것이 자연스럽다.

[어휘] on the way 오는[가는] 중에
upset[ʌpsét] 속상한, 마음이 상한
happen[hǽpən] 발생하다. 일어나다
answer the phone 전화를 받다
[선택지]
acting[ǽktiŋ] 연기

W I saw Amy on the way, and she looked very upset.
M I think I know why.
W Did something happen between you two?
M Well, she called me several times, but I didn't answer the phone.
W Why didn't you?
M I was busy playing computer games, so I didn't know she called me.
W I don't think that's why Amy is upset. Why don't you call her and ask why she called?
M Really? Maybe I should do that right now.

여 오는 길에 Amy를 만났는데 무척 화난 것 같더라.
남 난 왜 그러는지 알 것 같아.
여 너희 둘 사이에 무슨 일 있었어?
남 음. 걔가 전화를 몇 번 했는데 내가 못 받았거든.
여 왜 못 받았는데?
남 컴퓨터 게임을 하느라 바빠서 걔가 전화했는지 몰랐어.
여 그것 때문에 Amy가 화난 것 같진 않아. 걔한테 전화해서 왜 전화했었는지 물어보는 게 어때?
남 정말? 지금 바로 전화해야겠네.

① 난 게임하는 것을 좋아하지 않아.
② 동의해. 그녀의 연기가 정말 마음에 들었어.
③ 대신에 걔한테 줄 선물을 샀어.
④ 그래. 우리는 극장에서 즐거운 시간을 보냈어.

[해설] 놀이공원에 가는 대신에 집에서 영화를 보자고 제안하는 상황이다.

[어휘] final exam 기말고사
plan to-v ~할 계획이다
amusement park 놀이공원
weather forecast 일기 예보
chance[tʃæns] 가능성, 기회
change A's mind 마음을 바꾸다
instead of ~ 대신에

M The final exams are finished, and Mason and Chloe have some time to rest. They are planning to go to an amusement park tomorrow. However, the weather forecast says that there is a high chance of rain and it'll be cold with strong winds tomorrow. So, Mason changes his mind and wants to watch a movie at home instead of going to an amusement park. In this situation, what would Mason most likely say to Chloe?

Mason Chloe, why don't we watch a movie at home instead?

남 기말고사가 끝나서 Mason과 Chloe는 쉴 시간이 생겼다. 그들은 내일 놀이공원에 갈 계획이다. 하지만 일기 예보에서 내일 비 올 확률이 높고 강풍으로 추울 거라고 한다. 그래서 Mason은 마음을 바꿔서 놀이공원에 가는 대신 집에서 영화를 보길 원한다. 이러한 상황에서 Mason이 Chloe에게 할 말로 가장 적절한 것은 무엇인가?

Mason Chloe, 우리 대신 집에서 영화 보는 게 어때?

① 너는 따뜻한 옷을 입는 게 좋겠다.
② 우산 가져오는 거 잊지 마.
③ 너는 롤러코스터 타는 것을 좋아하니?
④ 너 놀이공원에 가 봤니?

01 ②	02 ④	03 ②	04 ⑤	05 ⑤	06 ④	07 ③
08 ③	09 ④	10 ④	11 ②	12 ①	13 ③	14 ②
15 ①	16 ①	17 ⑤	18 ④	19 ③	20 ⑤	

01 ②

해설 뼈다귀 모양의 이름표에 강아지 이름인 Happy가 쓰여 있고 그 밑에 전화번호를 쓰기로 했다.

어휘 name tag 명찰, 이름표
bone [boun] 뼈
change A's mind 마음을 바꾸다

W I made a name tag for my dog Happy. Look!
M It looks like a bone. It's very cute.
W Thanks. Actually, I wanted to make it in a heart shape, but I changed my mind. Happy really likes bones.
M He will love it. Oh, I think you should write your phone number under his name.
W That's a good idea. I'll write my number right away. [Pause] What do you think?
M It's perfect.

여 우리 강아지 Happy를 위해서 내가 만든 이름표야. 봐!
남 뼈다귀처럼 생겼네. 정말 귀엽다.
여 고마워. 실은 하트 모양으로 만들고 싶었는데 마음을 바꿨어. Happy가 뼈다귀를 정말 좋아하거든.
남 Happy가 좋아할 거야. 아, 강아지 이름 밑에 네 전화번호를 써넣는 게 좋을 것 같아.
여 좋은 생각이야. 지금 당장 내 전화번호를 적을게. [잠시 후] 어떻게 생각해?
남 완벽해.

02 ④

해설 종류(고양이), 털 색깔(회색), 나이(3개월), 이름(Scarlett)에 대한 언급은 있지만 먹이에 관한 언급은 없다.

어휘 fur[fəːr] 털
lovely[lʌ́vli] 사랑스러운
give birth to ~을 낳다
kitten[kítn] 새끼 고양이
name after ~의 이름을 따서 명명하다
actress[ǽktris] 여배우
suit[suːt] 어울리다

M Emily, what are you doing?
W I'm looking at pictures of my cat.
M Oh, do you have a cat?
W Yes. She has blue eyes with gray fur.
M Wow, she looks so lovely. How old is she?
W She is 3 months old. My aunt's cat gave birth to 2 kittens and she gave one of them to me.
M What's your cat's name?
W Scarlett. I named her after the famous actress Scarlett Johansson.
M I think the name suits her well.

남 Emily, 뭐하고 있니?
여 우리 고양이 사진을 보고 있어.
남 아, 너 고양이 기르니?
여 응. 회색 털이랑 파란 눈을 가지고 있어.
남 와, 정말 사랑스러워 보인다. 몇 살이야?
여 3개월이 되었어. 이모네 고양이가 새끼를 두 마리 낳았는데 한 마리를 나에게 주셨어.
남 고양이 이름이 뭐니?
여 Scarlett이야. 유명한 여배우인 Scarlett Johansson의 이름을 따서 이름 붙였어.
남 이름이 고양이에게 잘 어울리는 것 같다.

03 ②

해설 이미 예매한 공연의 시간을 3시에서 7시로 변경하고자 전화했다.

어휘 book[buk] 예매[예약]하다
change[tʃeindʒ] 바꾸다, 교환하다
available[əvéiləbl] 이용 가능한
original[ərídʒənəl] 원래의
I'm afraid so. 유감이지만 그렇습니다.

[Telephone rings.]
W Hello, Wonder Park Ticket. May I help you?
M Hello. I booked 2 musical tickets for *Ghost* last month.
W Okay. Is there a problem?
M I booked tickets for the 3 o'clock showing, but I'd like to change them to the 7 o'clock one. Are there any seats available?
W Oh, I'm sorry. Both showings are already sold out.
M I see. I think I have to keep my original tickets then.

[전화벨이 울린다.]
여 여보세요, Wonder Park Ticket입니다. 도와드릴까요?
남 여보세요. 제가 지난달에 뮤지컬 〈Ghost〉 표 두 장을 예매했는데요.
여 네. 무슨 문제라도 있나요?
남 3시 공연 표를 예매했는데 7시 공연으로 바꾸고 싶어서요. 가능한 좌석이 있을까요?
여 아, 죄송합니다. 두 개의 공연 모두 이미 매진되었습니다.
남 그렇군요. 원래의 표를 가지고 있어야겠네요.

W I'm afraid so.
M Thanks for your help.

여 그러셔야 할 것 같네요.
남 도와주셔서 감사합니다.

04 ⑤

[해설] 여자는 오후 3시와 4시 중에서 4시에 사용하겠다고 했다.

[어휘] reserve[rizə́:rv] 예약하다
tennis court 테니스 코트
make it 시간 맞춰 가다

[Telephone rings.]
M Hello, CS Sports Center. How may I help you?
W I'd like to reserve a tennis court for this Saturday.
M Okay. How long are you going to play?
W For one hour. Is there one available from 10 a.m. to 11 a.m.?
M Let me check. [Pause] Sorry, but they're all booked until noon. How about 2 p.m.?
W I can't make it then. Is it possible to use one at 3 p.m. or 4 p.m.?
M You can use one at 4 p.m.
W Great. I'll reserve it for then.

[전화벨이 울린다.]
남 여보세요, CS 스포츠센터입니다. 무엇을 도와드릴까요?
여 이번 주 토요일에 테니스 코트를 예약하고 싶은데요.
남 알겠습니다. 얼마나 오래 테니스를 치실 건가요?
여 1시간이요. 오전 10에서 11시 사이에 사용가능할까요?
남 확인해 볼게요. [잠시 후] 죄송하지만 정오까지는 예약이 모두 차 있어요. 오후 2시는 어떠세요?
여 그때는 시간이 안 돼요. 오후 3시나 4시에 사용 가능할까요?
남 오후 4시에 사용할 수 있어요.
여 잘됐네요. 그럼 그것을 예약할게요.

05 ⑤

[해설] 여자가 남은 음식을 포장해 달라고 부탁하는 상황이다.

[어휘] book[buk] 예약하다
delicious[dilíʃəs] 맛있는
satisfied[sǽtisfàid] 만족한
fresh[freʃ] 신선한
leftover[léftòuvər] 남은 음식

① W What did you have for lunch?
   M I ate potato pizza.
② W I'd like to make a reservation for 3 for 7 o'clock tonight.
   M Sorry, but we're fully booked for tonight.
③ W That pizza is delicious. How is your meal?
   M I'm not satisfied with my salad. It is not fresh.
④ W What would you like to drink?
   M I want a small coke.
⑤ W Excuse me. Could you put these leftovers into a box for me?
   M Sure. Please wait a moment.

① 여 점심으로 뭘 먹었니?
   남 포테이토 피자를 먹었어.
② 여 오늘 밤 7시에 세 명 자리를 예약하고 싶은데요.
   남 죄송하지만 오늘밤에는 예약이 꽉 찼습니다.
③ 여 이 피자 맛있어. 네 식사는 어떠니?
   남 샐러드가 마음에 안 들어. 신선하지 않거든.
④ 여 마실 것은 뭐로 드릴까요?
   남 콜라 작은 거 하나 주세요.
⑤ 여 실례합니다. 남은 음식을 싸주실 수 있나요?
   남 물론이죠. 잠시만 기다려 주세요.

06 ④

[해설] 이 장소에서 운동을 등록했다고 했고 여기서 얼마나 운동했는지 묻는 것으로 보아 대화 장소는 체육관임을 알 수 있다.

[어휘] expect[ikspékt] 기대하다
gym[dʒim] 체육관, 헬스 클럽
work out 운동하다
healthy[hélθi] 건강한

W Tony, I didn't expect to see you here.
M Oh, hi, Jenny. It's nice to see you out of school. Do you come here often?
W Yes. I'm a member of this gym. I've been working out here since last year.
M That's why you always look healthy and slim.
W Oh, thanks. How long have you been working out here?

여 Tony, 여기서 너를 볼 줄 생각도 못했어.
남 아, 안녕, Jenny. 학교 밖에서 보니 반갑다. 여기 자주 오니?
여 응. 이 체육관 회원이야. 작년부터 여기서 운동하고 있어.
남 그게 네가 항상 건강하고 날씬해 보이는 이유구나.
여 아, 고마워. 여기서 운동한 지 얼마나 됐니?

slim [slim] 날씬한
sign up ~에 등록하다
muscle [mʌ́səl] 근육

M Actually, I signed up here last week.
W Why did you start working out?
M Well, I want to get some muscles.

남 실은 지난주에 여기 등록했어.
여 왜 운동하기 시작했니?
남 음, 근육을 좀 만들고 싶거든.

---

07 ③

해설 토요일에 올 소포를 남자가 여자에게 받아달라고 부탁했다.

어휘 go fishing 낚시하러 가다
relax [rilǽks] 휴식을 취하다
ask A a favor A에게 부탁하다
package [pǽkidʒ] 소포
order [ɔ́ːrdər] 주문하다

W Honey, are you going fishing again on the weekend?
M Yes. Do you want to come with me?
W No, thanks. I'd rather stay home and relax.
M If you are going to stay home, can I ask you a favor?
W Sure. What is it?
M A package will arrive Saturday afternoon. Can you get it for me?
W Of course. Did you order something online?
M Yes, I ordered some books.

여 여보, 이번 주말에 또 낚시하러 갈 건가요?
남 네. 같이 갈래요?
여 아니요, 괜찮아요. 집에서 있으면서 쉬는 게 좋아요.
남 집에 있을 거면 하나 부탁해도 될까요?
여 그럼요. 뭔데요?
남 소포 하나가 토요일 오후에 도착할 거예요. 그것 좀 받아 주겠어요?
여 그럼요. 온라인으로 뭘 주문했어요?
남 네, 책을 몇 권 주문했어요.

---

08 ③

해설 회장 이름(Lily Collins), 모임 시간(매주 금요일 오후 2시부터 4시), 봉사 활동 장소(동물 보호소), 회원 가입 자격(15세 이상)에 대한 언급은 있지만 모임 장소에 대한 언급은 없다.

어휘 president [prézidənt] 회장
invite [inváit] 초대하다
care for ~을 돌보다
handle [hǽndl] 다루다
animal shelter 동물 보호소
volunteer [vὰləntíər] 자원봉사하다

W Hi, students! I'm Lily Collins, president of Love Pet Club. If you love animals, I'd like to invite you to join our club. We meet every Friday from 2 p.m. to 4 p.m. We learn how to care for and handle many kinds of pets. And we go to the animal shelter and volunteer on the last Friday of every month. Anyone who is 15 years of age or older can become a member. Please come and join us.

여 안녕하세요, 학생 여러분! 저는 Love Pet Club의 회장인 Lily Collins입니다. 만약 동물을 사랑하신다면 우리 동아리에 가입하시도록 초대하고 싶습니다. 우리는 매주 금요일 오후 2시부터 4시에 모입니다. 많은 종류의 반려동물들을 살피고 다루는 법을 배웁니다. 그리고 매달 마지막 금요일에는 동물 보호소에 가서 자원봉사를 합니다. 15세 이상이라면 누구나 회원이 될 수 있습니다. 오셔서 저희와 함께 하세요.

---

09 ④

해설 보드게임의 한 종류이며, 검은 돌과 흰 돌을 두 선수가 번갈아 두어 더 많은 범위를 차지하는 사람이 이기는 게임은 바둑이다.

어휘 invent [invént] 발명하다
gain [gein] 얻다
area [ériə] 범위
take turns to-v 교대로 ~을 하다
empty [émpti] 비어 있는

M This is a kind of board game. This was invented in China more than 3,000 years ago. In this game, the player who gains more area than the other player is the winner. The playing pieces, or stones, are white and black. One player uses the white stones and the other uses the black stones. The players take turns to place the stones on the empty places of a board.

남 이것은 일종의 보드게임이에요. 이것은 3천여 년 이상 전에 중국에서 발명되었어요. 이 게임에서 다른 선수보다 더 많은 범위를 차지하는 선수가 승자예요. 게임에 사용되는 조각 또는 돌은 흰색과 검은색이에요. 한 선수는 흰 돌을 사용하고 다른 선수는 검은 돌을 사용해요. 선수들은 보드의 비어 있는 곳에 번갈아서 돌을 놓아요.

10 ④

해설 좋아하는 영화의 장르를 물어보는 말에 팝콘과 콜라를 사겠다는 응답은 어색하다.

어휘 say hello to ~에게 안부 인사를 하다
cost[kɔːst] 비용이 들다
airport[ɛərpɔːrt] 공항
turn off 끄다

① M Please say hello to your parents for me.
  W Thank you, I will.
② M How much will it cost me to go to the airport?
  W If you go by bus, it will cost $10.
③ M Could you please turn off the TV?
  W Sorry, I didn't know you were studying.
④ M What kind of movies do you like best?
  W Then I'll buy popcorn and Coke.
⑤ M Are there any more trains for Gangnam today?
  W No. The last one just left a few minutes ago.

① 남 너희 부모님께 안부 전해 줘.
  여 고마워, 그럴게.
② 남 공항까지 가는 데 얼마의 비용이 들까요?
  여 버스를 타고 가면 10달러가 들 거예요.
③ 남 TV를 꺼 주겠니?
  여 미안. 네가 공부하고 있는 줄 몰랐어.
④ 남 어떤 종류의 영화를 가장 좋아하니?
  여 그럼 내가 팝콘과 콜라를 살게.
⑤ 남 오늘 강남행 열차가 더 있나요?
  여 아니요. 마지막 열차가 몇 분 전에 떠났어요.

11 ②

해설 빵집에서 케이크를 가져오는 걸 깜빡했다는 여자의 말에 남자가 바로 지금 가지러 가겠다고 했다.

어휘 almost[ɔ́ːlmoust] 거의
necktie[néktai] 넥타이
forget[fərɡét] 잊다
(forget-forgot-forgotten)
pick up (어디에서) ~을 찾아오다
bakery[béikəri] 빵집

M Mom, is there anything that I can help you with?
W Not really. I'm almost done. Look.
M Wow, it's a great birthday dinner. I'm sure Dad will be very happy.
W I hope so. Did you get a present for him?
M Yes. I got a necktie for him. Oh, where is the birthday cake?
W Oh no. I need to pick it up from Momo's Bakery.
M Don't worry. I'll do that right now.

남 엄마, 뭐 도와 드릴 거 있나요?
여 아니, 별로. 거의 끝났단다. 봐.
남 와, 근사한 생일 저녁상이네요. 아빠가 정말 행복해하실 것 같아요.
여 나도 그러길 바라. 아빠 선물은 준비했니?
남 네, 넥타이를 샀어요. 아, 생일 케이크는 어디 있어요?
여 이런. Momo 빵집에서 가져와야 해.
남 걱정 마세요. 제가 지금 당장 할게요.

12 ①

해설 2시의 치과 예약과 4시 30분의 기타 레슨 시간을 피해 정오에 만나기로 했다.

어휘 dentist[déntist] 치과
appointment[əpɔ́intmənt] 예약
probably[prɑ́bəbli] 아마
noon[nuːn] 정오, 낮 12시

M Do you want to go out and play badminton with me today?
W Sure, but I have a dentist appointment at 2 p.m.
M Will it take long?
W No, I'll probably be done by 3 p.m. Shall we meet at 4 p.m.?
M Sorry, I can't. I have to go to a guitar lesson at 4:30. How about playing before your dentist appointment?
W Okay. Let's meet at noon.
M That's fine.

남 오늘 나랑 나가서 배드민턴 칠래?
여 물론이지, 근데 오후 2시에 치과 예약이 있어.
남 오래 걸리니?
여 아니, 오후 3시면 끝날 거야. 오후 4시에 만날까?
남 미안하지만 안 돼. 4시 30분에 기타 레슨을 가야 하거든. 네 치과 예약 전에 치는 게 어때?
여 알겠어. 그럼 정오에 만나자.
남 그게 좋겠다.

13 ③

해설 2층의 가운데 구역과 입구와 가까운 곳을 제외한 곳을 예매한다고 했으므로 C구역을 선택할 것이다.

M Let's book the BTB concert tickets online. Where do you want to sit?
W I'd like to sit in one of the front sections close to the stage.

남 온라인으로 BTB 콘서트 표를 예매하자. 어디에 앉고 싶니?
여 무대와 가까운 앞쪽 구역 중 하나에 앉고 싶어.

M Well, the first floor only has a standing area. We have to stand and watch the concert there.

W Oh, I don't think I can stand for 3 hours. Then, let's sit in the central section on the second floor.

M Sure. [Pause] Oh, we're too late. All the seats in that section are already sold out. There are 2 sections left.

W Then this one seems better than the one near the entrance.

M Okay. Let's book tickets for this section.

남 그런데, 1층은 스탠딩 구역이야. 그곳에서는 서서 공연을 봐야 해.

여 아, 난 세 시간 동안 서 있을 수 없을 것 같아. 그럼, 2층의 가운데 구역에 앉자.

남 그래. [잠시 후] 아, 너무 늦었어. 그 구역의 좌석은 이미 매진되었어. 2개 남았어.

여 그럼, 입구 가까이에 있는 구역보다는 이 구역이 더 나아 보인다.

남 좋아. 이 구역에 있는 표를 예매하자.

14 ②

M Emily, is there something wrong with your right shoulder?

W Yes. It really hurts.

M What happened?

W Oh, I fell down hard during a bike ride yesterday.

M Did you see a doctor?

W Not yet. After school, I'll ask my mom to take me to the hospital.

M I hope you get well soon.

W Thank you.

남 Emily, 오른쪽 어깨에 무슨 문제라도 있니?

여 응. 정말 아파.

남 무슨 일이 있었니?

여 아, 어제 공원에서 자전거를 타다가 심하게 넘어졌거든.

남 병원에 갔다 왔니?

여 아니, 아직. 학교 끝나고 엄마에게 병원에 데려다 달라고 하려고.

남 빨리 나았으면 좋겠다.

여 고마워.

15 ①

W Attention all passengers for Flight 747 to Frankfurt. We will begin boarding in a minute. Please take out your tickets and passports. Passengers with first-class tickets may board first. Passengers in rows 10 through 25 will be the next to board. If you are in rows 26 to 40, please wait until the next announcement. Thank you very much for your cooperation.

여 Frankfurt 행 747 항공편의 모든 탑승객들에게 알립니다. 잠시 후 탑승을 시작할 것입니다. 비행기 표와 여권을 꺼내주세요. 1등급 석 표를 소지하신 승객분들은 먼저 탑승할 수 있습니다. 10열에서 25열 사이의 승객분들은 그 다음에 탑승할 것입니다. 26열에서 40열 사이라면 다음 안내까지 기다려주시기 바랍니다. 협조에 대단히 감사드립니다.

16 ①

W Excuse me. I'm looking for a handbag for my mom.

M How about this red one with a gold chain? It is very popular these days.

W It's nice. How much does it cost?

M The original price is $110, but now it's on sale.

W That sounds good. What is the sale price?

여 실례합니다. 엄마에게 드릴 핸드백을 찾고 있어요.

남 골드 체인이 달린 이 빨간 가방은 어떠세요? 요즘 무척 인기 있는 거예요.

여 멋지네요. 얼마인가요?

남 원래 가격은 50달러이지만 지금 할인 중이에요.

여 잘됐네요. 세일 가격은 얼마인가요?

gift-wrap [gift-ræp] 선물 포장하다
extra charge 추가 요금
for free 무료로, 무상으로

M It's $10 off the original price.
W Great. I'll take it.
M Would you like it gift-wrapped?
W Yes. Is there an extra charge for that?
M No, we do it for free.

남 원래 가격에서 10달러 할인됩니다.
여 좋네요. 그걸로 살게요.
남 선물 포장해 드릴까요?
여 네. 선물 포장하려면 추가 요금을 내야 하나요?
남 아니요, 무료로 해 드려요.

17 ⑤

해설 두 호텔 중에서 하나를 선택한 이유를 설명하는 응답이 이어져야 한다.

어휘 vacation [veikéiʃən] 휴가, 방학
prefer [prifə́:r] 더 좋아하다, 선호하다
expensive [ikspénsiv] 비싼
be located ~에 위치해 있다
[선택지]
face [feis] ~을 마주보다[향하다]

W Honey, what are you doing?
M I'm looking for a hotel for our vacation.
W Did you find a good hotel for us?
M Yes, I found 2 hotels that I want to stay at. One is called the Paradise Inn. The other is called Oasis Hotel. Which do you prefer?
W I don't know. Which one is more expensive?
M The Paradise Inn costs a little more because it's located at the beach.
W Then let's choose the Paradise Inn.
M Why do you want to stay at that hotel?
W I want to stay in a room facing the beach.

여 여보, 뭐하고 있어요?
남 휴가 때 머무를 호텔을 찾고 있어요.
여 괜찮은 호텔을 찾았나요?
남 네. 머물고 싶은 호텔을 두 군데를 찾았어요. 하나는 Paradise Inn이라는 곳이에요. 다른 하나는 Oasis 호텔이라는 곳이에요. 어떤 게 더 마음에 들어요?
여 모르겠네요. 어느 게 더 비싼가요?
남 해변가에 위치해서 Paradise Inn이 조금 더 비용이 들어요.
여 그럼 Paradise Inn으로 정해요.
남 왜 그 호텔에 머물고 싶어요?
여 해변을 마주하는 방에 머물고 싶어서요.

① 좀 쉬어야 해서요.
② 왜 안 돼요? 당신은 무엇이든지 할 수 있어요.
③ 긴 휴가를 보내게 되어 정말 신이 나요.
④ 좋아요. 해변 근처에 있는 호텔을 예약합시다.

18 ④

해설 세탁물을 언제 받을 수 있는지 묻는 여자의 말에 얼마나 걸리는지 설명하는 응답이 이어져야 한다.

어휘 dry-clean [drái-klí:n] 드라이클리닝하다
a pair of 한 벌의
pay [pei] 지불하다

M Hello, how may I help you?
W I'd like to have these clothes dry-cleaned.
M Okay. What do you have?
W I have 2 jackets and a pair of pants. How much is each one?
M $7 for each jacket and $5 for the pants.
W Should I pay now?
M No, you can pay later when you pick them up.
W It's Wednesday today. When can I get them?
M I think it'll take 3 days from today.

남 안녕하세요, 어떻게 도와드릴까요?
여 이 옷들을 드라이클리닝 해 주세요.
남 알겠습니다. 몇 벌인가요?
여 재킷 두 개와 바지 한 벌이에요. 각각 얼마지요?
남 재킷은 하나에 7달러이고, 바지는 5달러입니다.
여 지금 지불해야 하나요?
남 아니요, 나중에 찾아가실 때 내셔도 돼요.
여 오늘이 수요일이잖아요. 언제 찾아갈 수 있나요?
남 오늘부터 3일 정도 걸릴 거예요.

① 줄무늬 셔츠를 찾고 있어요.
② 모퉁이에서 그것들을 찾을 수 있어요.
③ 지난 수요일에 뭘 했나요?
⑤ 그래. 공항에서 너를 태우러 갈게.

19 ③

W Jiho, how was your weekend?
M I visited Busan with my family.
W Did you have a good time there?
M No. It was really boring!
W I thought there were many things to enjoy in Busan. Why was it so boring?
M I had a terrible stomachache on the first day.
W Oh, I'm sorry to hear that. So what did you do there?
M I stayed at a hotel and just watched TV all day while my family went sightseeing.
W That's too bad. I hope you have fun next time.

여 지호야, 주말 잘 보냈니?
남 가족과 함께 부산에 갔었어.
여 거기서 즐거운 시간을 보냈니?
남 아니. 정말 지루했어!
여 부산에는 즐길 거리가 많다고 생각했는데. 왜 그렇게 지루했니?
남 첫날에 배탈이 심하게 났거든.
여 그 말을 들으니 안됐구나. 그래서 넌 거기서 뭘 했는데?
남 우리 가족들이 관광할 동안 하루 종일 호 텔에서 TV만 보고 있었어.
여 안됐다. 다음에는 즐거운 시간을 갖게 되 길 바라.

① 멋지다! 네가 그것을 즐겼다니 기쁘다.
② 와, 넌 정말 멋진 휴가를 보냈구나!
④ 그 말을 들으니 안됐다. 그녀가 곧 회복하 기를 바라.
⑤ 알겠어. 어디를 관광하기를 원하니?

20 ⑤

M Angela feels tired, so she sits on a bench and takes a break. After a while, she finds out that there is wet paint on the bench. She stands up and tries to remove the paint off her pants. Then, a man comes to the bench and tries to sit down. She wants to tell him not to sit on it. In this situation, what would Angela most likely say to the man?

Angela Don't sit on the bench. The paint is still wet.

남 Angela는 피곤해서 벤치에 앉아 휴식을 취한다. 잠시 후 그녀는 벤치 위에 페인트 가 아직 마르지 않았다는 것을 알게 된다. 그녀는 바로 일어나서 바지에 묻은 페인트 를 없애려고 한다. 그리고 나서, 한 남자가 벤치로 와서 앉으려고 한다. 그녀는 그 남 자에게 앉지 말라고 말하려고 한다. 이러 한 상황에서 Angela가 그 남자에게 할 말 로 가장 적절한 것은 무엇인가?

Angela 벤치에 앉지 마세요. 페인트가 아직 마르지 않았어요.

① 저 여기에 앉아도 될까요?
② 우리 자리 좀 바꿔도 괜찮을까요?
③ 미술 숙제에 쓸 페인트가 좀 필요해요.
④ 도서관에서 제 자리를 맡아줄래요?

01 ⑤

해설 여자는 긴 바지에 주머니가 있고 리본 벨트가 있는 것을 사기로 했다.

어휘 shorts[ʃɔːrts] 반바지
a pair of pants 바지 한 벌
cheap[tʃiːp] 값이 싼

W Excuse me, where can I find girls' clothing?
M I'll show you where. Please follow me.
W Thank you. [Pause] These are all shorts. Do you <u>have</u> <u>any</u> <u>pants</u>?
M Yes, we do. Pants are over here.
W Great. I know it's summer, but my daughter needs a pair of pants.
M I understand. The ones <u>without</u> <u>any</u> <u>pockets</u> are on sale for $10.
W Oh, that's really cheap, but she needs <u>a</u> <u>pair</u> <u>with</u> <u>pockets</u>.
M Then how about the ones <u>with</u> <u>a</u> <u>ribbon</u> <u>belt</u>?
W They are really pretty. I'll take a pair of them.

여 실례지만, 여자 아이 옷은 어디에 있나요?
남 제가 어디인지 알려드릴게요. 저를 따라 오세요.
여 고마워요. [잠시 후] 이것들은 모두 반바지 네요. 긴 바지 있나요?
남 네, 있어요. 긴 바지는 이쪽에 있어요.
여 네. 여름인 건 알지만 제 딸이 긴 바지가 필요해서요.
남 그럴 수 있죠. 주머니가 없는 것들은 할인 해서 10달러입니다.
여 아, 정말 저렴하지만, 저희 애가 주머니가 있는 것을 원해요.
남 그럼 리본 벨트가 있는 건 어떠세요?
여 그거 정말 예쁘네요. 그걸로 한 벌 살게요.

02 ⑤

해설 여자는 남자에게 변경된 학부모 회 의 장소를 알려 주려고 전화했다.

어휘 parent meeting 학부모 회의
original[ərídʒənəl] 본래의
take place 열리다, 개최되다
auditorium[ɔːditɔ́ːriəm] 강당

[Telephone rings.]
M Hello.
W Hello. May I speak to Mr. Thompson?
M This is he. May I ask <u>who's</u> <u>calling</u>?
W Hi, Mr. Thompson. This is Sandy Johnson from Crossroad Middle School.
M Hi, Ms. Johnson. <u>Am</u> <u>I</u> <u>late</u> <u>for</u> the parent meeting?
W No, but I'm calling you about the meeting place.
M Isn't it at the cafeteria?
W That was the original plan, but the meeting <u>will</u> <u>take</u> <u>place</u> <u>in</u> the auditorium.
M Thank you for <u>letting</u> <u>me</u> <u>know</u>. I'll be there on time.

[전화벨이 울린다.]
남 여보세요.
여 여보세요. Thompson 씨 좀 바꿔 주시겠습 니까?
남 전데요. 누구신지요?
여 안녕하세요, Thompson 씨. Crossroad 중 학교의 Sandy Johnson입니다.
남 안녕하세요, Johnson 선생님. 제가 학부모 회의에 늦었나요?
여 아닙니다. 회의가 열리는 장소 때문에 전 화 드렸어요.
남 구내식당에서 하는 게 아닌가요?
여 원래는 그랬는데, 모임은 강당에서 진행될 거예요.
남 알려 주셔서 고맙습니다. 제시간에 가도록 할게요.

03 ⑤

해설 공항 카운터에서 체크인을 하기 위 해 남자가 여자에게 여권을 보여 달라고 하는 상황이다.

어휘 drop[drɑp] 떨어뜨리다
purse[pəːrs] 지갑
passport[pǽspɔːrt] 여권

① M Should I <u>start</u> <u>setting</u> <u>the</u> <u>table</u>?
W Yes, please. I'm almost done cooking.
② M Excuse me. You dropped your purse.
W I don't think <u>that's</u> <u>mine</u>.
③ M Do you need help with your backpack?
W Thank you so much. It's really heavy.

① 남 상을 좀 차릴까요?
여 그래요. 요리가 거의 다 끝나가거든요.
② 남 실례합니다. 지갑을 떨어뜨리셨네요.
여 그건 제 것이 아닌 것 같아요.
③ 남 제가 배낭을 들어드릴까요?
여 정말 고마워요. 아주 무겁거든요.

④ M Do you mind if I sit next to you?
　W I'm sorry, but someone's sitting here.
⑤ M Can you show me your passport?
　W Sure, let me get it out of my bag.

④ 남 옆에 앉아도 될까요?
　여 미안하지만, 여기 누가 앉을 거예요.
⑤ 남 여권을 보여 주시겠습니까?
　여 네, 가방에서 꺼낼게요.

04 ②

[해설] 놀이공원에 가기로 한 두 사람은 토요일과 일요일은 붐빌 것 같아 오전 수업만 하는 화요일에 가기로 했다.

[어휘] amusement park 놀이공원
think about v-ing ~할 것을 고려하다, ~할까 생각하다
crowded[kráudid] 붐비는, 혼잡한

W Have you been to the amusement park in Gyeongju?
M Not yet, but I've always wanted to visit there.
W I'm thinking about going there this Saturday with Kate. Do you want to come with us?
M Sure, but don't you think it's going to be crowded on Saturday?
W I guess you're right. Why don't we go on Tuesday next week?
M That's a good idea. We only have morning classes next Tuesday.
W Okay, then it's a plan.

여 경주에 있는 놀이공원에 가 봤어?
남 아직 안 가 봤지만, 항상 가 보고 싶었어.
여 이번 토요일에 Kate랑 거기에 갈까 생각 중이야. 너도 함께 갈래?
남 물론이지. 하지만 토요일에는 붐비지 않을까?
여 네 말이 맞는 것 같네. 우리 다음 주 화요일에 가는 게 어때?
남 좋은 생각이야. 다음 주 화요일에는 오전 수업만 있잖아.
여 좋아. 그럼 계획된 거다.

05 ⑤

[해설] 위치(5번가와 메인 스트리트가 만나는 모퉁이), 이름(Orange 카페), 개점한 시기(지난주), 애완동물 출입(가능)에 관해 언급했지만 직원 수에 대해서는 언급하지 않았다.

[어휘] avenue[ǽvənjùː] (도시의) 거리, ~가
pass by ~앞을 지나가다
experience[ikspíəriəns] 경험

W Have you been to the new cafe on 5th Avenue?
M Are you talking about the one on the corner of 5th Avenue and Main Street?
W Yes, it's called Orange Cafe.
M I've passed by it, but I've never been there before.
W It opened last week, and you can bring your pet there.
M How do you know so much about that cafe?
W I actually started working there yesterday.
M I see. I'm sure it'll be a very good experience for you.

여 5번가에 있는 새 카페에 가 봤어?
남 5번가와 메인 스트리트가 만나는 모퉁이에 있는 거 말하는 거니?
여 그래. Orange 카페라고 해.
남 그 옆을 지나치긴 했지만 그곳을 한번도 가 본 적은 없어.
여 지난주에 개점했고 그곳에 애완동물 데리고 와도 돼.
남 그 카페에 대해 어떻게 그렇게 잘 알아?
여 사실 난 어제 거기서 일하기 시작했거든.
남 그렇구나. 너에게 아주 좋은 경험이 될 거야.

06 ④

[해설] 타이어 교체 가격을 물어보면서 브레이크 점검을 요청하는 것으로 두 사람은 자동차 정비사와 손님임을 알 수 있다.

[어휘] tire[taiər] 타이어
flat tire 바람 빠진 타이어
replace[ripléis] 교체하다
brake[breik] 브레이크
examine[igzǽmin] 검사하다

W Can you take a look at my tires?
M Sure, do you have a flat tire?
W One of the front tires looks really flat.
M Let me check. [Pause] Oh, all of your tires need to be replaced. They're very old.
W Are they? How much would it cost to replace them?
M It's $100 each, so it'll be $400.

여 타이어 좀 봐 줄래요?
남 물론이죠, 타이어가 펑크났나요?
여 앞 타이어 하나가 바람이 많이 빠진 것 같아요.
남 확인해볼게요. [잠시 후] 아, 모든 타이어들을 교체해야 하네요. 너무 오래됐어요.
여 그래요? 모두 교체하는 데 얼마나 드나요?
남 하나에 100달러여서, 400달러입니다.

W Could you also take a look at the brakes?
M Yes, I'll examine them while I replace the tires.

여 브레이크도 좀 봐 주실래요?
남 네, 타이어를 교체하면서 점검해 드릴게요.

07 ⑤

해설 집까지 태워다 달라는 부탁에 벌써 집에 와 있다고 하는 응답은 어색하다.

어휘 get a good night's sleep
숙면을 취하다
at least 적어도
give A a ride A를 태워 주다

① M Would you like something to drink?
  W Yes, please. Can I have some milk?
② M I have to buy a new car. Mine is really old.
  W What kind of car do you want?
③ M Did you get a good night's sleep?
  W Yes, I slept like a baby.
④ M How often do you play tennis?
  W I play at least once a week.
⑤ M Could you give me a ride home?
  W Yes, I'm home already.

① 남 뭐 좀 마실래요?
  여 네. 우유를 주시겠어요?
② 남 새 차를 사야겠어. 내건 너무 낡았어.
  여 어떤 차를 원하니?
③ 남 잘 잤어?
  여 그래. 세상모르고 잤네.
④ 남 얼마나 자주 테니스를 치니?
  여 난 일주일에 적어도 한 번은 쳐.
⑤ 남 나 집까지 태워다 줄 수 있어?
  여 그래, 난 벌써 집에 와 있어.

08 ①

해설 여자는 남자에게 Sandy가 잠들 때까지 책을 읽어 달라고 부탁했다.

어휘 awake[əwéik] 깨어 있는
read[ri:d] (책을) 읽다; 읽어 주다
fall asleep 잠들다

W Honey, are you awake?
M Yes. I was about to read a book before going to bed.
W Can I ask you a favor?
M Sure. What is it?
W I have some e-mails to write, but I think it'll take some time.
M Okay. Do you need any help with that?
W No, that's okay. But Sandy is not sleeping at all. Can you read her some books until she falls asleep?
M Of course. I'll do that.

여 여보, 깨어 있나요?
남 네. 자러 가기 전에 책을 좀 읽으려고 했어요.
여 부탁 하나만 해도 돼요?
남 네. 뭔데요?
여 제가 작성해야 하는 이메일이 좀 있는데, 시간이 좀 걸릴 것 같아요.
남 알겠어요. 그거 하는 데 도움이 필요해요?
여 아뇨, 괜찮아요. 그런데 Sandy가 잠을 전혀 자지 않네요. 그 애가 잠들 때까지 책 좀 읽어줄래요?
남 물론이죠. 제가 할게요.

09 ②

해설 남자가 여자에게 꽃을 꺾어 주겠다고 하자 다른 사람도 꽃을 즐길 수 있게 꺾지 말라고 충고하고 있다.

어휘 unusually[ʌnjú:ʒuəli] 전에 없이
chilly[tʃíli] 쌀쌀한
lovely[lʌ́vli] 아름다운, 사랑스러운
pick[pik] 꺾다
beauty[bjú:ti] 아름다움

M I'm so happy that spring is finally here.
W I know. It was an unusually cold winter.
M Aren't you glad we came out to the park today?
W Yes, I am. I thought it'd still be a little chilly, but it's really warm.
M Look at all those beautiful flowers.
W Wow, they're so lovely.
M Let me pick one of the flowers for you.
W That's not a good idea. We should let other people enjoy their beauty, too.

남 드디어 봄이 와서 너무 좋아.
여 그래. 유난히 추운 겨울이었어.
남 오늘 공원에 나와서 즐겁지 않아?
여 아니, 즐거워. 아직 좀 쌀쌀할 줄 알았는데, 정말 따뜻하네.
남 저 예쁜 꽃들 좀 봐.
여 와, 정말 아름답다.
남 꽃 한 송이 꺾어 줄게.
여 그건 좋은 생각이 아니야. 다른 사람들도 꽃들의 아름다움을 즐길 수 있도록 해야 해.

10 ③

해설 남자는 100달러짜리 스케이트보드와 40달러짜리 헬멧만 구매하겠다고 했으므로 140달러를 지불할 것이다.

어휘 skateboard[skéitbɔ̀ːrd] 스케이트보드

expensive[ikspénsiv] 비싼(↔ cheap)

helmet[hélmit] 헬멧

protective[prətéktiv] 보호하는

M Excuse me. How much is this skateboard?
W Let me see. That's $100.
M Do you have a <u>less</u> <u>expensive</u> <u>one</u>?
W No, that's the cheapest model we have.
M Okay. I <u>also</u> <u>need</u> <u>a</u> <u>helmet</u>. How much is this one?
W That's $40. <u>You</u> <u>may</u> <u>want</u> <u>to</u> buy a pair of protective gloves, too.
M How much are they?
W They are $30 a pair.
M Hmm... It's all right. <u>I'll</u> <u>just</u> <u>get</u> the skateboard and the helmet.

남 실례합니다. 이 스케이트보드 얼마인가요?
여 잠시만요. 그건 100달러입니다.
남 더 싼 거 있어요?
여 아니요. 그게 저희가 갖고 있는 가장 싼 모델입니다.
남 좋아요. 헬멧도 필요한데요. 이건 얼마예요?
여 40달러입니다. 혹시 보호 장갑도 사면 좋을 거예요.
남 그건 얼마인가요?
여 한 켤레에 30달러입니다.
남 음… 괜찮아요. 그냥 스케이트보드랑 헬멧만 살게요.

11 ③

해설 여자가 피자를 주문하겠다고 하며 남자에게 쿠폰을 가져다 달라고 했다.

어휘 feel like v-ing ~하고 싶은 마음이 들다

eat out 외식하다

coupon[kúːpan] 쿠폰

M What should we eat for dinner tonight?
W I <u>don't</u> <u>feel</u> <u>like</u> <u>eating</u> Korean food.
M I can cook spaghetti if you want.
W Why don't we eat out? It's been a long time <u>since</u> <u>we</u> <u>ate</u> <u>out</u>.
M We could, but there's a baseball game I want to watch at 7.
W Okay, then I'll just order a pizza for us. I think we <u>have</u> <u>some</u> <u>coupons</u> for Johnny's Pizza. Can you <u>get</u> <u>those</u> <u>for</u> <u>me</u>?
M Sure. I will.

남 오늘 저녁에 뭐 먹을까요?
여 저는 한식은 먹고 싶지 않아요.
남 원한다면 제가 스파게티를 만들 수 있어요.
여 우리 외식하는 게 어때요? 외식한 지 꽤 됐잖아요.
남 그래도 되지만, 7시에 보고 싶은 야구 경기가 있어요.
여 좋아요, 그럼 제가 그냥 피자를 주문할게요. 우리 Johnny's 피자 쿠폰이 몇 개 있을 텐데요. 그것 좀 가져다줄래요?
남 그래요. 그럴게요.

12 ③

해설 위치(도심 한복판인 시청 바로 옆), 특징(건물이 독특하고 박물관이기도 하다), 기록물 관람 요일(수요일), 휴게실 위치(1층)에 대해 언급하고 있지만 개관 시간에 대한 언급은 없다.

어휘 be located 위치해 있다
unique[juːníːk] 독특한
not only A but also B A뿐만 아니라 B도
display[displéi] 전시하다
historical[histɔ́ːrikəl] 역사와 관련된
record[rékərd] 기록물
public[pʌ́blik] 일반 사람들
lounge[laundʒ] 휴게실, 라운지

W Welcome everyone to the New York City Library. We're located in the heart of the city, <u>right</u> <u>next</u> <u>to</u> the city hall. Unlike other libraries, this unique building is not only a library <u>but</u> <u>also</u> <u>a</u> <u>museum</u>. It keeps and displays various historical records of the city. The records are <u>open</u> <u>to</u> <u>the</u> <u>public</u> only on Wednesdays. Eating or drinking is not allowed in the library <u>except</u> <u>in</u> <u>the</u> <u>lounge</u> on the first floor.

여 뉴욕 시립 도서관에 오신 것을 환영합니다. 우리는 도심 한복판인 시청 바로 옆에 있습니다. 다른 도서관들과 달리 이 독특한 건물은 도서관일 뿐만 아니라 박물관이기도 합니다. 이곳에서는 도시의 다양한 역사 기록물을 보관하고 전시합니다. 그 기록물은 수요일에만 일반인에게 공개됩니다. 도서관에서는 1층 휴게실을 제외하고는 식사나 음료를 드실 수 없습니다.

13 ⑤

해설 로맨틱 코미디를 보기로 했고, 저녁 6시 전에는 영화를 보지 않는다고 했으며, 2D 영화를 보기로 했다.

어휘 **horror movie** 공포 영화
romantic comedy 로맨틱 코미디
dizzy[dízi] 어지러운
choice[tʃɔis] 선택

M What kind of movie do you want to watch, Michelle?
W I hate horror movies. Let's watch a romantic comedy.
M That sounds good to me.
W Let's have dinner at 6 before the movie.
M Okay. By the way, do you want to watch the movie on a 2D or a 3D screen?
W I get dizzy when I watch a movie on a 3D screen.
M Okay, then let's watch the movie on a 2D screen.
W All right. Then we have only one choice.

남 Michelle, 어떤 종류의 영화를 보고 싶니?
여 난 공포 영화를 싫어해. 로맨틱 코미디를 보자.
남 좋은 생각이야.
여 영화 보기 전에 6시에 저녁 먹자.
남 그래. 근데 영화를 2D 아니면 3D 화면으로 볼래?
여 나는 3D 화면으로 영화를 보면 어지러워.
남 좋아, 그럼 2D 화면으로 영화를 보자.
여 알았어. 그럼 우리에겐 선택할 게 하나밖에 없네.

14 ②

해설 열대 과일이며 주로 노란색이고 손으로 껍질을 벗겨 먹으면 되는 것은 바나나이다.

어휘 **tropical**[trápikəl] 열대의
thick[θik] 두꺼운
flesh[fleʃ] 과육
ripe[raip] (과일 등이) 익은
peel[piːl] 껍질을 벗기다

M This is a tropical fruit with a thick skin and a soft flesh. The color of this fruit is usually yellow when it is ripe and green when it is not ripe. Many people like to eat this fruit because it is low in calories and easy to eat. All you have to do is peel it with your hands.

남 이것은 껍질이 두껍고 과육이 부드러운 열대 과일이에요. 이 과일의 색깔은 주로 익으면 노랗고, 익지 않으면 녹색이에요. 이 과일은 칼로리가 낮고 먹기 쉽기 때문에 많은 사람들이 즐겨 먹어요. 손으로 껍질을 벗기기만 하면 돼요.

15 ②

해설 여자가 뮤지컬 티켓을 온라인으로 두 장 이상 사면 할인 받을 수 있다고 하자 남자가 당장 두 장을 사겠다고 했다.

어휘 **version**[vɔ́ːrʒən] 개작, 번안 (다른 예술 작품을 영화, 연극, 음악 작품으로 만드는 것)
expensive[ikspénsiv] 비싼
deal[diːl] 거래, 합의

M What are you doing this weekend, Jennifer?
W I'm going to see the musical *Cats* with my dad.
M Oh, I saw the movie last year.
W I did, too. And I really wanted to see the musical version of it.
M The musical is much more expensive than the movie, isn't it?
W Usually, yes. But if you buy 2 or more tickets online, you get 15 percent off.
M That's a good deal. I'll buy 2 tickets for me and my sister right now.

남 Jennifer, 이번 주말에 뭐 할 거야?
여 나는 아빠랑 뮤지컬 〈캣츠〉를 보러 갈 거야.
남 아, 나는 작년에 그 영화 봤어.
여 나도 봤어. 그리고 뮤지컬화 한 것으로 정말 보고 싶었어.
남 뮤지컬이 영화보다 훨씬 더 비싸지, 그렇지 않아?
여 보통은 그렇지. 근데 온라인에서 두 장 이상 티켓을 구매하면, 15% 할인 받아.
남 괜찮은 가격이네. 지금 당장 나랑 내 여동생이 볼 티켓 두 장을 사야겠어.

16 ③

해설 집들이 선물로 알람 시계를 사자고 제안하는 남자의 말에 여자가 동의했다.

어휘 **present**[prézənt] 선물
housewarming party 집들이

W We need to buy a present before we go to your uncle's housewarming party.
M How about buying some toilet paper?
W No, I don't want to do that. Let's get him something more meaningful.

여 너희 삼촌의 집들이에 가기 전에 선물을 사야 해.
남 화장지를 좀 사는 게 어때요?
여 아니, 그러고 싶진 않아. 좀 더 의미 있는 것을 가져가자.

toilet paper 화장지, 휴지
meaningful[míːniŋfəl] 뜻있는
toaster[tóustər] 토스터
alarm clock 알람 시계

M Okay, Mom. He said he needed a toaster.
W I already gave him our toaster because we never used it.
M Then let's get him an alarm clock. He's always late for everything.
W That's a great idea!
M Okay, let's go to the mall then.

남 그래요, 엄마. 삼촌이 토스터기가 필요하다고 했었어요.
여 토스터기는 우리가 사용하지 않아서 이미 삼촌에게 줬어.
남 그럼, 알람 시계를 사 드려요. 삼촌은 모든 일에 항상 늦잖아요.
여 그거 좋은 생각이다!
남 네, 그럼 쇼핑몰에 가요.

① 휴지 ② 토스터기 ③ 알람 시계
④ 양초 ⑤ 케이크

17 ②

해설 크리스마스 파티에 각자 음식을 가져오기로 했는데 무엇을 가져올 것인지 물었으므로 가져올 음식의 종류를 말하는 응답이 어울린다.

어휘 dress up as ~으로 분장하다
share[ʃɛər] 나누다
[선택지]
invitation[ìnvitéiʃən] 초대장

W When are we having our Christmas party?
M It's next Thursday. We only have 5 days left.
W I heard our teacher will dress up as Santa Claus.
M That's right. I can't wait!
W Oh, we should bring some food to share with our classmates, right?
M Yes. It'll be easier if everyone brings something.
W What are you going to bring, Jake?
M I'm going to bring a cheesecake.

여 크리스마스 파티는 언제 하지?
남 다음 주 목요일이야. 이제 5일밖에 안 남았어.
여 우리 선생님이 산타클로스로 분장할 거라고 들었어.
남 맞아. 정말 기대 돼!
여 아, 우리 반 친구들이랑 나눠 먹을 음식을 좀 가져와야 하지, 맞지?
남 그래. 모든 사람이 음식을 가져오면 수월할 거야.
여 Jake, 너는 뭘 가져올 거야?
남 나는 치즈케이크를 가져올 거야.

① 산타클로스는 실제로 존재하지 않아.
③ 네 여동생을 파티에 데려와도 돼.
④ 다음 주 목요일에 생일 파티를 할 거야.
⑤ 초대장을 모두 보내는 것을 기억할게.

18 ⑤

해설 남자가 호텔 시설에 대한 불만으로 내일 다른 곳으로 찾아봐야 하는지 물어보는 남자의 말에 여자는 지역에서 가장 저렴해서 괜찮다고 응답하는 게 적절하다.

어휘 bathroom[bǽθrù(ː)m] 욕실
staff[stæf] 직원
take a bath 목욕하다
[선택지]
come down with (감기 등에) 걸리다
area[ériə] 지역

M This is the worst hotel I've ever stayed in.
W What's wrong, honey? We just got here.
M There's no hot water in the bathroom.
W It's okay. I don't need hot water now. Let me talk to the staff tomorrow.
M I thought you wanted to take a bath.
W No. I'm just going to brush my teeth and go to bed. I'm really tired.
M I'm sorry. Do you want me to look for different hotels tomorrow?
W It's okay. This is the cheapest hotel in the area.

남 이곳은 내가 묵은 호텔 중 가장 최악이에요.
여 왜 그래요, 여보? 우린 방금 도착했잖아요.
남 욕실에 온수가 안 나와요.
여 괜찮아요. 지금은 더운 물이 필요 없어요. 내일 직원한테 얘기할게요.
남 당신이 목욕하고 싶어하는 줄 알았는데요.
여 아니에요. 그냥 양치하고 잘 게요. 너무 피곤하거든요.
남 미안해요. 내일 다른 호텔을 좀 찾아볼까요?
여 괜찮아요. 이곳은 지역에서 가장 저렴한 호텔이에요.

① 그래요. 우리 새 침대를 사야 해요.
② 내일 화장실을 고치면 돼요.
③ 감기가 오는 것 같아요.
④ 목욕을 하고 나면 한결 나아질 거예요.

19 ⑤

해설 남자에게 자신이 만든 과자를 선물한 여자가 나중에 과자 가게를 열고 싶다고 했으므로 자신이 단골손님이 되겠다고 응답하는 게 어울린다.

어휘 be into ~에 흥미가 많다
business[bíznis] 사업
[선택지]
promise[prámis] 약속하다
regular customer 단골손님

W I have something for your birthday, Michael.
M What is it? [Pause] Wow, these cookies are so cute. Where did you get them?
W I baked them myself.
M Really? I didn't know you were into baking.
W I became interested in baking about 2 years ago.
M Let me try one of them. [Pause] This is so good. I think you should start your own business.
W Thank you. I hope I can open my own cookie shop in the future.
M I promise that I will be a regular customer.

여 네 생일 선물을 준비했어, Michael.
남 그게 뭐야? [잠시 후] 와, 이 쿠키 정말 귀여워. 어디서 샀어?
여 내가 직접 구웠어.
남 그래? 나는 네가 빵 굽는 것에 흥미가 있는 줄 몰랐어.
여 한 2년 전에 빵 굽는 것에 빠지게 되었어.
남 하나 먹어 볼게. [잠시 후] 아주 맛있어. 네 사업으로 시작하는 게 좋을 것 같아.
여 고마워. 나중에 내 쿠키 가게를 열 수 있으면 좋겠어.
남 내가 너의 단골손님이 되겠다고 약속할게.

① 나는 지난 주말에 네 쿠키 가게에 갔었어.
② 그럼 너에게 쿠키를 더 구워 줘야겠다.
③ 네가 내 쿠키를 좋아한다는 말을 들으니 정말 기뻐.
④ 이 쿠키를 어디서 샀는지 말할 수 없어.

20 ⑤

해설 여자가 이미 사용한 샴푸를 가져와서 환불해 달라고 하고 있으므로 사용한 것은 환불해줄 수 없다는 말이 적절하다.

어휘 customer service desk 고객 서비스 창구
local[lóukəl] 지역의
shampoo[ʃæmpú:] 샴푸
empty[émpti] 빈
return[ritə́:rn] 반품하다
refund[ri(:)fʌ́nd] 환불

W Rachel works at the customer service desk at a local supermarket. One day, a woman comes up to the desk with a bottle of shampoo. The bottle is almost half empty. She says she wants to return the product and get a refund. Customers cannot return products that have already been used. In this situation, what would Rachel most likely say to the woman?

Reachel You can't return this because it's already been used.

여 Rachel은 동네 슈퍼마켓의 고객 서비스 창구에서 일한다. 어느 날, 한 여자가 샴푸 병을 들고 다가온다. 그 병은 거의 반이나 비어 있다. 그녀는 제품을 반품하고 환불 받고 싶다고 한다. 고객은 이미 사용한 제품은 반품할 수 없다. 이러한 상황에서 Rachel이 여자에게 할 말로 가장 적절한 것은 무엇인가?

Rachel 이미 사용하셔서 반품하실 수 없습니다.

① 당신을 전에 본 적이 없는 것 같아요.
② 일한 지 얼마나 되셨어요?
③ 그 드레스를 입으니 멋져 보여요.
④ 현금으로 지불하시겠습니까, 카드로 하시겠습니까?

01 ③	02 ①	03 ③	04 ④	05 ⑤	06 ②	07 ②
08 ④	09 ⑤	10 ③	11 ③	12 ⑤	13 ①	14 ②
15 ④	16 ⑤	17 ④	18 ③	19 ⑤	20 ⑤	

01 ③

해설 여자는 캐주얼화이면서 신발 끈이 없고 굽이 낮은 것을 산다고 했다.

어휘 sneakers[sníːkərs] 운동화
casual[kǽʒjuəl] 격식을 차리지 않는
leather[léðər] 가죽
shoelace[ʃúlèis] 신발 끈
heel[hiːl] 뒷굽

W Hi, I'm looking for a pair of shoes.
M You've come to the right place. What are you looking for?
W I need casual shoes.
M Okay. How about these leather ones?
W They have shoelaces. I'd prefer ones without shoelaces.
M Then these might be what you're looking for.
W They look good, but the heels are too high.
M How about these?
W They're perfect. I'll take them.

여 안녕하세요, 신발을 찾고 있어요.
남 잘 오셨습니다. 어떤 걸 찾으시나요?
여 캐주얼화가 필요해요.
남 알겠습니다. 이 가죽 신발은 어때요?
여 신발 끈이 있어요. 저는 신발 끈이 없는 것이 더 좋아요.
남 그럼, 이걸 찾으시는 것 같군요.
여 좋아 보이는데, 굽이 너무 높아요.
남 그럼 이건 어때요?
여 맘에 꼭 들어요. 이걸로 살게요.

02 ①

해설 학교에 지각한 남자는 아침을 먹을 시간이 없어서 여자에게 대신 사과를 씻어 달라고 부탁했다.

어휘 leave[liːv] 떠나다
put on ~을 신다

W You're going to be late for school if you don't hurry, James.
M What time is it, Mom?
W It's 7:30. Hurry up and eat your breakfast.
M Oh no. I'm already late.
W What do you mean? School starts at 8:30.
M Mr. Johnson asked me to come to school by 8 today.
W Oh, then you need to leave right now.
M Can you just wash an apple for me? I'll just eat that for breakfast.
W Okay, I'll do that while you put on your shoes.

여 서두르지 않으면 학교에 늦는다, James.
남 지금 몇 시예요, 엄마?
여 7시 30분이야. 빨리 아침을 먹으렴.
남 이런. 벌써 늦었네요.
여 무슨 소리니? 학교는 8시 30분에 시작하잖아.
남 Johnson 선생님이 저한테 오늘은 8시까지 학교에 오라고 하셨거든요.
여 아, 그럼 지금 당장 가야겠네.
남 그냥 사과 한 개만 씻어 주시겠어요? 아침으로 먹게요.
여 그래, 네가 신발을 신는 동안 그렇게 할게.

03 ③

해설 지하철에서 자리를 양보하자 곧 내리면서 사양하는 상황이다.

어휘 make a reservation 예약을 하다
restroom[réstrù(ː)m] 화장실
entrance[éntrəns] 출입구, 문
get off at ~에서 내리다
decide[disáid] 결정하다

① M Did you make a reservation?
　 W Yes, I reserved a table 2 days ago.
② M Where can I find the restroom?
　 W It's right next to the main entrance.
③ M Why don't you take my seat?
　 W It's okay. We're getting off at the next stop.
④ M Would you like one more piece?
　 W No, thank you. I've had enough to eat.
⑤ M Do you need more time to decide?
　 W Yes, can you come back in 5 minutes?

① 남 예약하셨나요?
　 여 네, 이틀 전에 자리를 예약했어요.
② 남 화장실이 어디인가요?
　 여 정문 바로 옆에 있어요.
③ 남 제 자리에 앉으시겠어요?
　 여 괜찮아요. 저희는 다음 정거장에서 내려요.
④ 남 한 조각 더 드실래요?
　 여 고맙지만 됐어요. 충분히 먹었어요.
⑤ 남 결정하는 데 시간이 더 필요하신가요?
　 여 네, 5분 후에 다시 오실래요?

04 ④

해설 두 사람은 금요일에 쇼핑몰에 가서 생일 선물을 사기로 했다.

어휘 chance[tʃæns] 기회

W When is John's birthday?
M It's January 7th, which is next Wednesday.
W So that's why he's having his birthday party this Saturday.
M That's right. You're going to the party, too, aren't you?
W Yes. Did you get a chance to buy a present for him?
M No, I am going to go to the mall after school on Friday.
W Oh, let's go to the mall together. I need to buy a present for him, too.
M That sounds good.

여 John의 생일이 언제니?
남 1월 7일, 다음 주 수요일이야.
여 그래서 이번 주 토요일에 생일 파티를 하는 거구나.
남 맞아. 너도 파티에 가는 거지, 그렇지 않니?
여 그래. John에게 줄 선물을 살 시간이 있었니?
남 아니, 금요일 방과 후에 쇼핑몰에 가려고.
여 아, 쇼핑몰에 같이 가자. 나도 걔한테 줄 선물을 사야 해.
남 좋아.

05 ⑤

해설 위치(남자의 집 근처), 음식 맛(좋음), 음식 가격(적당함), 특별 행사 품목(1달러짜리 특가 상품)에 대해 언급하고 있지만 주재료에 대한 언급은 없다.

어휘 reasonable[ríːzənəbl] 합리적인
price[prais] 가격
special deal 특가 상품
disagree[dìsəgríː] 동의하지 않다

W What's your favorite fast food restaurant?
M My favorite is Sandwich King. There's one near my house.
W Why do you like Sandwich King so much?
M The food there tastes good, and everything is at a reasonable price.
W Really? I think their sandwiches are too expensive.
M Do you know about their $1 special deals?
W Yes, I do. They are cheap, but you get what you pay for.
M Well, I'm with you on that.

여 네가 가장 좋아하는 패스트푸드점은 어디니?
남 나는 Sandwich King이 제일 좋아. 우리 집 근처에 하나 있어.
여 왜 Sandwich King이 그렇게 좋은데?
남 거기 음식이 맛있고, 가격도 모두 적당해.
여 그래? 나는 거기 샌드위치가 너무 비싼 것 같아.
남 그 가게에서 하는 1달러 특가 상품에 대해 알고 있니?
여 그래, 알아. 그건 싸긴 하지만, 싼 게 비지떡이야.
남 음, 그것에 대해서는 나도 동의해.

06 ②

해설 케이크로 유명한 곳이라 했으며, 케이크 외에 쿠키와 빵을 살 수 있는 곳은 제과점이다.

어휘 expect[ikspékt] 기대하다
be famous for ~로 유명하다

M Have you ever been here before, Linda?
W Yes, I have. I've bought some cookies here.
M How were they?
W They were okay. But they were not as good as I expected.
M That's because this place is actually famous for cakes.
W Are you going to buy a cake today?
M No, I'm actually picking up some bread for breakfast tomorrow.
W Oh, I should do that, too.

남 전에 여기 와 본 적 있어, Linda?
여 응, 있어. 나는 여기서 쿠키를 샀어.
남 어땠어?
여 괜찮았어. 하지만 기대했던 것만큼 좋지는 않았어.
남 이곳이 사실은 케이크로 유명해서 그래.
여 너는 오늘 케이크 살 거니?
남 아니, 내일 아침에 먹을 빵을 좀 살 거야.
여 아, 나도 그래야겠다.

07 ②

해설 남자가 피곤하다고(tired) 했는데 타이어들(tires)이 괜찮아 보인다고 했으

---

① M Don't worry. He'll get well soon.
W Thank you. I hope he will.

---

① 남 걱정하지 마. 그는 곧 나을 거야.
여 고마워. 그가 그렇게 됐으면 좋겠다.

므로 어색한 응답이다.

어휘 get well 병이 나아지다
tire[taiər] (고무로 만든) 타이어
quarter[kwɔ́:rtər] 15분; 4분의 1

② M I'm so tired that I can't move.
　W Your tires look just fine to me.
③ M Can you have her call me back?
　W Yes, as soon as she gets home.
④ M Excuse me. Do you have the time?
　W Yes, it's a quarter to 3.
⑤ M Would you like coffee or tea?
　W I'll have tea, please.

② 남 너무 피곤해서 움직일 수가 없어.
　여 네 타이어들은 괜찮아 보이는데.
③ 남 그녀에게 나한테 전화하라고 해 줄래?
　여 그래. 그녀가 집에 돌아오면 바로 할게.
④ 남 실례합니다. 지금 몇 시인지 아세요?
　여 네, 3시 15분 전입니다.
⑤ 남 커피로 하시겠습니까, 아니면 차로 하시겠습니까?
　여 차를 주세요.

08 ④

해설 바쁜 한 주를 보내고 나서 편하게 TV를 보고 있는 남자에게 여자가 개를 산책시켜 달라고 부탁했다.

어휘 feel like v-ing ~을 하고 싶다
deserve to-v ~ 받을 만하다
lazy[léizi] 게으른
walk[wɔːk] 산책시키다
fresh[freʃ] 맑은

W Are you still watching TV, Paul?
M It's Saturday, Mom. I don't have any homework to do.
W You've been watching TV for over 3 hours.
M I had a very busy week. I just don't feel like doing anything.
W Okay, I guess you deserve to be lazy for a day.
M Thanks, Mom.
W But can you at least walk the dog? He's been inside the house all day.
M Yes, I can do that. I want to get some fresh air, too.

여 Paul, 아직도 TV를 보고 있니?
남 토요일이잖아요, 엄마. 숙제가 하나도 없어요.
여 세 시간 넘게 TV를 봤잖아.
남 아주 바쁘게 한 주를 보냈거든요. 그냥 아무것도 하고 싶지 않아요.
여 그래. 넌 하루 동안 게으름을 피울 자격이 있는 것 같구나.
남 고마워요, 엄마.
여 그래도 최소한 개를 산책시킬 수 있겠니? 걔가 하루 종일 집 안에만 있었거든.
남 네, 그건 할 수 있어요. 저도 맑은 공기 좀 쐬고 싶어요.

09 ⑤

해설 아파트 단지 내 놀이터에서 아이들이 늦은 밤 소란스럽게 하는 것에 대한 민원이 있어서 놀이터 운영 시간을 조정한다는 안내 방송이다.

어휘 resident[rézidənt] 거주자, 주민
operating hour 운영 시간
playground[pléigràund] 놀이터
apartment complex 아파트 단지
management[mǽnidʒmənt] 운영진
complaint[kəmpléint] 불만
noise[nɔiz] 소음
in advance 미리
cooperation[kouàpəréiʃən] 협조

W Attention, residents. There is a change in operating hours of the playgrounds in our apartment complex. The management has received a lot of complaints about some children making loud noises on the playgrounds late at night. Starting tomorrow, the new operating hours of all the playgrounds will be from 10 a.m. to 9 p.m. We thank you in advance for your cooperation.

여 주민 여러분께 알려드립니다. 우리 아파트 단지 내 놀이터의 운영 시간이 변경됩니다. 몇몇 아이들이 늦은 밤 놀이터에서 시끄러운 소리를 내는 것에 대해 수많은 불만이 관리 사무소에 접수되었습니다. 내일부터 모든 놀이터의 새 운영 시간은 오전 10시부터 오후 9시까지입니다. 여러분의 협조에 미리 감사드립니다.

10 ③

해설 하루에 50달러인 차를 이틀 동안 빌리기로 했고, 하루 사용 요금이 10달러인 GPS 시스템을 장착하기로 했으므로 총 120달러를 내야 한다.

어휘 rent[rent] (돈을 내고) 빌리다
by myself 나 혼자

M Good morning. How can I help you?
W I'd like to rent a car for 2 days.
M What kind of car would you like to rent?
W I'll be traveling by myself, so I don't need a big car.
M Then this car will be big enough. It's $50 a day.

남 안녕하세요. 무엇을 도와드릴까요?
여 이틀 동안 차를 빌리고 싶어요.
남 어떤 차를 빌리고 싶으세요?
여 혼자 여행할 거니까 큰 차는 필요 없어요.
남 그럼 이 차로 충분할 거예요. 하루에 50달러입니다.

GPS system 위치 추적 시스템
extra charge 추가 요금

W Does it come with a GPS system?
M No, there is a $10 <u>extra charge per day</u> for a GPS system.
W Okay, I'll <u>get this car with</u> a GPS system for 2 days.

여 GPS 시스템도 함께 제공됩니까?
남 아니요, GPS 시스템을 쓰려면 하루에 10달러의 추가 요금을 내셔야 해요.
여 좋아요, 이틀 동안 GPS 시스템을 장착해서 이 차를 쓸게요.

11 ③

해설 여자가 머리가 아파서 저녁 약속에 늦는다고 부모님께 알리자고 했고 남자가 전화하겠다고 했다.

어휘 terrible[térəbl] 심한
headache[hédèik] 두통
medicine[médisn] 약
run late 늦다
cancel[kǽnsəl] 취소하다
lie down 눕다

M Are you ready, honey? We'll be late for dinner.
W I'm ready, John, but I have a terrible headache.
M Oh no. Do you want me to <u>bring you some medicine</u>?
W Yes, please. And I think we should tell your parents we're <u>running a little late</u>.
M We <u>can cancel dinner</u> if you're not feeling too well.
W I think I'll be fine if I just lie down for 10 minutes.
M Okay, <u>then I'll call them</u> and let them know.
W Yes, thank you.

남 준비됐어요, 여보? 우리 저녁 식사에 늦을 것 같아요.
여 전 준비됐어요, John. 하지만 머리가 너무 아프네요.
남 이런. 약을 좀 갖다 줄까요?
여 네, 부탁해요. 그리고 당신 부모님한테 우리가 좀 늦을 것 같다고 말씀드려야 할 것 같아요.
남 몸이 안 좋으면 저녁 식사는 취소해도 돼요.
여 10분만 누워 있으면 괜찮을 것 같아요.
남 알았어요, 그럼 제가 전화해서 알려드릴게요.
여 그래요. 고마워요.

12 ⑤

해설 교장 이름(Rick Kim), 설립 연도(2010년), 사용 언어(한국어와 영어), 모집 인원(100명)에 대해 언급했지만 개학 날짜에 대한 언급은 없다.

어휘 orientation session 오리엔테이션
principal[prínsəpəl] 교장
establish[istǽbliʃ] 설립하다
bilingual[bailíŋgwəl] 2개 국어를 병용하는
accept[əksépt] 받아들이다
apply[əplái] 지원하다

M Welcome to our orientation session, everyone. My name is Rick Kim, and <u>I am the principal</u> of this school. Sejong School was established in 2010, and it is <u>the first international</u> school in the state. Students will learn half of their subjects in Korean and the other half in English. <u>We're going to accept</u> 100 new students this year, and you can start applying on Monday the 20th.

남 여러분, 오리엔테이션에 오신 것을 환영합니다. 제 이름은 Rick Kim이고, 이 학교 교장입니다. 세종학교는 2010년에 설립되었으며, 주 최초의 국제 학교입니다. 학생들은 과목의 절반은 한국어로, 나머지 반은 영어로 배우게 됩니다. 올해 신입생을 100명 모집할 예정인데, 20일 월요일부터 지원할 수 있습니다.

13 ①

해설 화장실과 입구 근처를 제외한 방 중에서 부엌과 가까운 곳으로 하자고 했으므로 두 사람은 A방을 선택할 것이다.

어휘 restroom[réstrù(:)m] 화장실
entrance[éntrəns] 입구
noisy[nɔ́izi] 시끄러운
be able to ~을 할 수 있다

W I'm so excited to stay at Hanok Guesthouse.
M Me, too. Which room would you like to stay in?
W Well, I don't like <u>the rooms next to</u> the restroom.
M Okay. What about a room <u>near the entrance</u>? It will be easier to move around because we have many bags.

여 한옥 게스트하우스에 묵게 돼서 너무 신이 나네요.
남 저도요. 어느 방에서 묵고 싶어요?
여 음, 화장실 옆에 있는 방들은 별로네요.
남 알겠어요. 입구 근처 있는 방은 어때요? 우리가 가방이 많아서 움직이기 쉬울 거예요.
여 좋은 생각이 아닌 것 같아요. 너무 시끄러워서 잠을 잘 수 없을 거예요.

W I don't think that's a good idea. It could be really noisy, so we won't be able to sleep.
M I see. Then, we have 2 rooms left.
W How about the one near the kitchen? We can cook and eat faster.
M Great. Let's stay there then.

남 알겠어요. 그럼 방이 두 개 남았네요.
여 부엌 근처에서 묵는 게 어때요? 빨리 요리하고 먹을 수 있잖아요.
남 좋아요. 그러면 거기서 묵어요.

14 ②

해설 호주의 상징이며 새끼를 넣는 주머니가 있는 동물은 캥거루이다.

어휘 in fact 사실은
symbol[símbəl] 상징
appear[əpíər] 등장하다, 보이다
back leg 뒷다리
tail[teil] 꼬리
balance[bǽləns] 균형을 잡다
hop[hɑp] 깡충깡충 뛰다
pouch[pautʃ] (캥거루 등의) 새끼 주머니

W This animal is usually found in Australia. In fact, it is a symbol of Australia and even appears on some Australian money. This animal has large back legs, and it also has a long tail for balancing. It is the only large animal that moves by hopping. This animal is famous for having a pouch and keeping its babies in it.

여 이 동물은 호주에서 흔히 볼 수 있습니다. 사실, 이것은 호주의 상징이고 심지어 일부 호주 돈에 등장하기도 합니다. 이 동물은 뒷다리가 크고, 균형을 잡기 위한 긴 꼬리를 가지고 있습니다. 이것은 깡충깡충 뛰면서 움직이는 유일한 큰 동물입니다. 이 동물은 주머니를 가지고 있고 새끼를 그 안에 넣고 다니는 것으로 유명합니다.

15 ④

해설 여자는 내일 공원에서 날릴 연을 지금 만들 거라고 했다.

어휘 fly[flai] 날리다
kite[kait] 연
glue[glu:] 접착제

M It's such a beautiful day. Do you want to go to the park, Cindy?
W Now? Can we go tomorrow instead, Dad?
M Sure, we can. But it's going to be windy and cold tomorrow.
W I know. I want to fly a kite at the park tomorrow.
M Oh, that's why you asked me to get some glue this morning.
W Yes, I'm going to make a kite right now.
M Do you want me to help you?
W No, thanks, Dad. I want to do it by myself.

남 정말 날씨 좋다. Cindy, 공원에 가고 싶니?
여 지금요? 대신 내일 가도 될까요, 아빠?
남 그래. 그래도 되지. 하지만 내일은 바람이 불고 추워질 거라는데.
여 알아요. 저는 내일 공원에서 연을 날리고 싶어서요.
남 아, 그래서 오늘 아침에 나한테 접착제를 사다 달라고 한 거구나.
여 네, 지금 연을 만들 거예요.
남 내가 도와줄까?
여 고맙지만 괜찮아요, 아빠. 저 혼자 하고 싶어요.

16 ⑤

해설 여자는 5월 11일에 Riverside 고등학교와의 다음 경기를 앞두고 있다.

어휘 match[mætʃ] 경기, 시합
play against ~와 시합하다
confused[kənfjú:zd] 혼동하는

M Are you ready for the next tennis matches, Donna?
W I don't know. I still have to watch some more videos of the other team.
M Aren't you playing against the Newtown High School players on May 1st? That's only 3 days away.
W We already played against them on April 24th, Dad.
M Oh, I meant to say Riverside High School.
W We're playing against them on May 11th.
M I was confused about the dates and schools.

남 다음 테니스 경기 준비됐니, Donna?
여 모르겠어요. 아직 상대 팀의 비디오를 좀 더 봐야 해요.
남 5월 1일에 Newtown 고등학교 선수들과 경기하는 거 아니니? 3일밖에 안 남았어.
여 그 학교하고는 이미 4월 24일에 경기를 했어요, 아빠.
남 아, Riverside 고등학교라고 말하려고 했는데.
여 저희 학교는 5월 11일에 그 학교와 경기를 할 거예요.
남 내가 날짜와 학교를 혼동했구나.

17 ④

해설 놀이공원에서 탄 놀이 기구 중 어느 것이 가장 좋았냐고 묻는 말에 놀이 기구 중 좋았던 것을 말하거나 전부 맘에 든다는 식의 응답이 어울린다.

어휘 amusement park 놀이공원
amazing [əméiziŋ] 굉장한
ride [raid] (놀이공원에 있는) 놀이 기구
[선택지]
stop by ~에 들르다

W Have you been to Fantasy World, the new amusement park?
M Yes, I have. I went with my brother 2 weeks ago.
W It's an amazing place, isn't it?
M Yes, it's the best amusement park I've ever been to.
W Were you able to go on all the rides?
M Yes, we were very lucky.
W What was your favorite ride?
M It's hard to say. I liked all of them.

여 새로 생긴 놀이공원인 Fantasy World에 가 봤니?
남 응. 가 봤어. 2주 전에 동생과 함께 갔어.
여 정말 멋진 곳이지?
남 그래. 내가 가 본 놀이공원 중에서 가장 최고야.
여 놀이 기구를 전부 탈 수 있었니?
남 응. 우리는 아주 운이 좋았어.
여 어떤 놀이 기구가 가장 좋았니?
남 말하기 어렵네. 전부 다 맘에 들었거든.

① 너는 우리랑 같이 갔어야 했는데.
② 글쎄. 난 좋아하는 차가 없어.
③ 우리는 시청에 들러야 했어.
⑤ 아빠가 우리를 공원까지 태워다 주셨어.

18 ③

해설 비행기가 연착해서 같이 기다리는 걸 제안하는 남자의 말에 걱정하지 말라는 거절의 응답이 어울린다.

어휘 flight [flait] 비행기
departure time 출발 시각
delay [diléi] 지연시키다
[선택지]
connection [kənékʃən] 연결, 접속

M It's 9:30 right now. What time is your flight, Sally?
W The departure time is 10:30 a.m.
M I don't see any flights that are leaving at 10:30 a.m.
W That can't be right. Let me see.
M Are you flying American Air?
W Yes, Dad. It says the flight has been delayed. The new departure time is 11:30 a.m.
M Oh, I see. Do you want me to wait with you?
W Don't worry. I will be fine by myself.

남 지금 9시 30분이야. Sally, 몇 시 비행기지?
여 출발 시각은 오전 10시 30분이에요.
남 오전 10시 30분에 출발하는 비행기는 하나도 안 보이는데.
여 그럴 리가 없어요. 어디 봐요.
남 American Air를 타는 거니?
여 네, 아빠. 비행기가 연착되었다고 나오네요. 새 출발 시각은 오전 11시 30분이에요.
남 아, 그렇구나. 너랑 같이 기다려줄까?
여 걱정하지 마세요. 저 혼자도 괜찮아요.

① 저는 오늘 아침 10시에 일어났어요.
② 네, 저는 괜찮을 거예요. 비행기에서 잘 거예요.
④ 안 들려요. 연결 상태가 정말 안 좋아요.
⑤ 아뇨, 공항에서 저를 기다릴 필요 없어요.

19 ⑤

해설 피로 때문에 눈이 충혈된 여자에게 눈을 쉬게 해야 한다고 했으나 시험공부 때문에 쉴 수가 없다고 했으므로 시험보다 건강이 더 중요하다는 충고가 이어져야 어울린다.

어휘 take a look 보다
hurt [həːrt] 아프다; 해치다
pain [pein] 고통
plenty of 많은

W Dr. Jackson, my eyes are really red.
M Let me take a look. Do they hurt?
W No. I don't feel any pain. My eyes have been dry for the past few days.
M Have you been sleeping well?
W No, I haven't.
M That's why. Your eyes are telling you that you need to get plenty of rest.
W But I can't rest. There's a very important exam this Friday.

여 제 눈이 정말 빨개요, Jackson 선생님.
남 한번 볼게요. 눈이 아픈가요?
여 아뇨, 전혀 아프지 않아요. 눈이 건조해요.
남 잠은 잘 자고 있나요?
여 아뇨, 잠을 잘 못 자고 있어요.
남 그래서 그렇네요. 환자분의 눈이 충분한 휴식을 취해야 한다고 알려 주고 있잖아요.
여 하지만 전 쉴 수가 없어요. 이번 주 금요일에 아주 중요한 시험이 있거든요.

M Your health is more important than doing well on your exam.

남 시험을 잘 보는 것보다 건강이 더 중요해요.

① 죄송하지만 이번 주 금요일은 휴무입니다.
② 만약 당신이 깨어있을 수 없다면, 커피를 더 마셔요.
③ 잠을 너무 많이 자는 것도 건강에 해로울 수 있어요.
④ 눈의 통증을 줄일 수 있는 것을 줄게요.

20 ⑤

해설 Jennifer에게 회의가 늦게 시작하지 않도록 회의 전에 노트북 전원을 켜달라고 할 것이다.

어휘 debate club 토론 동아리
turn on ~을 켜다
remind[rimáind] 다시 한 번 알려주다, 상기시키다

M Tim is the leader of a debate club. He holds a club meeting at 4 p.m. every Wednesday. The meeting always starts 10 minutes late because one of the club members, Jennifer, forgets to turn on her computer. She needs to take notes on her computer, but everyone else always has to wait. So, Tim wants to remind her to check her computer before the meeting. In this situation, what would Tim most likely say to Jennifer?

Tim Jennifer, please turn on your computer before 4 o'clock.

남 Tim은 토론 동아리의 회장이다. 그는 매주 수요일 오후 4시에 동아리 회의를 연다. 동아리 회원 중 한 명인 Jennifer가 컴퓨터를 켜는 것을 잊어버리기 때문에 그 회의는 항상 10분 늦게 시작한다. 그녀는 회의에 대한 기록을 해야 하는데, 다른 사람들은 항상 기다려야 한다. 그래서 Tim은 회의가 시작하기 전에 컴퓨터를 켜야 한다는 것을 다시 한번 알려주려고 한다. 이러한 상황에서 Tim은 Jennifer에게 할 말로 가장 적절한 것은 무엇인가?

Tim Jennifer, 4시 전에 컴퓨터를 켜줘.

① 우리는 4시에 회의가 있어.
② 너를 소개 해줄래?
③ 너는 매일 운동을 해야 해.
④ Smith 선생님과 상담은 어땠어?

01 ②	02 ⑤	03 ①	04 ①	05 ③	06 ③	07 ③
08 ⑤	09 ②	10 ①	11 ⑤	12 ③	13 ③	14 ③
15 ①	16 ④	17 ⑤	18 ⑤	19 ②	20 ④	

01 ②

해설 여자는 별들이 그려진 셔츠를 구입하겠다고 했다.

어휘 over there 저쪽에
way[wei] (특정한) 방향, 쪽
in particular 특별히
unique[juːníːk] 독특한
play[plei] 연극

M Hello, how may I help you?
W Where can I find boys' shirts?
M Oh, they're right over there. This way, please.
W Thanks.
M Are you looking for anything in particular?
W I'm looking for a unique shirt. My son needs to wear it for his school play.
M Then, how about this one with flowers on it?
W It looks good, but this one with lots of stars on it would be better.
M I'm sure he'll like it, ma'am.
W I think so, too. I'll take it.

남 안녕하세요, 무엇을 도와드릴까요?
여 남자아이가 입을만한 셔츠는 어디에 있나요?
남 아, 바로 저쪽에 있어요. 이쪽으로 오세요.
여 고마워요.
남 특별히 찾으시는 것이 있나요?
여 독특한 셔츠를 찾고 있어요. 제 아들이 학교 연극에서 입어야 하거든요.
남 그럼, 꽃이 그려진 이건 어때요?
여 좋긴 하지만, 별이 많이 있는 이 셔츠가 더 좋을 것 같아요.
남 아드님이 분명 좋아할 겁니다.
여 저도 그렇게 생각해요. 이걸 살게요.

02 ⑤

해설 크기(6 사이즈), 가격(15달러), 재질(고무), 색상(검정색과 갈색)에 대해 언급했지만 무게에 대해서는 언급하지 않았다.

어휘 Welcome to ~. ~에 오신 것을 환영합니다.
basketball[bǽskitbɔ̀ːl] 농구 공
popular[pɑ́pulər] 인기 있는
grade[greid] 학년
enough[ináf] 충분한
be made of ~로 만들어지다
rubber[rʌ́bər] 고무

W Welcome to Richard's Sporting Goods. Can I help you find anything?
M I'm looking for a basketball.
W Sure, this is the most popular basketball we have.
M That is too big. I'm looking for something smaller. It's for my son in second grade.
W Then size 6 will be big enough. This one's only $15.
M Is it made of rubber?
W Yes, and it comes in 2 different colors, black and brown.
M Okay. I'll take a brown one.

여 Richard 스포츠 용품점에 오신 것을 환영합니다. 무엇을 찾으시나요?
남 농구공을 찾고 있어요.
여 네, 이게 여기서 가장 인기 있는 농구공이에요.
남 이건 너무 크네요. 좀 작은 것을 찾고 있거든요. 2학년인 아들한테 주려고요.
여 그러면 6사이즈면 충분하겠네요. 15달러밖에 안합니다.
남 고무로 만들어졌나요?
여 네, 두 가지 색상인 검정색과 갈색으로 나와요.
남 알겠습니다. 갈색으로 살게요.

03 ①

해설 이미 배달된 책상이 너무 커서 반품하고 환불을 받기 위해 전화했다.

어휘 furniture[fə́ːrnitʃər] 가구
purchase[pə́ːrtʃəs] 구매, 구매한 것
bed frame 침대 틀
deliver[dilívər] 배달하다
return[ritə́ːrn] 반환하다
get a refund 환불을 받다
shipping[ʃípiŋ] 배송

[Telephone rings.]
W Thank you for calling Jane's Furniture. How may I help you?
M I have a question about the purchase I made last week.
W Can I have your order number?
M Yes, it's 655789.
W Okay, let me check. [Pause] A bed frame and a desk were delivered 3 days ago.
M Yes, that's correct. Could I return the desk and get a refund for it?
W Is there anything wrong with the desk?

[전화벨이 울린다.]
여 Jane의 가구점에 전화 주셔서 감사드립니다. 무엇을 도와 드릴까요?
남 지난주에 구매한 것과 관련해서 물어볼 게 있어요.
여 주문 번호를 알려 주시겠어요?
남 네, 655789입니다.
여 알겠습니다, 확인해 보겠습니다. [잠시 후] 침대 틀과 책상은 3일 전에 배달되었네요.
남 네, 맞아요. 책상을 반품하고 환불을 받을 수 있을까요?
여 책상에 무슨 문제가 있나요?

M It is too big for my room.
W Okay. You can return it and get a refund. But you'll have to <u>pay for shipping</u>.
M That's not a problem.

남 책상이 제 방에 너무 커서요.
여 알겠습니다. 반품하시고 환불받으실 수 있어요. 하지만 배송료는 내셔야 할 겁니다.
남 괜찮습니다.

04 ①

[해설] 팬들이 참여하는 경기 전 행사를 위해 5시 30분보다 빨리 만나자고 하면서 4시 30분으로 약속 시간을 변경했다.

[어휘] final[fáinəl] 마지막의, 최종의
bus stop 버스 정류장
a little 약간, 조금
early[ə́ːrli] (계획보다) 일찍
pre-game[priː-géim] 경기 전의
participate in ~에 참여하다

W Hey, Peter. Are you excited about going to the baseball game tonight?
M Of course, I am. It's the final game of the season.
W We're meeting at 5:30 p.m. at the bus stop, right?
M Right. But I think we need to meet <u>earlier than that</u>.
W <u>How much earlier</u>? The game starts at 7, right?
M There are pre-game activities that all the fans can participate in. <u>They start at</u> 6 p.m.
W Really? Then <u>we should meet</u> at 4:30.
M That sounds good.

여 안녕, Peter. 오늘밤에 야구 경기 보러 가게 되어 신나니?
남 물론이지. 시즌 마지막 경기잖아.
여 우리가 오후 5시 30분에 버스 정류장에서 만나는 거 맞지?
남 맞아. 근데 우리 그것보다 더 일찍 만나야 할 것 같아.
여 얼마나 더 일찍? 경기는 7시에 시작하잖아, 그렇지?
남 팬들이 모두 참여할 수 있는 경기 전 행사들이 있어. 오후 6시에 시작하거든.
여 정말? 그럼 4시 30분에 만나야겠네.
남 그게 좋겠어.

05 ③

[해설] 콘서트를 관람한 뒤 집에 가려는 사람들의 줄을 보고 다음 열차를 탈 수 있을지 걱정하는 것으로 보아 지하철역임을 알 수 있다.

[어휘] crowded[kráudid] 붐비는
happen[hǽpən] (일이) 일어나다
every time ~ 할 때마다
wait in line 줄에 서서 기다리다
try to-v ~하려고 시도하다
get on (버스·기차 등을) 타다
probably[prábəbli] 아마도
run[rʌn] (교통편이) 운행되다

M Wow, it's so crowded in here.
W I know. This happens <u>every time there's a</u> concert at the stadium.
M Oh, is that why so many people are waiting in line?
W Yes. All these people are trying to get home after watching a boy group's concert.
M Will we be able to <u>get on the next train</u>?
W Probably not. If we can't, <u>we'll just get on</u> the one after that.
M <u>The train runs every</u> 5 minutes, right?
W Yes. We're lucky we only have 2 stops to go.

남 와. 여기 굉장히 붐비네.
여 맞아. 경기장에서 콘서트가 있을 때마다 일어나는 일이지.
남 아, 그래서 이렇게 많은 사람들이 줄을 서서 기다리고 있는 거야?
여 응. 이 사람들 모두가 보이 그룹 콘서트를 보고 나서 집에 가려고 하고 있어.
남 우리가 다음 열차를 탈 수 있을까?
여 아마도 안 될 걸. 만약 못 타면 그 다음 열차를 타게 되겠지.
남 열차가 5분마다 오지, 맞지?
여 응. 우린 두 정거장만 가면 되니 다행이야.

06 ③

[해설] 얼어 있는 웅덩이를 밟지 않도록 알려준 남자에게 감사의 말을 전하는 여자의 대화 내용이다.

[어휘] dozen[dʌ́zən] 한 다스, 12개짜리 한 묶음
Look out! 조심해!
step on ~을 밟다
park[pɑːrk] 주차하다
right here 바로 여기에

① M <u>How often do you</u> go swimming?
　 W I go swimming every day.
② M How much are these flowers?
　 W They are $20 a dozen.
③ M Look out! <u>Don't step on</u> the ice.
　 W Oh, thank you! I didn't see it.
④ M What would you like to drink?
　 W <u>I'll have</u> a glass of iced tea.
⑤ M Where can I park my car?
　 W You can <u>park it right here</u>.

① 남 너는 얼마나 자주 수영하러 가니?
　 여 나는 매일 수영하러 가.
② 남 이 꽃들이 얼마죠?
　 여 열두 송이 한 묶음에 20달러입니다.
③ 남 조심해요! 얼음을 밟지 마세요.
　 여 아, 고마워요! 못 봤네요.
④ 남 음료는 무엇으로 하시겠습니까?
　 여 아이스티 한 잔 주세요.
⑤ 남 차를 어디에 주차하면 될까요?
　 여 바로 여기에 주차하시면 됩니다.

07 ③

여자는 남자에게 집에 오는 길에 우편함을 확인해 달라고 부탁했다.

어휘 on A's way home A가 집에 오는 길에

get ~ done ~을 끝내다

schoolwork[skúlwə̀rk] 학교 공부, 학업

pick up ~을 사다

mailbox[méilbàks] 우편함

[Cell phone rings.]

M Hello.

W Hi, John. Are you <u>on your way</u> <u>home</u>?

M Yes, Mom. I should be home in about 10 minutes.

W Did you get all your schoolwork done?

M Yes, I <u>was able to</u> finish my report before I left.

W Good. I'll <u>start</u> <u>making</u> <u>dinner</u>.

M Do you want me to pick up anything from the supermarket?

W No. We have everything we need. Could you just <u>check the</u> <u>mailbox</u>?

M Okay, I will.

[휴대전화가 울린다.]

남 여보세요.

여 여보세요, John. 지금 집에 오고 있는 중이니?

남 네, 엄마. 10분 정도 후면 집에 도착할 거예요.

여 학교 공부는 다 끝냈니?

남 네, 나오기 전에 과제를 다 끝낼 수 있었어요.

여 잘했어. 저녁 준비를 시작해야겠구나.

남 슈퍼마켓에서 뭘 좀 사 올까요?

여 아니. 필요한 것은 다 있단다. 우편함만 좀 확인해 줄래?

남 알겠어요, 그럴게요.

08 ⑤

불 피우는 장소(표시되어 있는 곳), 주차 공간(각 야영지 마다 한 군데), 화장실 위치(세탁실 옆), 체크아웃 시각(낮 12시)에 대해 언급했지만 사용료에 대한 언급은 없다.

어휘 camper[kǽmpər] 야영객

announcement[ənáunsmənt] 알림

remind A of A에게 ~을 상기시켜 주다

marked[maːrkt] 표시된

parking spot 주차 공간

laundry room 세탁실

checkout[tʃ́ekaut] (호텔에서) 체크아웃

Make sure to-v. 반드시 ~하세요.

polite[pəláit] 예의 바른, 정중한

M Hello, campers. This is a short announcement reminding you of the rules for all the guests. Fires are allowed only <u>in</u> <u>marked</u> <u>areas</u>. Each campsite has one parking spot, and parking is <u>not allowed</u> <u>on</u> the grass. Bathrooms are located <u>next</u> <u>to the laundry room</u>. Please, remember that <u>the checkout time</u> is 12 p.m. Make sure to be polite to other campers, and I hope you enjoy your stay!

남 야영객 여러분, 안녕하세요. 모든 분들이 지켜야 할 규정을 간단하게 알려드리고자 합니다. 불은 표시된 지역에서만 사용하실 수 있습니다. 각 야영지마다 주차 공간이 한 군데씩 있으며 잔디밭에는 주차할 수 없습니다. 화장실은 세탁실 옆에 위치해 있습니다. 체크아웃 시각은 낮 12시라는 것을 기억해 주세요. 반드시 다른 야영객들에게 예의 있게 행동해주시고 여기 머무는 동안 즐거운 시간이 되기를 바랍니다!

09 ②

배드민턴을 칠 때 라켓을 사용해 네트 위로 보내는 것으로 깃털이 달린 원뿔 모양의 물체는 셔틀콕이다.

어휘 cone[koun] 원뿔

feather[féðər] 깃털

racket[rǽkit] 라켓

net[net] 네트

win a point 1점을 얻다[따다]

W This is shaped like a cone. It has a round end and 16 or more <u>feathers</u> <u>around the</u> <u>end</u>. It is used when you play badminton. In badminton, each player <u>hits</u> <u>this</u> <u>with</u> a racket and sends it <u>over</u> <u>the</u> <u>net</u> to the other player. If the other player <u>can't</u> <u>return it</u>, you win a point.

여 이것은 원뿔의 모양을 하고 있어요. 이것은 끝이 둥글고 그 주변으로 16개 이상의 깃털이 있고요. 이것은 배드민턴을 칠 때 쓰어요. 배드민턴 경기에서 각 선수들은 라켓으로 이것을 쳐서, 네트 너머의 상대 선수에게 보내요. 상대 선수가 이것을 돌려보내지 못하면 당신은 1점을 얻게 돼요.

10 ①

집에 도착하면 전화하겠다는 사람에게 자신의 전화기를 써도 된다고 허락하는 응답은 어색하다.

어휘 call[kɔːl] ~에게 전화하다
be raised 자라다
not ~ at all 전혀 ~ 아닌

① M I'll call you when I get home.
　 W Of course. You can use my phone.
② M Did you get my message?
　 W No, I didn't get it.
③ M Are you from Philadelphia?
　 W I was born and raised there.
④ M How often do you watch TV?
　 W I don't watch TV at all.
⑤ M Can I help you find anything?
　 W Yes, I'm looking for a green hat.

① 남 집에 도착하면 전화할게.
　 여 물론이지. 내 전화기를 써도 돼.
② 남 내 메시지 받았어?
　 여 아니, 못 받았어.
③ 남 Philadelphia에서 오셨나요?
　 여 저는 거기에서 태어나서 자랐어요.
④ 남 TV를 얼마나 자주 보나요?
　 여 저는 TV를 전혀 안 봐요.
⑤ 남 찾는 것을 도와 드릴까요.
　 여 네, 녹색 모자를 찾고 있어요.

11 ⑤

해설 남자는 동영상 제작이 어려워지자 대신 여자에게 포스터 디자인을 부탁했고 여자는 승낙했다.

어휘 less[les] 더 적은
toilet paper 화장지
think of v-ing ~할 것을 고려하다
bring A B A에게 B를 가져다주다

M Judy, can we talk about our project now?
W Sure. We are going to make a video about using less toilet paper, right?
M Yes. But we don't have enough time to make a video. So, how about changing our plan?
W Okay. What do you want to do?
M I'm thinking of making a poster instead. Can you design a poster? I brought you paper and a pencil.
W Sure. I'll do it now.
M Thanks.

남 Judy, 지금 우리의 프로젝트에 대해 얘기해 볼까?
여 좋아. 우리는 화장지를 적게 쓰는 것에 대한 동영상을 제작할 예정이지, 그렇지?
남 응. 그런데 동영상을 제작할 시간이 충분하지 않아. 그래서 계획을 바꾸는 게 어때?
여 그래. 너는 뭘 하면 좋겠어?
남 나는 대신에 포스터 제작을 고려하고 있어. 포스터 디자인을 해줄래? 내가 종이와 연필은 가져왔거든.
여 물론이지. 지금 할게.
남 고마워.

12 ③

해설 두 사람은 토요일에 7시보다 늦게 시작하고, 티켓 가격은 비싸지만 좋은 평을 받은 뮤지컬을 관람하기로 했다.

어휘 musical[mjúːzikəl] 뮤지컬
choose[tʃuːz] 선택하다
expensive[ikspénsiv] 비싼
review[rivjúː] 평론, 비평 기사

M Honey, let's go to a musical this weekend.
W Sure. I have time on Saturday.
M Great. I'll buy the tickets right now.
W Make sure to leave enough time for dinner before the musical starts.
M I will. The one we saw last month started at 7 p.m., right?
W Right. We need a later time.
M We have 2 musicals to choose from. Which one do you want to see?
W This musical is more expensive than that one, but I've read some good reviews about it.
M Okay. This one should be good then.

남 여보, 이번 주말에 뮤지컬 보러 가요.
여 좋아요. 저는 토요일에 시간이 있어요.
남 잘됐네요. 지금 당장 표를 살게요.
여 뮤지컬이 시작하기 전에 저녁을 먹을 수 있게 충분한 시간을 꼭 남겨 둬요.
남 그럴게요. 지난달에 본 것은 저녁 7시에 시작했어요, 그렇죠?
여 맞아요. 우리는 더 늦은 공연으로 해야 돼요.
남 우리가 선택할 수 있는 뮤지컬이 두 개가 있어요. 어느 것을 보고 싶어요?
여 이 뮤지컬이 저것보다 더 비싸지만 이 뮤지컬에 대해 좋은 비평 기사를 읽었어요.
남 알겠어요. 그럼 이 뮤지컬이 좋겠네요.

13 ③

해설 인터넷 뉴스에서는 산불이 2주 전인 10월 7일에 시작되었다고 했다.

M Did you see the news about the huge fire in California?
W Yes, I did. Wildfires often happen in autumn, but this one is really bad.

남 California에서 발생한 큰 화재에 대한 뉴스 봤어?
여 응. 봤어. 거기는 가을에 산불이 자주 발생하는데 이번 화재는 정말 심각해.

huge[hju:dʒ] 거대한
wildfire[waildfàiər] 산불, 들불
autumn[ɔ́:təm] 가을
terrible[térəbl] 끔찍한

M I know. It's terrible. Do you know when the fire started?

W I heard it started on October 7th.

M That's over 2 weeks ago. Didn't it start on October 14th?

W Well, the 7th is what I heard on the 8 o'clock news yesterday.

M Let's check the news on the Internet. [Pause] Oh, you're right. It started 2 weeks ago.

W It is really sad, isn't it?

남 맞아. 끔찍해. 화재가 언제 시작되었는지 아니?

여 10월 7일에 시작되었다고 들었어.

남 그렇다면 2주일도 넘었다는 말이네. 10월 14일에 시작되지 않았니?

여 글쎄. 7일이 내가 어제 8시 뉴스에서 들은 날짜야.

남 인터넷에서 뉴스를 확인해 보자. [잠시 후] 아, 네 말이 맞네. 2주일 전에 시작되었어.

여 정말로 슬픈 일이지, 그렇지 않아?

14 ③

해설 남자는 어제 배달된 새 책상을 하루 종일 조립했다고 했다.

어휘 pharmacy[fáːrməsi] 약국
medicine[médisn] 약
back[bæk] 허리; 등
kill[kil] 아파서 죽을 지경이 되게 만들다
order[ɔ́ːrdər] 주문하다
spend all day v-ing ~하느라 하루 종일을 보내다
put ~ together ~를 조립하다
feel better 회복되다

W Jack, are you going somewhere?

M I'm going to the pharmacy to get some medicine.

W Why? Are you feeling okay?

M No, I think I hurt my back. It's killing me.

W Oh no. What happened?

M I ordered a new desk a few days ago and it was delivered yesterday. So I spent all day putting it together.

W That sounds like a lot of work. I hope you feel better soon.

M Thanks.

여 Jack, 어디 가는 중이야?

남 약을 좀 사려고 약국에 가고 있어.

여 왜? 몸 괜찮니?

남 아니, 허리를 다친 것 같아. 아파 죽겠어.

여 이런. 어쩌다 그랬는데?

남 며칠 전에 새 책상을 주문했는데 어제 배달이 되었거든. 그걸 조립하느라 하루를 다 보냈어.

여 정말 일이 많았겠다. 빨리 회복됐으면 좋겠네.

남 고마워.

15 ①

해설 여름 야구 캠프에 대해 설명하면서 홍보하는 내용이다.

어휘 improve[imprúːv] 향상시키다
skill[skil] 기술
make friends 친구를 사귀다
most importantly 가장 중요한 것은
valuable[vǽljuːəbəl] 유익한, 귀중한
for the rest of A's life 삶의 남은 기간 동안, 죽을 때까지

M Hello, parents. Are you looking for a summer camp for your children? The JC Baseball Camp is a great place for young players to improve their skills, work hard and make new friends. Most importantly, they will learn valuable life skills they'll need for the rest of their lives. For more information, please visit our website, www.jcbaseballcamp.com.

남 학부모님들 안녕하세요. 여러분의 자녀들을 위한 여름 캠프를 찾으시나요? JC 야구 캠프는 어린 선수들이 기술을 향상시키고 열심히 운동하면서 새로운 친구들을 사귈 수 있는 아주 좋은 장소입니다. 가장 중요한 것은 어린 선수들이 앞으로 살아가는 동안 필요할 유익한 삶의 기술을 배우게 될 것입니다. 더 많은 정보가 필요하시면 저희 웹사이트 www.jcbaseballcamp.com. 을 방문해 주세요.

16 ④

해설 성인 2명(20달러), 어린이 2명(10달러)의 입장권 총금액은 30달러이며, 수요일인 오늘 10퍼센트 할인이 된다고 하였으므로, 여자는 27달러를 지불할 것이다.

어휘 natural history 자연사
adult[ədʌ́lt] 성인

M Welcome to the Natural History Museum. How may I help you?

W I'd like to buy tickets for 4 people, please.

M Are there any children under 12?

W Yes, there are 2 children.

M For adults, it's $10, and for children, it's $5.

남 자연사 박물관에 오신 것을 환영합니다. 무엇을 도와 드릴까요?

여 4명 입장권 네 장을 구매하고 싶어서요.

남 12세 미만의 어린이도 있나요?

여 네, 어린이 두 명이 있어요.

남 성인은 10달러이고, 어린이는 5달러입니다.

total[tóutl] 총액, 합계
offer[ɔ́(ː)fər] 제공하다
discount[dískaunt] 할인

W I see. What is the total?
M The total is $30. But on Wednesdays only, we offer a special discount on tickets. So today you get a 10% discount.
W That's great. Here is my card.

여 그렇군요. 그럼 총액이 얼마인가요?
남 총금액은 30달러입니다. 하지만 수요일에만 입장권 특별 할인을 제공합니다. 그래서 오늘 10퍼센트 할인을 받으실 거예요.
여 좋네요. 여기 제 카드예요.

17 ⑤

해설 남자가 가장 좋아하는 배우에 대해 왜 좋아하는지 묻는 여자의 말에 이유를 설명하는 응답이 이어져야 자연스럽다.

어휘 pick[pik] 고르다, 선택하다
blockbuster[blɑ́kbʌ̀stər] 블록버스터 (크게 성공한 책이나 영화)
handsome[hǽnsəm] 잘생긴, 멋진
[선택지]
recently[ríːsəntli] 최근에
donate[dóuneit] 기부하다
charity[tʃǽrəti] 자선 단체

W Who's your favorite actor, Andy?
M It's hard to pick just one. Hmm... I think I like Michael Smith best.
W He's one of my favorite actors, too.
M Did you see his blockbuster movie this summer?
W Of course, I did. I've seen all of his movies since 2010.
M Wow, you really do like him.
W Yes, I do. I think he's very handsome. Why do you like him so much?
M I like him because he donates to charities every year.

여 Andy, 네가 가장 좋아하는 배우는 누구니?
남 한 사람만 고르기 너무 힘든데. 음… Michael Smith가 가장 좋은 것 같아.
여 그는 내가 가장 좋아하는 배우 중 한 사람이기도 해.
남 이번 여름에 그가 나온 블록버스터 영화 봤니?
여 물론 봤지. 2010년 이후에 그가 나온 영화는 모두 봤거든.
남 와, 너는 그를 정말 좋아하는구나.
여 그래. 그는 정말 잘생긴 것 같아. 너는 왜 그를 그렇게 좋아하니?
남 나는 그가 매년 자선 단체에 기부하기 때문에 좋아해.

① 적어도 네가 그를 좋아하는 만큼 그를 좋아해.
② 최근에서야 그에 대해서 알게 되었어.
③ 그가 연기를 못 해서 좋아하지 않아.
④ 그는 잘생겼지만 그다지 좋은 사람은 아니야.

18 ⑤

해설 축제 때 쓸 마이크를 점검하다가 이상이 있음을 발견했으므로 새 마이크를 구하거나 고치는 것과 관련된 내용의 응답이 어울린다.

어휘 prepare[pripɛ́ər] 준비하다
do a final check 최종 점검을 하다
be done with ~을 끝내다
make sure 확인하다
work[wəːrk] (기계 등이) 작동되다
microphone[máikrəfòun] 마이크
[선택지]
fix[fiks] 고치다, 수리하다
right away 당장

M Have we finished preparing for our school festival?
W I'm not sure. Let's do a final check.
M Sure. How much time do we have left?
W We should be done preparing in about 10 minutes.
M You should make sure that the computer is working.
W Yes, it's working fine. Can you check the microphone for me?
M Okay. [Pause] There seems to be a problem with this microphone.
W Really? I'll ask Mr. Kim to bring a new one.

남 우리가 학교 축제를 준비하는 거 끝낸 거니?
여 잘 모르겠어. 최종 점검을 해 보자.
남 그러자. 시간이 얼마나 남았지?
여 10분 정도 후에 준비를 마쳐야 해.
남 너는 컴퓨터가 작동되고 있는지 꼭 확인하는 게 좋겠어.
여 응, 잘 작동되고 있어. 마이크 좀 확인해 볼래?
남 알겠어. [잠시 후] 마이크에 문제가 있는 것 같은데.
여 정말이야? 김 선생님께 새 것을 하나 갖다 달라고 해야겠다.

① 너는 컴퓨터를 고치는 방법을 아니?
② 완벽해! 우리가 드디어 준비를 끝냈어.
③ 너는 아직 시험을 끝마치기까지 10분이 있어.
④ 걱정하지 마. 내가 네 전화기를 당장 고칠 수 있어.

19 ②

[해설] 만우절에 하는 적절치 못한 언행이 다른 사람의 기분을 상하게 할 수 있다는 말에 대한 응답이므로 그러지 않도록 조심해야 한다는 말로 동의하는 내용이 어울린다.

[어휘] April Fools' Day 만우절
be aware of ~을 알고 있다
play a joke on ~에게 짓궂은 장난을 치다
luckily [lʌ́kili] 다행히도
stupid [stjúːpid] 어리석은
hurt A's feelings A의 기분을 상하게 하다
[선택지]
celebrate [séləbrèit] 기념하다

W Did you hear anything interesting at school today?
M No, I didn't. <u>Why</u> <u>do</u> <u>you</u> <u>ask</u>?
W Didn't you know? Today's April Fools' Day.
M Oh, I wasn't aware of that. Did anyone play a joke on someone at your school?
W No, <u>luckily</u> <u>nobody</u> <u>did</u>.
M Good. <u>We</u> <u>don't</u> <u>need</u> <u>any</u> jokes or stupid lies.
W I agree. It might <u>hurt</u> <u>someone's</u> <u>feelings</u>.
M Yes. We should be careful.

여 오늘 학교에서 재미있는 이야기를 들었니?
남 아니, 못 들었는데. 왜 물어봐?
여 너 몰랐니? 오늘이 만우절이잖아.
남 아, 난 몰랐어. 너네 학교에서는 누군가가 다른 사람에게 짓궂은 장난을 했니?
여 아니, 다행히 아무도 그러지 않았어.
남 좋은 일이야. 짓궂은 장난이나 어리석은 거짓말은 불필요해.
여 동의해. 사람들의 기분을 상하게 할 수 있잖아.
남 그래, 우리는 더욱 조심해야 해.

① 아니, 4월 1일이야.
③ 선생님들에게 장난을 치는 것은 불가능해.
④ 글쎄, 우리는 늘 만우절을 기념했어.
⑤ 즐거운 시간을 보내는 것이 진실을 말하는 것보다 더 중요해.

20 ④

[해설] 어떤 남자가 긴 줄에 서 있는 Jason의 앞으로 새치기를 했으므로 끝으로 가라고 말할 것이다.

[어휘] grocery [gróusəri] 식료품
usual [júːʒuəl] 평상시의, 보통의
before [bifɔ́ːr] ~ 전에
long weekend 긴 주말 연휴
annoyed [ənɔ́id] 짜증이 난
cashier [kæʃíər] 계산원
cut in line 새치기하다
[선택지]
go grocery shopping 장 보러 가다

W Jason goes grocery shopping at a big supermarket every Friday evening. Last Friday, there were <u>more</u> <u>people</u> <u>than</u> <u>usual</u> at the supermarket because it was right before a long weekend. He <u>was</u> <u>a</u> <u>little</u> <u>annoyed</u> because the waiting line for a cashier was too long. A few minutes later, a man with a small basket <u>cut</u> <u>in</u> <u>line</u> <u>before</u> him. In this situation, what would Jason most likely say to the man?

Jason Excuse me, <u>you need to go to the end of the line.</u>

여 Jason은 매주 금요일 저녁마다 대형 슈퍼마켓에 식료품을 사러 간다. 지난 금요일에는 긴 주말 연휴의 바로 전이여서 슈퍼마켓에 평소보다 사람들이 많았다. 계산원을 기다리는 줄이 너무 길었기 때문에, 그는 조금 짜증이 났다. 몇 분 후 작은 바구니를 든 남자가 그의 앞으로 새치기를 했다. 이러한 상황에서 Jason이 그 남자에게 할 말로 가장 적절한 것은 무엇인가?

Jason 실례합니다만, 줄 맨 끝으로 가셔야 해요.

① 근처에 슈퍼마켓이 있나요?
② 장 보러 어디로 가나요?
③ 당신이 여기에서 일한다는 것을 몰랐어요.
⑤ 그 바구니를 얼마 주고 샀나요?

01 ⑤	02 ⑤	03 ⑤	04 ④	05 ⑤	06 ②	07 ②
08 ③	09 ⑤	10 ④	11 ⑤	12 ③	13 ②	14 ⑤
15 ⑤	16 ②	17 ③	18 ⑤	19 ①	20 ①	

01 ⑤

해설 여자가 찾는 시계는 앞면이 둥근 디지털시계이며, K.J.Y.라는 머리글자가 쓰여져 있다.

어휘 diner[dáinər] 작은 식당
leave[li:v] 두고 오다
restroom[réstrù(:)m] 화장실
round[raund] 둥근
face[feis] (시계의) 앞면
initial[iníʃəl] (성명의) 머리글자
try A's best 최선을 다하다

[Telephone rings.]
M Thanks for calling Michelle's Diner. How may I help you?
W Hi. I had lunch there today, and I think I left my watch in the restroom.
M What does it look like?
W It's a digital watch, and it has a round face.
M We haven't found any watches yet, so can you call back tomorrow?
W Yes, I will. Oh, it also has my initials K. J. Y. on it.
M Okay, we'll try our best to look for your watch, ma'am.

[전화벨이 울린다.]
남 Michelle's Diner에 전화 주셔서 감사드립니다. 무엇을 도와 드릴까요?
여 안녕하세요. 오늘 거기에서 점심을 먹었는데요. 시계를 화장실에 두고 온 것 같아요.
남 어떤 모양인가요?
여 디지털시계이고요, 앞면이 둥근 모양이에요.
남 아직 들어온 시계가 없으니, 내일 다시 전화 주시겠어요?
여 네. 그러죠. 아, 그 위에 K.J.Y라는 제 이름의 머리글자도 있어요.
남 알겠습니다. 최선을 다해 시계를 찾아보겠습니다. 고객님.

02 ⑤

해설 국적(네덜란드), 사망 연도(1890년), 대표작(〈별이 빛나는 밤〉, 〈해바라기〉), 가족 관계(남동생)에 대해 언급했지만 종교에 대한 언급은 없었다.

어휘 Dutch[dʌtʃ] 네덜란드의
not ~ at all 전혀 ~하지 않은
alive[əláiv] 살아있는
painting[péintiŋ] 그림
starry[stá:ri] 별이 빛나는
sunflower[sʌnflàuər] 해바라기
close to ~와 친한
get married 결혼하다

W Do you have a favorite painter?
M Yes, my favorite painter is Vincent van Gogh. He's a Dutch painter.
W He is my favorite, too. It's too bad that he wasn't famous at all when he was alive.
M I know. He died in 1890, but his paintings became really popular 11 years later.
W Yes, that's right. So, which one of his paintings is your favorite?
M It's hard to choose one. I like The Starry Night and Sunflowers the most.
W I heard he was really close to his brother, but did he get married?
M No, he didn't. That's why he didn't have any children.

여 너는 제일 좋아하는 화가가 있니?
남 응. 내가 제일 좋아하는 화가는 Vincent van Gogh야. 그는 네덜란드 화가지.
여 그는 내가 제일 좋아하는 화가이기도 해. 그가 살아 있을 때 전혀 유명하지 않았다니 안됐어.
남 맞아. 그는 1890년에 사망했지만 그의 그림들은 11년 뒤에야 많은 인기를 얻게 됐지.
여 그래. 맞아. 그런데 그의 그림 중에서 어떤 걸 제일 좋아하니?
남 하나를 고르는 어려워. 나는 〈별이 빛나는 밤〉과 〈해바라기〉를 가장 좋아해.
여 그가 남동생과 아주 친했다고 들었는데 결혼은 했니?
남 아니. 하지 않았어. 그래서 아이가 없었지.

03 ⑤

해설 남자는 여자에게 커피숍에 있는 영화 촬영에 대해 설명하고, 같이 구경 가자고 제안하려고 전화했다.

어휘 bus terminal 버스 터미널
shoot a scene 장면을 찍다. 촬영하다
staff[stæf] 직원. 스태프

[Cell phone rings.]
W Hello.
M Hey, Samantha. It's Thomas.
W Hey, Thomas. What's up?
M Do you know the new cafe near the bus terminal?
W Sure. I went there once to meet my friends. What about it?

[휴대전화가 울린다.]
여 여보세요.
남 안녕, Samantha. 나 Thomas야.
여 안녕. Thomas. 무슨 일이야?
남 너 버스 터미널 근처에 새로 생긴 카페 아니?
여 당연하지. 친구들 만나러 그곳으로 한 번 갔었어. 그건 왜 묻는 거야?

M	I heard that Tom Cruise is coming to that cafe next week. He is going to shoot a scene there. We should go!	남	Tom Cruise가 다음 주에 그 카페로 온대. 그곳에서 영화 장면을 촬영할 거래. 우리도 가야 해!
W	But the cafe is going to be closed, isn't it?	여	근데 그 카페는 문을 닫겠지, 그렇지 않니?
M	Yes. But don't worry. My uncle is one of the movie staff. We can get near the cafe and watch.	남	그래. 근데 걱정하지 마. 우리 삼촌이 영화 직원 중 한 명이야. 우리 그 카페 근처에 가서 봐도 돼.
W	That's great! I hope we can see Tom Cruise.	여	정말 잘됐다! Tom Cruise도 볼 수 있었으면 좋겠어.

04 ④

해설 지하철 막차는 11시 30분에 떠난다고 했다.

어휘 head home 집으로 향해 가다
retirement[ritáiərmənt] 은퇴, 퇴직
miss[mis] (탈 것을) 놓치다
subway[sʌ́bwèi] 지하철
run[rʌn] (교통편이) 운행하다
until[əntíl] ~ 때까지
make sure 확실히 하다, 확인하다

M	It's getting really late. We should be heading home, Amy.	남	시간이 너무 늦어지고 있네. 집으로 가야 해, Amy.
W	Let's stay a little longer, Dad. It's your retirement party.	여	우리 조금 더 있어요, 아빠. 아빠의 퇴임 기념 파티잖아요.
M	It's already 10 p.m. We'll miss the last train.	남	벌써 밤 10시야. 마지막 열차를 놓치겠어.
W	The subway runs until at least 11 p.m.	여	지하철은 밤 11시까지는 운행해요.
M	Are you sure? We should check the subway schedule to make sure.	남	틀림없어? 확실히 하기 위해 지하철 스케줄을 확인해야겠네.
W	Okay, let's do that.	여	네, 그렇게 해요.
M	[Pause] Oh, the last train leaves here at 11:30 p.m.	남	[잠시 후] 아, 마지막 열차가 여기에서 밤 11시 30분에 떠나는구나.
W	See? Can we stay a little longer then?	여	그렇죠? 그럼 좀 더 있어도 될까요?
M	Yes, of course.	남	응. 물론이야.

05 ⑤

해설 여자가 다음에 방문할 때 의사가 여자의 치아 전체를 재점검할 예정이라고 한 것으로 보아 대화의 장소는 치과임을 알 수 있다.

어휘 total amount 총합계
comes out to be (합계가) ~이 되다
credit card 신용 카드
schedule[skédʒuːl] 일정을 잡다
work for ~ (시간이) ~에게 가능하다
at least 적어도, 최소한

M	Ms. Jensen, the total amount for your visit today comes out to be $67.	남	Jensen 씨, 오늘 진료 받으신 금액이 모두 합쳐서 67달러입니다.
W	Okay, I'll pay by credit card.	여	네, 신용 카드로 결제할게요.
M	We also need to schedule your next visit.	남	다음번에 오실 일정도 잡아야 합니다.
W	Right. The doctor said I need to come back in about 2 weeks.	여	맞아요. 의사 선생님이 대략 2주 정도 지나서 다시 와야 한다고 말씀하셨어요.
M	Will April 17th work for you?	남	4월 17일 괜찮으세요?
W	How long will my next visit take?	여	다음번에 오면 진료 시간이 얼마나 걸릴까요?
M	The doctor needs to check all of your teeth again. So it'll take at least an hour.	남	의사 선생님이 환자 분의 치아를 모두 다시 확인하셔야 해요. 그래서 적어도 한 시간은 걸릴 거예요.
W	I can come in at 4 p.m. on the 17th.	여	17일 오후 4시에 오겠습니다.
M	Okay, Ms. Jensen. We'll see you again on the 17th.	남	알겠습니다, Jensen 씨, 17일에 다시 뵙겠습니다.

06 ②

해설 낚시를 하고 있는 여자와 고기를 많이 잡았는지 묻고 있는 남자의 대화 내용이다.

① M	Have you been to Iceland?	① 남	아이슬란드에 가 본 적이 있니?
W	Yes, I have. It's a beautiful country.	여	응, 가 봤어. 아름다운 나라지.
② M	Did you catch a lot of fish?	② 남	고기 많이 잡았니?
W	Yes, I have caught 20 fish already.	여	응, 벌써 20마리나 잡았어.

<table>
<tr><td>어휘</td><td>Iceland[áislənd] 아이슬란드</td></tr>
</table>

어휘 Iceland[áislənd] 아이슬란드
look forward to ~을 기대하다
check[tʃek] 계산서

③ **M** Why don't we go fishing this weekend?
   W Sure. I'm really looking forward to it.
④ **M** Would you like some dessert?
   W No, thanks. Can I <u>have the check</u>, please?
⑤ **M** Did you clean your room?
   W No, I didn't. I'll do it tomorrow.

③ 남 이번 주말에 낚시하러 갈래?
   여 물론이지. 정말 기대하고 있어.
④ 남 디저트 드릴까요?
   여 아니요, 됐어요. 계산서 좀 갖다 주시겠어요.
⑤ 남 네 방을 청소했니?
   여 아니요, 안 했어요. 내일 할 거예요.

07 ②

해설 남자는 여자에게 어깨가 아프다고 하면서 어깨 마사지를 해 달라고 부탁했다.

어휘 happen[hǽpən] (일이) 일어나다
customer[kʌ́stəmər] 고객
by oneself 혼자서
shoulder[ʃóuldər] 어깨
massage[məsáːʒ] 마사지
hurt[həːrt] 아프다
a little bit 약간, 다소
have a seat 앉다, 착석하다

W How was your day, honey?
M I had <u>a really long day</u> at the office.
W Did something bad happen?
M Well, 3 people <u>didn't come to work</u> today, so I had to answer all the e-mails from customers by myself.
W Oh, I'm sorry to hear that. Is there anything I can do for you?
M <u>Could you give me</u> a shoulder massage? My shoulders hurt a little bit.
W Sure. <u>Have a seat</u> over here.

여 여보, 오늘 잘 보냈어요?
남 사무실에서 정말 긴 하루를 보냈어요.
여 안 좋은 일 있었어요?
남 음, 세 사람이 오늘 출근하지 않아서 고객이 보낸 모든 이메일에 혼자 답장을 해야 했어요.
여 아, 그 말을 들으니 마음이 아프네요. 내가 해 줄 일이 있을까요?
남 어깨 마사지를 좀 해 줄래요? 어깨가 좀 아프거든요.
여 물론이죠. 여기에 앉아 봐요.

08 ③

해설 기간(20일 ~ 26일), 읽어야 할 도서 종류(소설), 읽을 책의 분량(100페이지 이상), 초대 손님(유명 작가)에 대해 언급했지만 독후감 제출 방법에 대한 언급은 없다.

어휘 be required to-v ~하도록 요구되다, ~해야 한다
novel[návəl] 소설
celebrate[séləbrèit] 기념하다
guest[gest] 게스트, 손님
author[ɔ́ːθər] 작가

M Happy Friday, everyone. This is your English teacher Mr. Jenner speaking. Reading Week this year <u>starts on</u> Monday the 20th and <u>ends on</u> Sunday the 26th. All of you are required <u>to read a novel</u>. The book of your choice <u>has to be</u> at least 100 pages long. To celebrate this year's Reading Week, we will <u>have a surprise guest</u>, a famous author, visit on Wednesday.

남 즐거운 금요일입니다. 여러분. 저는 여러분의 영어 교사인 Jenner 선생님입니다. 올해의 독서 주간이 20일 월요일에 시작되어 일요일인 26일에 끝납니다. 여러분은 모두 소설 한 권을 읽어야 합니다. 여러분이 선택하는 책은 적어도 100페이지는 되어야 합니다. 올해의 독서 주간을 기념하기 위해 깜짝 게스트로 유명 작가 한 분이 수요일에 방문하십니다.

09 ⑤

해설 한 층에서 다른 층으로 데려다주고 계속해서 움직이지만, 문이 붙어있지 않은 것은 에스컬레이터이다.

어휘 get on (탈 것에) 타다
vehicle[víːikəl] 차량
move[muːv] 움직이다
moving[múːviŋ] 움직이는
object[ɔ́bdʒikt] 물건, 물체

W This is something that <u>you get on</u>, but it's not a vehicle. It takes you from <u>one floor to another</u>. You will see many of these in large buildings. For example, a department store has at least one of these on every floor. This <u>keeps moving</u>, so you need to be careful when you get on it. This moving object <u>has no doors</u>.

여 이것은 여러분이 타는 것이지만 차량은 아니에요. 이것을 여러분을 한 층에서 다른 층으로 데려다 줘요. 여러분은 큰 빌딩에서 이것들을 많이 보게 돼요. 예를 들어, 백화점에는 모든 층에 적어도 이것이 한 개 이상 있어요. 이것은 계속 움직이므로 여러분은 이것을 탈 때 조심해야 해요. 이 움직이는 물체에는 문이 없어요.

10 ④

① M How did you like the movie?
　 W I liked it a lot. It was really good.
② M I'm starving. What about you?
　 W I'm really hungry, too.
③ M My eyes are a bit tired now.
　 W Why don't you take a break?
④ M Do you have a runny nose?
　 W Yes, I run every morning.
⑤ M You shouldn't go to bed so late.
　 W I know. It is a bad habit.

① 남 그 영화 어땠니?
　 여 아주 좋았어. 정말 멋지던데.
② 남 난 몹시 배가 고파. 너는 어때?
　 여 나도 정말 배가 고파.
③ 남 지금 눈이 좀 피곤하네.
　 여 좀 쉬는 게 어때?
④ 남 너 콧물 나니?
　 여 응. 나 매일 아침에 달리기를 해.
⑤ 남 너무 늦게 잠자리에 들지 마라.
　 여 맞아요. 나쁜 버릇이예요.

11 ⑤

M It's raining now. Did you see my raincoat?
W Why do you need a raincoat, Dad?
M I just remembered what your mother said about rainy days.
W Oh, we should put the flower pots outside when it's raining, right?
M Yes, that's exactly what I'm going to do.
W Why don't you check the basement for your raincoat? I think I saw it there.
M Okay, I will. Thanks.

남 지금 비가 오네. 내 비옷을 봤니?
여 비옷이 왜 필요하세요, 아빠?
남 방금 네 엄마가 비 오는 날에 대해서 말한 게 생각났구나.
여 아, 비올 때 화분을 밖에 둬야 하죠, 그렇죠?
남 그래, 내가 하려고 하는 일이 바로 그거야.
여 지하실에서 비옷을 찾아보는 게 어때요? 제가 그곳에서 그걸 본 것 같아요.
남 그래, 그렇게 할게. 고맙구나.

12 ③

M You wanted to go to Yeosu this Saturday, right?
W Yes, but can we go to Mokpo instead? I heard it'll rain in Yeosu this weekend.
M Sure, what time do you want to get there?
W I want to have lunch there, so we should arrive at 12 p.m.
M Then we'll have to leave around 9 a.m.
W That's fine. Do you want to take economy or first class?
M Let's take first class. It's a lot more comfortable.
W I agree. It's more expensive, but it's definitely worth it.

남 이번 토요일에 너 여수에 가고 싶어 했지, 그렇지?
여 응. 우리 그런데 대신 목포에 가면 안 될까? 이번 주말에 여수에서 비가 올 거라고 들었거든.
남 좋아. 거기에 몇 시에 도착하고 싶어?
여 거기에서 점심 식사를 하고 싶거든, 그러니까 낮 12시에 도착해야겠지.
남 그럼 우리가 오전 9시경에 출발해야겠네.
여 좋아. 일반석으로 가고 싶어, 일등석을 타고 가고 싶어?
남 일등석으로 가자. 훨씬 편안하잖아.
여 네 말이 맞아. 더 비싸지만 분명히 그럴 만한 가치가 있어.

13 ②

[Telephone rings.]
M Thank you for calling Janet's Beauty Salon. How may I help you?
W Hi, I'd like to make an appointment for a haircut.

[전화벨이 울린다.]
남 Janet 미용실에 전화 주셔서 감사합니다. 무엇을 도와 드릴까요?
여 안녕하세요. 커트 예약을 하고 싶어요.

fully[fúlli] 완전히
book 예약하다
work for (날짜 등이) ~에게 가능하다
opening[óupəniŋ] 빈 자리, 공석

M	Okay. When would you like to come in?	남 알겠습니다. 언제 방문하시길 원하세요?
W	I'd like to <u>come in on</u> July 12th.	여 7월 12일에 가려고요.
M	I'm sorry, but Janet <u>is fully</u> <u>booked on</u> the 12th. Would July 10th work for you?	남 죄송하지만, 12일은 Janet 미용사님의 예약이 찼네요. 7월 10일은 괜찮으세요?
W	I don't think I can come in on the 10th. <u>How about</u> July 11th?	여 10일에는 갈 수 없을 것 같아요. 7월 11일은 어떤가요?
M	July 11th? There is <u>an opening</u> at 2 o'clock. Is that all right with you?	남 7월 11일이요? 2시 정각에 빈 시간이 있습니다. 괜찮으신가요?
W	That's perfect. Thank you very much.	여 아주 좋아요. 정말 고맙습니다.

14 ⑤

해설 주말에 여자는 쇼핑을 했고, 남자는 요리사인 누나와 함께 음식 축제에 갔다고 했다.

어휘 a good deal 좋은 거래, 싼 가격
food festival 음식 축제
chef[ʃef] (호텔·레스토랑 등의) 요리사
expert[ékspə:rt] 전문가

M	How was your weekend, Monica?	남 Monica, 주말 어떻게 보냈니?
W	It was good. I <u>went</u> <u>shopping</u> <u>with</u> my friends.	여 잘 보냈어. 친구들과 같이 쇼핑하러 갔거든.
M	Did you buy the boots you wanted?	남 너가 원하던 부츠를 샀니?
W	Yes, they were on sale, so I got a very good deal. Did you <u>do anything special</u> last weekend?	여 응. 부츠가 세일 중이어서 아주 싸게 잘 샀어. 너는 지난 주말에 특별히 한 게 있니?
M	Yes, I went to <u>a food festival</u> with my sister yesterday.	남 응. 나는 어제 누나와 같이 음식 축제에 갔어.
W	Your sister is a chef at a hotel restaurant, isn't she?	여 누나가 호텔 레스토랑에서 일하는 요리사지, 그렇지?
M	Yes, she's <u>an expert</u> in Chinese food.	남 응. 누나는 중국 요리 전문가야.

15 ⑤

해설 허리케인이 일어날 때를 대비해 행동 요령을 안내하는 내용이다.

어휘 hurricane[hə́:rəkèin] 허리케인
season[síːzn] (특정한 활동의) 시즌, 철
be aware of ~을 알다
guideline[gáidlàin] 가이드라인, 지침
blind[blaind] (창문에 치는) 블라인드
if necessary 필요하면
closet[klázit] 벽장
lie on 눕다

M	Hurricane season is here, and we all should be aware of what to do <u>when a</u> <u>hurricane</u> <u>happens</u>. During a hurricane, please follow these guidelines. <u>Stay inside</u> <u>and away</u> from windows and glass doors. You <u>must close all doors</u> and keep curtains and blinds closed. If necessary, stay in a small room or a closet. You could also <u>lie on the floor</u> under a table.	남 허리케인 시즌이 돌아와서 우리는 허리케인이 일어날 시 어떻게 해야 하는지 알아야 합니다. 허리케인 동안에는 이 지침을 따라주시기 바랍니다. 내부에 머물러 있으면서 창문과 유리로 된 문에서 떨어져 주세요. 모든 문을 닫아야 하며, 커튼과 블라인드도 닫아야 합니다. 필요하면 작은 방이나 옷장 안에 머무르십시오. 테이블 아래 바닥에 누우셔도 됩니다.

16 ②

해설 매트리스와 침대 틀을 구매한 가격은 총 2,000달러이며, 여기서 30퍼센트 할인된다고 했으므로 여자가 지불할 총금액은 1,400달러이다.

어휘 advertisement[ædvərtáizmənt] 광고
mattress[mǽtris] 매트리스
bed frame 침대 틀
discount[dískaunt] 할인

M	Welcome to Mattress King. How may I help you?	남 Mattress King을 찾아 주셔서 감사드립니다. 어떻게 도와드릴까요?
W	I saw the advertisement about <u>your</u> <u>special sale</u> event.	여 특별 세일 행사 광고를 보았어요.
M	Oh, yes. If you buy a mattress and a bed frame together, you will get a 30% discount <u>on the total price</u>.	남 아, 그러셨군요. 매트리스와 침대 틀을 함께 같이 구입하시면 총 가격에서 30%를 할인 받게 됩니다.
W	That sounds great. How much is this mattress?	여 그거 좋네요. 이 매트리스 가격이 얼마죠?
M	That mattress is $1,000.	남 그 매트리스는 1,000달러입니다.

W	How about this bed frame?	여	이 침대 틀은요?
M	That bed frame is also $1,000.	남	그 침대 틀도 1,000달러입니다.
W	Okay, I'll get this <u>bed</u> <u>frame</u> <u>and</u> <u>the</u> <u>mattress</u>, too.	여	좋아요. 이 침대 틀하고 매트리스도 살게요.
M	Okay. <u>You will get</u> the 30% discount.	남	알겠습니다. 고객님은 30% 할인을 받으실 겁니다.

17 ③

[해설] 주유소가 멀지 않다는 표지판이 있다는 여자의 말에 안도하는 응답이 이어져야 적절하다.

[어휘] on the road 여행[이동] 중인
stop by ~에 들르다
gas station 주유소
be about to-v 막 ~ 하려는 참이다
be low on ~이 부족하다, 얼마 안 남다
run out of ~이 다 떨어지다
gas[gæs] 휘발유, 가솔린
sign[sain] 표지판, 간판

W	How long have we been on the road, Dad?
M	I think it's been about 2 hours.
W	<u>Can</u> <u>we</u> <u>stop</u> <u>by</u> a gas station? I need to go to the restroom.
M	Sure. I was about to look for a gas station because <u>we're</u> <u>low</u> <u>on</u> <u>gas</u>.
W	<u>What</u> <u>happens</u> <u>if</u> we run out of gas?
M	I hope that doesn't happen.
W	Look! The sign over there says there's a gas station within 3 kilometers.
M	Oh, good. <u>I was getting really worried.</u>

여 우리가 출발한 지 얼마나 되었어요, 아빠?
남 대략 두 시간쯤 된 것 같구나.
여 주유소에 좀 들를 수 있나요? 화장실에 가야겠어요.
남 그러자. 휘발유가 얼마 남지 않아서 주유소를 찾으려던 참이었단다.
여 휘발유가 다 떨어지면 어떻게 되나요?
남 그런 일은 일어나지 않았으면 좋겠네.
여 봐요! 저쪽에 있는 표지판에 주유소가 3킬로미터 이내에 있다고 하네요.
남 아, 잘됐구나. <u>나는 정말로 걱정하고 있었거든.</u>

① 좋았어! 두 시간 뒤에 깨워 줄게.
② 우리는 늦었으니까 계속 가야 해.
④ 우리는 주유소 말고 화장실을 찾아야 해.
⑤ 좋아, 내가 역에 도착하면 전화할게.

18 ⑤

[해설] 강의 스타일이 어떤지 의견을 묻는 남자의 말에 강의에 대한 자신의 의견을 말하는 응답이 가장 적절하다.

[어휘] semester[siméstər] 학기
European[jùərəpíən] 유럽의
almost[ɔ́ːlmoust] 거의
impossible[impάsəbl] 불가능한
[선택지]
graduate[grǽdʒuət] 졸업하다
organized[ɔ́ːrgənàizd] 체계적인, 조직화된

M	How's your semester coming along, Kate?
W	I think I'm doing <u>better</u> <u>than</u> <u>I</u> <u>did</u> last semester.
M	That's good. <u>You're</u> <u>taking</u> Mr. Kim's European history class, right?
W	Yes, I am. Didn't you take that class last year?
M	I did, and I got a B+.
W	I heard that <u>it's</u> <u>almost</u> <u>impossible</u> to get an A in that class.
M	I heard that, too. <u>What</u> <u>do</u> <u>you</u> <u>think</u> about his teaching style?
W	<u>He's not that interesting, but his class is very organized.</u>

남 학기 잘 보내고 있니, Kate?
여 지난 학기보다는 더 잘하고 있는 것 같아.
남 잘됐구나. 너 김 선생님의 유럽사 강의를 듣고 있지, 그렇지?
여 응, 맞아. 너는 그 강의를 작년에 수강하지 않았니?
남 수강했지, 그리고 B+를 받았어.
여 그 수업에서 A학점을 받는 것은 거의 불가능하다고 들었는데.
남 나도 그렇게 들었어. 그분의 강의 스타일은 어떤 것 같니?
여 <u>그 선생님은 그다지 재미있지는 않지만 그 수업은 아주 체계적이야.</u>

① 내가 올해에 졸업을 할 수 없을 거야.
② 나는 다음 학기에 그의 강의를 수강할 거야.
③ 나는 유럽사를 공부한 적이 전혀 없어.
④ 너는 다른 역사 강의를 수강하는 게 좋을 것 같아.

19 ①

M Do you like noodles, Mary?
W Yes, I love noodles.
M I love noodles, too. In fact, I eat noodles much more often than I eat bread or rice.
W Really? What kind of noodles do you like?
M My favorite is Korean cold noodles. What about you?
W My favorite is Vietnamese rice noodles. Have you tried Vietnamese noodles before?
M Of course, I have. I cook them at home quite often.
W I didn't know you cooked. Where did you learn to cook them?
M I learned it from my mom.

남 너 국수 좋아하니, Mary?
여 응. 나는 국수를 아주 좋아해.
남 나도 국수를 정말 좋아해. 사실, 나는 빵이나 밥보다 국수를 훨씬 더 자주 먹고 있어.
여 정말? 어떤 종류의 국수가 좋은데?
남 내가 가장 좋아하는 것은 한국의 냉면이야. 너는?
여 나는 베트남 쌀국수가 가장 좋아. 전에 베트남 국수 먹어 본 적 있니?
남 물론 먹어 봤지. 집에서 꽤 자주 만드는 걸.
여 네가 요리를 한다는 건 몰랐네. 베트남 쌀국수 요리법을 어디에서 배웠어?
남 난 그걸 엄마한테 배웠어.

② 나는 빵을 굽는 것이 훨씬 어렵다고 생각해.
③ 대부분의 사람들은 밥이 국수보다 낫다고 하지.
④ 내가 베트남에 갔을 때 정말 더웠어.
⑤ 쌀국수는 다른 국수들보다 맛이 훨씬 좋아.

20 ①

W Jake wants a bicycle for his birthday present. Jake's father will buy him any bicycle he wants this weekend. Jake has not found the perfect bicycle for himself yet. One day, he sees his friend Terry with his bicycle. Jake really likes Terry's bicycle and wants to find out where he bought it. In this situation, what would Jake most likely say to Terry?

Jake Where did you get your bicycle?

여 Jake는 생일 선물로 자전거를 받고 싶어 한다. Jake의 아버지는 이번 주말에 그가 원하는 어떤 자전거라도 사 주려 한다. Jake는 자신에게 맞는 완벽한 자전거를 아직 찾지 못했다. 어느 날, 그는 친구 Terry와 그의 자전거를 본다. Jake는 Terry가 탄 자전거가 정말 갖고 싶어서 그가 어디에서 샀는지 알아내고 싶어 한다. 이러한 상황에서 Jake가 Terry에게 할 말로 가장 적절한 것은 무엇인가?

Jake 네 자전거 어디에서 샀니?

② 아버지가 너에게 선물을 사 주셨니?
③ 나에게 자전거 타는 법을 가르쳐 줄 수 있니?
④ 네 자전거가 내 것보다 더 비싸니?
⑤ 생일 선물로 무엇을 받고 싶니?

01 ④	02 ④	03 ③	04 ③	05 ③	06 ④	07 ④
08 ②	09 ⑤	10 ④	11 ⑤	12 ④	13 ③	14 ⑤
15 ②	16 ④	17 ②	18 ⑤	19 ②	20 ③	

01 ④

해설 긴 바지가 같이 있고 곰들이 그려져 있는 잠옷에 실내화까지 구매한다고 했다.

어휘 pajamas[pədʒɑ́ːməz] 잠옷
prefer[prifə́ːr] 더 좋아하다, 선호하다
pants[pænts] 바지
dinosaur[dáinəsɔ̀ːr] 공룡
on sale 할인 중인
slipper[slípər] 실내화

M Welcome to Good House. Can I help you find anything?
W Yes, please. I'm looking for women's pajamas.
M Do you have anything in mind?
W Hmm... I prefer the ones with pants.
M Okay. How about these ones with dinosaurs on them?
W They're cute, but I don't like dinosaurs. Oh, these ones have bears on them.
M They are popular. They're also on sale for $30.
W Great. I'll take them.
M Okay. Would you like the ones with slippers? They are just $5 more.
W Yes, please.

남 Good House에 오신 것을 환영합니다. 찾으시는 것을 도와 드릴까요?
여 네. 여성용 잠옷을 찾고 있어요.
남 생각해 둔 게 있으세요?
여 흠… 전 바지랑 같이 있는 것이 더 좋아요.
남 알겠습니다. 공룡이 그려진 이건 어떠세요?
여 귀엽지만, 전 공룡을 좋아하지 않아서요. 아, 이건 곰이 그려져 있네요.
남 그것도 인기가 있어요. 할인되어 30달러이기도 하고요.
여 좋네요. 이걸로 살게요.
남 알겠습니다. 실내화랑 같이 있는 걸로 드릴까요? 5달러만 더 내시면 돼요.
여 네, 주세요.

02 ④

해설 출생지(이탈리아), 사망한 나이(67세), 대표 작품(《모나리자》, 《최후의 만찬》), 다양한 직업(화가, 엔지니어, 발명가)에 대해 언급했지만 성격에 관해서는 언급되지 않았다.

어휘 be born 태어나다
create[kriéit] 만들어 내다
painting[péintiŋ] 그림
including[inklúːdiŋ] ~을 포함하여
supper[sʌ́pər] 저녁 식사
inventor[invéntər] 발명가
talented[tǽləntid] 재능 있는

W What are you reading, Mike?
M I'm reading a book on Leonardo da Vinci.
W Oh, I know him. He was born in Italy, right?
M Yes. He died when he was 67.
W He created many famous paintings, including *The Mona Lisa* and *The Last Supper*.
M I know. Did you know that he was also a great engineer and an inventor?
W Really? I didn't know that. He was so talented.

여 뭘 읽고 있니, Mike?
남 Leonardo da Vinci에 대한 책을 읽고 있어.
여 아, 나 그 사람 알아. 이탈리아에서 태어났지, 그렇지?
남 응. 그는 67세 때 사망했어.
여 그는 〈모나리자〉와 〈최후의 만찬〉을 포함해 아주 많은 그림을 그렸지.
남 맞아. 그가 뛰어난 엔지니어이면서, 발명가였다는 걸 알고 있었니?
여 정말? 재능이 아주 뛰어났구나.

03 ③

해설 남자는 이번 주 금요일 대신 다음 주 금요일로 여행 일정을 변경해 달라고 요청하기 위해 전화했다.

어휘 set up 짜다, 마련하다
be supposed to-v ~하기로 되어 있다
make a change 변경하다
certainly[sə́ːrtnli] 확실히, 틀림없이

[Telephone rings.]
W World Travel. This is Linda Shaw speaking.
M Hello, Ms. Shaw. This is Paul Kay.
W Good morning, Mr. Kay. How can I help you?
M I'm calling about the travel plans I made yesterday.

[전화벨이 울린다.]
여 World Travel입니다. Linda Shaw입니다.
남 안녕하세요, Shaw 씨. 저는 Paul Kay이라고 합니다.
여 안녕하세요, Kay 씨. 무엇을 도와드릴까요?
남 어제 제가 예약한 여행 일정 때문에 전화 드렸어요.

W Yes. I remember helping you to set up those plans.
M I'm supposed to leave for France this Friday, but something happened.
W Would you like to make a change?
M Yes, please. Can I leave next Friday instead?
W I can certainly make that change for you, sir.

여 네. 제가 그 일정 짜는 걸 도와드렸던 게 기억나네요.
남 이번 주 금요일에 프랑스로 출발하기로 했는데요, 일이 좀 생겼어요.
여 일정을 변경하고 싶으세요?
남 네, 부탁드려요. 대신 다음 주 금요일에 떠나도 될까요?
여 고객님에 맞춰 당연히 그렇게 변경해 드릴 수 있습니다.

04 ③

해설 일행이 다섯 명 이상일 경우 6시 30분에만 예약이 가능하다는 여자의 말에 남자는 괜찮다고 했다.

어휘 reservation[rèzərvéiʃən] 예약
book[buk] 예약하다
available[əvéiləbl] 이용할 수 있는
party[pɑ́ːrti] 일행
early[ə́ːrli] 일찍; 이른

[Telephone rings.]
W Thanks for calling Top Restaurant. How may I help you?
M Hello. Do you take reservations for Friday evening?
W I'm sorry, sir. Friday evening is fully booked.
M Then, can I make a reservation for 7 p.m. on Thursday?
W Of course. How many will it be for?
M It's for 8 people.
W I'm terribly sorry, but the only time available for a party of 5 or more is 6:30 p.m.
M Oh, that's fine. We can get there a little earlier.
W Thank you so much for your understanding.

[전화벨이 울린다.]
여 Top 레스토랑에 전화 주셔서 고맙습니다. 무엇을 도와드릴까요?
남 안녕하세요. 금요일 저녁 예약을 받나요?
여 죄송합니다. 고객님. 금요일 저녁은 예약이 다 찼습니다.
남 그러면 목요일 저녁 7시로 예약할 수 있을까요?
여 물론입니다. 몇 분이 오실 건가요?
남 여덟 명입니다.
여 정말 죄송합니다만, 일행이 다섯 명이거나 그 이상일 경우 저녁 6시 30분에만 가능합니다.
남 아, 괜찮습니다. 조금 더 일찍 도착할 수 있어요.
여 이해해 주셔서 정말 감사드립니다.

05 ③

해설 청구서 발송지를 수정하고 돈을 계좌에 넣어 달라고 하는 상황으로 보아 대화의 장소가 은행임을 알 수 있다.

어휘 update[ʌpdéit] 수정[갱신]하다
billing address 청구서 발송지
ID(= identification)[áidìː] 신분증
driver's license 운전면허증
last[læst] 지난, 가장 최근의
credit card bill 신용 카드 청구서
by mail 우편으로
bank account 예금 계좌

M Can I help the next person, please?
W Hi. I'd like to update my billing address.
M Of course. May I see your ID?
W Yes. Here is my driver's license.
M Thanks. Can you write down your new address here?
W Of course. [Pause] Here you are.
M It looks like your last credit card bill was already sent to the old address by mail.
W That's fine. My parents live there. I'll pick it up later.
M Okay. Your address has been updated. Is there anything else?
W Oh, can you put this money into my bank account, too?
M Sure.

남 다음 분 도와드릴까요?
여 안녕하세요. 제 청구서 발송지를 수정하고 싶습니다.
남 알겠습니다. 신분증을 보여 주시겠어요?
여 네. 여기 제 운전면허증이에요.
남 감사합니다. 여기에 새 주소를 적어 주시겠어요?
여 물론이죠. [잠시 후] 여기 있습니다.
남 지난 신용 카드 청구서가 이미 우편으로 예전 주소로 보내진 것 같네요.
여 괜찮아요. 제 부모님이 그곳에 살고 계세요. 나중에 제가 찾으면 돼요.
남 알겠습니다. 고객님의 주소가 수정되었습니다. 더 필요하신 게 있으세요?
여 아, 이 돈도 제 계좌에 넣어 주실래요?
남 물론이죠.

06 ④

해설 사진을 찍어 달라고 부탁하고, 이를 승낙하는 상황이다.

어휘 oak tree 오크 나무
steal[stiːl] 훔쳐 가다
(steal-stole-stolen)
Certainly. 그럼요, 물론이지요.
pass[pæs] 건네주다
pepper[pépər] 후추

① M What kind of tree is that?
　 W I think that's an oak tree.
② M Can I help you find anything?
　 W Yes, where can I find cameras?
③ M I think someone stole my backpack.
　 W Why don't you call the police?
④ M Could you take a picture of us?
　 W Certainly.
⑤ M Could you pass the pepper, please?
　 W Sure, here you are.

① 남 저게 무슨 나무지?
　 여 오크 나무인 것 같아.
② 남 찾는 것을 도와드릴까요?
　 여 네, 카메라는 어디에 있나요?
③ 남 누군가 내 배낭을 훔쳐 간 것 같아요.
　 여 경찰에 전화하지 그러니?
④ 남 저희 사진 좀 찍어 줄래요?
　 여 물론 그러죠.
⑤ 남 후추 좀 건네줄래요?
　 여 그러죠, 여기 있어요.

07 ④

해설 남자는 여자에게 엄마에게 줄 생일 카드를 만들어 달라고 부탁했다.

어휘 lesson[lésən] 수업
surprise[sərpráiz] 놀라게 하다
forget[fərgét] 잊어버리다
(forget-forgot-forgotten)

W What are you doing, Dad?
M I'm making a birthday cake for your mom.
W Really? Where did you learn to do that?
M I took baking lessons for the last 6 months after work. I wanted to surprise your mom.
W Do you want me to help you with anything?
M Yes, could you make a birthday card for her? I forgot to get a card.
W Sure. I can do that.

여 아빠, 뭐 하세요?
남 네 엄마에게 줄 생일 케이크를 만들고 있단다.
여 정말요? 만드는 거 어디에서 배우셨어요?
남 퇴근 후에 지난 6개월 동안 제빵 수업을 들었어. 네 엄마를 놀라게 해 주고 싶었거든.
여 제가 뭘 좀 도와 드릴까요?
남 엄마에게 줄 생일 카드를 좀 만들어 줄래? 카드 사오는 것을 잊었구나.
여 네. 제가 할 수 있어요.

08 ②

해설 개관 시기(2006년 1월 28일), 입장료(무료), 주차료(10달러), 소장품(유럽의 회화, 조각품, 사진)에 관해 언급했지만 위치에 관해서는 언급되지 않았다.

어휘 visual art 시각 예술
purpose[pə́ːrpəs] 목적
be open to ~에게 개방되어 있다
without[wiðáut] ~ 없이
admission fee 입장료
charge[tʃɑːrdʒ] (요금을) 청구하다
parking fee 주차 요금
a great number of 다수의, 많은
sculpture[skʌ́lptʃər] 조각품

M Welcome everyone to the Payne Museum. This museum opened on January 28, 2006, and its purpose is to teach others about the visual arts. It's open to everyone without any admission fees. We do, however, charge a parking fee of $10. The Payne Museum has a great number of European paintings, sculptures, and photos by world-famous artists. I hope you enjoy your visit.

남 Payne 박물관을 찾아 주신 여러분, 환영합니다. 이 박물관은 2006년 1월 28일에 개관했으며 사람들에게 시각 예술에 대해 가르치는 것이 목적입니다. 이 박물관은 입장료 없이 누구에게나 열려 있습니다. 하지만 주차료로 10달러를 받고 있습니다. Payne 박물관은 세계적으로 유명한 예술가들이 만들어 낸 다수의 유럽의 회화, 조각품, 그리고 사진들을 소장하고 있습니다. 여러분들의 즐거운 방문이 되기 바랍니다.

09 ⑤

해설 둥글고 빨간색을 띠고 있으며 과일인지 채소인지에 대해서는 논란이 있고 디저트보다는 요리의 재료로 더 잘 쓰이는 것은 토마토이다.

W This is something that we eat. It's usually round and red. Everybody agrees that this is good for us, but not everybody agrees whether this is a fruit or a vegetable.

여 이것은 우리가 먹는 것입니다. 이것은 보통 둥글고 빨갛습니다. 이것이 우리에게 좋다는 것에는 누구나 동의하지만 이것이 과일인지 채소인지에 대해서는 모두가 동

어휘 usually [júːʒuəli] 주로, 대개
be good for ~에 좋다
agree [əgríː] 동의하다
whether A or B A인지 B인지
consider [kənsídər] ~로 간주하다
dessert [dizə́ːrt] 디저트, 후식
various [vériəs] 다양한
such as 예를 들어 ~ 같은

Some people consider this a vegetable because this <u>doesn't</u> <u>taste</u> <u>sweet</u> <u>like</u> other fruits. So, people don't usually eat this as a dessert. Instead, they cook this <u>in</u> <u>various</u> <u>ways</u> such as in a soup or sauce.

의하지는 않습니다. 어떤 사람들은 이것이 다른 과일들처럼 달콤한 맛이 나지 않기 때문에 채소로 간주합니다. 그래서, 사람들은 대개 이것을 디저트로 먹지 않습니다. 대신에 이것을 수프나 소스와 같이 다양한 방법으로 요리합니다.

10 ④

해설 문을 열어 두라는 요청에 영업시간을 안내하는 것은 어색하다.

어휘 call [kɔːl] ~에게 전화하다
ring [riŋ] (종·벨 등이) 울리다
leave [liːv] (어떤 상태로) 있게 만들다;
그대로 두다

① M　Did you call your mother?
　W　I did, but <u>she</u> <u>didn't</u> <u>answer</u>.
② M　Do you like to watch TV?
　W　I like it a lot.
③ M　The phone's ringing, Cindy.
　W　Okay. I'll get it.
④ M　Can you <u>leave</u> <u>the</u> <u>door</u> <u>open</u>?
　W　No. We're open from 10 to 7 every day.
⑤ M　<u>Could</u> <u>I</u> <u>speak</u> <u>to</u> Ms. Taylor?
　W　This is she. How can I help you?

① 남　네 어머니에게 전화했니?
　여　했는데, 전화를 받지 않으셨어.
② 남　TV 보는 거 좋아하니?
　여　아주 좋아해.
③ 남　전화벨이 울리고 있어, Cindy.
　여　알겠어. 내가 받을게.
④ 남　문을 좀 열어 둘 수 있나요?
　여　아니요. 저희는 매일 10시에서 7시까지 문을 엽니다.
⑤ 남　Taylor 씨와 통화할 수 있을까요?
　여　전데요. 무엇을 도와 드릴까요?

11 ⑤

해설 남자는 카메라를 찾는 여자에게 자신의 가방에 있으니 가져다주겠다고 했다.

어휘 smell [smel] ~한 냄새가 나다
wake A up A를 깨우다
guess [ges] 추측하다
print out 출력하다
bring A over to B A를 B에게로 갖고 오다

M　The coffee smells really nice, honey.
W　Did you sleep well? I didn't want to <u>wake</u> <u>you</u> <u>up</u>.
M　I did. I guess I was really tired.
W　I'm sure you were. <u>You</u> <u>drove</u> <u>over</u> 10 hours yesterday.
M　It was a great trip, wasn't it?
W　Yes, it was. Did you <u>see</u> <u>my</u> <u>camera</u>? I'm going to print out some of the pictures we took.
M　Your camera is in my backpack. <u>I'll</u> <u>bring</u> <u>it</u> <u>over</u> to you.
W　Thanks.

남　커피 냄새가 정말 좋네요, 여보.
여　잘 잤어요? 깨우고 싶지 않았어요.
남　잘 잤어요. 내가 정말 피곤했던 것 같아요.
여　틀림없이 피곤했을 거예요. 어제 10시간 넘게 운전했잖아요.
남　멋진 여행이었죠, 그렇지 않아요?
여　네, 멋진 여행이었죠. 내 카메라 봤어요? 우리가 찍은 사진들 중에서 몇 장을 출력하려고요.
남　당신 카메라는 내 배낭 안에 있어요. 바로 가져다줄게요.
여　고마워요.

12 ④

해설 남자는 화면이 6인치이고, 저장 공간이 64GB인 빨간색 스마트폰을 구입하겠다고 했다.

어휘 in particular 특별히
screen [skriːn] 화면
inch [intʃ] 인치
storage [stɔ́ːridʒ] 저장, 보관

W　How may I help you?
M　I'd like to buy a smartphone. Can you help me choose one?
W　Of course. <u>Are</u> <u>you</u> <u>looking</u> <u>for</u> something in particular?
M　I want the screen to be big. My old smartphone had a 5-inch screen, and it was <u>too</u> <u>small</u> <u>for</u> <u>me</u>.

여　어떻게 도와드릴까요?
남　저 스마트폰을 하나 사려고 해요. 하나 고르는 데 도와주시겠어요?
여　물론이죠. 특별히 찾는 게 있으신가요?
남　전 화면이 컸으면 좋겠어요. 제 예전 스마트폰이 5인치 화면이 있었는데, 그건 저한테 너무 작았거든요.

space[speis] 공간
model[mɑːdl] (상품의) 모델, 디자인

| W | I see. How about storage space? | 여 | 그렇군요. 저장 공간은요? |

W I see. How about storage space?
M I don't take many pictures or videos. So, I don't <u>need more than</u> 64GB.
W All right. How about this model? It comes in two different colors, black and red.
M This model is perfect for me. I'll <u>take the red one</u>.

여 그렇군요. 저장 공간은요?
남 전 사진이나 비디오를 많이 찍지 않아요. 그래서 공간은 64GB보다 더 필요하지 않아요.
여 알겠습니다. 이 모델은 어떠세요? 그건 두 가지 다른 색상인 검은색과 빨간색으로 나와요.
남 이 모델이 저에게 딱 맞겠네요. 전 빨간색인 걸 살게요.

13 ③

해설 로봇 경진 대회가 6월 5일에서 7일까지 열릴 예정인데 여자는 6월 6일에 참가할 예정이다.

어휘 enter[éntər] 참가하다
competition[kàmpitíʃən] 대회, 시합
yet[jet] 아직
take place 개최되다
be held 개최되다
attend[əténd] 참가하다

M I heard you're going to enter the robot competition. Are you ready for it, Michelle?
W I'm not ready yet, but I will be.
M Isn't the competition <u>taking place on</u> June 5th? That's tomorrow.
W Yes. But it's held for 3 days from June 5th to 7th.
M Right. So, <u>when will you attend</u> the competition?
W <u>I'll be there</u> on June 6th.
M I see. Well, I hope you'll win!
W Thanks.

남 로봇 경진 대회에 참가한다고 들었어. 준비가 됐니, Michelle?
여 아직 준비가 안 됐지만, 그렇게 될 거야.
남 대회가 6월 5일에 열리지 않아? 바로 내일이잖아.
여 그래. 근데 6월 5일부터 7일까지 3일 동안 열리거든.
남 맞다. 그래서 넌 언제 대회에 참가하는 거야?
여 나는 6월 6일에 참가할 거야.
남 그렇구나. 음, 네가 우승하길 바랄게!
여 고마워.

14 ⑤

해설 남자는 어제 드론으로 학교 교정을 촬영했다고 했다.

어휘 edit[édit] 편집하다
by oneself 혼자서
post[poust] 게시하다
shoot[ʃuːt] 촬영하다
film[film] 촬영하다, 찍다
use[juːz] 이용하다
drone[droun] 드론, 무인 항공기
entire[intáiər] 전체의
campus[kǽmpəs] 교정, 교내
this[ðis] 이 정도로, 이렇게

W What are you doing, Rick?
M I'm editing a video.
W Wow, it's our school! Did you take <u>the video by yourself</u>?
M Yes. I took it to post on my blog.
W I see. Where did you learn how to shoot videos?
M I learned it from my father.
W Cool. So, <u>how did you film</u> our school campus?
M I used my drone to <u>shoot the entire campus</u> yesterday.
W Wow, I didn't know our school was this beautiful.

여 뭐 하고 있니, Rick?
남 동영상을 편집하고 있어.
여 와, 이건 우리 학교잖아! 동영상을 너 혼자 찍었니?
남 응. 내 블로그에 올리려고 찍었지.
여 그렇구나. 동영상을 촬영하는 방법은 어디에서 배웠니?
남 우리 아버지한테서 배웠어.
여 멋지다. 그런데, 우리 학교 교정을 어떻게 촬영했니?
남 교정 전체를 촬영하기 위해 어제 드론을 사용했어.
여 와, 우리 학교가 이렇게 아름다운 줄은 몰랐네.

15 ②

해설 현장 학습이 궂은 날씨로 인해 연기되고 대신 평소대로 수업을 진행하기로 했다는 내용을 공지하고 있다.

어휘 principal[prínsəpəl] 교장
field trip 현장 학습

M Hello, students. This is your principal speaking. I wanted to tell you that our field trip to the City Fire Department this Friday <u>is delayed due to</u> bad weather. Because of this change, classes on Friday will <u>be held as usual</u>. I'll let you know when we

남 학생 여러분, 안녕하세요? 교장입니다. 이번 주 금요일에 시 소방서로 가려던 현장 학습 계획이 날씨 때문에 연기된다는 것을 알려 주고자 합니다. 이 같은 변경 때문에, 금요일 수업은 평소처럼 진행될 것입니다. 현장 학습 일정이 다시 잡히는 대로 알려

fire department 소방서
be delayed 연기되다
due to ~ 때문에
as usual 평소처럼
reschedule[rì:skédʒuːl] 일정을 다시
짜다

reschedule the trip. Thank you all for your attention.

드리겠습니다. 주목해 줘서 고맙습니다.

16 ④

[해설] 처음 세 시간 동안은 시간당 10달러이므로 두 대를 빌리면 총 60달러이다.

[어휘] rent[rent] (돈을 내고) 빌리다
electric[iléktrik] 전기의
sign[sain] 표지판
raise[reiz] (가격 등을) 올리다
then[ðen] 그러면

M Hi, I'd like to rent an electric bicycle.
W Okay. How long are you going to rent it?
M For 3 hours.
W Sure. It's $10 an hour.
M Oh, this sign here says that it's $8 an hour to rent a bicycle.
W That was last year, but the price was raised to $10 this year.
M All right. I'll rent 2 bicycles for 3 hours then.
W Sure.

남 안녕하세요. 전기 자전거를 빌리고 싶어요.
여 네. 얼마 동안 빌리실 건가요?
남 세 시간 동안이요.
여 알겠습니다. 시간당 10달러입니다.
남 아, 여기 표지판에는 자전거 빌리는 데 한 시간에 8달러라고 되어 있는데요.
여 그건 작년에 그랬고요, 가격이 올해에 10달러로 올랐습니다.
남 그렇군요. 그러면 세 시간 동안 두 대를 빌리겠습니다.
여 그러세요.

17 ②

[해설] 지금 바로 숙소 예약을 해달라는 부탁에 이를 수락하면서 지금 온라인으로 예약하겠다는 대답이 가장 적절하다.

[어휘] participate[pɑ:rtísəpèit] 참가하다
expect[ikspékt] 기대하다
[선택지]
online[ɔ́nlàin] 온라인으로
cancel[kǽnsəl] 취소하다

M Amy, I need to talk to you about our club trip to Gyeongju this Saturday.
W Oh, did something happen?
M We have more people participating than we expected, so we have to make a reservation for a bigger room.
W Okay. I know a place that can take more than 20 people. And it's cheap.
M That's good. Can you make a reservation right now? We don't have much time.
W No problem. I'll do it online now.

남 Amy, 이번 주 토요일에 경주로 동아리 여행하는 것에 대해 얘기를 좀 해야 해.
여 아, 무슨 일 생겼어?
남 우리가 예상했던 것보다 참가하는 사람이 많아. 그래서 더 큰 방을 예약해야 해.
여 알겠어. 20명 이상을 수용할 수 있는 장소를 알아. 그리고 가격도 저렴하거든.
남 잘됐다. 지금 당장 예약을 할 수 있니? 시간이 많지 않거든.
여 문제 없어. 지금 온라인으로 할게.

① 더 작은 곳을 예약하고 싶어.
③ 넌 이미 아침 식사를 하지 않았니?
④ 이 호텔은 다른 곳보다 비싸.
⑤ 호텔에 전화해서 예약을 취소해야겠어.

18 ⑤

[해설] 친구에게 사과하라고 충고하는 여자의 말에 대한 응답으로 남자의 상황상 이미 사과를 했거나 하겠다는 말이 이어져야 자연스럽다.

[어휘] have a fight with ~와 싸우다
promise[prάmis] 약속하다
break[breik] 고장 내다
(break-broke-broken)

W Did you have a fight with Chris yesterday?
M How do you know that, Mom?
W Your sister told me this morning. So, what happened between you and Chris?
M I thought Chris broke my bike and lied about it. So we had an argument.
W Did he really break it?
M No. Actually, the bike wasn't broken at all. I was wrong. I should have believed him.

여 너 어제 Chris와 싸웠니?
남 그걸 어떻게 아세요, 엄마?
여 네 여동생이 오늘 아침에 말해줬어. 그래서 너랑 Chris 사이에 무슨 일이 있었니?
남 Chris가 제 자전거를 고장 내고 거짓말하는 줄 알았어요. 그래서 말다툼했어요.
여 정말 그 애가 고장 냈니?
남 아니요. 사실 그 자전거는 고장 나지 않았어요. 제가 틀렸어요. 걔 말을 믿었어야 했는데.

have an argument 말다툼하다
believe[bilíːv] 믿다
apologize[əpάlədʒàiz] 사과하다

W Chris must be very upset. You should call and apologize to him.
M I already did, but he didn't accept my apology.

여 Chris가 너무 화가 났겠네. 그 애한테 전화해서 사과해야 하겠구나.
남 이미 했는데, 걔가 제 사과를 받아주지 않았어요.

① 사흘 전에 그를 만났어요.
② 죄송해요, 전화했어야 했는데.
③ 죄송하지만, 전 연설을 잘 못 해요.
④ 다른 사람의 비밀을 말하는 건 좋은 게 아니에요.

19 ②

해설 고등학교 진학에 대해 좀 더 생각할 시간을 달라는 남자의 말에 이어서 시간을 충분히 가지라는 응답이 가장 자연스럽다.

어휘 for a second 잠시
worried[wə́ːrid] 걱정하는
far from ~에서부터 먼
[선택지]
take[eik] 데려다 주다; 가지다

W Can I talk to you for a second, Rick?
M Sure, Mom. What's up?
W Your teacher called earlier today.
M Oh, I didn't know that. What did she say?
W She told me to think about sending you to Horton Science High School.
M Horton Science High School? I don't know if I'm good enough to go there.
W Well, I think you will be fine there. But I'm worried that the school is far from the house.
M I see. Well, can you give me more time to think about it?
W Of course. Take as long as you need.

여 잠시 얘기 좀 해도 되니, Rick?
남 물론이죠, 엄마. 무슨 일이세요?
여 네 선생님께서 오늘 전화하셨단다.
남 아, 전 몰랐어요. 선생님께서 뭐라고 하셨어요?
여 너를 Horton 과학 고등학교로 보내는 거에 대해 생각해보라고 하시더구나.
남 Horton 과학 고등학교요? 제가 그곳에 갈 정도로 잘 하는지 모르겠어요.
여 음, 넌 그곳에서 잘 할 것 같아. 하지만 집에서 학교가 멀어서 걱정되는구나.
남 그렇군요. 음, 제가 그것에 대해 생각할 시간을 좀 주시겠어요?
여 물론이지. 네가 필요한 만큼 충분히 시간을 가지렴.

① 알았다. 그곳으로 차로 데려다 줄게.
③ 너는 분명히 학교에서 최선을 다할 거야.
④ 너는 지금 숙제를 끝내야 해.
⑤ 저녁 먹으러 어디로 갈지 정해야 해.

20 ③

해설 식당에서 늘 주문했던 음식을 주문했는데, 다른 음식이 나온 상황이다.

어휘 diner[dáinər] 작은 식당
order[ɔ́ːrdər] 주문하다
a slice of 한 조각
this morning 오늘 아침에
server[sə́ːrvər] 웨이터

W Claire eats her breakfast at the same diner every morning. She needs to be at work by 9:30, so she arrives at the diner at 8:50 every morning. She always orders a cup of coffee and a slice of apple pie. This morning, she ordered the same thing, but the server brought her a slice of cherry pie. In this situation, what would Claire most likely say to the server?

Claire I'm afraid that's not what I ordered.

여 Claire는 매일 아침 같은 식당에서 아침 식사를 한다. 그녀는 9시 30분까지 출근해야 해서 식당에 매일 아침 8시 50분에 도착한다. 그녀는 늘 커피 한 잔과 애플파이 한 조각을 주문한다. 오늘 아침, 그녀는 같은 것을 주문했지만 웨이터가 그녀에게 체리파이 한 조각을 갖다 주었다. 이러한 상황에서 Claire가 웨이터에게 할 말로 가장 적절한 것은 무엇인가?

Claire 이건 제가 주문한 게 아닌 것 같아요

① 내가 일을 어떻게 시작하는지 보여 줄게요.
② 당신은 9시 30분까지 출근해야 하나요?
④ 이것은 내가 먹어 본 애플파이 중에서 가장 최고예요.
⑤ 오늘 어떤 종류의 커피를 드시나요?

01 ③	02 ④	03 ②	04 ③	05 ③	06 ⑤	07 ⑤
08 ③	09 ⑤	10 ④	11 ②	12 ②	13 ④	14 ②
15 ⑤	16 ④	17 ③	18 ②	19 ③	20 ⑤	

01 ③

해설 곰 그림이 그려진 티셔츠를 이용해서 새로 장미 그림을 그려 넣은 가방이다.

어휘 eco-friendly[iːkoufréndli] 환경 친화적인

W What is that?
M I made an eco-friendly bag, Mom.
W Did you <u>make</u> <u>that</u> <u>with</u> one of your T-shirts?
M Yes, I did. You can <u>see</u> <u>the</u> <u>bear</u> from the T-shirt here.
W <u>What</u> <u>about</u> <u>the</u> <u>rose</u>? Did you draw it?
M I did.
W Why didn't you <u>write</u> <u>your</u> <u>name</u> on it?
M This is for my girlfriend Sara, not me.

여 그게 뭐니?
남 친환경 재활용 가방을 만들었어요, 엄마.
여 네 티셔츠 중에서 하나로 만들었니?
남 네, 그랬죠. 여기 티셔츠의 곰 그림이 보이잖아요.
여 장미는? 네가 그렸니?
남 제가 그렸어요.
여 왜 그 위에 네 이름을 쓰지 않았니?
남 이건 제가 아니라 제 여자 친구 Sara에게 줄 거예요.

02 ④

해설 위치(California 북부), 명소(UC Berkeley 대학), 날씨(아주 좋음), 도시 이름의 유래(18세기 아일랜드의 철학자 George Berkeley)에 관해 언급했지만 인구수에 관해서는 언급하지 않았다.

어휘 be famous for ~로 유명하다
close to ~에 가까운
be named after ~을 따서 이름 짓다
century[séntʃəri] 세기
Irish[áiəriʃ] 아일랜드의
philosopher[filásəfər] 철학자

W Have you been to Berkeley?
M No, I haven't. <u>Where</u> <u>is</u> <u>it</u>?
W It's in Northern California. <u>It's</u> <u>famous</u> <u>for</u> the University of California, Berkeley.
M Isn't San Francisco in Northern California too?
W Yes, Berkeley is very close to San Francisco.
M Then the weather <u>must</u> <u>be</u> <u>really</u> <u>good</u> in Berkeley.
W Yes, the weather is really nice there. Oh, and the city <u>is</u> <u>named</u> <u>after</u> the 18th-century Irish philosopher George Berkeley.
M That's very interesting.

여 Berkeley에 가 본 적이 있니?
남 아니, 안 가 봤어. 어디에 있는데?
여 북부 캘리포니아 지역에 있어. UC Berkeley 대학으로 유명해.
남 San Francisco도 북부 캘리포니아 지역에 있지 않니?
여 아니, Berkeley는 San Francisco에서 아주 가까워.
남 그러면 Berkeley의 날씨는 틀림없이 좋겠네.
여 응, 거기 날씨는 정말 좋아. 아, 그 도시는 18세기 아일랜드의 철학자 George Berkeley의 이름을 따서 지어졌어.
남 정말 흥미롭네.

03 ②

해설 남자가 취업하게 되어 여자가 사는 곳 근처로 이사를 가게 되었다는 소식을 전하기 위해 전화했다.

어휘 graduate from ~을 졸업하다
college[kálidʒ] 대학
share with ~와 공유하다
offer[ɔ(ː)fər] 제안하다
fantastic[fæntǽstik] 환상적인, 굉장한

[Cell phone rings.]
W Hello.
M Aunt Mary, this is Tim.
W Tim? Oh, it's so nice to hear your voice again. <u>How</u> <u>have</u> <u>you</u> <u>been</u>?
M I've been great. How have you and Uncle Jack been doing?
W We've been just fine. I heard that you'll be graduating from college in June.
M Yes, I will, and I <u>have</u> <u>great</u> <u>news</u> to share with you.
W Really? What is it?

[휴대전화가 울린다.]
여 여보세요.
남 Mary 이모, 저 Tim이에요.
여 Tim이라고? 아, 너의 목소리를 다시 들으니 너무 좋구나. 어떻게 지냈니?
남 아주 잘 지내고 있어요. 이모하고 Jack 이모부는 어떻게 지내셨어요?
여 우린 잘 지내고 있어. 네가 6월에 대학을 졸업한다고 들었어.
남 네, 그래요. 그리고 알려 드릴 좋은 소식이 있어요.
여 정말? 뭔데?

M I'll start working at a bank in Atlanta this summer.

W That's great. You'll be very close to where we live, then.

M That's right. I'll be seeing you a lot more often.

남 Atlanta에 있는 한 은행에서 올 여름에 일을 시작할 거예요.

여 그거 잘됐구나. 그러면 우리가 사는 곳에서 아주 가까운 곳에 있게 되겠네.

남 맞아요. 훨씬 더 자주 뵙게 되겠네요.

04 ③

해설 여자는 배드민턴 연습이 4시에 있어서 현재 시각인 2시 30분으로부터 한 시간 뒤인 3시 30분에 일어나겠다고 했다.

어휘 take a nap 낮잠 자다
past[pæst] 지난
completely[kəmplíːtli] 완전히

W I'm going to take a nap, Dad.

M Okay. Do you want me to wake you up in an hour?

W Hmm... It's 2:30 right now, so can you wake me up at 4:30?

M You won't be able to sleep at night if you take a 2-hour nap.

W But I'm really tired right now. I haven't been sleeping well for the past few days.

M Don't you have badminton practice at 4:00 today?

W Oh, you're right. I completely forgot about that. I should get up in an hour, then.

여 아빠, 저 낮잠 좀 잘게요.

남 그래. 한 시간 뒤에 깨워 줄까?

여 글쎄요. 지금이 2시 30분이니까 4시 30분에 깨워 주실 수 있나요?

남 두 시간 동안 낮잠을 자면 밤에 잠을 잘 수가 없을 텐데.

여 하지만 지금 정말 피곤해요. 지난 며칠 동안 잠을 잘 못 잤거든요.

남 오늘 4시에 배드민턴 연습이 있지 않니?

여 아, 맞아요. 완전히 잊고 있었네요. 그러면, 한 시간 뒤에 일어나야겠어요.

05 ③

해설 남자는 입장에 필요한 신분증을 가져오지 않았고 공연을 보지 못하게 되어 짜증이 난 상태이다.

어휘 under the name of ~라는 이름으로
ID(= identification)[áidì:] 신분증
theater[θí(:)ətər] 극장
book[buk] 예매하다
miss[mis] 놓치다
show[ʃou] 보여주다; 공연, 쇼

M Hello. I have 2 tickets under the name of Jackson Kim.

W Okay. May I see your ID, please?

M Sure. [Pause] Oh no. I think I left my ID at home. Can I just get the tickets?

W I'm afraid you can't. We need to check your ID to let you enter the theater.

M Can I show you my friend's ID instead?

W No. We need to see your ID because you booked the tickets.

M I can't believe I forgot my ID. Now we'll miss the show.

W I'm sorry, but there's nothing we can do.

남 안녕하세요, Jackson Kim이라는 이름으로 티켓 2장이 있는데요.

여 알겠습니다. 신분증을 보여주시겠어요?

남 네. [잠시 후] 이런. 제 신분증을 집에 두고 온 것 같네요. 그냥 티켓을 받아도 될까요?

여 죄송하지만 그럴 수 없습니다. 극장에 들어가시려면 저희가 신분증을 확인해야 합니다.

남 제 친구의 신분증을 대신 보여드려도 되나요?

여 아니요. 고객님께서 티켓을 예매하셨기 때문에 고객님의 신분증을 봐야 합니다.

남 신분증을 잊어버리고 왔다니 믿기지 않네요. 이제 공연을 놓치겠어요.

여 유감이지만, 저희가 도와드릴 수 있는 게 없네요.

① 겁먹은   ② 질투하는   ③ 짜증이 난
④ 만족스러운   ⑤ 감사하는

06 ⑤

해설 길거리에서 노래를 부르는 여자를 보고 여자가 판매하는 CD를 사려고 하는 상황이다.

① M Have you seen my pencil case?
　 W Yes, I put it in your backpack.

② M Do you offer guitar lessons here?
　 W No, sir. We only offer piano lessons.

① 남 내 필통 봤니?
　 여 응, 내가 네 가방에 넣었어.

② 남 여기서 기타 강습을 해 주나요?
　 여 아니요, 고객님. 저희는 피아노 강습만 합니다.

어휘 backpack[bǽkpæk] 가방, 배낭
offer[ɔ́(:)fər] 제공하다
soar throat 아픈 목, 인후염
lose[lu:z] 잃어버리다
shortly[ʃɔ́:rtli] 곧, 금방

③ **M** Excuse me. What time is it right now?
　　W I'm sorry. I don't know the time.
④ **M** I have a sore throat. I think I'm losing my voice.
　　W I see. The doctor will be with you shortly.
⑤ **M** She sings so well, doesn't she?
　　W Yes, she does. Let's buy one of her CDs.

③ 남 실례합니다. 지금이 몇 시죠?
　　여 죄송합니다. 몇 시인지 모르겠어요.
④ 남 목이 아파요. 목소리가 안 나오는 것 같아요.
　　여 그렇군요. 의사 선생님이 곧 봐주실 거예요.
⑤ 남 그녀는 노래를 잘 부르네, 그렇지 않니?
　　여 응, 잘 부르네. 그녀의 CD를 하나 사자.

07 ⑤

해설 여자가 정원을 돌보자고 하면서 남자에게 정원에 물 주기를 부탁했다.

어휘 now that ~이니까, ~이므로
water[wɔ́:tər] (화초 등에) 물을 주다
pick up 줍다
leaves[li:vz] leaf(나뭇잎)의 복수형
branch[bræntʃ] 나뭇가지
get to ~을 시작하다, ~에 착수하다
right away 곧바로

W The weather's been really nice these days.
M I know. It's been really warm and sunny.
W When was the last time it rained or snowed?
M I think it rained about 2 weeks ago.
W Now that spring is finally here, we should start taking care of our garden.
M Yes, we should.
W Can you water the garden today? I'll pick up the leaves and branches.
M Sure, I'll get to it right away.

여 요즘 날씨가 정말 좋네요.
남 맞아요. 정말 따뜻하고 화창해요.
여 마지막으로 비나 눈이 내린 때가 언제였죠?
남 2주 전에 비가 왔던 것 같아요.
여 봄이 마침내 왔으니 우리 정원을 돌보는 일을 시작해야겠어요.
남 네, 그래야겠어요.
여 오늘 정원에 물을 좀 줄 수 있어요? 제가 잎이랑 가지를 주울게요.
남 물론이죠, 지금 바로 시작할게요.

08 ③

해설 위치(3번가와 Palm 가 사이), 운영 시간(오전 10시 ~ 오후 10시), 강사 수 (30명 이상), 수업료 할인율(10%)에 대해서는 언급되었지만 악기 종류에 관해서는 언급되지 않았다.

어휘 be located ~에 위치해 있다
avenue[ǽvənjù:] 거리
provide[prəváid] 제공하다
level[lévəl] 수준
over[óuvər] ~이 넘는, ~ 이상의
instructor[instrʌ́ktər] 강사

W Do you want to improve your musical skills? You should come to the Lesson Paradise. We are located at the corner of 3rd street and Palm Avenue. We're open every day from 10 a.m. to 10 p.m. We provide music lessons for all levels and ages, and we have over 30 instructors. If you sign up now, you'll get a 10% discount on lessons. If you have any questions, we'll be more than happy to answer them.

여 음악적 솜씨를 향상시키고 싶으신가요? Lesson Paradise로 오셔야 합니다. 저희는 3번가와 Palm 가의 교차 지점에 있습니다. 저희는 매일 오전 10시부터 오후 10시까지 엽니다. 저희는 모든 레벨과 연령대를 위한 음악 강좌를 제공하며 저희는 30명이 넘는 강사를 보유하고 있습니다. 지금 신청하시면, 수업료 10% 할인을 받을 수 있습니다. 질문이 있으시면 저희가 기꺼이 답해 드리겠습니다.

09 ⑤

해설 얼굴에 착용하는 것으로 코와 입을 가리고, 감기에 걸릴 때 특히 착용하게 되는 것은 마스크이다.

어휘 completely[kəmplí:tli] 완전히
cover[kʌ́vər] 덮다, 가리다
including[inklú:diŋ] ~을 포함하여
reason[rí:zən] 이유
stylish[stáiliʃ] 멋진
flu[flu:] 독감

M This is something that you wear on your face. It can completely cover your face, or it can cover only part of your face, including the nose and the mouth. People wear this for many reasons. Some people wear this because they think this is stylish, and others wear this to keep themselves warm in the winter. But it is important that you wear this if you have a cold or the flu.

남 이것은 당신이 얼굴에 착용하는 물건이다. 이것은 당신의 얼굴을 완전히 덮거나 코나 입을 포함한 얼굴의 일부만을 덮을 수 있다. 사람들은 이것을 여러 가지 이유로 착용한다. 어떤 사람들은 멋있다고 생각해서 이것을 착용하고, 다른 사람들은 겨울에 몸을 따뜻하게 유지하기 위해 착용한다. 하지만 감기나 독감에 걸리면 이것을 착용하는 것이 중요하다.

10 ④

해설 졸려서 잠자리에 들자고 하는 사람에게 알았다면서 커피를 타 주겠다고 말하는 것은 어색하다.

어휘 do the dishes 설거지하다
sleepy[slí:pi] 졸린

① M Can I see you in my office?
　 W Sure, I'll be right there.
② M Hello, is anybody home?
　 W Yes, I'm coming.
③ M Should I do the dishes?
　 W Yes, that would be great.
④ M I'm sleepy. Can we go to bed?
　 W Okay, I'll make you a cup of coffee.
⑤ M Do you like chocolate cake?
　 W No, I don't like sweet things.

① 남 제 사무실에서 볼 수 있을까요?
　 여 좋아요, 제가 바로 거기에 갈게요.
② 남 안녕하세요, 집에 누구든 계시나요?
　 여 네, 갑니다.
③ 남 내가 설거지를 해야 하니?
　 여 응, 그게 좋을 것 같아.
④ 남 저 졸리네요. 우리 자러 갈까요?
　 여 그래요, 제가 커피를 타 줄게요.
⑤ 남 초콜릿 케이크 좋아하니?
　 여 아니, 난 단 것을 좋아하지 않아.

11 ②

해설 쇼핑몰로 출발하기 전에 옷부터 갈아입는다고 했다.

어휘 give A a ride A를 태워 주다
mall[mɔːl] 쇼핑몰
camping[kǽmpiŋ] 캠핑
change A's clothes 옷을 갈아입다

W Are you busy now, Dad?
M No, it's all right. Do you need something?
W Can you give me a ride to the mall if you have time?
M Sure. What are you getting at the mall?
W I need to pick up a few things for my camping trip next week.
M I see. Let's leave in 10 minutes.
W All right. Then I'll change my clothes first.

여 지금 바쁘세요, 아빠?
남 아니, 괜찮단다. 뭔가가 필요하니?
여 시간이 있으시면, 저 쇼핑몰까지 태워 주실 수 있으세요?
남 물론이지. 쇼핑몰에서 뭘 사려고 하니?
여 다음 주 캠핑 여행에 필요한 걸 좀 사려고요.
남 그렇구나. 10분 뒤에 출발하자.
여 알겠어요. 그러면 먼저 옷부터 갈아 입을 게요.

12 ②

해설 목요일에, 3시 30분 이후에 있는 수업 중에서 악기를 배우는 수업이 아닌 것을 선택했다.

어휘 end[end] 끝나다
instrument [ínstrəmənt] 악기

M Mom, I need to decide which class to take after school.
W You have swimming lessons on Tuesday, so it'll have to be on Thursday.
M You're right. Should I take a 4 o'clock or 5 o'clock class?
W Well, what time does your last class end on Thursdays?
M It ends at 3:30 p.m. So any class after 3:30 is good.
W Why don't you take the guitar class? You like music, don't you?
M I do, but I'm taking piano lessons. I don't want to learn another instrument right now.
W Okay, then you have only one choice.

남 엄마, 방과 후에 어느 수업을 들을 지 결정해야 해요.
여 너는 화요일에 수영 레슨이 있으니까 목요일이어야겠네.
남 맞아요. 4시 수업을 들어야 할까요, 아니면 5시 수업을 들어야 할까요?
여 글쎄. 목요일에 마지막 수업이 몇 시에 끝나니?
남 오후 3시 30분에 끝나요. 그러니까 3시30분 이후에는 어떤 수업도 가능해요.
여 기타 수업을 듣는 게 어떠니? 너 음악 좋아하잖아, 그렇지 않니?
남 좋아하죠, 하지만 피아노 강좌를 듣고 있잖아요. 당장은 다른 악기를 배우고 싶지 않아요.
여 알겠어, 그러면 선택할 것이 하나뿐이네.

13 ④

해설 16일 이후인 18일로 배달 날짜를 재조정했다.

[Telephone rings.]
W Hello.
M Hello. May I speak to Tara Taylor, please?
W This is she. Who's calling?

[전화벨이 울린다.]
여 여보세요.
남 여보세요. Tara Taylor 씨 좀 바꿔 주시겠어요?
여 전데요. 누구시죠?

어휘 electronics[ilèktrániks] 전자 기기

delivery[dilívəri] 배달

go away 집을 떠나다, 어디를 가다

M I'm calling from Best Electronics. You bought a TV last week from us.
W That's right. Is there something wrong?
M I'm very sorry, but the delivery date has to be changed.
W Really? To when?
M The date has to be either August 12th or 14th.
W I see. Both dates are not good for me. I'm going away for a few days. Any day after the 16th would be better.
M Then how about the 18th?
W That sounds good.

남 Best Electronics에서 전화드립니다. 지난 주에 TV를 구매하셨죠?
여 맞아요. 뭐가 잘못 되었나요?
남 죄송하지만, 배달 날짜가 변경되어야 합니다.
여 정말요? 언제로요?
남 8월 12일이나 14일이 되어야 할 것 같습니다.
여 그렇군요. 둘 다 안 될 것 같아요. 제가 며칠 동안 어디를 갈 예정이거든요. 16일 이후에 아무 날짜가 더 좋을 것 같아요.
남 그러면 18일은 어떠세요?
여 그게 좋을 것 같네요.

14 ②

해설 어제 배가 아파서 병원에서 진료를 받았다고 했다.

어휘 for a minute 잠시

stomachache[stʌ́məkèik] 복통, 배 아픔

doctor's note 소견서, 진단서

hand in 제출하다

M Mrs. Robinson, may I talk to you for a minute?
W Of course, Jake. What is it?
M Well, could you give me more time to finish my history homework?
W Was it too difficult for you?
M That's not it. I haven't started it yet.
W Oh, did something happen?
M Yes, Mrs. Robinson. I had a terrible stomachache yesterday and went to see the doctor. Here is the doctor's note.
W I see. Then can you finish it and hand it in tomorrow?
M Sure, I will. Thank you very much.

남 Robinson 선생님, 잠시 이야기 좀 할 수 있을까요?
여 물론이지, Jake. 무슨 일이니?
남 제 역사 숙제를 끝낼 시간을 좀 더 주실 수 있나요?
여 너한테 너무 어려웠니?
남 그건 아니고요. 아직 시작하지 못했거든요.
여 아, 무슨 일 있었니?
남 네, Robinson 선생님. 제가 어제 배가 너무 아파서 진료를 받았어요. 여기 의사 소견서예요.
여 알겠다. 그럼 그것을 끝내서 내일 제출할 수 있니?
남 물론 그렇게 할게요. 정말 감사합니다.

15 ⑤

해설 시장이 학교를 방문해 교내 식당에서 식사를 할 예정이므로 점심시간에 예의 바르게 행동하도록 요청하는 내용이다.

어휘 interrupt[ìntərʌ́pt] 방해하다

mayor[méiər] 시장

run around 뛰어다니다

loudly[láudli] 크게

keep it down 조용히 하다

as much as possible 가능한 한

W Hello, everyone. I'm sorry to interrupt your class, but I have an important announcement to make. At noon today, the mayor of our city will be visiting our school. He's going to have lunch with some of our teachers in the cafeteria. I know that many of you run around and speak loudly during lunchtime, but try to keep it down as much as possible. Thank you.

여 여러분, 안녕하세요. 수업을 방해해서 미안하지만 발표할 중요한 내용이 있습니다. 오늘 정오에 우리 시의 시장님이 학교를 방문할 예정입니다. 시장님은 교내 식당에서 우리 학교의 선생님 몇 분과 점심 식사를 할 예정입니다. 나는 여러분 중 많은 사람들이 점심시간에 뛰어다니고 크게 말하는 걸 잘 알고 있지만 가능한 한 조용히 하도록 노력해 주세요. 감사합니다.

16 ④

해설 40달러짜리 티셔츠 두 개를 구입하면 세 번째 티셔츠는 무료라고 했으므로 여자는 티셔츠 총 세 개를 두 개의 가격으로 구매하여 총 80달러를 지불할 것이다.

M Hi, do you need any help?
W Yes, how much are these T-shirts?
M They are $20 each.
W Oh, that's a reasonable price. How about these?

남 안녕하세요, 도와드릴까요?
여 네, 이 티셔츠들은 얼마죠?
남 하나에 20달러입니다.
여 아, 가격이 괜찮군요. 이것들은요?

M Those are $40 each. They are a little more expensive, so we <u>have a special sale</u> on them.

W <u>What kind of sale</u> do you have on them?

M If you buy two of them, you can get <u>the third one for</u> free.

W That's good. Then I'll get 2 <u>of these</u> T-shirts.

남 그것들은 40달러씩입니다. 그것들은 조금 더 비싸서 특별 할인을 하고 있어요.

여 어떤 할인인데요?

남 두 개를 구입하시면 세 번째 티셔츠는 무료로 드립니다.

여 좋습니다. 그럼 이 티셔츠를 두 개 살게요.

17 ③

해설 필기도 하고 열심히 공부했으니 시험에 떨어지지 않을 것이라는 남자의 말에 노트가 도움이 되었으면 좋겠다고 응답하는 것이 가장 적절하다.

어휘 starve[staːrv] 굶주리다
already[ɔːlrédi] 벌써
anyway[éniwèi] 하여간, 어쨌든
serious[síəriəs] 진지한
fail[feil] (시험에) 낙제하다, 떨어지다
take notes 필기하다

M I'm starving. Why don't we go and get something to eat, Judy?

W <u>Is it already</u> lunchtime?

M Yes, it's 12:30. You've been <u>studying for over</u> 3 hours already.

W We came to the library at 10:30, James.

M Did we? Anyway, you're too serious about studying.

W I have to be. I don't want to <u>fail my science test</u> again.

M You won't. You <u>took notes and studied</u> really hard for it.

W I hope these notes help me pass the test.

남 나 배고파 죽겠어. 가서 뭘 좀 먹지 않을래, Judy?

여 벌써 점심시간이야?

남 응. 12시 30분이야. 너는 벌써 세 시간 넘게 공부했어.

여 우리는 10시 30분에 도서관에 왔어, James.

남 그래? 어쨌든 넌 공부에 대해 너무 진지해.

여 나는 그래야 돼. 과학 시험에 또 낙제하고 싶지 않거든.

남 그렇게 되지 않을 거야. 필기도 했고 열심히 공부했잖아.

여 <u>이 노트들이 시험에 통과하도록 도와줬으면 좋겠어.</u>

① 나는 과학책을 책상에 놓고 왔어.
② 너는 왜 책을 그렇게 깨끗하게 쓰니?
④ 오늘 너는 내 과학책을 빌릴 수 있어.
⑤ 나는 점심을 먹으면서 책 읽는 것을 좋아해.

18 ②

해설 물을 마시는 필터로 사용할 수 있는 책을 아프리카로 보내면 좋겠다는 여자의 말에 그렇게 하려고 했다는 응답이 가장 자연스럽다.

어휘 drinkable[dríŋkəbl] 마실 수 있는, 마셔도 되는
tear out 뜯다, 뜯어내다
filter[fíltər] 필터, 여과기
helpful[hélpfəl] 도움이 되는
send[send] 보내다
village[vílidʒ] 마을
[선택지]
exactly[igzǽktli] 정확히, 틀림없이
no one ~ 아무도 ~ 아니다
at least 적어도, 최소한

W That's an interesting title for a book, *Drinkable Book*. What is that about?

M Well, it's not a book we can read. There's something very special about it.

W Really? <u>What's so special</u> about this book?

M You use the book to drink water.

W What? You <u>can drink this book</u>?

M No. You can tear out a page of this book and use it <u>as a water filter</u>.

W Oh, it would be <u>helpful to send</u> drinkable books to villages in Africa.

M Right. That's exactly what I'm going to do.

여 〈마실 수 있는 책〉이라, 아주 재미있는 책 제목이네. 어떤 내용이니?

남 음, 그건 우리가 읽을 수 있는 책이 아니야. 그 책에는 뭔가 특별한 게 있어.

여 정말? 이 책이 뭐가 그렇게 특별한데?

남 물을 마시기 위해 이 책을 사용해.

여 뭐라고? 이 책을 마실 수 있다고?

남 아니. 이 책 한 장을 뜯어내서 물 필터로 사용할 수 있어.

여 아, 마실 수 있는 책들을 아프리카의 마을에 보내면 도움이 되겠네.

남 맞아. 그게 바로 내가 하려고 하는 일이야.

① 아니, 나는 이 책을 읽고 싶지 않아.
③ 아니, 우리는 이미 깨끗한 물을 충분히 갖고 있어.
④ 글쎄, 아무도 이 책을 마실 수 없어.
⑤ 응, 나는 적어도 여덟 잔의 물을 마셔야 해.

19 ③

해설 유명해지려면 어떻게 하는 게 좋을지 의견을 물어보는 남자의 말에 손흥민 선수만큼 열심히 노력하는 것이 필요하다고 조언하는 응답이 자연스럽다.

어휘 amazing[əméiziŋ] 놀라운
all over 곳곳에
proud of ~이 자랑스러운
doubt[daut] 의심
famous[féiməs] 유명한
[선택지] not ~ at all 전혀 ~ 아닌
in person 직접, 몸소
first of all 무엇보다도
impossible[impásəbl] 불가능한

M Did you see the amazing goal by Son Heung-min?
W Yes, I did. It's all over the news.
M I'm so proud of him. He's one of the best soccer players in the world.
W There's no doubt about that. What a great soccer player he is!
M I wish I could become as famous as he is.
W Well, you're only 16 years old. You still have time.
M You think so? What do you think I should do to become famous?
W You need to work as hard as he does.

남 손흥민의 놀라운 골 장면을 봤니?
여 응, 봤지. 온통 그 뉴스뿐이던 걸.
남 나는 그가 정말 자랑스러워. 그는 세계 최고의 축구 선수 중 한 명이야.
여 그건 의심의 여지가 없어. 그는 정말 대단한 축구 선수야!
남 나도 그처럼 유명해질 수 있다면 좋겠어.
여 글쎄, 너는 겨우 열 여섯살이잖아. 아직 시간이 있어.
남 그렇게 생각해? 내가 어떻게 해야 유명해질 것 같니?
여 너도 그가 하는 만큼 열심히 노력해야 해.

① 너는 그를 만날 수 있어.
② 나는 그가 전혀 유명하다고 생각하지 않아.
④ 지난밤에 뉴스 보는 것을 잊었어.
⑤ 축구 선수가 유명해지는 것은 불가능해.

20 ⑤

해설 다른 사람들에게 피해를 줄 수 있기 때문에 밤늦게 음악을 연주하는 것을 자제하도록 조언해야 하는 상황이다.

어휘 outdoor[áutdɔ̀ːr] 실외의, 옥외의
go camping 캠핑하러 가다
once every other week 2주일에 한 번
for a while 잠시 동안
take out ~을 꺼내다
midnight[mídnàit] 자정
camper[kǽmpər] 야영객
bother[báðər] 성가시게 하다

M David loves outdoor activities, and he goes camping once every other week. He usually goes camping with one of his friends, and this week he goes with James. After dinner, they talk for a while, and David is getting ready to go to sleep. Then, James takes out his guitar and starts playing. It is after midnight, and David is worried that he will wake other campers. In this situation, what would David most likely say to James?

David It's too late. You shouldn't be playing the guitar.

남 David는 야외 활동을 아주 좋아해서 2주일에 한 번씩 캠핑을 간다. 그는 대개 친구 중 한 명과 같이 캠핑을 가는데, 이번 주에는 친구 James와 같이 간다. 저녁 식사 후, 그들은 잠시 이야기를 나누고 David는 잠자리에 들 준비를 한다. 그 때, James가 기타를 꺼내 연주하기 시작한다. 자정이 지났고 David는 그가 다른 야영객들을 깨울까봐 걱정한다. 이러한 상황에서 David가 James에게 할 말로 가장 적절한 것은 무엇인가?

David 너무 늦었어. 기타를 치면 안 돼.

① 저녁 식사를 요리하는 거 즐거웠니?
② 전에도 캠핑을 간 적이 있니?
③ 가장 좋아하는 야외 활동이 뭐니?
④ 기타 연주 하는 것을 언제 처음 배웠니?

01 ⑤	02 ④	03 ②	04 ③	05 ⑤	06 ②	07 ③
08 ①	09 ④	10 ⑤	11 ②	12 ③	13 ①	14 ①
15 ①	16 ②	17 ④	18 ①	19 ④	20 ①	

01 ⑤

해설 크리스마스트리 모양이고, 맨 아래에 'Merry Christmas'라고 쓰여 있는 카드이다.

어휘 **look like** ~처럼 보이다
cute[kjuːt] 귀여운
space[speis] 공간
inside[ìnsáid] 내부에
front[frʌnt] 앞면, 앞부분
bottom[bátəm] 아래

M I bought a Christmas card for our parents, Jane. Let's write in it together.
W Good. Oh, it looks like a Christmas tree.
M Yes, I thought it looked cute.
W It does, but do you think it has enough space for us to write on?
M Yes, it's big enough to write something inside.
W Good. Can we write anything on the front?
M No, it already says "Merry Christmas" at the bottom of the card. So we can't write anything.
W Oh, okay.

남 부모님께 드릴 크리스마스카드를 샀어, Jane. 같이 쓰자.
여 좋아. 아, 크리스마스트리 모양 같네.
남 응, 귀여운 것 같았거든.
여 귀여워. 그런데 우리가 적을 수 있는 공간이 충분할까?
남 응, 안에 뭔가를 적기엔 충분히 커.
여 좋았어. 앞쪽에도 쓸 수 있을까?
남 아니, 카드 아래쪽에 'Merry Christmas'라고 이미 쓰여 있어. 그래서 우리는 아무 것도 쓸 수가 없어.
여 아, 알겠어.

02 ④

해설 두께(아주 두꺼움), 냄새(바닐라 냄새가 남), 맛(달지 않음), 재료(꿀)에 관해 언급했지만 가격에 대한 언급은 없었다.

어휘 **try**[trai] 먹어 보다
thick[θik] 두꺼운
taste[teist] ~ 맛이 나다

W Are you making pancakes for breakfast, Dad?
M Yes, I am. Try these pancakes.
W [Pause] They're very thick and smell like vanilla.
M They do, don't they? Do you like them?
W They taste very different. They are not sweet enough.
M I knew you would say that.
W Why do they taste different?
M That's because I used honey instead of sugar.

여 아빠, 아침 식사로 먹을 팬케이크를 만들고 있어요?
남 응, 맞아. 이 팬케이크를 먹어 보렴.
여 [잠시 후] 아주 두껍고 바닐라 냄새가 나네요.
남 그래, 그렇지? 마음에 드니?
여 맛이 완전 다르네요. 달지 않아요.
남 네가 그렇게 말할 줄 알았어.
여 맛이 왜 다른 거죠?
남 설탕 대신에 꿀을 사용했거든.

03 ②

해설 남자는 몸이 좋지 않아서 여자와의 약속을 취소하려고 전화했다.

어휘 **almost**[ɔ́ːlmoust] 거의
take long 오래 걸리다
actually[ǽktʃuəli] 사실은
some other time 다른 어느 때에
get well 건강을 회복하다

[Cell phone rings.]
W Hello.
M Hi, Sarah.
W Will, are you already there? I'm almost ready. It won't take long to get there.
M No. I'm still at home.
W Oh, that's good. Can we meet 30 minutes later?
M Actually, I was calling to ask you if we could meet some other time.
W Of course. That's not a problem. Did something happen?

[휴대전화가 울린다.]
여 여보세요.
남 안녕, Sarah.
여 Will, 벌써 도착했어? 나도 거의 다 준비됐어. 그곳에 도착하기까지 그리 오래 걸리지 않을 거야.
남 아니야. 나 아직 집이야.
여 아, 잘됐네. 우리가 30분 후에 만나도 될까?
남 사실은, 우리가 다른 날 만나도 될 지 물어보려고 전화한 거야.
여 물론이지. 문제없어. 무슨 일 생겼니?

M I'm not feeling well, and I think I should get some rest.
W Okay, I understand. I hope you get well soon.

남 몸이 좋지 않아서 좀 쉬어야 할 것 같아.
여 그래, 알겠어. 빨리 나아지길 바랄게.

04 ③

해설 6시 이후 아무 때나 괜찮다는 여자의 말에 남자는 6시 30분을 제안했고 여자는 이를 수락했다.

어휘 go bowling 볼링 치러 가다
meet up with A (뭔가를 하려고) A를 만나다
grab something to eat 간단히 [재빨리] 먹다

W What are you doing tonight, Mike?
M Nothing special. How about you?
W Do you want to go bowling with me? I'm meeting up with my friends at 7:30 p.m.
M Sure. That sounds fun. What time should we meet?
W I can meet anytime after 6:00 p.m.
M Why don't we meet at 6:30 then? Let's grab something to eat before we go bowling.
W Okay. Where do you want to meet?
M Let's meet at Central Station.

여 오늘 밤에 뭘 할 계획이니, Mike?
남 특별한 것 없어. 너는?
여 나와 함께 볼링 치러 갈래? 저녁 7시 30분에 친구들이랑 만나기로 했거든.
남 그래. 재미있겠다. 우리 몇 시에 만날까?
여 오후 6시 이후에는 언제라도 좋아.
남 그럼 6시 30분에 만날까? 볼링 치러 가기 전에 간단히 뭘 좀 먹자.
여 알겠어. 어디에서 만날까?
남 Central 역에서 만나자.

05 ⑤

해설 남자는 음료를 주문하려고 하고, 여자에게 자리를 맡아달라고 하는 것으로 보아 두 사람이 있는 곳은 커피숍임을 알 수 있다.

어휘 right now 지금 당장은
upstairs[ʌ́pstέərz] 위층으로

M What do you want to drink, Rebecca?
W I don't need anything right now.
M Then can you find a table while I order mine?
W All the tables are taken on the first floor, so I'll check the second floor.
M Okay. Are you sure you don't need anything?
W Yes, I'm sure. I drank too much coffee this morning.
M Okay. I'll go upstairs after I order my drink.

남 뭘 마시고 싶니, Rebecca?
여 지금은 아무것도 마시고 싶지 않아.
남 그럼 내가 마실 음료를 주문하는 동안 자리를 맡아 줄래?
여 1층은 모든 자리가 찼어, 그러니 2층을 알아볼게.
남 좋아. 너 정말 아무것도 마시지 않을 거지?
여 그럼, 확실해. 나는 오늘 아침에 커피를 너무 많이 마셨거든.
남 알겠어. 내 음료를 주문한 뒤에 위층으로 올라갈게.

06 ②

해설 아무도 앉아 있지 않아서 의자를 가져가도 되는지 물어보는 상황이다.

어휘 still[stil] 아직도
work on ~에 노력을 들이다
Do you mind if I ~? 제가 ~해도 될까요?
Go ahead. 어서 하세요.
move[mu:v] 옮기다
on sale 할인 중인
discount[dískaunt] 할인

① M Excuse me. Are you finished?
   W No, I'm still working on it.
② M Do you mind if I take this chair?
   W Go ahead. No one's sitting there.
③ M Do you want me to move this table?
   W Yes, please. It is too heavy for me.
④ M It's time to go to bed, honey.
   W Okay, can you read me a book?
⑤ M Is this chair on sale?
   W Yes, you get a 15% discount on that chair.

① 남 실례합니다. 다 하셨나요?
   여 아뇨, 아직 작업하는 중입니다.
② 남 이 의자를 가져가도 될까요?
   여 어서 가져가세요. 아무도 앉을 사람 없어요.
③ 남 이 테이블을 옮겨 드릴까요?
   여 네, 부탁드려요. 제게는 너무 무겁네요.
④ 남 잘 시간이야, 얘야.
   여 알겠어요. 책 좀 읽어 주실래요?
⑤ 남 이 의자 할인 중인가요?
   여 네, 그 의자는 15% 할인됩니다.

07 ③

해설 여자는 남자에게 계란을 삶아달라고 부탁했다.

어휘 invite[inváit] 초대하다
set the table 상을 차리다
later[léitər] 나중에
boil[bɔil] 삶다
for sure 확실히

M Are you still cooking, honey?
W Yes, but I'm almost done.
M I'm sorry I invited so many people.
W It's okay. The more, the better.
M Is there anything I can do to help? Do you want me to set the table?
W No, I'll do that later. But can you boil some eggs for me?
M Of course. That's something I know how to do for sure.

남 여보, 아직도 요리하고 있는 중이에요?
여 네, 하지만 거의 다 끝났어요.
남 내가 너무 많은 사람을 초대해서 미안해요.
여 괜찮아요. 사람이 많을수록 더 좋아요.
남 내가 도울 수 있는 일이 있을까요? 상을 차릴까요?
여 아니요, 그건 내가 나중에 할게요. 계란 좀 삶아 줄 수 있어요?
남 물론이죠. 그건 내가 방법을 확실히 알고 있는 일이죠.

08 ①

해설 무게(28킬로그램 미만), 사용법(하루에 20분씩 타기), 가격(200달러), 구매방법(60분 이내에 전화하기)에 관해 언급되었지만 이름에 대한 언급은 없었다.

어휘 stay fit 건강을 유지하다
consider v-ing ～하는 것을 고려하다
weigh[wei] 무게가 ～이다
less[les] 더 적게
equipment[ikwípmənt] 장비
product[prádəkt] 제품
within[wiðín] ～ 이내에, ～ 안에
miss[mis] 놓치다
opportunity[àpərtjú:nəti] 기회

W Hello, everyone. If you'd like to stay fit during wintertime, consider buying an exercise bike from us. Our exercise bike is 100 centimeters tall and weighs less than 28 kilograms. All you have to do is ride this bike for 20 minutes a day. This amazing piece of equipment is only $200, and the only way to buy this product is by calling us within the next 60 minutes. So, hurry and don't miss this great opportunity.

여 여러분, 안녕하세요. 여러분이 겨울 동안 건강을 유지하고 싶으시면, 실내 운동용 자전거를 사는 것을 고려해 보세요. 저희 실내 운동용 자전거는 높이가 100센티미터이고 무게는 28킬로그램이 되지 않습니다. 여러분이 한 일은 하루에 20분 동안 이 자전거를 타는 것이 전부입니다. 이 놀라운 장비는 200달러밖에 하지 않는데, 이 제품을 구입할 수 있는 유일한 방법은 앞으로 60분 이내에 저희에게 전화하시는 겁니다. 그러니 서두르셔서 이 좋은 기회를 놓치지 마세요.

09 ④

해설 두 사람이 또는 두 사람으로 구성된 두 팀이 중앙에 네트가 있는 실내 혹은 실외 코트에서 라켓과 함께 보통 노란색 고무공으로 하는 경기는 테니스이다.

어휘 usually[jú:ʒuəli] 주로, 대개
individual[ìndəvídʒuəl] 개인, 사람
in order to ～하기 위해
indoor[índɔːr] 실내의
outdoor[áutdɔːr] 야외의, 옥외의

M This is a sport that is usually played by 2 individuals. It can also be played by 2 teams, and each team has only 2 players. In order to play this sport, you need to have a ball and a racket. The ball is made of rubber and is usually yellow in color. This sport can be played on an indoor or outdoor court which has a net in the middle.

남 이것은 보통 두 사람이 하는 운동입니다. 또한 두 팀으로 나누어 경기하기도 하는데 각 팀에 단 두 사람이 있습니다. 이 경기를 하기 위해서 당신은 공 한 개와 라켓 한 개가 필요합니다. 공은 고무로 만들어져 있고 보통 노란색을 띕니다. 이 경기는 중앙에 네트가 있는 실내 혹은 실외 코트에서 행해집니다.

10 ⑤

해설 이름을 묻는 질문에 음식을 주문하는 것은 어색하다.

어휘 check[tʃek] 계산서
cousin[kʌ́zən] 사촌
times[taimz] ~ 번, ~ 회

① M Can I have the check, please?
   W Yes, I'll bring it right away.
② M Is that your sister in the picture?
   W No, she's my cousin.
③ M Be careful. The coffee is really hot.
   W Thank you. I'll just drink it later.
④ M How many times have you read this book?
   W I have read it more than 5 times.
⑤ M May I have your name?
   W Yes, I'll have the T-bone steak.

① 남 계산서 좀 갖다 주시겠어요?
   여 네, 바로 가져다 드리겠습니다.
② 남 사진에 있는 사람이 네 여동생이니?
   여 아니, 그녀는 내 사촌이야.
③ 남 조심해. 커피가 정말 뜨거워.
   여 고마워. 나중에 마실게.
④ 남 이 책을 몇 번 읽었니?
   여 다섯 번 이상 읽었어.
⑤ 남 성함을 알려주시겠습니까?
   여 네, T-bone 스테이크 주세요.

11 ②

해설 여자가 파티 장소를 예약해달라고 부탁하자 남자는 바로 하겠다고 했다.

어휘 be stressed out 스트레스를 받다
prepare for ~을 준비하다
(all) by oneself 혼자서
book[buk] 예약하다

M You look tired, Erica. Is everything all right?
W I've been really stressed out about the class party next week.
M You're not preparing for that party all by yourself, are you?
W Yes, I am. Everyone else in my class is busy with other work.
M But that's too much work for one person. I can help if you want.
W Then can you call and book a room for the party for me? I'll give you the number.
M Okay. I will do it now.

남 Erica, 너 피곤해 보인다. 괜찮니?
여 다음 주에 있을 학급 파티 때문에 정말 스트레스가 많았어.
남 너 혼자 그 파티 준비를 다 하는 것은 아니잖아, 그렇지?
여 아니, 내가 다 하고 있어. 모두 다 다른 일로 바쁘거든.
남 그래도 한 사람이 하기엔 너무 많은 일이야. 네가 원하면 내가 도울게.
여 그럼 전화해서 파티 장소를 예약해 줄래? 내가 전화번호를 줄게.
남 응. 지금 할게.

12 ③

해설 싱가포르에서 일주일 동안 머물기로 하였으며, 좋은 호텔을 포함한 가격이 더 비싼 여행 패키지를 선택했다.

어휘 decide on ~에 대해 결정하다
vacation package 휴가 패키지여행
botanic garden 식물원
option[ápʃən] 선택, 선택권
[선택지]
destination[dèstənéiʃən] 목적지
duration[djuréiʃən] 지속 기간

M Honey, let's decide on our summer vacation package today.
W Sure. Where do you want to go?
M How about Singapore? I want to visit the Botanic Gardens.
W I want to go there, too. How long are we going to stay there?
M How about staying at least a week?
W Great. Then we only have 2 options to choose from.
M Why is this one more expensive than the other one?
W That's because this one includes a much nicer hotel.
M Let's choose this package then. I want to stay at a good hotel.
W That sounds good.

남 여보, 오늘 여름 휴가 패키지를 결정해요.
여 네. 어디에 가고 싶어요?
남 싱가포르는 어때요? 식물원에 가보고 싶거든요.
여 나도 거기 가고 싶어요. 얼마나 머무를 예정이에요?
남 적어도 일주일 머무르는 게 어때요?
여 좋아요. 그러면 선택할 수 있는 건 두 가지뿐이네요.
남 왜 이건 다른 것보다 비싼 거죠?
여 그건 훨씬 더 좋은 호텔을 포함해서 그래요.
남 그러면 이 패키지로 선택해요. 좋은 호텔에 머물고 싶네요.
여 좋은 것 같아요.

13 ①

해설 올해 추석은 목요일인 10월 1일이며 추석 연휴가 시작되는 날은 9월 30일이라고 했다.

어휘 holiday[hάlədèi] 휴일
place[pleis] 집
during[djúəriŋ] ~ 동안
entire[intáiər] 전체의

M When is Chuseok this year?
W It's October 1st. That's a Thursday.
M That's perfect! Then we have a 5-day holiday this year.
W You're right. The Chuseok holiday starts on September 30th.
M Do you have any plans for the long holiday?
W My grandmother's birthday is October 4th, so we'll stay at her place during the entire holiday.

남 올해는 추석이 언제지?
여 10월 1일이야. 그날은 목요일이야.
남 잘됐다! 그럼 올해는 휴일을 5일 동안 갖게 되는 거네.
여 맞아. 추석 휴일은 9월 30일에 시작해.
남 긴 휴일 동안에 계획이 있니?
여 할머니 생신이 10월 4일이거든. 그래서, 휴일 내내 할머니 댁에 있을 거야.

14 ①

해설 남자는 어제 직업 박람회에 갔다고 했다.

어휘 graduate from ~을 졸업하다
university[jù:nəvə́:rsəti] 대학교
right away 곧바로
either ~ or ... ~아니면 …
mechanic[məkǽnik] 정비사
engineer[èndʒiníər] 기술자, 수리공
job fair 직업 박람회
find out 알게 되다, 알아내다

W What do you want to do after you graduate from high school?
M Well, I'm not going to university. I'm planning to get a job right away.
W Really? What kind of job do you want to have?
M I want to be either a mechanic or an engineer.
W Wow, you already decided what to become. That's amazing.
M I went to a job fair yesterday, and I found out a lot about myself.
W I'd like to go there, too.

여 너는 고등학교를 졸업한 후에 뭐하고 싶니?
남 글쎄, 대학교에 가지는 않을 거야. 바로 취직할 계획이거든.
여 정말? 어떤 직업을 갖고 싶은데?
남 정비사 아니면 기술자가 되고 싶어.
여 와, 넌 이미 뭐가 될지 결심했구나. 대단하다.
남 어제 직업 박람회에 갔는데 내 자신에 대해 많은 것을 알게 됐거든.
여 나도 거기에 가고 싶다.

15 ①

해설 추수 감사절에 칠면조를 먹을 수 없는 사람들을 위해 특별 메뉴로 칠면조 요리를 준비했다고 알려 주는 방송 내용이다.

어휘 attention[əténʃən] 주의, 주목
Thanksgiving[θæ̀ŋksgíviŋ] 추수 감사절
away[əwéi] (시간 · 공간적으로) 떨어져 있는
be able to-v ~할 수 있다
turkey[tə́:rki] 칠면조
for various reasons 여러 가지 이유로
serve[sə:rv] (음식을) 차려 내다

W May I have your attention, please? As you all know, Thanksgiving is only a week away. I'm sure most of you will have a big Thanksgiving dinner with friends and family. But some of you may not be able to enjoy eating turkey for various reasons. So we have prepared our own turkey and will serve it as a special lunch today. I hope you enjoy it!

여 여러분, 주목해 주시겠어요? 모두 알다시피, 추수 감사절이 일주일밖에 남지 않았습니다. 여러분 중 대부분은 친구들이나 가족과 함께 성대한 추수 감사절 저녁 식사를 하겠지요. 하지만 여러분 중 일부는 여러 가지 이유로 칠면조를 먹는 즐거움을 누리지 못할 수도 있어요. 그래서 우리만의 칠면조를 준비했고 오늘 특별 점심 메뉴로 제공할 것입니다. 칠면조를 맛있게 드시기 바랍니다!

16 ②

해설 50달러짜리 축구공 한 개와 10달러짜리 양말 두 켤레를 구입하였으므로 남자가 지불할 금액은 70달러이다.

어휘 less[les] 덜하게, 더 적게
quality[kwάləti] 품질
about[əbáut] 거의
per[pər] ~당
payment[péimənt] 결제, 지불

M Excuse me. How much is this soccer ball?
W That one is $80.
M Wow, it's expensive. Do you have any less expensive ones?
W Sure. This ball is $50. The quality is about the same.
M That's good. I'll take that then. I also need some pairs of soccer socks.
W Of course. These ones are $10 per pair.
M Great. I'll take 2 pairs with the ball.
W Okay. I'll help you with the payment over there.

남 실례합니다. 이 축구공은 얼마인가요?
여 그건 80달러입니다.
남 와, 비싸네요. 덜 비싼 것도 취급하시나요?
여 물론입니다. 이 공은 50달러예요. 품질은 거의 같아요.
남 좋아요. 그럼 그걸로 살게요. 저 축구 양말도 좀 필요해요.
여 네. 이것들은 한 켤레당 10달러입니다.
남 좋네요. 공이랑 같이 두 켤레 살게요.
여 알겠습니다. 저쪽에서 결제 도와드릴게요.

17 ④

해설 우쿨렐레 연주법을 어떻게 배웠는지 묻고 있으므로 인터넷 동영상을 보고 배웠다는 응답이 적절하다.

어휘 carry[kǽri] 들고 다니다
ukulele[jùːkəléili] 우쿨렐레 (현악기의 일종)
string[striŋ] (악기의) 줄, 현
[선택지]
teach oneself 독학하다
on the Internet 인터넷을 통해
string instrument 현악기

W What are you carrying, Sam?
M This is a ukulele.
W I thought it was a guitar. That's a big ukulele.
M Yes, it is. There are about 5 different sizes, and this is the biggest size.
W Ukuleles only have 4 strings, right?
M Yes, they do, and guitars have 6 strings. So, ukuleles are much easier to play than guitars.
W Where did you learn to play the ukulele?
M I taught myself by watching videos on the Internet.

여 네가 들고 다니는 것이 뭐니, Sam?
남 이건 우쿨렐레야.
여 기타인줄 알았어. 그건 큰 우쿨렐레네.
남 응. 맞아. 크기가 다섯 가지 정도 있는데, 이게 가장 큰 거야.
여 우쿨렐레는 줄이 네 개뿐이지, 그렇지?
남 응. 맞아. 그리고 기타는 줄이 여섯 개지. 그래서, 우쿨렐레는 기타보다 훨씬 치기 쉬워.
여 우쿨렐레 연주하는 법을 어디에서 배웠니?
남 인터넷에서 동영상을 보면서 독학했어.

① 나는 중국에서 처음 우쿨렐레를 샀어.
② 대부분의 기타 가게들은 우쿨렐레도 취급해.
③ 우쿨렐레를 연주하기에는 내 체구가 너무 크다고 생각했어.
⑤ 현악기는 피아노보다 연주하기가 쉬워.

18 ①

해설 중학교 시절에 대해 졸업을 앞두고 남자가 친구 사귀는 것과 공부에 대해 아쉬운 점을 말하고 있으므로 여자도 아쉬운 점을 구체적으로 말하는 것이 자연스럽다.

어휘 differently[dífərəntli] 다르게
natural[nǽtʃərəl] 자연스러운, 당연한
regret[rigrét] 후회

W I can't believe we're graduating in 3 weeks.
M I know. It feels like just yesterday that I started middle school.
W We had a great time, didn't we? It was the best 3 years of my life.
M I had a great time, but I wish I had done a few things differently.
W It's only natural to have a few regrets, Paul.

여 3주 뒤에 우리가 졸업한다니 믿어지지 않아.
남 그러게. 중학교에 다니기 시작한 게 바로 어제 같아.
여 우리는 즐거운 시간을 보냈어, 그렇지 않니? 내 인생 중 최고의 3년이었지.
남 나는 즐거웠지만 몇 가지를 다르게 했다면 하는 아쉬운 것들이 있어.
여 후회할 일들이 생기는 건 아주 당연해, Paul.

M I don't think I've made enough friends or studied hard enough.
W I wish I had studied a little harder, too.

남 친구도 충분히 못 사귀었고 공부도 열심히 하지 않은 것 같아.
여 나도 조금 더 열심히 공부했더라면 좋았을 거야.

② 내 인생의 3년을 낭비한 느낌이야.
③ 중학교는 정말 어려운 시기였어.
④ 너는 고등학교에서 더 많은 돈을 벌 거야.
⑤ 네 졸업식에 참석하지 못해서 미안해.

19 ④

해설 너무 늦게 자지 않았으면 하는 여자의 말에 지금 보고 있는 동영상만 보고 바로 자겠다는 남자의 응답이 가장 적절하다.

어휘 past[pæst] (시간이) 지나서
be supposed to-v ~하기로 되어 있다
school night 학교 가는 날의 전날 밤
online[ɔ́nlain] 온라인으로
experiment[ikspérəmənt] 실험
stay up late 늦게까지 자지 않고 있다
[선택지]
upload[ʌ́plòud] 업로드하다

W Are you still sitting at your computer, Jack? It's past your bedtime.
M Okay, Mom. I'll go to bed in 5 minutes.
W You know you're not supposed to play computer games on school nights.
M I wasn't playing games. I was watching something online.
W What were you watching?
M Something for science class tomorrow. This video is about a science experiment.
W Okay, but I still don't want you to stay up late.
M I understand. I'll go to sleep after this video.

여 아직도 컴퓨터 앞에 앉아 있니, Jack? 잠잘 시간 지났는데.
남 알겠어요, 엄마. 5분 뒤에 자러갈게요.
여 학교 가기 전날 밤에는 컴퓨터 게임을 하지 않기로 한 것을 알잖니.
남 게임을 하고 있지 않았어요. 온라인으로 뭘 좀 보고 있었어요.
여 무엇을 보고 있었니?
남 내일 과학 수업에 필요한 거예요. 이 동영상은 과학 실험에 관한 거예요.
여 알았다. 하지만 네가 늦게까지 잠을 안 자고 있는 건 여전히 원치 않아.
남 알아요. 이 동영상만 보고 잘게요.

① 아니요, 제가 가장 좋아하는 과목은 과학이에요.
② 잘했어. 너는 잠을 좀 자야 해.
③ 너무 많이 게임을 하면 안 돼.
⑤ 지난달부터 이 동영상들을 업로드했어요.

20 ①

해설 떨어진 지갑을 주워서 여자에게 건네는 상황이다.

어휘 regular customer 단골손님
drop[drɑp] 떨어뜨리다
wallet[wɑ́lit] 지갑
grab[græb] 붙잡다.
run after ~을 따라가다. 뒤쫓다
be about to-v ~하려던 참이다
catch up to ~을 따라잡다
[선택지]
believe[bilíːv] 생각하다. 여기다

M Patrick is a regular customer at a cafe near the bus stop. He drinks his coffee while he waits for his bus to work. One day, he orders his coffee and starts to drink it. Then he sees a woman drop her wallet and leave the cafe. Patrick grabs the wallet and runs after her. When she is about to get on a bus, he finally catches up to her. In this situation, what would Patrick most likely say to the woman?

Patrick Excuse me, I believe this is yours.

남 Patrick은 버스정류장 근처에 있는 카페의 단골손님이다. 그는 직장으로 가는 버스를 기다리는 동안 커피를 마신다. 어느 날, 그는 커피를 주문하고 그것을 마시기 시작한다. 그리고 나서 그는 한 여자가 지갑을 떨어뜨리고 카페를 나서는 것을 본다. Patrick은 그 지갑을 들고 그녀를 따라간다. 그녀가 버스에 타려던 참에, 그는 드디어 그녀를 따라잡는다. 이러한 상황에서 Patrick이 그 여자에게 할 말로 가장 적절한 것은 무엇인가?

Patrick 실례합니다. 이건 당신 거 같아요

② 버스에서 뛰면 안 됩니다.
③ 커피 한 잔 드시겠어요?
④ 운전면허증을 보여주시겠습니까?
⑤ 이 버스는 도서관으로 가요.

01 ④	02 ⑤	03 ⑤	04 ④	05 ②	06 ④	07 ③
08 ①	09 ⑤	10 ②	11 ④	12 ①	13 ③	14 ⑤
15 ①	16 ③	17 ⑤	18 ④	19 ③	20 ⑤	

01 ④

[해설] 둥근 모양에 'Happy Birthday, Kate'라고 쓰인 케이크를 구매할 것이다.

[어휘] heart-shaped[háːrtʃèipt] 하트 모양의
round[raund] 둥근 모양의
minute[mínit] (시간 단위) 분

W Hello, how may I help you?
M Hi, I'm looking for a birthday cake for my daughter.
W Sure. We have many different kinds here.
M I like this heart-shaped one. Can you write my daughter's name on it?
W I'm sorry, but this cake is too small to write anything on it.
M I see. How about this one?
W Yes, this round one is big enough.
M If you could write "Happy Birthday, Kate" on the cake, that would be great.
W No problem. Just give me a few minutes.

여 어서 오세요. 무엇을 도와 드릴까요?
남 안녕하세요. 딸에게 줄 생일 케이크를 찾고 있어요.
여 그러시군요. 저희는 여기에 여러 가지 종류를 갖추고 있지요.
남 이 하트 모양이 맘에 드네요. 위에 딸의 이름을 써 줄 수 있나요?
여 죄송하지만 이 케이크는 너무 작아서 제가 그 위에 아무것도 쓸 수가 없네요.
남 알겠어요. 이건 어떤가요?
여 네, 이 둥근 케이크는 크기가 충분하네요.
남 'Happy Birthday, Kate'라고 케이크 위에 써 주시면 아주 좋을 것 같아요.
여 그럴게요. 몇 분만 기다리세요.

02 ⑤

[해설] 개최 요일(이번 주 토요일), 시작 장소(경기장), 종료 시각(밤 11시 30분), 참가비(무료)에 관해 언급되었지만 참가자 의상에 대해서는 언급되지 않았다.

[어휘] lantern[lǽntərn] 랜턴
participate in ~에 참가하다
parade[pəréid] 가두 행진, 퍼레이드
stadium[stéidiəm] 경기장
pretty[príti] 상당히
completely[kəmplíːtli] 완전히
free[friː] 무료인
show up 나타나다

W What are you making, Jake?
M I'm making a lantern.
W Are you going to participate in the Lantern Parade this Saturday?
M Yes, I am. It starts at the sports stadium and ends at the city hall.
W What time does the parade start?
M It starts at 7 p.m. and ends at 11:30 p.m.
W It ends pretty late. How much do you have to pay to participate?
M It's completely free. You just need to show up with your own lantern.

여 무엇을 만들고 있니, Jake?
남 랜턴을 만들고 있어.
여 이번 주 토요일에 열리는 랜턴 퍼레이드에 참가하려고?
남 그래, 맞아. 그 퍼레이드는 경기장에서 시작해서 시청에서 끝나.
여 퍼레이드는 몇 시에 시작하니?
남 오후 7시에 시작해서 11시 30분에 끝나.
여 상당히 늦게 끝나는구나. 참가하려면 얼마를 내야 하니?
남 완전히 무료야. 각자 자신의 랜턴을 갖고 나타나기만 하면 돼.

03 ⑤

[해설] 진료를 받으러 온 환자가 문이 잠겨있다며 병원에 들어가는 방법을 묻기 위해 전화했다.

[어휘] entrance[éntrəns] 입구
lock[lak] 잠그다
be located 위치해 있다
through[θruː] ~을 통해
employee[implɔííː] 직원, 종업원

[Telephone rings.]
W Riverside Hospital, how can I help you?
M Hi, I have a 3:30 appointment with Dr. Taylor. I'm at the entrance, but the door is locked.
W Are you on Peachtree Street right now?
M Yes, I am. Isn't that where you're located?
W You're at the back entrance. The front entrance is on Elm Street.
M Do I have to enter through the front entrance?

[전화벨이 울린다.]
여 Riverside 병원입니다. 무엇을 도와 드릴까요?
남 안녕하세요, 3시 30분에 Taylor 선생님과 진료 예약이 되어 있어요. 제가 입구에 있는데요, 문이 잠겨 있네요.
여 지금 Peachtree 가에 계신가요?
남 네, 그래요. 병원이 거기에 있지 않나요?
여 지금 후문에 계시네요. 정문은 Elm 가에 있어요.
남 정문을 통해서 들어가야 하나요?

W Yes, sir. The back entrance is for employees only.
M I see. Then I'll go through the front entrance.

여 그렇습니다. 후문은 직원들 전용이에요.
남 알겠습니다. 그럼 정문으로 들어갈게요.

04 ④

해설 친구가 1시까지 일해야 해서 12시 기차를 오후 2시로 변경했다고 했다.

어휘 pack[pæk] 짐을 싸다
already[ɔːlrédi] 이미, 벌써
catch[kætʃ] (차를) 잡아타다

W Paul, what are you still doing at home?
M I'm not done packing yet.
W But it's already 11 o'clock. You should be leaving for the station soon.
M I know, Mom. Don't worry. I still have enough time.
W Don't you have a 12 o'clock train to catch?
M No, I changed my train ticket to 2 o'clock in the afternoon.
W Why did you do that?
M My friend Jake said he had to work until 1 o'clock today.
W Okay. Then you'll have time for lunch, too.

여 Paul, 아직 집에서 뭐하고 있니?
남 아직도 짐을 챙기는 걸 끝내지 못했어요.
여 벌써 11시 정각이야. 곧 역으로 출발해야 하잖아.
남 알아요, 엄마. 걱정 마세요. 시간이 아직 충분해요.
여 12시 정각 기차를 타야 하지 않니?
남 아뇨, 기차표를 오후 2시 정각으로 바꿨어요.
여 왜 그랬니?
남 제 친구 Jake가 오늘 1시까지 일을 해야 한다고 했거든요.
여 알았어. 그럼 점심을 먹을 시간이 있겠구나.

05 ②

해설 여자는 휴대전화가 고장이 나게 된 계기를 설명하고, 남자는 내부를 확인해야 한다고 말하는 상황으로 보아 대화 장소는 휴대전화 수리점임을 알 수 있다.

어휘 pool[puːl] 수영장
remove[rimúːv] 제거하다
turn on (스위치 등을) 켜다
inside[insáid] 내부
chance[tʃæns] 가능성
work[wəːrk] 작동하다
would rather ~ than …하기보다는 ~하겠다
repair[ripɛ́ər] 수리하다
give it a try 한번 해 보다

W Can you check this for me?
M Sure. What's wrong with it?
W I dropped it in the pool. So I removed the battery and let the cell phone dry for a few days.
M Oh, I see. What else did you do?
W I tried to turn it on. But the cell phone wouldn't start.
M I have to open it and check the inside. But there is a chance that your cell phone might not work again.
W I understand, but I'd rather get it repaired than buy a new one.
M All right. I'll give it a try.

여 이것을 좀 점검해 주시겠어요?
남 물론 해 드리죠. 어디가 문제인가요?
여 그걸 수영장에 떨어뜨렸거든요. 그래서 배터리를 빼고 휴대전화를 며칠 동안 말렸어요.
남 아, 그렇군요. 그 밖에 하신 게 있나요?
여 전원을 켜보려고 했어요. 하지만 휴대전화가 작동하지 않았어요.
남 열어 보고 내부를 점검해야겠네요. 하지만 고객님의 휴대전화가 다시 작동을 하지 않을 수도 있어요.
여 이해하지만 새것을 사는 것보단 차라리 이걸 수리했으면 해요.
남 그러시군요. 한번 해 보겠습니다.

06 ④

해설 화장지가 어디에 있는지 물어보는 남자에게 다 떨어졌다고 응답하는 상황이다.

어휘 cold[kould] 추위를 느끼는
toilet paper 화장지
out of ~이 없는
take a break (잠시) 휴식을 취하다

① M Can you open the window?
　W Sorry, I can't. I'm a little cold.
② M What would you like to order?
　W Can you give me a minute? I'm not ready yet.
③ M Could you give me the menu?
　W Of course, sir. Here it is.
④ M Where can I find toilet paper?
　W I'm sorry. We're out of toilet paper right now.

① 남 창문 좀 열어 주시겠어요?
　여 미안하지만 안돼요. 제가 약간 추워서요.
② 남 무엇을 주문하시겠습니까?
　여 잠깐만 시간을 주시겠어요? 아직 준비가 안 되었어요.
③ 남 메뉴판 좀 주시겠어요?
　여 그럼요, 고객님. 여기 있습니다.
④ 남 화장지가 어디에 있나요?
　여 죄송합니다. 화장지가 지금 떨어졌네요.

⑤ **M** Do you want to play another game?
　　W No, I need to take a break.

⑤ 남　다른 게임을 하고 싶니?
　　여　아니. 난 좀 쉬어야겠어.

07　③

[해설] 남자는 여자에게 자신의 야구 방망이가 어디에도 보이지 않는다고 하면서 찾아 달라고 부탁했다.

[어휘] finally[fáinəli] 마침내, 드디어
half an hour 30분
find A ~ A에게 ~을 찾아 주다
basement[béismənt] 지하실

W The rain has finally stopped.
M I know. The sun is out again, so I'm going to the park.
W Are you going to play baseball with your friends today?
M Yes, I'm meeting with them in half an hour.
W Then you should hurry up and finish your lunch.
M Okay, I will. Oh, can you find me my baseball bat? I don't see it anywhere.
W Okay. I'll go and check the basement first.

여　비가 드디어 멈췄구나.
남　그래요. 해가 다시 났네요. 그래서 공원에 가려고 해요.
여　오늘 친구들과 야구 시합을 할 거니?
남　네. 30분 뒤에 친구들을 만날 거예요.
여　그러면 서둘러서 점심 식사를 끝내야겠네.
남　알겠어요. 그럴게요. 아, 제 야구 방망이를 좀 찾아 주실래요? 어디에도 보이지 않아서요.
여　그래. 먼저 지하실에 가서 확인해 볼게.

08　①

[해설] 개장 시간(오전 6시 ~ 오후 10시), 휴무일(일요일), 등록 조건(강사에게 레벨 테스트 받기), 등록 기간(매달 1일 ~ 5일)에 관해 언급되었지만 위치에 대해서는 언급되지 않았다.

[어휘] take lessons 강습을 받다
instructor[instrʌ́ktər] 강사
register[rédʒistər] 등록하다

M Welcome to Swim Boston, everyone. If you want to become a better swimmer, you've come to the right place. We're open from 6 a.m. to 10 p.m. from Monday to Saturday. We're closed on Sundays. If you want to take swim lessons, you must take a level test with one of our instructors. Anyone who wants to take lessons needs to register between the 1st and 5th of each month.

남　Swim Boston에 오신 것을 환영합니다. 여러분. 수영을 더 잘하고 싶으시다면 여러분은 제대로 찾아오신 겁니다. 저희는 월요일부터 토요일까지 아침 6시에서 밤 10시까지 엽니다. 일요일에는 문을 닫습니다. 수영 강습을 원하시면 저희의 강사들 중 한 분에게 레벨 테스트를 받아야 합니다. 강습을 원하시는 분은 매달 1일에서 5일 사이에 등록을 하셔야 합니다.

09　⑤

[해설] 뿌리채소로 비타민 A가 풍부해 눈에 좋고 달콤한 맛이 나며 말이나 토끼가 즐겨 먹는 채소는 당근이다.

[어휘] vegetable[védʒitəbl] 야채
stick[stik] 막대기
be rich in ~이 풍부하다
flavor[fléivər] 맛
though[ðou] 비록 ~일지라도

W This is a root vegetable that looks like a stick. This is very rich in vitamin A, so it can keep our eyes healthy. Many people like to put this vegetable in many dishes because it has a sweet flavor. Though many children don't like this very much, animals like horses and rabbits enjoy it.

여　이것은 막대기처럼 보이는 뿌리채소이다. 이것은 비타민 A가 아주 풍부해서 우리의 눈을 건강하게 지켜 줄 수 있다. 많은 사람들이 달콤한 맛 때문에 이 야채를 많은 요리에 넣는다. 이것을 그다지 좋아하지 않는 어린이들이 많지만 말이나 토끼와 같은 동물들은 이것을 즐겨 먹는다.

10　②

[해설] 오늘 밤에 무엇을 하고 싶은 지 묻는 질문에 대해 먹고 싶은 음식을 말하는 응답은 어색하다.

① **M** It's 4:15. You're late again.
　　W I thought the meeting was at 4:30.
② **M** What would you like to do tonight?
　　W I'd like a cheeseburger and a coke.

① 남　4시 15분이야. 너 또 늦었구나.
　　여　모임이 4시 30분인 줄 알았어.
② 남　오늘 밤에 뭘 하고 싶니?
　　여　치즈 버거 하나와 콜라 한 잔을 원해요.

어휘 terrible[térəbl] 끔찍한
fever[fíːvər] 열
temperature[témpərətʃər] 체온, 기온
press[pres] 누르다
abroad[əbrɔ́ːd] 해외에서, 해외로

③ **M** I feel terrible and I think I <u>have a fever</u>.
　W Let me take your temperature.
④ **M** Could you take a picture of us?
　W Sure. Do I <u>press this button</u>?
⑤ **M** <u>Have you been to</u> Rome in Italy?
　W No, I've never been abroad.

③ 남 나 몸이 안 좋고 열이 있는 것 같아.
　여 네 체온을 재 볼게.
④ 남 저희의 사진을 좀 찍어 주시겠어요?
　여 그러죠. 이 버튼을 누르면 되나요?
⑤ 남 이탈리아의 로마에 가본 적 있니?
　여 아니, 나는 해외에 나가 본 적이 없어.

11 ④

해설 여행을 가자고 제안하는 여자에게
남자는 어디로 가면 좋을지를 안다고 하
면서 묵을 장소부터 찾아보겠다고 했다.

어휘 go hiking 하이킹[등산]가다
that way 그런 식으로
go on a trip 여행을 가다
go away 집을 떠나다
exactly[igzǽktli] 정확히

W Dad, why don't we do something fun together more often?
M We went hiking last weekend. Wasn't it fun?
W Well, it was <u>more like exercising</u>.
M Oh, I didn't see it that way. Do you want to go to the movies this weekend then?
W How about <u>going on a trip</u>?
M That's a good idea. We <u>can go away</u> for a few days.
W Great! Mom will love that, too.
M In fact, I know exactly where we should go. I'll look for <u>a place to stay</u>.

여 아빠, 우리 재미있는 걸 좀 더 자주 하면 어때요?
남 지난 주말에 하이킹을 갔잖아. 재미없었니?
여 음, 운동하는 느낌이 더 컸어요.
남 아, 나는 그렇게 생각하지 않았는데. 그럼 이번 주말에 영화 보러 갈래?
여 여행을 가는 건 어때요?
남 좋은 생각이야. 며칠 동안 갔다 올 수 있지.
여 신난다! 엄마도 정말 좋아하실 거예요.
남 사실, 나는 우리가 어디로 가면 좋을 지 잘 알고 있거든. 묵을 곳을 찾아볼게.

12 ①

해설 유선이고, 검은색이며 60달러 미만
의 이어폰을 선택했다.

어휘 wired[waiərd] 유선의
wireless[wáiərlis] 무선의
convenient[kənvíːnjənt] 편리한
have ~ in mind ~을 마음에 두다
particular[pərtíkjulər] 특정한, 특별한
bright[brait] (색상이) 밝은, 선명한
spend[spend] (비용·시간 등을) 쓰다
[선택지]
wire[waiər] 선, 줄

M Excuse me. Can you help me choose earphones?
W Of course. Would you like wired ones or wireless ones?
M I heard wireless ones are really convenient. But I <u>prefer wired ones</u>.
W Sure. Do you have any particular color in mind?
M Black. I don't want my earphones <u>to be too bright</u>.
W I understand. There are 2 models to choose from.
M Hmm... I don't want to <u>spend more than</u> $60.
W Then these ones are <u>the perfect earphones</u> for you.

남 실례합니다. 저 이어폰 고르는 것 좀 도와 주실래요?
여 물론이죠. 선이 있는 것이 좋으세요, 무선으로 된 것이 좋으세요?
남 무선 이어폰이 정말 편리하다고 들었어요. 근데 전 유선 이어폰이 더 좋아요.
여 네. 특별히 마음에 두신 색상이 있으세요?
남 검은색이요. 제 이어폰이 너무 밝지 않은 게 좋아서요.
여 알겠습니다. 고를 수 있는 모델이 두 가지 남았어요.
남 음… 60달러 이상 쓰고 싶지 않아요.
여 그러면 이게 고객님에게 맞는 이어폰이네요.

13 ③

해설 영화제는 10월 10일보다 3일 이른
7일에 시작한다고 했다.

어휘 grandparent[grǽndpɛ̀ərənt]
조부[모]

M What are you doing this weekend, Rachel?
W I'm going to Busan with my family.
M Are you visiting your grandparents in Busan?

남 이번 주말에 뭘 할 예정이니, Rachel?
여 가족과 함께 부산에 가려고 해.
남 부산에 계신 조부모님을 방문할 거니?

international[intərnǽʃənəl] 국제의
festival[féstivəl] 축제, 기념제
weekday[wíkdèi] 평일
run[rʌn] (어느 기간 동안) 계속되다

W Yes, we are, and we're <u>also going to</u> the Busan International Film Festival on Saturday the 10th.
M Oh, right. The festival is held <u>in October every year</u>, isn't it?
W Yes. This year <u>it will start</u> on the 7th.
M Really? Why does it <u>start on a weekday</u>?
W The festival runs for 10 days, so it <u>will end on Friday</u> the 16th.
M Oh, I see. I hope you have fun!

여 응, 그럴 거야. 하지만 우리는 토요일인 10일에 부산 국제 영화제에도 가려고 해.
남 맞다. 벌써 10월이구나. 영화제가 이번 주말에 시작하니?
여 아니, 사실은 사흘 일찍 7일에 시작해.
남 정말? 왜 주 중에 시작하지?
여 축제가 10일 동안 계속되고 그래서 금요일인 16일에 끝날 예정이야.
남 아, 알겠네. 재미있는 시간을 보내기 바랄게!

14 ⑤

해설 남자는 어제 친구가 개업한 도넛 가게에 가서 친구를 도와줬다고 했다.

어휘 donut[dóunət] 도넛
near[niər] ~ 근처에
get a discount 할인을 받다

W The meeting was really long today.
M I know. I couldn't <u>keep my eyes open</u>.
W Do you want to go and get some coffee?
M Yes. Let's go to the donut place near the subway station.
W The donut place? I've <u>never heard of it</u> before. Is it new?
M Yes. One of my friends <u>opened it yesterday</u>. I went there <u>and helped him</u>.
W That's great. Can we get a discount?
M Of course. <u>I'll buy some</u> donuts for you.

여 오늘 회의가 정말 길었네요.
남 맞아요. 저는 눈을 뜨고 있을 수가 없었어요.
여 가서 커피 좀 마실래요?
남 그래요. 지하철역 근처에 있는 도넛 가게로 가요.
여 도넛 가게요? 전에 들어본 적이 없는데. 새로 생긴 곳인가요?
남 네. 어제 제 친구 중 한 명이 그 가게를 개업해서 가서 도와줬거든요.
여 잘됐네요. 도넛을 할인받을 수 있나요?
남 물론이죠. 제가 도넛을 좀 사드릴게요.

15 ①

해설 좋은 구직자를 찾는 데 효과적이라고 하면서 구인 앱을 홍보하는 내용이다.

어휘 efficient[ifíʃənt] 효과적인, 효율적인
app(= application)[æp] 지원서, 신청서; 어플리케이션
as a result 결과적으로
have a better chance to-v
~할 가능성이 높다
filter[fíltər] 여과하다, 거르다
tool[tu:l] 도구, 장치
in no time 즉시

M Hello, listeners. Have you been looking for a more efficient way to <u>find new employees</u>? <u>Download</u> <u>our new app</u> "Find Employees Fast" and you will be able to find more people. As a result, you will have a better chance <u>of finding great people</u> for your job. The smart filtering tools in our app will help you <u>get the right employee</u> in no time!

남 청취자 여러분, 안녕하세요. 새 직원을 구하는 보다 효과적인 방법을 찾고 계신가요? 그렇다면 저희의 새로운 앱 '직원 빨리 찾기'를 다운로드하면 더 많은 사람들을 찾을 수 있을 겁니다. 그 결과로, 여러분의 직장에 맞는 훌륭한 지원자를 찾게 될 가능성이 높아질 것입니다. 우리 앱의 똑똑한 필터 도구가 적합한 직원을 즉시 찾을 수 있도록 도울 겁니다!

16 ③

해설 1달러짜리 베이글을 12개의 가격으로 13개를 살 수 있다고 하자, 여자는 13개를 구매하겠다고 했으므로 지불할 금액은 12달러이다.

어휘 bagel[béigəl] 베이글 (도넛같이 생긴 딱딱한 빵)

M Good morning, and welcome to Rick's Bagels.
W How much are these plain bagels?
M One plain bagel is $1.
W Okay, I'll get 10 of them.
M If you want 10 plain bagels, you <u>might as well buy</u> a dozen of them.

남 안녕하세요, Rick's Bagels에 오신 것을 환영합니다.
여 이 플레인 베이글은 얼마죠?
남 플레인 베이글 하나에 1달러입니다.
여 알겠어요. 10개 주세요.
남 플레인 베이글 10개를 원하시면 한 다스를 사는 게 낫습니다.

plain[plein] 첨가물을 넣지 않은
might as well-v ~하는 편이 낫다
dozen[dʌ́zən] 12개(짜리 묶음), 다스
baker's dozen 13개(짜리 묶음)

W Why is that?
M Because you get 13 bagels for the price of 12 bagles.
W Does that mean I get one more bagle?
M Yes, that's right. It's called a baker's dozen.
W That sounds good. I'll get a baker's dozen then.

여 왜 그렇죠?
남 베이글 12개 가격으로 13개를 살 수 있기 때문입니다.
여 베이글을 하나 더 얻는다는 뜻인가요?
남 네, 맞습니다. 그것이 제빵사의 한 다스라고 불리는 거예요.
여 좋아요. 그럼 제빵사의 한 다스를 구입할게요.

17 ⑤

[해설] Taylor가 언제 한국에 방문할 지 남자의 생각을 묻는 여자의 말에 가능한 빨리 한국에 올 거라고 대답하는 것이 자연스럽다.

[어휘] latest[léitist] 최근의, 최신의
suddenly[sʌ́dnli] 갑자기
cancel[kǽnsəl] 취소하다
disappointing[dìsəpɔ́intiŋ]
실망스러운
be in the hospital 입원해 있다
recover[rikʌ́vər] 회복하다
[선택지]
reservation[rèzərvéiʃən] 예약
as soon as ~ 하자마자

W I can't believe this is happening.
M What's wrong, Samantha?
W Have you heard the latest news about Taylor's world tour concerts?
M Oh, yes. They suddenly got canceled. How disappointing!
W I know. She was supposed to come to Korea next week.
M I heard she's in the hospital in Japan now. I hope she recovers soon.
W When do you think she'll be able to come to Korea?
M I'm sure she'll come as soon as she can.

여 이런 일이 일어나고 있다는 것이 믿어지지 않아.
남 무슨 일인데, Samantha?
여 Taylor의 월드 투어 콘서트에 관련된 최근 뉴스 들었어?
남 아, 들었어. 콘서트들이 갑자기 취소되었지. 너무 실망스러웠어!
여 맞아. 그녀가 다음 주에 한국에 오기로 되어 있었어.
남 지금 일본에 입원해 있다고 들었어. 그녀가 곧 회복되면 좋겠어.
여 그녀가 언제 한국에 올 수 있을 거라고 생각하니?
남 분명히 그녀는 가능한 한 빨리 올 거야.

① 나는 그녀가 지난주에 한국에 있었다고 들었어.
② 당신은 예약을 취소할 수 없어요.
③ 대신 그녀는 다음 주에 중국에 갈 예정이야.
④ 너랑 같이 콘서트에 간다면 좋을 텐데.

18 ④

[해설] 운동회 경기에 참가하는지 묻는 남자의 말에 참가한다는 말과 함께 구체적으로 어떤 경기에 참가하는지 답하는 응답이 가장 자연스럽다.

[어휘] final match 최종 결승전
semi-final match 준결승전
Good luck on ~. ~에 대해 행운이 있기를 빌어.
[선택지]
cheer for ~를 응원하다
relay race 릴레이 경주, 계주

M Sports day is this Friday, right?
W Yes, it is. Are you participating in any event?
M Yes. I'm on the soccer team for my class.
W Is your team going to play in the final match this Friday?
M Oh, we're having our semi-final match after school today. We have to win today to go to the finals.
W Wow, your team must be really good. Good luck on your match today.
M Thank you. How about you? Are you participating in any event?
W Yes, I am. I'm running in the relay race.

남 운동회가 이번 주 금요일이야. 맞지?
여 응, 맞아. 참가하기로 한 경기가 있니?
남 나는 우리 반 축구팀에 있어.
여 너희들 이번 금요일에 결승전에서 경기하니?
남 아, 오늘 방과 후에 준결승전을 해. 결승전에 가려면 오늘 이겨야 하거든.
여 와, 너희 팀 정말 잘하는구나. 오늘 너희 경기에 행운이 있기를 빌게.
남 고마워. 너는 어때? 어떤 경기라도 참여할 거니?
여 응, 나는 릴레이 경주에서 달리기를 할 예정이야.

① 너는 내가 아는 가장 빠른 달리기 선수야.
② 이번 주 금요일에 너를 응원할게.
③ 나는 오늘 방과 후에 너를 태우러 올 수 없어.
⑤ 아니, 나는 너희 시합에 갈 수 없을 거야.

19 ③

해설 드론으로 마을 전체를 촬영할 수 있다는 여자의 말에 사진이 잘 나오기를 바란다는 응답이 이어지는 것이 자연스럽다.

어휘 peaceful[píːsfəl] 평화로운
village[vílidʒ] 마을, 부락
whole[houl] 전체의, 전부의
drone[droun] 드론 (지상에서 조종하는 무인 항공기)
[선택지]
turn out ~한 결과가 되다
get on 탑승하다
fly[flai] 비행하다

W This place is so beautiful, isn't it?
M It really is. I've never been to such a beautiful and peaceful place as this before.
W Did you take many pictures of the village?
M I took a few, but I need to go to a higher place.
W Why do you need to do that?
M I want to take a picture of the whole village.
W Well, that's why I brought this drone. We can take pictures of the whole village with this here.
M That's great. I hope the pictures turn out great.

여 이곳은 정말 아름다워, 그렇지 않니?
남 정말 그래. 나는 이곳처럼 아름답고 평화로운 곳에 와 본 적이 없어.
여 마을 사진을 많이 찍었니?
남 몇 장 찍었는데, 더 높은 위치로 가야겠어.
여 왜 그래야 하는데?
남 마을 전체가 나오는 사진을 찍고 싶거든.
여 음, 그래서 내가 이 드론을 갖고 왔지. 이걸로 여기서 마을 전체가 나오는 사진을 찍을 수 있어.
남 잘됐다. 사진들이 잘 나왔으면 좋겠네.

① 미안, 그 마을이 어디에 있는지 모르겠어.
② 드론을 띄우기 위해 더 높은 곳으로 가자.
④ 내가 그 드론의 사진을 찍어 줄까?
⑤ 나는 이미 마을 전체 사진을 몇 장 찍었어.

20 ⑤

해설 세탁기 사용법에 대해서 여자에게 물어보려고 하는 상황이다.

어휘 coin laundry 셀프서비스 세탁소
recently[ríːsəntli] 최근에
move from ~에서 이사하다
particular[pərtíkjulər] 특정한, 특별한
how to-v ~하는 방법
laundry[lɔ́ːndri] 세탁물
washing machine 세탁기
look around 주위를 둘러 보다

W Paul is in a coin laundry. He has recently moved from a different city and has never been to this particular coin laundry. He needs to wash all his blankets but does not know how to use big washing machines. He looks around to see if he can get some help. Then he finds a woman putting her laundry in one of the big washing machines. In this situation, what would Paul most likely say to the woman?

Paul Excuse me, can you show me how to use this washing machine?

여 Paul은 셀프서비스 세탁소에 있다. 그는 최근에 다른 도시에서 이사 왔는데 이 특별한 셀프서비스 세탁소에는 와 본 적이 없다. 그는 자기의 담요를 모두 세탁해야 하지만 큰 세탁기를 사용하는 법을 모른다. 그는 도움을 얻을 수 있는지를 알아보기 위해 주변을 둘러본다. 그때 한 여자가 큰 세탁기 중 하나에 담요들을 넣고 있는 것을 발견한다. 이러한 상황에서 Paul이 그 여자에게 할 말로 가장 적절한 것은 무엇인가?

Paul 실례합니다. 이 세탁기 사용법 좀 알려 주시겠어요?

① 당신의 담요를 모두 어디에서 샀죠?
② 이 세탁기는 가격이 얼마죠?
③ 이 도시에 얼마나 오래 사셨나요?
④ 이 셀프서비스 세탁소가 오늘 언제 문을 닫나요?

01 ④	02 ②	03 ⑤	04 ⑤	05 ④	06 ④	07 ⑤
08 ④	09 ②	10 ⑤	11 ⑤	12 ④	13 ④	14 ②
15 ①	16 ②	17 ④	18 ②	19 ④	20 ⑤	

01 ④

해설 독특한 디자인을 찾고 있는 남자는 손이 그려진 것을 사겠다고 했다.

어휘 sleep mask 수면 안대
particular[pərtíkjulər] 특별한
pressure[préʃər] 압박
unique[juːníːk] 독특한

W Hello. May I help you?
M Yes, please. I'm looking for a sleep mask for travelers. I can't sleep well on planes.
W Is there any particular design you want?
M Well, I want one that doesn't put pressure on my eyes while I sleep.
W Okay. Is there anything else?
M I want one with a unique design.
W Then how about these ones with the pictures of eyes or glasses on them?
M They're not bad, but I think that one with hands on it is better. I'll take that one.

여 안녕하세요. 도와드릴까요?
남 네. 여행자를 위한 수면 안대를 찾고 있어요. 비행기에서는 잠을 잘 못 자서요.
여 특별히 원하는 디자인이 있으신가요?
남 음, 제가 자는 동안 눈을 압박하지 않는 것이었으면 좋겠어요.
여 알겠습니다. 그 외에 다른 게 있나요?
남 그리고 독특한 디자인을 원해요.
여 그렇다면 눈이나 안경 그림이 그려진 이것들은 어떠세요?
남 나쁘진 않지만 손이 그려진 저게 더 좋은 것 같아요. 저걸 살게요.

02 ②

해설 주소(Pine 가 120번지), 층수(2층), 침실 개수(2개), 마당(넓고 수영장이 있음)에 대해 언급했지만, 지붕에 대해서는 언급하지 않았다.

어휘 two-story house 2층집
downstairs[dáunstéərz] 아래층에
upstairs[ʌ́pstéərz] 위층에, 2층에

M Look. This is a picture of my new house.
W Oh, where do you live now?
M At 120 Pine Street.
W It's a two-story house, isn't it?
M Yes. Downstairs, there are a living room, a kitchen and a guest room.
W How about upstairs?
M There are 2 bedrooms and a bathroom.
W Do you have a yard?
M Yes, I have a big yard. And there's a small swimming pool in it.
W Nice! I'd like to visit your house sometime.

남 봐. 이건 우리 새 집 사진이야.
여 아, 지금 어디 사는데?
남 Pine 가 120번지에 살아.
여 2층집이네, 그렇지?
남 응. 아래층에는 거실과 부엌과 손님방이 있어.
여 위층은?
남 침실 두 개와 욕실이 있어.
여 마당이 있니?
남 응. 큰 마당이 있어. 그리고 거기에 작은 수영장도 있어.
여 멋지겠다! 나중에 너희 집에 한번 가보고 싶어.

03 ⑤

해설 Chris가 휴대전화를 받지 않자, 집 전화번호를 물어보기 위해 남자가 여자에게 전화를 걸었다.

어휘 borrow[bárou] 빌리다
text message 문자 메시지

[Cell phone rings.]
W Hello.
M Hi, Jane. This is Paul. Do you know where Chris is?
W I think he's at home now. He has to study for an exam.
M I called him on his cell phone to borrow his book, but he didn't answer. Do you know his home number?
W Let me check. *[Pause]* Yes, I have his home number. Do you want it?

[휴대전화가 울린다.]
여 여보세요.
남 안녕, Jane. 나 Paul이야. Chris가 어디 있는지 아니?
여 지금 집에 있는 것 같아. 걔는 시험공부를 해야 하잖아.
남 책을 빌리려고 걔 휴대전화로 전화를 걸었는데 받지를 않네. 걔네 집 전화번호 아니?
여 확인해볼게. *[잠시 후]* 응. 나 걔네 집 전화번호 있어. 알려줄까?

| M | Yes, please. Can you send it to me by text message right away? | 남 | 응, 부탁해. 지금 바로 문자로 보내 줄 수 있어? |
| W | Sure. | 여 | 물론이지. |

04 ⑤

<u>해설</u> 토요일은 3시, 일요일은 7시 공연 중에서 두 사람은 일요일 공연을 보기로 했다.

<u>어휘</u> on sale 판매 중인
book[buk] 예매[예약]하다
online[ɔ́nlàin] 온라인의
showing[ʃóuiŋ] 공연, 상영

M	The tickets for Teen Music Fest are on sale now.	남	Teen Music Fest 티켓이 지금 판매 중이야.
W	Let's book the tickets online right away.	여	지금 바로 온라인으로 예매하자.
M	Okay. [Pause] There are still tickets left for 3 o'clock on Saturday and 7 o'clock on Sunday.	남	그래. [잠시 후] 토요일 3시와 일요일 7시 티켓이 아직 남아 있어.
W	Really? I want to go to the festival on Saturday. How about you?	여	정말? 나는 토요일 페스티벌에 가고 싶은데. 너는 어때?
M	Oh, I have a swimming lesson this Saturday until 5. Can we go to the festival on Sunday evening?	남	아, 이번 주 토요일 5시까지 수영 강습이 있어. 일요일 저녁 페스티벌에 갈 수 있니?
W	Sure. Sunday is fine with me.	여	그래. 일요일도 좋아.
M	Then I'll get 2 tickets for the 7 o'clock showing.	남	그럼 7시 공연의 티켓을 두 장 살게.
W	Okay. I can't wait to go to the festival!	여	그래. 빨리 페스티벌에 가고 싶다!

05 ④

<u>해설</u> 음식이 너무 덜 익었다고 불만을 표시하고 있는 상황이다.

<u>어휘</u> convenient[kənví:njənt] 편리한
Vietnamese[viètnə:mí:z] 베트남의
rare[rɛər] 살짝 익힌

① M	You can book that restaurant online.	① 남	그 식당은 온라인으로 예약할 수 있어.
W	Oh, I see. How convenient!	여	아, 그래. 정말 편리하네!
② M	What would you like to drink?	② 남	음료는 뭐로 하시겠습니까?
W	I'd like a glass of mango juice.	여	망고주스 한 잔 주세요.
③ M	Shall we try that new Vietnamese restaurant?	③ 남	새로 생긴 베트남 식당에 가 볼까?
W	Sure. I hope there isn't a long line right now.	여	좋아. 지금 줄이 길지 않았으면 좋겠다.
④ M	Are you enjoying your meal?	④ 남	식사 맛있게 하고 계신가요?
W	Not really. This steak is too rare for me.	여	그렇지 않아요. 이 스테이크가 너무 덜 익었어요.
⑤ M	Do you mind if I sit here?	⑤ 남	여기에 앉아도 되나요?
W	Sorry, but I'm waiting for my friend.	여	미안하지만, 친구를 기다리고 있어요.

06 ④

<u>해설</u> 여자가 태국 요리책을 추천해 달라고 했고 남자가 책을 추천해주며 할인 중이라고 설명하는 것으로 보아 대화 장소는 서점이다.

<u>어휘</u> Thai[tai] 태국의
cookbook[kúkbùk] 요리책
recommend[rèkəménd] 추천하다
beginner[bigínər] 초보자
choice[tʃɔis] 선택

M	Hello. How may I help you?	남	안녕하세요. 무엇을 도와드릴까요?
W	I'm looking for a Thai cookbook. Can you recommend one?	여	태국 요리책을 찾고 있어요. 한 권 추천해 주실래요?
M	Okay. Have you ever cooked Thai food?	남	그러죠. 태국 음식을 만들어 본 적 있으세요?
W	No, I haven't, but I love eating Thai food.	여	아니요. 만들어 본 적은 없지만 태국 음식 먹는 걸 좋아해요.
M	Well, we have some Thai cookbooks for beginners. Come this way, please.	남	음, 초보자를 위한 태국 요리책이 몇 권 있어요. 이쪽으로 오세요.
W	[Pause] Oh, how about this one? This book looks good to me.	여	[잠시 후] 아, 이 책은 어떤가요? 이 책이 저에게 맞을 것 같아요.

M　Good choice. And it's 20% off now.
W　Great! Thank you so much. I'll take it.

남　잘 고르셨어요. 그리고 그 책은 지금 20% 할인 중이에요.
여　잘됐네요! 정말 고마워요. 이걸로 살게요.

07 ⑤

[해설] 남자는 우산과 비옷 챙기는 것을 잊었다고 하며 여자에게 우산을 찾아 달라고 부탁했다.

[어휘] miss[mis] ~을 빼먹다, 놓치다
exchange[ikstʃéindʒ] 환전하다
pack[pæk] 짐을 싸다
closet[klázit] 옷장

W　Billy, are you ready for your trip tomorrow?
M　Yes, but I feel like I'm missing something.
W　Oh, where did you put your passport?
M　It's in my backpack.
W　Good. Did you exchange money?
M　No, but I'm going to do that at the airport.
W　Okay. You checked the weather in Rome before you packed your clothes, right?
M　Of course, I did. [Pause] Oh, I forgot to pack an umbrella and a raincoat. Can you find me a small umbrella?
W　Sure. Your raincoat should be in the closet.
M　Okay. Thanks, Mom.

여　Billy, 내일 여행 갈 준비됐니?
남　네, 하지만 뭔가 빠뜨린 것 같아요.
여　아, 여권은 어디에 두었니?
남　그건 제 배낭 안에 있어요.
여　잘했다. 환전은 했니?
남　아니요, 하지만 공항에서 할 거예요.
여　좋아. 옷을 챙기기 전에 로마의 날씨는 확인했지?
남　물론 그렇게 했어요. [잠시 후] 아, 우산과 비옷 챙기는 것을 잊었네요. 작은 우산 좀 찾아 주실래요?
여　그럴게. 네 비옷은 옷장에 있을거야.
남　알겠어요. 고마워요, 엄마.

08 ④

[해설] 위치(뉴욕), 건물 설계자(Frank Lloyd Wright), 건물 외형(찻잔처럼 보임), 일일 투어(미술관 교육자들이 진행함)에 관해 언급되었지만 주요 전시물에 대한 언급은 없다.

[어휘] work of art 미술 작품
architect[á:rkətèkt] 건축가
shape[ʃeip] 모양
teacup[tíkəp] 찻잔
sculpture[skʌ́lptʃər] 조각품
educator[édʒukèitər] 교육자

M　Welcome to the Guggenheim Museum in New York. You'll find beautiful works of art here, but the building itself is a work of art. Frank Lloyd Wright, an American architect, designed the building to be such a unique shape. The outside looks like a teacup. If you go inside, you'll feel like you're walking in a big sculpture. If you want to know more about this museum, join the daily tour led by museum educators.

남　뉴욕의 Guggenheim 미술관에 오신 걸 환영합니다. 여러분은 이곳에서 아름다운 미술 작품들을 볼 수 있지만, 건물 자체도 예술 작품입니다. 미국 건축가인 Frank Lloyd Wright가 이 건물을 이처럼 독특한 모양으로 설계했습니다. 바깥은 찻잔처럼 보입니다. 안으로 들어가면 마치 커다란 조각품 안을 걷는 듯한 느낌을 받을 것입니다. 이 미술관에 대해 더 많은 것을 알고 싶다면, 미술관 교육자들이 이끄는 일일 투어에 참여해 보세요.

09 ②

[해설] 입출국할 때 신분을 확인할 수 있는 문서이며 사진, 국적, 도장 찍을 자리 등이 있는 것은 여권이다.

[어휘] official document 공문서
identify[aidéntəfài] (본인임을) 확인하다
contain[kəntéin] 포함하다
nationality[næ̀ʃənǽləti] 국적
blank[blæŋk] 백지의, 공백의
abroad[əbrɔ́:d] 해외로
apply for ~을 신청하다
city hall 시청, 시 당국

W　This is an official document that identifies you. This contains your photo, name, date of birth, your nationality, and some blank pages for stamps. If you don't have this when you're planning a trip abroad, you have to go to a city hall and apply for this. When you leave your country and enter another country at an airport, you must show this.

여　이것은 당신의 신분을 확인해 주는 공문서이에요. 이것에는 사진, 이름, 생년월일, 국적, 그리고 도장을 찍게 될 빈 페이지가 몇 장 들어 있어요. 해외여행을 계획하고 있는데 이것이 없다면, 시청에 가서 신청해야 해요. 공항에서 나라를 떠나거나 다른 나라에 들어갈 때는 이것을 보여 줘야 해요.

10 ⑤

해설 캠프가 어땠는지 묻는 말에 하이킹을 좋아하는 이유를 말하는 것은 어색하다.

어휘 surprise[sərpráiz] 놀라움
invention[invénʃən] 발명품
play[plei] 연극
go hiking 하이킹을 하다
wild[waild] 야생의

① M Hi, Sandy. What a surprise!
   W Hi, Jimin. I'm glad we're in the same class.
② M I think chocolate is the greatest invention.
   W I agree. It makes me feel good.
③ M You look so worried.
   W I'm nervous that I might make a mistake in the school play.
④ M Ben won first prize on the quiz show.
   W Really? I'm so happy for him.
⑤ M How did you like the camp?
   W I like to go hiking because I can see wild birds.

① 남 안녕, Sandy. 놀랍다!
   여 안녕, 지민아. 우리가 같은 반이 돼서 너무 좋아.
② 남 나는 초콜릿이 가장 위대한 발명품이라고 생각해.
   여 동의해. 나를 기분 좋게 하거든.
③ 남 너 정말 걱정돼 보여.
   여 학교 연극에서 실수를 할까 봐 긴장돼서 그래.
④ 남 Ben이 퀴즈 쇼에서 1등을 했어.
   여 정말? 너무 잘 됐다.
⑤ 남 캠프는 어땠어?
   여 나는 산새를 볼 수 있기 때문에 하이킹 가는 걸 좋아해.

11 ⑤

해설 여자가 남자의 땅콩버터를 먹어서 더러워진 개를 목욕시키라고 했고 남자가 그러겠다고 했다.

어휘 jar[dʒɑːr] (특히 잼을 담아 두는) 병
peanut butter 땅콩버터
make a mess 엉망으로 만들다
fault[fɔːlt] 잘못
go around 돌아다니다

M Mom, where is Buddy? I want to take him for a walk.
W I think I saw him go into your bedroom.
M Oh no! I left a jar of peanut butter on my desk.
W Hurry before he makes a mess in your room.
M It's too late. Look at him. He has peanut butter all over his face.
W It's your fault to leave peanut butter in your room. You should give him a bath now. I don't want Buddy to go around with peanut butter on him.
M Okay, I will.

남 엄마, Buddy 어디에 있어요? 산책시키려고요.
여 네 방에 들어가는 걸 본 것 같구나.
남 이런! 저 책상 위에 땅콩버터를 올려두었어요.
여 방을 엉망으로 만들기 전에 서두르렴.
남 너무 늦었어요. 걔를 보세요. 얼굴 전체에 땅콩버터가 묻어있어요.
여 네 방에 땅콩버터를 둔 네 잘못이지. 지금 목욕시키는 게 좋겠구나. 땅콩버터를 얼굴에 묻힌 채로 돌아다니지 않았으면 좋겠어.
남 알겠어요, 그렇게 할게요.

12 ④

해설 두 사람은 요리 리얼리티 쇼를 보기로 하였으며, 5시 20분에 시작한다고 했다.

어휘 drama[drάːmə] 드라마
reality show 리얼리티 쇼
run[rʌn] 운영하다
pop-up[pάpʌ̀p] 임시 매장의
channel[tʃǽnəl] (텔레비전의) 채널
remote control 리모컨, 원격 조정

M What's on TV right now?
W My Girl. It's really interesting. Let's watch it.
M No, thanks. I don't like watching dramas.
W Okay. There's a good reality show later.
M What is it?
W It's Kim's Kitchen and it's a popular show. A famous chef runs a pop-up Korean restaurant in Turkey.
M I like reality cooking shows. Let's watch that instead. What time is it on?
W It's on at 5:20.
M Oh, it's 5:15 now. What channel is the show on?
W It's on channel 6. I'll change the channel with the remote control.

남 지금 TV에서 하고 있는 프로가 뭐야?
여 〈My Girl〉이야. 정말 재미있어. 같이 보자.
남 아니, 안 볼래. 나는 드라마는 별로 보고 싶지 않아.
여 알았어. 나중에 재미있는 리얼리티 쇼를 해.
남 그게 뭔데?
여 〈Kim's Kitchen〉이고 인기 프로야. 한 유명한 요리사가 터키에서 잠시 동안 한식당을 운영하는 거야.
남 나는 요리하는 리얼리티 쇼를 좋아해. 대신 그걸 보자. 그건 언제 방영되니?
여 5시 20분에 방영해.
남 아, 지금 5시 15분이야. 그 쇼는 채널 몇 번에서 방영하니?
여 채널 6번에서 해. 내가 리모컨으로 채널을 바꿀게.

13 ④

해설 남자가 찾고 있는 신간 구역은 역사책 구역의 옆에 있고, 잡지 구역의 근처에 위치해있다.

어휘 mystery novel 추리 소설
recommend[rèkəménd] 추천하다
big fan 열혈 팬
new arrival 신착품, 새로 온 물품
section[sékʃən] 구역; 부문
magazine[mӕgəzíːn] 잡지

M Hello, Ms. Lee.

W Hi, Ben. How may I help you?

M I want to read a mystery novel. Can you recommend a good book?

W Sure. There's Steve King's new book, *The Dark House*.

M Great! I'm a big fan of his. Where can I find the book?

W It's in the "New Arrivals" section. The section is next to the "History Books" section.

M Is it close to the "Children's Books" section?

W No. You have to go to the one near the "Magazine" section.

M Thank you for your help. I hope the book is still there.

남 안녕하세요, 이 선생님.

여 안녕, Ben. 무엇을 도와줄까?

남 추리 소설을 읽고 싶어요. 좋은 책을 좀 추천해 주시겠어요?

여 물론이지. Steve King의 새 책 〈The Dark House〉가 있어.

남 좋아요! 저는 그의 열혈 팬이거든요. 그 책은 어디서 찾으면 되나요?

여 '신간' 구역에 있어. 그 구역은 '역사책' 구역의 옆에 있어.

남 그건 '어린이 도서' 구역과 가깝나요?

여 아니. '잡지 구역' 근처에 있는 곳으로 가야해.

남 도와주셔서 감사해요. 그 책이 아직 거기 있었으면 좋겠네요.

14 ②

해설 여자는 어제 배구를 하다가 오른손을 다쳤다고 했다.

어휘 favor[féivər] 부탁
hurt[həːrt] ~를 다치다
volleyball[válibɔːl] 배구
instead[instéd] 대신에

M Sena, can you do me a favor?

W What is it?

M I'm going to participate in the K-pop contest next week.

W That's great, Paul!

M So, can you play the guitar while I sing in the contest?

W I'd love to, but I can't. I hurt my right hand while I was playing volleyball yesterday.

M Oh, that's too bad.

W Why don't you ask Hajun instead? He's good at playing the guitar, too.

남 세나야, 부탁 좀 들어줄래?

여 뭔데?

남 내가 다음 주에 K-pop 경연대회에 참가할 거야.

여 멋지다, Paul!

남 그래서, 대회에서 노래할 때 네가 기타를 쳐 줄 수 있니?

여 그러고 싶은데 할 수가 없어. 어제 배구를 하다가 오른손을 다쳤거든.

남 아, 안됐네.

여 대신 하준이에게 부탁해 보면 어떨까? 걔도 기타를 잘 치잖아.

15 ①

해설 오늘만 저렴한 가격에 판매되는 제품의 할인에 대해 알리는 내용이다.

어휘 shopper[ʃápər] 쇼핑하는 손님
organically[ɔːrgӕnikəli] 유기 재배로
in addition 게다가
a variety of 여러 가지의
available[əvéiləbl] 이용할 수 있는

M Hello, shoppers. Here's some great news! Today is Joe's Supermarket's Special Price Day. Fresh organically grown fruits and vegetables are on sale. A bag of oranges is only $2. A bag of delicious apples is $3. In addition, we are selling a variety of other products at very low prices. These amazing prices are available only for today. Enjoy shopping!

남 안녕하세요, 쇼핑객 여러분. 좋은 소식이 있습니다! 오늘은 Joe's 슈퍼마켓의 특별 가격의 날입니다. 유기농으로 재배한 신선한 과일과 채소를 할인해 드립니다. 오렌지 한 봉지는 2달러밖에 안 됩니다. 맛있는 사과 한 봉지는 3달러입니다. 그 밖에도, 다양한 제품들을 아주 싼 가격에 판매하고 있습니다. 이 놀라운 가격은 오늘만 가능합니다. 즐거운 쇼핑이 되기를 바랍니다!

16 ②

남자는 배터리 수명이 길지 않아도 된다며 배터리 수명이 5시간인 600달러 짜리를 구입했다.

laptop[læptàp] 노트북 컴퓨터
screen[skri:n] 화면
difference[dífərəns] 차이
model[mádl] (상품의) 모델
battery life 배터리 수명

M Excuse me, how much is this laptop?
W That's $800.
M Do you have any cheaper ones?
W Sure. The ones with smaller screens are cheaper. This is $600, and that is $700.
M What's the difference between the two models?
W The one that is $600 has a 5-hour battery life, and the other one has a 7-hour battery life.
M I see. I don't need a long battery life. I'll take the cheaper one.
W That's a very good choice.

남 실례합니다만, 이 노트북은 얼마죠?
여 800달러입니다.
남 더 저렴한 건 없나요?
여 있지요. 화면이 더 작은 건 더 저렴해요. 이 것은 600달러이고, 저것은 700달러입니다.
남 두 모델의 차이가 뭔가요?
여 600달러짜리는 배터리 수명이 5시간이고, 다른 건 배터리 수명이 7시간입니다.
남 그렇군요. 저는 배터리 수명이 긴 것은 필요 없어요. 더 저렴한 걸로 할게요.
여 아주 잘 선택하셨어요.

17 ④

호주의 날에 하는 여러 행사 중에서 어떤 것을 가장 좋아하느냐고 물었으므로 그날 하는 행사 중 하나를 말하는 것이 적절한 응답이다.

National Foundation Day 개천절
public holiday 공휴일
event[ivént] 행사
include[inklú:d] 포함하다
street parade 가두 행진
firework[faiərwə́:rk] 불꽃놀이

M I have no school tomorrow.
W Really? Why not?
M It's the National Foundation Day of Korea.
W Oh, I see. We also have Australia Day. It's on January 26th.
M Is that a public holiday in Australia, too?
W Yes. There's no school or work. Everyone has a day off.
M What events do you have?
W The events include a street parade, a concert, and fireworks.
M That sounds exciting. What's your favorite part?
W I love the fireworks best. I always watch them.

남 나는 내일 학교에 안 가.
여 정말? 왜 안 가는데?
남 한국의 개천절이거든.
여 아, 그렇구나. 우리도 호주의 날이 있어. 그 날은 1월 26일이야.
남 그 날 호주에서도 공휴일이니?
여 응. 학교나 직장도 쉬어. 모두가 쉬는 날이 지.
남 어떤 행사를 하니?
여 거리 행진, 콘서트, 불꽃놀이 등의 행사가 있어.
남 재미있겠다. 네가 가장 좋아하는 건 뭐야?
여 나는 불꽃놀이를 제일 좋아해. 항상 그걸 봐.

① 한국에서는 그 날 뭐 하니?
② 나는 그날이 정말 기다려져.
③ 그래서 너는 내일 뭐 하니?
⑤ 학교에 갈 필요가 없기 때문이야.

18 ②

속도위반으로 걸린 남자가 여자로부터 면허증을 돌려받은 후에 가도 되는지 묻는 말이 이어져야 가장 자연스럽다.

driver's license 운전면허증
speed[spi:d] 과속 운전을 하다
ticket[tíkit] (교통 법규 위반) 딱지
speed limit 제한 속도

W Excuse me, sir. Let me see your driver's license.
M Here you are, Officer. What did I do wrong?
W You were speeding.
M I was speeding?
W Yes. I'm going to have to give you a ticket.
M Oh no. How fast was I going?
W You were going 90 kilometers per hour. This road has a speed limit of 60 kilometers per hour.

여 실례합니다. 선생님. 운전면허증을 보여주세요.
남 여기 있어요, 경관님. 제가 뭘 잘못했나요?
여 과속 운전을 했습니다.
남 제가 과속했다고요?
여 네. 딱지를 끊겠습니다.
남 이런. 제가 얼마나 빨리 가고 있었나요?
여 시속 90km로 가셨어요. 이 도로는 제한 속도가 시속 60 km입니다.

M I'm sorry. I didn't know that.
W [Pause] Here's your license. Drive carefully.
M I will. Can I go now?

남 미안합니다. 몰랐어요.
여 [잠시 후] 여기 면허증 있습니다. 조심해서 운전하세요.
남 그럴게요. 이제 가도 될까요?

① 이제 그게 뭔지 알겠어요.
③ 알겠어요. 안전벨트를 맬게요.
④ 딱지를 떼는 것은 불공평해요.
⑤ 도와주셔서 정말 감사합니다.

19 ④

M What's the matter? Are you all right?
W I was just thinking about my presentation from yesterday's class.
M What about it?
W Well, I think I made so many mistakes.
M Don't worry about it. I didn't notice them at all.
W I don't know. I wish I could turn back time and do it again.
M Have you heard "Today is a gift" before?
W No. What does that mean?
M It means you should focus on today.

남 무슨 일이야? 너 괜찮니?
여 그냥 어제 수업에서 했던 발표를 생각하고 있었어.
남 그거에 대해 어떤 거?
여 음. 너무 많이 실수를 한 거 같아.
남 걱정하지 마. 난 전혀 알지 못했어.
여 모르겠어. 난 시간을 되돌려서 다시 하고 싶어.
남 '오늘은 선물이다'라고 전에 들어본 적 있니?
여 아니. 그게 무슨 뜻이야?
남 그건 현재에 집중해야 한다는 의미야.

① 그것에 대해 잊어버릴 수가 없어.
② 그에게 완벽한 선물이 될 거야.
③ 네 조언은 항상 나에게 도움이 돼.
⑤ 발표를 도와줘서 너무 고마워.

20 ⑤

W Jacob comes home from school at 3 o'clock and finds his mother in the living room. She is not supposed to be home until 7 p.m., but she is home already. He notices that she is drinking hot tea and wearing a thick sweater. He thinks that she is not feeling well. So he wants to ask her if there is anything to make her feel better. In this situation, what would Jacob most likely say to his mom?

Jacob Mom, do you want me to get you anything?

여 Jacob은 3시에 학교에서 집으로 돌아와 엄마가 거실에 있는 것을 본다. 엄마는 오후 7시까지는 집에 오지 않을 텐데, 벌써 집에 와 있다. 그는 엄마가 따뜻한 차를 마시고 두꺼운 스웨터를 입고 계신다는 것을 알게 된다. 그는 엄마가 몸이 좋지 않다고 생각한다. 그래서 그는 엄마를 낫게 해줄 만한 것이 있는지 물어보고 싶다. 이러한 상황에서 Jacob이 엄마에게 할 말로 가장 적절한 것은 무엇일까?

Jacob 엄마, 뭘 좀 가져다 드릴까요?

① 우리 외식할까요?
② 음료는 뭐로 마실래요?
③ 제가 옆에 앉아도 될까요?
④ 저녁 식사로 뭘 먹을까요?

01 ③	02 ⑤	03 ①	04 ②	05 ④	06 ③	07 ③
08 ⑤	09 ④	10 ④	11 ④	12 ③	13 ④	14 ③
15 ①	16 ③	17 ②	18 ②	19 ⑤	20 ⑤	

01 ③

해설 가죽 끈을 여러 번 감고 매듭을 묶었으며 하트 장식이 있는 팔찌이다.

어휘 bracelet[bréislit] 팔찌
craft[kræft] 수공예
leather[léðər] 가죽
wrap[ræp] 감다
strap[stræp] 끈
wrist[rist] 손목
knot[nɑt] 매듭
decoration[dèkəréiʃən] 장식
cool[kuːl] 멋진, 근사한

M Maya, this is a gift for you.
W Wow, what a pretty bracelet! Where did you buy it?
M I made it myself in our craft club.
W Really? How did you make it?
M After wrapping the leather strap a few times around my wrist, I tied a knot and cut it. And I added a heart decoration you like.
W That sounds easy, but you made the world's coolest bracelet.
M I'm glad you like it.

남 Maya, 이건 널 위한 선물이야.
여 와, 정말 예쁜 팔찌구나! 어디서 샀어?
남 내가 공예 동아리에서 직접 만들었어.
여 정말? 어떻게 만들었어?
남 가죽 끈을 손목에 맞게 몇 번 감은 후에, 매듭을 묶고 잘랐어. 그리고 네가 좋아하는 하트 장식을 달았지.
여 쉬운 것 같지만, 세상에서 가장 멋진 팔찌를 만들었네.
남 네가 맘에 들어 하니까 기뻐.

02 ⑤

해설 제목(〈Turandot〉), 줄거리(중국 공주와 그녀를 사랑하게 되는 용감한 왕자의 이야기), 작곡가(Giacomo Puccini), 공연 요일(이번 주 토요일)에 관해 언급되었지만 공연 장소에 대한 언급은 없었다.

어휘 opera[ápərə] 오페라
princess[prínsis] 공주
prince[prins] 왕자
fall in love with ~와 사랑에 빠지다
compose[kəmpóuz] 작곡하다
composer[kəmpóuzər] 작곡가

W Luke, what are you going to do this weekend?
M I'm going to watch the opera Turandot.
W Turandot? What is it about?
M It's about a Chinese princess and a brave prince who falls in love with her.
W That sounds interesting. Who composed it?
M Giacomo Puccini. He was a famous Italian composer.
W Cool. I want to see an opera someday.
M Oh, really? Then why don't you join me this Saturday?
W I'd love to, but I can't. I have other plans this weekend.
M Okay. Maybe next time.

여 Luke, 이번 주말에 뭐 할 거야?
남 나는 오페라 〈Turandot〉을 볼 거야.
여 〈Turandot〉라고? 어떤 내용이야?
남 중국 공주와 그녀를 사랑하게 되는 용감한 왕자의 이야기야.
여 재미있겠다. 누가 작곡했니?
남 Giacomo Puccini. 그는 유명한 이탈리아 작곡가였어.
여 좋다. 언젠가 오페라를 꼭 보고 싶어.
남 아, 정말? 그럼 이번 주 토요일에 나랑 같이 가지 않을래?
여 그러고 싶지만 그럴 수가 없어. 이번 주말에 다른 계획이 있거든.
남 알았어. 다음에 가기로 하자.

03 ①

해설 내일 미세 먼지가 심해서 축구 경기를 미루자는 말을 하려고 전화했다.

어휘 fine dust 미세 먼지
level[lévəl] 수준, 농도
outdoor[áutdɔ̀ːr] 야외의
be supposed to-v ~하기로 되어 있다
text[tekst] (휴대전화로) 문자를 보내다

[Cell phone rings.]
W Hello.
M Hi, Kate. It's Harry. Did you hear the weather forecast for tomorrow?
W No, I didn't. What did it say?
M It said the fine dust level will be very high and outdoor activities should be limited.
W Oh no. We're supposed to play soccer tomorrow.
M Yes. I think we'd better play another day.

[휴대전화가 울린다.]
여 여보세요.
남 Kate, 안녕. Harry. 내일 일기 예보 들었어?
여 아니, 못 들었어. 뭐라고 했는데?
남 미세 먼지 농도가 매우 높을 거라서 야외 활동을 제한해야 한다고 했어.
여 이런. 우리 내일 축구하기로 했잖아.
남 그래. 다른 날 하는 게 좋을 것 같아.
여 맞아. 그러면 다른 멤버들에게 알려야겠

W You're right. Then we should let the other members know.

M I'll text the other members of our team right now.

W That would be good.

네.

남 지금 내가 다른 멤버들에게 문자 보낼게.

여 그게 좋겠어.

04 ②

해설 3시 영화는 모두 매진되어서 대신 3시 30분에 시작하는 영화를 보기로 했다.

어휘 girlhood[gɚlhud] 소녀 시절
sold out (표가) 매진된
space[speis] 우주
jump shot 점프 슛
action[ǽkʃən] (영화 속의) 액션

W Can I get 2 tickets for *Girlhood* for 3 o'clock?

M I'm afraid we're all sold out for 3 o'clock, but there are some seats left for 5:30.

W We don't want to wait so long to see it.

M We have a few other movies playing around 3. They are *Space* and *Jump Shot*.

W Oh, we'll watch one of them, then.

M If you like action, I recommend *Jump Shot*. It starts at 3:30.

W That sounds perfect. I'd like 2 tickets for *Jump Shot*, please.

M Okay.

여 〈Girlhood〉 3시 티켓 두 장 살 수 있을까요?

남 죄송하지만 3시 것은 다 매진되었고, 5시 30분 자리가 좀 있어요.

여 그걸 보려고 너무 오래 기다리고 싶지는 않아요.

남 3시쯤에 상영하는 다른 영화가 몇 편 있어요. 〈Space〉와 〈Jump Shot〉이에요.

여 아, 그럼 그중 하나를 볼게요.

남 액션을 좋아한다면 〈Jump Shot〉을 추천할게요. 3시 30분에 시작해요.

여 좋은 것 같네요. 〈Jump Shot〉 티켓 두 장 주세요.

남 알겠습니다.

05 ④

해설 자전거를 타다 돌부리에 걸려 넘어진 여자를 보고 남자가 괜찮냐고 묻는 상황이다.

어휘 repair shop 수리점
nearby[nìərbái] 가까이에
helmet[hélmit] 헬멧
stone[stoun] 돌
parking space 주차 공간

① **M** Are there any bike repair shops nearby?

　W The closest one is just around the corner.

② **M** Can I try your new bike?

　W Sorry, but it's not my bike. It's my brother's.

③ **M** You should wear a helmet when you ride a bike.

　W Okay. Then I'll go back inside to get one.

④ **M** Oh no! Are you okay?

　W I think so. I didn't see that stone and hit it.

⑤ **M** We need to make a bicycle parking space at school.

　W That's a good idea.

① 남 근처에 자전거 수리점이 있니?

　여 가장 가까운 것은 바로 저 모퉁이 부근에 있어.

② 남 네 새 자전거를 한번 타 봐도 될까?

　여 미안하지만, 내 자전거가 아니야. 우리 오빠 거야.

③ 남 자전거 탈 때 헬멧을 써야 해.

　여 알았어. 안에 들어가서 갖고 올게.

④ 남 저런! 괜찮아?

　여 괜찮은 것 같아. 저 돌을 미처 보지 못하고 부딪혔네.

⑤ 남 우리는 학교에 자전거 주차 공간을 만들어야 해.

　여 좋은 생각이야.

06 ③

해설 깁스를 푸는 시기를 알려주고 이후 치료 프로그램을 권하는 상황으로 보아 두 사람이 대화하는 장소는 병원임을 알 수 있다.

어휘 take off (옷 등을) 벗다

W Well, your arm is much better now.

M Oh, that's good news. When will you take off my cast?

W I will remove it in a week if you don't hurt yourself again.

M Yes, I'll be careful.

여 자, 네 팔이 이제 아주 좋아졌네.

남 아, 그거 반가운 소식이네요. 언제 깁스를 풀어 주실 건가요?

여 네가 다시 다치지만 않으면 일주일 뒤에 풀어 줄게.

남 네, 조심할게요.

cast[kæst] 깁스
remove[rimúːv] 제거하다
for a while 한동안
physical therapy 물리 치료

W It won't be easy to use your arm for a while after the cast is off.
M Then what should I do?
W I recommend that you do a physical therapy program here.
M Okay, I will. Thank you so much.

여 깁스를 푼 뒤 한동안은 팔을 쓰기가 쉽지 않을 거야.
남 그럼 어떻게 해야 하나요?
여 여기서 하는 물리 치료 프로그램에 참여하는 걸 추천할게.
남 네, 그럴게요. 정말 감사합니다.

07 ③

해설 남자는 여자에게 한 상자에 5개씩 쿠키를 넣어 포장해달라고 부탁했다.

어휘 bake sale (자선 모금을 위한) 빵 [과자] 판매
day-care center 어린이집

W Bill, are you baking cookies? Can I try one?
M Go ahead. [Pause] What do you think?
W Wow, it's really good. It's better than any other cookie.
M Thanks. I'm glad you like it.
W You're baking so many cookies. Are you having a bake sale?
M No, they're for the children at the day-care center.
W Oh, I see. Do you need any help?
M Sure. Please put the cookies in the gift boxes. 5 cookies in each box.
W Okay.

여 Bill, 쿠키를 굽고 있니? 하나 먹어 봐도 돼?
남 먹어 봐. [잠시 후] 어때?
여 와, 이거 정말 맛있다. 다른 어떤 쿠키보다도 맛있는 걸.
남 고마워. 네가 좋아하니까 기쁘네.
여 쿠키를 정말 많이 만들고 있네. 쿠키 판매를 할 거니?
남 아니, 어린이집에 있는 아이들에게 줄 거야.
여 아, 그렇구나. 내가 좀 도와줄까?
남 좋지. 선물 상자에 쿠키를 넣어 줘. 한 상자에 5개씩.
여 알았어.

08 ⑤

해설 설립자(Kyle Weiss와 그의 형제), 설립 계기(2006년 독일 월드컵 때 아프리카의 축구 팬들을 만나 축구의 가치를 인식함), 설립 시기(2006년 월드컵이 지난 2년 후), 주요 활동(축구를 할 수 있는 장비와 안전한 운동장 제공)에 관해 언급되었지만, 참여 방법에 대한 언급은 없었다.

어휘 realize[ríːəlàiz] 알게 되다, 깨닫다
value[vǽljuː] 가치
skill[skil] 기술
create[kriéit] 만들다
organization[ɔ̀ːrɡənizéiʃən] 조직, 단체
provide[prəváid] 제공하다
equipment[ikwípmənt] 장비

M Hi, I'm Kyle Weiss. At the 2006 World Cup games in Germany, I met some soccer fans from Africa. During that time, I realized that soccer helps people come together and teaches kids important values and life skills. So, 2 years after the German World Cup, I created an organization with my brother to build soccer fields for children in Africa. We provide a safe field with equipment to play soccer. I hope you will help us at FUNDaFIELD.

남 안녕하세요, 저는 Kyle Weiss입니다. 2006년 독일 월드컵 때 아프리카의 축구 팬들을 만났어요. 그 기간 동안 축구가 사람들이 하나가 되게 하는 것을 돕고 아이들에게 중요한 가치와 삶의 기술을 가르쳐준다는 것을 깨닫게 되었어요. 그래서 독일 월드컵 지난 2년 후에 저는 제 형제와 함께 아프리카 어린이들을 위한 축구장을 만드는 단체를 설립했어요. 저희는 축구를 할 수 있는 장비와 함께 안전한 운동장을 제공합니다. 여러분들이 FUNDaFIELD에 도움을 주기를 바랍니다.

09 ④

해설 꽃을 옮겨 다니면서 식물이 씨앗과 과일을 맺도록 돕고 꿀을 만들어내는 곤충은 꿀벌이다.

어휘 insect[ínsekt] 곤충
collect[kəlékt] 모으다
fine[fain] 미세한, 고운

W These are flying insects, and they help flowers, fruits, and vegetables grow. When they collect food, they go from flower to flower. They also carry fine powder from one flower to another flower. This helps plants bear seeds and fruits. They are called social insects because they live

여 이것은 날아다니는 곤충이며, 꽃과 과일, 채소의 성장을 돕는다. 그것이 음식을 모을 때, 꽃에서 꽃으로 옮겨 다닌다. 그것은 또한 한 꽃에서 다른 꽃으로 미세한 가루를 운반한다. 이렇게 함으로써 식물이 씨앗과 과일을 맺도록 돕는다. 그것은 공동체로서 함께 살고 일하기 때문에 사회적

powder[páudər] 가루
bear[bɛər] (식물이 꽃이나 열매를) 피우다[맺다]
seed[siːd] 씨앗
social[sóuʃəl] 사회적인
community[kəmjúːnəti] 공동체
trip[trip] 이동, 오고감
produce[prədjúːs] 생산하다
amount[əmáunt] (무엇의) 양

and work together as a community. Each of them makes hundreds of trips to produce a small amount of honey.

곤충이라고 불린다. 그들은 각자 소량의 꿀을 만들기 위해 수백 번씩 이동한다.

10 ④

해설 K-pop 음악을 좋아하는 이유를 물었는데 한국 음식을 먹고 싶다고 응답하는 것은 어색하다.

어휘 dessert[dizə́ːrt] 후식
rap[ræp] 랩 음악
modern[mádərn] 현대의, 근대의

① M What would you like to have for dessert?
  W I'd like to have some apple pie.
② M Why don't we go fishing tomorrow?
  W That's a good idea.
③ M Can you tell me how old the tree is?
  W It's about 120 years old.
④ M Why do you like K-pop?
  W I'd like to eat some Korean food.
⑤ M Need any help, ma'am?
  W Yes, please. Where's the Museum of Modern Art?

① 남 후식으로 뭘 드시겠어요?
  여 애플파이로 할게요.
② 남 우리 내일 낚시하러 가지 않을래?
  여 좋은 생각이야.
③ 남 그 나무가 몇 살인지 알려 줄래?
  여 120년 정도 됐어.
④ 남 너는 왜 K-pop을 좋아하니?
  여 난 한국 음식을 좀 먹고 싶어.
⑤ 남 도움이 필요하시나요?
  여 네. 현대 미술관이 어디인가요?

11 ④

해설 시계를 교환하기 위해 신청서를 작성해야 한다고 말하면서 여자가 남자에게 펜을 건네는 상황으로 보아 남자는 교환 신청서를 작성할 것이다.

어휘 battery[bǽtəri] 배터리
run out 다 떨어지다
have a look (한 번) 보다
satisfied[sǽtisfàid] 만족한
return[ritə́ːrn] 반품하다
exchange[ikstʃéindʒ] 교환하다
fill out (양식 등을) 채우다
form[fɔːrm] 양식

W Hello, sir. What can I do for you?
M I bought this smartwatch only 2 weeks ago, but the battery is running out very fast.
W May I have a look at it?
M Here you are.
W [Pause] I'm sorry, but I think it'll take a few days to fix it.
M Well, I'm not satisfied with the watch. I'd like to return it.
W You can't return it, but you can exchange it for a new one.
M I see. Then I'd like to exchange it for a new one, please.
W Of course. You need to fill out this form. Here is a pen.
M Thanks.

여 안녕하세요. 무엇을 도와드릴까요?
남 이 스마트워치는 불과 2주 전에 구입했는데 배터리가 너무 빨리 닳아요.
여 제가 한 번 볼까요?
남 여기 있습니다.
여 [잠시 후] 죄송하지만, 고치는 데 며칠 걸릴 것 같아요.
남 음, 저 이 시계가 마음에 들지 않네요. 반품하고 싶어요.
여 반품할 수는 없지만 새것으로 교환은 가능합니다.
남 그렇군요. 그럼 새 것으로 바꿔 주세요.
여 그러죠. 이 양식을 작성해 주세요. 여기 펜 있습니다.
남 고맙습니다.

12 ③

해설 여자는 남자에게 7시에 일어나면 된다고 했다.

어휘 prepare[pripέər] 준비하다

M Mom, what time are we going to visit grandmother tomorrow?
W We're going to leave around 9 in the morning.
M Aren't we going to make a birthday cake for her?

남 엄마, 우리 내일 할머니 댁에 몇 시에 가요?
여 아침 9시쯤에 출발할 거야.
남 할머니 생신 케이크를 만들어 드리지 않을 건가요?

W Yes. I'm going to bake it before we go.
M Should I get up early to help you?
W I'd be happy if you could help me.
M What time should I get up?
W I'm going to get up around 6 o'clock to prepare for baking. You can get up at 7 and help me make the cake.
M Okay. Good night, Mom.

여 만들어야지. 가기 전에 내가 만들려고 해.
남 제가 일찍 일어나서 도와드릴까요?
여 도와준다면 나야 좋지.
남 제가 몇 시에 일어날까요?
여 만드는 걸 준비하기 위해 6시쯤에 일어날 거야. 너는 7시에 일어나서 케이크 만드는 거 도와주면 돼.
남 그럴게요. 안녕히 주무세요, 엄마.

13 ④

해설 여자는 가방을 맡길 물품 보관함을 찾고 있으며, 그것은 구내식당과 화장실 사이에 있다고 했다.

어휘 locker[lάkər] 물품 보관함, 로커
cafeteria[kæfətíəriə] 구내식당

W Excuse me.
M Hello. How can I help you?
W Is it okay to take this backpack with me in here?
M I'm afraid large bags are not allowed in the museum.
W I see. Are there any lockers I can leave my backpack in?
M Sure. Do you see the cafeteria on your right?
W Yes.
M The lockers are between the cafeteria and the restroom.
W I see. Thank you so much.

여 실례합니다.
남 안녕하세요. 무엇을 도와드릴까요?
여 이 배낭을 이곳 안에 가지고 들어가도 되나요?
남 죄송하지만 박물관 안에는 큰 가방을 가지고 들어갈 수 없어요.
여 알겠습니다. 그럼 제 배낭을 둘 수 있는 물품 보관함이 있나요?
남 네. 오른쪽에 구내식당이 보이나요?
여 네.
남 보관함은 저 식당과 화장실 사이에 있어요.
여 알겠습니다. 정말 고맙습니다.

14 ③

해설 남자는 어제 태권도 연습을 하다가 안경을 깨뜨렸다고 했다.

어휘 step on ~을 밟다
break[breik] 깨뜨리다, 부수다
(break-broke-broken)
practice[prǽktis] 연습하다

W Ouch! You stepped on my foot again.
M Oh, I'm sorry. Are you okay?
W Yes, but this is the second time you did that today.
M I can't see well because I'm not wearing my glasses today.
W What happened to your glasses?
M I broke my glasses while practicing Taekwondo yesterday. I'm going to get new glasses this afternoon.
W I see. You should be careful until then.

여 아야! 네가 또 내 발을 밟았어.
남 아, 미안해. 괜찮아?
여 응, 하지만 오늘 두 번째 밟은 거야.
남 오늘 안경을 쓰지 않아서 잘 안 보여서 그래.
여 네 안경은 어떻게 되었는데?
남 어제 태권도 연습을 하다가 안경이 깨졌어. 오늘 오후에 새 안경을 사러 갈 거야.
여 그렇구나. 그때까지 조심해야겠네.

15 ①

해설 강도의 인상 착의를 알려 주면서 신고를 독려하고 있다.

어휘 search for ~을 찾다
rob[rab] ~에서 강탈하다
release[rilíːs] (대중들에게) 공개하다
medical mask 의료용 마스크
average build 보통 체구
robber[rάbər] 도둑, 강도

M Good evening and welcome to DBS News. The police are searching for 2 men who robbed a mobile phone store this morning on East Broad Street. Police released a video showing one of the men. The man is wearing a medical mask and is about 180 centimeters tall. He is of average build and has long blond hair. If you have any information about the robbers, please call the police.

남 안녕하십니까, DBS 뉴스에 오신 것을 환영합니다. 경찰은 오늘 아침 East Broad 가에서 휴대전화 가게를 턴 두 남자를 찾고 있습니다. 경찰은 남자들 중 한 명의 모습이 담긴 영상을 공개했습니다. 이 남성은 의료용 마스크를 쓰고 있으며 키는 180cm 정도입니다. 그는 보통 체구에 긴 금발머리를 하고 있습니다. 강도들에 대한 정보가 있다면 경찰에 신고해 주십시오.

16 ③

해설 음식값 총 25달러에 배달료 5달러를 추가하여 총 30달러를 지불할 것이다.

어휘 original[ərídʒənəl] 원래의
mashed potato 으깬 감자
delivery[dilívəri] 배달
charge[tʃɑːrdʒ] 요금; (요금을) 청구하다
extra[ékstrə] 추가의
in total 모두 합해서

[Telephone rings.]

W Hot Chicken. Can I take your order?
M Yes, I'd like a 12-piece original chicken with mashed potatoes and a green salad.
W All right. It comes to $25.
M Is that with or without delivery charge?
W Without. We charge an extra $5 for the delivery. What's your address, please?
M It's 30 Lake Street, apartment 7.
W Okay. Is your phone number 3232-7740?
M That's correct.
W It'll be $30 in total, and your food will be there in 40 minutes.
M Thank you.

[전화벨이 울린다.]

여 Hot Chicken입니다. 주문하시겠습니까?
남 네, 오리지널 치킨 열두 조각에 으깬 감자와 그린샐러드를 주세요.
여 알겠습니다. 25달러입니다.
남 그건 배달료가 포함되어 있나요 아님 아닌가요?
여 포함되지 않았어요. 저희는 배달료 5달러를 따로 받습니다. 주소가 어떻게 되시죠?
남 Lake 가 30번지, 아파트 7호입니다.
여 알겠습니다. 그리고 전화번호는 3232-7740인가요?
남 맞아요.
여 총 금액은 30달러이고, 40분 뒤에 음식이 도착할 겁니다.
남 고맙습니다.

17 ②

해설 세 가지 차의 색을 알려주며 어떤 색 차를 원하느냐고 물었으므로 그중 원하거나 원하지 않는 색을 말하는 응답이 자연스럽다.

어휘 used car 중고차
automatic[ɔ̀ːtəmǽtik] 자동의
go over ~을 넘다
[선택지]
brand-new[brǽndnjuː] 아주 새로운, 신품의

M Hello. How may I help you?
W I'm looking for a used car.
M Okay. Do you want an automatic car?
W Yes, please. It's easier for me to drive.
M Okay. How much are you planning to spend?
W I don't want to go over $7,000.
M What about the color? The 3 most popular colors are black, white, and gray.
W I don't want a black car.

남 안녕하세요. 무엇을 도와드릴까요?
여 중고차를 찾고 있어요.
남 알겠습니다. 자동 변속기 차를 원하십니까?
여 네. 그게 제가 운전하기 더 쉽거든요.
남 알겠습니다. 얼마를 쓰실 생각이세요?
여 7,000달러는 넘지 않았으면 해요.
남 색상은요? 가장 인기 있는 세 가지 색은 검은색, 흰색, 그리고 회색입니다.
여 저는 검은색 차는 원하지 않아요.

① 좀 더 싼 것을 원해요.
③ 그럼 이게 당신한테 딱 맞는 차입니다.
④ 저는 신형 차를 사려고 해요.
⑤ 요즘 어떤 색 차가 인기인가요?

18 ②

해설 공포 영화나 멜로 영화를 좋아하지 않는다는 남자에게 액션 영화를 권했으므로 그 영화가 좋은지 싫은지를 응답해야 자연스럽다.

어휘 horror[hɔ́ːrər] 공포
romantic movie 멜로 영화
[선택지]
be into ~에 관심이 많다, 빠지다

M Emma, why don't we stay at home and watch a movie tonight?
W Well, I'd rather go out to the theater.
M Okay. What movie would you like to watch?
W How about *Friday the 13th*?
M No way! You know I don't like horror movies.
W I'm sorry. I forgot. Then, how about *Forever Love*?
M I don't enjoy romantic movies, either. Is there anything else?
W Well, then how about an action movie? *My Spy* is also playing.

남 Emma, 우리 오늘 저녁에 집에 있으면서 영화나 한 편 보는 게 어때?
여 글쎄, 극장에 가는 게 더 좋을 것 같은데.
남 알겠어. 어떤 영화를 보고 싶니?
여 〈Friday the 13th〉은 어때?
남 절대 안 돼! 내가 공포 영화를 싫어하는 거 알잖아.
여 미안해. 깜박했어. 그렇다면 〈Forever Love〉는 어때?
남 나는 멜로 영화도 좋아하지 않아. 다른 건 없을까?
여 음, 그러면 액션 영화는 어때? 〈My spy〉가 상영 중이야.

M I think that works for me.

남 그게 나한테 딱 좋은 것 같아.

① 표 두 장은 16달러입니다.
③ 빨리 그 콘서트를 보고 싶어!
④ 나는 멜로 영화를 좋아하지 않아.
⑤ 나 요즘 공포 영화에 푹 빠졌거든.

19 ⑤

[해설] 플라스틱 제품 사용을 줄이기 위해 각자의 컵을 사용하는 것을 제안하는 남자의 말에 동의하거나 반대하는 응답이 이어져야 적절하다.

[어휘] plastic[plǽstik] 플라스틱으로 된; 플라스틱

waste[weist] 쓰레기
shocked[ʃɑːkt] 충격을 받은
suffer[sʌ́fər] 고통 받다
reduce[ridjúːs] 줄이다
reuse[riːjúːz] 재사용하다
product[prɑ́dəkt] 제품
instead of ~ 대신에
[선택지]
take actions 조치를 취하다

M Sandy, did you see the TV program *A Plastic Ocean*?

W Yes, I did. I learned that plastic waste is very dangerous to sea animals from that program.

M Me, too. I was really shocked to see sea animals suffer.

W We have to do something to save them.

M You're right. How can we reduce plastic waste?

W We should reuse plastic products to use less of them.

M Sure. We can also use our own cups instead of plastic ones.

W Good idea. Taking simple actions like these can help.

남 Sandy, 너 텔레비전 프로그램 〈Plastic Ocean〉 봤니?

여 응, 봤어. 그 프로그램에서 플라스틱 쓰레기가 해양 동물들에게 아주 위험하다는 것을 알게 되었어.

남 나도 그걸 배웠어. 나는 해양 동물들이 고통 받는 것을 보고 정말 충격 받았어.

여 우리가 그 동물들을 구하기 위해 무언가를 해야 해.

남 네 말이 맞아. 어떻게 하면 플라스틱 쓰레기를 줄일 수 있을까?

여 플라스틱 제품을 덜 사용하기 위해 재사용하는 것은 어때?

남 그래. 우리는 또 플라스틱 컵 대신 자신의 컵을 사용하면 되잖아.

여 좋은 생각이야. 이런 간단한 행동을 하는 것이 도움이 될 수 있어.

① 내가 도와줄까?
② 우리가 바다를 위해 무엇을 해야 할까?
③ 좋아. 파티에 필요한 컵을 더 구해보자.
④ 그리고 손을 씻는 것도 중요하지.

20 ⑤

[해설] 우승에 대한 부담감 때문에 초조해하는 Ben에게 운동회 자체를 즐기라고 얘기하는 것이 적절하다.

[어휘] sports day 운동회 날
look forward to ~을 기대하다
runner[rʌ́nər] 주자
relay race 릴레이 경주
relax[rilǽks] 긴장을 풀다
[선택지]
enjoy oneself 즐기다

W Sports Day is next Wednesday. Emily is looking forward to it, but Ben isn't. He is very nervous and worried because he's the last runner in the relay race. He's also afraid that his team will lose because of him. So, Emily wants to tell him Sports Day is not about winning. She wants Ben to relax a little and enjoy the fun event. In this situation, what would Emily most likely say to Ben?

Emily You should enjoy yourself on Sports Day.

여 다음 주 수요일은 운동회 날이다. Emily는 그날이 매우 기다려지는데, Ben은 그렇지 않다. 그는 릴레이 경주에서 마지막 주자라서 매우 초조해하고 걱정하고 있다. 그는 자신 때문에 팀이 질까 봐도 두렵다. 그래서 Emily는 그에게 운동회는 이기는 것이 중요하지 않다고 말하고 싶어 한다. 그녀는 Ben이 조금 긴장을 풀고 그 재미있는 행사를 즐기기를 원한다. 이러한 상황에서 Emily가 Ben에게 할 말로 가장 적절한 것은 무엇인가?

Emily 너는 운동회를 즐겨야 해.

① 아주 잘 했어.
② 나는 경주를 위해 최선을 다할 거야.
③ 그 경주에 대해 듣게 되어 유감이야.
④ 나는 네가 더 열심히 연습해야 한다고 생각해.

01 ③

해설 남자는 얼굴이 그려진 티셔츠 디자인을 제안했고, 여자도 동의했다.

어휘 decide[disáid] 결정하다
sleeve[sli:v] 소매
unique[ju(:)ní:k] 독특한

W Dad, can you help me decide on the design for my class T-shirt? We're going to wear the T-shirt on Sports Day in June.
M Sure. Let me see what designs you have.
W How about this red one with short sleeves?
M Wasn't the class T-shirt last year red? How about this one with a star on it?
W It's not bad, but I want something more unique.
M How about this one with faces on the front? You can change those to the faces of your classmates.
W That's a great idea!

여 아빠, 저희 반 티셔츠 디자인 결정하는 것 좀 도와주실래요? 우리가 6월 운동회 때 입으려고요.
남 물론이지. 어떤 디자인이 있는지 보여줘.
여 이 빨간색 반팔은 어떠세요?
남 작년에 반 티셔츠가 빨간색 아니었니? 별이 있는 이건 어때?
여 나쁘지 않지만, 좀 더 독특했으면 좋겠어요.
남 앞에 얼굴들이 그려진 이건 어때? 그걸 너희 반 친구들의 얼굴로 바꿀 수 있잖아.
여 그것 참 좋은 생각이네요!

02 ①

해설 남자는 여자에게 추리소설을 몇 권 추천해달라고 했다.

어휘 as well 또한
big fan 열혈 팬
mystery[místəri] 추리, 미스터리
be made into ~로 만들어지다
original author 원작자
recommend[rèkəménd] 추천하다
lend[lend] 빌려주다

[Cell phone rings.]
W Hello.
M Hi, Becky. I had a great time with you yesterday. Did you enjoy the movie as well?
W Yes. I am a big fan of mystery movies.
M Since I watched the movie, I started thinking about reading the books by Agatha Christie, the original author.
W That sounds great. Many of her novels have been made into movies, too.
M I know you're a big fan of her. Can you recommend some of her books?
W Of course. I've read all of her mystery books. And I can also lend you some books I have.
M Thanks. I'm sure I'll like her books, too.

[휴대전화가 울린다.]
여 여보세요.
남 안녕, Becky. 어제 너와 좋은 시간을 보냈어. 너도 그 영화 재미있게 봤니?
여 응. 난 추리 영화 열혈 팬이거든.
남 그 영화를 본 후로 원작자인 Agatha Christie가 쓴 책을 읽을 생각을 하게 되었어.
여 그거 좋다. 그 작가의 소설도 영화로도 만들어졌어.
남 네가 그 작가의 열혈 팬이라고 알고 있어. 나한테 책을 몇 권 추천해 줄 수 있니?
여 물론이지. 나는 그 작가의 추리소설을 모두 읽었거든. 그리고 내가 가지고 있는 책 몇 권을 빌려줄 수도 있어.
남 고마워. 나도 분명히 그 작가의 책을 좋아하게 될 거야.

03 ②

해설 학교에 늦은 여자가 남자에게 차를 태워달라고 하는 상황이다.

어휘 give A a ride A를 태워주다
wake up (잠에서) 깨다

① W Dad, I'm a bit hungry.
　 M Do you want me to make a pizza for you?
② W I'm late for school. Could you give me a ride, please?
　 M Sure. Get in the car.

① 여 아빠, 배가 좀 고파요.
　 남 내가 피자를 만들어 줄까?
② 여 학교에 늦었어요. 저 좀 태워다 주실 수 있나요?
　 남 그래. 차에 타렴.

③ W Do you mind if I open the window?
   M No, not at all.
④ W Why don't you take a walk every day?
   M Okay. I'll think about it.
⑤ W Dad, is something wrong? You look tired.
   M I woke up too early this morning.

③ 여 창문을 열어도 될까요?
   남 그럼.
④ 여 매일 산책하시는 게 어떨까요?
   남 알았어. 생각해 볼게.
⑤ 여 아빠, 무슨 일 있어요? 피곤해 보여요.
   남 오늘 아침에 너무 일찍 일어났어.

04 ④

해설 여자는 자신의 생일이 있기도 하고 부모님과 휴가를 갈 수 있어서 8월을 가장 좋아한다고 했다.

어휘 present[préznt] 선물
reason[ríːzn] 이유
off[ɔːf] (근무일을) 쉬는
vacation[veikéiʃən] 정기 휴가

W Jake, what's your favorite month?
M Hmm... Let's see. I think I like July best.
W Why?
M My birthday is July 10th. I get a lot of presents and have a fun party on that day.
W Really? My birthday is on the 10th, too. But August 10th.
M I see. Then is August your favorite month of the year?
W Yes, but there's another reason why I like August best.
M What is it?
W That's the month when my parents get a week off. So we go on vacation then.

여 Jake, 네가 가장 좋아하는 달은 언제니?
남 음… 글쎄. 나는 7월이 가장 좋은 것 같아.
여 왜?
남 내 생일이 7월 10일이거든. 이날 선물도 많이 받고 즐거운 파티도 하잖아.
여 정말? 내 생일도 10일인데. 하지만 8월 10일이야.
남 그렇구나. 그러면 네가 가장 좋아하는 달은 8월이겠네?
여 맞아, 하지만 내가 8월을 가장 좋아하는 또 다른 이유가 있어.
남 그게 뭔데?
여 그 달은 우리 부모님이 일주일 동안 쉬는 달이야. 그래서 우리는 그때 휴가를 가거든.

05 ⑤

해설 원작(F. Scott Fitzgerald의 동명 소설), 배경(1922년 뉴욕 롱아일랜드의 한 마을), 주인공(Jay Gatsby와 Daisy), 결말(비극)에 관해 언급되었지만 상영 시간에 관한 언급은 없었다.

어휘 based on ~에 근거하여
neighbor[néibər] 이웃사람
main character 주인공
end in ~로 끝나다
tragedy[trǽdʒədi] 비극
scene[siːn] 장면

W The beautiful movie *The Great Gatsby* is based on F. Scott Fitzgerald's 1925 novel of the same name. The movie tells the story of neighbors from a town on New York's Long Island in 1922. The main character Jay Gatsby, who is very rich, falls in love with Daisy, but their love ends in tragedy. After the movie is over, you will never forget the party scenes in the movie.

여 이 아름다운 영화 〈위대한 개츠비〉는 F. Scott Fitzgerald의 1925년 동명의 소설을 원작으로 하고 있습니다. 이 영화는 1922년 뉴욕 롱아일랜드의 한 마을 이웃들의 이야기입니다. 대부호인 주인공 Jay Gatsby는 Daisy와 사랑에 빠지지만 그들의 사랑은 비극으로 끝납니다. 영화가 끝난 후에도 당신은 영화 속 파티 장면을 절대 잊지 못할 겁니다.

06 ④

해설 관광 지도를 요청하고, 가보고 싶은 곳에 대해 정보를 얻고 있는 것으로 보아 관광 안내원과 관광객이 나누는 대화임을 알 수 있다.

어휘 tourist map 관광 지도
flea market 벼룩시장
specific[spisífik] 특정한
accessories[æksésəriz] 액세서리

W Hello. How may I help you?
M Hi. I'd like to get a tourist map of the city.
W Are there any special places you want to go?
M Yes. I want to visit some flea markets.
W Oh, there are many flea markets held in London. The biggest one in London is Portobello Market. It opens every day.
M That sounds great. Do you know any

여 안녕하세요. 무엇을 도와드릴까요?
남 안녕하세요. 이 도시의 관광 지도를 얻고 싶어요.
여 특별히 가보고 싶은 곳이 있나요?
남 네. 벼룩시장에 가보고 싶어요.
여 런던에는 벼룩시장이 많아요. 런던에서 가장 큰 것은 Portobello 마켓이지요. 그곳은 매일 열어요.
남 좋군요. 옷과 액세서리에 특화된 곳도 아

specific ones for clothes and accessories?

W Then go to Black Lane Market. It's open today.

M How can I get there?

W Just keep walking until you see a subway station. Then turn right at the corner, and the market should be there.

세요?

여 그럼 Black Lane 마켓으로 가 보세요. 오늘 열려요.

남 그곳은 어떻게 가나요?

여 지하철역이 보일 때까지 계속 걸어가세요. 그런 다음 모퉁이에서 우회전하면 거기 시장이 있을 거예요.

07 ②

해설 학교에 어떻게 가는지 묻는 말에 일찍 학교에 간다는 응답은 어색하다.

어휘 model airplane 모형 비행기
disappointed[dìsəpɔ́intid] 실망한
audition[ɔːdíʃən] 오디션
traffic light 신호등

① M I'm going to enter the model airplane contest.
  W Me, too. I'm looking forward to it.
② M How do you go to school?
  W I go to school early in the morning.
③ M You look disappointed.
  W I failed the audition for the school band.
④ M How do I get to the bank?
  W Go down this road and turn left at the traffic light.
⑤ M Do you have any brothers or sisters?
  W Yes, I have 2 brothers and a sister.

① 남 나 모형 비행기 대회에 나갈 거야.
  여 나도. 정말 기다려져.
② 남 너는 학교에 어떻게 가니?
  여 나는 아침 일찍 학교에 가.
③ 남 너 실망한 것 같구나.
  여 학교 밴드 오디션에서 떨어졌어.
④ 남 은행에 어떻게 가나요?
  여 이 길을 따라 내려가다가 신호등에서 좌회전하십시오.
⑤ 남 너는 형제자매가 있니?
  여 응, 나는 두 명의 형제와 한 명의 여동생이 있어.

08 ④

해설 여자는 남자에게 제시간에 약 먹는 것을 잊지 말라는 말을 Mark에게 전해달라고 했다.

어휘 answer[ǽnsər] 응답하다
take a nap 낮잠 자다
medicine[médisn] 약
on time 제시간에

[Cell phone rings.]

M Hello?

W Hi, James. This is Mark's mom. Is he with you?

M Oh, hello, ma'am. Yes, he is. We're studying for the exam together. Do you need something?

W No, I called him on his cell phone, but he wasn't answering.

M Oh, he's taking a nap now. I'll wake him up.

W No, you don't have to.

M Then I'll let him know that you called when he wakes up.

W Sure. Also, tell him not to forget to take his medicine on time.

[휴대전화가 울린다.]

남 여보세요?

여 안녕, James. Mark 엄마야. Mark는 너랑 같이 있니?

남 아, 안녕하세요. 네, 여기 있어요. 같이 시험공부를 하고 있어요. 무슨 용건이 있으세요?

여 아니, Mark한테 휴대전화로 전화를 했는데 받지를 않는구나.

남 아, 걔가 지금 낮잠을 자고 있어요. 제가 깨울게요.

여 아냐, 그럴 필요 없단다.

남 그럼 걔가 일어나면 전화하셨다고 할게요.

여 그래. 그리고, 걔한테 제시간에 약 먹는 거 잊지 말라고 전해주렴.

09 ③

해설 여자가 농악 리듬에 맞춰 춤추고 있는 사람들과 함께 하자고 제안하자 남자는 신나겠다며 동의하고 있다.

어휘 traditional[trədíʃənəl] 전통적인

W Peter, do you hear the music coming from over there?

M Yes. Is it Korean traditional music?

W Yes, it's called nongak.

M Nongak? Can you explain more about it?

여 Peter, 저쪽에서 들려오는 음악 들려?

남 응. 한국 전통 음악이니?

여 그래. 농악이라고 해.

남 농악? 좀 더 설명해 줄래?

explain[ikspléin] 설명하다
perform[pərfɔ́ːrm] 공연하다, 연주하다
cheer up ~을 격려하다
wish[wiʃ] 기원하다
harvest[háːrvist] 수확
rhythm[ríðm] 리듬

W Sure. It's a form of traditional farmers' music. It has been performed to cheer up farmers and to wish <u>for a good harvest</u>.

M I see. I like the sound of it.

W Look! Many people are dancing to the rhythm together. <u>Why don't we join them</u>, too?

M <u>That sounds exciting</u>! Why not?

여 그래. 그건 전통적인 농부들의 음악의 한 형태야. 농부들을 격려하고 풍년을 기원하기 위해 공연되어 왔어.

남 그렇구나. 나는 저 음악이 마음에 들어.

여 봐! 많은 사람들이 리듬에 맞춰 함께 춤을 추고 있어. 우리도 저들과 함께 하는 게 어때?

남 그거 신나겠다! 좋지.

10 ⑤

해설 감자튀김을 곁들인 핫도그가 5달러이고 콜라 큰 것이 2달러이므로 총금액 7달러를 지불할 것이다.

어휘 fries(= French fries)[fraiz] 감자튀김
be supposed to-v ~하기로 되어 있다
lunchtime[lʌ́ntʃtàim] 점심시간
correct[kərékt] 정확한

W Hello, I'd like a hot dog with fries.

M Okay. <u>Your total comes to</u> $5.

W $5? Isn't it supposed to be $4?

M That's only <u>during lunchtime</u>.

W Okay, I see. Oh, how much is a large drink?

M The large one is $2.

W All right. <u>Then I'll take</u> a large coke.

M Let me <u>check your order</u>. One hot dog with fries and one large drink, correct?

W That's right.

여 안녕하세요, 감자튀김을 곁들인 핫도그 하나 주세요.

남 네. 모두 5달러입니다.

여 5달러요? 원래 4달러 아닌가요?

남 그건 점심시간에만 해당됩니다.

여 네, 그렇군요. 아, 음료 큰 것은 얼마인가요?

남 큰 것은 2달러입니다.

여 네. 그럼 콜라 큰 걸로 할게요.

남 주문을 확인해 보겠습니다. 감자튀김을 곁들인 핫도그 하나와 음료 큰 것 하나, 맞나요?

여 맞아요.

11 ①

해설 여자는 남자에게 자신이 쓸 기사에 사용할 사진을 골라 달라고 했다.

어휘 article[áːrtikl] 기사
endangered[indéindʒərd] 멸종위기에 처한
in the near future 가까운 미래에
choose[tʃuːz] 고르다

W Paul, are you busy now? Can you help me with something?

M I'm not busy at all. What do you need help with?

W I <u>need a picture for</u> my article in the school newspaper.

M What is your story about?

W It's about endangered animals. We <u>may not be able to</u> see some animals in the near future.

M I see. I am interested in saving them, too.

W Great. I need to <u>choose only one picture</u> out of these four. Which one should I pick?

M Let me see.

여 Paul, 너 지금 바쁘니? 뭐 좀 도와줄래?

남 전혀 바쁘지 않아. 무슨 도움이 필요한데?

여 학교 신문에 쓸 내 기사에 사진이 필요해.

남 어떤 내용인데?

여 멸종위기 동물에 관한 거야. 가까운 미래에 일부 동물들을 볼 수 없을지도 모르거든.

남 그렇구나. 나도 그들을 구하는 데 관심 있어.

여 좋아. 이 네 장 중에서 한 장만 골라야 해. 어떤 걸 고를까?

남 한번 볼게.

12 ③

해설 서식지(세계의 거의 모든 바다), 개체 수(1만에서 2만 5천 마리 정도), 멸종 이유(사람들이 사냥해서), 보호 대책(보존 프로그램을 지지하고 고래로 만든 제품은 피해야 함)에 관해 언급되었지만 먹이에 관한 언급은 없었다.

M Hello. I'd like to tell you why we save blue whales and how. Blue whales are the largest animals in the world. They <u>live in almost</u> all the oceans of the world. They were numerous in the past, but today only between 10,000 and 25,000 of <u>them are left</u>. That's because people have <u>hunted</u>

남 안녕하세요. 저는 왜 우리가 흰긴수염고래를 구해야 하는지, 그리고 어떻게 구할 수 있는지에 대해 말하려고 해요. 흰긴수염고래는 세계에서 가장 큰 동물이에요. 그들은 세계의 거의 모든 바다에 살지요. 과거에는 수가 많았는데, 오늘날에는 1만에서 2만 5천 마리 정도만 남았어요. 사람들이

blue whale 흰긴수염고래
numerous[njúːmərəs] 다수의
hunt[hʌnt] 사냥하다
support[səpɔ́ːrt] (정책 등을) 지지하다,
후원하다
conservation[kὰnsərvéiʃən] 보호, 보존
avoid[əvɔ́id] 피하다

them for oil, food, and clothing. To protect them, we should support conservation programs and avoid any products made of whales.

기름이나 음식, 옷을 얻으려고 그들을 사냥해 왔기 때문이에요. 이들을 보호하려면 보존 프로그램을 지지하고 고래로 만든 제품은 사용을 피해야 해요.

13 ①

해설 Shakespeare 극장이 아닌 곳에서 공연하며, 저녁 7시 전에 끝나는 연극 중 더 싼 것을 고르면 된다.

어휘 famous[féiməs] 유명한
theater[θí(ː)ətər] 극장
mind[maind] 상관하다, 신경쓰다
choose[tʃuːz] 고르다
choice[tʃɔis] 선택

W Jack, do you want to go and see a play today?
M There are 2 famous theaters in town. Which one should we go to?
W I've already been to the Shakespeare Theater. Can we go to the other one today?
M Of course, I don't really mind.
W I also need to get home by 7 p.m. today. Will we have enough time?
M Yes, the plays are about 2 hours long.
W I see. Then you can choose which one to watch. I don't really mind either one.
M Okay, then let's choose the cheaper one.
W Good choice.

여 Jack, 오늘 연극 보러 갈래?
남 시내에 유명한 극장이 두 개 있어. 어느 쪽으로 갈까?
여 난 이미 Shakespeare 극장에 가 봤어. 오늘은 다른 곳으로 가도 될까?
남 물론이지. 나는 상관없어.
여 그리고 오늘 저녁 7시까지 집에 가야 하는데, 시간이 될까?
남 응, 연극은 2시간 정도 걸려.
여 알았어. 그러면 어떤 걸 볼지 네가 선택해. 난 어느 것이든 상관없거든.
남 좋아, 그럼 더 싼 걸로 보자.
여 잘 선택했어.

14 ②

해설 추석에 반달 모양으로 만들어 속에 깨 등을 넣어 쪄서 먹는 한국 전통 음식이며, 솔잎에 쪄서 소나무 냄새가 나는 것은 송편이다.

어휘 Thanksgiving Day 추수감사절
half-moon[hǽːfmúːn] 반달
shape[ʃeip] 모양
fill[fil] 채우다
sesame seed 참깨
chestnut[tʃésnʌt] 밤
steam[stiːm] (음식을) 찌다
pine needles 솔잎
translate[trænsléit] 번역하다

W This is a traditional Korean food. We make and eat this on the Korean Thanksgiving Day, Chuseok. It has a half-moon shape, and it is filled with sesame seeds, sugar, chestnuts, or beans. You steam this on pine needles. That's why this smells like pine trees. Its name comes from the use of pine trees and it translates to "pine cakes."

여 이것은 한국 전통 음식이에요. 우리는 한국의 추수감사절인 추석에 이것을 만들어 먹어요. 반달 모양을 하고 있으며, 참깨나 설탕, 밤 또는 콩으로 속을 채워요. 이것은 솔잎 위에 쪄요. 그래서 소나무 냄새가 나요. 그것의 이름은 소나무를 사용하는 것에서 유래했고, '소나무 케이크'로 번역돼요.

15 ②

해설 이사를 가는 친구 때문에 우울한 여자에게 남자가 사진집을 만들 것을 제안했고 여자도 동의해서 바로 만들기로 했다.

어휘 quiet[kwáiət] 조용한
promise[prάmis] 약속하다

M Sura, is something wrong? You're very quiet today.
W I'm feeling very sad. My best friend Jamie is moving to Toronto next week.
M I'm sorry to hear that.
W We promised to have video chats online every day, but I'll still miss her.

남 수라야, 무슨 일 있어? 오늘 별로 말이 없네.
여 나 정말 슬퍼. 내 가장 친한 친구인 Jamie가 다음 주에 토론토로 이사를 가.
남 저런, 안 됐구나.
여 우리는 매일 화상 채팅을 하기로 약속했지만, 나는 그래도 걔가 그리울 거야.

chat[tʃæt] 채팅, 잡담
miss[mis] 그리워하다; 놓치다
meaningful[míːninfəl] 의미 있는

M Then why don't you make Jamie a photo book full of her and your pictures?
W That's a good idea. I'm sure it will be a meaningful gift.
M Let's make it right now. I'll help you.
W Thanks.

남 그러면 Jamie에게 그녀와 너의 사진들로 채운 사진집을 만들어주는 게 어때?
여 좋은 생각이야. 정말 의미 있는 선물이 될 것 같아.
남 지금 바로 그것을 만들어 보자. 내가 도와줄게.
여 고마워.

16 ④

해설 여자는 파란색 블라우스로 교환해 달라고 했다.

어휘 blouse[blaus] 블라우스
purple[pə́ːrpl] 보라색의
medium[míːdiəm] 중간

M Hello, ma'am. How may I help you?
W I got this blouse as a gift yesterday, but the color doesn't look good on me.
M Oh, I see. This blouse comes in 3 other colors.
W Great. Does it come in orange?
M I'm sorry, but there are yellow, purple, and blue ones. How about this purple one?
W It looks good, but I think blue would be better. Do you have a blue one in medium?
M Of course. I'll be right back with it.

남 안녕하세요. 고객님. 무엇을 도와드릴까요?
여 이 블라우스를 어제 선물로 받았는데 색이 저한테 잘 어울리지 않아요.
남 아, 그렇군요. 이 블라우스는 세 가지의 다른 색이 있어요.
여 잘됐네요. 오렌지색 있나요?
남 죄송하지만, 노랑, 보라, 파란색이 있어요. 이 보라색은 어때요?
여 그것도 좋아 보이지만, 파란색이 더 좋을 것 같아요. 파란색으로 중간 크기 있어요?
남 물론이죠. 제가 바로 가지고 오겠습니다.

17 ①

해설 시험 때문에 받는 스트레스가 오히려 도움이 된 이유를 묻는 남자의 말에 이어 스트레스가 어떤 도움을 주었는지 알려주는 응답이 적절하다.

어휘 stress[stres] 스트레스를 주다; 스트레스
helpful[hélpfəl] 도움이 되는
[선택지]
pressure[préʃər] 압박

W Are you studying, Henry? Have some of these cookies.
M Thanks, Mom. I'm studying for the science test, but I'm so worried.
W I understand. I used to feel that way before exams, too.
M Really? You did well in school, didn't you?
W I tried my best, but exams always stressed me out. But a little stress was helpful for me.
M Why do you say that?
W Because it made me try harder.

여 공부하는 중이니, Henry? 이 쿠키 좀 먹어.
남 고마워요, 엄마. 과학 시험 공부 중인데 너무 걱정돼요.
여 이해해. 나도 시험 전이면 그런 기분이 들곤 했어.
남 정말요? 엄마는 공부를 잘하셨잖아요, 그렇지 않나요?
여 나는 최선을 다했지만 시험 때문에 항상 스트레스를 받았어. 하지만 약간의 스트레스는 나에게 도움이 되었단다.
남 왜 그렇게 말씀하세요?
여 그게 나를 더 노력하게 만들었기 때문이야.

② 그것에 대해 걱정하지 않아도 된다.
③ 내 자신에게 너무 많은 압박을 가했거든.
④ 걱정하지 마. 너는 과학을 잘하잖아.
⑤ 운 좋게도 좋은 친구들이 많았기 때문이야.

18 ④

해설 디저트로 아이스크림을 주문했는데 아이스크림은 없다고 했으므로 다른 디저트 종류를 주문하는 응답이 어울린다.

어휘 fresh[freʃ] 신선한
mushroom[mʌ́ʃru(ː)m] 버섯

W Good evening, sir. Can I take your order?
M Good evening. I'd like some pasta with fresh mushrooms.
W Okay. Would you like a drink with that?
M Yes, please. I'd like some water with lemon.

여 안녕하십니까, 선생님. 주문하시겠습니까?
남 안녕하세요. 저는 신선한 버섯이 들어간 파스타를 먹을게요.
여 네. 그것과 함께 음료도 하시겠습니까?
남 네. 그럴게요. 레몬을 넣은 물을 마실게요.

mango[mǽŋɡou] 망고
dessert[dizə́:rt] 디저트, 후식

W Okay. Anything else?
M Could I have some bread and cheese?
W Yes, of course. Is that all then?
M I'd like some mango ice cream for dessert.
W I'm sorry, but there isn't any ice cream here.
M Then I'd like some chocolate cake.

여 알겠습니다. 더 주문하실 거 있나요?
남 빵과 치즈를 먹을 수 있을까요?
여 네, 그럼요. 그럼 이게 전부신가요?
남 디저트로 망고 아이스크림을 먹을게요.
여 죄송하지만 여기에 아이스크림은 없습니다.
남 그럼 초콜릿 케이크를 먹을게요.

① 아뇨, 괜찮아요. 목마르지 않아요.
② 계산서 좀 주시겠습니까?
③ 저는 이 파스타가 마음에 안 들어요.
⑤ 딸기 아이스크림 있어요?

19 ⑤

해설 여자가 같이 여행을 간다면 재밌을 것이라는 남자의 말에 초대해 줘서 고맙다는 응답이 이어지는 것이 가장 적절하다.

어휘 go on vacation 휴가를 가다
break[breik] 휴가, 방학
peaceful[píːsfəl] 잔잔한, 평화로운
wave[weiv] 파도
scenery[síːnəri] 경치
awesome[ɔ́ːsəm] 기막히게 좋은, 근사한

M Amy, where are you going to go on vacation this summer break?
W I'm not sure yet. What about you?
M I'm going to go to Ulleung-do with my friends. It's known for its peaceful blue waves and beautiful scenery.
W I heard that, too. That's where I've always wanted to go.
M Then would you like to come with us?
W Wow! That sounds awesome. Are you sure it's okay to join you and your friends?
M Of course. It will be a lot of fun.
W Great. Thanks for inviting me.

남 Amy, 이번 여름방학에 어디로 휴가를 갈 예정이니?
여 아직 잘 모르겠어. 너는 어때?
남 나는 친구들과 울릉도에 갈 거야. 잔잔한 푸른 물결과 아름다운 경치로 유명한 곳이지.
여 나도 그렇다고 들었어. 내가 항상 가고 싶었던 곳이야.
남 그럼 우리랑 같이 갈래?
여 와! 좋아. 너랑 네 친구들과 함께 가도 정말 괜찮아?
남 물론이지. 아주 재미있을 거야.
여 좋아. 초대해 줘서 고마워.

① 아니, 갈 수 없어. 다음 기회로 미루자.
② 즐거운 여행이 되길 바랄게.
③ 내가 같이 가기를 바라니?
④ 미안하지만 다른 계획이 있어.

20 ③

해설 함께 영화를 본 은지에게 영화가 어땠는지 의견을 묻고 싶어 하는 상황이다.

어휘 thrilling[θríliŋ] 스릴 넘치는
on the edge of A's seat (영화·이야기 따위에) 매료되어
throughout[θruːáut] ~ 동안 쭉[내내]
character[kǽriktər] 등장인물
special effects 특수 효과
amazing[əméiziŋ] 놀라운
wonder[wʌ́ndər] 궁금해 하다

M Jason is a huge fan of action movies. He watched the new movie that he had waited for with Eunji today. The thrilling action movie kept him sitting on the edge of his seat throughout it. The main characters were great and the special effects were amazing. Jason loved the movie, but he wonders if Eunji liked it. In this situation, what would Jason most likely say to Eunji?

Jason How did you like the movie?

남 Jason은 액션 영화의 열렬한 팬이다. 그는 오늘 은지와 함께 기다려 왔던 새 영화를 봤다. 스릴 넘치는 그 액션 영화는 영화 내내 그를 매료시켰다. 주인공들도 멋졌고 특수효과도 놀라웠다. Jason은 이 영화가 좋았지만 은지도 좋아했는지 궁금하다. 이러한 상황에서 Jason이 은지에게 할 말로 가장 적절한 것은 무엇인가?

Jason 이 영화 어땠어?

① 내가 팝콘 살게.
② 액션 영화 좋아하니?
④ 우리 내일 영화 보는 게 어때?
⑤ 너는 그 영화를 몇 번이나 봤니?

01 ②	02 ④	03 ⑤	04 ④	05 ③	06 ②	07 ③
08 ④	09 ②	10 ④	11 ③	12 ③	13 ②	14 ②
15 ⑤	16 ⑤	17 ⑤	18 ④	19 ①	20 ②	

01 ②

해설 정사각형 모양이며 가장자리에 꽃으로 띠를 두른 것을 구입하겠다고 했다.

어휘 tray[trei] 쟁반
round[raund] 둥근 모양의
these days 요즘
prefer A to B B보다 A를 더 좋아하다
square[skwɛər] 정사각형 모양의
band[bænd] 띠(모양의 것), 줄무늬
edge[edʒ] 가장자리, 테두리

M Hello, ma'am. Can I help you?
W Hello. I'm looking for a tray.
M Round ones are popular these days. What do you think of this round one with the word "Happy" in the center?
W Hmm… I prefer square ones to round ones.
M I see. Then how about this one with flowers in the center?
W Actually, this is not bad, but do you have any square ones with a band of flowers around the edge?
M Oh, you must be looking for something like this.
W This is perfect. I'll take it.

남 안녕하세요, 고객님. 도와 드릴까요?
여 안녕하세요, 쟁반을 찾고 있어요.
남 둥근 것이 요즘 아주 인기예요. 가운데에 'Happy'라는 단어가 있는 이 둥근 것은 어떠세요?
여 음… 전 둥근 것보다 정사각형 모양이 더 좋아요.
남 알겠습니다. 그럼 가운데에 꽃이 있는 이건 어떠세요?
여 사실은 나쁘지 않아요, 하지만 가장자리에 꽃으로 띠를 두른 것은 없나요?
남 아, 이런 것을 찾으시는 군요.
여 이거면 딱이네요. 이걸 살게요.

02 ④

해설 어제 맡긴 자동차 수리가 언제 끝나는지 확인하기 위해 전화했다.

어휘 auto[ɔ́ːtou] 자동차
repair shop 수리점, 정비 공장
repair[ripɛ́ər] 수리하다; 수리
complete[kəmplíːt] 완료된
around[əráund] 대략
come by 잠깐 들르다

[Telephone rings.]
W Johnny's Auto Repair Shop, what can I do for you?
M Hello, I'm Larry Jackson. I took my car there yesterday afternoon to get it repaired. Is the repair complete?
W Let me check. *[Pause]* Oh, Mr. Jackson, it seems like your car is under repair now.
M I see. When should I come in?
W Your car should be ready later this afternoon, around 5 p.m.
M Okay. How late are you open today?
W We're open until 6 p.m.
M All right. I'll come by around 5:30.

[전화벨이 울린다.]
여 Johnny's 자동사 수리점입니다, 무엇을 도와 드릴까요?
남 안녕하세요, Larry Jackson이라고 합니다. 제 차를 어제 오후에 갖고 가서 수리를 맡겼거든요. 수리가 끝났나요?
여 확인해 보겠습니다. *[잠시 후]* 아, Jackson 씨, 고객님 차가 지금 수리 중인 것 같네요.
남 알겠습니다. 언제 가면 될까요?
여 고객님 차는 오늘 오후 늦게 5시 쯤 준비가 될 것 같습니다.
남 알겠어요. 오늘 언제까지 문을 여나요?
여 저희는 오후 6시까지 문을 엽니다.
남 알겠습니다. 5시 30분경에 들르겠습니다.

03 ⑤

해설 여자가 음악을 키워도 되는지 묻는 말에 노트북으로 작업 중인 남자는 집중을 해야 한다며 거절하는 상황이다.

어휘 turn down (소리 등을) 줄이다
loud[laud] 시끄러운
aisle seat 통로 쪽 좌석
window seat 창가 쪽 좌석

① W Can you turn down the volume? I can't hear the TV.
　M I'm sorry. I didn't know it was that loud.
② W Can I get you something to drink?
　M I'd like a Coke, please.
③ W Would you like an aisle seat or a window seat?

① 여 소리 좀 줄여 주시겠어요? TV 소리를 들을 수가 없네요.
　남 미안합니다. 그렇게 시끄러운 줄 몰랐어요.
② 여 마실 것 좀 갖다 드릴까요?
　남 콜라로 부탁해요.
③ 여 통로 쪽 좌석이 좋으세요, 창문 쪽 좌석이 좋으세요?

ATM(= automated teller machine) 현금 자동 입출금기
Do you mind if ~? ~해도 될까요?
turn up (소리, 온도 등을) 높이다, 올리다
concentrate[kάnsəntrèit] 집중하다

M A window seat, please.
④ W Excuse me, can you tell me how to use the ATM?
M Don't worry, I'll help you.
⑤ W Do you mind if I turn up the music?
M Sorry, but I'm trying to concentrate.

남 창문 쪽 좌석으로 주세요.
④ 여 실례합니다. ATM 사용하는 방법 좀 알려 줄 수 있나요?
남 걱정 마세요, 제가 도와 드릴게요.
⑤ 여 음악 소리를 좀 키워도 괜찮을까요?
남 죄송합니다만, 집중을 좀 하려고 하고 있거든요.

04 ④

해설 Ted's 피자집의 피자가 맛있다고 했지만, 여자는 스파게티를 먹겠다고 했다.

어휘 eat out 외식하다
go grocery shopping 식료품을 사러 가다
grocery store 식료품 가게
serve[səːrv] (음식을) 제공하다, 차려 내다
other than ~ 이외에

W There is nothing to cook with in the kitchen. Do you want to eat out?
M Sure. Maybe we should go grocery shopping after dinner.
W Then let's go to one of the restaurants around the grocery store.
M Okay. We could go to a Japanese or an Indian restaurant.
W Well, is there anything else?
M Let me think. How about Ted's Pizza? The pizza is really good there.
W Does the restaurant serve anything other than pizza?
M There are spaghetti and steaks, too.
W I'll have spaghetti then.

여 부엌에서 요리할 재료가 없네. 나가서 먹고 싶어요?
남 좋아요. 저녁 식사 후에 식료품을 사러 가야겠군요.
여 그럼 식료품 가게 주변에 있는 레스토랑 중에서 한 곳을 가요.
남 알겠어요. 일식이나 인도 레스토랑에 가면 되겠네요.
여 글쎄, 다른 곳은 있어요?
남 생각해 볼게요. Ted's 피자집은 어때요? 피자가 아주 맛있어요.
여 거기에서 피자 외에 다른 것도 나오나요?
남 스파게티와 스테이크도 있어요.
여 그럼 스파게티를 먹어야 겠네요.

05 ③

해설 목적지(로마), 비행 시간(11시간 25분), 비행 속도(시속 520마일), 날씨(좋음)에 관해 언급되었지만, 도착 예정 시각에 관한 언급은 없었다.

어휘 captain[kǽptən] (비행기의) 기장
crew[kruː] 승무원
aboard[əbɔ́ːrd] 탑승한
flying time 비행 시간
altitude[ǽltətjùːd] 고도
feet[fiːt] 피트 《길이의 단위》
mile[mail] 마일 《길이의 단위》
ahead[əhéd] 앞으로, 앞에
relax[rilǽks] 긴장을 풀다
rest[rest] 나머지
flight[flait] 비행

M Good evening, ladies and gentlemen. This is your captain speaking. The crew would like to welcome you all aboard. Our flying time to Rome today will be 11 hours and 25 minutes. We're flying now at an altitude of 43,000 feet and our airspeed is 520 miles an hour. The weather ahead is good, so relax and enjoy the rest of the flight. Thank you.

남 신사 숙녀 여러분, 안녕하세요. 기장입니다. 저희 승무원들은 탑승하신 여러분 모두를 환영합니다. 오늘 로마까지 비행 시간은 11시간 25분이 소요될 것입니다. 우리는 지금 고도 43,000 피트의 높이로 비행하고 있고 비행 속도는 시속 520마일입니다. 앞으로의 날씨가 좋을 것 같으니 편안히 남은 비행 여정을 즐겨 주시기 바랍니다. 감사합니다.

06 ②

해설 새로 카드를 잃어버려 신청하고, 발급된 카드를 이 은행에서 찾을 수 있다는 남자의 말로 보아 두 사람의 관계는 은행원과 고객임을 알 수 있다.

M Good afternoon. How may I help you?
W Hello. I need to get a new card.
M I see. Do you have an account with our bank?

남 안녕하세요, 무엇을 도와드릴까요?
여 안녕하세요. 카드를 새로 발급받아야 해요.
남 그러시군요. 저의 은행에 계좌가 있으신가요?

어휘 account[əkáunt] 계좌
wallet[wálit] 지갑
fill out (서식을) 작성하다
form[fɔːrm] 서식
business day 영업일

W Yes. I lost my wallet and everything in it. So, I'd like to order the same card I had.
M I see. Then can you fill out this form?
W All right. How long will it take to get a new card?
M If you choose to pick it up at this bank, it'll take 2 to 3 business days.

여 네. 지갑과 그 안에 든 것을 모두 다 잃어 버렸어요. 그래서, 갖고 있던 것과 같은 카드를 주문하려고요.
남 알겠습니다. 그러면 이 서식을 작성해 주시겠어요?
여 그러죠. 새 카드를 받으려면 얼마나 걸릴 까요?
남 이 은행에서 받아 가기로 하신다면 영업일 기준으로 2, 3일 걸릴 겁니다.

07 ③

해설 직업을 묻는 말에 가끔 자신의 개를 산책시킨다는 대답은 어색하다.

어휘 usually[júːʒuəli] 대개, 주로
for a living 생계 수단으로
walk[wɔːk] (동물을) 산책시키다; 걷다
run late 늦다

① **M** How often do you practice the piano?
   W I usually practice 3 or 4 times a week.
② **M** Have you been to Paris before?
   W No, but I hope to visit there one day.
③ **M** What do you do for a living?
   W Well, I sometimes walk my dog.
④ **M** Are you running late?
   W Yes, there are only 10 minutes left until class.
⑤ **M** Why don't you join the music club?
   W Sure. I've always wanted to learn to sing.

① 남 피아노 연습을 얼마나 자주 하니?
   여 보통 1주일에 서너 번 해.
② 남 전에 파리에 가 본 적이 있니?
   여 아니, 하지만 언젠가 거기를 방문하기를 바래.
③ 남 직업이 뭔가요?
   여 음, 전 가끔 저희 개를 산책시켜요.
④ 남 늦었니?
   여 응, 수업까지 10분밖에 남지 않았어.
⑤ 남 음악 동아리에 가입하는 것이 어떠니?
   여 좋아. 나는 항상 노래 부르는 방법을 배우고 싶었거든.

08 ④

해설 여자는 남자에게 휴가를 가는 곳의 경치 사진을 찍어달라고 부탁했다.

어휘 go on vacation 휴가를 가다
beach[biːtʃ] 바닷가, 해변
South Pacific 남태평양
scenery[síːnəri] 경치

W Tom, where are you going on vacation this summer?
M I'm going to a beach in the South Pacific.
W Really? Are you doing anything special?
M Not really. I just want to relax and enjoy the scenery.
W I see. Oh, can you do me a favor?
M What is it? I hope it's an easy one.
W Can you take pictures of the beautiful scenery there? I want to put them in my magazine.
M No problem. You know I am good at taking pictures.

여 Tom, 이번 여름에 어디로 휴가를 가니?
남 남태평양에 있는 해변으로 갈 예정이야.
여 정말? 특별한 어떤 일을 할 거니?
남 그건 아니고, 그저 긴장을 풀고 경치를 즐기고 싶어.
여 그렇구나. 아, 부탁 좀 들어 줄 수 있니?
남 뭔데? 쉬운 일이면 좋겠는데.
여 그곳의 아름다운 경치 사진을 좀 찍을 수 있어? 내 잡지에 사진들을 좀 넣고 싶어서 그래.
남 문제 없지. 내가 사진 찍는 데 재주가 있잖아.

09 ②

해설 여자가 남자에게 방을 매일 조금씩 청소하고 정돈하라며 충고했다.

어휘 mess[mes] 엉망인 상태
everywhere[évrihwɛ̀ər] 어디에나
in a minute 곧
trash[træʃ] 쓰레기
organized[ɔ́ːrɡənàizd] 정돈된

W Jack! Look at your room.
M What about my room, Mom?
W It's a mess. Your dirty clothes are everywhere.
M I'll put them in the laundry room in a minute.
W And all this trash?
M I'll put it in the can and clean the room.

여 Jack! 네 방을 좀 봐라!
남 제 방이 뭐가 어때서요, 엄마?
여 엉망이잖아. 네 더러운 옷들이 곳곳에 널려 있구나.
남 세탁실에 곧 그것들을 둘게요.
여 그러면 이 쓰레기들 전부는?
남 쓰레기통에 넣고 방을 청소할게요.

organize[ɔ́ːrɡənàiz] 정돈하다
make a habit of ~하는 습관을 들이다

W It's very important to keep your room clean and organized. It's also good for your health.
M But there is too much to clean.
W You should make a habit of cleaning and organizing a little each day.

여 방을 깨끗하고 정돈된 상태로 유지하는 건 아주 중요하단다. 네 건강에도 좋아.
남 하지만 너무 많아서 다 치울 수가 없어요.
여 너는 매일 조금씩 청소하고 정돈하는 습관을 들여야 한단다.

10 ④

[해설] 성인 요금 6달러짜리 티켓 두 장과 8세 이하 어린이 요금 3달러짜리 티켓 한 장을 구매하겠다고 했으므로 여자가 지불할 금액은 총 15달러이다.

[어휘] tour[tuər] 여행, 관광
adult[ədʌ́lt] 성인, 어른
under[ʌ́ndər] ~ 미만인
run[rʌn] (버스, 기차 등이) 운행하다
once[wʌns] 한 번
get to 도착하다

W How much are the tickets for the tour bus?
M $6 for adults and $3 for children under 8.
W How often does the tour bus run on Sundays?
M It runs once every hour. The next one leaves at 4 o'clock.
W How long does it take to get to the K-Tower?
M About an hour and a half. Would you like a ticket?
W Yes. I want tickets for 2 adults and a child, please.
M All right.

여 투어 버스 티켓이 얼마죠?
남 성인은 6달러이고 8세 미만 어린이는 3달러입니다.
여 일요일에는 투어 버스가 얼마나 자주 다니죠?
남 매 시간 한 번 다닙니다. 다음 버스는 4시에 출발합니다.
여 K-Tower까지 가는 데 얼마나 걸리죠?
남 대략 1시간 30분 걸립니다. 티켓 드릴까요?
여 네. 성인 두 명, 어린이 한 명 티켓을 주세요.
남 알겠습니다.

11 ③

[해설] 책이 반납되면 문자 메시지로 알려 주겠다며 대출 예약 서식을 작성하라는 여자의 말에 남자는 알겠다고 했다.

[어휘] geographic[dʒìːəɡrǽfik] 지리(학)적인
magazine[mæ̀ɡəzíːn] 잡지
be supposed to-v ~해야 한다
fill out (서식을) 작성하다
form[fɔːrm] 서식
text message 문자 메시지

W Hi, can I help you?
M Yes. Do you have the latest *World Geographic*?
W I'll check for you. *[Pause]* I'm afraid it won't be here until next week. Somebody else already borrowed it.
M Oh no! I really need it now.
W It's one of the most popular magazines in this library.
M Hmm... What am I supposed to do now?
W Fill out this form. We'll send you a text message as soon as we have it back.
M Okay.

여 안녕하세요, 도와 드릴까요?
남 네. 〈World Geographic〉 최신호 있어요?
여 확인해 드릴게요. *[잠시 후]* 어쩌죠, 다음 주까지는 여기에 없을 거예요. 다른 누군가가 이미 대출했어요.
남 이런! 지금 꼭 필요한데.
여 이 도서관에서 가장 인기 있는 잡지 중 하나예요.
남 음… 이제 어떻게 해야 하죠?
여 이 서식을 작성하세요. 반납되면 바로 문자 메시지를 보내 드릴게요.
남 알겠습니다.

12 ③

[해설] 위치(페루), 건설 시기(서기 1450년경), 발견 시기(1911년), 발견자(Hiram Bingham)에 관해 언급되었지만, 건설 목적에 관한 언급은 없었다.

[어휘] Inca[íŋkə] 잉카 제국, 잉카 사람
researcher[risə́ːrtʃər] 조사자, 연구자
AD[éidí] 서기, 기원 후
above sea level 해발

W Machu Picchu is an Inca city in Peru. Many researchers believe that the city was built around 1450 AD. It is about 2,430 meters above sea level. For centuries, it was buried in the jungle. In 1911, it was discovered by American historian Hiram Bingham and became known to the world. Machu Picchu has been one of the most famous tourist

여 Machu Picchu는 페루에 있는 잉카의 도시이다. 많은 연구원들은 이 도시가 서기 1450년경에 세워졌다고 믿고 있다. 이곳의 높이는 해발 약 2,430미터이다. 이곳은 수 세기 동안 정글 속에 묻혀 있었다. 1911년에 미국인 역사학자 Hiram Bingham에 의해 발견되어 세상에 알려졌다. Machu Picchu는 발견된 이후 세계에서 가장 유명한 관광 명소 중 하나가 되었다.

century[séntʃəri] 세기, 100년
bury[béri] 묻다, 매장하다
discover[diskʌ́vər] 발견하다
historian[histɔ́ːriən] 역사가
become known 유명해지다
tourist attraction 관광 명소
discovery[diskʌ́vəri] 발견

attractions in the world ever since its discovery.

13 ②

[해설] 기초반 중에서 월요일을 제외한 오전 강좌를 선택하겠다고 했다.

[어휘] table tennis 탁구
level[lévəl] 수준, 레벨
beginner[bigínər] 초보자
basic[béisik] 초급의, 기초적인
except[iksépt] ~을 제외하고
prefer to ~하는 것을 더 좋아하다
[선택지]
intermediate[ìntərmíːdiət] 중급의
advanced[ədvǽnst] 고급의

W Hello, I'd like to take table tennis lessons here at the sports center.
M Okay. What level are you going to take?
W Well, since I'm a beginner, I have to choose the basic one.
M For basic, you have to come 3 times a week.
W Well, I can come any days except Mondays.
M Okay. Would you prefer to come in the morning or afternoon?
W In the morning, please.
M All right.

여 안녕하세요, 여기 스포츠 센터에서 탁구 강습을 받고 싶습니다.
남 알겠습니다. 어떤 레벨을 수강할 예정이세요?
여 글쎄요, 초보자니까 기초반을 선택해야 하겠네요.
남 기초반은 일주일에 세 번 나오셔야 합니다.
여 음, 월요일을 제외하고 어느 요일에도 올 수 있어요.
남 네. 오전에 나오는 것이 더 좋으세요, 아니면 오후가 더 좋으세요?
여 오전으로 부탁해요.
남 알겠습니다.

14 ②

[해설] 건축 재료, 가구, 무기는 물론 음식 재료 등으로까지 쓰이고 있고, 줄기는 단단하고 판다가 아주 좋아하는 식물은 대나무이다.

[어휘] diameter[daiǽmitər] 지름
be used to-v ~하는 데 사용되다
building material 건축 재료
furniture[fə́ːrnitʃər] 가구
tool[tuːl] 도구, 연장
even[íːvən] 심지어
weapon[wépən] 무기
food ingredient 식재료
stem[stem] 줄기
light[lait] 가벼운

M This is a plant. This can grow over 30 meters tall and be 30 centimeters in diameter. This is often used to make building materials, furniture, tools, and even weapons. Young ones are often used as a food ingredient. Stems of this are hard and light. People in many Asian countries use them to cook food like rice and soup. Pandas love to eat as much as 18 kilograms of it each day.

남 이것은 식물이에요. 이것은 높이가 30미터 이상으로 자랄 수 있고 지름이 30센티미터까지도 될 수 있어요. 이것은 종종 건축 재료, 가구, 연장, 심지어 무기를 만드는 데에도 사용돼요. 이것의 어린 것은 종종 음식의 재료로 사용되기도 하지요. 이것의 줄기는 단단하고 가벼워요. 많은 아시아 국가의 사람들은 이것을 이용해 밥이나 국 같은 음식을 요리해 왔어요. 판다는 매일 18킬로그램이나 되는 양의 이것을 먹는 것을 아주 좋아해요.

15 ⑤

[해설] 호텔 이용이 처음이기 때문에, 여자가 대신 프런트 데스크에 연락하여 남자의 요청 사항을 전달하겠다고 했다.

[어휘] wake-up call 모닝콜
front desk (호텔 등의) 프런트, 안내 데스크

[Telephone rings.]
W Room service. How can I help you?
M I'd like to order a hamburger, please.
W Of course, sir. It'll be ready in 20 minutes. Is there anything else?
M I also would like a wake-up call at 5:30 tomorrow morning.

[전화벨이 울린다.]
여 룸서비스입니다. 무엇을 도와 드릴까요?
남 햄버거를 하나 주문하고 싶어요.
여 알겠습니다. 고객님. 20분 후에 준비되겠습니다. 다른 것도 있으세요?
남 내일 아침 5시 30분에 모닝콜도 좀 부탁할게요.

towel[táuəl] 수건
since ~이기 때문에
clerk[klərk] 직원
request[rikwést] 요구
right away 당장, 바로

W I'm sorry. For wake-up calls, you have to call the front desk.
M I see. I also need some towels. Should I call the front desk about that, too?
W Yes. But since it's your first time, I'll let the front desk clerk know about your request right away.
M Thank you very much.

여 죄송합니다. 모닝콜에 대해서는 프런트에 전화하셔야 합니다.
남 알겠습니다. 수건도 좀 필요해요. 이것에 대해서도 프런트에 전화해야 하나요?
여 네. 하지만 처음이시니까 제가 프런트 직원에게 고객님의 요청 사항을 바로 알려 주겠습니다.
남 감사합니다.

16 ⑤

해설 두 사람은 오후 4시에 만나기로 했다.

어휘 advertise[ǽdvərtàiz] 광고하다
have an appointment 약속이 있다

[Telephone rings.]
W Hello.
M Hello. I'm calling about the 3-bedroom apartment you advertised.
W Of course. What time would you like to come and see it?
M I'd like to be there at 1 o'clock tomorrow afternoon.
W I'm sorry, but I have an appointment at 1:30 tomorrow afternoon.
M How about 3 o'clock then?
W Sorry. There will be no one home around 3 o'clock. Is 4 o'clock okay?
M That's fine with me. See you then.

[전화벨이 울린다.]
여 여보세요.
남 여보세요. 광고하신 방 세 개짜리 아파트 때문에 전화 드렸습니다.
여 그러시군요. 몇 시에 와서 보고 싶으세요?
남 내일 오후 1시에 갔으면 합니다.
여 죄송하지만, 내일 오후 1시 30분에 약속이 있거든요.
남 그럼 3시는 어떠세요?
여 죄송해요. 3시쯤에는 집에 아무도 없을 것 같아요. 4시는 괜찮을까요?
남 좋습니다. 그 때 뵙죠.

17 ⑤

해설 메시지를 남기면서 언제든지 전화 해도 된다는 남자의 말에 이어서 여자는 메시지를 전달하겠다는 응답이 이어져야 가장 적절하다.

어휘 law office 법률 사무소, 변호사 사무소
at the moment 지금
leave[li:v] 남기다
arrive in ~에 도착하다
any time 언제라도
[선택지]
look forward to ~을 고대하다
You have the wrong number. 전화 잘못 거셨습니다.

[Telephone rings.]
W Hello. This is Anderson's Law Office. How can I help you?
M Hello. May I speak to Mr. David Greene, please?
W I'm afraid he's not here at the moment.
M Can I leave him a message?
W Sure. May I have your name, please?
M Eric Koppel. Please tell him I am going to arrive in Berlin at 8 p.m. tomorrow.
W All right. Does he have your number?
M Yes, he does. He can call me any time.
W I'll give him the message as soon as he's back.

[전화벨이 울린다.]
여 여보세요. Anderson 법률 사무소입니다. 무엇을 도와 드릴까요?
남 여보세요. David Greene 씨와 통화할 수 있을까요?
여 지금은 자리에 안 계십니다.
남 메시지를 남겨도 될까요?
여 네. 성함이 어떻게 되세요?
남 Eric Koppel이라고 합니다. 제가 내일 저녁 8시에 베를린에 도착할 예정이라고 전해 주세요.
여 알겠습니다. Greene 씨가 당신의 전화번호를 알고 있나요?
남 네. 아무 때나 저에게 전화해도 됩니다.
여 그가 돌아오는 대로 메시지를 전해 드릴게요.

① 그가 누구에게 전화하면 될까요?
② 당신에게 그의 전화번호를 알려 드릴게요.
③ 당신의 방문을 기대하고 있습니다.
④ 죄송하지만 전화 잘못 거셨네요.

18 ④

해설 바이올린 연주하는 걸 계속 연습한 다면 그것을 즐기게 될 것이라고 조언하는 여자에게 여자의 말이 맞길 바란다고 응답하는 것이 상황상 가장 자연스럽다.

어휘 find[faind] ~라고 여기다, 생각하다

boring[bɔ́:riŋ] 따분한, 지겨운
confident[kánfədənt] 자신감이 있는
continue[kəntínju:] 계속하다
give up 포기하다
[선택지]
should have p.p. ~했어야 했다
successful[səksésfəl] 성공한, 성공적인

W How are your violin lessons going?
M My teacher says I'm getting better, but I'm not sure.
W How long have you been taking lessons?
M For 6 months.
W Do you enjoy playing the violin?
M No, I find it boring and difficult. I'm not confident that I should continue to take lessons.
W You shouldn't give up yet. Keep practicing and you'll be able to enjoy playing the violin.
M Thanks. I hope you're right.

여 바이올린 레슨이 어떻게 되어 가고 있니?
남 선생님은 내가 나아지고 있다고 말씀하시는데 나는 잘 모르겠어.
여 레슨을 받은 지는 얼마나 되었니?
남 6개월 되었지.
여 바이올린 연주하는 걸 즐기니?
남 아니, 난 그게 따분하고 어려운 것 같아. 레슨을 계속 받아야 하는지 자신이 없어.
여 아직 포기해서는 안 돼. 계속 연습하면 바이올린 연주를 즐길 수 있게 될 거야.
남 고마워. 네 말이 맞기를 바래.

① 자신감을 가져.
② 아니, 나는 훌륭한 피아니스트가 될 거야.
③ 맞아, 너는 성공할 거야.
⑤ 너는 연습을 더 일찍 시작했어야 했어.

19 ①

해설 좋은 가격에 옷을 산 남자에게 어디서 샀는지 묻는 상황으로 보아, 여자도 그곳에서 쇼핑하고 싶다는 응답이 가장 자연스럽다.

어휘 still[stil] 아직도, 여전히
item[áitəm] 품목
[선택지]
in total 총계해서
had better ~하는 게 낫다
not ~ anymore 더 이상 ~ 아닌
look good on ~에게 어울리다

M How do I look in my new T-shirt?
W Wow, you look wonderful. How much was your shirt?
M It was just $10.
W That's a very good price.
M I think so, too. It's still on sale now. And I also got some other items, too.
W Where did you get them?
M At the new shopping mall across the street.
W I'd like to go shopping there, too.

남 새 티셔츠 입으니까 어때 보여?
여 와, 멋져 보이네. 얼마 주고 샀어?
남 겨우 10달러야.
여 정말 좋은 가격이다.
남 나도 그렇게 생각해. 아직도 세일 중이야. 그리고 나는 다른 품목들도 좀 샀지.
여 그것들을 어디에서 샀어?
남 길 건너에 있는 새 쇼핑몰에서.
여 나도 거기에 쇼핑하러 가고 싶다.

② 새 쇼핑몰이 어디에 있니?
③ 너는 전부 얼마를 쓴 거니?
④ 너는 더 이상 쇼핑 하러 가지 않는 게 좋겠어.
⑤ 그 새 티셔츠는 나한테 어울리지 않아.

20 ②

해설 우산을 가져오지 않은 Amy에게 같이 쓰자고 제안하는 상황이다.

어휘 without[wiðáut] ~ 없이
heavy rain 폭우
expect[ikspékt] 예상하다
share[ʃɛər] ~을 같이 쓰다
[선택지]
mine[main] 나의 것
clear up (날씨가) 개다

W Amy comes to school without an umbrella. When she sees Bill carrying an umbrella, she asks him if it'll rain. Bill says heavy rain is expected later this afternoon. Amy gets worried because she has no one to bring her an umbrella. So Bill wants to tell her he can share his umbrella with her since it's big enough. In this situation, what would Bill most likely say to Amy?

Bill You can share mine if you want.

여 Amy가 우산 없이 학교에 간다. 그녀는 Bill이 우산을 가지고 다니는 것을 보자 비가 올지를 그에게 묻는다. Bill은 오늘 오후 늦게 폭우가 예상된다고 말한다. 수미는 그녀에게 우산을 가져다 줄 사람이 아무도 없어서 걱정이 된다. 그래서 Bill은 우산이 충분히 크기 때문에 그녀와 우산을 같이 쓸 수 있다고 그녀에게 말하고 싶어 한다. 이러한 상황에서 Bill이 Amy에게 할 말로 가장 적절한 것은 무엇인가?

Bill 원한다면 내 우산을 같이 써도 좋아.

① 안녕, 내일 보자.
③ 걱정하지 마, 곧 날씨가 갤 거야.
④ 나의 좋은 친구가 되어 줘서 고마워.
⑤ 너 왜 우산 안 가져 왔니?

01 ③	02 ②	03 ③	04 ⑤	05 ⑤	06 ③	07 ④
08 ⑤	09 ⑤	10 ②	11 ⑤	12 ②	13 ②	14 ②
15 ⑤	16 ④	17 ①	18 ⑤	19 ③	20 ⑤	

01 ③

해설 줄무늬 매트가 비싸지만, 순면으로 만들어졌고 더 두꺼워서 오래 사용할 거라는 남자의 말에 여자는 동의하면서 그것을 구입하기로 결정했다.

어휘 mat[mæt] 매트, 깔개
shelf[ʃelf] 선반
reasonable[ríːzənəbl] 합리적인
striped[straipt] 줄무늬의
prefer[prifɔ́ːr] 선호하다
be made of ~으로 만들어지다
cotton[kátn] 면
thick[θik] 두꺼운
last[læst] 오래가다, 지속되다
cash register 계산대, 금전 등록기

W Let's go in here. I need a mat for our bathroom.
M Okay. They have many kinds of mats on the shelf.
W I like this flower design. It's soft and the price is reasonable.
M That one is good. But I like this striped one better.
W But it's more expensive. Why do you prefer it?
M It's made of 100% cotton and it's thicker. So I think it'll last longer.
W I see what you mean. Should we get the striped one then?
M Yes. I think we'll use it for a long time.
W All right. Let's take this to the cash register.

여 여기 들어가요. 욕실용 매트가 하나 필요해요.
남 알았어요. 선반에 다양한 종류의 매트가 있네요.
여 이 꽃 디자인이 마음에 들어요. 부드럽고 가격도 합리적이에요.
남 그거 좋네요. 하지만 나는 이 줄무늬 매트가 더 좋아요.
여 그건 더 비싸잖아요. 왜 그게 더 좋아요?
남 순면으로 만들어졌고 더 두꺼워요. 그래서 더 오래갈 것 같아요.
여 무슨 말인지 알겠어요. 그럼 우리가 줄무늬 매트를 사야 할까요?
남 네. 우린 그걸 오랫동안 사용할 수 있을 거예요.
여 알겠어요. 이걸 계산대로 가져가요.

02 ②

해설 여자는 자신의 차와 트럭이 충돌한 사고를 신고하려고 전화했다.

어휘 report[ripɔ́ːrt] 알리다
accident[ǽksidənt] 사고
describe[diskráib] 설명하다
crash into ~와 충돌하다
hurt[həːrt] 다친
injured[índʒərd] 부상을 입은
ambulance[ǽmbjuləns] 구급차

[Telephone rings.]
M Nine-one-one. What's your emergency?
W I want to report an accident.
M Can you describe the accident?
W A truck has just crashed into my car!
M Are you hurt?
W No, but my husband is injured.
M Where did it happen?
W At the corner of Pearl Street and 10th Street.
M What's your name?
W Mary Adams.
M All right. I'll send an ambulance right away.

[전화벨이 울린다.]
남 911입니다. 무슨 응급 상황인가요?
여 사고를 알리려고요.
남 사고에 대해 설명해 주시겠습니까?
여 방금 트럭이 제 차와 충돌했어요!
남 다치셨나요?
여 저는 아니고, 제 남편이 다쳤어요.
남 사고가 어디서 일어났나요?
여 Pearl 가와 10번가가 만나는 모퉁이에서요.
남 성함이 어떻게 되십니까?
여 Mary Adams입니다.
남 알겠습니다. 지금 바로 구급차를 보내겠습니다.

03 ③

해설 여자가 전구를 바꿔 끼우려는데 천장에 손이 닿지 않아서 남자에게 도움을 청하는 상황이다.

어휘 engine[éndʒin] 엔진
loud[laud] 시끄러운
noise[nɔiz] 소음

① W Is this seat taken?
　 M No, it isn't. Go ahead.
② W What's the matter with it?
　 M It's the engine. It's making a loud noise.
③ W Could you give me a hand, please?
　 M Yes, of course.

① 여 여기 자리 있나요?
　 남 아니요, 어서 앉으세요.
② 여 그것에 무슨 문제가 있나요?
　 남 문제는 엔진이네요. 시끄러운 소리가 나고 있어요.
③ 여 저를 도와주시겠어요?
　 남 네, 물론이지요.

give ~ a hand 도와주다
tool[tuːl] 도구

④ W This Christmas tree is so beautiful.
  M I know. These small lights make it very beautiful.
⑤ W Can you teach me how to use this tool?
  M Sure. Let me take a look first.

④ 여 이 크리스마스트리가 아주 아름다워요.
  남 그러네요. 이 작은 전구들이 그것을 매우 아름답게 만드네요.
⑤ 여 이 도구 사용법을 가르쳐 주실래요?
  남 물론이죠. 먼저 한 번 볼게요.

04 ⑤

해설 두 사람은 일요일에 만나서 테니스를 치기로 했다.

어휘 volunteer[vὰləntíər] 봉사 활동하다
nursing home 양로원
reserve[rizə́ːrv] 예약하다
tennis court 테니스 코트

[Cell phone rings.]
W Hello.
M Hello, Susan. This is Eric.
W Hi, Eric. What's up?
M I'm planning to play tennis this Friday. Do you want to join me?
W Sorry, I can't. I'm going to volunteer at a nursing home. How about this Saturday?
M Saturday? I have other plans that day. Is Sunday okay with you?
W Sunday sounds perfect.
M Great! I'll call you back later tonight after I reserve a tennis court.

[휴대전화가 울린다.]
여 여보세요.
남 안녕, Susan. 나 Eric이야.
여 안녕, Eric. 무슨 일이야?
남 나 이번 금요일에 테니스를 치려고 해. 같이 할래?
여 미안하지만 안 될 것 같아. 양로원에서 봉사 활동하거든. 이번 토요일은 어때?
남 토요일? 나 그날 다른 계획이 있어. 너 일요일은 괜찮니?
여 일요일은 좋은 것 같아.
남 좋아! 테니스 코트 예약하고 오늘 밤 나중에 다시 전화할게.

05 ⑤

해설 출시일(2020년 3월), 크기(베이직, 플러스, 울트라), 기능(100배 크게 볼 수 있는 카메라 기능), 색상(검은색, 흰색, 파란색, 빨간색, 회색)에 관해 언급되었지만, 가격에 관한 언급은 없었다.

어휘 introduce[ìntrədjúːs] 소개하다
based on ~에 근거하여
amazing[əméiziŋ] 놀라운
times[taimz] …배가 되는, …배
model[mάdl] 모델
regret[rigrét] 후회하다

W Let me introduce our new smartphone, the Rainbow 20. It came out in March 2020. There are 3 models based on size: basic, plus, and ultra. It has an amazing camera. You can see things 100 times larger. Rainbow 20 has 5 colors: black, white, blue, red, and gray. All models are 30% off today only. Buy one. You won't regret it!

여 저희의 새로운 스마트폰인 Rainbow 20을 소개하겠습니다. 2020년 3월에 출시되었습니다. 크기를 기준으로 베이직, 플러스, 그리고 울트라의 세 가지 모델이 있습니다. 이것은 놀라운 카메라를 가지고 있습니다. 사물을 100배 더 크게 볼 수 있습니다. Rainbow 20에는 검은색, 흰색, 파란색, 빨간색, 그리고 회색의 다섯 가지 색상이 있습니다. 모든 모델은 오늘만 30퍼센트 할인됩니다. 하나 구입하세요. 후회하지 않으실 겁니다!

06 ③

해설 더 좋은 버전의 스마트폰이 다음 주에 출시된다고 설명하면서 다음 주까지 기다렸어야 했다고 말하는 것으로 보아 여자는 새로 스마트폰을 구매한 것을 후회하고 있다는 것을 알 수 있다.

어휘 smartphone[smάːrtfoun] 스마트폰
satisfied[sǽtisfaid] 만족하는
version[və́ːrʒn] (이전의 것과 다른) -판 [형태]

M I heard you got a new smartphone. Can I see it?
W Sure. Here it is.
M Aren't you excited to have a new one?
W Not really. I'm not really satisfied with it.
M This one doesn't look so bad. Why are you not satisfied with it?
W Well, a better version of this phone is coming out next Friday. It comes with much more space and a better camera.
M When did you get yours?

남 네가 스마트폰을 새로 샀다고 들었어. 봐도 될까?
여 물론이지. 여기 있어.
남 새것을 갖게 되어 기분이 좋지 않니?
여 별로. 그걸로 그렇게 만족하지 않아.
남 이것도 그렇게 나쁘지 않은 것 같은데. 그걸로 왜 만족하지 않아?
여 음, 이 전화기의 더 좋은 버전이 다음 주 금요일에 출시되거든. 더 큰 저장 공간이랑 더 좋은 카메라를 가지고 나온대.
남 네 것은 언제 샀니?

come out 나오다, 출시되다
space[speis] (이용할 수 있는) 공간

W I got this a week ago. I <u>should've waited</u> <u>until</u> next week.

여 일주일 전에 이걸 샀어. 다음 주까지 기다렸어야 하는데.

① 지루한 ② 질투하는 ③ 후회하는
④ 신이 난 ⑤ 놀란

07 ④

해설 줄에 서 있는 건지 묻는 말에, 아니라고 하면서 노란 선 밖으로 물러서 달라는 대답은 어색하다.

어휘 make oneself at home 편히 쉬다
lovely[lʌ́vli] 예쁜, 사랑스러운
be in line 줄을 서다
behind[biháind] ~의 뒤에
close[klous] 아슬아슬한
cross[krɔːs] 건너다

① **M** My sister is very sick.
　　W I'm sorry to hear that.
② **M** Please <u>make yourself at home</u>.
　　W Thanks. Your house is very lovely.
③ **M** Would you like something to <u>drink with</u> <u>your meal</u>?
　　W Yes, please. I'll have a glass of water.
④ **M** <u>Are you in line</u>?
　　W No. Please stand behind the yellow line.
⑤ **M** That was close!
　　W You'd better be careful when <u>you cross</u> <u>the street</u>.

① 남 제 여동생이 매우 아파요.
　여 그 말을 들으니 유감이에요.
② 남 편하게 있어요.
　여 고마워요. 집이 매우 예쁘네요.
③ 남 식사와 함께 마실 것을 드릴까요?
　여 네. 물 한 잔 주세요.
④ 남 줄을 서신 건가요?
　여 아니요. 노란 선 뒤에 서 주세요.
⑤ 남 큰일 날 뻔 했어요!
　여 길을 건널 때 조심하는 게 좋겠어요.

08 ⑤

해설 여자는 자판기가 좀 더 건강한 음료들로 채워져야 한다면서 남자에게 회의 때 논의해달라고 부탁했다.

어휘 moment[móumənt] 잠깐, 잠시
suggest[səgdʒést] 제안하다
vending machine 자판기
soft drinks 청량음료
add[æd] 추가하다
discuss[diskʌ́s] 논의하다
staff meeting 직원 회의
mention[ménʃən] 언급하다

W Excuse me, Mr. Pine. Do you have a moment?
M Sure, Lisa. Come on in.
W There is something I'd like to <u>suggest for</u> <u>our company</u>.
M Okay. What is it?
W There are many vending machines in our office building. However, they only have coffee and soft drinks.
M I see. Would you like to <u>add something</u> <u>else</u>?
W I think those vending machines should have more healthy drinks like juice. <u>Would</u> <u>you discuss</u> this at the next staff meeting?
M Of course. <u>I'll mention it</u> at the next meeting.

여 실례합니다, Pine 씨. 시간 좀 있으세요?
남 네, Lisa. 들어와요.
여 우리 회사에 제안하고 싶은 것이 있어요.
남 좋아요. 그게 뭐죠?
여 우리 사무실 건물에 자판기가 많이 있잖아요. 하지만 커피와 청량음료만 있어요.
남 그렇군요. 다른 것을 추가하고 싶으신가요?
여 자판기에 주스 같은 더 건강한 음료가 있어야 할 것 같아요. 다음 직원 회의에서 논의해 주시겠어요?
남 물론이에요. 다음 회의에서 그것에 대해 언급할게요.

09 ⑤

해설 여자는 남자에게 가서 다른 친구들을 만나자고 제안했다.

어휘 graduate from ~을 졸업하다
slim[slim] 날씬한
work out 운동하다
lose weight 체중이 줄다
contact lenses 콘택트렌즈

W Hi, David. It's been a long time since we last met.
M I know. Almost 10 years <u>have passed</u> <u>since</u> we graduated from middle school.
W Time really flies, right?
M It sure does.
W You look slimmer now than in middle school. Do you work out often?

여 안녕, David. 우리가 마지막으로 만난 지 오래되었구나.
남 그러게. 우리가 중학교를 졸업한 이후로 거의 10년이 지났네.
여 시간이 정말 빨라, 그렇지?
남 정말 그래.
여 너는 중학교 때보다 지금 더 날씬해 보여. 운동 자주 하니?

age[eidʒ] 나이를 먹다

M Yes. I lost a lot of weight. And I <u>have grown taller</u> since then.
W Wow, that's great. And you don't wear glasses any longer.
M I'm wearing contact lenses instead. You look great, too. You <u>haven't aged</u> at <u>all</u>.
W Thanks. <u>Let's go and meet</u> the others. I can't wait to see them all.

남 응. 나는 몸무게가 많이 줄었어. 그리고 그때 이후로 키가 더 컸지.
여 와, 잘됐다. 그리고 안경을 더 이상 쓰지 않는구나.
남 대신에 콘택트렌즈를 끼고 있어. 너도 멋져 보여. 전혀 나이를 먹지 않았네.
여 고마워. 가서 다른 애들을 만나자. 빨리 걔네 모두를 보고 싶어.

10 ②

해설 30달러인 앨범을 세일 중이라 절반 가격으로 살 수 있다고 했으므로, 여자가 지불할 금액은 15달러이다.

어휘 expensive[ikspénsiv] 비싼
on sale 할인 중인
half[hæf] 절반
cool[ku:l] 좋은, 멋진

W Tomorrow is my sister's birthday. I want to buy a present for her.
M <u>How about a music album</u>? She likes music.
W Right. Maybe I'll get her the second album of John Mendes. He is her favorite singer.
M Isn't it expensive? <u>You said it was</u> $30.
W It was, but it's on sale now. I can get it <u>for half price</u>.
M Oh, that's cool!
W I know. My sister will be so happy when she sees the album.

여 내일이 내 여동생의 생일이야. 나는 동생에게 줄 선물을 사고 싶어.
남 음악 앨범 어떠니? 걔는 음악을 좋아하잖아.
여 맞아. 아마 John Mendes의 두 번째 앨범을 살거야. 내 동생이 정말 좋아하는 가수이거든.
남 그거 비싸지 않니? 네가 30달러라고 했잖아.
여 그랬지. 그런데 지금 세일 중이야. 절반 가격으로 살 수 있어.
남 아, 그거 좋은데!
여 맞아. 내 여동생이 그 앨범을 보면 매우 기뻐할 거야.

11 ⑤

해설 여자는 남자의 제안에 따라 테니스 수업을 신청하겠다고 했다.

어휘 gym[dʒim] 체육관
sign up for ~을 신청하다
decide[disáid] 결정하다

M Where are you going?
W I'm going to the gym <u>to sign up for</u> a class.
M What class are you planning to take next month?
W Well, I'm deciding between badminton and tennis.
M Why don't we take a swimming class together?
W I took a swimming class last month. It was interesting, but I don't want <u>to take it again</u>.
M How about signing up for <u>a tennis class</u>? I took it last month, and it was fun.
W All right. I'll go and sign up for it.

남 너 어디 가니?
여 나는 수업을 신청하러 체육관에 가는 중이야.
남 다음 달에 무슨 수업을 들을 계획이니?
여 음, 배드민턴과 테니스 중에서 결정할까 해.
남 우리 수영 수업을 함께 듣는 건 어때?
여 나는 지난달에 수영 수업을 들었어. 재미있었지만, 다시 듣고 싶지는 않아.
남 테니스 수업을 신청하는 게 어때? 작년에 수강했는데 재미있었거든.
여 알겠어. 가서 그 수업을 신청할게.

12 ②

해설 장소(올림픽 공원), 준비물(점심, 입장료, 마실 물), 출발 시간(9시 30분), 옷차림(편안한 옷)에 관해 언급되었지만, 놀이 활동에 관한 언급은 없었다.

어휘 entrance fee 입장료

M Good morning, everyone. Don't forget that tomorrow is <u>the school picnic at</u> Olympic Park. Please bring your own lunch and $3 <u>for the entrance fee</u>. Please come to school by 9:20. The buses <u>will leave at</u> 9:30. Don't be late! You don't need to

남 안녕하세요, 여러분. 내일은 올림픽 공원으로 학교 소풍을 가는 날임을 잊지 마세요. 각자 점심과 입장료로 3달러를 가져오세요. 9시 20분까지 학교에 오세요. 버스는 9시 30분에 떠날 거예요. 늦지 마세요! 교복을 입을 필요는 없어요. 편안한 옷을

late[leit] 늦은
school uniform 교복
comfortable[kʌ́mftəbl] 편한

wear school uniforms. You can come in comfortable clothes. Oh, don't forget to bring some drinking water. See you tomorrow!

입고 오면 됩니다. 아, 마실 물을 가져오는 걸 잊지 마세요. 내일 봅시다!

13 ②

해설 여자는 시카고로 가는 직항 비행기 표 중에서 12시 이전에 출발하고 가격이 저렴한 항공편을 구매하겠다고 했다.

어휘 direct flight 직항편
stopover[stápòuvər] (여행 중 두 지점 사이에 잠시) 머묾, 경유; 도중 하차지, 경유지
noon[nuːn] 정오
cheap[tʃiːp] 저렴한, 값이 싼

M How may I help you?
W I'd like to get a ticket to Chicago from Los Angeles on July 4th.
M Of course. Would you prefer a direct flight?
W Yes, please. I don't want a stopover. It will take too much time.
M Okay. Would you like to leave in the morning or afternoon?
W Anything before noon is fine with me.
M It seems like there are 2 flights with 2 different prices.
W I'll go with the cheaper one, please.

남 어떻게 도와 드릴까요?
여 7월 4일에 로스앤젤레스에서 시카고로 가는 표를 사려고요.
남 네. 직항편을 선호하시나요?
여 네, 부탁해요. 저는 경유를 원하지 않아요. 너무 많은 시간이 걸리거든요.
남 알겠습니다. 오전에 떠나시겠어요, 오후에 떠나시겠어요?
여 정오 이전에는 어떤 시간이든 괜찮아요.
남 가격이 다른 두 개의 항공편이 있는 것 같네요.
여 더 저렴한 항공편으로 갈게요.

14 ②

해설 이 건물에 많은 의자가 있는 방들이 있으며, 사람들이 와서 연극 같은 것을 볼 수 있다고 했으므로, 극장에 대한 설명이다.

어휘 gather[gǽðər] 모이다
such as ~와 같은
play[plei] 연극
turn off (전원을) 끄다
disturb[distə́ːrb] 방해하다

W This is a building. In the building, there are rooms with many chairs for people to sit. People usually gather in this building to watch something such as a play. During that time, everyone has to turn off their cell phones, be quiet and try not to disturb others.

여 이것은 건물입니다. 건물에는 사람들이 앉을 수 있는 의자들이 많이 있는 방들이 있습니다. 사람들은 보통 이 건물에 모여서 연극 같은 것을 봅니다. 그 시간 동안에, 모두 휴대전화를 끄고, 조용히 하면서 다른 사람들을 방해하지 않도록 해야 합니다.

15 ⑤

해설 여자는 주말에 스케이트보드를 타러 가자는 남자의 제안을 받아들였다.

어휘 blue[bluː] 우울한
hate[heit] 싫어하다
cheer up 격려하다
hurt[həːrt] 다치게 하다
get hurt 다치다
protective gear 보호 장비
once[wʌns] 한 번

M What's the matter with you?
W I feel so blue. I go to work early in the morning and I come home late at night every day.
M I have an idea to make you feel better.
W Oh, really? What's that?
M Let's go skateboarding this weekend.
W You know how much I hate doing that.
M When you feel bad, doing something different might cheer you up.
W I don't know how to skateboard. I could hurt myself.
M You won't get hurt if you wear protective gear. What is important is that you have some fun on the weekend.
W Okay. Just this once.

남 무슨 일이 있니?
여 너무 우울해. 아침 일찍 출근해서 매일 밤 늦게 집에 와.
남 너의 기분을 나아지게 할 좋은 생각이 있어.
여 아, 정말? 그게 뭔데?
남 이번 주말에 스케이트보드를 타러 가자.
여 너 내가 그런 거 하는 거 얼마나 싫어하는지 알잖아.
남 네가 기분이 안 좋을 때, 다른 뭔가를 하는 게 널 기운내게 할지도 모르잖아.
여 나는 스케이트보드를 타는 방법조차 몰라. 다칠 수 있잖아.
남 보호 장비를 착용하면 다치지 않을 거야. 중요한 건 주말에 즐거운 시간을 보내는 거야.
여 좋아. 이번 한 번만이야.

16 ④

해설 영화는 7시 30분에 시작해서 2시간 반 동안 상영하므로, 영화가 끝나는 시각은 10시이다.

어휘 go on a date 데이트하러 가다
worry[wə́:ri] 걱정하다
go to the movies 영화 보러 가다
make sure 반드시 하다
until[əntíl] ~까지
run[rʌn] 상영하다

W Dad, I'm going out tonight.
M With whom? Are you going on a date?
W I am. Don't worry. He's a nice person.
M What are you going to do tonight? Are you going to the movies?
W Yes. But before that, we're going to have dinner at an Italian restaurant.
M Okay. Make sure you come home by 8:00.
W 8:00? The movie doesn't start until 7:30.
M How long does the movie run?
W For 2 and a half hours.
M Okay. Be back by 11:00.
W I will. Thanks, Dad.

여 아빠, 저 오늘밤에 외출할 거예요.
남 누구랑? 데이트하러 가는 거니?
여 네. 걱정 마세요. 그는 좋은 사람이에요.
남 오늘밤에 뭘 할 거니? 영화 보러 갈 거니?
여 네. 하지만 그 전에, 우리는 이탈리안 식당에서 저녁을 먹을 거예요.
남 알았다. 8시까지는 꼭 집에 와라.
여 8시요? 영화가 7시 30분이 되서야 시작해요.
남 영화 상영 시간은 얼마나 되니?
여 2시간 반이요.
남 좋아. 11시까지는 집에 와라.
여 알겠어요. 감사해요, 아빠.

17 ①

해설 4시에 회의해도 괜찮은지 묻는 남자의 말에 이어서 이를 수락하거나 거절하는 응답이 이어져야 한다.

어휘 review[rivjú:] 검토하다
sales plan 판매 계획
half an hour 30분
schedule[skédʒu:l] 일정
meeting[mí:tiŋ] 회의

M Carol, we need to review our sales plan.
W Okay. How long do we need to talk?
M Maybe half an hour.
W Let me check my schedule. Is Thursday okay?
M Sure. Do you want to meet in the morning or in the afternoon?
W In the afternoon. I'm a little busy in the morning.
M Can we meet at 2:00 p.m.?
W I already have another meeting then.
M Then, will 4:00 be okay?
W That's fine with me. See you then.

남 Carol, 우리의 판매 계획을 검토해야 해요.
여 알겠어요. 얼마나 오래 이야기해야 하나요?
남 아마 30분쯤이요.
여 제 일정을 살펴볼게요. 목요일 괜찮나요?
남 좋아요. 만나기에 오전이 더 좋으세요, 아니면 오후가 더 좋으세요?
여 오후요. 제가 오전에는 좀 바빠서요.
남 오후 2시에 만날 수 있을까요?
여 그때는 이미 다른 회의가 있어요.
남 그러면, 4시는 괜찮아요?
여 저는 좋아요. 그때 봐요.

② 미안하지만, 저는 휴식 시간이 없어요.
③ 좋아요, 몇 시가 좋은가요?
④ 우리의 상품을 팔 수 있는 좋은 계획이 있어요.
⑤ 저는 내일 아침에 다른 약속이 있어요.

18 ⑤

해설 언제 복사가 끝나는지 묻는 여자의 말에 소요되는 시간을 알려주는 응답이 이어져야 자연스럽다.

어휘 make a copy 복사하다
document[dάkjumənt] 서류
page[peidʒ] 페이지, 쪽
cost[kɔ:st] 비용이 들다
per[pər] ~당[마다]
be ready 준비되다
[선택지]
attend[əténd] 참석하다

W Excuse me, I'd like some help, please.
M What can I do for you?
W I'd like to make some copies.
M No problem. How many copies do you want?
W I'd like 5 copies of these documents.
M How many pages are there?
W 10. How much does it cost?
M It is 10 cents per page.
W When will they be ready? I have a class at 1 o'clock.
M They'll be ready in 20 minutes.

여 실례지만, 좀 도와주세요.
남 무엇을 도와드릴까요?
여 복사를 좀 하고 싶은데요.
남 좋습니다. 복사를 몇 부 원하시나요?
여 이 서류를 5부 복사하고 싶어요.
남 몇 페이지나 되나요?
여 10페이지요. 비용이 얼마인가요?
남 페이지 당 10센트입니다.
여 언제 준비될까요? 제가 1시에 수업이 있어서요.
남 20분 안에 준비될 겁니다.

① 모두 해서 5달러입니다.
② 그 회의에 참석할게요.
③ 신용카드로 지불할게요.
④ 1시까지 여기 있을 겁니다.

19 ③

해설 책상 서랍 안을 확인했는지 묻는 남자의 말에 확인 여부를 말하는 응답이 이어져야 한다.

어휘 passport[pǽspɔːrt] 여권
on business 업무로
sudden[sʌ́dn] 갑작스러운
find out 알게 되다
business trip 출장
drawer[drɔːr] 서랍

W Do you know where my passport is?
M Your passport? Where are you going?
W I have to go to India next week on business, and I can't find my passport.
M Next week? This is so sudden.
W I know. I only found out about the business trip this morning.
M Then, when are you coming back?
W On Tuesday. Anyway, do you remember where I put it?
M Did you look in the desk drawer?
W That's the first place I checked.

여 내 여권이 어디에 있는지 알아요?
남 당신 여권이요? 어디 가요?
여 다음 주에 업무 차 인도에 가야 하는데, 내 여권을 찾을 수가 없어요.
남 다음 주요? 너무 갑작스러운데요.
여 맞아요. 오늘 아침에 출장 여행에 대해서 알았어요.
남 그러면, 언제 돌아와요?
여 화요일에요. 어쨌든, 내가 어디에 여권을 두었는지 기억해요?
남 책상 서랍 안을 봤어요?
여 내가 가장 먼저 확인한 곳이 거기예요.

① 미안해요, 저는 당신을 몰라요.
② 아무도 그것이 어디에 있는지 몰라요.
④ 네, 책상 서랍 안에 그것을 둘게요.
⑤ 다음번에는 책상 서랍을 반드시 잠그세요.

20 ⑤

해설 집에 혼자 있는 상황에서 문을 열어주는 게 불안하여 문 앞에 물건을 두고 가달라고 말하고 싶은 상황이다.

어휘 alone[əlóun] 혼자서
suddenly[sʌ́dnli] 갑자기
deliver[dilívər] 배달하다
marketplace[márkətpleis] 시장
uneasy[ʌníːzi] 불안한
delivery man 배달원

M Sophia is home alone because her family has gone out. Suddenly, someone rings the bell at Sophia's home. Sophia asks who he is. He's delivering a package from an online marketplace and asking her to open the door. Sophia feels uneasy about opening the door, so she decides to tell him to leave the package by the door. In this situation, what would Sophia most likely say to the delivery man?

Sophia   Please leave it in front of the door.

남 Sophia는 가족들이 밖에 나가서 혼자 집에 있다. 갑자기 누군가 Sophia의 집 초인종을 누른다. Sophia는 그가 누구인지 묻는다. 그는 온라인 마켓에서 온 소포를 배달하는 중인데, 문을 열어주기를 요청한다. Sophia는 문을 열어 주기가 불안해서 문 앞에 두고 가달라고 말하려고 한다. 이러한 상황에서, Sophia가 배달원에게 할 말로 가장 적절한 것은 무엇인가?

Sophia 문 앞에 그것을 두고 가주세요.

① 좋아요! 들어오세요.
② 전부 해서 얼마인가요?
③ 왜 더 일찍 오지 않았어요?
④ 죄송하지만, 환불 받기를 원해요.

01 ②	02 ②	03 ①	04 ⑤	05 ④	06 ④	07 ⑤
08 ②	09 ③	10 ②	11 ⑤	12 ③	13 ⑤	14 ④
15 ⑤	16 ③	17 ③	18 ②	19 ②	20 ③	

01 ②

[해설] 여자가 주문한 소파는 검은색에 짧은 다리가 있는 소파이다.

[어휘] next to ~의 옆에
perfect[pə́:rfikt] 딱 좋은, 완벽한
order[ɔ́:rdər] 주문하다
thin[θin] 가는, 얇은
mistake[mistéik] 실수

M Where do you want to put this sofa?
W In the living room, please. Next to the window would be perfect.
M No problem.
W Wait! This is not the sofa I ordered. It's not even the same color. I ordered a black one.
M Are you sure?
W Yes. I ordered a sofa with short legs. This one has long, thin legs. This is not the right sofa.
M I'm sorry. It seems like there has been a mistake.
W Please take this one back and bring me the one I ordered.

남 이 소파를 어디에 놓고 싶으세요?
여 거실에 놔주세요. 창문 옆이 딱 좋겠어요.
남 그러죠.
여 잠깐만요! 이건 제가 주문한 소파가 아닌데요. 심지어 같은 색도 아니네요. 전 검은색 소파를 주문했어요.
남 확실하세요?
여 네. 저는 짧은 다리가 있는 소파를 주문했어요. 이 소파는 길고 가는 다리잖아요. 이것은 맞는 소파가 아니에요.
남 죄송합니다. 무슨 실수가 있었던 것 같네요.
여 이 소파를 다시 가져가시고, 제가 주문한 걸 가져다주세요.

02 ②

[해설] 여자는 남자가 남긴 메시지를 확인하고 테니스 라켓을 팔기 위해 남자에게 전화했다.

[어휘] racket[rǽkit] 라켓
put up 게시하다, 내붙이다
for sale 팔려고 내놓은
in good shape 상태가 좋은
once[wʌns] 한 번

[Cell phone rings.]
M Hello.
W Hello, is this Brian Jones?
M Yes, this is he. Who's calling?
W I'm Jenny Davis. You left a message about the tennis racket I put up for sale.
M That's right. Is it in good shape?
W It's as good as new. I only used it once.
M How much do you want for it?
W It's $70.
M $70? It's a little more expensive than I thought.
W Well, how about $60?
M Okay. I'll buy it.

[휴대전화가 울린다.]
남 여보세요.
여 여보세요, Brian Jones이신가요?
남 네, 전데요. 전화 거신 분은 누구세요?
여 저는 Jenny Davis입니다. 당신이 제가 팔려고 내놓은 테니스 라켓을 사고 싶다는 메시지를 남기셨는데요.
남 맞아요. 그거 상태가 좋은가요?
여 새것만큼 좋아요. 딱 한 번 사용했거든요.
남 얼마를 원하세요?
여 70달러요.
남 70달러요? 제가 생각했던 것보다 조금 더 비싸네요.
여 음, 60달러는 어떠세요?
남 좋아요. 그걸 살게요.

03 ①

[해설] 미용실에서 가운을 입은 남자가 의자에 앉아 있고, 여자가 머리를 어떻게 자르고 싶은지 묻는 상황이다.

[어휘] hair cut 이발, 머리 깎기
machine[məʃíːn] 기계
fitting room 탈의실
put on ~을 입다

① W How would you like your hair cut?
   M I want to cut it short.
② W Do you know how to use this machine?
   M Sorry. You have to ask somebody else.
③ W I like your new hairstyle.
   M Thank you. I'm glad you like it.
④ W Where is the fitting room?
   M It's over there.

① 여 머리를 어떻게 잘라드릴까요?
   남 짧게 자르고 싶어요.
② 여 이 기계를 어떻게 사용하는지 아시나요?
   남 죄송해요. 다른 분에게 물어보셔야 해요.
③ 여 새 머리 스타일이 마음에 들어요.
   남 감사합니다. 마음에 드신다니 기쁘네요.
④ 여 탈의실은 어디 있나요?
   남 저쪽에 있어요.

gown[gaun] 가운

⑤ W Can I get my hair cut?
　 M Sure. Would you put on a gown and sit here?

⑤ 여 머리 좀 잘라 주실래요?
　 남 그럼요. 가운을 입고 여기 앉으시겠어요?

04 ⑤

해설 두 사람은 금요일 저녁에 식사를 하기로 했다.

어휘 skip[skip] 건너뛰다
final exam 기말고사
busy[bízi] 바쁜

M I heard that you're going back to Korea soon. Would you like to go out for dinner before you go?
W That's a great idea, but let's skip Monday. I have to study for the final exam.
M Me, too, but I am free on Tuesday. How about going out that night?
W I am afraid I can't. I'm going out for dinner with Nancy. How about Wednesday night?
M I have a meeting for the band club. Are you busy on Friday night?
W No. I'm free.
M Let's meet then. I'll take you to the best restaurant in town.
W Okay.

남 네가 곧 한국으로 돌아간다고 들었어. 가기 전에 저녁 먹으러 나가는 거 괜찮아?
여 좋은 생각이지만, 월요일은 건너뛰자. 기말고사 공부를 해야 돼.
남 나도 그래, 하지만 화요일은 한가해. 그날 밤에 나가는 거 어때?
여 나는 안 될 것 같아. Nancy와 저녁 먹으러 나갈 거야. 수요일 밤에는 어때?
남 나는 밴드 동아리 모임이 있어. 금요일 밤에는 바빠?
여 아니. 한가해.
남 그럼 그때 만나자. 동네에서 제일 좋은 식당으로 데려갈게.
여 알겠어.

05 ④

해설 개장일(5월 1일), 위치(Blue City), 부대 시설(여러 상점들), 영업 시간(매일 오전 9시부터 오후 10시까지)에 관해 언급되었지만, 입장료에 관한 언급은 없었다.

어휘 experience[ikspíəriəns] 경험하다
be located in ~에 위치해 있다
theme park 테마 파크
a variety of 다양한
excitement[iksáitmənt] 신남, 흥분
come true 실현되다

M Do you want to experience something exciting? Come to Sky World. It opened on May 1st. It's located in Blue City, which has a beautiful lake. You'll find 2 theme parks and a variety of shops here. You can have fun, and shop in here, too. It's open every day from 9 a.m to 10 p.m. Experience a lot of fun and excitement in this place where dreams come true.

남 당신은 신나는 것을 경험하고 싶습니까? Sky World로 오세요. 5월 1일에 문을 열었습니다. 이곳은 아름다운 호수가 있는 Blue City에 위치하고 있습니다. 여러분은 여기서 두 개의 테마 파크와 다양한 상점들을 찾을 수 있습니다. 여러분은 이 안에서 재미있게 놀고, 쇼핑할 수도 있습니다. 이곳은 오전 9시부터 오후 10시까지 매일 개장합니다. 꿈이 실현되는 이곳에서 많은 재미와 신나는 일들을 경험하세요.

06 ④

해설 남자가 여자에게 딱 맞는 아파트를 찾았다며 그 아파트에 대해 설명하는 것으로 보아 두 사람은 부동산 중개인과 고객임을 알 수 있다.

어휘 third floor 3층
clean[kli:n] 깨끗한
view[vju:] 전망

[Telephone rings.]
W Hello.
M Hi. This is Jack. I'm calling about the apartment you are looking for.
W Hi, Jack. Did you find any good places?
M Yes, I think I may have found you the perfect apartment.
W Really? Tell me about it.
M It's on Sunshine Street. And it's on the third floor.
W Is it new?

[전화벨이 울린다.]
여 여보세요.
남 안녕하세요. 저는 Jack인데요. 찾으시는 아파트 때문에 전화 드렸어요.
여 안녕하세요, Jack. 좋은 집을 좀 찾으셨나요?
남 네, 당신에게 딱 맞는 아파트를 찾은 것 같아요.
여 정말요? 집에 대해 말해주세요.
남 Sunshine 가에 있고요. 그리고 3층이에요.
여 새 집인가요?

M No. It's not very new, but the floors and walls have been changed recently.
W Does it look nice?
M Yes, it does. It is very clean. It also has a very nice view of the park.

남 아니요. 아주 새 집은 아니지만, 바닥과 벽을 최근에 바꿨어요.
여 집이 좋아 보이나요?
남 네. 그래 보여요. 아주 깨끗해요. 또한 공원 전망이 매우 멋져요.

07 ⑤

[해설] 우리 팀이 이길 거라고 확신한다는 말에 걱정하지 말라고 격려하면서 그럴 리가 없다고 반대로 확신하는 응답은 어색하다.

[어휘] Help yourself to ~. ~을 마음껏 드세요.
Do you mind if ~? ~해도 될까요?
not mind 신경 쓰지 않다

① M Go ahead. Help yourself to this soup.
　 W No, thanks. I've had more than enough.
② M What time shall we meet?
　 W How about 10 o'clock?
③ M Do you mind if I sit here?
　 W No, I don't mind at all.
④ M I'm looking for White Hospital.
　 W It's two blocks from here.
⑤ M I'm sure that our team will win.
　 W Don't worry about it. It can't be.

① 남 먼저 드세요. 이 수프를 마음껏 드세요.
　 여 아니요. 괜찮아요. 실컷 먹었어요.
② 남 우리 몇 시에 만날까요?
　 여 10시 어때요?
③ 남 여기에 앉아도 될까요?
　 여 네, 그러세요.
④ 남 저는 White 병원을 찾고 있어요.
　 여 여기서 두 블록 거리예요.
⑤ 남 우리 팀이 이길 거라고 확신해요.
　 여 걱정 마세요. 그럴 리가 없어요.

08 ②

[해설] 남자가 실수로 Smith 씨의 소포에 다른 고객의 서류를 넣어서, 소포를 받으면 다시 보내 달라고 부탁했다.

[어휘] do A a favor A의 부탁을 들어주다
package[pǽkidʒ] 소포
mistake[mistéik] 실수
client[kláiənt] 고객
document[dάkjumənt] 서류
return fee 반송 수수료

[Telephone rings.]
W Hello.
M Hello. I'm Tom Collins. Is Mr. Smith in?
W I'm sorry. He just went out.
M When will he be back?
W He won't be back today. Would you like to leave a message?
M No, but would you do me a favor?
W What is it?
M I sent a package to Mr. Smith but there's been a mistake. I put another client's document in it. When the package arrives, would you send it back to me?
W Okay. But will you pay the return fee?
M Of course. Thank you.

[전화벨이 울린다.]
여 여보세요.
남 여보세요. 저는 Tom Collins라고 합니다. Smith 씨 계신가요?
여 죄송합니다. 방금 나갔네요.
남 언제쯤 돌아오실까요?
여 오늘은 돌아오지 않을 거예요. 메시지를 남기시겠어요?
남 아니요, 하지만 부탁 하나만 들어주시겠어요?
여 뭔데요?
남 제가 Smith 씨에게 소포를 보냈는데 실수가 있었거든요. 다른 고객의 서류를 그 안에 넣었어요. 소포가 도착하면, 그걸 저에게 다시 보내주시겠어요?
여 알겠습니다. 하지만 반송 수수료는 그쪽에서 부담하실 거죠?
남 물론입니다. 감사합니다.

09 ③

[해설] 남자는 여자에게 전시회에 같이 갈 수 있는지 물었지만, 여자는 미술에 관심이 없다면서 거절했다.

[어휘] by the way 그런데
nearby[nìərbái] 근처에
exhibition[èksəbíʃən] 전시회
downtown[dáuntáun] 시내
gallery[gǽləri] 미술관

M Hi, Sally.
W Oh, it's Harry, right?
M Yeah. We met at Daniel's birthday party last Friday night.
W Oh, I remember. You sang for Daniel that day. By the way, what brings you here?
M I'm going to meet a friend at a restaurant nearby.
W I see. Have a good time.

남 안녕, Sally.
여 아, Harry구나, 맞지?
남 응. 우리는 지난 금요일 밤 Daniel의 생일 파티에서 만났잖아.
여 아, 기억나. 너는 그날 Daniel을 위해 노래를 불렀지. 그런데, 무슨 일로 여기에 온 거야?
남 근처에 있는 식당에서 친구를 만날 거야.
여 그렇구나. 즐거운 시간 보내.

volunteer work 자원 봉사
animal shelter 동물보호소

M	Thanks. Oh, wait. Do you have any plans this Saturday? There's a great exhibition downtown at a gallery.
W	Sorry. I have <u>volunteer work</u> at an animal shelter that day.
M	How about this Sunday? We <u>could have</u> <u>lunch</u> and then see the exhibition.
W	<u>I'm sorry</u>, I'm not interested in art.

남	고마워. 아, 잠깐만. 이번 토요일에 혹시 계획이 있니? 시내의 미술관에서 훌륭한 전시회를 하거든.
여	미안. 나는 그날 동물보호소에서 자원 봉사활동이 있어.
남	그럼 이번 일요일은 어때? 점심을 먹고 난 다음에 그 전시회를 볼 수 있어.
여	미안해. 나는 미술에 관심이 없어.

10 ②

[해설] 여자는 7개의 오렌지를 6개의 오렌지 가격에 샀으며, 오렌지는 개당 2달러이므로 12달러를 지불할 것이다.

[어휘] fresh[freʃ] 신선한
for free 무료로
shopping bag 장바구니
plastic bag 비닐봉지

M	May I help you?
W	Yes, please. I want some oranges.
M	Here they are. They're very fresh and sweet.
W	How much are they?
M	One is $2. Buy 6, and you'll get 1 <u>for free</u>.
W	Do you mean I get 7 oranges <u>for the price</u> <u>of 6</u> oranges?
M	<u>That's right</u>.
W	Then I'll have 7 oranges, please.
M	Of course. Did you <u>bring a shopping</u> <u>bag</u>?
W	No. Please put them in a plastic bag. Here is the money.
M	Thank you.

남	도와드릴까요?
여	네. 저는 오렌지를 좀 원해요.
남	여기 있습니다. 아주 싱싱하고 달아요.
여	얼마입니까?
남	한 개에 2달러입니다. 여섯 개 사시면, 한 개를 그냥 드려요.
여	7개를 6개의 가격에 살 수 있다는 말씀이세요?
남	맞습니다.
여	그러면 오렌지 7개 주세요.
남	네. 장바구니를 가지고 오셨나요?
여	아니요. 비닐봉지에 담아 주세요. 여기 돈 드릴게요.
남	감사합니다.

11 ⑤

[해설] 여자가 마음에 드는 신발의 맞는 사이즈가 있는지 찾아봐 달라고 부탁했고, 남자는 창고에서 찾아보겠다고 했다.

[어휘] rack[ræk] 선반, 받침대
out of stock 품절이 되어
look up 찾아보다
stockroom[stάkrùːm] 창고
try on 신어[입어] 보다

M	May I help you?
W	Yes. Do you <u>have these shoes</u> in a size 6?
M	I'm not sure. If you can't find them on the rack, they may be <u>out of stock</u>.
W	I really like these shoes. I'm sorry, but could you please look them up?
M	Sure. I'll <u>look for them</u> in the stockroom.
W	Thanks. I'd like to <u>try on a pair</u> if you have them.
M	Okay. I'll be right back.

남	도와드릴까요?
여	네. 이 신발로 사이즈 6이 있나요?
남	확실하지 않네요. 진열대 위에 없으면, 품절되었을 거예요.
여	저는 이 신발이 정말 마음에 들어요. 죄송하지만, 한 번 찾아봐 주시겠어요?
남	네. 제가 창고에서 찾아볼게요.
여	고마워요. 그 사이즈가 있으면, 신어 볼게요.
남	알겠어요. 곧 돌아올게요.

12 ③

[해설] 행사 기간(5월 31일~6월 10일), 할인 품목(대부분의 의류품), 할인율(20~50%), 사은품(우산)에 관해 언급되었지만, 제외 품목에 관한 언급은 없었다.

[어휘] clear out 처분하다
item[άitəm] 물품, 품목
clothing store 옷 가게
reduce[ridjúːs] 낮추다, 인하하다
goods[gudz] 상품
customer[kʌ́stəmər] 고객

W	May I have your attention, please? Starting May 31st, we are going to <u>clear</u> <u>out</u> our spring items. This sale <u>will end on</u> June 10th. Most clothing stores will reduce <u>the price of all goods</u>, from socks to jackets, by 20 to 50%. Customers who spend over $100 will <u>get a free umbrella</u>. If you want to know more about the sale, visit the customer service center.

여	안내 말씀드리겠습니다. 5월 31일부터, 저희는 봄 물품들을 처분할 예정입니다. 이 할인은 6월 10일에 끝납니다. 대부분의 옷 가게에서 양말부터 재킷까지 모든 상품들의 가격을 20에서 50퍼센트로 낮출 겁니다. 100달러 이상 구입하는 고객들에게는 무료로 우산을 드립니다. 할인에 대해 더 알고 싶으시면, 고객 서비스 센터를 방문해 주십시오.

13 ⑤

해설 두 사람은 Blue Square에서 하는 공연 중 더 저렴한 〈Dolphin Show〉를 보기로 했고, 현재 시각인 2시 30분 이후의 공연을 보기로 했다.

어휘 aquarium[əkwέəriəm] 수족관
brochure[brouʃúər] 책자, 팸플릿
popular[pápulər] 인기 있는
option[ápʃən] 선택사항
choose[tʃu:z] 고르다
fantastic[fæntǽstik] 환상적인
in addition 게다가
later[léitər] 더 뒤의, 더 늦은

M Wow! This aquarium is very large. I've never been to such a large aquarium before.
W Me neither. There are a lot of things to see.
M Oh, look! There is the list for the shows here at Blue Square.
W How about watching the "Mermaid Show"? It's the most popular show here.
M Can we watch something else? I want to see sea animals.
W Then, what are our options?
M There are 2 shows to choose from. They are "Dolphin Show"and "Fish in Wonderland".
W I've always wanted to see the "Dolphin Show." I heard it's fantastic. In addition, it's a little cheaper than "Fish in Wonderland."
M Let me see. It's 2:30. So let's watch the later show.

남 와! 이 수족관은 정말 크구나. 나는 전에 이렇게 큰 수족관에 가 본 적이 없거든.
여 나도 그래. 볼 게 많네.
남 아, 봐! 여기 Blue Square에서 하는 공연 팸플릿이야.
여 〈Mermaid Show〉를 보는 게 어때? 여기에서 가장 인기 있는 공연이래.
남 우리 다른 걸 볼까? 난 해양 동물들이 보고 싶거든.
여 그러면, 우리의 선택사항이 뭐가 있니?
남 고를 수 있는 공연이 두 개 있어. 〈Dolphin Show〉랑 〈Fish in Wonderland〉야.
여 난 항상 〈Dolphin Show〉를 보고 싶었어. 환상적이라고 들었거든. 게다가, 〈Fish in Wonderland〉보다 약간 저렴해.
남 어디 보자. 지금 2시 30분이야. 그러니까 더 뒤의 공연을 보자.

14 ④

해설 조용하고 깨끗하며, 많이 먹지 않고, 혼자 사는 사람들이 선호하는 애완동물이지만, 털에 알레르기가 있는 사람들이 기를 수 없으며, 자신의 주인을 하인으로 여기는 동물은 고양이다.

어휘 alone[əlóun] 혼자서
allergic[ələ́:rdʒik] 알레르기가 있는
interestingly[íntərəstiŋli] 흥미롭게도
owner[óunər] 주인
servant[sə́:rvənt] 하인

M They are wonderful pets because they are lovely and cute. They are also quiet and clean. They don't like eating much, so they are not expensive to have around. People who live alone prefer them. Some people are allergic to their hair, so they can't have them. Interestingly, they think their owners are their servants. Having them can make your home a happy place.

남 그들은 사랑스럽고 귀여워서 멋진 애완동물이다. 그들은 조용하고 깨끗하기도 하다. 그들은 많이 먹는 것을 좋아하지 않아서, 곁에 두기에 비용이 많이 들지 않는다. 혼자 사는 사람들이 그들을 선호한다. 어떤 사람들은 그들의 털에 알레르기가 있어서, 그들을 기를 수 없다. 흥미롭게도, 그들은 자신의 주인이 그들의 하인이라고 생각한다. 그들을 기르는 것은 당신의 집을 행복한 곳으로 만들 수 있다.

15 ⑤

해설 여자는 남자가 추천한 에어로빅 프로그램을 신청하겠다고 했다.

어휘 new year's resolution 새해 결심
get in shape 좋은 몸 상태를 유지하다
fit[fit] (몸이) 탄탄한, 건강한
recommend[rèkəménd] 추천하다
opinion[əpínjən] 의견
be determined to-v ~하기로 결심하다
swimming suit 수영복

W Would you like to exercise with me?
M Good idea. My new year's resolution is to get in shape.
W Get in shape? You're already in good shape.
M Yes, but I'm going to enter a Taekwondo competition next fall. I have to lose more weight.
W I want to be fit, too. I need your advice. Can you recommend an exercise to me?
M In my opinion, an aerobic program would be good for you.
W Then I'll sign up for it. I am determined to look good in my swimming suit this summer.

여 나랑 같이 운동할래?
남 좋은 생각이야. 나의 새해 결심은 좋은 몸을 만드는 거야.
여 좋은 몸을 만든다고? 너는 이미 좋은 체형인데.
남 그래. 하지만 이번 가을에 태권도 대회에 나가거든. 몸무게를 줄여야 해.
여 나도 몸이 탄탄하고 싶어. 네 조언이 필요해. 나에게 운동을 추천해 줄래?
남 내 의견으로는, 에어로빅 프로그램이 너에게 좋을 거야.
여 그러면 그걸 신청할 게. 나는 올 여름에 수영복 차림의 멋진 모습을 보이도록 결심했거든.

16 ③

해설 여자는 오후 3시쯤 일을 시작한다고 했다.

어휘 around[əráund] ~쯤
on weekdays 주중에
exactly[igzǽktli] 정확히
report[ripɔ́ːrt] 보도하다
finish[fíniʃ] 끝나다

M How do you spend your day?
W Well, I get up around 10 on weekdays. Then I read the newspaper and have lunch at about noon.
M Really? What time do you go to work?
W I start working at 3 p.m.
M You start working so late. What do you do exactly?
W I report the weather on an evening news show.
M I'm sorry, I didn't know that. When do you go home?
W I finish at 11 p.m.

남 당신은 하루를 어떻게 보내시나요?
여 음, 주중에는 10시쯤 일어나요. 그 다음에 신문을 읽고 정오쯤에 점심을 먹어요.
남 정말이요? 몇 시에 일하러 가시나요?
여 오후 3시에 일하기 시작해요.
남 너무 늦게 일을 시작하네요. 정확히 무슨 일을 하시나요?
여 저는 저녁 뉴스에서 날씨를 보도해요.
남 미안해요, 저는 그걸 몰랐어요. 집에 언제 가시나요?
여 밤 11시에 끝나요.

17 ③

해설 언제 재킷이 준비되는지 묻는 남자의 말에 세탁소에 언제 오면 되는지 말하는 응답이 이어져야 자연스럽다.

어휘 stain[stein] 얼룩
get A out A를 제거하다, 빼다
tough[tʌf] 어려운
cost[kɔːst] 비용이 들다
extra[ékstrə] 추가로
pay[pei] 지불하다
[선택지]
convenient[kənvíːnjənt] 편리한
stop by 들르다

M How may I help you?
W Hi, my jacket has a stain on it. Can you get the stain out?
M Let me see. [Pause] Hmm... It is a tough one, and it might cost extra. Is that okay with you?
W Of course. It's my favorite jacket, so it doesn't matter how much it costs.
M Okay. It'll take some time though.
W No problem.
M Please write down your name and your phone number here.
W Sure. [Pause] When will it be ready?
M You should come back next Friday.

남 어떻게 도와드릴까요?
여 안녕하세요, 제 재킷에 얼룩이 있어요. 얼룩을 제거할 수 있나요?
남 어디 봅시다. [잠시 후] 음… 빼기 어려운 얼룩이라서 추가로 비용이 들 수 있습니다. 괜찮으신가요?
여 물론이죠. 제가 아끼는 재킷이라서 얼마든 상관없습니다.
남 알겠습니다. 시간이 좀 걸릴 수 있습니다.
여 괜찮습니다.
남 여기에 이름과 전화번호를 적어주시겠어요?
여 네. [잠시 후] 그게 언제 다 될까요?
남 다음 금요일에 오시면 됩니다.

① 편한 시간이 언제야?
② 미안해, 내가 이번 토요일에 바빠.
④ 7시에 우리 집에 들러줘.
⑤ 집 앞으로 그걸 가지러 올래?

18 ②

해설 어제 주문한 음식이 오지 않았다는 여자의 말을 듣고 요금을 취소하겠다는 응답이 이어져야 적절하다.

어휘 check out (호텔에서 비용을 지불하고) 체크아웃하다[나가다]
bill[bil] 계산서
strange[streindʒ] 이상한
amount[əmáunt] 금액
expect[ikspékt] 예상하다, 기대하다

W Good morning. I'd like to check out. My room number is 703.
M Just one moment. Oh, I got it. Are you Natalie Brown?
W Yes.
M Here's your room bill.
W Hmm, this is strange. The amount is higher than I expected.
M I believe you had room service yesterday.
W I ordered breakfast yesterday morning, but I canceled it a few minutes later.

여 안녕하세요. 체크아웃을 하고 싶은데요. 객실 번호는 703호입니다.
남 잠시만요. 아, 찾았습니다. Natalie Brown 이시죠?
여 네.
남 여기 객실 요금 계산서입니다.
여 음, 이거 이상한데요. 금액이 제 예상보다 더 많아요.
남 어제 룸서비스를 받으신 거 같은데요.
여 어제 아침에 아침 식사를 주문했는데, 몇 분 후에 취소했어요.

[선택지]
cancel[kǽnsəl] 취소하다
charge[tʃɑːrdʒ] 요금
extend[iksténd] 연장하다
stay[stei] 체류 (기간), 방문
according to ~에 따르면

M I'm sorry. I'll give you the new bill.

남 죄송합니다. 새 요금 계산서를 드릴게요.

① 오전 11시까지 체크아웃을 하셔야 합니다.
③ 아, 죄송합니다, 체류를 연장해드릴 수 없습니다.
④ 유감스럽게도 손님 예약을 찾을 수 없습니다.
⑤ 이것에 따르면, 네 번의 통화를 하셨습니다.

19 ②

해설 방금 한 말을 되묻는 남자의 말에 여자가 다시 말해주는 것이 자연스럽다.

어휘 directly[diréktli] 직접
step in 들어오다

[Cell phone rings.]
W Hello.
M Hello. Is this Susan?
W No. This is Susie. Who's this?
M Oh, Susie. This is Andy. Can I talk to Susan?
W Sorry, she's not in now.
M Is she expected home soon?
W Maybe in about an hour. Shall I have her call you back?
M Yes. I'd rather speak to her directly.
W [Pause] Oh, I think she just stepped in.
M What did you say?
W I said she just came in.

[휴대전화가 울린다.]
여 여보세요.
남 여보세요. Susan이니?
여 아니요. Susie에요. 누구시죠?
남 아, Susie. 나 Andy야. Susan 좀 바꿔줄래?
여 미안하지만, 언니는 지금 여기 없어요.
남 Susan이 집에 곧 올 예정이니?
여 아마 한 시간쯤 후에요. 다시 전화 걸라고 할까요?
남 그래. Susan과 직접 통화하고 싶거든.
여 [잠시 후] 아, 언니가 방금 들어온 것 같아요.
남 뭐라고 그랬어?
여 언니가 방금 들어왔다고 말했어요.

① 그 말을 들으니 유감이에요.
③ 언니가 다른 전화를 받고 있어요.
④ 언니가 오빠와 통화하고 싶대요.
⑤ 왜 저에게 그것에 대해 말하지 않았어요?

20 ③

해설 Tiffany가 John에게 만나기로 한 시간을 7시 20분으로 바꾸자고 말해야 하는 상황이다.

어휘 theater[θí(ː)ətər] 극장
find out 알게 되다
watch[wɑtʃ] 돌보다

W John and Tiffany are friends in middle school. John asks Tiffany to go to the movies with him because he has 2 free movie tickets. So they agree to meet at the theater at 7 p.m. Tiffany comes home, but she finds out she has to watch her sister until 7 p.m. Now Tiffany decides to call John and tell him to meet at 7:20 instead. In this situation, what would Tiffany most likely say to John?

Tiffany Can we change the time to 7:20?

여 John과 Tiffany는 중학교 친구이다. John이 무료 영화 티켓이 두 장이 생겨서 Tiffany 에게 영화를 보러 가자고 한다. 그래서 그들은 오후 7시에 영화관에서 만나기로 한다. Tiffany는 집으로 오지만 오후 7시까지 동생을 돌봐줘야 한다는 것을 알게 된다. 지금 Tiffany는 John에게 전화해서 대신 7시 20분에 만나자고 말하려고 한다. 이러한 상황에서 Tiffany가 John에게 할 말로 가장 적절한 것은 무엇인가?

Tiffany 우리 시간을 7시 20분으로 바꿔도 될까?

① 가고 싶지만, 그럴 수 없어.
② 너의 여동생에게 무슨 일 있어?
④ 지금 온라인으로 표를 구매해.
⑤ 오늘 저녁에 영화 한 편 보는 게 어때?

01 ④	02 ③	03 ⑤	04 ③	05 ④	06 ①	07 ⑤
08 ①	09 ③	10 ④	11 ②	12 ⑤	13 ②	14 ③
15 ④	16 ④	17 ③	18 ①	19 ②	20 ④	

01 ④

해설 자리에 앉아서 발뒤꿈치를 들어 올리는 운동이다.

어휘 hurt[həːrt] 아프다
muscle[mʌ́səl] 근육
lift[lift] 들어 올리다
heel[hiːl] 뒤꿈치
hold[hould] 유지하다
position[pəzíʃən] 자세
repeat[ripíːt] 반복하다

W Ouch!
M What's the matter?
W I was standing all day long, and my legs really hurt.
M Why don't you do exercises to relax your leg muscles?
W Okay. What exercises should I do?
M Take a seat and lift both of your heels.
W Okay.
M Then hold that position for 15 seconds and repeat it 3 times.
W Oh, my legs feel better. Thanks.

여 아야!
남 무슨 일이야?
여 하루 종일 서 있었더니 다리가 정말 아파.
남 다리 근육을 푸는 운동을 하지 그래?
여 좋아. 어떤 운동을 해야 하는데?
남 자리에 앉아서 발뒤꿈치를 전부 들어.
여 알았어.
남 그리고 15초 동안 그 자세를 유지하고 그걸 세 번 반복해.
여 아, 다리가 한결 낫네. 고마워.

02 ③

해설 여자는 알람 시계가 작동하지 않아서, 새 시계를 사는 주말까지 모닝콜을 해달라고 남자에게 부탁했다.

어휘 alarm clock 알람 시계
go off 울리다
even though ~할지라도
set[set] (시간을) 맞추다
perhaps[pərhǽps] 아마
wake-up call 모닝콜
appreciate[əpríːʃièit] 감사하다

W I was late for work today.
M Again?
W I overslept. My alarm clock didn't go off this morning, even though I set it last night.
M Your clock never works. Perhaps you should buy a new one.
W You're right. I'll buy a new one this weekend.
M What will you do until this weekend?
W Since my alarm clock doesn't work, can you give me a wake-up call until then?
M Okay. I'll wake you up at 6 in the morning.
W I'd really appreciate that.

여 나 오늘 회사에 지각했어.
남 또?
여 늦잠을 잤어. 알람 시계가 지난밤에 맞춰놓았는데도 오늘 아침에 울리지 않았거든.
남 네 시계는 항상 작동하지 않네. 어쩌면 너는 새 걸 사는 게 좋겠어.
여 네 말이 맞아. 이번 주말에 새 시계를 살 거야.
남 주말까지는 어떻게 할 거야?
여 내 알람 시계가 작동하지 않으니까, 그때까지 네가 모닝콜을 해줄래?
남 알겠어. 아침 6시에 깨워줄게.
여 정말 고마워.

03 ⑤

해설 여자가 강아지를 남자의 집에 데리고 와서 잠시 돌봐달라고 부탁하는 상황이다.

어휘 gentle[dʒéntl] 순한
prefer[prifə́ːr] 선호하다
raise[reiz] 기르다
be away 떨어져 있다, 부재 중이다

① W What are you looking for?
   M I'm looking for my dog.
② W What kind of dog do you want?
   M I like gentle ones. They are easy to take care of.
③ W What kind of pet would you prefer the most?
   M Dogs are the best.
④ W Have you ever raised a dog?
   M No, I haven't.

① 여 무엇을 찾고 있나요?
   남 제 개를 찾고 있어요.
② 여 어떤 종류의 개를 원하세요?
   남 저는 순한 개를 좋아해요. 돌보기 쉽거든요.
③ 여 어떤 종류의 애완동물을 가장 선호하시나요?
   남 개가 가장 좋아요.
④ 여 개를 길러본 적이 있으세요?
   남 아니요, 없어요.

⑤ **W** Would you mind looking after my dog while I'm away?
M No, not at all.

⑤ 여 제가 없는 동안 제 개를 돌봐주시겠어요?
남 네, 그러죠.

04 ③

해설 여자는 기타를 빌리기 위해 수요일 오전 10시에 남자의 집으로 가기로 했다.

어휘 borrow[bárou] 빌리다
come over 들르다
stop by (~에) 잠시 들르다

W Sam, can I borrow your guitar?
M Sure. But it's at home. You have to come over to get it. Is that all right?
W That's fine. Can I stop by your house at 5 p.m. on Tuesday?
M Oh, sorry. I won't be home at that time.
W Then how about 4:30 p.m. on Wednesday?
M 4:30 p.m.? I have to meet Jake at 4.
W Well, how about earlier the same day? 10 a.m.?
M That sounds good.
W Okay. See you then.

여 Sam, 네 기타를 좀 빌려도 될까?
남 물론이지. 근데 그건 집에 있어. 가지러 집에 와야 하는데. 괜찮아?
여 괜찮지. 화요일 오후 5시에 너의 집에 들러도 되니?
남 아, 미안해. 나는 그 시간에 집에 없을 거야.
여 그러면 수요일 오후 4시 30분은 어때?
남 오후 4시 30분? 나는 4시에 Jake를 만나야 해.
여 음, 같은 날 더 일찍은 어때? 오전 10시?
남 좋은 것 같아.
여 알았어. 그때 보자.

05 ④

해설 침실의 개수(3개), 주차장 유무(차고가 있음), 주변 시설(병원, 쇼핑센터), 주변 환경(안전하고 조용함)에 관해 언급되었지만, 층수에 관한 언급은 없었다.

어휘 terrific[tərífik] 아주 좋은, 멋진
garage[gərá:dʒ] 차고
renovate[rénəvèit] 개조하다, 보수하다
far from ~에서 먼
surroundings[səráundiŋz] 주변 환경

M Hello, Mrs. Baker. I've found a house you will want to buy.
W Oh, terrific! What's it like?
M It has 3 bedrooms and 2 bathrooms. There is also a big garage, so you can park your car in there.
W That sounds good.
M The house has been renovated, so it is as good as new.
W All right. Then, what about the hospital and the shopping center?
M They're not far from the house. The house is also in very safe and quiet surroundings.
W Okay. Could I see it tomorrow afternoon?
M Sure.

남 안녕하세요, Baker 부인. 당신이 사고 싶어 할 집을 찾았습니다.
여 아, 잘됐어요! 어떤 집이에요?
남 침실이 세 개이고 욕실이 두 개가 있어요. 차고도 있어서 그 안에 주차할 수 있어요.
여 좋네요.
남 개조되어서 새것만큼 좋아요.
여 좋아요. 그러면, 병원과 쇼핑센터는 어떤가요?
남 집에서 멀지 않아요. 또 그 집은 매우 안전하고 조용한 주변 환경에 있어요.
여 알겠어요. 내일 오후에 그 집을 볼 수 있을까요?
남 물론이죠.

06 ①

해설 방이 있는지 물어보는 여자에게 투숙객이 평상시보다 많아 2인실밖에 없다고 설명하는 남자의 말로 보아 두 사람이 대화하는 장소는 호텔임을 알 수 있다.

어휘 available[əvéiləbl] 이용 가능한
reservation[rèzərvéiʃən] 예약
front desk (호텔 등의) 프런트[안내 데스크]
conference[kánfərəns] 회의, 학회
hold[hould] 열다, 개최하다

M Hello, ma'am. How may I help you?
W Hello. Is there any room available for tonight?
M Oh, do you not have a reservation?
W No, I don't. I called about a month ago, but the front desk said we didn't need one.
M During this time of year, that's usually true. However, because of a conference being held near here, we have more guests than usual. Are you alone?

남 안녕하세요. 어떻게 도와 드릴까요?
여 안녕하세요. 오늘 밤에 이용 가능한 방이 있나요?
남 아, 예약을 하지 않으셨나요?
여 네, 안 했어요. 한 달 전쯤에 전화했는데, 프런트에서 예약할 필요가 없다고 하더군요.
남 일 년 중 이맘때는 보통 그렇습니다. 하지만, 이 근처에서 열리는 회의 때문에, 평소보다 손님이 더 많네요. 혼자이신가요?

guest[gest] 손님, 투숙객
at the moment 지금

W No. My husband is bringing our 2 daughters.
M I'm sorry, but all we have at the moment is a room for 2. Would you like to stay anyway?
W Well, it's better than spending the night in our car.

여 아니요. 제 남편이 두 딸을 데리고 오고 있어요.
남 죄송하지만, 지금 남아 있는 방은 전부 2인실입니다. 그래도 머무시겠습니까?
여 음, 자동차에서 밤을 보내는 것보다 낫겠죠.

07 ⑤

[해설] 졸업 후에 하고 싶은 일을 물었는데, 할머니를 만나러 공항에 갈 거라는 계획을 말하는 응답은 어색하다.

[어휘] leave for ~로 떠나다
bored[bɔːrd] 지루한
take a walk 산책하다
someday[sʌ́mdèi] 언젠가
graduate from ~을 졸업하다
airport[ɛ́ərpɔ̀ːrt] 공항

① W How do you like your new home?
   M I love it! It's near my school.
② W What time are you leaving for China?
   M At 3 o'clock this afternoon.
③ W I'm bored. Let's do something.
   M Okay. How about taking a walk in the park?
④ W Have you ever been to London?
   M No, I haven't. I really want to visit there someday.
⑤ W What do you want to do after you graduate from school?
   M I am planning to meet my grandmother at the airport.

① 여 네 새 집이 맘에 드니?
   남 아주 좋아! 학교 근처에 있거든.
② 여 몇 시에 중국으로 떠나니?
   남 오늘 오후 3시.
③ 여 나 지루해. 뭐라도 하자.
   남 알겠어. 공원에서 산책하는 게 어때?
④ 여 런던에 가 본 적 있니?
   남 아니, 없어. 언젠가는 정말 거기에 가보고 싶어.
⑤ 여 학교 졸업 후에 뭐 하고 싶니?
   남 나는 공항으로 우리 할머니를 만나러 갈 계획이야.

08 ①

[해설] 남자는 힘든 하루를 보내서 녹초가 됐다고 하면서, 여자에게 설거지를 대신해 달라고 부탁했다.

[어휘] stay up 깨어 있다
practice[præktis] 연습
rough[rʌf] 힘든
do the dishes 설거지하다
turn[təːrn] 차례
deal[diːl] 거래, 합의

W You look tired. What's the matter?
M I stayed up until 3 a.m. studying for the exam. I got up early in the morning and went to school. Then I took the exam from 9 to 11. Then I had basketball practice from 1 to 3.
W It sounds like you had a rough day.
M Yes. Could you do the dishes tonight? I know it's my turn, but I am too tired.
W Sure. You can do them for me tomorrow night.
M It's a deal. Thanks.

여 너 피곤해 보여. 무슨 일이야?
남 시험공부를 하느라 새벽 3시까지 자지 않았어. 아침 일찍 일어나서 학교에 갔지. 9시부터 11시까지는 시험이 있었고, 그 다음에 1시부터 3시까지 농구 연습을 했어.
여 네가 힘든 하루를 보낸 것 같네.
남 응. 오늘 밤에 설거지를 해줄래? 내 차례라는 건 알지만, 내가 너무 피곤해.
여 그래. 네가 내일 밤에 나 대신에 설거지하면 돼.
남 그렇게 하자. 고마워.

09 ③

[해설] 학교 도서관에서 개최하는 시 쓰기 대회에 대해 홍보하는 안내 방송이다.

[어휘] poem[póuəm] 시
subject[sʌ́bdʒikt] 주제
post[poust] 게시하다
reward[riwɔ́ːrd] 상, 보상
application form 신청서

W Good morning, students. Our school library is going to hold a Poem Writing Contest. Students will have to write 3 poems on the subjects posted on our school website. Three winners will be chosen, and each of them will receive a gift card as a reward. If you want to join this contest, please bring your application form to the library office. Thank you.

여 안녕하세요, 학생 여러분. 우리 학교 도서관에서 시 쓰기 대회를 개최합니다. 학생들은 학교 웹사이트에 게시된 주제로 3편의 시를 써야 합니다. 세 명의 수상자가 선정되며, 각각의 수상자는 상으로 기프트 카드를 받을 것입니다. 이 대회에 참가하려면, 신청서를 도서관 사무실에 제출하십시오. 감사합니다.

10 ④

해설 10퍼센트 할인하는 50달러짜리 신발을 두 켤레를 구매했으므로 90달러를 지불해야 한다.

어휘 off[ɔːf] 할인하여
wrap[ræp] 포장하다
separately[sépərətli] 따로따로, 개별적으로

M May I help you?
W Yes, please. I'm looking for a pair of shoes.
M Okay, ma'am. Take your time.
W How much are those red ones?
M They're $50, but they are <u>on sale for</u> 10% off.
W Do you have them <u>in another color</u>, too?
M We also have them in black.
W All right. I'll take <u>one pair in black</u>, and one in red.
M <u>Should I wrap them</u> separately?
W Yes, please.

남 도와 드릴까요?
여 네. 신발을 찾고 있는데요.
남 알겠습니다. 손님. 천천히 고르세요.
여 저 빨간색 신발은 얼마예요?
남 50달러입니다. 하지만 10퍼센트 할인하여 판매 중입니다.
여 그걸로 다른 색깔도 있나요?
남 검은색도 있습니다.
여 좋아요. 검은색으로 하나, 빨간색으로 하나 살게요.
남 전부 따로 포장해야 하나요?
여 네.

11 ②

해설 남자는 탑승 10분 전에 기차표를 집에 두고 온 것 같다면서 표를 다시 사 오겠다고 했다.

어휘 get ready 준비하다
be about to-v 막 ~하려고 하다
board[bɔːrd] 탑승하다
a bit 조금

W Peter, <u>get the tickets ready</u>. We are about to board.
M Okay. Wait a minute.
W What's the matter?
M I can't find the tickets.
W Oh no! The train leaves in 10 minutes. I <u>gave them to you</u> this morning, remember?
M Yes. I put them in the pocket of my jacket and now <u>they're not there</u>.
W Look again.
M I'm afraid I left them at home. <u>I'll buy new tickets</u> now.

여 Peter, 표 준비해요. 막 탑승하려고 해요.
남 알겠어요. 잠시만요.
여 무슨 일이에요?
남 표를 찾을 수가 없어요.
여 이런! 10분 후에 기차가 출발해요. 오늘 아침에 내가 당신에게 표를 준 거 기억해요?
남 네. 내 재킷 주머니에 표를 넣었는데 지금 거기에 없네요.
여 다시 봐요.
남 집에 두고 온 것 같아요. 내가 지금 표를 새로 사 올게요.

12 ⑤

해설 개최 장소(학교 본관 앞), 개최 날짜(9월 7일), 행사 목적(미술을 공부하고 싶어 하는 가난한 어린이들을 돕기 위해), 판매 품목(책과 옷 같은 중고품)에 관해 언급되었지만, 간식 메뉴에 관한 언급은 없었다.

어휘 president[prézədənt] 회장
flea market 벼룩 시장
be held 개최하다
main building 본관
prepare[pripέər] 준비하다
raise money 모금하다
used goods 중고품
such as ~ 같은
cafeteria[kæfətíəriə] 구내식당

M Hello, students. I'm Robert Clark, the president of the Art Club. I'm happy to introduce the Parkwoods Flea Market. It will be <u>held in front of</u> the main building at the school on September 7th. We've prepared this event in order <u>to raise money for</u> poor children who want to study art. <u>We'll sell used goods</u> such as books and clothes at this event. You can <u>also buy some snacks</u> in the cafeteria. Please come and get some good things at a low price. Thank you.

남 안녕하세요, 학생 여러분. 미술 동아리 회장 Robert Clark입니다. Parkwoods 벼룩 시장을 소개하게 되어서 기쁩니다. 그것은 9월 7일에 학교 본관 앞에서 열립니다. 저희는 미술을 공부하고 싶어 하는 가난한 어린이들을 위한 돈을 모으기 위해 이 행사를 준비했습니다. 이 행사에서 우리는 책과 옷 같은 중고품을 팔 것입니다. 여러분은 구내식당에서 간식을 사 먹을 수도 있습니다. 오셔서 저렴한 가격에 좋은 물건들을 사세요. 감사합니다.

13 ②

해설 리모델링이 필요하지 않고 카페 옆과 화장실 옆이 아닌 곳을 사용하기로 했다.

어휘 corner[kɔ́ːrnər] 구석
rent[rent] 임대료
remodeling[rimάdəliŋ] 개보수, 리모델링
lover[lʌvər] …애호가
crowded[kráudid] 붐비는
all day long 하루 종일
noisy[nɔ́izi] 시끄러운
restroom[réstrù(ː)m] 화장실

M Emily, which room is good for our office?
W How about Room A? I think it's quiet because it's in the corner.
M The rent is cheap, too. But the room looks old. We would need to spend some money on remodeling.
W What about using one of the rooms next to the cafe? You're a coffee lover.
M But the cafe is crowded and music plays all day long. So those rooms may be noisy.
W You're right. Then, we have 2 rooms left, Room B and Room D.
M Let's not take the room next to the restroom.
W Okay.

남 Emily, 우리 사무실로 어떤 방이 좋아요?
여 방 A는 어때요? 구석에 있기 때문에 조용할 것 같아요.
남 임대료도 싸네요. 하지만 방이 오래된 것 같아요. 리모델링에 돈을 써야 할 거예요.
여 카페 옆에 있는 방들 중 하나를 쓰는 게 어때요? 당신은 커피를 좋아하잖아요.
남 하지만 카페는 붐비고 하루 종일 음악을 틀어요. 그래서 그 방들은 시끄러울 거예요.
여 맞아요. 그러면 B방과 D방 두 방이 남았네요.
남 화장실 옆에 있는 방은 얻지 맙시다.
여 좋아요.

14 ③

해설 무색무취의 액체이고, 식물과 동물의 생명에 있어서 필수적이며, 섭씨 0도에서 얼고 100도에서 끓는 것은 물이다.

어휘 clear[kliər] 맑은, 깨끗한
liquid[líkwid] 액체
necessary[nésəsèri] 필수적인
almost[ɔ́ːlmoust] 거의
freeze[friːz] 얼다
boil[bɔil] 끓다
in fact 사실
a third 3분의 1
make up 구성하다
human body 인체

W This is a clear liquid. It has no color and no smell. It is very necessary for most plant and animal life. Without this, almost all of the living things on earth would die. It freezes at 0°C and boils at 100°C. In fact, this covers a third of the earth. Also, this makes up a large part of living things. About 60 to 70 percent of the human body is this. Because this is necessary for life, it's important that we keep it clean.

여 이것은 많은 액체예요. 색깔과 냄새가 없어요. 그것은 대부분의 식물과 동물의 생명에게 매우 필수예요. 이것이 없으면, 지구상의 거의 모든 생물은 죽을 거예요. 섭씨 0도에서 얼고 100도에서 끓어요. 사실, 이것은 지구의 3분의 1을 뒤덮어요. 또한, 생물의 많은 부분을 구성해요. 사람 몸의 약 60~70퍼센트가 이것이에요. 생명에 필수이기 때문에, 우리가 그것을 깨끗이 유지하는 것이 중요해요.

15 ④

해설 주말 내내 비가 올 거라는 예보를 들었는데 확실히 하기 위해 날씨를 다시 확인해보라는 남자의 말에 여자는 그렇게 하겠다고 했다.

어휘 hike[haik] 하이킹[도보 여행]을 하다
mention[ménʃən] 언급
mistaken[mistéikən] 잘못 알고 있는
make sure 확실히 하다

W Larry, I'm going hiking in the mountains this weekend. Do you want to come?
M This weekend? Are you sure?
W Is there something wrong?
M I heard that it will rain all weekend.
W Well, I checked the weather a few days ago, but there was no mention of rain this weekend.
M I might be mistaken. You'd better check it again to make sure.
W You're right. I'll do that right now.

여 Larry, 나 이번 주말에 등산하러 갈 거야. 너도 갈래?
남 이번 주말에? 확실해?
여 뭐가 잘못됐니?
남 근데 주말 내내 비가 올 거라고 들었어.
여 음, 며칠 전에 날씨를 확인했지만, 이번 주말에는 비에 대한 언급은 없었어.
남 내가 잘못 알았을 수도 있어. 확실히 하기 위해서 다시 확인하는 게 좋을 거야.
여 네 말이 맞아. 지금 바로 그렇게 할게.

16 ④

解説 남자는 4월 25일 다음 날에 영화를 보자고 제안했고, 여자가 그 날 티켓을 구매하겠다고 했으므로 두 사람이 영화를 볼 날짜는 4월 26일이다.

語彙 actually[金ktʃuəli] 사실
make it 만나다

[Cell phone rings.]
W Hello.
M Hi, Cindy. It's Mark.
W Hi, Mark. What's up?
M Did you buy the tickets to the movie for this Wednesday?
W Not yet. Why?
M Actually, I don't think I can make it on that day. I forgot April 25th is my grandmother's birthday.
W That's okay. Are you free the next day?
M Yes. Do you want to see the movie on that day instead?
W Sure. Then I will buy the tickets for Thursday.
M Okay. See you on Thursday.

[휴대전화가 울린다.]
여 여보세요.
남 안녕, Cindy. 나 Mark야.
여 안녕, Mark. 무슨 일이야?
남 이번 주 수요일에 볼 영화표를 샀니?
여 아직. 왜?
남 사실, 그날 만날 수 없을 거 같아. 4월 25일이 우리 할머니 생신이라는 걸 깜빡했어.
여 괜찮아. 그 다음 날은 한가하니?
남 응. 대신에 그날 영화를 볼래?
여 좋아. 그러면 내가 목요일 표를 살게.
남 알겠어. 목요일에 보자.

17 ③

解説 박물관으로 가는 버스를 타는 곳과 운행 시간에 대해 설명해주는 남자에게 고맙다고 인사하는 것이 가장 적절하다

語彙 catch[kætʃ] (버스 등을) 타다
across[əkrɔ́:s] 건너서
cross[krɔ(:)s] 건너다
crosswalk[krɔ́:swɔ̀:k] 횡단보도
run[rʌn] 운행하다
[선택지]
had better+v ~하는 것이 낫다
appreciate[əprí:ʃièit] 감사하다
be used to+명사 ~하는 데 익숙하다
traffic jam 교통 체증

W Excuse me. I'd like to go to the National Museum of Korea. How can I get there?
M Then you need to take bus number 400.
W Where can I take that bus?
M You can catch it over there across the street.
W Right on that corner?
M Yes. You can cross the street at the crosswalk.
W Thanks a lot.
M It runs about every 15 minutes, so you shouldn't have to wait too long.
W That's good. I appreciate your help.

여 실례합니다. 국립 중앙 박물관에 가고 싶은데요. 그곳으로 어떻게 가나요?
남 그러면 400번 버스를 타셔야 합니다.
여 그 버스를 어디서 탈 수 있나요?
남 길 건너 저쪽에서 그것을 탈 수 있어요.
여 바로 저 모퉁이에서요?
남 네. 횡단보도로 길을 건너시면 돼요.
여 정말 감사합니다.
남 버스가 15분쯤마다 오니까, 너무 오래 기다리지는 않을 거예요.
여 잘됐네요. 도와주셔서 감사합니다.

① 버스는 얼마나 자주 오나요?
② 그 버스를 타지 않으시는 게 좋겠어요.
④ 박물관에 가 본 적이 있나요?
⑤ 괜찮아요. 저는 아침 교통 체증에 익숙해요.

18 ①

解説 비행기 출발 시각과 탑승구 번호를 물었으므로 이를 알려주는 응답이 가장 적절하다.

語彙 seating preference 선호하는 좌석
aisle[ail] 통로
extra legroom 다리를 펼 여분의 공간
possible[pásəbl] 가능한
emergency exit 비상 출입구
boarding pass 탑승권

M May I see your passport, please?
W Here you go.
M Do you have a seating preference, Ms. Anderson?
W I'd like an aisle seat. One with extra legroom, if possible.
M I have a seat next to the emergency exit.
W Oh, that would be good!
M Here's your boarding pass.
W Thank you. What is the departure time and gate number?

남 여권을 보여주시겠어요?
여 여기 있습니다.
남 선호하는 좌석이 있습니까, Anderson 씨?
여 통로 쪽 좌석을 원해요. 가능하면, 다리를 펼 공간이 있는 것으로요.
남 음… 비상 출입구 옆에 좌석이 있습니다.
여 아, 그거 좋겠군요!
남 여기 탑승권입니다.
여 감사합니다. 출발 시각과 탑승구 번호가 어떻게 되지요?

departure[dipá:rtʃər] 출발

gate[geit] 탑승구

[선택지]

check-in counter 체크인 카운터(공항의 탑승 수속 창구)

depart[dipá:rt] 떠나다

platform[plǽtfɔ:rm] (역의) 승강장

lounge[laundʒ] 휴게실

M It'll board at Gate 202 at 5:30.

남 5시 30분에 202번 게이트에서 탑승하실 겁니다.

② 탑승 수속대에서 만납시다.

③ 손님 기차는 7번 승강장에서 출발할 겁니다.

④ 4시간 30분 걸릴 겁니다.

⑤ 30분 동안 휴게실에서 기다리는 게 좋을 겁니다.

19 ②

해설 진료 시간을 물었으므로 이를 알려주는 응답이 이어져야 가장 적절하다.

어휘 closing time 문 닫는 시간

office hours 진료 시간, 근무 시간

[선택지]

through[θru:] (…부터) …까지

M Excuse me. Where's Dr. Miller's office?
W It's on the fifth floor.
M Is there an elevator here?
W Yes. Go this way, and the elevator is on the left.
M Thanks.
W No problem. But you should hurry. It's almost closing time.
M What are their office hours?
W 9 to 5, Monday through Friday.

남 실례합니다. Miller 선생님 진료실이 어디죠?
여 5층에 있습니다.
남 여기 엘리베이터가 있나요?
여 네, 이 길로 가시면, 왼쪽에 엘리베이터가 있습니다.
남 감사합니다.
여 천만에요. 하지만 서두르시는 게 좋아요. 거의 문을 닫을 시간이에요.
남 진료 시간이 어떻게 되는데요?
여 월요일부터 금요일까지, 9시에서 5시요.

① 지금은 8시 30분이에요.
③ 그러고 싶지만, 저는 지금 가야 해요.
④ 그는 제 시간에 거기 갈 수 있을 거예요.
⑤ 저는 바빠요. 나중에 병원에 갈게요.

20 ④

해설 몸이 아파도 수학시험을 걱정하는 Ben에게 하루 정도는 쉬어도 괜찮다고 말하는 상황이다.

어휘 take notes 필기하다

dizzy[dízi] 어지러운

no matter how 아무리 ~하더라도

fall behind 뒤떨어지다, 뒤처지다

[선택지]

subject[sʌ́bdʒikt] 과목

skip[skip] (일을) 거르다, 빼먹다

M Ben is not doing well in math class. To get better grades in math class, he listens to the teacher and takes notes on everything. This morning, when he wakes up, he starts to feel dizzy. His mother tells him to stay home today. However, Ben wants to go to school no matter how sick he is. He is very worried about a math test next week. He is afraid that if he misses a math class, he will fall behind again. His mother is worried about him, so she decides to tell him not to worry about the test. In this situation, what would Ben's mother most likely say to Ben?

Ben's mother It's okay to skip math for one day.

남 Ben은 수학 시간에 잘하지 못한다. 수학 수업에서 더 좋은 성적을 얻기 위해, 그는 선생님 말씀을 듣고, 모든 것을 필기한다. 오늘 아침에 일어났을 때, 그는 어지럽기 시작했다. 그의 어머니는 오늘은 집에 머물라고 말한다. 하지만 Ben은 아무리 아프더라도 학교에 가고 싶어 한다. 그는 다음 주에 있을 수학 시험에 대해 걱정한다. 그는 수업을 놓치면 다시 뒤처질까봐 두려워한다. 그의 어머니는 그를 걱정해서, 시험에 대해서는 걱정하지 말라고 말하려고 한다. 이러한 상황에서 Ben의 어머니는 Ben에게 할 말로 가장 적절한 것은 무엇인가?

Ben의 어머니 하루 동안 수학을 빼먹어도 괜찮단다.

① 나중에 다시 전화해도 되니?
② 수학은 나도 가장 좋아하는 과목이란다.
③ 시험을 대비하여 열심히 공부해야 한단다.
⑤ 어제 수업에서 필기한 노트를 빌려도 될까?

실전 모의고사 20 p. 218

01 ①	02 ②	03 ④	04 ②	05 ⑤	06 ④	07 ③
08 ①	09 ④	10 ②	11 ④	12 ④	13 ⑤	14 ②
15 ⑤	16 ④	17 ⑤	18 ⑤	19 ③	20 ③	

01 ①

해설 바닥에 앉아 다리를 쭉 뻗은 뒤에 최대한 허리를 굽혀서 팔을 뻗고 다리를 붙잡는 자세이다.

어휘 back[bæk] 허리, 등
straight[streit] 똑바로
extend[iksténd] 뻗다, 내밀다
grab[græb] 붙잡다
bend[bend] 굽히다
waist[weist] 허리
relax[rilǽks] (근육 등의) 긴장이 풀리다
position[pəzíʃən] 자세
repeat[ripíːt] 반복하다

W Ugh, my back really hurts.
M I know an easy and good stretch for you.
W Okay. What is that?
M First sit on the floor with both legs out straight.
W And then?
M Extend your arms. Then grab your feet by bending at the waist.
W Oh, my back feels better already.
M Hold this position for 30 seconds and repeat this three times.

여 으, 등이 너무 아프네.
남 내가 쉽고도 좋은 운동을 알고 있어.
여 알았어. 그게 뭔데?
남 우선 두 다리를 쭉 뻗고 바닥에 앉아.
여 그러고 나서는?
남 허리를 최대한 굽힌 채로 팔을 뻗어서 발을 붙잡아.
여 아, 내 등이 긴장이 풀리는 게 느껴진다.
남 이 자세를 30초간 유지하고 세 번 반복해.

02 ②

해설 여자가 수학과 과학을 혼자 공부하기가 어렵다고 하면서 남자에게 함께 공부하자고 부탁했다.

어휘 on your's mind (걱정 등이) 마음에 있는[걸리는]
mid-term[mídtəːrm] 중간의
fully[fúlli] 완전히
prepare[pripɛ́ər] 준비하다
several[sévərəl] 몇 개의
hard[haːrd] 어려운, 힘든

M Hey, what's on your mind?
W The mid-term exams. I'm not fully prepared yet.
M Well, you still have 3 days.
W Yeah, but 3 days are not enough to study for several classes.
M Which classes are the most difficult for you?
W Math and science. It's really hard for me to study alone. Can you study with me?
M Of course. I hope I can help you.
W You will. I am really worried about those exams.
M Don't worry so much. Just study hard and you'll do well.

남 야, 뭐가 마음에 걸리니?
여 중간고사. 나는 아직 완전히 준비하지 못했어.
남 음, 아직 3일 남았잖아.
여 그래, 하지만 몇 과목을 공부하기에 3일은 충분하지 않아.
남 너는 어느 과목이 가장 어렵니?
여 수학과 과학. 혼자 공부하는 게 정말 어려워. 나와 함께 공부할 수 있니?
남 물론이지. 내가 너에게 도움이 될 수 있으면 좋겠네.
여 그럴 거야. 난 저 시험들이 정말 걱정돼.
남 너무 걱정하지 마. 그냥 열심히 공부해. 그러면 잘 할 거야.

03 ④

해설 소포를 보내고 싶다는 남자에게 여자가 저울 위에 소포를 올려달라고 하는 상황이다.

어휘 package[pǽkidʒ] 소포
by air 항공으로
scale[skeil] 저울

① M Could you pick up the box?
W Of course. Here you are.
② M What are you doing now?
W I'm writing a letter to my parents.
③ M How do you want to send the package?
W I'd like to send it by air.
④ M I'd like to send this package.
W Could you please put the package on the scale?

① 남 상자 좀 집어 주시겠어요?
여 물론이죠. 여기 있습니다.
② 남 지금 무엇을 하고 계신가요?
여 부모님께 편지를 쓰고 있어요.
③ 남 소포를 어떻게 보내시겠어요?
여 항공 우편으로 보내고 싶어요.
④ 남 이 소포를 보내고 싶은데요.
여 저울 위에 소포를 올려 주시겠어요?

⑤ M Where can I send the package?

W There is a post office <u>on the second floor</u>.

⑤ 남 소포를 어디에서 보낼 수 있을까요?

여 2층에 우체국이 있어요.

04 ②

해설 남자가 화요일에 자전거를 타도되는지 묻자, 여자는 그날은 특별한 일이 없다고 말하면서 허락했다.

어휘 dentist[déntist] 치과 의사
appointment[əpɔ́intmənt] 약속
special[spéʃəl] 특별한

M Mom, can I play some computer games this week?

W <u>When do you want</u> to play computer games?

M Maybe on Wednesday, after school.

W Well, you shouldn't do it on that day. You <u>have a piano lesson</u>.

M What about Monday?

W Monday? You have a dentist's appointment.

M Then <u>what about</u> Tuesday?

W <u>That should be fine</u>. I don't think you have anything special to do on that day.

남 엄마, 저 이번 주에 컴퓨터 게임을 좀 해도 돼요?

여 컴퓨터 게임을 언제 하고 싶니?

남 아마도 수요일 방과 후예요.

여 음, 그날에 하면 안 돼. 너 피아노 수업이 있잖아.

남 월요일은 어때요?

여 월요일? 너 치과 진료 예약이 있어.

남 그럼, 화요일은 어때요?

여 괜찮을 거야. 그날에는 해야 할 특별한 일은 없는 것 같네.

05 ⑤

해설 디자인(꽃모양이 있는 터틀넥), 색깔(분홍색, 노란색, 녹색), 가격(50달러), 재료(양모)에 관해 언급되었지만, 사이즈에 대한 언급은 없었다.

어휘 turtleneck[tə́ːrtlnèk] 터틀넥(목이 긴 스웨터의 깃)
look good on ~와 잘 어울리다
made of ~로 만들어진
wool[wul] 양털, 양모

W Oh, that sweater looks good.

M That turtleneck sweater with flowers? Girls really love it.

W I think <u>the one in pink</u> would look good on my daughter. How much is it?

M It's $50. It's on sale now.

W It's a little expensive.

M It is very warm because <u>it's made of wool</u>.

W Do you have it in a different color?

M <u>It comes in</u> pink, yellow, and green.

W I'll take 2, one in pink and one in yellow.

M Okay. I'll <u>put them in a bag</u>.

여 아, 저 스웨터는 좋아 보이네요.

남 저 꽃이 있는 터틀넥 스웨터요? 여자아이들이 그 스웨터를 정말 좋아해요.

여 제 딸에게 분홍색 스웨터가 잘 어울릴 것 같아요. 얼마인가요?

남 50달러예요. 지금 세일 중입니다.

여 조금 비싸네요.

남 양모로 만들어져서 매우 따뜻해요.

여 그걸로 다른 색이 있나요?

남 분홍색, 노란색, 녹색이 있어요.

여 분홍색으로 하나 그리고 노란색으로 하나, 두 개를 살게요.

남 알겠습니다. 가방에 넣어 드리겠습니다.

06 ④

해설 소파를 구입하려는 여자에게 남자가 혜택에 대해 설명하는 것으로 보아 두 사람은 가구점에서 대화하는 것을 알 수 있다.

어휘 deal[diːl] 거래
comfortable[kʌ́mfərtəbl] 편안한
leather[léðər] 가죽
for free 무료로
regret[rigrét] 후회하다

M This sofa set is on sale this week. It's a very good deal.

W It's really nice and so comfortable.

M And for only $300 more, you <u>can get it in</u> leather.

W Leather! I've always wanted a leather sofa.

M If you buy it today, you'll get <u>this coffee table for free</u>.

W I really need a coffee table, too.

M You won't find a deal <u>like this anywhere else</u>.

W Okay, <u>I'll take it</u>.

M Great! You won't regret it.

남 이 소파 세트는 이번 주에 세일을 합니다. 아주 좋은 가격이죠.

여 정말 멋지고, 아주 편안하네요.

남 그리고 300달러만 더 내시면, 그 소파를 가죽으로 하실 수 있어요.

여 가죽이요! 저는 항상 가죽 소파를 원했어요.

남 오늘 사시면, 이 커피 탁자를 공짜로 받으실 겁니다.

여 전 커피 탁자도 정말 필요해요.

남 이런 거래는 어디에서도 찾으실 수 없을 거예요.

여 알겠어요, 그걸 살게요.

남 잘하셨어요! 후회하지 않으실 거예요.

07 ③

① M Ann, will you do me a favor?
  W Sure, what is it?
② M I'm really nervous about going on the stage.
  W Don't be. You're the best singer in our school.
③ M Can I ask you a question?
  W Sure, I can. Thanks for helping me.
④ M Excuse me, can you tell me the way to Pearl Bookstore?
  W Sorry, but I'm a visitor here, too.
⑤ M What do you want to be in the future?
  W I'm interested in math, so I want to be a math teacher.

① 남 Ann, 나를 도와줄래?
  여 물론이지, 그게 뭔데?
② 남 나는 무대 위에 오르는 게 정말 긴장이 돼.
  여 긴장하지 마. 너는 우리 학교에서 가장 노래를 잘하잖아.
③ 남 질문 하나 해도 돼?
  여 물론. 도와줘서 고마워.
④ 남 실례합니다, Pearl 서점에 가는 길을 알려주시겠어요?
  여 죄송하지만, 저도 여기 방문객이라서요.
⑤ 남 너는 미래에 무엇이 되고 싶니?
  여 나는 수학에 관심이 있어서, 수학 교사가 되고 싶어.

08 ①

[Cell phone rings.]
M Hello.
W Hello, Robin. It's me. Where are you?
M I am still in the supermarket.
W Great! Did you find everything on the shopping list I gave you?
M Everything except milk. I am on my way to pick it up.
W Great. Actually, I'm calling because I forgot to add sugar on the list. We're running out of it. Can you get a bag?
M Of course. Anything else?
W That will be all. Thanks.

[휴대전화가 울린다.]
남 여보세요.
여 여보세요, Robin. 난데요. 당신 어디에요?
남 나 아직 슈퍼마켓에 있어요.
여 잘됐어요! 내가 당신에게 준 쇼핑 목록에 있는 것 다 찾았어요?
남 우유만 빼고 다요. 그것을 가지러 가는 중이에요.
여 좋아요. 사실, 내가 목록에 설탕을 추가하는 걸 깜빡해서 전화했어요. 설탕이 다 떨어져 가요. 한 봉지 사다 줄래요?
남 네. 다른 건요?
여 그게 다예요. 고마워요.

09 ④

W Do you enjoy outdoor sports? Why don't you join our bike club? You can ride your bike and make new friends. Also, we can breathe in fresh air! We are looking for new members now! Anyone who is interested in bike riding can join. If you want to join, come to the school playground at 4 o'clock tomorrow. We meet every Saturday to ride our bikes. Oh, and one more thing. You must have your own bike.

여 야외 스포츠를 즐기십니까? 저희 자전거 동아리에 가입하는 게 어떠신가요? 여러분은 자전거를 타면서 새로운 친구들을 사귈 수 있습니다. 또한, 신선한 공기를 마실 수 있습니다! 우리는 지금 새로운 회원들을 찾고 있습니다! 자전거 타기에 관심이 있는 분은 누구라도 가입할 수 있습니다. 가입을 원하시면, 내일 4시에 학교 운동장으로 오세요. 우리는 자전거를 타기 위해 매주 토요일에 만납니다. 아, 하나 더요. 본인의 자전거가 있어야 합니다.

10 ②

70달러짜리 방에 객실 세금이 10 퍼센트가 추가되므로 77달러를 지불할 것이다.

어휘 reserve[rizə́:rv] 예약하다
available[əvéiləbl] 이용할 수 있는
tax[tæks] 세금

[Telephone rings.]

W Hello. Sunnyside Hotel. How may I help you?

M I'd like to reserve a room on the 21st of March.

W Okay. Let me check for a moment. [Pause] Well, we have only one room available.

M How much is it?

W It's $100, plus a 10% room tax.

M Oh, that's too expensive for me. Do you have a cheaper room available?

W We have a few rooms available on the 20th.

M How much are they?

W They are $70, plus the 10% room tax.

M Okay, I'd like one of those.

[전화벨이 울린다.]

여 여보세요. Sunnyside 호텔입니다. 어떻게 도와 드릴까요?

남 3월 21일에 방을 하나 예약하고 싶어서요.

여: 알겠습니다. 잠시 확인해 볼게요. [잠시 후] 음, 이용 가능한 방이 딱 하나 있네요.

남 얼마인가요?

여 100달러인데, 10퍼센트 객실 세금이 붙어요.

남 아, 저에게는 너무 비싸네요. 더 저렴한 방이 있나요?

여 20일에 방이 몇 개 있어요.

남 얼마인가요?

여 70달러인데, 10퍼센트 객실 세금이 붙어요.

남 좋아요, 그것들 중 하나로 할게요.

11 ④

해설 여자는 건전지가 맨 위 서랍 안에 있을 것이라고 했으므로, 남자는 그곳을 확인하여 건전지를 가져다 줄 것이다.

어휘 battery[bǽtəri] 건전지
be replaced 교체되다
extra[ékstrə] 여분의
drawer[drɔ́:r] 서랍

M There is something wrong with this clock.

W What's the problem?

M Well, it just stopped.

W Really? Let me have a look. Maybe the battery needs to be replaced.

M Do you have any extra batteries?

W I may have some in one of my desk drawers.

M Which drawer should I look in?

W Try the top drawer. The batteries should be in there.

남 이 시계에 문제가 좀 있어요.

여 뭐가 문제인데요?

남 음, 그냥 멈췄어요.

여 그래요? 내가 한 번 볼게요. 아마 건전지가 교체되어야 할 거 같아요.

남 당신 여분의 건전지를 가지고 있어요?

여 내 책상 서랍 중 하나에 몇 개 있을 거예요.

남 어느 서랍을 봐야 하나요?

여 맨 위의 서랍을 봐요. 건전지가 그 안에 있을 거예요.

12 ④

해설 날짜(5월 10일), 장소(서울아트센터), 공연자(유명한 가수들과 연주자들), 행사 목적(도움이 필요한 아프리카의 아이들을 위해)에 관해 언급되었지만, 관람료에 대한 언급은 없었다.

어휘 be held 열리다, 개최되다
performer[pərfɔ́:rmər] 연주자
perform[pərfɔ́:rm] 공연하다
in need 도움이 필요한
die of ~로 죽다
hunger[hʌ́ŋgər] 굶주림, 기아
meaningful[mí:niŋfəl] 의미 있는

M Hello. The Seoul Charity Concert will be held on Sunday, May 10th at the Seoul Art Center. Many famous singers and performers from around the world will perform in this concert. It's held for African children in need. Many children there are sick or dying of hunger. Your help is needed, more than ever. So come and join us for this meaningful event.

남 안녕하세요. 서울 자선 콘서트가 5월 10일 일요일에 서울아트센터에서 열립니다. 전 세계의 많은 유명한 가수들과 연주자들이 이 콘서트에 공연할 겁니다. 이 콘서트는 도움이 필요한 아프리카 아이들을 위해 개최됩니다. 그곳의 많은 아이들이 병들거나 굶주림으로 죽어가고 있습니다. 어느 때보다 더 여러분의 도움이 필요합니다. 그러므로 오셔서 이 의미 있는 행사에 참여하세요.

13 ⑤

해설 3층 엘리베이터에서 내려서 오른쪽으로 가다가 화장실을 지나서 오른쪽에 있다고 했다.

어휘 art supplies 미술 도구
complex[kámpleks] 복합 건물, 단지
get off ~에서 내리다
past[pæst] ~을 지나서
restroom[réstrù(:)m] 화장실

W Excuse me. Do you know any good place to buy art supplies?
M Yes, there's a new place, Art Complex, on the 3rd floor of this building.
W This is my first time visiting this building. Where is it on the 3rd floor?
M Get off the elevator and turn right. Keep walking past the restroom. You'll see it on the right.
W I see. Thank you so much.
M Don't mention it.

여 실례합니다. 미술 도구를 살 만한 좋은 곳을 아시나요?
남 네, 이 건물의 3층에 Art Complex라고 새로 생긴 곳이 있어요.
여 저는 이 건물에 처음 방문해서요. 3층 어디에 있나요?
남 엘리베이터에서 내려서 오른쪽으로 가세요. 화장실을 지나서 계속 걸어가세요. 그곳이 오른쪽에 보일 거예요.
여 알겠어요. 정말 감사합니다.
남 천만에요.

14 ②

해설 돈을 넣고 원하는 상품을 누르면 그것을 꺼낼 수 있는 기계는 자동판매기이다.

어휘 machine[məʃíːn] 기계
everywhere[évriʰwɛ̀ər] 어디에서나
product[prádəkt] 상품
coin[kɔin] 동전
paper bill 지폐
such as ~ 같은

W This is a machine, and you can see it everywhere. It's so easy to use this machine. First, just put your money in it. Second, push the button of the product you want. Then, take it out from the machine. You can use either coins or paper bills to buy from this. You can get lots of things, such as coffee, juice, snacks, and even some food.

여 이것은 기계이고, 어디에서나 볼 수 있어요. 이 기계를 사용하는 것은 매우 쉬워요. 먼저, 돈을 그 안에 넣으세요. 둘째, 원하는 상품의 버튼을 누르세요. 그 다음에, 기계에서 상품을 꺼내세요. 동전이나 지폐 중 어느 것이나 사용하여 이것으로부터 구입할 수 있어요. 커피, 주스, 간식, 심지어는 음식 같은 많은 것들을 살 수 있어요.

15 ⑤

해설 남자가 간식으로 샌드위치와 오렌지 주스를 먹겠다고 하자, 여자는 바로 샌드위치를 만들어주겠다고 했다.

어휘 snack[snæk] 간식
refrigerator[rifrídʒərèitər] 냉장고
free like v-ing …할 마음이 나다

M Mom, I'm a little hungry. Can I have a snack?
W There are some strawberries and milk in the refrigerator.
M I don't feel like having fruit or milk. Can I have something else?
W Would you like to have a sandwich and orange juice?
M Yes, please. The sandwiches that you make are really good.
W Wait a minute. I'll make you one right away.
M Thank you.

남 엄마, 저 배가 좀 고파요. 간식 먹어도 되나요?
여 냉장고에 딸기와 우유가 좀 있어.
남 과일이나 우유를 먹고 싶지 않아요. 다른 걸 먹을 수 있나요?
여 샌드위치와 오렌지 주스 좀 먹을래?
남 네, 주세요. 엄마가 만드는 샌드위치는 정말 맛있거든요.
여 잠깐 기다려라. 바로 하나 만들어줄게.
남 고맙습니다.

16 ④

해설 여자는 1월 3일에 평창에 도착했고, 일주일 동안 그곳에 있었으며, 이틀 후에 집에 간다고 했으므로, 1월 12일에 집에 돌아올 것이다.

[Cell phone rings.]
M Hello.
W Hi, Peter. It's me, Julia.
M Oh, Julia! Are you enjoying your winter vacation in Pyeongchang?

[휴대전화가 울린다.]
남 여보세요.
여 안녕, Peter. 나야, Julia.
남 아, Julia! 평창에서 겨울 방학을 즐기고 있니?

어휘 snowboard[snóubɔ̀ːrd] 스노보드를 타다

sheep ranch 양떼 목장

look forward to ~을 기대하다

arrive[əráiv] 도착하다

W Of course, I am. I went snowboarding yesterday. Today, I'll visit a sheep ranch. I'm looking forward to it.
M That's great! How long have you been there?
W I arrived here on January 3rd and I've been here for a week.
M When will you come back to Gwangju?
W I'll be home in 2 days.
M Okay. See you soon.

여 물론, 그렇지. 어제 스노보드 타러 갔었어. 오늘 양떼 목장을 방문할 거야. 너무 기대가 돼.
남 좋구나! 거기에 얼마나 있었지?
여 나는 1월 3일에 여기에 도착했고, 일주일 동안 여기에 있었어.
남 언제 광주에 돌아올 거니?
여 이틀 후에 집에 갈 거야.
남 알았어. 곧 보자.

17 ⑤

해설 테이블이 날 때까지 휴게실에서 기다리겠다는 남자의 말에 테이블이 준비되면 부르겠다는 응답이 가장 적절하다.

어휘 party[páːrti] 일행
at the moment 바로 지금
wating time 대기 시간
lounge[laundʒ] 휴게실

W Good evening. Did you make a reservation?
M I'm afraid we didn't.
W How many are in your party?
M There are 4 of us.
W I'm sorry, but we are full at the moment.
M How long do we have to wait?
W The waiting time for a table is about 20 minutes. Is that okay?
M Then we'll wait in the lounge.
W Okay. I'll call you when your table's ready.

여 안녕하세요. 예약하셨습니까?
남 유감스럽게도 하지 못했어요.
여 일행이 모두 몇 분이신가요?
남 저희는 네 명입니다.
여 죄송하지만, 현재 모두 자리가 찼습니다.
남 얼마나 기다려야 하나요?
여 테이블 대기 시간은 약 20분입니다. 괜찮으시겠습니까?
남 그러면 휴게실에서 기다리겠습니다.
여 네. 손님 테이블이 준비되면 부르겠습니다.

① 이제 주문하시겠어요?
② 테이블을 바꾸시겠습니까?
③ 네. 그것을 주방으로 되돌려 보내겠습니다.
④ 계산서에 실수가 있는 것 같은데요.

18 ⑤

해설 용돈의 일부를 저금하고, 기부하고 책을 사겠다는 여자의 말에 돈을 현명하게 쓴다고 말하는 응답이 가장 적절하다.

어휘 allowance[əláuəns] 용돈
owe[ou] (돈을) 빚지고 있다
pile up 쌓이다
saving[séiviŋ] 저금
donate[dóunèit] 기부하다
rest[rest] 나머지

W Dad, please give me my allowance. Today is Monday.
M Oh, I forgot about that. How much do I owe you?
W $100.
M $100? Do I owe you that much?
W You keep forgetting to give me my allowance, and it keeps on piling up.
M What are you planning to do with the money?
W I'm going to put some in the bank, donate some to poor people, and use the rest to buy books.
M That sounds like a perfect way to spend money.

여 아빠, 용돈 주세요. 오늘은 월요일이니까요.
남 아, 깜빡 잊었구나. 얼마를 줘야 하지?
여 100달러요.
남 100달러라고? 그렇게 많이 줘야 해?
여 아빠가 제게 용돈 주는 것을 계속 잊어버리셔서 쌓인 거예요.
남 그 돈으로 무엇을 할 계획이니?
여 은행에 좀 넣고, 어려운 사람들에게 기부를 좀 하고, 나머지를 책을 사는 데 사용할 거예요.
남 돈을 쓰는 데 가장 완벽한 방법인 것 같구나.

① 그 말을 들으니 유감이야.
② 왜 그렇게 말하는 거니?
③ 부탁 하나 들어줄래?
④ 나는 네가 어떻게 돈을 쓰는지 모르겠어.

19 ③

해설 구매했던 재킷을 반품하겠다는 남자의 말에 환불해 주겠다고 응답하는 것이 가장 적절하다.

어휘 exchange[ikstʃéindʒ] 교환하다
either[íːðər] (둘 중) 어느 하나
tight[tait] 꼭 끼는
receipt[risíːt] 영수증
[선택지]
refund[rifʌ́nd] 환불(금)
final price 최종 가격

W　May I help you?
M　I got this jacket last week, and I <u>was wondering if</u> I could return or exchange it.
W　You can do either. May I ask why?
M　I really like this jacket, but <u>it's a little tight</u>.
W　All right. *[Pause]* Here, try this one. It's a little larger.
M　Thanks. This is good, but it seems to be a little longer.
W　I'm afraid <u>that's the last one</u> in that style and size.
M　Then I guess I <u>have to return it</u>. I have the receipt right here.
W　<u>Okay. I will give you a refund.</u>

여　도와드릴까요?
남　저는 지난주에 이 재킷을 구입했는데, 반품하거나 교환할 수 있는지 궁금해요.
여　둘 다 가능해요. 이유를 물어도 되나요?
남　저는 이 재킷이 정말 마음에 들지만, 약간 끼어서요.
여　알겠어요. *[잠시 후]* 여기, 이걸 입어보세요. 약간 더 큰 사이즈예요.
남　감사합니다. 좋지만, 약간 좀 긴 것 같네요.
여　유감이지만 그 유형과 사이즈로는 그게 마지막 물건입니다.
남　그러면 재킷을 반품해야 할 것 같아요. 여기 영수증 있습니다.
여　<u>알겠습니다. 환불해 드리겠습니다.</u>

① 네, 파란색 재킷을 사겠습니다.
② 네, 그건 가장 인기 있는 제품입니다.
④ 물론이죠. 새 것으로 교환해 드리겠습니다.
⑤ 죄송하지만, 그것이 최저로 드릴 수 있는 가격입니다.

20 ③

해설 새벽 4시에 일어나서 출근할 때까지 조금도 쉬지 않고 운동하는 Tim에게 휴식을 취할 것을 조언하는 상황이다.

어휘 weight training 웨이트 트레이닝
gym[dʒim] 체육관
take a break 휴식을 하다
rest[rest] 휴식

W　Tim always gets up around 4 o'clock. He usually <u>runs for an hour</u>. Then he does his weight training for 2 hours <u>at the gym near</u> his house. After that, he comes home, takes a shower, and eats breakfast. After he reads the newspaper, he goes to work at 9 o'clock. He <u>doesn't take a break</u> during this time. His wife Kate is really worried that he is <u>not getting enough rest</u>. In this situation, what would Kate most likely say to Tim?

Kate　<u>I think you should get some rest.</u>

여　Tim은 항상 4시쯤에 일어난다. 그는 보통 한 시간 동안 달린다. 그 다음에 그는 집 근처의 체육관에서 두 시간 동안 웨이트 트레이닝을 한다. 그 후에, 그는 집에 와서, 샤워를 하고, 아침을 먹는다. 신문을 읽은 후, 9시에 출근한다. 이 시간 동안 그는 휴식을 취하지 않는다. 그의 아내 Kate는 그가 충분한 휴식을 하지 않아 걱정한다. 이러한 상황에서, Kate가 Tim에게 할 말로 가장 적절한 것은 무엇인가?

Kate　당신은 좀 쉬어야 할 것 같아요.

① 당신은 더 열심히 일하는 게 좋겠어요.
② 당신은 지금 몸매가 좋아요.
④ 공원에서 함께 조깅할까요?
⑤ 더 일찍 체육관에 가는 게 어때요?

01 ③	02 ③	03 ⑤	04 ③	05 ③	06 ④	07 ②
08 ⑤	09 ①	10 ②	11 ⑤	12 ③	13 ④	14 ⑤
15 ②	16 ②	17 ①	18 ⑤	19 ④	20 ⑤	

01 ③

[해설] 남자가 구입할 재킷은 지퍼가 두 개 있고, 후드와 주머니가 없다.

[어휘] hood[hud] 후드, (외투 등에 달린) 모자
try on 입어 보다
put on ~을 입다
zipper[zípər] 지퍼
pocket[pákit] 호주머니

M Can I get some help?
W Sure, what can I do for you?
M I really like this jacket, but do you have this style <u>with</u> a <u>hood</u>?
W Let me see. *[Pause]* Is this what you're looking for?
M Thank you. Let me try it on.
W I think you would look better if you put on <u>the</u> <u>one</u> <u>without</u> a hood.
M Really? What do you think about this one then? This one has 2 zippers.
W That one's actually the most popular style.
M There's no hood, and there are <u>no</u> <u>pockets</u>, <u>either</u>.
W That's true. That's <u>what</u> <u>young</u> <u>people</u> <u>like</u> these days.
M Okay, I'll take this.

남 좀 도와주시겠어요?
여 네, 무엇을 도와드릴까요?
남 이 재킷이 정말 마음에 드는데, 이런 스타일로 후드가 달린 거 있나요?
여 한번 볼게요. *[잠시 후]* 이게 찾으시는 건가요?
남 고마워요. 입어 볼게요.
여 후드가 없는 옷을 입어보면 더 괜찮을 것 같은데요.
남 그래요? 그럼 이건 어떨 것 같아요? 이건 지퍼가 두 개네요.
여 그게 사실 가장 인기 있는 스타일입니다.
남 후드도 없고, 주머니도 없네요.
여 맞아요. 요즘 젊은 사람들은 그런 걸 좋아하거든요.
남 좋아요, 그럼 이걸로 할게요.

02 ③

[해설] 정식 명칭(One More Generation), 설립자(Carter Ries와 Olivia Ries), 설립 목적(멸종 위기에 처한 동물 보호), 활동 내용(플라스틱 쓰레기를 줄이는 인식을 높임)에 관해 언급되었지만 설립 연도에 대한 언급은 없었다.

[어휘] organization[ɔ̀ːrɡənizéiʃən] 단체, 조직
stand for ~을 나타내다[의미하다]
generation[dʒènəréiʃən] 세대, 대
non-profit[nànpráfit] 비영리적인
endangered[indéindʒərd] 멸종 위기에 처한
cheetah[tʃíːtə] 치타
raise[reiz] 끌어올리다
awareness[əwɛ́ərnis] 인식
reduce[ridjúːs] 줄이다
waste[weist] 쓰레기, 폐기물
die from ~로 죽다

W Have you heard of an organization called OMG?
M Does OMG <u>stand</u> <u>for</u> <u>anything</u>?
W Yes, it stands for One More Generation.
M Oh, I've heard of it. It's a non-profit organization that 2 kids started, right?
W Right, their names are Carter and Olivia Ries.
M What is the organization for?
W It's for <u>protecting</u> <u>endangered</u> <u>animals</u> like wild cheetahs in South Africa.
M What does the organization do to save animals?
W People there try to raise awareness <u>to</u> <u>reduce</u> <u>plastic</u> <u>waste</u>.
M Really? Why is that important?
W Because many animals die <u>from</u> <u>eating</u> <u>plastic</u> <u>waste</u>.
M Oh, I see.

여 OMG라는 단체에 대해 들어본 적 있어?
남 OMG가 나타내는 게 있어?
여 그래, One More Generation을 나타내.
남 아, 들어봤어. 두 아이가 시작한 비영리단체지, 그렇지?
여 맞아, 그들의 이름은 Carter와 Olivia Ries 남매야.
남 어떤 단체야?
여 남아프리카의 야생 치타처럼 멸종 위기에 처한 동물들을 보호하는 곳이야.
남 그 단체는 동물을 구하기 위해 뭘 하니?
여 그곳 사람들은 플라스틱 쓰레기를 줄이는 인식을 높이기 위해 노력해.
남 그래? 그게 왜 중요한데?
여 왜냐하면 많은 동물들이 플라스틱 쓰레기를 먹고 죽거든.
남 아, 그렇구나.

03 ⑤

남자는 연기된 회의 일정에 대해 논의하기 위해 전화했다.

어휘 **set up** 준비하다
delay[diléi] 미루다, 연기하다

[Cell phone rings.]
W Hello.
M Hello, Michelle? This is Jake.
W Hi, Jake. How are you?
M I'm good. Thanks. How are you feeling?
W I'm feeling much better.
M Great. I'm calling to ask you when it would be good to <u>set</u> <u>up</u> <u>our</u> <u>meeting</u> <u>with</u> Mr. Taylor.
W I'm sorry that you had to delay the meeting with him.
M It's perfectly fine.
W I should be able to <u>go</u> <u>to</u> <u>work</u> <u>on</u> <u>Friday</u>.
M Will 3 p.m. on Friday work for you?
W Yes, <u>that'll</u> <u>work</u> <u>for</u> <u>me</u>. I'll see you then.

[휴대전화가 울린다.]
여 여보세요.
남 여보세요, Michelle? 나 Jake예요.
여 안녕하세요, Jake. 잘 지내요?
남 잘 지내요. 고마워요. 몸은 좀 어때요?
여 훨씬 나아졌어요.
남 잘됐어요. Taylor 씨와의 미팅을 언제 잡는 게 좋을지 물어보려고 전화했어요.
여 그와의 미팅을 미뤄야 해서 미안해요.
남 괜찮아요.
여 저는 금요일에 출근할 수 있을 것 같아요.
남 금요일 오후 3시면 괜찮을까요?
여 네, 그날 괜찮아요. 그때 봐요.

04 ③

해설 결혼식은 3시에 시작하지만 2시 30분에 만나기로 했다.

어휘 **remember**[rimémbər] 기억하다
get married 결혼하다
wedding[wédiŋ] 결혼(식)
ceremony[sérəmòuni] 식
wedding hall 결혼식장

W Do you remember my older sister Rachel?
M Of course, I do. Isn't she <u>getting</u> <u>married</u> this month?
W Yes, her wedding is this Saturday. Do you want to come?
M Sure. What time is the ceremony?
W <u>It</u> <u>starts</u> <u>at</u> 3 p.m. at Grace Wedding Hall.
M Okay. Can I go there and meet you at 2?
W You don't have to come too early. <u>Let's</u> <u>meet</u> <u>at</u> 2:30 in front of the wedding hall.
M Sure. See you then.

여 너 우리 언니 Rachel 기억하니?
남 물론, 기억하지. 이번 달에 결혼하시지 않니?
여 그래. 결혼식이 이번 토요일에 있어. 너도 올래?
남 갈게. 몇 시 결혼식이야?
여 Grace 웨딩홀에서 3시에 시작해.
남 알겠어. 2시에 거기로 가서 널 만나면 될까?
여 너무 일찍 올 필요는 없어. 웨딩홀 앞에서 2시 30분에 만나자.
남 그래. 그때 보자.

05 ③

해설 탁자를 배달하는 사람에게 탁자 놓을 곳을 알려주는 상황이다.

어휘 **on sale** 세일 중인
discount[dískaunt] 할인
break[breik] 휴식(시간)
project[prádʒekt] 과제; 프로젝트

① M Did you order pizza, ma'am?
   W Yes, can you put it <u>on</u> <u>the</u> <u>table</u>, please?
② M Excuse me. Are TVs on sale?
   W Yes, you get a 20% <u>discount</u> <u>on</u> <u>all</u> <u>TVs</u>.
③ M Where do you want this table?
   W Can you put it in the living room <u>next</u> <u>to</u> <u>the</u> <u>sofa</u>?
④ M I'm tired. I can't run any more.
   W Why don't you take a 5-minute break?
⑤ M Did you finish your art project?
   W No, <u>I'll</u> <u>finish</u> <u>it</u> after dinner tonight.

① 남 피자 주문하셨나요, 손님?
   여 네, 테이블 위에 올려 주시겠어요?
② 남 실례합니다만. TV가 세일 중인가요?
   여 네, 모든 TV를 20% 할인합니다.
③ 남 이 테이블 어디에 놓을까요?
   여 거실 소파 옆에 놓아주시겠어요?
④ 남 나 피곤해. 더 이상은 못 뛰겠어.
   여 5분 정도 쉬는 게 어때?
⑤ 남 미술 과제는 다 끝냈니?
   여 아니. 오늘 저녁 식사 후에 끝낼 거야.

06 ④

해설 공룡 장난감의 위치를 알려주고 선물 포장도 가능하다는 내용으로 보아 두 사람은 장난감 가게에서 대화를 나누고 있음을 알 수 있다.

어휘 dinosaur[dáinəsɔ̀ːr] 공룡
whole[houl] 전체의
section[sékʃən] 부분, 부문
gift-wrapping[gíftræpiŋ] 선물용 포장
counter[káuntər] 계산대

M Excuse me. Do you have any dinosaurs here?

W Yes, of course. We have a whole section for dinosaurs.

M Can you show me where they are?

W Sure, follow me, please.

M [Pause] Oh, there they are. You have so many different toys to choose from.

W Yes, we do. Who is the dinosaur for?

M It's for my little brother. His birthday is tomorrow.

W We also offer gift-wrapping service for $1. It's at the customer service near the counter.

M All right. Thank you for your help.

남 실례합니다만, 여기 공룡이 있나요?

여 네, 물론이지요. 공룡만 있는 구역이 있어요.

남 그것들이 어디에 있는지 알려주시겠어요?

여 네, 저를 따라오세요.

남 [잠시 후] 아, 저기 있네요. 고를 수 있는 장난감이 아주 많군요.

여 네, 그렇죠. 공룡은 누구를 주려는 것인가요?

남 제 동생이요. 내일이 걔 생일이거든요.

여 1달러에 선물 포장 서비스도 받을 수 있어요. 계산대 근처에 있는 고객 서비스 센터에서요.

남 알겠어요. 도와줘서 고마워요.

07 ②

해설 남자는 여자에게 양동이에 물을 채워 달라고 부탁했다.

어휘 promise[prámis] 약속하다; 약속
fill[fil] 채우다
bucket[bʌ́kit] 양동이

W Where are you going, Bill?

M I'm going outside to wash the car, Mom.

W What? Why would you do that?

M I promised Dad something and I am trying to keep it.

W What kind of promise did you make?

M I promised that I'd wash the car if I didn't do well on my math exam.

W Oh, I see. Can I give you a hand?

M Yes, please. Can you fill this bucket with water, please?

W Okay. I'll do that right now.

여 Bill, 어디 가니?

남 엄마, 저 세차하러 밖에 나가려고요.

여 뭐라고? 왜 네가 그것을 하니?

남 아빠와 약속을 해서, 그 약속을 지키려고요.

여 어떤 약속을 했는데?

남 제가 수학 시험을 잘 못 보면 세차하겠다고 약속했거든요.

여 아, 그랬구나. 내가 도와줄까?

남 네. 이 양동이에 물을 채워 주실래요?

여 알았어. 그걸 바로 지금 할게.

08 ⑤

해설 시작 시각(정오), 집합 장소(본관 앞), 종료 시각(12시 30분), 다음 훈련 날짜(6월 10일)에 관해 언급되었지만 훈련 담당자에 관한 언급은 없었다.

어휘 principal[prínsəpəl] 교장
remind[rimáind] 상기시키다
fire drill 소방[화재 대피] 훈련
alarm[əláːrm] 경보음
gather[gǽðər] 모이다
take place 일어나다

M Good morning, students. This is your principal speaking. I want to remind all of you that we're having a fire drill at noon today. When you hear the alarm, all of you need to leave your classrooms and gather in front of the main building. You'll be asked to go back into your classrooms when the drill ends at 12:30. The next fire drill will take place on June 10th. That's the only message I have for you this morning. I hope you have a great day.

남 학생 여러분, 좋은 아침입니다. 저는 교장입니다. 오늘 정오에 소방 훈련이 있다는 것을 여러분 모두에게 상기시키려고 해요. 경보음이 들리면 모두 교실을 나와 본관 앞에 모여야 합니다. 훈련이 12시 30분에 끝나면 다시 교실로 들어가게 될 것입니다. 다음 소방 훈련은 6월 10일에 실시됩니다. 오늘 아침에 전할 말은 이것뿐입니다. 좋은 하루 보내세요.

09 ①

해설 한 팀에 9명이 하는 팀 경기이며 배트와 공, 글러브가 필요하고 공을 치고 4개의 베이스를 모두 터치하면 득점이 되는 것은 야구이다.

어휘 **bat**[bæt] 방망이, 배트; (배트로) 공을 치다

score a point 득점하다

home plate (야구의) 본루

base[beis] (야구 등의) 베이스, –루

pitcher[pítʃər] 투수

batter[bǽtər] 타자

inning[íniŋ] 《야구》 (9회 중의 한) 회

W This is a team sport. In order to play this sport, you need to have at least <u>a bat</u>, <u>a ball</u>, and gloves. You score a point when you bat at home plate and touch all 4 bases. The person who <u>throws the ball</u> is called a pitcher, and the person who <u>hits the ball</u> is called a batter. There are 9 <u>players</u> <u>on</u> <u>each</u> <u>team</u>, and they play 9 innings. This is a very popular sport in many countries, such as Korea, Japan, Taiwan, and the U.S.

여 이건 팀 스포츠이다. 이 운동을 하려면 최소한 배트, 공, 글러브가 있어야 한다. 본루에서 공을 치고 4개의 베이스를 모두 닿으면 득점이 된다. 공을 던지는 사람을 투수라 하고, 공을 치는 사람을 타자라 한다. 각 팀에 9명의 선수가 있고, 그들은 9회를 경기한다. 이것은 한국, 일본, 대만, 그리고 미국과 같은 많은 나라에서 매우 인기 있는 스포츠이다.

10 ②

해설 이 대화에서 in private은 '개인적으로, 은밀히'를 의미하므로 개인적으로 이야기할 수 있는지 묻는 질문에 사립학교에 다녔다는 응답은 어색하다.

어휘 **dry**[drai] 말리다, 닦다

in private 다른 사람이 없는 데서, 은밀히

private school 사립학교

keep in shape 건강을 유지하다

interrupt[ìntərʌ́pt] 방해하다

① **M** Will you dry the dishes, please?
　W Of course. Let me get a <u>towel for that</u>, first.
② **M** Could I speak to you in private?
　W Yes, <u>I went to</u> a private school.
③ **M** How do you <u>keep in shape</u>?
　W I try to run 30 minutes every day.
④ **M** Did you want to talk to me?
　W Yes, do you have a minute?
⑤ **M** I'm sorry. Did I interrupt you?
　W No, you didn't. I <u>was just leaving</u>.

① 남 접시 좀 말려 줄래?
　여 그럴게. 우선 수건부터 가져올게.
② 남 개인적으로 얘기 좀 할 수 있을까?
　여 그래, 난 사립학교에 다녔어.
③ 남 어떻게 건강을 유지하니?
　여 난 매일 30분씩 달리려고 노력해.
④ 남 나랑 얘기하고 싶었어?
　여 네, 시간 좀 내주시겠습니까?
⑤ 남 미안해. 내가 방해했니?
　여 아니, 넌 그러지 않았어. 막 떠나려던 참이었어.

11 ⑤

해설 남자가 농장 일을 해보고 싶었다고 하자 여자가 농장 자원 봉사자로 등록하는 방법을 알려주었고 남자는 당장 하겠다고 했다.

어휘 **volunteer**[vàləntíər] 자원 봉사자; 자원 봉사를 하다

farm[fɑːrm] 농장

plant[plænt] (씨앗 등을) 심다

feed[fiːd] 먹이를 주다 (feed-fed-fed)

sign up 등록하다

website[websait] 웹사이트

information[ìnfərméiʃən] 정보

M How was your weekend, Samantha?
W It was great. I volunteered to work at a farm.
M That sounds interesting. What did you do there?
W I planted tomatoes and potatoes <u>and fed the animals</u>.
M I've always wanted to do that, too. How did you volunteer there?
W Oh, it's not difficult <u>to find volunteer work</u> at a farm.
M Really? I didn't know that.
W Just <u>sign up as a volunteer</u> on the website helpingfarmers.org, and you'll get a list of places to volunteer.
M Thanks for the information. I'll <u>do that right now</u>.

남 주말 어땠어, Samantha?
여 정말 좋았어. 나는 농장에서 자원봉사를 했어.
남 그거 흥미롭네. 거기서 뭘 했니?
여 나는 토마토와 감자를 심고 동물들에게 먹이를 주었어.
남 나도 언제나 그걸 해보고 싶었는데. 거기서 어떻게 자원봉사를 하게 됐니?
여 아, 농장에서 하는 봉사활동을 찾는 건 어렵지 않아.
남 그래? 나는 그걸 몰랐네.
여 helpingfarmers.org 웹사이트에서 자원 봉사자로 등록하기만 하면, 자원 봉사할 수 있는 곳들의 목록이 나올 거야.
남 알려줘서 고마워. 지금 당장 해볼게.

12 ③

해설 국제선을 이용할 것이 아니기 때문에 공항에 일찍 가지 않아도 된다고 해서 12시 셔틀버스를 타기로 했다.

어휘 shuttle bus 셔틀버스
at least 적어도
departure[dipáːrtʃər] 출발
international flight 국제선

W How are we getting to the airport tomorrow, Dad?

M I'm planning to drive there.

W Why don't we take the shuttle bus since we only have 2 bags?

M That's a good idea. We can take the 12 o'clock shuttle.

W Our plane leaves at 2 o'clock, Dad. Why don't we take the 11 o'clock shuttle?

M It only takes about 30 minutes to get to the airport. Besides, we don't have to go to the airport that early. We're only going to Jeju-do.

W I thought we had to arrive at the airport at least 2 hours before the departure time.

M That's for an international flight.

W Oh, I see. Then I guess we don't have to leave so early.

여 아빠, 우리 내일 공항에는 어떻게 가요?

남 공항까지 내가 운전해서 가려고.

여 작은 가방 두 개밖에 없는데 셔틀버스를 타는 게 어때요?

남 좋은 생각이야. 12시 셔틀버스를 탈 수 있어.

여 우리 비행기가 2시에 떠나요, 아빠. 11시 셔틀을 타는 게 어때요?

남 공항까지는 30분 정도밖에 걸리지 않잖아. 게다가 그렇게 일찍 공항에 갈 필요는 없어. 우리는 단지 제주도에 가는 거잖아.

여 출발 시간 2시간 전에 공항에 도착해야 하는 줄 알았어요.

남 그건 국제선 비행기의 경우야.

여 아, 그렇군요. 그럼 그렇게 일찍 출발할 필요는 없겠네요.

13 ④

해설 스크린에서 가깝지 않고 입구에서 멀지 않은 곳에 앉기로 했다.

어휘 decide[disáid] 결정하다
section[sékʃən] 구역
unfortunately[ʌnfɔ́ːrtʃənitli] 유감스럽게도, 불행하게도
screen[skriːn] 화면
neck[nek] 목

M We're still going to the movies this Saturday, right?

W Yes. I'll buy the tickets right away.

M I was actually doing that now. We just need to decide where to sit.

W Oh, I see. One section is already full.

M Yes, unfortunately. You don't want to sit close to the screen, do you?

W No, I don't. My neck hurts if I sit too close to the screen.

M Okay, then we only have 2 sections to choose from.

W I don't want to sit too far from the entrance. It might not be easy to go to the restroom during the movie.

M Okay. Let's sit there.

남 이번 주 토요일에도 영화 보러 가는 거지, 맞지?

여 맞아. 내가 바로 티켓을 살게.

남 사실 지금 그걸 하고 있었어. 우리가 어디 앉을지만 정하면 돼.

여 아, 그렇구나. 벌써 한 구역은 꽉 찼네.

남 유감스럽게도 그러네. 스크린에 가까이 앉고 싶지는 않지, 그렇지?

여 그래, 싫어. 스크린에 너무 가까이 앉으면 목이 아파.

남 좋아. 그럼 선택할 수 있는 구역은 두 군데 뿐이네.

여 입구에서 너무 먼 곳은 앉고 싶지 않아. 영화 도중에 화장실에 가기 쉽지 않을 거야.

남 알았어. 저기에 앉자.

14 ⑤

해설 여자는 어제 밴드 오디션을 봤다고 했다.

어휘 keyboard[kíːbɔ̀ːrd] 키보드, 건반
drummer[drʌ́mər] 드럼 연주자
audition[ɔːdíʃən] 오디션을 보다

M You seem to be in a good mood today, Aunt Ann.

W Well, I'm just waiting for a phone call from someone.

M A phone call? From who? Your boyfriend?

W No. He is busy with work right now.

M You met your boyfriend in college, right?

W Yes, we were in the school band.

M Right, you played the keyboard and he was the drummer.

남 오늘 기분이 좋아 보이시네요, Ann 이모.

여 음, 그냥 누군가에게 올 전화를 기다리고 있거든.

남 전화요? 누구한테요? 남자친구 분이요?

여 아니야. 남자친구는 지금 일이 바빠.

남 이모는 남자친구 분을 대학교에서 만나셨죠, 그렇죠?

여 그래, 우린 학교 밴드에 있었지.

남 맞아요, 이모는 키보드를 연주했고 남자친구는 드러머였고요.

W That's right. Actually, I auditioned for a very famous band yesterday, and I think it went really well.

M Oh, that's who you are waiting for a phone call from.

W Yes. If everything goes well, I'll start playing the keyboard for the band next week.

M I'm sure you'll get it.

여 맞아. 실은, 내가 어제 아주 유명한 밴드에 오디션을 봤는데 아주 잘 될 것 같아.

남 아, 그래서 거기서 올 전화를 기다리고 있는 거군요.

여 그래. 일이 잘되면, 다음 주에 밴드와 키보드를 연주를 하게 될 거야.

남 이모는 분명히 뽑힐 거예요.

15 ②

해설 휴가로 집을 비운 동안 문단속을 잘하고 보안 시스템을 작동해서 범죄로부터 자신과 이웃을 보호하라는 안내 방송이다.

어휘 neighbor[néibər] 이웃
relative[rélətiv] 친척
possible[pásəbl] 가능성 있는
break-in[bréikìn] 방송 침입
activate[ǽktəvèit] 작동시키다
security system 보안 장치
neighborhood[néibərhùd] 인근, 이웃
secure[sikjúər] 단단히 보안 장치를 하다

M Hello, neighbors. I understand that many of you are planning on visiting your parents and relatives outside the city during the holiday season. So, I want to remind you of how to protect your homes against possible break-ins while you're away. Please make sure to close all your windows, lock all the doors, and activate your home security system. We try our best to keep our neighborhood safe for everyone. You should also do your part by securing your homes as best as you can.

남 안녕하세요, 이웃 여러분. 많은 분들이 휴가철에 부모님과 도시 바깥의 친척들을 방문할 계획인 것으로 알고 있습니다. 그래서, 집을 비운 동안 발생할 수 있는 침입으로부터 집을 보호하는 방법을 상기시키려고 합니다. 모든 창을 닫고 문을 모두 잠그고 가정 보안 시스템을 켜 두십시오. 우리는 모두를 위해 동네를 안전하게 지키기 위해 최선을 다하겠습니다. 여러분도 최대한 집의 보안을 단단히 하는 역할을 다해 주시기 바랍니다.

16 ②

해설 입장료는 성인은 100달러, 어린이 요금은 50달러이며, 여자는 성인 두 명과 어린이 한 명 입장에서 가족 할인 10%를 받을 수 있으므로 총 225달러를 지불해야 한다.

어휘 admission price 입장료
adult[ədʌ́lt] 성인, 어른
discount[dískaunt] 할인
purchase[pə́ːrtʃəs] 구매하다

[Telephone rings.]

M Thank you for calling Kids' World. How may I help you?

W Hi, I have some questions about your admission prices.

M Sure. The admission for adults is $100, and the admission for children under 13 is $50.

W I have a 4-year-old son. Do I have to pay for him?

M No, ma'am. There is no admission for anyone who's 5 or younger.

W I also have a 10-year-old daughter. Do you have any special discounts for families?

M Yes, we do. We have a 10% discount for families with children between 6 and 12.

W Great! My family can get the discount, right?

M Yes, then you'll pay for 2 adults and 1 child. And you'll get a 10% discount.

W Perfect. Can I purchase the tickets over the phone?

M Sure. I can help you with that.

[전화벨이 울린다.]

남 Kids' World에 전화 주셔서 감사합니다. 무엇을 도와드릴까요?

여 안녕하세요, 입장료에 대해 물어보려고요.

남 네. 성인 입장료는 100달러, 13세 미만 어린이 입장료는 50달러입니다.

여 4살인 아들이 있는데요. 그 애 입장료도 지불해야 하나요?

남 아닙니다. 5세 이하는 입장료가 없습니다.

여 10살인 딸도 있어요. 가족 특별 할인이 있나요?

남 네, 있습니다. 6세와 12세 아이가 있는 가족에게 10퍼센트 할인을 해 줍니다.

여 잘됐네요! 우리 가족은 할인을 받을 수 있겠네요, 맞죠?

남 네, 그럼 어른 두 명과 어린이 한 명의 값을 내면 됩니다. 그리고 10퍼센트 할인을 받고요.

여 좋아요. 전화로 입장권을 구매할 수 있나요?

남 그럼요, 도와드리죠.

17 ①

W How was your weekend, Mike?
M It was awesome. How was yours?
W I just stayed at home. I wasn't feeling too well. What did you do?
M I went fishing with my dad on Saturday.
W Really? I've never gone fishing before.
M Oh, if you want, I can ask my dad to take you next time.
W That would be great! Where did you go fishing on Saturday?
M We went to a river near my grandparents' house.
W How many fish did you catch?
M Unfortunately, it wasn't my lucky day.

여 주말은 어땠어, Mike?
남 정말 멋졌어. 너는 어땠니?
여 난 그냥 집에 있었어. 몸이 별로 안 좋았어. 너는 무엇을 했는데?
남 토요일에 아빠랑 낚시하러 갔어.
여 그래? 나는 전에 낚시하러 간 적이 없어.
남 아, 원한다면 다음에 아빠한테 너를 데려가 달라고 부탁할 수 있어.
여 그거 좋겠다! 토요일에 낚시하러 어디로 갔었니?
남 조부모님 댁 근처에 있는 강에 갔었어.
여 물고기를 몇 마리나 잡았어?
남 불행히도 그날은 운 좋은 날이 아니었어.

② 문제없어. 나중에 따라갈게.
③ 이것은 내가 잡아 본 물고기 중 가장 큰 것이야.
④ 너희 부모님에게 함께하자고 해도 돼.
⑤ 감기에 걸려서 하루 종일 집에 있었어.

18 ⑤

M I heard there's a very famous restaurant near your house.
W Are you talking about Joe's Mexican Restaurant?
M Yes, that's the name. You've been there, right?
W Of course, I have.
M How's the food? Is it really good?
W It's the best Mexican restaurant I've ever been to.
M Is the food really that good? I can't wait to try it.
W You'll love it.
M All right, then there's only one way to find out. Let's go there right now.
W But we can't go there unless we have a reservation.

남 너희 집 근처에 아주 유명한 식당이 있다고 들었어.
여 Joe's Mexican Restaurant을 말하는 거야?
남 그래, 그 이름이야. 너 가 봤지?
여 물론 가 봤어.
남 음식은 어때? 정말 맛있어?
여 내가 가 본 최고의 멕시칸 식당이야.
남 음식이 정말 그렇게 맛있어? 빨리 먹어보고 싶네.
여 너는 정말 좋아할 거야.
남 좋아. 그럼 알 수 있는 방법은 한 가지 밖에 없지. 당장 그곳에 가자.
여 하지만 거기는 예약하지 않으면 갈 수 없어.

① 나는 멕시코 음식을 먹어 본 적이 없어.
② 너는 정말 과식하는 것을 멈춰야 해.
③ 우선 그 식당이 어디 있는지 알아봐야겠다.
④ 나는 더 맛있는 멕시코 음식을 먹을 수 있는 곳을 알아.

19 ④

해설 이웃집에서 소란스러울 것이라고 미리 양해를 구했다는 여자의 말에 미리 얘기하지 그랬냐는 응답이 가장 적절하다.

어휘 stand[stænd] 참다
noise[nɔiz] 소음
run around 뛰면서 돌아다니다
pajama party 파자마 파티
apologize[əpálədʒàiz] 사과하다
in advance 미리
[선택지]
pajamas[pədʒáːməz] 잠옷

W Where are you going, honey? It's almost 10 p.m.
M I <u>can't stand this noise</u> any more.
W Are you going to talk to the Wilsons about the noise?
M Yes, I am. They shouldn't <u>let their children run</u> around like that after 9 p.m.
W No, don't. Mrs. Wilson <u>came by this afternoon</u> and told me that this would happen.
M What do you mean?
W It's her youngest daughter's birthday today, and they're having a pajama party.
M Oh, that makes more sense.
W Mrs. Wilson also brought us this cake and <u>apologized in advance</u>.
M Well, you should have told me that sooner.

여 여보, 어디 가요? 거의 밤 10시예요.
남 이 소음을 더 이상 참을 수가 없어요.
여 Wilson 씨네 가서 소음에 대해 얘기하려고요?
남 네, 그러려고요. 밤 9시 넘어서 아이들이 그렇게 뛰어다니게 해서는 안 되잖아요.
여 그러지 마세요. Wilson 아주머니께서 오늘 오후에 저희 집에 들러서 이렇게 될 거라고 말해주셨어요.
남 무슨 말이에요?
여 오늘이 막내딸 생일인데, 파자마 파티를 할 거라고요.
남 아, 이해가 되네요.
여 Wilson 아주머니가 이 케이크를 가지고 와서 미리 사과하셨어요.
남 <u>아, 더 일찍 말해주지 그랬어요.</u>

① 잠옷이 어디 있는지 모르겠어요.
② 그 집 아이들이 잠든 것 같아요.
③ 알겠어요, 그녀에게 소음에 대해 사과할게요.
⑤ 이 케이크를 굽는 데 얼마나 걸렸어요?

20 ⑤

해설 유아용 식사 의자를 요청했지만 식사가 다 나왔는데도 가져오지 않아서, 다시 한 번 더 요청하는 상황이다.

어휘 crowded[kráudid] 붐비는
finally[fáinəli] 마침내
high chair 유아용 식사 의자
serve[səːrv] (식당에서 음식을) 제공하다

W Sean is going out for dinner with his family today. They go to his favorite Korean restaurant, which <u>is always crowded</u> on Fridays. They have to wait for over an hour to get a table. He and his family finally sit down, and he <u>asks for a high chair</u> for his 5-year-old son. The waiter says that he will be right back with a high chair, <u>but doesn't bring one</u>. All the food is served, but the waiter <u>still doesn't bring them</u> a high chair. In this situation, what would Sean most likely say to the waiter?

Sean Excuse me, <u>when are we getting the high chair we asked for?</u>

여 Sean은 오늘 가족과 함께 저녁을 먹으러 나간다. 그들은 그가 가장 좋아하는 한국 식당에 가는데, 그곳은 금요일이면 항상 붐빈다. 그들은 자리가 날 때까지 한 시간이 넘게 기다려야 한다. 그와 그의 가족은 마침내 자리에 앉았고, 그는 다섯 살짜리 아들을 위해 유아용 식사 의자를 부탁한다. 웨이터는 유아용 의자를 가지고 금방 돌아오겠다고 하지만 가져오지 않는다. 음식이 다 나오지만 웨이터는 여전히 유아용 의자를 가져오지 않는다. 이러한 상황에서 Sean이 웨이터에게 할 말로 가장 적절한 것은 무엇인가?

Sean 실례합니다만, <u>우리가 요청한 유아용 의자는 언제 받을 수 있나요?</u>

① 메뉴판 좀 주시겠습니까?
② 이것은 우리가 주문한 음식이 아니에요.
③ 왜 우리 음식이 아직 나오지 않나요?
④ 우리랑 같이 저녁 먹을래요?

고난도 모의고사 02

p. 242

01 ④	02 ③	03 ③	04 ①	05 ⑤	06 ①	07 ③
08 ④	09 ①	10 ⑤	11 ⑤	12 ③	13 ④	14 ②
15 ②	16 ⑤	17 ①	18 ⑤	19 ⑤	20 ①	

01 ④

해설 앞바퀴가 뒷바퀴보다 큰 모델이며 보조 바퀴가 있고 바구니가 있는 자전거를 사려고 한다.

어휘 front wheel 앞바퀴
back wheel 뒷바퀴
training wheel 보조 바퀴
attach[ətǽtʃ] 달다, 붙이다

M Hello, how can I help you?
W I'm looking for a bicycle for my daughter. She's turning 7 next month.
M Okay, then this should be the right size for her.
W Is the front wheel bigger than the back wheel?
M Yes, it is. This is a very popular model.
W Okay, do you have that model with training wheels?
M Sure, this one has 2 small wheels attached to the back wheel.
W It has a basket, too. Can we take the training wheels off later?
M Of course, you can.
W Good! I'll take this one.

남 안녕하세요, 무엇을 도와드릴까요?
여 딸에게 줄 자전거를 찾고 있어요. 다음 달에 7살이 되거든요.
남 네, 그럼 이게 따님에게 크기가 맞을 거예요.
여 앞바퀴가 뒷바퀴보다 크네요?
남 네, 그렇죠. 이게 아주 인기 있는 모델이에요.
여 좋아요, 보조 바퀴가 달린 이 모델 있나요?
남 네, 이건 뒷바퀴에 두 개의 작은 바퀴가 달려 있어요.
여 바구니도 있군요. 나중에 보조 바퀴를 떼어 낼 수도 있나요?
남 물론 됩니다.
여 좋습니다! 이걸로 할게요.

02 ③

해설 점포 위치(우체국 바로 옆), 서비스 품질(서비스 품질이 아주 좋음), 인터넷 요금(한 달에 30달러), 인터넷 속도(정말 빠름)에 관해 언급되었지만 특별 할인 행사에 관한 언급은 없었다.

어휘 provider[prəváidər] 제공자
quality[kwáləti] 품질
charge[tʃɑːrdʒ] (요금을) 청구하다
switch[switʃ] 바꾸다
speed[spiːd] 속도

W I need to find a new Internet provider.
M What's wrong with the one you have right now?
W It's too slow. I'm going to check out the new store right next to the post office.
M You mean K Mobile? That's my Internet provider.
W Really? I heard the quality of its service is really good.
M Yes, and I only pay $30 a month for the Internet service.
W Wow! That's $10 less than what I'm paying.
M Then you should switch because the Internet speed is really fast.
W I should have talked to you about my Internet provider sooner.

여 나는 새 인터넷 제공회사를 찾아야 해.
남 지금 쓰고 있는 거에 문제 있어?
여 너무 느려. 우체국 바로 옆에 새로 생긴 가게에 가 봐야겠어.
남 K 모바일을 말하는 거야? 그거 내가 쓰고 있는 인터넷 제공회사야.
여 그래? 그 서비스 품질이 아주 좋다고 들었어.
남 응, 그리고 난 인터넷 서비스 비용으로 한 달에 30달러만 지불해.
여 와! 지금 내가 내는 것보다 10달러가 더 싸네.
남 그렇다면 인터넷 속도도 정말 빠르니까 바꾸는 게 좋겠다.
여 더 빨리 내 인터넷 제공회사에 대해 너한테 얘기했어야 했는데.

03 ③

해설 남자는 배달원의 실수로 가구를 잘못 배달했다고 사과하기 위해 전화했다.

어휘 manager[mǽnidʒər] 매니저, 점장

[Telephone rings.]
W Hello.
M Hello, my name is Rick Price, and I'm the store manager of Best Furniture. May I speak to Ms. Miller?

[전화벨이 울린다.]
여 여보세요.
남 안녕하세요, 제 이름은 Rick Price이고, 베스트 가구 매장의 매니저입니다. Miller 씨 좀 바꿔 주시겠습니까?

furniture[fə́ːrnitʃər] 가구
mistake[mistéik] 실수
exactly[igzǽktli] 정확히, 바로
delivery[dilívəri] 배달
sincerely[sinsíərli] 진심으로
apologize[əpάlədʒàiz] 사과하다

W Hi, Mr. Price. This is she. I was just about to call the store. I think there's been a mistake.
M Yes, Ms. Miller. That's exactly why I am calling you.
W I told the delivery person that we didn't order a table, but he wouldn't listen.
M I sincerely apologize for the delivery mistake, Ms. Miller.
W When will I be getting the desk I ordered?
M It will be delivered to you tomorrow, ma'am.
W All right. Please make sure that I get the right furniture this time.

여 안녕하세요, Price 씨. 전데요. 막 그 가게에 전화하려던 참이었어요. 착오가 있었던 것 같아요.
남 네, Miller 씨. 그래서 전화했어요.
여 제가 배달원에게 우리는 테이블을 주문하지 않았다고 말했는데, 듣지 않았어요.
남 배달 실수에 대해 진심으로 사과드립니다, Miller 씨.
여 제가 주문한 책상은 언제 받을 수 있나요?
남 내일 배달될 겁니다.
여 알겠어요. 이번에는 확실히 제대로 된 가구를 받게 해주세요.

04 ①

해설 내일 오후 7시 예약을 하지 못해서 식당에 일찍 가서 자리가 나기를 기다리자며 오후 5시에 만나기로 했다.

어휘 time flies 시간이 쏜살같다
reservation[rèzərvéiʃən] 예약

W I can't believe it's Christmas again.
M I know. Time flies.
W What time is our dinner reservation tomorrow? Is it at 7 p.m.?
M Actually, I couldn't reserve a table for us tomorrow. I called too late.
W That's okay. We can get there early and wait for a table.
M Do you want to meet at the restaurant at 6 p.m.?
W Shouldn't we go earlier than that? How about 5 p.m.?
M That might be a little too early. We will be seated at 5:30.
W That's fine. I don't mind eating dinner early.
M Okay, then let's do that.

여 또 다시 크리스마스라니 믿을 수가 없어.
남 그러게. 세월 참 빠르다.
여 내일 저녁 예약이 몇 시야? 오후 7시인가?
남 사실, 내일 우리 테이블을 예약할 수 없었어. 내가 너무 늦게 전화했거든.
여 괜찮아. 그곳에 일찍 도착해서 기다리면 돼.
남 그럼, 저녁 6시에 식당에서 만날래?
여 그보다 더 일찍 가야 하지 않을까? 오후 5시는 어때?
남 그건 좀 너무 이른 것 같아. 우리가 5시 30분에 자리에 앉게 될 거야.
여 괜찮아. 나는 저녁을 일찍 먹는 것도 상관없어.
남 그래. 그럼 그렇게 하자.

05 ⑤

해설 문 앞에 서 있는 남자가 유모차를 끌고 있는 여자에게 문을 잡고 있겠다고 말하는 상황이다.

어휘 stair[stɛər] 계단
department store 백화점
for a second 잠시 동안
hold[hould] 잡다
appreciate[əprí:ʃièit] 고마워하다

① M Are you going to take the elevator?
   W No, I'm taking the stairs.
② M Do you work here at the department store?
   W Yes, I've been working here since 2010.
③ M Does your child know how to read?
   W Yes, he reads by himself every day.
④ M Can I talk to you for a second?
   W Sure, let me just finish this phone call.
⑤ M Do you want me to hold the door for you?
   W That would be great. I appreciate that.

① 남 엘리베이터를 탈 건가요?
   여 아니, 계단으로 갈 거예요.
② 남 이곳 백화점에서 일하세요?
   여 네, 2010년부터 여기서 일하고 있어요.
③ 남 아이가 읽을 줄 아나요?
   여 네, 그 애는 매일 혼자 책을 읽어요.
④ 남 잠깐 얘기 좀 할 수 있을까요?
   여 그러죠, 이 전화만 바로 끊을게요.
⑤ 남 제가 문을 잡아드릴까요?
   여 그러면 좋겠어요. 고맙습니다.

06 ①

[해설] 여자가 처음 보는 과일에 대한 설명을 듣고 먹고 싶다고 하며 가서 가격을 물어보겠다고 했으므로 두 사람은 과일가게에 있음을 알 수 있다.

[어휘] watermelon[wɔ́:tərmèlən] 수박
certainly[sə́:rtnli] 분명히
honeydew melon 허니듀 멜론, 감로 멜론
honey[hʌ́ni] 꿀
delicious[dilíʃəs] 맛있는

M Margaret, do you know what that is?
W I'm not sure. Is it a watermelon?
M Well, it is a type of melon, but it is certainly not a watermelon.
W I knew it was too small to be a watermelon. What is it then?
M It's called a honeydew melon.
W I guess it's really sweet since its name has the word "honey" in it.
M Yes, it is sweet. It's one of my favorite fruits, and it's a really popular fruit in this country.
W Let's get one. I want to try it.
M Sure. I think you'll love them since they're so delicious.
W I can't wait to try it. I'll ask the lady how much it is.

남 Margaret, 저게 뭔지 알아?
여 잘 모르겠어. 저거 수박이야?
남 음, 그건 멜론의 일종이지만, 확실히 수박은 아니야.
여 수박이라기엔 너무 작다는 건 알아. 그럼 뭐지?
남 허니듀 멜론이라고 해.
여 이름에 '꿀'이라는 말이 들어 있으니까 아주 달콤할 것 같은데.
남 맞아. 달콤해. 내가 가장 좋아하는 과일 중 하나인데, 이 나라에서 아주 인기 있는 과일이야.
여 하나 사자. 먹어보고 싶어.
남 그래. 아주 맛있으니까 너도 좋아할 것 같아.
여 빨리 먹어보고 싶어. 저 여자 분에게 얼마인지 물어 볼게.

07 ③

[해설] 여자는 처음 만들어보는 파스타의 맛이 괜찮은지 남자에게 소스 맛을 봐 달라고 부탁했다.

[어휘] creamy[krí:mi] 크림이 든
garlic[gɑ́:rlik] 마늘
recipe[résəpi] 요리법
taste[teist] 맛이 나다; 맛보다
sauce[sɔːs] 소스

M Something smells good. What are you cooking, Mom?
W I'm cooking creamy garlic pasta.
M I don't think we've ever had that at home.
W You're right. I'm making this for the first time.
M Where did you get the recipe from?
W One of my friends showed me how to make this the other day.
M Well, I hope it tastes as good as it smells.
W Can you taste the sauce to see if it's any good?
M Yes, but I'm sure it's good. You've always been a good cook.
W Thanks.

남 뭔가 좋은 냄새가 나요. 엄마, 무슨 요리를 하고 있어요?
여 크림 마늘 파스타를 만들고 있어.
남 우리 집에서 그런 건 먹어본 적이 없는 것 같은데요.
여 맞아. 처음 만드는 거야.
남 요리법은 어디서 구했어요?
여 내 친구 중 한 명이 요전 날 이걸 만드는 방법을 보여줬어.
남 음, 냄새만큼 맛이 있었으면 좋겠어요.
여 맛이 괜찮은지 소스 맛을 좀 봐 줄래?
남 네, 근데 분명히 맛있을 거예요. 엄마는 늘 요리를 잘하시잖아요.
여 고마워.

08 ④

[해설] 개최 횟수(10회), 대회 일시(토요일 오전 8시), 총 코스 거리(5킬로미터), 참가 복장(편한 옷, 운동화)에 관해 언급되었지만 우승 상품에 관한 언급은 없었다.

[어휘] sign up 등록하다
annual[ǽnjuəl] 일 년마다의
race[reis] 경주, 달리기
participate[pɑːrtísəpèit] 참가하다
take place 열리다
comfortable[kʌ́mfərtəbl] 편한
concern[kənsə́ːrn] 우려

M Hello, everyone. If you haven't signed up for our 10th annual school race yet, you must do so by 9 a.m. tomorrow in order to participate in the event. It will take place this Saturday, and the first group will start at 8 a.m. You will only run 5 kilometers as this is a short race. Make sure to wear comfortable clothes and running shoes. However, you are not allowed to wear jeans. If you have any questions or concerns about the race, please don't hesitate to email me.

남 안녕하세요, 여러분. 제10회 연례 학교 달리기 대회에 아직 신청하지 않았다면 내일 오전 9시까지 등록을 해야 행사에 참가할 수 있습니다. 달리기는 이번 주 토요일에 열리며, 첫 번째 그룹은 오전 8시에 출발합니다. 이것은 단축 달리기이기 때문에 5킬로미터만 달릴 것입니다. 반드시 편한 옷을 입고 러닝화를 착용하도록 해요. 하지만, 청바지를 입는 건 안 됩니다. 달리기 대회에 관해 궁금한 점이나 우려되는 일이 있으시면 주저하지 말고 저한테 이메일을 보내세요.

해설 비행 물체이지만 조종사나 승객이 없고 군사적 목적 외에 물건 배달 상업적 목적이나 사람들의 취미로도 쓰이는 것은 드론이다.

어휘 object[ɔ́bdʒikt] 물체
passenger[pǽsəndʒər] 승객
military[mílitèri] 군사의
purpose[pə́ːrpəs] 목적
bomb[bɑm] 폭탄
enemy[énəmi] 적
territory[térətɔ̀ːri] 영토
commercial[kəmə́ːrʃəl] 상업의

M This is a flying object that comes in various sizes and shapes. This can <u>look like an airplane</u>, but this has no pilots or passengers. This can <u>be used for</u> military purposes such as dropping a bomb in enemy territory, but this can also be used for commercial purposes such as <u>delivering products to homes</u>. Many people like to fly one of these objects <u>as a hobby</u>, too. You can learn to fly one by yourself, or you can take lessons at a special school.

남 이것은 다양한 크기와 모양으로 생산되는 비행 물체이다. 그것은 비행기처럼 보일 수 있지만, 조종사나 승객이 없다. 적의 영토에 폭탄을 투하하는 것 같은 군사적 목적으로 사용할 수 있지만, 가정에 물건을 배달하는 것과 같은 상업적 목적으로도 사용할 수 있다. 또한 많은 사람들이 취미로 이 물건 중 하나를 날리는 것을 좋아한다. 당신은 이것을 날리는 법을 혼자서 익힐 수도 있고, 특수학교에서 강습을 받을 수도 있다.

해설 우체국이 어디 있는지 물었는데 내일 사무실에서 그것을 보내겠다고 응답하는 것은 어색하다.

어휘 quit[kwit] 그만두다
post[poust] 발송하다

① M Do you think I <u>should quit my job</u>?
　 W I would if I were you.
② M Could I talk to you for a second?
　 W Can it wait? I'm busy right now.
③ M I'll call you as soon as I'm done.
　 W <u>There's no hurry</u>.
④ M I don't think I can eat any more.
　 W You <u>don't have to</u> finish it then.
⑤ M Do you know where the post office is?
　 W Sure, <u>I'll post it at</u> my office tomorrow.

① 남 내가 직장을 그만둬야 한다고 생각해?
　 여 내가 너라면 그랬을 거야.
② 남 잠깐 얘기 좀 할 수 있을까?
　 여 기다려줄래? 나 지금 바쁘거든.
③ 남 일이 끝나는 대로 전화할게.
　 여 서두를 필요 없어.
④ 남 더는 못 먹을 것 같아.
　 여 그러면 다 먹으려고 할 필요 없어.
⑤ 남 우체국이 어디 있는지 아세요?
　 여 네, 내일 사무실에서 그것을 보낼게요.

해설 온라인으로 청소기를 주문하면 이틀 걸린다는 여자의 말에 남자는 그렇게 하겠다고 했다.

어휘 vacuum cleaner 진공청소기
cordless[kɔ́ːrdlis] 무선의
in stock 재고로
probably[prɑ́bəbli] 아마
place an online order 온라인으로 주문하다
ship[ʃip] 운송하다, 배송하다
extra charge 추가 요금

M Excuse me, do you know where I can find vacuum cleaners?
W Yes, you'll find them next to the TVs.
M Do you have cordless vacuum cleaners?
W Oh, we just <u>sold the last one</u> we had in stock.
M When do you think you'll <u>have them in the store</u> again?
W We'll probably have them in about 10 days.
M That's not good. I'm having a party at my place this weekend.
W If you <u>place an online order</u> right now, it'll be shipped to your place in 2 days.
M Will there be an extra charge for shipping?
W No, shipping is always free.
M Great! Then I'll <u>order one online</u>. I should be able to use it before the party.

남 실례합니다만, 진공청소기가 어디 있는지 아시나요?
여 네, TV 옆에서 볼 수 있을 겁니다.
남 무선의 진공청소기 있나요?
여 아, 마지막 하나 남아있던 것이 방금 전에 팔렸네요.
남 언제쯤 다시 가게에 들어올 것 같나요?
여 아마 10일쯤 후에 들어오게 될 겁니다.
남 그럼 안 되는데. 이번 주말에 우리 집에서 파티를 하려고 하거든요.
여 지금 바로 온라인으로 주문하면 이틀 후에 집으로 배송될 겁니다.
남 배송비가 추가되나요?
여 아니요, 배송은 항상 무료입니다.
남 좋아요! 그러면 인터넷으로 주문할게요. 파티하기 전에 그것을 사용할 수 있겠네요.

12 ③

해설 남자는 9시 30분과 11시 30분 강습 중 더 이른 강습을 듣겠다고 했다.

어휘 register [rédʒistər] 등록하다
yoga [jóugə] 요가
currently [kə́ːrəntli] 지금
wait list 대기자 명단
sign up 신청하다, 등록하다

[Telephone rings.]

W Thanks for calling California Fitness. How may I help you?

M Hi, I'd like to register for one of your yoga classes.

W Sure. We have classes that start at 9:30 a.m. and 11:30 a.m.

M Don't you have a class that starts at 10:30 a.m.?

W Yes, we do, but that class is currently full.

M Can you add me to the wait list for that class?

W Sure, but it may take over a month before you can sign up.

M Oh, I don't want to wait that long.

W Then you'll have to choose between the 2 classes.

M Okay, then I'll just sign up for the earlier class.

[전화벨이 울린다.]

여 캘리포니아 피트니스에 전화 주셔서 감사합니다. 무엇을 도와드릴까요?

남 안녕하세요. 요가 강습에 등록하고 싶어요.

여 네. 오전 9시 30분과 오전 11시 30분에 시작하는 강습이 있습니다.

남 오전 10시 30분에 시작하는 강습은 없나요?

여 네, 있긴 하지만 그 수업은 현재 다 찼네요.

남 그 수업 대기자 명단에 저를 추가해줄래요?

여 물론이죠. 그렇지만 등록하기까지 한 달 이상 걸릴 수도 있어요.

남 아, 그렇게 오래 기다리고 싶지는 않네요.

여 그렇다면, 두 수업 중 하나를 선택해야 합니다.

남 알겠어요. 그러면 더 일찍 하는 강습에 등록할게요.

13 ④

해설 화장실과 푸드 트럭 근처가 아니면서 편의점 근처인 곳을 찾으면 된다.

어휘 pack [pæk] 꾸리다
convenience store 편의점

M This is such a beautiful park, isn't it?

W It's an amazing park. I don't know how they made that lake in the middle of this city.

M I don't, either, but I'm glad that we have it.

W Where should we have our picnic?

M Well, we shouldn't be near the restroom.

W I agree. We packed enough sandwiches, right?

M Yes, we have more than enough food.

W Then we don't really have to be near the food trucks.

M That's right. It would be better to be near the convenience store.

W Okay, then there's only one place left.

남 여긴 정말 아름다운 공원이야, 그렇지?

여 정말 멋진 공원이야. 나는 이 도시 한복판에 어떻게 이 호수를 만들었는지 모르겠어.

남 나도 몰라, 하지만 호수가 생기게 되어서 기뻐.

여 어디서 피크닉을 할까?

남 음, 화장실 근처는 안 돼.

여 나도 동의해. 샌드위치는 충분히 싸왔지?

남 그래, 음식은 충분히 가지고 왔어.

여 그렇다면 우리는 정말로 푸드 트럭 근처에 있을 필요가 없네.

남 맞아. 편의점 근처에 있는 게 나을 거야.

여 좋아, 그럼 한 곳밖에 안 남았네.

14 ②

해설 여자는 어제 벼룩시장에 가서 머그컵과 유리잔들을 샀다고 했다.

어휘 coworker [kóuwə̀ːrkər] 동료
housewarming [háuswɔ̀ːrmiŋ] 집들이
mug [mʌg] 머그컵
flea market 벼룩시장
exotic [igzátik] 이국적인, 이국 정서의

M You have such a beautiful apartment, Janice.

W Thanks, Mike. I'm so glad that all our coworkers were able to come.

M Yes, everyone was looking forward to coming to your housewarming party.

W And thank you so much for the coffeemaker. Where did you get it?

M Oh, I bought it at the shopping mall near my house.

남 Janice, 당신은 정말 멋진 아파트를 가지고 있군요.

여 고마워요, Mike. 동료들이 모두 올 수 있어서 정말 기뻐요.

남 그래요, 모두들 이 집들이에 오기를 고대하고 있었어요.

여 그리고 커피메이커 정말 고마워요. 그거 어디서 샀어요?

남 아, 우리 집 근처 쇼핑몰에서 샀어요.

W Can you take me there some time? I need to get a few things for my apartment.

M Sure. By the way, where did you get all these interesting mugs and glasses?

W I went to a flea market yesterday and bought most of them there.

M Really? They look very exotic.

여 다음에 나 좀 데려다 줄 수 있어요? 아파트에 필요한 몇 가지 물건을 사야 해서요.

남 그래요. 그런데, 이 재미있는 머그잔과 유리잔들은 어디서 다 구했어요?

여 어제 벼룩시장에 가서 그곳에서 거의 다 샀어요.

남 정말요? 그것들은 정말 이국적인 거 같아요.

15 ②

해설 겨울방학 동안 독감에 걸리지 않기 위해 해야 할 일들을 알려주고 있다.

어휘 prevent[privént] ~을 막다
flu[fluː] 독감
avoid[əvɔ́id] 피하다
contact[kántækt] 접촉

M Hello, everyone. Today is the last day of school as winter break starts next week. Before I let you go today, I wanted to tell you about what you can do to prevent yourself from getting the flu. First, you should wash your hands often. Second, you should avoid touching your eyes, nose, or mouth. Lastly, try to avoid close contact with people who are sick. And if you get sick, it is very important that you stay at home. I hope all of you have a great winter break!

남 안녕하세요, 여러분. 다음 주에 겨울방학이 시작되기 때문에 오늘은 학교에 오는 마지막 날입니다. 오늘 여러분을 보내기 전에 독감에 걸리지 않기 위해 할 수 있는 일을 알려주려고 합니다. 먼저 손을 자주 씻어야 합니다. 둘째, 눈, 코, 입을 만지면 안됩니다. 마지막으로, 아픈 사람들과는 가깝게 접촉하지 않도록 하십시오. 그리고 만약 아프면, 집에 머무는 것이 매우 중요합니다. 여러분 모두가 멋진 겨울 방학을 보내길 바랍니다!

16 ⑤

해설 500달러짜리 패키지여행인데, 200달러인 비행기 표를 추가하고 방을 혼자 써야 해서 50달러의 추가 요금을 내야 하므로 총 750달러를 지불하게 된다.

어휘 package tour 패키지여행
include[inklúːd] 포함하다
purchase[pə́ːrtʃəs] 사다
by oneself 혼자서
charge[tʃɑːrdʒ] 청구하다

[Telephone rings.]

M The Greatest World Tour. How can I help you?

W Hi, I'm calling about the Vietnam package tour that I saw in the newspaper.

M Yes, that's our most popular package tour.

W Is it $500 per person?

M Yes, that's correct, but the $500 doesn't include the airline ticket.

W If I buy an airline ticket from you, it'll be $200 extra, right?

M Right, but you can purchase your ticket from the airline directly.

W I see. I'll be traveling by myself, so I only need one room.

M Oh, then you'll be charged an extra $50.

W I see. I'll sign up for one person, and I'll buy an airline ticket from you, too.

[전화벨이 울린다.]

남 The Greatest World Tour입니다. 무엇을 도와드릴까요?

여 안녕하세요, 신문에서 본 베트남 패키지여행 때문에 전화했어요.

남 네, 그게 저희의 가장 인기 있는 패키지여행입니다.

여 1인당 500달러인가요?

남 네, 맞아요, 하지만 500달러에 비행기 표는 포함되어 있지 않아요.

여 제가 거기서 비행기표를 사면 200달러가 더 들겠죠, 맞죠?

남 맞아요, 하지만 항공사에서 직접 표를 구매하셔도 돼요.

여 알겠습니다. 저는 혼자 여행할 거니까 방을 혼자 써야 해요.

남 아, 그러면 50달러를 추가하셔야 해요.

여 알겠어요. 한 사람 신청하고, 거기서 비행기 표도 살게요.

17 ①

해설 여자가 지금 사용하는 방에 문제가 있는지 물었으므로 문제가 무엇인지 설명하는 내용이 와야 적절하다.

어휘 front desk 프런트, 안내 데스크

[Telephone rings.]

M This is the front desk. How may I help you?

W Hi, my name is Kathy Smith, and I'm in room 1705.

[전화벨이 울린다.]

남 프런트 데스크입니다. 무엇을 도와드릴까요?

여 안녕하세요, 제 이름은 Kathy Smith이고, 1705호에 묵고 있어요.

delay[diléi] 지연
receive[risíːv] 받다
bucket[bʌ́kit] 양동이, 통
vacancy[véikənsi] 빈 방
[선택지]
request[rikwést] 요구, 요청
specific[spisífik] 구체적인, 분명한

M Yes, Ms. Smith. We're going to get you the ice you <u>asked</u> <u>for</u> <u>in</u> <u>a</u> <u>moment</u>. We're very sorry for the delay.

W Oh, I just received the bucket of ice. Thank you.

M You're very welcome. Is there anything else I can do for you?

W Would it be possible <u>for</u> <u>me</u> <u>to</u> <u>move</u> to a different room?

M If there are any vacancies, you can move. But it will take a while for me to check.

W Well, can you <u>please</u> <u>check</u> <u>right</u> <u>away</u>? I don't think I can stay in this room any longer.

M Oh, is there <u>something</u> <u>wrong</u> <u>with</u> <u>your</u> <u>room</u>?

W I think someone smoked in this room.

남 네, Smith 씨. 부탁하신 얼음은 잠시 후에 가져다드릴게요. 늦어져서 죄송합니다.

여 아, 방금 얼음 한 통을 받았어요. 고맙습니다.

남 천만에요. 저희가 해 드릴 다른 일이 또 있나요?

여 다른 방으로 옮겨도 될까요?

남 빈 방이 있으면 옮겨서도 됩니다. 하지만 확인하는 데는 시간이 좀 걸려요.

여 음, 지금 바로 확인해 줄 수 있나요? 이 방에 더 이상 머물 수 없을 것 같아서요.

남 아, 방에 무슨 문제가 있나요?

여 이 방에서 누군가 담배를 피운 것 같아요.

② 당신의 요구는 내 것만큼 구체적이지 않군요.

③ 왜 제가 부탁한 얼음을 받지 못하고 있죠?

④ 이 방에서 3박 예약하려고 해요.

⑤ 이 방은 바다의 경치가 멋지군요.

18 ⑤

해설 영어를 잘하는 남자에게 영어를 배우기 위해 무엇을 했냐고 물었으므로 영어를 익힌 방법을 말하는 게 적절하다.

어휘 support[səpɔ́ːrt] 지지하다
overnight[òuvərnáit] 하룻밤 사이에
shocked[ʃɑkt] 깜짝 놀란
thankful[θǽŋkfəl] 감사하는
[선택지]
fluently[flúːəntli] 유창하게

W Welcome to England, Justin. How was your concert last night?

M It was great. A lot of <u>fans</u> <u>came</u> <u>out</u> and supported me.

W You've become one of the most famous singers in the world almost overnight.

M I'm just <u>as</u> <u>shocked</u> <u>as</u> everyone else, and I'm really thankful to all my fans in the world.

W You're 23 years old and <u>you've</u> <u>never</u> <u>lived</u> <u>in</u> an English-speaking country. Is that right?

M That is correct. I've been living in Korea ever since I was born.

W Yet, you speak English so well. <u>What</u> <u>did</u> <u>you</u> <u>do</u> to learn English?

M I watched many movies and TV shows in <u>English</u>.

여 영국에 온 걸 환영합니다, Justin. 어젯밤 콘서트는 어땠어요?

남 정말 좋았어요. 많은 팬들이 와서 호응해 주셨어요.

여 당신은 거의 하룻밤 사이에 세계에서 가장 유명한 가수 중 한 명이 되었어요.

남 저도 다른 사람들처럼 놀랐고, 세계의 모든 제 팬들에게 정말 감사하고 있어요.

여 당신은 23살이고, 영어권 국가에서 살아본 적이 없어요. 그렇죠?

남 맞아요. 저는 한국에서 태어나고 쭉 거기서 살아왔어요.

여 그런데도 영어를 아주 잘하네요. 영어를 배우기 위해 무엇을 했나요?

남 저는 영어로 된 영화와 TV 쇼를 많이 봤어요.

① 맞아요, 저는 제 노래로 유명해졌어요.

② 저는 프랑스어를 더 유창하게 말하고 싶어요.

③ 저는 K-pop 음악을 공부하려고 한국에 왔어요.

④ 저는 어렸을 때 3년 동안 영국에서 살았어요.

19 ⑤

해설 남자와 여자는 투표할 나이가 됐지만 정치에 관심이 없어서 후보자가 누군지도 모른다고 했으므로 이제 투표하게 되었으니 정치에 관심을 가지자고 충고하는 내용이 어울린다.

어휘 vote[vout] 투표하다
at least 적어도
law[lɔː] 법
election[ilékʃən] 선거
candidate[kǽndidèit] 후보자
pay attention 관심을 갖다
politics[pálətiks] 정치

W How old are you, William?
M I'm turning 18 next month.
W Are you going to vote in April?
M Don't I have to be at least 19 in order to vote?
W No, the law has been changed. You only have to be 18 to vote.
M I didn't know that. You turned 18 last month, right?
W Yes, I can vote in April, too.
M Do you know whom you're going to vote for in this election?
W That's the problem. I know I can vote, but I don't know whom I should vote for.
M I don't know any of the candidates. I've never paid any attention to politics.
W We'd better start paying attention now that we can vote.

여 William, 너 몇 살이지?
남 다음 달에 18살이 돼.
여 4월에 투표할 거야?
남 투표하려면 적어도 19살은 되어야 하지 않니?
여 아니, 법이 바뀌었어. 투표하려면 18살이면 돼.
남 그건 몰랐어. 너는 지난달에 18살이 되었지?
여 맞아, 나도 4월에 투표할 수 있어.
남 이번 선거에서 네가 누구를 뽑아야 할지 알고 있니?
여 그게 문제야. 투표할 수 있다는 건 알지만 누구에게 투표해야 할지는 모르겠어.
남 난 후보자들 중 아무도 몰라. 나는 정치에 관심을 둬 본 적이 없거든.
여 이제 우리도 투표할 수 있으니 관심을 갖기 시작하는 게 좋겠어.

① 내가 누구에게 투표했는지 이미 말했어.
② 나는 18살이어서 투표할 수 없을 거야.
③ 내가 투표한 후보는 훌륭한 사람이야.
④ 내가 너라면 후보자 중 아무에게나 투표할 텐데.

20 ①

해설 남자는 자신의 차를 막고 있는 트럭을 빨리 치우기 위해서 트럭에서 책상을 꺼내는 중인 여자를 도우려는 상황이다.

어휘 gym[dʒim] 체육관
moving truck 이삿짐 트럭
block[blɑk] 막다
move[muːv] 옮기다

W Peter sees a moving truck in front of his apartment building. It's blocking his car and he needs to use his car soon. He looks around to find the driver of the truck but does not see anyone. He comes back after taking a shower and sees a young woman trying to take a desk out of the truck by herself. He wants to help her move the desk before he asks her to move her truck. In this situation, what would Peter most likely say to the woman?

Peter Can I help you with the desk?

여 Peter는 그의 아파트 건물 앞에 있는 이삿짐 트럭을 본다. 그 트럭이 그의 차를 막고 있고 곧 차를 사용해야 한다. 그는 트럭 운전자를 찾기 위해 주위를 둘러보지만 아무도 보이지 않는다. 그는 샤워를 마치고 돌아왔는데 이 때 혼자 트럭에서 책상을 꺼내려는 젊은 여자를 본다. 그는 그녀에게 트럭을 옮겨달라고 부탁하기 전에 그녀가 책상을 옮기는 것을 도와주고 싶다. 이런 상황에서 Peter가 여자에게 뭐라고 말할까?

Peter 책상 옮기는 거 도와드릴까요?

② 벌써 체육관에서 돌아왔어요?
③ 이건 제가 주문한 책상이 아닌 것 같아요.
④ 차 좀 빌려 줄래요? 제가 늦어서요.
⑤ 죄송하지만, 제가 트럭 운전사예요.

| 01 ③ | 02 ③ | 03 ① | 04 ⑤ | 05 ② | 06 ④ | 07 ⑤ |
| 08 ⑤ | 09 ③ | 10 ② | 11 ③ | 12 ① | 13 ④ | 14 ① |
| 15 ① |

서답형 1 Staff   서답형 2 talent   서답형 3 stranger

---

01 ③

해설 여자는 신발 모양의 장난감을 사겠다고 했다.

어휘 chicken-shaped 치킨 모양의
chew[tʃuː] 씹다

M Hello. May I help you?
W Yes, please. I want to buy a toy for my dog.
M How about these balls? Many dogs like to play with balls.
W He already <u>has a few balls</u>.
M Okay. This chicken-shaped one <u>which makes a sound</u> is popular.
W He doesn't like that kind of toy.
M What does your dog like to do?
W He likes to <u>chew on my shoes</u>.
M Then how about this shoe-shaped toy? You won't have to worry about your shoes any more.
W Great! <u>I'll take it</u>.

남 안녕하세요. 도와드릴까요?
여 네. 우리 개가 쓸 장난감을 사려고요.
남 이 공들은 어때요? 많은 개들이 공을 가지고 노는 것을 좋아하죠.
여 공은 이미 몇 개 가지고 있어요.
남 네. 소리를 내는 이 닭 모양의 장난감이 인기가 있어요.
여 우리 개는 그런 장난감을 좋아하지 않아요.
남 그 개는 무엇을 하는 것을 좋아하나요?
여 제 신발을 물어뜯는 걸 좋아해요.
남 그럼 이 신발 모양의 장난감은 어떠세요? 손님의 신발 때문에 더는 걱정할 필요가 없겠죠.
여 좋군요! 이걸 살게요.

---

02 ③

해설 체크아웃을 하고 공항 가는 셔틀버스에 대한 안내를 받을 수 있는 곳은 호텔 접수대이다.

어휘 check out 체크아웃하다
satisfying[sǽtisfàiiŋ] 만족스러운
minibar[mínibàːr] (호텔 객실 등의) 소형 냉장고
bill[bil] 계산서
airport shuttle 공항 셔틀버스

M Good morning. May I check out?
W Sure. Was <u>your stay satisfying</u>?
M Yes, it was very nice.
W That's great. Did you <u>have anything from</u> the minibar?
M No, I didn't.
W Okay. Here's your bill.
M Thanks. By the way, I need to <u>go to the airport</u>.
W I see. A free airport shuttle is leaving in half an hour.
M Great. <u>I'll take the shuttle</u>. Thank you so much.

남 안녕하세요. 체크아웃해도 될까요?
여 그러시죠. 만족하게 머무셨나요?
남 네, 아주 좋았어요.
여 잘 됐네요. 미니바에서 드신 게 있나요?
남 아뇨, 없어요.
여 알겠습니다. 여기 계산서입니다.
남 감사합니다. 그런데 제가 공항으로 가야 해요.
여 알겠습니다. 30분 후에 무료 공항 셔틀이 출발할 겁니다.
남 잘 됐네요. 셔틀을 탈게요. 정말 감사합니다.

---

03 ①

해설 마음에 들어 하는 가방을 남자가 생일선물로 사 주겠다고 해서 여자는 행복해 한다.

어휘 popular[pápjulər] 인기 있는
wonder[wʌ́ndər] 궁금해 하다
reasonable[ríːzənəbl] 적당한, 비싸지 않은

W Dad, look at that bag in the window. Isn't it nice?
M Oh, it's very nice.
W That's the most popular style these days.
M But I think it's <u>too small for</u> you.
W That's okay. I need a small bag. I wonder how much it is.

여 아빠, 저 진열된 가방 좀 보세요. 예쁘지 않아요?
남 아, 아주 멋지구나.
여 저게 요즘 가장 인기 있는 스타일이에요.
남 하지만 너한테는 너무 작은 것 같구나.
여 괜찮아요. 저는 작은 가방이 필요해요. 가격이 얼마일지 궁금하네요.

M Why don't we go in and check it out? If the price is reasonable, I'll buy it <u>as your</u> <u>birthday present</u>.

W Really? Thank you so much, Dad. <u>You're</u> <u>the best</u>.

남 들어가서 확인해 볼까? 가격이 적당하다면 너의 생일선물로 사주마.

여 정말요? 정말 고마워요, 아빠. 아빠가 최고예요.

① 행복한　　② 두려워하는　③ 자랑스러운
④ 충격 받은　⑤ 실망한

04 ⑤

해설 식당은 운영하지 않는다고 했다.

어휘 simply[símpli] 단순히
herb[ə:rb] 허브
located[lóukeitid] ~에 위치한
run[rʌn] 운영하다

W Welcome to Siam Thai Cooking School. We are not just a cooking school where you simply cook and eat. You can also learn <u>how to grow vegetables</u> and herbs here. The school is located in <u>the center</u> <u>of</u> the old town of Chiang Mai. We have 2 courses. A full-day course is 8 hours long, and a half-day course is 4 hours long. We <u>don't run restaurants</u>. We're sure you will never forget your time here.

여 Siam Thai 요리 학교에 오신 것을 환영합니다. 우리는 단순히 요리하고 먹어보는 요리 학교가 아닙니다. 여러분은 이곳에서 채소와 허브를 키우는 방법도 배울 수 있습니다. 이 학교는 치앙마이 구시가지 중심에 있습니다. 우리는 두 개의 과정을 운영합니다. 종일 과정은 8시간이고 반나절 과정은 4시간 걸립니다. 우리는 식당은 운영하지 않습니다. 여러분은 여기서 보낸 시간을 절대 잊지 못할 것이라고 확신합니다.

05 ②

해설 여자는 기침을 하고 목이 아픈 남자에게 목이 좋아지려면 카페인이 든 음료를 줄여야 한다고 조언했다.

어휘 cough[kɔ(:)f] 기침을 하다
throat[θrout] 목
sore[sɔ:r] 아픈
energy drink 에너지 드링크, 강장 음료
focus on ~에 집중하다
contain[kəntéin] 포함하다
caffeine[kæfí:n] 카페인
cut down on ~을 줄이다

W What's wrong?

M I cough a lot and sometimes <u>my throat</u> <u>gets sore</u>, Doctor.

W [Pause] Hmm, you don't have a fever. Do you drink a lot of coffee or energy drinks?

M I always drink energy drinks to <u>focus on</u> <u>my studies</u>.

W Those drinks contain a lot of caffeine, and too much caffeine can <u>hurt your body</u>.

M Oh, I didn't know that.

W You need to <u>cut down on drinks</u> with caffeine in them so that your throat can get better.

M I see. Thank you, Doctor.

여 어디가 불편하신가요?

남 기침을 많이 하고 가끔 목이 아파요, 선생님.

여 [잠시 후] 흠, 열은 없네요. 커피나 에너지 드링크를 많이 마시나요?

남 네. 공부에 집중하려고 항상 에너지 드링크를 마시고 있어요.

여 그 음료에는 카페인이 아주 많아요. 그리고 카페인을 너무 많이 섭취하면 몸에 안 좋아요.

남 아, 몰랐어요.

여 목이 좋아지려면 카페인이 든 음료를 줄여야 해요.

남 알겠습니다. 감사합니다, 의사 선생님.

06 ④

해설 조리 실습을 시작하기 전에 알아두어야 할 사항들을 알려주고 있다.

어휘 traditional[trədíʃənl] 전통적인
keep in mind 명심하다
sharp[ʃɑ:rp] 날카로운
creativity[kriːeitívəti] 창의력

M Hello, everyone. Today you're going to make traditional Korean rice cake. Make groups of 4 people and sit around the tables. <u>Before you cook</u>, there are a few things I want you to <u>keep in mind</u>. First, make sure you wash your hands. Second, be careful when you <u>use something</u> <u>sharp</u>. Lastly, <u>use your creativity</u> when you cook. All right, let's start.

남 안녕하세요, 여러분. 오늘은 한국 전통 떡을 만들 겁니다. 네 명이 한 조가 되어 조리대에 둘러앉으세요. 요리하기 전에, 여러분이 몇 가지 명심해야 할 것이 있어요. 첫째, 반드시 손을 씻으세요. 둘째, 날카로운 것을 사용할 때는 조심하세요. 마지막으로, 요리할 때 창의력을 발휘하세요. 좋습니다. 시작하지요.

해설 개집을 만드는 것이 아니라 개집을 청소하는 활동을 한다.	[Telephone rings.] M Thanks for calling Happy Dog. What can I help you with? W Hi, I'd like to join your volunteer project with dogs. M Why do you <u>want to join us</u>? W When I saw some poor dogs on TV, I wanted to help them. M We work at the Animal Center <u>every Saturday from</u> 10 a.m. to 4 p.m. Is that okay? W Sure. What can I do there? M You can walk the dogs, give them <u>a bath</u>, and <u>clean their houses</u>. W No problem. I'll do my best. M Thank you for joining us. See you this Saturday.	[전화벨이 울린다.] 남 Happy Dog에 전화 주셔서 감사합니다. 무엇을 도와드릴까요? 여 안녕하세요, 개들과 함께 하는 자원 봉사 프로젝트에 함께하고 싶어요. 남 왜 저희와 함께하고 싶으신 거죠? 여 TV에서 불쌍한 개들을 보았을 때, 그들을 돕고 싶었어요. 남 우리는 매주 토요일 오전 10시부터 오후 4시까지 동물센터에서 일해요. 괜찮나요? 여 네. 제가 거기서 무엇을 하면 되나요? 남 개들을 산책시키고, 목욕시키고, 개집을 청소하면 돼요. 여 문제없어요. 최선을 다할게요. 남 함께해 주셔서 고맙습니다. 이번 주 토요일에 봐요.

어휘 volunteer[vàləntíər] 자원 봉사
poor[puər] 불쌍한

해설 Michael은 서로 목표가 다른 상사와 사이가 좋지 않아서 일을 그만뒀다고 했다.	W Hey, Peter! I heard Michael quit his job. Is that true? M I didn't know that. Where did you hear that? W I heard that from his friend. M Did Michael work overtime? W I don't think so. He <u>left work on time</u> every day. M Then <u>what made him quit</u> his job? W I heard he worked hard and his salary was good, but he didn't <u>get along with</u> his boss. M Did Michael do something wrong? W <u>Their goals were totally different</u>. His boss wanted to focus on sales, and Michael wanted to focus on quality.	여 이봐, Peter! Michael이 일을 그만뒀다고 들었어. 사실이니? 남 나도 몰랐어. 그 말은 어디서 들었어? 여 그의 친구한테 들었어. 남 Michael이 야근을 많이 했니? 여 그런 것 같지 않아. 그는 매일 정시에 퇴근했거든. 남 그러면 왜 그가 그만두었을까? 여 그가 열심히 일했고 급여도 좋았지만, 그의 상사와 좋지 않았다고 들었어. 남 Michael이 뭔가 잘못을 했니? 여 그들의 목표가 완전히 달랐대. 그의 상사는 판매를 중요시했고, Michael은 품질을 중요시했거든.

어휘 quit[kwit] 그만두다
overtime[óuvərtàim] 규정 외 노동 시간
on time 시간을 어기지 않고, 정각에
salary[sǽləri] 월급
get along with ~와 잘 지내다
boss[bɔ(ː)s] 상사
goal[goul] 목표
totally[tóutəli] 완전히
sale[seil] 판매
quality[kwáləti] 품질

해설 여자는 남자에게 한옥마을을 안내해 준 것에 대해 고맙다는 말을 하려고 전화했다.	[Cell phone rings.] M Hello. W Hi, Jiho. <u>I'm on the train</u>. My train is leaving in 10 minutes. M Great. I hope you <u>enjoyed your trip here</u>. W I really enjoyed it. M Which place did you like most in my town? W I liked the Jeonju Hanok Village most. I enjoyed walking around in hanbok.	[휴대전화가 울린다.] 남 여보세요. 여 안녕, 지호. 나 기차에 있어. 기차가 10분 후에 출발해. 남 잘 됐네. 이곳에서의 여행이 즐거웠다면 좋겠네. 여 정말 즐거웠어. 남 우리 동네에서 어디가 제일 좋았니? 여 나는 전주 한옥마을이 가장 좋았어. 한복을 입고 즐겁게 돌아다녔지.

어휘 walk around 이리저리 걷다
show around ~에게 구경시켜 주다

M Yes, that was a lot of fun!
W I'm calling to thank you for showing me around.
M I enjoyed it, too.

남 그래, 정말 재미있었어!
여 안내해 줘서 고맙다는 말을 하려고 전화했어.
남 나도 즐거웠는걸.

10 ②

해설 여자는 학교에 가지 않고 아빠와 점심을 먹은 후, 뮤지컬을 보았고, 집에 와서 자기 전에 개를 산책시켰다.

어휘 anniversary[æ̀nəvə́ːrsəri] 기념일
take ~ off ~(동안)을 쉬다
amazing[əméiziŋ] 굉장한

W I had fun today. I had no school because today is my school's 30th anniversary. My dad and I decided to see a musical, so he took the afternoon off for me. Before watching the musical, we had lunch together. I had pasta and it was delicious! Then we went to see the musical and it was amazing. We both liked it very much. When we came home, I felt a little tired. But before I went to bed, I walked my dog.

여 저는 오늘 재미있게 놀았어요. 우리 학교가 30주년 개교기념일이라서 학교에 가지 않았거든요. 아빠와 저는 뮤지컬을 보기로 했고, 아빠는 저를 위해 오후에 휴가를 내셨어요. 뮤지컬을 보기 전에 우리는 함께 점심을 먹었어요. 전 파스타를 먹었는데 맛있었어요! 그러고 나서 뮤지컬을 보러 갔었는데 정말 멋졌어요. 우리 둘 다 아주 좋아했어요. 집에 돌아왔을 때, 저는 조금 피곤했어요. 하지만 잠들기 전에, 우리집 개를 산책시켰어요.

11 ③

해설 비행기가 착륙하기 직전 도착지 상황을 알려주고 탑승구에 도착할 때까지의 주의 사항을 안내하고 있다.

어휘 international airport 국제공항
temperature[témpərətʃər] 기온
degree[digríː] (온도 단위인) 도
Celsius[sélsiəs] 섭씨
from now on 지금부터
fasten[fǽsən] 매다

M Good afternoon, everyone. We are now arriving at Istanbul International Airport. It is 4:30 in the afternoon. It is raining here and the temperature is 25 degrees Celsius. You can't use the restroom from now on. Please make sure you stay in your seats and fasten your seat belts until we get to the gate. Thank you.

남 좋은 오후입니다, 여러분. 우리는 지금 이스탄불 국제공항에 도착하고 있습니다. 지금 시각은 오후 4시 30분입니다. 지금 이곳에는 비가 내리고 있고, 기온은 섭씨 25도입니다. 지금부터는 화장실 사용을 할 수 없습니다. 탑승구에 도착할 때까지 자리에 그대로 앉아서 안전벨트를 매고 계십시오. 감사합니다.

12 ①

해설 서로의 탓을 하면서 얘기할 시간이 없다는 여자의 말에 동의하며 얼른 뛰자는 응답이 이어지는 것이 자연스럽다.

어휘 not ~ any more 더 이상 ~ 않다
fault[fɔːlt] 과실, 잘못
stop for ~을 위해 들르다
wish[wiʃ] 바라다

W Hurry up, Leo.
M One minute. I can't run any more.
W We don't have much time left. The movie starts in 15 minutes.
M This is your fault. You said it would be better to walk there.
W You said you were hungry, too. We shouldn't have stopped for a hamburger.
M I wish we could fly to the theater.
W Come on. We don't have time to talk about that.
M You're right. Let's just run.

여 서둘러, Leo.
남 1분만. 더 이상 뛸 수가 없어.
여 우리 시간이 별로 없어. 영화는 15분 후에 시작해.
남 다 네 잘못이야. 네가 거기까지 걸어가는 게 낫다고 했잖아.
여 너도 배가 고프다고 했잖아. 햄버거를 먹으러 들르지 말았어야 했는데.
남 우리가 극장까지 날아갈 수 있으면 좋을 텐데.
여 빨리 와. 그런 이야기할 시간 없어.
남 네 말이 맞아. 그냥 뛰자.

② 나는 그 영화를 빨리 보고 싶어.
③ 우리가 표를 구해서 다행이야.
④ 네 말을 듣지 않아서 미안해.
⑤ 알았지? 우리는 버스를 타지 말았어야 했어.

13 ④

해설 산은 오르기 어렵지 않다는 남자의 말에 여자는 남자의 제안을 받아들이고 약속을 정하는 응답이 이어지는 것이 적절하다.

어휘 scenery[síːnəri] 경치
dangerous[déindʒərəs] 위험한
[선택지]
hiking[háikiŋ] 하이킹, 도보 여행
meet up (~와) 만나다

M Anna, what are you going to do this Sunday?
W I'm not sure yet. What about you?
M I'm going to go hiking with my brother. Do you want to join us?
W I'd love to. Where are you going?
M We're going to Bukhan Mountain. The scenery there is really beautiful this time of year.
W That sounds great. But I'm not good at hiking. Will that be okay?
M Of course. The mountain is not so difficult to climb and it is not dangerous. And my brother and I will be with you.
W Okay. What time should I meet up with you?

남 Anna, 이번 일요일에 뭐 할 거야?
여 아직 확실하지 않아. 너는 어때?
남 나는 형과 하이킹을 갈 거야. 우리랑 같이 갈래?
여 나도 그러고 싶어. 어디로 갈 거야?
남 북한산으로 갈 거야. 일 년 중 이맘때면 그곳 풍경이 정말 아름답거든.
여 좋을 것 같아. 그런데 나는 등산을 잘 못하는데. 괜찮을까?
남 물론이지. 그 산은 오르기 그다지 어렵지 않고 위험하지도 않아. 그리고 우리 형이랑 내가 너랑 같이 있을 거잖아.
여 좋아. 너희랑 몇 시에 만날까?

① 그럼 다음에 가자.
② 하이킹 코스는 얼마나 걸리니?
③ 오늘 오후에 소풍가는 게 어때?
⑤ 도봉산에 갈까 생각 중이야.

14 ①

해설 디자이너가 되고 싶다는 딸의 꿈을 처음 알게 된 엄마가 어려운 길을 택한 것에 대해 우려하고 있으므로 최선을 다하겠다는 말로 자신의 의지를 보이는 것이 적절하다.

어휘 for the first time 처음으로
surprised[sərpráizd] 놀란
focus more on ~에 더 중점을 두다

W When you graduate from middle school, you want to go to a design high school. You tell your mother about it for the first time. Your mother is very surprised to hear that because she thought you were interested in science. She says that it's not easy to become a designer, so you should focus more on science rather than design. However, you hope that your mother allows you to go to a design school. In this situation, what would you say to your mother?

여 당신은 중학교를 졸업하면 디자인 고등학교에 가고 싶어 한다. 당신은 엄마에게 그런 생각을 처음 이야기한다. 엄마는 당신이 과학에 관심이 있다고 생각했기 때문에 그 말을 듣고 매우 놀란다. 엄마는 디자이너가 되는 것이 쉽지 않기 때문에 디자인보다는 과학에 더 중점을 두는 게 좋겠다고 말한다. 하지만, 당신은 엄마가 디자인 학교에 가는 것을 허락하기를 바란다. 이러한 상황에서 당신은 엄마에게 뭐라고 말할 것인가?

① 최선을 다하겠다고 약속할게요.
② 엄마는 저를 이해하지 못할 거예요.
③ 엄마가 하신 말씀 다시 해 주시겠어요?
④ 저는 분명히 훌륭한 과학자가 될 거예요.
⑤ 저는 노래하고 춤추는 법을 배울 거예요.

15 ①

해설 두 아이가 찾아다니던 파랑새가 먼 곳이 아닌 집 마당에 있었듯이 행복은 먼 곳이 아니라 가까이에 있다고 말하고 있다.

어휘 happiness[hǽpinis] 행복
set out 출발하다, 나서다
surprisingly[sərpráiziŋli] 놀랍게도
backyard[bǽkjɑ̀ːrd] 마당

M Where do you find happiness? Here's the story of 2 children who set out to find a bluebird. They travel all over the world for a long time, but they can't find it. Surprisingly, however, when they return home, they find it in their own backyard. The story explains that happiness is found when you stop looking for it. Happiness is not far away, but within you.

남 당신은 어디에서 행복을 찾나요? 여기 파랑새를 찾기 위해 나선 두 아이의 이야기가 있습니다. 그들은 오랫동안 세계 곳곳을 여행하지만 그것을 찾지 못합니다. 하지만 놀랍게도, 그들이 집으로 돌아왔을 때, 그들은 자신의 집 뒷마당에서 그것을 발견합니다. 이 이야기는 여러분이 행복을 찾으려는 것을 멈췄을 때 비로소 찾게 된다는 것을 설명해 줍니다. 행복은 멀리 있는 것이 아니라 여러분 안에 있거든요.

① 행복은 늘 당신 가까이에 있다.
② 아이들은 항상 우리를 웃게 만든다.
③ 여행은 우리의 마음을 노래하게 한다.
④ 일을 즐기는 것을 잊지 마라.
⑤ 우리는 얻기 힘든 것을 얻었을 때, 행복하다.

서답형 1 Staff

[해설] 4시부터 5시 30분까지는 직원들 휴식 시간이다.

[어휘] operating hour 운영[영업] 시간
staff[stæf] 직원

[Telephone rings.]

M Oliver's Restaurant. How may I help you?

W What are your operating hours on Friday?

M We are open from 11 a.m. to 9 p.m. on weekdays and take last orders at 8 p.m.

W How about on the weekend?

M From 11 a.m. to 10:30 p.m. on Saturdays. But we are closed on Sundays.

W I see. Can I make a reservation for 3 people at 5 o'clock this Saturday?

M I'm sorry. We take an hour and a half off for the staff at 4 p.m.

W Then how about 5:30?

M Okay. May I have your name?

[전화벨이 울린다.]

남 Oliver 레스토랑입니다. 무엇을 도와드릴까요?

여 금요일 영업시간이 어떻게 됩니까?

남 평일은 오전 11시부터 오후 9시까지 영업하며 오후 8시에 마지막 주문을 받습니다.

여 주말은 어떤가요?

남 토요일 오전 11시부터 저녁 10시 30분까지입니다. 하지만 일요일에는 쉽니다.

여 알겠습니다. 이번 주 토요일 5시에 세 사람 예약할 수 있나요?

남 죄송합니다. 저희는 오후 4시부터 한 시간 반 동안 직원들이 휴식을 취합니다.

여 그럼 5시 30분은 어떤가요?

남 좋습니다. 성함을 말씀해 주시겠어요?

서답형 2 talent

[해설] 40세 넘어서 마침내 작가로서의 꿈을 이룬 박완서의 예를 들면서 자신의 재능과 꿈을 믿으면 꿈이 이루어진다는 말을 하고 있다.

[어휘] novelist[návəlist] 소설가
collection[kəlékʃən] 모음집
poverty[pávərti] 가난
talent[tǽlənt] 재능
finally[fáinəli] 마침내, 결국
come true 실현되다, 이루어지다
someday[sʌ́mdèi] 언젠가

W Have you ever read a novel written by Park Wansuh? She was one of the greatest novelists in Korea. She wrote 15 novels and 10 short story collections after she became a writer at the age of 40. When she was young, she could not show her special talent in writing because of war and poverty. However, she believed in her talent and dream, so she finally became a famous writer. If you believe in what you are good at and what you want to do, you can make your dreams come true someday.

Question: What does the woman suggest to make your dreams come true?

➡ She suggests that we believe in our talent and dreams to make our dreams come true.

여 박완서가 쓴 소설을 읽어본 적이 있나요? 그녀는 한국에서 가장 위대한 소설가 중 한 명이었어요. 그녀는 40세에 작가가 된 후에 15편의 소설책과 10편의 단편집을 냈어요. 그녀가 젊었을 때는 전쟁과 가난 때문에 글 쓰는 특별한 재능을 발휘할 수 없었지요. 하지만 그녀는 자신의 재능과 꿈을 믿었기 때문에 마침내 유명한 작가가 되었어요. 여러분이 자신이 잘하는 것과 하고 싶은 것을 믿고 있다면, 언젠가는 여러분의 꿈을 이룰 수 있어요.

질문: 여자는 여러분이 꿈을 이루기 위해 무엇을 할 것을 제안하나요?

➡ 그녀는 우리가 꿈을 이루기 위해서는 우리의 재능과 꿈을 믿을 것을 제안합니다.

서답형 3 stranger

해설 낯선 사람에게는 판단을 받거나 다시 볼 염려가 없기 때문에 개인적인 문제들을 이야기하기 쉽다는 사람의 심리를 말하고 있다.

어휘 personal[pə́rsənl] 개인적인
detail[díːteil] 사소한 일
emotion[imóuʃən] 감정
stranger[stréindʒər] 모르는 사람
effect[ifékt] 효과
conversation[kànvərséiʃən] 대화
judge[dʒʌdʒ] 판단하다
experience[ikspíəriəns] 경험

M Why do so many people share personal details, thoughts, and emotions online with people they've never met? Why do some people tell complete strangers about their problems? This is called the "stranger on the train" effect. It's about 2 people meeting on the train, having a personal conversation, and leaving without seeing each other ever again. That's because they don't have to worry about being judged or seeing them the next day. They even feel better because of this experience.

Sometimes, it's easier to tell a stranger something very personal.

남 왜 그렇게 많은 사람들이 만난 적도 없는 사람들과 개인사나 생각, 감정 등을 온라인에서 공유할까요? 왜 어떤 사람들은 전혀 모르는 사람들에게 자신의 문제를 말할까요? 이것을 '기차에서 만난 이방인' 효과라고 합니다. 기차 안에서 두 사람이 만나 개인적인 대화를 나누고 떠난 뒤 다시 만나지 않는다는 얘기지요. 이것은 그들이 판단을 받거나 다음날 그들을 볼 염려가 없기 때문입니다. 그들은 심지어 이러한 경험을 하고 나서 기분이 나아집니다.

때때로, 낯선 사람에게 매우 개인적인 것을 말하는 것이 더 쉽다.

01 ④	02 ①	03 ②	04 ④	05 ④	06 ③	07 ⑤
08 ④	09 ②	10 ③	11 ③	12 ⑤	13 ④	14 ④
15 ③						

서답형 1 <u>lessons</u>   서답형 2 <u>fiction</u>   서답형 3 <u>jogging</u>

01 ④

해설 남자는 정사각형 시계를 사겠다고 했다.

어휘 triangle[tráiæŋgl] 삼각형
narrow[nǽrou] 좁은
common[kámən] 흔한
square[skwεər] 정사각형
perfect[pə́ːrfikt] 완벽한, 딱 맞는

M Emma, what clock would look good in my office?
W I think the triangle one <u>would</u> <u>be</u> <u>good</u>. What do you think?
M I don't like the design. What about the long, narrow one?
W It <u>looks</u> <u>too</u> <u>big</u> <u>for</u> your office.
M You're right. Since the office is small, maybe I should get a small one.
W Yes. These round ones are not bad. How about <u>getting</u> <u>one</u> <u>of</u> <u>these</u>?
M They are too common. I wanted to get something different this time.
W How about this square one then? It would be <u>perfect</u> <u>for</u> <u>your</u> <u>office</u>.
M Okay. I'll get it.

남 Emma, 어떤 시계가 내 사무실에 어울릴까?
여 삼각형 시계가 좋을 거라고 생각해. 너는 어떻게 생각해?
남 나는 디자인이 마음에 안 들어. 길고 좁은 시계는 어때?
여 사무실에 비해 너무 커 보여.
남 네 말이 맞아. 사무실이 작기 때문에, 아마 작은 시계를 사야 할 거야.
여 응. 이 둥근 시계들이 나쁘지 않네. 이것들 중 하나를 사는 게 어때?
남 그것들은 너무 흔해. 이번에는 다른 것을 사고 싶었어.
여 그럼 이 정사각형 시계는 어때? 네 사무실에 딱일 거 같아.
남 좋아. 그것을 살게.

02 ①

해설 여자가 남자에게 책을 찾는 것을 도와주면서 찾는 책들이 품절이라고 말하는 걸로 보아 두 사람이 대화하는 장소는 서점임을 알 수 있다.

어휘 list[list] 목록
sold out 다 팔린, 품절인
mean[miːn] 의미하다
at the moment 지금

M Excuse me. I'm <u>looking</u> <u>for</u> <u>these</u> <u>books</u>. Can you help me find them, please?
W Yes, of course. Let me see your list.
M Here it is. I was only able to find one of the 3 books that I was looking for.
W I'm sorry, I can't <u>read</u> <u>this</u> <u>title</u>. What does it say?
M It's <u>a</u> <u>book</u> <u>called</u> *How to Become a Good Teacher*.
W Let me check if we have these books.
M Thank you.
W [Pause] Sorry, but these books <u>are</u> <u>sold</u> <u>out</u>.
M Does that mean you don't have them at the moment?
W I'm <u>afraid</u> <u>so</u>.

남 실례합니다. 이 책들을 찾고 있는데요. 찾는 걸 도와주실래요?
여 네, 그럼요. 당신의 목록을 보여주세요.
남 여기 있어요. 제가 찾고 있는 세 권 중에서 한 권만 찾을 수 있었어요.
여 죄송합니다. 이 제목을 읽을 수가 없네요. 뭐라고 하신 거죠?
남 〈좋은 선생님이 되는 법〉이라는 책이에요.
여 저희한테 이 책들이 있는지 찾아볼게요.
남 감사합니다.
여 [잠시 후] 죄송하지만, 이 책들은 품절되었네요.
남 지금 그것들이 없다는 말씀이신가요?
여 유감스럽게도 그렇습니다.

03 ②

해설 남자는 심판들의 많은 실수로 자신이 응원하는 축구팀이 경기에서 졌다면서 화가 난 상황이다.

어휘 fair[fεər] 공정한
referee[rèfəríː] 심판

W Paul, did you catch the soccer match last night?
M I did. The game was not <u>fair</u> <u>at</u> <u>all</u>. The referees made so many mistakes.
W No, they didn't. They were completely right.

여 Paul, 지난밤에 축구 경기 봤니?
남 봤어. 그 경기는 전혀 공정하지 않았어. 심판들이 아주 많은 실수를 했어.
여 아니, 그러지 않았어. 그들은 아주 옳았어.

completely[kəmplíːtli] 전적으로
fair and square 정정당당하게
one-sided[wʌ́nsáidid] 편파적인, 일방적인
judgment[dʒʌ́dʒmənt] 판정, 판단
replace[ripléis] 교체하다

M They made mistakes and it should have been <u>our team that won</u>.
W Why do you say that? The other team won fair and square.
M Do you remember the last game? We <u>lost that game</u> because of the referee's one-sided judgment.
W You're right about that game, but not about this one.
M No way. Those referees must be replaced!

남 그들이 실수를 했고 우리 팀이 이겼어야 했어.
여 왜 그렇게 말해? 상대 팀은 정정당당하게 이겼어.
남 지난 번 경기 기억해? 우리는 심판의 편파적인 판정 때문에 그 경기에서 졌어.
여 그 경기에 관해서는 네 말이 맞지만, 이번 경기에 관해서는 아냐.
남 말도 안돼. 그 심판들은 반드시 교체되어야 해!

① 자랑스러운 ② 화가 난 ③ 신이 난
④ 걱정스러운 ⑤ 실망한

04 ④

[해설] 회원의 입장료는 7달러이고 비회원의 입장료는 10달러라고 했다.

[어휘] good old days 좋았던 옛 시절
each day 매일
star[staːr] (영화에서) 주연을 맡다
admission[ədmíʃən] 입장

M Hello. We have the Golden Cinema event at ABC Theater this week. You can enjoy movies <u>from the good old days</u>. During the week, there will be 2 <u>movies playing each day</u>. Tonight, the first is *Casablanca*. It starts at 7:00 and ends at 8:40. The second is *Breakfast at Tiffany's*, starring Audrey Hepburn. It starts at 9:00 and ends at 10:55. The admission <u>price for members</u> is $7, and it is $10 for non-members. Doors open at 30 minutes <u>before the first movie starts</u>.

남 안녕하세요. 이번 주에 ABC 극장에서 Golden Cinema 행사가 있습니다. 여러분은 좋았던 옛 시절의 영화를 즐길 수 있습니다. 일주일 동안, 매일 두 편의 영화가 상영될 겁니다. 오늘 밤, 첫 영화는 〈카사블랑카〉입니다. 7시에 시작하여 8시 40분에 끝납니다. 두 번째 영화는 Audrey Hepburn 주연의 〈티파니에서 아침〉입니다. 9시에 시작하여 10시 55분에 끝납니다. 회원의 입장료는 7달러이고, 비회원은 10달러입니다. 극장 문은 첫 영화 상영 30분 전에 엽니다.

05 ④

[해설] 남자가 부모님의 큰 기대에 자신이 부응할 수 없을 거 같다고 걱정하자, 여자는 자신을 너무 힘들게 하지 말라고 조언하고 있다.

[어휘] troubling[trʌ́bliŋ] 괴롭히는, 애 먹이는
once[wʌns] 일단 ~하면
get ~ off your chest (마음을 짓누르던) ~을 털어놓다
live up to (기대에) 부응하다
expectation[èkspektéiʃən] 기대
no matter what 무슨 일이 있어도
be hard on ~을 심하게 대하다

W Tony, is something troubling you?
M No, everything's fine, Ms. Brown.
W Well, you <u>don't seem to focus</u> in school or talk to anybody in class. Is there anything I can help you with?
M I think this is my own problem to solve.
W I understand that it is <u>not easy to be</u> open and talk about what's on your mind at first. But once you get it off your chest, you'll feel so much better.
M All right. Here it goes. *[Pause]* My parents <u>expect too much from</u> me. I feel like I can't live up to their expectations.
W Your parents will love you no matter what. Please don't <u>be so hard on</u> yourself.

여 Tony, 너를 괴롭히는 게 있니?
남 아뇨, 다 괜찮아요, Brown 선생님.
여 음, 네가 학교에서 집중하거나 수업 중에 다른 사람과 말하지 않는 거 같구나. 내가 도와줄 게 있니?
남 이건 제가 해결해야 할 문제인 것 같아요.
여 처음에는 마음을 열고 무슨 생각을 하는지 말하는 게 쉽지 않다는 것을 이해해. 하지만 일단 그것을 털어놓으면, 훨씬 더 좋아질 거야.
남 알겠어요. 말씀드릴게요. *[잠시 후]* 부모님은 저에게 너무 많은 것을 기대하세요. 저는 그분들의 기대에 부응할 수 없을 거 같아요.
여 너의 부모님은 무슨 일이 있어도 너를 사랑할 거야. 자신을 너무 힘들게 하지 마렴.

06 ③

[해설] 나이든 사람들의 인구가 점점 늘어나서 젊은 사람들보다 수적으로 많아질 거라는 내용이다.

W The world is getting older and older. Not the planet, but <u>the people living on it</u>. A new report shows that the global

여 세계는 점점 더 나이가 들어가고 있습니다. 지구가 아니라, 그곳에 살고 있는 사람들 말입니다. 한 새로운 보고서는 나이든

planet[plǽnit] 행성, 지구
global population 세계 인구
increase[inkríːs] 증가하다
researcher[risə́ːrtʃər] 연구원
great[greit] 많은
billion[bíljən] 십억
elderly[éldərli] 연세가 드신
outnumber[àutnʌ́mbər] 수적으로 우
세하다
impact[ímpækt] 영향
society[səsáiəti] 사회

population of older people is increasing faster than ever. Today, there are about 700 million people aged 65 or older. However, researchers predict the number will be greater than 1.5 billion by 2050. They also say the elderly will soon outnumber the young. This will have a big impact on society.

사람들의 세계 인구는 그 어느 때보다도 더 빠르게 늘고 있음을 보여줍니다. 오늘날, 65세 이상 사람들은 대략 7억 명입니다. 하지만, 연구원들은 그 수가 2050년까지 15억 명이 넘을 것이라고 예측합니다. 그들은 또한 곧 나이든 사람들이 젊은 사람들보다 수적으로 많아질 것이라고 말합니다. 이것은 사회에 커다란 영향을 줄 겁니다.

07 ⑤

해설 포스터에는 9시까지 학교에 오라고 되어있는데, 남자는 8시까지 학교에 도착해야 한다고 했다.

어휘 poster[póustər] 포스터
activity[æktívəti] 활동
competition[kàmpətíʃən] 경연대회
extra[ékstrə] 여분의
arrive at ~에 도착하다

M Look at this poster. We're going to go to a Winter Ski Camp.
W Yay! It says it's on January 15th and 16th.
M It will be a fun event. It's held at White Resort.
W What can we do there?
M We can learn to ski and snowboard. And there are special activities like a dance competition, face painting, and a campfire.
W Oh, they all sound very interesting. What do we need to take?
M We must bring extra clothes and gloves.
W Does it say how and when we should go there?
M We will go to the resort by school bus. We must arrive at school by 8.

남 이 포스터를 봐. 우리는 겨울 스키 캠프에 가게 될 거야.
여 야호! 1월 15일과 16일이라고 나오네.
남 재미있는 행사일 거야. White Resort에서 열리네.
여 우리가 거기서 뭘 할 수 있니?
남 우리는 스키와 스노보드를 배울 수 있어. 그리고 춤 경연대회, 얼굴 페인팅, 그리고 캠프파이어 같은 특별한 활동들이 있어.
여 아, 전부 다 아주 재미있겠는데. 우리가 뭘 가져가야 하니?
남 여분의 옷과 장갑을 가져가야 해.
여 우리가 어떻게, 언제 거기에 간다고 되어 있니?
남 우리는 학교 버스로 리조트에 갈 거야. 우리는 8시까지 학교에 도착해야 해.

08 ④

해설 남자는 병원에서 아이들에게 책을 읽어주거나 영어 책을 한국어로 번역하는 일을 하기로 했으므로, 봉사활동을 하기 위해서 왔음을 알 수 있다.

어휘 ad(= advertisement)[æd] 광고
mention[ménʃən] 언급하다, 말하다
translate A into B A를 B로 번역하다

W Hello. What can I do for you?
M My name is Daniel. I called earlier this week about the ad.
W Oh, that's right. I'm Janet. We talked over the telephone.
M Nice to meet you, Janet. So what do you want me to do?
W Today, could you read some books to the children?
M No problem. Is there anything else?
W That's all for today. Oh, you mentioned you speak Korean, correct?
M Yes. Do you want me to teach Korean, too?
W No. There are a few kids who speak Korean in this hospital. If you can, can you translate English books into Korean for them?
M Sure. That's not a problem.

여 안녕하세요. 어떤 일로 오셨나요?
남 제 이름은 Daniel이에요. 저는 이번 주 초에 그 광고에 대해 전화했는데요.
여 아, 맞아요. 저는 Janet이에요. 우리는 전화로 이야기했죠.
남 만나서 반가워요, Janet. 그래서 제가 어떤 일을 하면 될까요?
여 오늘, 아이들에게 책을 좀 읽어주실래요?
남 네. 그밖에 다른 것이 있나요?
여 오늘은 그게 다예요. 아, 한국어를 한다고 하셨죠, 맞죠?
남 네. 제가 한국어도 가르치기를 원하시나요?
여 아니요. 이 병원에는 한국어를 하는 아이들이 몇 명 있어요. 가능하다면, 그들을 위해 영어 책을 한국어로 번역해줄 수 있나요?
남 그럼요. 그건 문제가 되지 않아요.

해설 잡지사 직원인 남자는 여자의 언니인 Maggie Jones에게 인터뷰를 요청하기 위해서 전화했다.

어휘 magazine[mǽgəzíːn] 잡지
wonder[wʌ́ndər] 궁금하다
interview[íntərvjùː] 인터뷰하다
business[bíznis] 업무, 일
take care of ~을 돌보다, 처리하다

[Telephone rings.]
W Hello.
M Hello. Is this Maggie Jones?
W No, this is Olivia, her sister. May I ask who's calling?
M This is Matt Cooper, and I work for *Happy Life* magazine. I was wondering if I could interview Ms. Jones.
W Well, you're going to have to ask her yourself, but she's not here at the moment.
M Could you tell me when she'll be back?
W She has some personal business to take care of. Please try calling back at the beginning of next week.
M Okay. Thank you.

[전화벨이 울린다.]
여 여보세요.
남 여보세요. Maggie Jones인가요?
여 아니요, 여동생인 Olivia예요. 누구신지 물어도 될까요?
남 저는 Matt Cooper이고, 〈Happy Life〉 잡지사에서 일해요. Jones 씨를 인터뷰할 수 있을까 해서요.
여 음, 그녀에게 직접 물어보셔야 할 텐데, 지금은 여기 없네요.
남 언제 돌아오실지 말씀해 주실 수 있나요?
여 그녀가 처리할 개인적인 업무가 좀 있어요. 다음 주 초에 다시 전화해 보세요.
남 알겠습니다. 감사합니다.

---

10 ③

해설 토요일에는 사파리 공원에 갔고, 일요일 오후에는 보트를 타고 새를 구경했으며, 일요일 저녁에는 모닥불에 둘러앉아 시간을 보냈다고 했다.

어휘 fantastic[fæntǽstik] 환상적인
hippo[hípou] 하마
crocodile[krákədàil] 악어
wildlife[wáildlàif] 야생 동물
share[ʃɛər] 공유하다
campfire[kǽmpfàiər] 모닥불
campground[kǽmpgràund] 캠프장
surround[səráund] 둘러싸다
pine tree 소나무

M Last weekend, I had a fantastic time with my family. On Saturday, I went to a safari park to see hippos, crocodiles, lions, elephants, and other wildlife. On Sunday afternoon, we took a boat trip on a beautiful lake. I saw hundreds of birds there. I took many pictures of the birds. And in the evening on that day, we shared experiences of the day around a campfire on a campground surrounded by tall pine trees. It was a really good trip.

남 지난 주말, 저는 가족과 함께 환상적인 시간을 보냈어요. 토요일에, 저는 하마, 악어, 사자, 코끼리와 다른 야생 동물을 보기 위해 사파리 공원에 갔어요. 일요일 오후에, 우리는 아름다운 호수에서 보트 여행을 했어요. 그곳에서 수백 마리의 새를 보았어요. 저는 새 사진을 여러 장 찍었어요. 그리고 그날 저녁에, 우리는 키 큰 소나무로 둘러싸인 캠프장의 모닥불 주위에서 하루의 경험을 공유했어요. 정말 즐거운 여행이었어요.

---

11 ③

해설 열차 운행이 취소되어서 다른 승강장에서 탑승하라고 안내하는 방송이다.

어휘 attention[əténʃən] 주의
announcement[ənáunsmənt] 알림
passenger[pǽsəndʒər] 승객
platform[plǽtfɔːrm] 승강장, 플랫폼
announce[ənáuns] 방송으로 알리다
due to ~ 때문에
engine checkup 엔진 점검
board[bɔːrd] 승차[탑승]하다
depart from ~에서 출발하다
apologize[əpálədʒàiz] 사과하다
inconvenience[ìnkənvíːnjəns] 불편

M May I have your attention, please? This announcement is for passengers who are waiting on Platform 4. We are sorry to announce that the 6:30 train to Incheon has been canceled. This is due to an engine checkup. Please do not board this train on Platform 4. We ask you to catch the 6:40 train to Incheon at Platform 7 instead. Once again, the 6:40 train to Incheon will depart from Platform 7. We apologize for the inconvenience. Thank you for your understanding.

남 잠시 안내 말씀드리겠습니다. 4번 승강장에서 기다리시는 승객들에게 알려드립니다. 인천행 6시 30분 열차가 운행이 취소되었음을 알려드리게 되어 죄송합니다. 엔진 점검으로 운행 취소되었습니다. 4번 승강장에서 이 기차에 승차하지 마시기 바랍니다. 대신 7번 승강장에서 인천으로 가는 6시 40분 열차를 이용해 주시기 바랍니다. 다시 한번, 6시 40분 인천행 열차가 7번 승강장에서 출발하겠습니다. 불편을 드려 죄송합니다. 이해해주셔서 감사합니다.

12 ⑤

해설 현재 통화 중이라서 잠시 기다릴 건지 묻는 여자의 말에 나중에 전화해 달라고 전해달라는 응답이 가장 적절하다.

어휘 employee[implɔíí:] 직원
hold on (전화상으로 상대방에게 하는 말로) 기다리다
moment[móumənt] 잠깐

[Telephone rings.]
W Hello.
M Hello. Is this Star Travel?
W Yes, it is.
M I'd like to speak to an employee there.
W Who would you like to speak to?
M I'd like to speak to Ms. Parker, please.
W May I ask who's calling?
M My name is Christian Russell.
W Hold on, please. [Pause] Sorry, Mr. Russell. She's on another line. Would you like to wait a moment?
M No, that's okay. Can you tell her to call me back?

[전화벨이 울린다.]
여 여보세요.
남 여보세요. Star Travel이죠?
여 네, 그렇습니다.
남 거기 직원과 통화하고 싶어요.
여 누구와 통화하고 싶으신가요?
남 Parker 씨 좀 바꿔주세요.
여 전화거신 분은 누구시죠?
남 제 이름은 Christian Russell입니다.
여 잠시 만요. [잠시 후] 죄송합니다. Russell 씨. 그녀가 통화중인데요. 잠시 기다리시겠습니까?
남 아니요, 괜찮습니다. 그녀에게 전화해 달라고 전해주실래요?

① 감사해요! 최선을 다할게요.
② 그녀를 방문할 충분한 시간이 없어요.
③ 미안하지만, 저는 여기 처음이에요.
④ 바로 그녀의 집 앞에서 그녀를 기다리고 있을게요.

13 ④

해설 무료 급식소에서 일하는 것이 힘들겠다는 남자의 말에 자원 봉사를 함으로써 기분이 좋아진다는 응답이 가장 적절하다.

어휘 soup kitchen 무료 급식소
provide[prəváid] 제공하다
meal[mi:l] 식사
volunteer[vàləntíər] 자원 봉사하다

M Do you have any plans for this weekend?
W Yes, I have to go to a soup kitchen.
M A soup kitchen? What is that?
W It's a place that provides meals for free.
M Do you volunteer there?
W Yes, I do.
M What kind of work do you do?
W Well, I make sandwiches or I cut up vegetables, things like that.
M Wow, that sounds like hard work.
W It is, but it makes me feel good.

남 이번 주말에 무슨 계획 있니?
여 응, soup kitchen에 가야 해.
남 soup kitchen? 그게 뭔데?
여 무료로 식사를 제공해주는 곳이야.
남 너 거기서 자원 봉사하니?
여 응, 그래.
남 어떤 종류의 일을 하니?
여 음, 샌드위치를 만들거나 야채를 써는 그런 일이야.
남 와, 그거 힘들겠다.
여 힘들지만 그 일을 하면 내 기분이 좋아져.

① 물론, 넌 놓칠 리가 없어.
② 좋아, 널 도와줄게.
③ 좀 쉬는 게 어떠니?
⑤ 응, 모퉁이에 하나 있어.

14 ④

해설 식당에서 친구로 착각하고 다른 남자의 어깨에 손을 얹어 깜짝 놀라게 한 상황이므로 그 남자에게 사과의 말을 하는 것이 가장 적절하다.

어휘 be supposed to-v ～하기로 되어 있다

W You are supposed to meet your friend Bill at a restaurant in the shopping mall. But you are already 15 minutes late. When you step into the restaurant, you see Bill eating a hamburger and French fries. So you think you will surprise him from behind. Then you put your hand on Bill's

여 당신은 쇼핑몰에 있는 식당에서 친구 Bill을 만나기로 한다. 하지만 이미 15분 늦었다. 식당 안으로 들어설 때, 당신은 Bill이 햄버거와 감자튀김을 먹고 있는 것을 본다. 그래서 당신은 Bill 뒤에서 그를 놀라게 해주려고 생각한다. 그래서 당신은 Bill의 어깨에 손을 올리고 그를 놀라게 한다. 그러나

step into ~로 발을 들여놓다

surprise[sərpráiz] 놀라게 하다

shoulder[ʃóuldər] 어깨

find out 알게 되다

somebody else 누군가 다른 사람

[선택지]

mistake[mistéik] 오해하다, 잘못 판단

하다 (mistake-mistook-mistaken)

shoulder and surprise him. But you find out it is somebody else, not Bill. In this situation, what would you say to the man?

여 B에이 아니라 다른 사람이라는 것을 알게 된다. 이러한 상황에서 당신은 그 남자에게 뭐라고 말하겠는가?

① 절 도와주셔서 감사합니다.

② 식사는 마음에 드십니까?

③ 오랫동안 당신을 보지 못했습니다.

④ 미안합니다. 당신을 제 친구로 오해했어요.

⑤ 오래 기다리게 해서 죄송합니다.

15 ③

해설 컴퓨터 키보드가 화장실 변기보다 더 더럽고 키보드에서 나온 세균들이 배탈을 유발할 수 있다는 연구 결과를 언급하면서 정기적으로 키보드를 깨끗이 닦아야 한다는 내용이다.

어휘 harmful[háːrmfəl] 해로운

company[kʌ́mpəni] 회사

bacteria[bæktíəriə] 박테리아

result[rizʌ́lt] 결과

shocking[ʃákiŋ] 충격적인

toilet seat 변기

germ[dʒəːrm] 세균

cause[kɔːz] 유발하다

upset stomach 배탈

regularly[régjulərli] 정기적으로

W Your computer keyboards could be harmful for your health. A company asked some researchers to check 30 keyboards in their offices for bacteria. The results were shocking. They showed the keyboards were 5 times dirtier than a toilet seat. The researchers said the germs from the keyboards could easily cause an upset stomach. Thus, you should clean your keyboards regularly in order to stay healthy.

여 당신의 컴퓨터 키보드는 당신의 건강에 해로울 수 있습니다. 한 회사가 몇몇 연구원들에게 그들의 사무실에 있는 30개의 키보드에 박테리아가 있는지 검사해 달라고 요청했습니다. 그 결과는 충격적이었습니다. 그 결과에서 키보드들이 화장실 변기보다 5배가 더 더럽다는 것을 보여주었습니다. 연구원들은 키보드에서 나온 세균들이 쉽게 배탈을 유발할 수 있다고 말했습니다. 그러므로, 건강을 유지하기 위해서 정기적으로 키보드를 깨끗이 닦아야 합니다.

① 새로운 키보드를 구입해라.

② 키보드를 사용하지 마라.

③ 키보드를 자주 닦아라.

④ 키보드에서 떨어져 있어라.

⑤ 키보드를 사용하기 전에 장갑을 착용해라.

서답형 1 lessons

해설 강습을 포함하여 한 달에 7만 원이라고 했다.

어휘 sign up for ~을 신청하다

fill out 작성하다

form[fɔːrm] 양식

including[inklúːdiŋ] ~을 포함하여

overcome[òuvərkʌ́m] 극복하다

fear[fiər] 두려움

get in shape 좋은 몸매를 가지다

W Can I sign up for your swimming class?

M Sure. I'll ask you some questions to fill out this form. Have you learned to swim before?

W No. I've always wanted to, but I'm afraid of water.

M You must be a beginner.

W That's right. When do you have classes?

M The classes are on Mondays, Wednesdays, and Fridays. But you may use the pool every day. It's 70,000 won a month including the lessons.

W I'll take the class on Wednesdays.

M Okay. Why do you want to learn swimming?

W I want to overcome my fear of water. Also, it'll help me get in shape.

여 수영 강습을 신청할 수 있나요?

남 그럼요. 이 양식을 작성하기 위해 몇 가지 물어볼게요. 전에 수영하는 법을 배운 적이 있나요?

여 아니요. 항상 배우고 싶었지만, 물이 두려워요.

남 초보자이시군요.

여 맞아요. 수업은 언제 있나요?

남 월요일, 수요일, 그리고 금요일에 있어요. 하지만 매일 수영장을 이용하셔도 됩니다. 강습을 포함하여 한 달에 7만 원입니다.

여 전 수요일에 수업을 들을 게요.

남 알겠어요. 수영을 왜 배우고 싶은가요?

여 물에 대한 제 두려움을 극복하고 싶어요. 좋은 몸매를 갖도록 해줄 수도 있고요.

서답형 2 fiction

해설 창의력을 개발하는 데 도움을 줄 수 있기 때문에 소설을 읽는 것도 실제 사건이나 사실에 대한 책을 읽는 것만큼 중요하다고 했다.

어휘 real[rí:əl] 실제의
event[ivént] 사건
fact[fækt] 사실
scientific[sàiəntífik] 과학적인
limit[límit] 제한하다
fiction[fíkʃən] 소설
non-fiction 비소설
develop[divéləp] 개발하다
creativity[krì:eitívəti] 창의성
essential[isénʃəl] 필수적인
imagination[imæ̀dʒənéiʃən] 상상
necessary[nésəsèri] 필수의
as well 또한

M Books about real events, real people, and facts are important as they can teach us about history, important people that we should know about, and scientific facts. However, we should <u>not limit our choice</u> of books. So I suggest you should also read fiction. <u>Fiction is as important as</u> non-fiction because it can help us to <u>develop our creativity</u>. Of course, knowing history and facts is essential in life, but imagination and creativity <u>are necessary for us</u> to dream about the future as well.

> **Question:** What does the man suggest to develop creativity?

➡ He suggests that we should read <u>fiction</u> in order to develop creativity.

남 실제 사건, 실제 인물, 그리고 사실에 관한 책들은 우리에게 역사, 우리가 알아야 할 중요한 인물, 그리고 과학적 사실에 대해 가르쳐 줄 수 있으므로 중요합니다. 하지만, 우리는 책 선택에 제한을 두면 안 됩니다. 그래서 저는 우리가 소설도 읽을 것을 제안합니다. 소설은 우리가 창의력을 개발하는 데 도움을 줄 수 있기 때문에 비소설만큼 중요합니다. 물론, 역사와 사실을 아는 것이 삶에 있어서 필수적이지만, 상상력과 창의력도 우리가 미래에 대한 꿈을 꾸는 데 필수적입니다.

> 질문: 남자는 창의력을 개발하기 위해서 무엇을 제안합니까?

➡ 그는 창의력을 개발하기 위해서 <u>소설</u>을 읽을 것을 제안합니다.

서답형 3 jogging

해설 일과 현대적인 도시 환경 속에서 압박감을 받는 현대인의 삶에서 달리기가 치료제가 될 수 있다고 했다.

어휘 interest[íntərèst] 관심
instead of ~ 대신에
pressure[préʃər] 압박
modern[mádərn] 현대의
urban[ə́:rbən] 도시의
environment[inváiərənmənt] 환경
look upon as ~로 여겨지다
medicine[médisn] 약, 치료제
alone[əlóun] 혼자서
moreover[mɔːróuvər] 게다가
everywhere[évrihwὲər] 모든 곳에서
relieve[rilíːv] (고통 등을) 없애[덜어] 주다

W There has been increasing interest in health. Today, <u>we work sitting down</u>, using our brains instead of our bodies. Every day, we find ourselves under pressure from our jobs and just living in a modern urban environment. In this sense, <u>running can be looked</u> upon as medicine. Also, while a person <u>is jogging</u>, he has time to enjoy himself alone. Moreover, it can <u>be done almost everywhere</u>, and you don't have to spend a lot of money to do it.

> You should remember that jogging can be considered a medicine to relieve your stress.

여 건강에 대한 관심이 증가하고 있습니다. 오늘날, 우리는 앉아서 일을 하며, 우리의 몸 대신에 머리를 사용합니다. 매일, 우리는 일로부터 오는 압박감 속에 있고, 현대적인 도시 환경 속에서 그냥 살아가고 있는 자신을 발견합니다. 이런 점에서, 달리기는 치료제로 여겨질 수 있습니다. 또한, 사람이 조깅을 하고 있는 동안에, 혼자서 즐길 수 있는 시간을 갖게 됩니다. 게다가, 조깅은 거의 모든 곳에서 할 수 있고, 조깅을 하기 위해서 많은 돈을 쓸 필요가 없습니다.

> 조깅은 스트레스를 풀기 위한 치료제로 여겨질 수 있다는 것을 기억해야 한다.